P9-DUZ-157

Preface

The field of abnormal psychology is inherently controversial because we lack a clear delineation between normal and abnormal behavior. Most phenomena in the realm of abnormal psychology fall along continua; the point on a continuum at which behavior moves from being considered "normal" to being considered "abnormal" varies considerably and is influenced by a number of factors. Consider the example of an active boy's behavior. His running around impulsively and shouting out aimless comments would be viewed as normal behavior on a playground but abnormal behavior in a quiet classroom. In a classroom setting, his behavior might be referred to as impulsive and hyperactive, possibly prompting his teacher to refer him to a mental health professional for therapy and medication to help him settle down and pay attention. Although such referrals are commonplace in American schools, some people contend that we pathologize the normal behavior of children when we view their high levels of energy as mental disorders. This is but one of the debates about which you will read in this book, and it is a good example of the kind of controversy found in the field of mental health.

There are many complex issues that arise in the field of abnormal psychology; in this book you will read about 20 controversial matters with which mental health experts struggle. Part 1 explores debates pertaining to the classification of mental disorders by considering whether or not the current diagnostic system is conceptually flawed and whether or not it is biased against women. Part 2 looks at psychological conditions and treatments about which there has been vehement disagreement in recent years, with some experts expressing intense skepticism about the validity of specific clinical problems and interventions that have been in the spotlight. Moving on to issues pertaining to treatment, Part 3 looks at the trend toward biological interventions for an array of psychological problems and mental disorders. Part 4 explores pertinent social issues that interface with the field of abnormal psychology. The final part features a set of debates about ethical and legal issues that pertain to the field of mental health.

Most students who enroll in a course in abnormal psychology begin the semester with the belief that they will be learning about problems that affect "other people," rather than themselves. In a short period of time, however, they come to realize that they are reading about conditions that have much more personal salience than they had anticipated. Sooner or later, they recognize conditions that they or someone close to them have experienced, and their interest in the topic intensifies. In all likelihood, you will have a similar reaction as you read this book. To capture the essence of each debate, you will find it helpful to connect yourself in a personal way to the issue under consideration; you might imagine yourself dealing with the issue personally, or as the relative of a client with the particular problem, or even as a professional trying to provide mental health assistance.

Plan of the book To assist you in understanding the significance of each issue, every issue begins with an *introduction* that provides important background about the issue and summarizes the perspective in each of the pieces. Points and counterpoints are enumerated to help you appreciate the specific areas of disagreement between the two pieces. Each issue concludes with a set of *challenge questions* that can serve as the basis for further thought or discussion on the topic as well as a list of suggested additional readings. In addition, Internet site addresses (URLs) have been provided on the *On the Internet* page at the beginning of each part, which should prove useful as starting points for further research on the issues. At the back of the book is a listing of all the *contributors to this volume* with a brief biographical sketch of each of the prominent figures whose views are debated here.

Changes to this edition This third edition of *Taking Sides: Clashing Views on Controversial Issues in Abnormal Psychology* includes some important changes from the second edition. Three new issues have been included, and one issue has been updated. New to this edition are the following: "Should Abstinence Be the Goal for Treating People with Alcohol Problems?" (Issue 8), "Are Antipsychotic Medications the Treatment of Choice for People with Psychosis?" (Issue 10), and "Should Psychologists Prescribe Medication?" (Issue 13). Issue 11, "Is Ritalin Overprescribed?" has been updated to include more recent publications. There are eight new readings in all. Furthermore, six of the issues are now placed within a new conceptual unit, Part 3, entitled "The Trend toward Biological Intervention."

A word to the instructor An *Instructor's Manual With Test Questions* (multiple-choice and essay) is available through the publisher for the instructor using *Taking Sides* in the classroom. A general guidebook, *Using Taking Sides in the Classroom,* which discusses methods and techniques for integrating the procon approach into any classroom setting, is also available. An online version of *Using Taking Sides in the Classroom* and a correspondence service for *Taking Sides* adopters can be found at http://www.dushkin.com/usingts/.

Taking Sides: Clashing Views on Controversial Issues in Abnormal Psychology is only one title in the Taking Sides series. If you are interested in seeing the table of contents for any of the other titles, please visit the Taking Sides Web site at http://www.dushkin.com/takingsides/.

Acknowledgments Special gratitude goes to the research assistants who played such important roles in the preparation of this volume. For this edition, Justin Smith did a masterful job researching and developing three of the issues: "Should Abstinence Be the Goal for Treating People with Alcohol Problems?" (Issue 8), "Are Antipsychotic Medications the Treatment of Choice for People with Psychosis?" (Issue 10), and "Is Ritalin Overprescribed?" (Issue 11). In his role as senior editorial assistant, Justin also proceeded line by line through the second edition in order to update all components of the volume. In addition to meeting all his responsibilities

TAKING SIDES

Clashing Views on Controversial

Issues in Abnormal Psychology

THIRD EDITION

Selected, Edited, and with Introductions by

Richard P. Halgin
University of Massachusetts–Amherst

McGraw-Hill/Dushkin
A Division of The McGraw-Hill Companies

To my wonderful wife, Lucille, whose love and support provide me with immeasurable amounts of energy, and to our children, Daniel and Kerry, whose values and achievements have been inspiring.

Photo Acknowledgment
Cover image: Chad Baker/Getty Images

Cover Art Acknowledgment
Maggie Lytle

Copyright © 2005 by McGraw-Hill/Dushkin,
A Division of The McGraw-Hill Companies, Inc., Dubuque, Iowa 52001

Copyright law prohibits the reproduction, storage, or transmission in any form by any means of any portion of this publication without the express written permission of McGraw-Hill/Dushkin and of the copyright holder (if different) of the part of the publication to be reproduced. The Guidelines for Classroom Copying endorsed by Congress explicitly state that unauthorized copying may not be used to create, to replace, or to substitute for anthologies, compilations, or collective works.

Taking Sides ® is a registered trademark of McGraw-Hill/Dushkin

Manufactured in the United States of America

Third Edition

1234567890DOCDOC0987654

Library of Congress Cataloging-in-Publication Data
Main entry under title:
Taking sides: clashing views on controversial issues in abnormal psychology/selected, edited, and with introductions by Richard P. Halgin.—3rd ed.
Includes bibliographical references and index.
1. Psychology, Pathological. I. Halgin, Richard P., *comp.*
616.89

0-07-291709-1
ISSN: 1527-604X

Printed on Recycled Paper

with efficiency, intelligence, and editorial sophistication, Justin has also opened the door to the consideration of important topics, such as the appropriate treatment for alcoholism and psychosis. Eric Nguyen, who had developed the issue "Does Evolution Explain Why Men Rape? (Issue 15) for the second edition, also played an important role for this edition by researching and developing the issue entitled "Should Psychologists Prescribe Medication?" (Issue 13). Justin Smith and Eric Nguyen did wonderful work building upon the contributions to the first and second editions by Joseph Greer, Kerry Halgin, Molly Burnett, Sandro Piselli, and Diana Rancourt, all of whom have been conscientious and careful in their research endeavors, insightful and sophisticated in their conceptualizations, and thoughtful and courteous in their interactions.

Thanks also to Ted Knight and the staff at McGraw-Hill/Dushkin. Ted's inspiration and wise direction continue to play a pivotal role in this edition, as he has continued to provide invaluable advice and thoughtful reflections about ways to make this edition an excellent resource for faculty and students.

Richard P. Halgin
University of Massachusetts–Amherst

Contents In Brief

Contents

Psychiatrist Frank W. Putnam contends that the diagnosis of multiple personality disorder meets the standards for the three basic forms of validity: content validity, construct validity, and criterion-related validity. Psychiatrist Paul R. McHugh denies the validity of multiple personality disorder, asserting that this condition is a socially created behavioral disorder induced by psychotherapists.

Psychiatrist Edward M. Hallowell asserts that an appreciation for the complexity of attention deficit disorder (ADD) can provide valuable understanding about the workings of the brain and how this disorder affects the lives of millions of people. Educational consultant and former special education teacher Thomas Armstrong contends that the diagnosis of ADD has been blown out of proportion by the public and the professional community and is, in fact, a questionable diagnosis.

Science writers Robert Mathias and Patrick Zickler argue that MDMA has skyrocketed in popularity and that insufficient attention has been paid to the physical and psychological risks associated with its use. June Riedlinger, an assistant professor of clinical pharmacy, and Michael Montagne, a professor of pharmacy, contend that the risks associated with MDMA use have been exaggerated and that there are legitimate therapeutic uses for this substance.

Psychiatrist E. Joanne Angelo contends that women who have abortions are at risk of developing a lasting, serious syndrome consisting of several emotional and behavioral problems. Social activist Joyce Arthur asserts that a general consensus has been reached in the medical and scientific communities that most women who have abortions experience little or no psychological harm.

Psychologist Robert Resnick endorses the recommendation that psychologists be given prescription privileges in order to expand psychopharmacological availability to people needing medication. Psychologist William Robiner and his colleagues object to the notion of granting prescription privileges to psychologists, and express several concerns pertaining to training and competence.

Physician Max Fink asserts that electroconvulsive therapy (ECT) is an effective intervention whose use has been limited as a result of social stigma and philosophical bias, which have been reinforced by intimidation from the pharmaceutical and managed care industries. Leonard R. Frank, editor and cofounder of the Network Against Psychiatric Assault, criticizes the use of ECT because of its disturbing side effects, some of which he personally has suffered, and asserts that its resurgence in popularity is economically based.

PART 4 SOCIAL ISSUES 257

Psychology and communication researchers L. Rowell Huesmann and Jessica Moise assert that there is a clear relationship between aggression and children's viewing of media violence, and they point to several theoretical explanations for this connection. Psychology professor Jonathan L. Freedman disagrees with the conclusion of researchers that there is a relationship between aggression and children's viewing of media violence, and he argues that many conclusions in this area are based on methodologically flawed studies.

Sociology professor Diana E. H. Russell considers pornography profoundly harmful because it predisposes men to want to rape women and undermines internal and social inhibitions against acting out rape fantasies. Law professor Nadine Strossen contends that there is no credible research to support the claim that sexist, violent imagery leads to harmful behavior against women.

Psychology professors Judith Wallerstein and Julia Lewis, and Sandra Blakeslee, a science and medicine correspondent for the *New York Times,* assert that children of divorced parents suffer emotional damage that impedes normal growth and functioning and permanently alters their lives. Professor of psychology E. Mavis Hetheringon and writer John Kelly dismiss some of what they view as myths of the divorce culture, stating that divorce is not necessarily detrimental to all children but can, in fact, provide opportunities for growth for the children as well as the parents involved in the divorce.

Evolutionary biologist Randy Thornhill and evolutionary anthropologist Craig T. Palmer assert that the reasons why men rape are misunderstood. They contend that, rather than an act of gratuitous violence, rape can be understood as a biologically determined behavior in which socially disenfranchised men resort to this extreme act in order to gain access to women. Journalist Susan Brownmiller argues that rape is an exemplification of the male-female struggle in which men humiliate and degrade women in a blunt and ugly expression of physical power.

Rhea K. Farberman, director of public communications for the American Psychological Association, makes the case that mental health professionals should be called upon to assess terminally ill people who request hastened death in order to ensure that decision making is rational and free of coercion. Psychiatrists Mark D. Sullivan, Linda Ganzini, and Stuart J. Youngner argue that the reliance on mental health professionals to be suicide gatekeepers involves an inappropriate use of clinical procedures to disguise society's ambivalence about suicide itself.

Psychologist Mark A. Yarhouse asserts that mental health professionals have an ethical responsibility to allow individuals to pursue treatment aimed at curbing same-sex attraction, stating that doing so affirms the client's dignity and autonomy. Psychologist Douglas C. Haldeman criticizes therapy involving sexual reorientation, insisting that there is no evidence that such treatments are effective and that they run the risk of further stigmatizing homosexuality.

Introduction

What's "Abnormal" About Abnormal Psychology?

Richard P. Halgin

The field of abnormal psychology lends itself well to a discussion of controversial issues because of the inherent difficulty involved in defining the concept of "abnormal." The definition of abnormality is contingent on a myriad of influences that include cultural, historical, geographical, societal, interpersonal, and intrapersonal factors. What is considered everyday behavior in one culture might be regarded as bizarre in another. What was acceptable at one point in time might seem absurd in contemporary society. What seems customary in one region, even in one section of a large city, might be viewed as outrageous elsewhere. Even on a very personal level, one person's typical style of emotional expression might be experienced by another person as odd and disruptive. This introductory essay looks at some of the complex issues involved in defining and understanding abnormality and, in doing so, will set the stage for the controversial issues that follow. With this theoretical foundation, you will be better equipped to tackle the thorny issues in this volume and to develop an approach for reaching your own conclusions about these controversies.

Defining Abnormality

One of the best ways to begin a discussion of the complexity of defining abnormality is by considering our own behavior. Think about an outlandish costume that you wore to a Halloween party and the fun you had engaging in this completely normal behavior. Now imagine wearing the same costume to class the following day, and think about the reactions you would have received. What seemed so normal on the evening of October 31 would have been considered bizarre on the morning of November 1. Only a day later, in a different context, you would have been regarded as abnormal, and your behavior would have been viewed as both disturbed and disturbing. Consider another example: Recall a time in which you were intensely emotional, perhaps weeping profusely at a funeral. If you were to display similar emotionality a few days later in a class discussion, your behavior would cause considerable stir, and your classmates would be taken aback by the intensity of your emotions. Now consider a common behavior that is completely acceptable and expected in American culture, such as shaking a person's hand upon meeting. Did you know that in some cultures such behavior is regarded as rude and unacceptable? These simple examples highlight the ways in which the concept of "normal" is contingent on many factors. Because of the wide variability in definitions of what is abnormal, psychologists have spelled out criteria that can be used in determining abnormal human behavior. These criteria fall into four categories: distress, impairment, risk to self or other people, and socially and culturally unacceptable behavior.

Distress

I begin with the most personal criterion of abnormality because the experience of inner emotional distress is a universal phenomenon and a powerful way in which every person at some point in life feels different from everyone around them. Distress, the experience of emotional pain, is experienced in many ways, such as depression, anxiety, and cognitive confusion. When people feel any of these responses to an extreme degree, they feel abnormal, and they typically look for ways to alleviate their feelings of inner pain. Some of the issues in this book illustrate the various ways in which different people respond to similar life events. For example, Issue 6 explores the emotional impact of abortion on women who undergo this procedure, with the controversy focusing on the extent to which abortion might evoke intense experiences of lasting emotional distress.

Impairment

People who are intensely distressed are likely to find it difficult to fulfill the everyday responsibilities of life. When people are very depressed or anxious, they typically have a difficult time concentrating on their studies, attending to their work responsibilities, or even interacting with other people. Impairment involves a reduction in a person's ability to function at an optimal or even an average level. Although distress and impairment often go hand in hand, they do not always; a person can be seriously impaired but feel no particular distress. This is often the case with substance abuse, in which people are incapable of the basic tasks of physical coordination and cognitive clarity but feel euphoric. Some of the debates in this book address the issue of impairment and the difficulty in assessing the extent to which people are impaired. For example, Issue 19 focuses on physician-assisted suicide, with particular attention to the role of mental health professionals in determining a person's competency to choose suicide. One aspect of the controversy pertains to the issue of whether or not a terminally ill person is too impaired to make a rational life-ending decision.

Risk to Self or Others

Sometimes people act in ways that cause risk to themselves or others. In this context, risk refers to danger or threat to the well-being of a person. In the case of suicide or self-mutilating behavior, the personal risk is evident. In the case of outwardly directed violence, rape, or even emotional exploitation, the risk is to other people. Although the issue of risk to self or others might not seem controversial on the surface, there are many facets of risk that provoke debate. For example, does an individual have the right to engage in self-injurious, perhaps even life-ending, behavior, or does society have a right, even a responsibility, to intervene? The choice of suicide, even by terminally ill people, has prompted heated debate in our society, but so have less-extreme issues, such as the choice to view pornography. The issue of pornography is especially controversial because some experts believe that viewing sexually explicit—particularly sexually violent—stimuli places individuals at risk of engaging in the violent behaviors that they observe in pornographic media. This controversy, addressed in Issue 16, raises not only questions pertaining to risk to other people but also question of whether or not indulgence in pornography might result in personal psychological risk.

Socially and Culturally Unacceptable Behavior

Another criterion for defining abnormality pertains to the social or cultural context in which behavior occurs. In some instances, behavior that is regarded as odd within a given culture, society, or subgroup is common elsewhere. For example, some people from Mediterranean cultures believe in a phenomenon called *mal de ojo*, or "evil eye," in which the ill will of one person can negatively affect another. According to this belief, receiving the evil eye from a person can cause a range of disturbing physical and emotional symptoms; consequently, individuals in these cultures often take steps to ward off the power of another person's evil eye. Such beliefs might be regarded as strangely superstitious, almost delusional, in American culture, but they are considered common elsewhere. Even more subtle contexts can influence the extent to which a behavior is defined as abnormal, as illustrated by the example of the Halloween costume mentioned previously. This book features issues related to social and cultural variables, such as whether media violence promotes violent behavior in young people (Issue 15) and whether divorce is detrimental to children (Issue 17).

What Causes Abnormality?

In trying to understand why people act and feel in ways that are regarded as abnormal, social scientists consider three dimensions: biological, psychological, and sociocultural. Rather than viewing these dimensions as independent, however, experts discuss the relative contribution of each dimension in influencing human behavior, and they use the term *biopsychosocial* to capture these intertwining forces. In the context of abnormality, the biopsychosocial conceptualization of human behavior conveys the sense that abnormal behavior arises from a complex set of determinants in the body, the mind, and the social context.

Biological Causes

During the past several decades scientists have made tremendous progress in discovering ways in which human behavior is influenced by a range of biological variables. In the realm of abnormal psychology, the contributions of the biological sciences have been especially impressive, as researchers have developed increasing understanding of the ways in which abnormal behavior is determined by bodily physiology and genetic makeup. As is the case with many medical disorders, various mental disorders, such as depression, run in families. Mental health researchers have made great efforts to understand why certain mental illnesses are passed from one generation to another and also to understand why certain disorders are not inherited even in identical twin pairs when one of the twins has the condition and the other does not.

In addition to understanding the role of genetics, mental health experts also consider the ways in which physical functioning can cause or aggravate the experience of psychological symptoms. Experts know that many medical conditions can cause a person to feel or act in ways that are abnormal. For example, a medical abnormality in the thyroid gland can cause wide variations in mood and emotionality. Brain damage resulting from a head trauma, even a slight one, can result in bizarre behavior and intense emotionality. Similarly, the use of drugs or alcohol can cause people to act in extreme ways that neither they nor those who know them well would have ever imagined. Even exposure to environmental stimuli, such as toxic substances or allergens, can cause people to experience disturbing emotional changes and to act in odd or bizarre ways. Several issues in this book explore conditions in which biology plays a prominent causative role. For example, attention deficit disorder (ADD) is regarded as a disorder of the brain that interferes with a person's ability to pay attention or to control behavior (see Issue 4).

Psychological Causes

Biology does not tell the entire story about the causes of mental disorders; many forms of emotional disturbance arise as a result of troubling life experiences. The experiences of life, even seemingly insignificant ones, can leave lasting marks on a person. In cases in which an experience involves trauma, such as rape or abuse, the impact can be emotionally disruptive throughout life, affecting a person's thoughts, behaviors, and even dreams.

In trying to understand the psychological causes of abnormality, social scientists and mental health clinicians consider a person's experiences. Not only do they focus on interpersonal interactions with other people that may have left a mark, but they also consider the inner life of the individual— thoughts and feelings that may cause distress or impairment. Some conditions arise from distorted perceptions and faulty ways of thinking. For example, highly sensitive people may misconstrue innocent comments by acquaintances that cause obsessional worry about being disliked or demeaned. As a result, these people may respond to their acquaintances in hostile ways that perpetuate interpersonal difficulties and inner distress.

For several of the issues in this book, psychological forces play a significant causative role. For example, Issue 3 considers the personality disturbances of people who have suffered traumatic life experiences and the controversies surrounding the possibility that trauma might be repressed or might cause the development of multiple personalities.

Sociocultural Causes

The term *sociocultural* refers to the various circles of social influence in the lives of people. The most immediate circle is composed of people with whom we interact in our immediate environment; for college students, this includes roommates, classmates, and coworkers. Moving beyond the immediate circle are people who inhabit the extended circle of relationships, such as family members back home or friends from high school. A third circle is composed of the people in our environments with whom we interact minimally and rarely by name, such as residents of our community or campus, whose standards, expectations, and behaviors influence our lives. A fourth circle is the much wider culture in which people live, such as American society.

Abnormal behavior can emerge from experiences in any of these social contexts. Troubled relationships with a roommate or family member can cause intense emotional distress. Involvement in an abusive relationship may initiate an interpersonal style in which the abused person becomes repeatedly caught up with people who are hurtful or damaging. Political turmoil, even on a relatively local level, can evoke emotions ranging from intense anxiety to incapacitating fear.

This book discusses several conditions in which sociocultural factors are significant. For example, Issue 2 focuses on the potential role of gender bias in the diagnosis of mental disorders. Other issues address the ways in which pornography may be responsible for the extent of violence against women (Issue 16) and the ways in which violence in young people may be rooted in media violence (Issue 15).

The Biopsychosocial Perspective

From the discussion so far, it should be evident that most aspects of human behavior are determined by a complex of causes involving an interaction of biological, psychological, and sociocultural factors. As you read about the clinical conditions and mental disorders discussed in this book, it will be useful for you to keep the biopsychosocial perspective in mind, even in those discussions in which the authors seem narrowly focused. For example, a condition may be put forth as being biologically caused, leading the reader to believe that other influences play little or no role. Another condition may be presented as being so psychologically based that it is difficult to fathom the role that biology might play in causing or aggravating the condition. Other issues may be discussed almost exclusively in sociocultural terms, with minimal attention to the roles of biological and psychological factors. An intelligent discussion in the field of abnormal psychology is one that explores the relative importance of biological, psychological, and sociocultural influences. An intelligent discussion in the field of abnormal psychology is also one that avoids reductionistic thinking, in which simplistic explanations are offered for complex human problems.

Why We View Behavior as "Abnormal"

In addition to understanding how to define abnormality and what causes abnormal behavior, it is important to understand how members of society view people who are abnormal and how this view affects people with emotional problems and mental disorders. Many people in our society discriminate against and reject mentally disturbed people. In so doing, they aggravate one of the most profound aspects of dealing with mental disorder—the experience of stigma. A stigma is a label that causes certain people to be regarded as different and defective and to be set apart from mainstream members of society. Today, several decades after sociologist Erving Goffman brought the phenomenon of stigma to public attention, there is ample evidence in American society that people with mental disorders are regarded as different and are often deprived of the basic human right to respectful treatment.

It is common for people with serious psychological disorders, especially those who have been hospitalized, to experience profound and long-lasting emotional and social effects. People who suffer from serious psychological problems tend to think less of themselves because of these experiences, and they often come to believe many of the myths about themselves that are perpetuated in a society that lacks understanding about the nature of mental illness and psychological problems.

Although tremendous efforts have been undertaken to humanize the experiences of people with psychological problems and mental disorders, deeply rooted societal reactions still present obstacles for many emotionally distressed people. Controversies continue to rage about the systems of diagnosis and assessment used by mental health professionals, about the validity of certain clinical conditions, and about the efficacy of various psychotherapeutic and medical interventions. As you read both sides of the debates in this book, it is important that you keep in mind the strong personal beliefs that influence, and possibly bias, the statements of each writer and to consider the ways in which various societal forces are intertwined with the comments of the author.

The most powerful force within the field of mental health during the twentieth century was the medical model, upon which many forms of intervention are based. This book frequently mentions a system of diagnosis developed by the American Psychiatric Association that has been revised several times during the past 50 years. This system is published in

20

a book called the *Diagnostic and Statistical Manual of Mental Disorders*. The most recent version is the fourth edition, which is commonly abbreviated *DSM-IV*. In this medical model diagnostic system, mental disorders are construed as diseases that require treatment. There are both advantages and disadvantages to this approach.

Not only does *DSM-IV* rely on the medical model, but it also uses a categorical approach. A categorical approach assumes that diseases fit into distinct categories. For example, the medical disease pneumonia is a condition that fits into the category of diseases involving the respiratory system. In corresponding fashion, conditions involving mood fit into the category of mood disorders, conditions involving anxiety fit into the category of anxiety disorders, and so on. However, as the authors of *DSM-IV* admit, there are limitations to the categorical approach. For one thing, psychological disorders are not neatly separable from each other or from normal functioning. For example, where is the dividing line between normal sadness and clinical depression? Furthermore, many disorders seem linked to each other in fundamental ways. In a state of agitated depression, for example, an individual suffers from both anxiety and saddened mood.

Several of the conditions and interventions discussed in this book have been debated for years. As you read about these issues, it will be helpful for you to keep in mind the context in which these debates have arisen. Some debates arise because of turf battles between professions. For example, psychiatrists may be more inclined to endorse the diagnostic system of the American Psychiatric Association (*DSM-IV*) and to support biological explanations and somatic interventions for mental disorders. Psychologists, on the other hand, may urge mental health professionals to take a broader point of view and to proceed more cautiously in turning to biological explanations and causes.

The Influence of Theoretical Perspective on the Choice of Intervention

Although impressive advances have been achieved in determining why people develop various mental disorders, understanding of how best to treat their conditions remains limited and also powerfully influenced by the ideological biases of many clinicians and researchers. For much of the twentieth century, various interventions emerged from markedly different schools of thought, each approach being tied to one of the three major realms—biological, psychological, or sociocultural. But how are biological, psychological, and sociocultural frameworks used in determining choice of intervention?

Within the biological perspective, disturbances in emotions, behavior, and cognitive processes are viewed as being caused by abnormalities in the functioning of the body, such as the brain and nervous system or the endocrine system. Treatments involve a range of somatic therapies, the most common of which is medication, the most extreme of which involves psychosurgery. Several issues in this book focus on debates about reliance on biological explanations and interventions, such as the issues on ADD

(Issue 4), psychosurgery (Issue 12), rape (Issue 18), and electroconvulsive therapy (Issue 14).

The realm of psychological theories contains numerous approaches, although three schools of thought emerged as most prominent during the second half of the twentieth century: psychodynamic, humanistic, and behavioral. Proponents of the psychodynamic perspective emphasize unconscious determinants of behavior and recommend the use of techniques involving exploration of the developmental causes of behavior and the interpretation of unconscious influences on thoughts, feelings, and behavior. This is pertinent to the debate over repressed memories (Issue 7), which involves clinicians who believe that people are inclined to "forget" traumatic experiences in order to defend themselves from the disruptive anxiety they would otherwise experience.

At the core of the humanistic perspective is the belief that human motivation is based on an inherent tendency to strive for self-fulfillment and meaning in life. Humanistic therapists use a client-centered approach in which they strive to treat clients with unconditional positive regard and empathy. Mental health professionals are called upon to act in ways that are more client-centered as they deal with issues ranging from distress about sexual orientation (Issue 20) to matters involving a client's choice to end life due to a debilitating illness (Issue 19).

According to the behavioral perspective, abnormality is caused by faulty learning experiences, with a subset of behavioral theory focusing on cognitive functions, such as maladaptive thought processes. Because behaviorists and cognitive theorists believe that disturbance results from faulty learning or distorted thinking, intervention focuses on teaching clients more adaptive ways of thinking and behaving. Some of the discussions in this book focus on the ways in which behavioral and cognitive approaches might be preferable to medical approaches to conditions such as ADD (Issue 4) and distress related to sexual orientation (Issue 20).

Clinicians working within sociocultural models emphasize the ways that individuals are influenced by people, social institutions, and social forces. According to this viewpoint, psychological problems can emerge from social contexts ranging from the family to society. In a corresponding vein, treatments are determined by the nature of the group. Thus, problems rooted within family systems would be treated with family therapy; societal problems caused by discrimination or inadequate care of the mentally ill would be dealt with through enactment of social policy initiatives. Several issues in this volume touch upon sociocultural influences, such as the effects of pornography (Issue 16), the prevalence of divorce (Issue 17), and the most appropriate intervention for treating alcoholism (Issue 8).

Keeping the Issues in Perspective

In evaluating the content of the writings in this book, it is important to keep in mind who the writers are and what their agendas might be. Most of the contributors are distinguished figures in the fields of mental health, ethics, and law. They are regarded as clear and influential thinkers who have important messages to convey. However, it would be naive to think that any writer, particularly when addressing a controversial topic, is free of bias.

It is best to read each issue with an understanding of the forces that might influence the development of a particular bias. For example, as physicians, psychiatrists have been trained in the medical model, with its focus on biological causes for problems and somatic interventions. Non-physician mental health professionals may be more inclined to focus on interpersonal and intrapersonal causes and interventions. Lawyers and ethicists are more likely to be further removed from questions of etiology, focusing instead on what they believe is justified according to the law or right according to ethical standards.

As you read about the issues facing mental health clinicians and researchers, you are certain to be struck by the challenges that these professionals face. You may also be struck by the powerful emotion expressed by the authors who discuss their views on topics in this field. Because psychological stresses and problems are an inherent part of human existence, many discussions about abnormal psychology are emotionally charged. At some point in life, most people have a brush with serious emotional problems, either directly or indirectly. This is a frightening prospect for many people, one that engenders worried expectations and intense reactions. By acknowledging our vulnerability to disruptive emotional experiences, however, we can think about the ways in which we would want clinicians to treat us. As you read the issues in this book, place yourself in the position of an individual in the process of being assessed, diagnosed, and treated for an emotional difficulty or mental disorder.

Before you take a side in each debate, consider how the issue might be personally relevant to you at some point in life. You may be surprised to discover that you respond in different ways to issues that might have special salience to yourself, as opposed to random people somewhere else. By imagining yourself being personally affected by a professional's controversial opinion regarding one or more of the debates in this book, you will find yourself immersed in the discussions about issues for which there is no clear right or wrong.

On the Internet . . .

DSM-IV Questions and Answers

At this site, the American Psychological Association provides questions and answers concerning the *DSM-IV*.

http://www.psych.org/clin_res/dsm/faq81301.cfm

Gender Issues and Patient Care

This paper, developed by the Canadian Psychological Association in conjunction with the American Psychiatric Association, discusses the importance of being aware of possible gender bias in patient care.

http://www.cpa-apc.org/PublicationsPosition_Papers/
Gender.asp

PART 1

Classification and Diagnosis

*I*n recent decades mental health experts have devoted considerable effort to developing a system for the classification and diagnosis of mental disorders. The system that is currently in use is called the Diagnostic and Statistical Manual of Mental Disorders, 4th ed. This comprehensive book, which provides a list and description of all mental disorders, has engendered considerable controversy, with some critics asserting that the system is seriously flawed and others contending that it contains biases, particularly about women.

- Is the *DSM-IV* a Useful Classification System?

- Is There Gender Bias in the *DSM-IV*?

ISSUE 1

Is the *DSM-IV* a Useful Classification System?

YES: Allen Frances, Michael B. First, and Harold Alan Pincus, from "DSM-IV: Its Value and Limitations," *Harvard Mental Health Letter* (June 1995)

NO: Herb Kutchins and Stuart A. Kirk, from "DSM-IV: Does Bigger and Newer Mean Better?" *Harvard Mental Health Letter* (May 1995)

ISSUE SUMMARY

YES: Psychiatrists Allen Frances, Michael B. First, and Harold Alan Pincus contend that although the *Diagnostic and Statistical Manual of Mental Disorders*, 4th ed. (*DSM-IV*) has certain limitations, it represents a vast improvement over previously used systems and incorporates the most up-to-date knowledge available.

NO: Professor of social work Herb Kutchins and professor of social welfare Stuart A. Kirk assert that the American Psychiatric Association's diagnostic system, particularly the current edition, *DSM-IV*, is so flawed that its utility should be seriously questioned.

When making a diagnosis, mental health professionals use standard terms and definitions, which are contained in the *Diagnostic and Statistical Manual of Mental Disorders (DSM)*. Since the publication of the first edition of this manual in 1952 by the American Psychiatric Association (APA), there have been several revisions: *DSM-II, DSM-III, DSM-III-R,* and *DSM-IV*. With each revision the authors of the *DSM* have tried to incorporate the most current knowledge about each mental disorder and have relied increasingly on empirical methods in their efforts to increase the reliability and validity of diagnostic labels.

For the first edition of the *DSM*, leading psychiatrists in the APA made the first systematic attempt to spell out diagnostic criteria for mental disorders. Although their efforts were well intentioned, mental health practitioners soon came to realize that these diagnostic criteria were vague and unreliable. The authors of the second edition, which was published in 1968, made an important change in the system when they based the system on the *International Classification of Diseases (ICD)*. Although the authors of the second edition made an effort to avoid theoretical bias, it soon became apparent that this system was actually based on psychoanalytic concepts. The publication of *DSM-III* in 1980 was heralded as a major improvement over its predecessors because this volume contained more precise rating criteria and better definitions for disorders. In 1987 the revision *DSM-III-R* was published as an interim manual until a more complete overhaul, *DSM-IV*, could be published in 1994.

Although the efforts of the APA to develop an efficient and reasonable diagnostic system might seem noncontroversial, each edition has provoked a storm of controversy and vehement debate. Certain issues have taken on the aura of political campaigns, with vocal activists lobbying on behalf of emotionally charged issues. For example, in 1980 the authors of *DSM-III* removed homosexuality from the list of psychological disorders, following 10 years of debate, with the realization that it was absurd to pathologize people on the basis of sexual orientation. In that same edition posttraumatic stress disorder was added in response to pressure from Vietnam veterans who urged mental health professionals to recognize the constellation of symptoms experienced by thousands of survivors of traumatic events, such as combat.

Allen Frances, Michael B. First, and Harold Alan Pincus are prominent psychiatrists who were centrally involved in the development of *DSM-IV*. In the following selection, they assert that the current version of the *DSM* consists of a clear and comprehensive summary of the most up-to-date knowledge available, which coincides with international classification systems for all medical disorders.

Herb Kutchins and Stuart A. Kirk are outspoken critics of the APA's diagnostic manuals. They view the *DSM* as a highly politicized money-making publication that is laden with problems of reliability and validity. In the second selection, Kutchins and Kirk assert that *DSM-IV* is complicated and imprecise and lacks a unified theoretical framework.

POINT

- *DSM-IV* provides a comprehensive summary of what is known about mental disorders, and it is simple and clear to use.
- Decisions about controversial diagnoses have been made by relying on open discussion and empirical data rather than mere opinion.
- *DSM-IV* relies on empirical data and represents an important advance from earlier editions.
- *DSM-IV* represents the most careful and comprehensive scientific analysis of diagnoses ever conducted.

COUNTERPOINT

- *DSM-IV* is an excessively complicated manual, it is too long, and it lacks important features needed to make the system user-friendly.
- Decisions about controversial diagnoses have been unduly influenced by political forces.
- *DSM-IV* lacks a consistent conceptual framework, with inadequate articulation of the underlying principles.
- Scientific standards pertaining to reliability and validity have been compromised in *DSM-IV*.

Allen Frances, Michael B. First, and Harold Alan Pincus

 YES

DSM-IV: Its Value and Limitations

Our years of work on *DSM-IV* [*Diagnostic and Statistical Manual of Mental Disorders,* 4th ed.] have made us acutely aware of its imperfections, and we want to discuss them here. But first we will respond to the criticisms of [Herb] Kutchins and [Stuart A.] Kirk, which are superficial and easily refuted. They complain, first, that *DSM-IV* is too long and complex. It is longer than *DSM-III-R* [a revised version of *DSM-III*], but that is because we have tried to provide a fuller summary of what is known about mental disorders. Psychiatric diagnosis is inherently complex. Our goal was not to make it simple but to make it clear, and we believe we have succeeded fairly well. The manual had to be long to serve its purpose; most readers use it as a reference and expect it to be detailed and authoritative. To meet their needs, we expanded the discussion of ways to distinguish a disorder from others that resemble it (differential diagnosis). We also added more information on variations associated with age, gender, and culture; on physical examinations and laboratory findings; and on common comorbid (accompanying) medical and psychiatric conditions.

Kutchins and Kirk say that *DSM-IV* lacks the support of a consistent conceptual framework or adequate scientific evidence. Here they offer two inconsistent complaints. While questioning the scientific credibility of *DSM-IV,* they long for the days when *DSM* was influenced by theoretical formulations that were not (and could not possibly be) based on empirical data. In fact, the field lacks a widely accepted overarching theory (or theories) confirmed by scientific data. But the preparation of *DSM-IV* benefitted from the impressive amount of data now available to inform diagnostic decisions.

The empirical review took place in three stages. In the first stage 150 work groups identified issues from the published literature on mental disorders, and each group laid out these issues for review by 50 to 100 experts. In the second stage 45 sets of data derived from earlier studies were reanalyzed to answer questions addressed inadequately in the published literature. In the final stage 12 focused field trials with new patients compared various ways of defining mental disorders for reliability and utility. All the issues and options under consideration were widely known to the research and

From Allen Frances, Michael B. First, and Harold Alan Pincus, "DSM-IV: Its Value and Limitations," *Harvard Mental Health Letter,* vol. 11, no. 12 (June 1995). Copyright © 1995 by The President and Fellows of Harvard College. Reprinted by permission of The Harvard Medical School Health Publications Group.

clinical communities. A *DSM-IV* options book was published in 1991 to stimulate further suggestions and data. As Kutchins and Kirk note, we succeeded in avoiding angry controversies—not, as they imply, by some political maneuver, but by relying on open discussion and empirical data rather than mere opinion.

Carefully Done

Kutchins and Kirk incorrectly state that the DSM task force "barely mentioned reliability." In fact, no more careful and comprehensive analysis of the reliability of psychiatric diagnoses has ever been conducted. In the focused field trials more than 6,000 patients were evaluated at 70 sites by several hundred raters. Kutchins and Kirk have apparently confused these field trials, completed several years ago during the preparation of *DSM-IV*, with a different reliability project that is now under way. This project was never intended to influence the making of *DSM-IV*. Its aim is to develop a videotape library of diagnostic interviews so that the reliability of *DSM-IV* diagnoses can be evaluated consistently at various times and places throughout the world, in clinical practice as well as research settings. The project will attempt to determine how reliability is influenced by the identity of the clinician, the nature of the material presented, and the diagnostic criteria themselves. . . .

Kutchins and Kirk are also inaccurate in their account of the relationship between *DSM-IV* and ICD, the international classification of general medical disorders. *DSM-IV* is fully compatible, not only with the ICD-9-CM system now used in the United States, but also with the ICD-10 revision that will eventually be implemented. Compatibility with ICD-10 was in fact one of the requirements we set for *DSM-IV*. The United States Government has now delayed the implementation of ICD-10 until well after the year 2000, mainly because it will be expensive to reprogram the medical records systems and analyze the impact of these changes on Medicare payments. Therefore we have worked hard to insure that all *DSM-IV* codes are valid under ICD-9-CM as well as ICD-10.

The genuine limitations of *DSM-IV* are less trivial than those inaccurately described by Kutchins and Kirk. We have discussed those limitations in great detail in earlier publications, in *DSM-IV* itself, and in the *DSM-IV Guidebook*. . . . We will summarize some of the most important points here.

First, the manual does not provide a definition that clearly distinguishes mental disorders from normality and that works in every clinical situation. The term "mental disorder," as opposed to "physical disorder," implies an anachronistic mind-body dualism, but we have persisted in using the term because we cannot find an adequate substitute. No definition adequately specifies the boundaries of this concept in all situations, but in that respect it resembles many other concepts in medicine and science. The definition of mental disorder given in *DSM-IV* is not intended to determine which disorders should be included in the manual or where the line should be drawn between a mental disorder and a life problem.

Limited Understanding

DSM-IV is also inherently limited by its status as a descriptive system. It is not based on a deep understanding of mental disorders because in most cases we lack that understanding. Some *DSM-IV* diagnoses, such as dementia of the Alzheimer's type, are well enough understood to be called established diseases. A few other diagnoses have a causal rather than a purely descriptive basis: those that involve the direct physiological effect of a substance or medical condition (such as alcohol intoxication) and those that involve a reaction to stress (such as posttraumatic stress disorder). Still other diagnoses, such as the simple phobias, are no more than single symptoms.

But most disorders defined in *DSM-IV* are syndromes—symptoms that commonly occur together and are grouped in order to facilitate research, education, and treatment. The purpose is to identify patterns that share such features as degree of impairment, course of illness, family history, biological markers, comorbid disorders, and response to treatment. The predictive power of these associations makes a syndromal classification useful. Descriptive definitions of syndromes do not necessarily represent independent disease entities; they reflect the state of medical understanding at the time they are drafted, and require regular revision as that understanding evolves. Our aim is to define mental disorders in ways that correspond ever more closely to the underlying causes of pathology and targets of treatment. *DSM-IV* is an imperfect but indispensable tool for that purpose.

Another limitation of *DSM-IV* is inherent in the fact that, like all systems of medical diagnosis, it makes use of categories based on sets of criteria with defining features. This categorical approach to classification works best when all members of a class are nearly alike, the boundaries between classes are clear, and the different classes are mutually exclusive. But such categories necessarily impose artificial boundaries on a natural continuum, and some experts would prefer a dimensional model instead. Dimensional systems make use of features that can be measured quantitatively and work well in describing phenomena that are distributed continuously, without clear boundaries. This approach improves the reliability of diagnosis, and it preserves some information that is lost when everything must be classified in one category or another. But so far dimensional systems have not taken root in medicine, partly because dimensional descriptions are less vivid and familiar than categorical ones, and partly because there is no agreement on which dimensions to use. Dimensional approaches may become more widely accepted as we learn more about them.

Providing Guidance

DSM-IV should not be used as a book of recipes or taken as literally as some fundamentalists take the Bible. It is true that excessively flexible and idiosyncratic application of *DSM-IV* categories would reduce its usefulness as a common language for communication among professionals. But its classifications, criteria, and descriptions are meant to be used as guidelines, not applied mechanically. *DSM-IV* should be employed only by professionals with appropriate training and experience who are guided by clinical judgment. For example, a certain diagnosis may be justified even if not all the required symptoms are present, as long as the symptoms that are present are persistent and severe. Clinical judgment partially compensates for the lack of clear boundaries separating mental disorders from one another and from normality. It is often needed in deciding whether the patient's impairment or distress is sufficient to constitute a mental disorder, and to determine which *DSM-IV* category comes closest to describing the symptoms. Although the use of clinical judgment necessarily limits the reliability of diagnoses, there is no adequate alternative.

DSM-IV will often recommend multiple diagnoses for a single patient. Since the publication of *DSM-III* in 1980 new categories have repeatedly been introduced, old ones have been divided up, and criteria that exclude diagnoses have been removed. Thus many patients now meet the criteria for more than one mental disorder. This development is not objectionable as long as it is clearly understood that the diagnoses are tools for communication and research, not necessarily descriptions of independent disease entities or pathological processes. When a patient meets criteria for more than one diagnosis, they may be related in any of the following ways:

1. Condition A causes or predisposes to condition B;
2. Condition B causes or predisposes to condition A;
3. An underlying condition C causes or predisposes to both condition A and condition B;
4. Conditions A and B are part of a more complex unified syndrome that is yet to be defined;
5. Conditions A and B seem to occur together often because their definitions overlap;
6. Condition A and condition B often occur together by chance, because both are common.

The flaws in *DSM-IV* reflect the limitations of our present scientific knowledge about mental health and illness. The manual will eventually be superseded as new knowledge is acquired through the powerful tools of neuroscience and clinical research. *DSM-IV* may appear somewhat quaint and primitive once we understand more deeply the nature and causes of psychiatric disorders, but it will have fulfilled its intended function by facilitating the growth of that understanding.

DSM-IV: Does Bigger and Newer Mean Better?

The *Diagnostic and Statistical Manual of Mental Disorders,* Fourth Edition (*DSM-IV*) is the 1994 revision of a dull, complex, technical compendium of psychiatric conditions compiled by the American Psychiatric Association (APA). It contains no major discoveries or innovations, no basically new approach to mental illness. In fact, the APA has made every effort to avoid controversial departures from current psychiatric practice. Yet the publication of this manual was a major news event reported on the front page of *The New York Times*. To understand what is happening, we must look at the historical context.

Consistent, credible diagnosis has always been a problem in the field of mental health, and the APA published the first edition of *DSM* in 1952 in order to standardize psychiatric nomenclature. In 1968 it published a revision of the manual, *DSM-II,* that was designed to conform with the system used in the International Classification of Diseases (ICD). This was necessary because of an international agreement to use ICD as the official reporting system for all illnesses.

Everyone was dissatisfied with *DSM-II*. Few clinicians used it to plan treatment, and many researchers doubted its scientific value. In fact, the basic credibility of psychiatric diagnosis was under attack. In one study of state hospital patients, schizophrenia was found to have been substantially overreported. When outside experts evaluated the patients, many were rediagnosed as suffering from mood disorders. In another experiment a psychologist arranged to have sane people committed to a mental hospital by faking a single symptom. Once hospitalized, they dropped even that pretense without being unmasked by staff members (although other patients recognized the deception).

The APA soon had to confront a series of critics who complained that diagnostic decisions in *DSM* were influenced by political considerations. Gay activists objected to listing homosexuality as a mental illness, and in 1973 the APA decided to drop it from *DSM-II*. The decision was challenged and ultimately confirmed by a referendum of the membership in 1974. Meanwhile, Vietnam veterans were demonstrating for the adoption of the diagnosis of

From Herb Kutchins and Stuart A. Kirk, "DSM-IV: Does Bigger and Newer Mean Better?" *Harvard Mental Health Letter*, vol. 11, no. 11 (May 1995). Copyright © 1995 by The President and Fellows of Harvard College. Reprinted by permission of The Harvard Medical School Health Publications Group.

posttraumatic stress disorder so that they could qualify for psychiatric benefits. They finally succeeded with the publication of *DSM-III*. The irony was
that in the very act of remedying two genuine grievances, the APA confirmed the charges of political influence on the formulation of diagnoses.

Getting Specific

In order to improve the scientific and professional value of the manual, a
task force began work on a revision in the mid-'70s. When the new edition,
DSM-III, was published in 1980 it contained a number of important new features. A major innovation was the introduction of specific criteria for each
diagnosis instead of brief, vague descriptions. Another innovation was a
multiaxial system consisting of five dimensions. Diagnosticians were asked
to record clinical conditions (Axis I), personality and developmental disorders (Axis II), medical conditions (Axis III), the severity of psychosocial
stressors (Axis IV), and the patient's highest level of adaptive functioning
(Axis V). The editors of *DSM-III* also made an effort to confirm the reliability
of psychiatric diagnoses. If a classification system is to be useful for clinical or
research purposes, different clinicians must be able to agree on the diagnosis
of a given patient. The *DSM-III* task force claimed that most of its diagnoses
were highly reliable, although the evidence for this claim is questionable.

The new edition was heralded as a revolution in mental health practice
and a "paradigm shift" in psychiatric thinking. Despite its size, complexity,
and high price, it was an astonishing success—partly because insurance companies and government agencies that had become major sources of financing
for mental health services demanded use of its diagnostic system.

Only three years after the publication of *DSM-III*, the APA initiated
what was at first described as a minor revision that would rectify mistakes
and incorporate new research findings. When the revision was published
as *DSM-III-R* in 1987, it retained the basic design of *DSM-III*, but there
were changes in more than half of the diagnoses, and no studies of the
overall reliability of the new manual. The rush to revise the text aborted
efforts of independent investigators to evaluate the usefulness of *DSM-III*
in clinical practice, since research on the older version was now moot and
an evaluation of *DSM-III-R* would be premature.

Meanwhile a new series of embarrassing public confrontations occurred, this time with feminists who objected to the inclusion of three new
diagnoses: self-defeating personality disorder, paraphiliac rapism (later
replaced by sadistic personality disorder), and what is now called premenstrual dysphoric disorder (PDD). Although the developers of the manual
insisted that the new diagnoses had a scientific basis, they placed them in
an appendix labeled "Needing Further Study." (Two of the diagnoses have
been dropped from *DSM-IV* because of insufficient scientific evidence; PDD
is still reserved for further study.)

After the publication of *DSM-III-R*, the APA almost immediately started
work on the present edition, and Allen Frances, who was appointed to
oversee the revision process, announced that the publication of *DSM-III-R*

had been a mistake. The APA says that the newest edition, *DSM-IV,* is easier to use than older ones, but the claim is difficult to justify. *DSM-IV* is a volume of more than 900 pages, 50% longer than *DSM-III-R,* yet it adds only 13 new diagnoses and eliminates eight old ones. It no longer includes the index of symptoms that allowed users of *DSM-III-R* to move quickly from clinical observations to diagnoses. An appendix comparing *DSM-IV* to *DSM-III-R* is far less clear and precise than similar appendices in previous revisions. An appendix reviewing the mental disorders listed in the International Classification of Diseases has been dropped; this will make it more difficult to translate diagnoses between the two systems.

Confusing the Issue

The instructions for use of *DSM-IV* are often excessively complicated. For example, the chapter on substance-related disorders has been lengthened from 62 to 98 pages, and these disorders are also included in other parts of the manual. The change necessitates a time-consuming hunt for the appropriate diagnosis, and it may heighten disagreement among clinicians, thereby reducing reliability. A similar problem exists with respect to mental disorders that result from general medical conditions. These were previously called "organic," but the editors of the manual did not want to imply that other psychiatric disorders lacked an organic basis. They dropped the term "organic" and dispersed many of the medically-related conditions to various parts of the manual. This reorganization only complicates the task of locating these disorders; it does not resolve the underlying conceptual issue.

Its developers regard the new manual as more "user-friendly" mainly because they have simplified the operational criteria (the long lists of symptoms used to identify each disorder), and the use of the multiaxial system is no longer required. Certain criteria have been eliminated and instructions for applying the criteria have sometimes been simplified, although many other procedures have been made more complicated. But *DSM-IV* has also relaxed the rules to allow greater individual discretion. Users are told that they may employ clinical judgment to make a diagnosis even when the criteria have not been fully satisfied. Sacrificing precision in this way may seem convenient to some clinicians, but in the long run it could lead to lower reliability and sloppier practice. It would be a mistake to return to the days when there were no clear standards for psychiatric diagnoses. Although the manual should not be used mechanically, winking at the diagnostic criteria and ignoring the multiaxial system are not good alternatives.

Making Changes

The developers of *DSM-IV* acknowledged that many diagnoses in older versions lacked adequate scientific support, and they announced that extensive research would go into the revision. They now argue that the new manual has a more solid scientific basis than any previous one. Certainly more researchers and investigations have been involved; the names of more than 1,000 contributors occupy 26 pages of the manual. But all that activity does not necessarily guarantee scientific credibility. One fundamental deficiency of the manual is the lack of a consistent conceptual framework. *DSM-I* was strongly influenced by Freudian theories, and it described psychiatric disorders as reactions—schizophrenic reactions, affective reactions, psychoneurotic reactions, and so on. Although the scheme was not entirely consistent, it was at least related to a set of theoretical assumptions.

In later editions *DSM* has moved increasingly away from psychoanalytical thinking. The terms "reaction" and later, "neurosis" have been dropped, and the medical aspects of diagnosis have been increasingly emphasized. *DSM-IV* continues this trend, but underlying principles are not adequately articulated, and the resulting hodgepodge lacks a consistent rationale. Three hundred diagnoses, a larger number than ever before, are divided into 16 categories. Some of these categories are based on the presumed cause of the disorder, some on shared symptoms, and some on the patient's age. There is no consistent rationale for placing a disorder in one category rather than another.

Standards of reliability also continue to be a problem. Although reliability was the main scientific concern in developing *DSM-III*, the DSM-IV Task Force barely mentioned it when their work began. The APA belatedly proposed reliability trials for only 10 diagnoses. This research, which is now in progress, has been criticized because it is inadequate to test the overall reliability of the manual in everyday practice. Even if it does produce useful data, it obviously cannot affect *DSM-IV.* The approach appears to be one suggested in *Alice in Wonderland*—"sentence first, verdict afterward."

Another basic concern is the standard for evaluating the validity of diagnoses. The APA announced that new diagnoses had to meet more rigorous scientific tests for inclusion in *DSM-IV*. But most of the diagnoses have been carried over from earlier editions, and the APA admits that many of them do not meet the new standards. As a result, we cannot be sure which diagnoses have a solid scientific basis.

Because of the disruption that revisions of *DSM* cause in research and practice, and because of all the unsettled questions about the new revision, many professionals complained that the release of *DSM-IV* was premature. In response to critics who said that *DSM-IV* was rushed to publication, the APA repeatedly claimed that it had to publish a new edition to conform to the 1992 revision of the International Classification of Diseases, ICD-10. But ICD-10 has not yet been adopted by the United States. The latest estimate is that this will not happen until 2003. *DSM-IV,* like *DSM-III-R,* is keyed to ICD-9-CM. ICD-10 uses a very different coding system, and an appendix to *DSM-IV* covers some of the ICD-10 codes. When ICD-10 is recognized in this country, users will have to consult the main body of *DSM-IV* for a diagnosis before turning to that appendix. Even this cumbersome, confusing procedure does not entirely solve the problem. There are hundreds of directions that involve the use of ICD-9-CM throughout

DSM-IV, and instructions about ICD-10 are incomplete and inadequate. Thus the manual will be obsolete when ICD-10 is adopted. Clinicians might have to abandon *DSM-IV* entirely and rely on ICD-10—unless the APA decides to publish another revision of *DSM.*

The APA manuals, so far, are a great success story, but we might consider the lesson of another such story, the triumph of the American automobile. After World War II Detroit seemed to have found the secret of unlimited sales by making each model bigger and more streamlined, with more accessories than the previous one. But the bigger cars were more expensive and harder to operate; they broke down more easily, consumed more energy and created more pollution. When American automakers ignored these problems, consumers stopped buying their cars.

DSM-IV is not only bigger than ever but has its own set of accessories— a "library" that includes a casebook, five projected volumes of research reports, several volumes describing clinical interviewing techniques, a study guide, a glossary, a computerized version of the manual, and more. We doubt that the road to continued success for psychiatry is a series of manuals, each in a new color coordinated with accessories, each bigger than the last, and each with built-in obsolescence that insures demand for the next model. Unless the APA confronts the issues discussed here, *DSM* may be cruising toward the same junkyard as the great fishtailed, portholed, chrome-grilled dinosaurs that were once regarded as the pinnacle of American ingenuity.

CHALLENGE QUESTIONS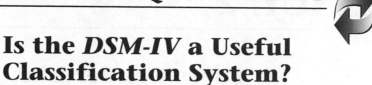

Is the *DSM-IV* a Useful Classification System?

1. To what extent should the authors of the next edition of the *DSM* be concerned with vehemently expressed opinions about particular diagnostic labels?
2. What role does a diagnostic system such as that in *DSM-IV* play in the stigmatization of mental illness?
3. Compare the description of a particular diagnosis (e.g., schizophrenia) in an earlier *DSM* with the *DSM-IV* diagnostic criteria for that disorder. How would you characterize the changes that have been made in terms of clarity and usefulness?
4. To what extent does the linking between mental disorders and the *International Classification of Diseases* "medicalize" emotional problems?
5. What issues would you urge the American Psychiatric Association to consider as work is begun on *DSM-V*?

Suggested Readings

Barron, J. W. (Ed.) (1998). *Making diagnosis meaningful: Enhancing evaluation and treatment of psychological disorders.* Washington, DC: American Psychological Association.

Kutchins, H., & Kirk, S. A. (1997). *Making us crazy. DSM: The psychiatric bible and the creation of mental disorders.* New York, NY: The Free Press.

Sarbin, T. R. (1997). On the futility of psychiatric diagnostic manuals (DSMs) and the return of personal agency. *Applied & Preventative Psychology, 6,* 233–243.

Thakkar, J., & Ward, T. (1998). Culture and classification: The cross-cultural application of the DSM-IV. *Clinical Psychology Review, 18*(5), 501–529.

Tucker, G. J. (1998). Putting DSM-IV in perspective. *American Journal of Psychiatry, 155*(2), 159–161.

ISSUE 2

Is There Gender Bias in the *DSM-IV*?

YES: Terry A. Kupers, from "The Politics of Psychiatry: Gender and Sexual Preference in DSM-IV," in Mary Roth Walsh, ed., *Women, Men, and Gender: Ongoing Debates* (Yale University Press, 1997)

NO: Ruth Ross, Allen Frances, and Thomas A. Widiger, from "Gender Issues in DSM-IV," in Mary Roth Walsh, ed., *Women, Men, and Gender: Ongoing Debates* (Yale University Press, 1997)

ISSUE SUMMARY

YES: Forensic psychiatric consultant Terry A. Kupers asserts that several phenomena pertaining to gender and sexuality are pathologized in the diagnostic system of the *Diagnostic and Statistical Manual of Mental Disorders,* 4th ed. (*DSM-IV*).

NO: Ruth Ross, Allen Frances, and Thomas A. Widiger, coeditors of the American Psychiatric Association's *DSM-IV Sourcebook,* disagree with the notion of bias associated with gender and sexuality.

During the last few decades of the twentieth century, Americans became acutely aware of ways in which discrimination and bias pertaining to gender and sexuality have influenced culture. Much has been written about the ways in which societal disadvantages experienced by women have been emotionally costly. Some contend that it should come as no surprise that women are more likely than men to be diagnosed with mental disorders and are also more likely to seek professional help for their psychological problems. However, the issues of psychiatric diagnosis and help-seeking behavior are multifaceted, and sometimes they involve subtle bias.

Researchers and clinicians have been particularly interested in understanding the reasons why women are more likely than men to be assigned particular diagnoses, such as mood and personality disorders. Some experts have questioned whether or not there is a gender bias that results in feminine personality characteristics being perceived as pathological. Take the case of dependent personality disorder, a diagnosis with characteristics involving an excessive need to be taken care of, which leads to submissive, clinging behaviors and feelings of insecurity. Some theorists contend that women have been socialized to yield control to men and to develop a style of dependency. At some other point along the continuum of dependency, such behavior can be labeled as pathological, and the dependent individual is assigned the diagnosis of a personality disorder.

Terry A. Kupers argues in the following selection that the field of psychiatry has been influenced in overt and covert ways such that various political causes have been advanced, with the result being that society's concept of mental health, as well as categories of mental disorder, have been socially constructed. In other words, people in positions of power (in the case of psychiatry, mostly men) determine what constitutes mental disorder among those over whom they have power. For example, Kupers notes that just when middle-class women are entering the workplace in record numbers, increasing attention is being given to the emotionally charged label "premenstrual syndrome." According to Kupers, those in power can pathologize just about any characteristic noted among those who are not in power. Thus, excessive emotionality in women can be characterized as pathological, and so can excessive assertiveness.

In the second selection, Ruth Ross, Allen Frances, and Thomas A. Widiger acknowledge that a number of psychiatric disorders have markedly different rates of occurrence in women and men, but they are uncertain about whether these differences are actual or attributable to various biases. They note that a disorder such as dependent personality disorder involves stereotypical feminine traits, which could be mislabeled as personality disorder in a biased system, but they assert that the diagnosis actually involves maladaptive variants of these stereotypic feminine traits. Ross and her colleagues argue that the *DSM-IV* development process was characterized by serious attempts to base decisions on a fair and balanced interpretation of the available data pertaining to gender issues in diagnosis.

POINT

- The *DSM-IV* categories of mental disorder are socially constructed by people in power who determine what constitutes mental disorder in those over whom they have power.

- *DSM-IV* pathologizes normal phenomena found in women (e.g., menstrual cycles) while ignoring male characteristics that could just as easily be pathologized.

- The authors of *DSM-IV* yielded to pressures from feminist psychiatrists and psychologists who argued that certain diagnoses stigmatized and blamed victims of domestic abuse.

- Gender differences in the diagnosis of many conditions are well established and reflect diagnostic biases.

COUNTERPOINT

- The *DSM-IV* development process involved serious attempts to base decisions on fair and balanced interpretations of available data on gender-related issues in diagnosis.

- *DSM-IV* cautions against the imposition of gender-biased assumptions, especially when diagnosing personality disorders.

- The authors of *DSM-IV* relied on a thorough empirical study of controversial diagnoses (e.g., self-defeating personality disorder) before making a determination to drop these labels.

- There is no reason to believe that the appearance of given disorders should be spread equally between genders.

Terry A. Kupers  **YES**

The Politics of Psychiatry: Gender and Sexual Preference in DSM-IV

The fourth edition of the *Diagnostic and Statistical Manual of Mental Disorders* (DSM-IV), published by the American Psychiatric Association (APA) in 1994, contains the official list of diagnostic categories. It is touted as an improvement over previous editions, more precise in its descriptions of mental disorders, more rigorous in its criteria for establishing diagnoses. There is some effort to take gender and sexual orientation into consideration, as well as race and ethnicity. And there are claims of greater objectivity on account of the improvements, the detail, and the attention to cultural contexts. But is the new edition really an improvement, or merely a more rigorous rationalization for pathologizing nonmainstream behaviors and attitudes? And how successful have the authors been in transcending past gender biases? A meaningful discussion of these questions requires reading between the lines as well as attending to the social and historical context.

A Longer, More Detailed List of Diagnostic Categories

The first thing to note about the DSM-IV is its size, 886 pages. DSM-I (APA, 1952) contained 130 pages; DSM-II (APA, 1968) contained 134 pages; DSM-III (APA, 1980) contained 481 pages. (A revised DSM-III, DSM-III-R, was published in 1987, but I will leave it out of this summary for simplicity's sake.) In each edition there are new disorders, new groupings of disorders, some deletions, and various revisions in the way well-established disorders are viewed.

For instance, with the publication of the third edition in 1980, Panic Disorder, Post-traumatic Stress Disorder, Social Phobia, and Agoraphobia were added. The last two diagnoses had been lumped under the category Phobias in DSM-II; in DSM-III they, along with Panic Disorder and PTSD, became subtypes of the group of Anxiety Disorders. And with the publication of DSM-III some names were changed, for instance Manic-Depressive

From Terry A. Kupers, "The Politics of Psychiatry: Gender and Sexual Preference in DSM-IV," in Mary Roth Walsh, ed., *Women, Men, and Gender: Ongoing Debates* (Yale University Press, 1997), pp. 340–347. Originally published in *masculinities*, vol. 3, no. 2 (1995). Copyright © 1995 by *masculinities*. Reprinted by permission.

Disorder (DSM-II) became Bipolar Disorder (DSM-III); and some categories were dropped, notably homosexuality.

Again, in DSM-IV, there are new categories (Substance-Induced Anxiety Disorder, Sibling Relational Problem, Physical and Sexual Abuse of Adult); there are name changes (Multiple Personality Disorder becomes Dissociative Identity Disorder); there are new groupings (Gender Identity Disorders subsumes what used to be three groupings: Gender Identity Disorder of Childhood, of Adolescence, and of Adulthood); and there are deletions (Passive-aggressive Personality Disorder, Transsexualism). Relatively few new categories were added to DSM-IV, the emphasis being on more detail in the descriptions, presumably to increase inter-rater reliability. And the fourth edition makes the diagnostic categories relatively less exclusive so that one does not need to be as careful to rule out one category in order to pin down the diagnosis of another. Consequently a given individual is more likely to be assigned two or more "comorbid" diagnoses, for instance Obsessive Compulsive Disorder with Depression or with Alcohol Dependence.

Two Explanations for a Longer, More Detailed DSM

Why has the DSM grown thicker, the list of disorders longer? There are two basic explanations, one built upon a positivist notion of scientific progress, the other on the notion that our concepts of mental health and mental disorder are socially and historically constructed.

According to the positivist model, which underlies the stance of orthodox psychiatry and rationalizes its current turn toward biologism (for a critique see Cohen, 1993), advancing technology, and newer research findings permit us to discover mental disorders which always existed, but went undetected until now because our understanding of the brain and mental functioning was not as sophisticated as it is today. Joel Kovel (1980) says it well: "Psychiatry's self-image (is) of a medical profession whose growth is a matter of increasing mastery over a phenomenon, mental illness, which is supposed to be always present, a part of nature passively awaiting the controlling hand of science" (p. 72). The emphasis in DSM-IV on extensive reviews of clinical and research literatures and the conduct of field trials with revised diagnostic categories reflect this assumption. The goal is to see how much consistency can be achieved among diagnosticians.

Then there is the rush to develop "Treatment Guidelines," keyed to DSM-IV categories. For instance, the APA recently released its "Practice Guidelines for the Treatment of Patients with Bipolar Disorder" (APA, 1994b). Treatment guidelines provide medical centers and third-party payers with a rationale for allowing some benefits and disallowing others. Thus scientific truth is defined in terms of consensus among certain clinicians, mainly psychiatrists who have clout in the APA, about the proper diagnosis and treatment of each disorder.

Confident that their opinions about the existence of mental disorders constitute a science that is advancing rapidly and unfalteringly, psychiatrists and their collaborators are not very likely to uncover the biases and social interests that determine the path of their scientific endeavors, for instance the fact that a significant part of their research is funded by pharmaceutical companies that would like very much to see them identify mental disorders for which the treatment of choice is a pharmaceutical agent.

The social/historical model holds that "the disorder and the remedy are both parts of the same social process, and that they form a unity subject to the total history of the society in which they take place" (Kovel, 1980, p. 72). Our concept of mental health as well as our categories of mental disorder are socially constructed, and people in power determine what constitutes mental disorder among those they have power over (Conrad, 1980; Foucault, 1965). Jean Baker Miller (1976), building on [G. W. F.] Hegel's Master/Slave dialectic, points out that in the interest of continuing domination, the dominant group is the model for "normal human relationships" while the subordinate group is viewed as inferior in one way or another (Blacks are intellectually inferior, women are "ruled by emotion"). Thomas and Sillen (1974) point out that slaves who ran away from their owners' plantations in the antebellum South received the diagnosis "drapetomania," literally, "flight-from-home madness" (p. 2).

Elizabeth Packard's husband declared in 1860 that her disagreement with his religious views was evidence of insanity; and because the laws of Illinois as well as the male asylum psychiatrist were on his side, he was able to have her locked in an asylum (Chesler, 1972). Hughes (1990) uncovers some of the gender biases in the testimony of families who had a member admitted to an asylum in late nineteenth-century Alabama. To skip to the present, is it merely coincidental that just when middle-class women are entering the workplace in record numbers, premenstrual syndrome is declared a form of mental disorder?

Social theory provides two related answers to the question of why the DSM grows longer and more detailed in successive editions. First, the growth of the mental health industry depends on the expansion of the list of diagnostic categories. The number of psychiatrists, psychologists, and psychotherapists has grown considerably in recent years, as has the variety of psychotropic medications. As clinicians examine and treat a larger proportion of the citizenry, more diagnoses are needed to justify the whole endeavor. I will return to this point in the section on childhood disorders.

Second, our consciousness and everyday lives have become increasingly regimented and administered over the past century, and as a result the average citizen is permitted fewer eccentricities before deviance is declared. The Industrial Revolution required a disciplined workforce capable of sufficient delayed gratification to endure long hours at hard labor for less than fair wages. Those who could not work had to be marginalized as criminals, beggars, or lunatics. This was the period when great leaps were made in the description of such psychotic conditions as dementia praecox, later to be renamed schizophrenia. Since the explosive growth of consumerism in the 1920s, newer, milder diagnoses are needed for those who are capable of working, who buy into the promise of ad campaigns that the purchase of one commodity after another will lead to happiness, and yet are unable to attain the kind of happiness portrayed in advertisements and films. The successful but still unhappy people must be neurotic; perhaps they need psychoanalysis, psychotherapy, a tranquilizer, or an antidepressant.

While the positivist model directs our attention toward the gathering of ever more empirical data analyses, the social/historical model permits us to understand the way social interests determine our views on psychopathology as well as our views on what constitutes scientific progress.

About Homosexuality

The debate about homosexuality in the late 1960s and early 1970s included mass demonstrations at annual meetings of the APA. The straight male leadership was forced to back down, voting in 1973 to delete the category of homosexuality from the official list of mental disorders. The change was reflected in the next edition, DSM-III, in 1980.

But the stigmatization did not end there. The official list of mental disorders is merely the tip of the iceberg when it comes to pathologizing. Psychoanalysts and psychotherapists pathologize constantly, deciding, for instance, when to intervene in the patient's story and make an interpretation. There is the decision to interpret something and not to interpret something else, and the clinician's views about normalcy and pathology determine her or his choices. In the 1920s, analysts repeatedly interpreted penis envy in women (for a summary of psychoanalytic views on gender, see Connell, 1994). Why did they not choose instead to interpret the pathology in men's defensive need to exclude women from the halls of power? In the 1960s, analysts interpreted the radical activism of young adults as a sign of psychopathology. Why did they not interpret the inactivism of others (including themselves) in the face of great social upheavals (Kupers, 1993b)?

I do not believe there is anything inherently wrong with pathologizing certain human characteristics. Sedgwick (1982) argues convincingly that the attempt by libertarians and radical therapists in the sixties to get rid of the entire concept of mental illness was misguided at best. The question is which human traits shall be pathologized. Throughout the history of the mental health professions, why has homosexuality consistently been the target for pathologizing while homophobia has never appeared among the list of mental disorders? The unstated biases reflected in these choices do not disappear just because one category of mental disorder is deleted.

Still, in the struggle to transcend homophobia, it is a positive development when homosexuality is removed from the list of mental disorders. In its place, in DSM-III (1980), a new category was added, Ego-Dystonic Homosexuality, designed for gays and lesbians who would prefer to be straight but were having trouble converting their desires. Since this category became, in practice, a substitute for the category of homosexuality, its deletion in DSM-IV is another positive step—likely motivated by the presence of more women and gays on the task force and work groups that developed DSM-IV. The APA even calls for all professional organizations and individuals "to do all that is possible to decrease the stigma related to homosexuality" (APA, 1993, p. 686).

But the pathologization of homosexuality remains. Consider this statement, made two years after the APA decided to stop diagnosing homosexuality, by Otto Kernberg (1975), a prominent psychoanalyst:

> We may classify male homosexuality along a continuum that differentiates the degree of severity of pathology of internalized object relations. First, there are cases of homosexuality with a predominance of genital, oedipal factors, in which the homosexual relation reflects a sexual submission to the parent of the same sex as a defense against oedipal rivalry. . . . In a second and more severe type, the male homosexual has a conflictual identification with an image of his mother and treats his homosexual objects as a representation of his own infantile self. . . . In a third type of homosexual relation, the homosexual partner is "loved" as an extension of the patient's own pathological grandiose self. . . . This, the most severe type of homosexual involvement, is characteristic of homosexuality in the context of narcissistic personality structure proper, and constitutes the prognostically most severe type of homosexuality. (pp. 328–29)

I am not aware of any disclaimer of this formulation by Kernberg, who is listed as an adviser to the authors of DSM-IV. Even though the diagnosis of homosexuality is no longer officially sanctioned, a clinician, following Kernberg and other prominent experts, might assign a gay man the DSM-IV diagnoses Gender Identity Disorder, Sexually Attracted to Males (APA, 1994a, p. 534) with Narcissistic Personality; or Transvestic Fetishism (p. 530) with Narcissistic Personality Disorder; and other clinicians would get the point. There is also continuing debate about whether the goal in treating homosexuals should be conversion to heterosexuality (Socarides, Kaufman, Gottlieb, & Isay, 1994). In other words, long after the category is removed from the official list and the APA advocates destigmatization, prominent clinicians continue to pathologize homosexuality while showing no interest in creating a category for homophobia.

Women's Disorders

Women have evolved a strong voice within establishment psychiatry. The list of contributors to DSM-II (1968) contains the names of thirty-seven men and three women, whereas the equivalent list for DSM-IV (1994a) contains the names of twenty-six men and eleven women. (It is not as easy to determine how many gays and lesbians were involved.) As a result, there were rancorous debates about the pathologization of women's experiences and characteristics prior to the publication of DSM-IV. Two proposed diagnostic categories were at issue: "Self-defeating Personality" (for women who find themselves repeatedly victimized by abusive men) and "Late Luteal Phase Dysphoric Disorder" (the luteal phase of the menstrual cycle begins at ovulation and ends at menses, and this diagnosis is synonymous with PMS). Feminist psychiatrists and psychologists argued that the former diagnosis stigmatized and blamed the victims of domestic abuse (Caplan, 1987). They prevailed: Self-defeating Personality was not included in DSM-IV. Meanwhile the categories Sexual Abuse of Adult (APA, 1994a, p. 682) and Physical Abuse of Adult (p. 682) were added to the official list, permitting the clinician to diagnose pathology in the perpetrator.

In regard to Late Luteal Phase Dysphoric Disorder, the question was why pathologize the woman's natural cycles? Why not pathologize instead men's need to avoid all signs of emotion and dependency while maintaining an obsessively steady pace (Spitzer et al., 1989)? I coined the term "pathological arrhythmicity" for this disorder in men (Kupers, 1993a). The debate about PMS was not as intense as the one about Self-defeating Personality. Some women clinicians claimed that a category for PMS might serve to increase sensitivity among male colleagues to the experiences of women. The debate ended in compromise: Premenstrual Dysphoric Disorder is included in an appendix of DSM-IV designated ". . . For Further Study."

But remember, the official manual is merely the tip of the iceberg when it comes to pathologizing. Penis envy was never an official diagnostic category, yet it was frequently diagnosed. Phyllis Chesler (1972) explains how the diagnosis of Hysteria in women has served to maintain their subordination: "Both psychotherapy and marriage enable women to express and defuse their anger by experiencing it as a form of emotional illness, by translating it into hysterical symptoms: frigidity, chronic depression, phobias, and the like" (p. 122). Hysteria is a rare diagnosis today, and women are more likely diagnosed Borderline Character Disorder, Multiple Personality Disorder (there is intense debate about the existence of this disorder, connected with the debate about "recovered memories" of childhood molestation), or Somatization Disorder. Judith Herman (1992) points out that among women assigned these modern diagnostic substitutes for hysteria are a significant number who were molested as girls, but these diagnoses divert attention away from the early traumas and focus the clinician's attention instead on the woman's personal flaws. She proposes that instead of diagnosing Borderline Character Disorder and Somatization Disorder in so many women today, we consider the diagnosis "Complex Post-traumatic Stress Disorder," the residual condition resulting from repeated childhood sexual and physical abuse. Thus far Complex PTSD has not made its way into the DSM.

Another relevant critique of the way women's characteristics are selectively pathologized comes from the staff of the Stone Center at Wellesley College (Jordan, Kaplan, Miller, Stiver, & Surrey, 1991). They believe that this culture's overvaluation of autonomy and independence leaves something to be desired in terms of community and the capacity to be intimate, and that a very male notion of independence and autonomy is at the core of traditional clinical descriptions of psychopathology. Women are pathologized because of their emphasis on connection and interdependence. They call for a redrawing of the line between psychopathology and mental health so that women's need for connection and community will be viewed as an admirable trait rather than a symptom.

The APA has not heeded this group's call. The category Dependent Personality Disorder remains in DSM-IV and is assigned disproportionately to women, while no equivalent category has been devised to describe the male dread of intimacy and dependency. The description of Dependent Personality Disorder contains the very bias that clinicians from the Stone Center are concerned about. Consider this sentence: "Individuals with this disorder have difficulty initiating projects or doing things independently" (APA, 1994a, p. 666). Often there is a choice between two contrasting ways to handle problems at work: one way being for the individual to come up with a totally independent solution and get credit for doing so at promotion time; another being for several coworkers to brainstorm, work together to figure out a solution collectively, and share the credit. It is as if official psychiatry has decided that individual action is preferred and the search for collaborative solutions (more usual for women workers in today's corporate culture) is pathological. Thus, in spite of improvements in DSM-IV regarding gender bias, many problems remain.

What About the Men?

I have already mentioned several diagnoses that might be included in a DSM but are not: homophobia, "pathological arrhythmicity," and the dread of dependency. There are other male behaviors we might wish to pathologize: dependence on pornography, workaholism, friendlessness, the need for sexual conquests, the tendency to react to aging by deserting one's same-age female partner and taking up with someone the age of one's children, and so forth.

There is a brief and very telling statement about the gender distribution of each mental disorder in DSM-IV. Disorders diagnosed more frequently in males include Conduct Disorder in boys and adolescents, Obsessive-Compulsive Personality Disorder (distinct from Obsessive-Compulsive Disorder, or OCD, which is distributed equally between the sexes), Narcissistic Personality Disorder, Paraphilias, Antisocial Personality Disorder, Intermittent Explosive Disorder, and Pathological Gambling. A comparable list of conditions diagnosed more often in women includes Histrionic Personality Disorder, some forms of Depression, Eating Disorders, Dissociative Identity Disorder, Kleptomania, Panic Disorder, Somatization Disorder, Agoraphobia, and Borderline Personality Disorder.

Could there be a clearer reflection of gender stereotypes? But why are the same qualities that compose the stereotypes—the unfeeling, action-oriented, sexually aggressive, misbehaving male; and the emotional, dependent, weight-conscious, frightened, and sickly woman—so much the basis for pathologizing each gender? Perhaps the diagnostic categories serve to create an upper limit for the very characteristics that are socially encouraged in each gender. Boys are encouraged to be active, rough, aggressive, sexually adventurous, steady, and rational. But when boys become too aggressive they are assigned the diagnosis Conduct Disorder or Intermittent Explosive Disorder, when men become too steady and rational they are diagnosed Obsessive-Compulsive Personality Disorder, when men break the rules too badly in the sexual realm they are considered Paraphiliacs, and so forth. It is a little like the college and pro football teams that encourage players to be hyperaggressive and then have to discipline some of them when they draw negative publicity by raping women after a game. The mental disorders typically assigned to men, like the fines assigned for the overly aggressive football players, serve to keep the lid on the very behaviors that are being encouraged. Similarly, women are encouraged from early childhood to be emotional and connected with others, but if they are too emotional they are diagnosed Histrionic Personality Disorder, and if they are too connected they are diagnosed Dependent Personality Disorder. There is little if any support for creating new, improved forms of masculinity and femininity in DSM-IV.

Childhood Disorders and the Shaping of Gender

The main thing to notice about the section of DSM-IV on childhood and adolescent disorders is that the list of disorders is growing. In DSM-II (1968) there were two subsections containing a total of seven disorders, whereas in DSM-IV (1994a) there are ten subsections and thirty-two disorders. Most of the enlargement occurred between DSM-II and DSM-III, the authors of DSM-IV beingn more interested in providing detailed descriptions for established disorders than in adding new ones to the official list. Still, the number of children who see mental health professionals and undergo psychotherapy or receive psychotropic medications is growing, and children are being taken to see professionals at younger ages.

Consider three childhood disorders from the list in DSM-IV: Attention Deficit/Hyperactivity Disorder (ADHD), Oppositional Defiant Disorder, and Gender Identity Disorder. What if Oscar Wilde had been given one or more of these diagnoses when he was six or eight years old? What if Ritalin had been prescribed to limit his energy level or he had been given Prozac to control his nonconformist notions about gender and sexuality? What if there had been a way at that time to predict which children might become gay or antisocial (research of this kind is proliferating today), and preventive treatment had been instituted? Would Wilde's vision have been the same, would he have created great literature? This is not to say that Wilde was mentally disordered, or that mental disorder is a prerequisite for works of genius. Rather I am selecting Wilde to illustrate the point that earlier diagnosis and treatment of mental disorders in children runs the risk of stigmatizing unusual men and women, creating less tolerance for experimentation in the realm of gender roles, and thereby limiting the historical possibilities for transforming gender relations.

Of course, in some children, for instance those who compulsively pull out their hair or those who cannot sit still long enough to finish a classroom assignment, professional intervention can have positive effects. I am not arguing that any particular child should be denied examination and treatment. But when children in unprecedented numbers are taken to see professionals, there are social ramifications. One is that approaches to social problems are reduced to the search for psychopathology in individual children. For instance, consider the difficulty teachers have maintaining order in classrooms containing ever-larger numbers of students as budgets for public instruction decline. The teacher cannot reduce the size of the class, but he or she can tell the parents of problematic children that their kids suffer from ADHD and need to be taking Ritalin. In general, it is when we despair about the prospects for social transformation—e.g., making public education a higher social priority—that we tend to reduce social problems to the pathology of individuals. Breggin and Breggin (1994) outline the dangers of this development, though they tend to polarize the discussion by minimizing the positive contributions of child psychiatry and psychotherapy.

Of course, there is money to be made from the quest for earlier detection of mental disorders in children. An even more alarming implication is that society has embarked on the early correction of all deviations from the "straight" path of development. As our lives as workers and consumers become more routinized, and as the gap between the rich and the poor grows wider, concerned parents begin to wonder if their children are going to be among the winners or the losers. This motivates them to watch for early signs of mental disorder and hurry their children off to a mental health professional at the first sign of hyperactivity, school failure, impulsive behavior, or gender impropriety.

There are class and race differences. Diagnosing children in the inner city with Conduct Disorder and Oppositional Defiant Disorder does not usually lead to quality treatment (the public mental health service system is shrinking rapidly); but the diagnoses do serve to rationalize the fact that low-income, inner city children are less likely than their middle-class cohorts to find fulfilling work and are more likely to wind up behind bars. People actually begin to believe it is the psychopathology of poor people, not social inequity, that causes unemployment and criminality. As we pathologize more "off-beat" qualities, we are inadvertently tightening the bounds around what is considered "normal" behavior for boys and girls. Nothing is said about this social inequity in DSM-IV, and this silence is quite worrisome.

Conclusion

The DSM-IV is definitely an improvement over previous editions. There is more participation by women in the work groups. Homosexuality has been deleted from the list of disorders, as has DSM-III's Ego-Dystonic

Homosexuality; the proposal to add Self-defeating Personality has been defeated; and there are sections on racial and ethnic differences (that do not go far enough toward correcting racial bias in the diagnostic process . . .). Meanwhile, the DSM grows longer, the descriptions of mental disorders become more codified, and psychiatry has little or nothing to say about the social ramifications of its pathologizing.

Traditional psychiatry looks backward, diagnosing mental illness in those who do not fit yesterday's prescribed social roles. Emotionality as well as assertiveness in women, rebellion on the part of minority members, and homosexuality have all been pathologized. As previously stigmatized groups gain power within the mental health professions, diagnoses are modified. DSM-IV reflects admirable progress in terms of the inclusion of diverse groups and the concerted effort to minimize gender bias and homophobia wherever it can be identified. Still, the fourth edition of DSM continues to pathologize deviation from yesterday's gender roles.

Instead of a longer, more detailed list of mental disorders, we need a system of psychopathology that is informed by a vision of a better society. We could begin by envisioning that society, one in which gender equality reigns and there is no homophobia or any other form of domination. Then, by extrapolating backward from that vision, we could pathologize the qualities that would make a person dysfunctional in that more equitable and just social order. Racism, misogyny, and homophobia would head the list of psychopathologies. This kind of pathologizing might even serve to bring about the vision. Unfortunately, far from solving the problems of gender bias and homophobia, the improvements in DSM-IV will serve largely to appease potential dissenters as the mental health professions evolve an ever more conformist manual of psychopathology.

References

American Psychiatric Association. (1952). *Diagnostic and statistical manual of mental disorders*. Washington, D.C.: Author.

American Psychiatric Association. (1968). *Diagnostic and statistical manual of mental disorders* (2nd ed.). Washington, D.C.: Author.

American Psychiatric Association. (1980). *Diagnostic and statistical manual of mental disorders* (3rd ed.). Washington, D.C.: Author.

American Psychiatric Association. (1993). Position statement on homosexuality. *American Journal of Psychiatry, 150,* 686.

American Psychiatric Association. (1994a). *Diagnostic and statistical manual of mental disorders* (4th ed.). Washington, D.C.: Author.

American Psychiatric Association. (1994b). Practice guideline for the treatment of patients with bipolar disorder. *American Journal of Psychiatry, 151,* Supplement, 1–36.

Breggin, P. R., & Breggin, G. R. (1994). *The war against children.* New York: St. Martin's Press.

Caplan, P. J. (1987). The psychiatric association's failure to meet its own standards: The dangers of self-defeating personality disorder as a category. *Journal of Personality Disorders, 1,* 178–182.

Chesler, P. (1972). *Women and madness.* New York: Avon.

Cohen, C. (1993). The biomedicalization of psychiatry: A critical overview. *Community Mental Health Journal, 29,* 509–522.

Connell, R. W. (1994). Psychoanalysis on masculinity. In H. Brod & M. Kaufman (Eds.), *Theorizing masculinities* (pp. 11–38). Thousand Oaks, Calif.: Sage.

Conrad, P. (1980). On the medicalization of deviance and social control. In D. Ingleby (Ed.), *Critical psychiatry* (pp. 102–119). New York: Pantheon.

Foucault, M. (1965). *Madness and civilization.* New York: Pantheon.

Herman, J. (1992). *Trauma and recovery: The aftermath of violence—From domestic abuse to political terror.* New York: Basic Books.

Hughes, J. S. (1990). The madness of separate spheres: Insanity and masculinity in Victorian Alabama. In M. C. Carnes & C. Griffen (Eds.), *Meanings of manhood: Constructions of masculinity in Victorian America* (pp. 67–78). Chicago: University of Chicago Press.

Jordan, J., Kaplan, A., Miller, J. B., Stiver, I. P., and Surrey, J. L. (1991). *Women's growth in connection: Writings from the Stone Center.* New York: Guilford Press.

Kernberg, O. F. (1975). *Borderline conditions and pathological narcissism.* New York: Jason Aronson.

Kovel, J. (1980). The American mental health industry. In D. Ingleby (Ed.), *Critical psychiatry* (pp. 72–101). New York: Pantheon.

Kupers, T. A. (1993a). *Revisioning men's lives: Gender, intimacy and power.* New York: Guilford.

Kupers, T. A. (1993b). Psychotherapy, neutrality and the role of activism. *Community Mental Health Journal, 29,* 523–534.

Miller, J. B. (1976). *Toward a new psychology of women.* Boston: Beacon Press.

Sedgwick, P. (1982). *Psychopolitics: Laing, Foucault, Goffman, Szasz and the future of mass psychiatry.* New York: Harper & Row.

Socarides, C. W., Kaufman, B., Gottlieb, F., & Isay, R. (1994). Letters about reparative therapy. *American Journal of Psychiatry, 151,* 157–59.

Spitzer, R. L., Severino, S. K., Williams, J. B., & Parry, B. L. (1989). Late luteal phase dysphoric disorder and DSM-III-R. *American Journal of Psychiatry, 146,* 892–897.

Thomas, A., & Sillen, S. (1974). *Racism and psychiatry.* Secaucus, N.J.: Citadel.

NO

Ruth Ross, Allen Frances, and Thomas A. Widiger

Gender Issues in DSM-IV

How to Understand Differences in Gender Prevalences

A number of psychiatric disorders have markedly different rates of occurrence in women and men. It is not clear whether these differences are inherent to actual differences in psychopathology between women and men or are the artifactual result of biases in ascertainment, definition, or assessment (Brown 1986; Davidson and Abramovitz 1980; Deaux 1985; Earls 1987; Hamilton et al. 1986; Kaplan 1983; Lewine et al. 1984; Loring and Powell 1988; Russell 1985; Sherman 1980; Smith 1980; Snyder et al. 1985; Widiger and Nietzel 1984; Widiger and Settle 1987; Widiger and Spitzer 1991; Widom 1984; Zeldow 1984). Gender differences in treatment seeking or referral patterns may explain the different gender ratios that occur in community samples as opposed to more selected clinical samples. For example, there is a higher ratio of women with major depressive disorder in clinical than in epidemiological samples, perhaps because women are more likely to recognize and admit to depression. In contrast, there is a higher ratio of men with schizophrenia in clinical than in epidemiological samples, perhaps because men with schizophrenia are more disruptive and likely to require treatment intervention. However, there also appear to be data supporting the view that a higher rate of major depression in women is a real and not artifactual finding. Biases in definition may also play a role in gender differences in prevalence. There may also be gender differences in prevalence because of biases in the evaluator that may lead to misinterpretation of the diagnostic criteria. It is likely that there are also real differences in prevalence, at least for certain disorders (e.g., conduct disorder, antisocial personality disorder) that reflect real differences between women and men.

Gender and the Personality Disorder Criteria

Another extremely controversial issue has been the question of a possible gender bias within the DSM-III-R criteria sets, particularly for the diagnoses of histrionic personality disorder and dependent personality

From WOMEN, MEN AND GENDER: Ongoing Debates, edited by Mary Roth Walsh, pp. 348–357. Copyright © 1997 by Yale University Press. Reprinted by permission.

disorder (Hirschfeld et al. 1991, 1996; Pfohl 1996). Both of these personality disorders are diagnosed much more frequently in women than in men. Histrionic personality disorder and dependent personality disorder appear to involve, at least in part, stereotypic feminine traits (Kaplan 1983; Sprock et al. 1990; Walker 1994) that could be mislabeled as personality disorder in a gender-biased system. In contrast, others have argued that histrionic personality disorder and dependent personality disorder are diagnosed more frequently in women than in men not because of definition or assessment bias but precisely because these personality disorders involve maladaptive variants of stereotypic feminine traits, just as antisocial personality disorder and obsessive-compulsive personality disorder involve maladaptive variants of stereotypic masculine traits and are diagnosed more frequently in men (Widiger and Spitzer 1991; Widiger et al. 1994b; Williams and Spitzer 1983). There is no reason to assume that each personality disorder will occur with an equal frequency across genders. To the extent that some personality traits are more prevalent or predominant within one gender (e.g., Eagly and Crowley 1986; Eagly and Steffen 1986), one might expect personality disorders that represent maladaptive or excessive variants of these traits to be more prevalent within that gender. However, concerns about a possible gender bias are also understandable. The DSM-III/DSM-III-R personality disorder criteria were constructed, for the most part, by males with little input from systematic empirical research. It would not be surprising to find that male clinicians would have a lower threshold for the attribution of maladaptive feminine traits than for the attribution of maladaptive masculine traits.

It is also important to ensure that empirically derived criteria sets do not impel or exaggerate gender differences through research that is confined largely to one gender. This risk is perhaps easiest to demonstrate in the case of antisocial personality disorder. As a matter of convenience, studies on antisocial personality disorder have often been confined to males; as a result, the diagnostic criteria that performed best within these studies are criteria that work best for males with this disorder. For example, it is possible that the DSM-III-R criteria for antisocial personality disorder, with such behaviors as forcing someone into a sexual activity before age fifteen or beating one's spouse after the age of fifteen, were biased toward the manner in which males expressed antisocial personality traits. More males than females may indeed have antisocial personality disorder, but to the extent that the diagnostic criteria were based on research confined to male subjects, the criteria set may result in the underdiagnosis of females with this disorder. Moreover, there is evidence that antisocial personality traits in females may be misdiagnosed as histrionic (Ford and Widiger 1989; Hamilton et al. 1986).

The DSM-IV Personality Disorders Work Group addressed this problem in a variety of ways. The DSM-IV field trials on antisocial personality disorder were analyzed separately for males and for females to assess whether any proposed revisions would be detrimental to the diagnosis of antisocial personality disorder in females. In addition, individual criteria were revised to be more gender neutral. For example, the DSM-III-R histrionic personality disorder item "is inappropriately sexually seductive in appearance or behavior" (American Psychiatric Association 1987, p. 349) was revised to "interaction with others is often characterized by inappropriate sexually seductive or provocative behavior" (American Psychiatric Association 1994, p. 657). This item was revised to emphasize seductive or provocative behavior rather than just appearance, because normal sexual attractiveness can be readily confused with sexual seductiveness and because females may be more likely to be perceived as sexually seductive in appearance given the social pressure concerning physical attractiveness in females. Provocative or seductive behavior is perhaps less prone to gender-biased attributions than seductive appearance. Likewise, the criteria set for conduct disorder was revised in part to include antisocial behaviors that tend to occur in females (e.g., staying out at night despite parental prohibitions before age thirteen).

Gender variations in the expression of personality disorders are also discussed in the "Specific Culture, Age, and Gender Features" sections of the texts for these disorders. For example, in the discussion of histrionic personality disorder, it is noted that

> the behavioral expression of histrionic personality disorder may be influenced by sex role stereotypes. For example, a man with this disorder may dress and behave in a manner often identified as "macho" and may seek to be the center of attention by bragging about athletic skills, whereas a woman, for example, may choose very feminine clothes and talk about how much she impressed her dance instructor. (American Psychiatric Association 1994, p. 656)

The text discussions also caution against the imposition of gender-biased assumptions when making personality disorder diagnoses—for example, noting that "there has been some concern that antisocial personality disorder may be underdiagnosed in females, particularly because of the emphasis on aggressive items in the definition of conduct disorder" (American Psychiatric Association 1994, p. 647) or cautioning in the text for dependent personality disorder that "societies may differentially foster and discourage dependent behavior in males and females" (American Psychiatric Association 1994, p. 667).

To the extent that there are clearly established gender variations in the expression of a personality disorder (or any disorder), the authors of the future DSM-V may eventually consider developing separate criteria sets for each gender. This is already done for gender identity disorder, in which such differences are inherent in the disorder itself. However, there is currently insufficient research to support such an approach in DSM-IV.

Self-Defeating Personality Disorder

The inclusion of the self-defeating personality disorder (originally called masochistic personality disorder) in the appendix to DSM-III-R generated substantial controversy (Caplan 1987, 1991; Rosewater 1987; Walker 1987,

1994). In considering whether to continue to include self-defeating personality disorder in the DSM-IV appendix, the conceptual and empirical foundation for this proposed disorder was thoroughly studied by the DSM-IV Personality Disorders Work Group and by the Task Force on DSM-IV. As a culmination of its review process, the Personality Disorders Work Group recommended that self-defeating personality disorder not be included in the main body or the appendix of DM-IV (Widiger, in press).

The literature review for self-defeating personality disorder (Fiester, 1996) indicated that this newly proposed diagnosis has received very little research attention and that there have been only a few investigations of real patients (the few available studies have focused more on surveys or the diagnosis of illustrative written case examples). The work group was also concerned about the inherent difficulty of accurately diagnosing self-defeating personality disorder in the presence of a harsh environmental context or when other psychiatric disorders are present. The clinical studies suggested that self-defeating personality disorder would overlap a great deal with the eleven other personality disorders that are included in DSM-III-R. This is a serious problem because most clinicians and researchers believe that we are already burdened by the inclusion of too many personality disorders in DSM-III-R, creating a system that is cumbersome to use in clinical and research practice and usually results in multiple diagnoses.

However useful the concept of masochism remains in the practice of psychotherapy, the work group discussions revealed that there are structural problems that prevent the simple translation of the psychodynamic construct of masochism to the psychiatric diagnosis of personality disorder. The criteria set of self-defeating personality disorder was an attempt to provide a descriptive operationalization of the psychodynamic construct that unconscious forces may lead to a masochistic pattern of interpersonal relationships and behaviors. The analytic literature has attributed this masochistic pattern to a variety of unconscious motivations, including self-punishment consequent to superego pathology; an external reenactment of introjected early sadomasochistic relationships; self-directed aggression as a defense against sadism; and pathological narcissism. In the psychotherapy situation, the evaluation of these unconscious motivations usually requires a careful and prolonged assessment of the patient's transferential attitudes and behaviors in the treatment relationship. This judgment depends on a good deal of psychodynamic expertise and inference and usually can be confirmed only by the patient's masochistic treatment behavior, not just by the evaluation of problems presented in the diagnostic interview. The self-defeating personality disorder criteria represented an attempt to draft a set of behavioral and interpersonal criteria that would capture the surface manifestations of the presumed unconscious motivation for masochistic behavior. This turned out to be an inherently impossible task. One cannot convert this particular psychodynamic construct inferring unconscious masochistic motivation into a behavioral (and less inferential) criteria set that is not confounded by the individual's interactions with the environment. This effort failed because it cannot be done, not just because of any deficiencies in the specific self-defeating personality disorder criteria that were selected. It was not simply a matter of studying and improving the existing criteria set. The basic issue is that much "self-defeating" behavior occurs for reasons other than the specific "masochistic" unconscious motivations that are meant to be at the heart of the self-defeating personality disorder concept. It is usually impossible within the context of a general psychiatric evaluation to determine whether the individual's pattern of self-defeating behavior is an expression of unconscious motivation that would play out over and over again regardless of the environment in which the individual exists or whether the "self-defeating" pattern of behavior is an understandable and perhaps adaptive result of the need to survive in a harsh and punishing environment.

In addition many mental disorders are characterized by behaviors and symptoms that are "self-defeating" in their effect but not "masochistic" in their unconscious motivations. This is particularly true for chronic depression but is also true for many other psychiatric disorders. The concept of self-defeating personality disorder is inherently confounded with self-defeating aspects that are secondary consequences of other mental disorders. There were also no studies to document that the diagnosis described a behavior pattern that was not already adequately represented by an existing Axis I or Axis II diagnosis. Although self-defeating behaviors are encountered commonly enough in clinical practice, it is not clear that the self-defeating personality disorder diagnosis is specific in capturing the central or predominant pathology in most of these cases.

Another major concern that was factored into the consideration of the proposed self-defeating personality disorder diagnosis was that the diagnosis might be used to blame victims of (spouse) abuse for their own victimization (Fiester 1991; Widiger, 1995; Widiger and Frances 1989). The proposed criteria set did provide an exclusion criterion such that the items would not be considered present if they occurred exclusively in response to or in anticipation of being physically, sexually, or psychologically abused. However, many of the instruments that were developed to assess self-defeating personality disorder failed to consider this exclusion criterion, and many victims are reluctant to acknowledge the presence of actual abuse. The research on self-defeating personality disorder often failed to consider the occurrence and influence of victimization on the diagnosis (e.g., Spitzer et al. 1989), and the research on victimization has failed to assess adequately for the role and influence of self-defeating personality traits (e.g., Walker 1984).

Although there undoubtedly are individuals with self-defeating personality patterns, the utility and validity of the construct as a psychiatric diagnosis has not yet been established, and the Personality Disorders Work Group concluded that its provision within an appendix to DSM-IV would provide the diagnosis with a credibility or recognition that it did not yet warrant. A diagnosis that has the potential for misuse should be held to an especially high standard of validation before it is given any official credibility. Nevertheless, the concept of self-defeating unconscious motivations is sometimes useful in understanding or treating individuals encountered in clinical practice.

Sadistic Personality Disorder

Sadistic personality disorder was included in the appendix to DSM-III-R based almost completely on anecdotal case reports. In considering whether to continue to include this proposed diagnosis in the DSM-IV appendix, the Personality Disorders Work Group undertook a literature review on sadistic personality disorder (Fiester and Gay 1991). The group found that little research on sadistic personality disorder had been done and that the only published studies were by the original proponents of the disorder (i.e., Fiester and Gay 1991; Gay, in press; Spitzer et al. 1991). Based on the lack of systematic research supporting this diagnosis and the potential for misuse, the Personality Disorders Work Group recommended that it not be included in the appendix to DSM-IV (Widiger 1995).

Premenstrual Dysphoric Disorder

As mentioned earlier, the inclusion of late luteal phase dysphoric disorder, as it was then called, in the appendix to DSM-III-R produced one of the more heated controversies surrounding the publication of DSM-III-R (Chait 1986; Eckholm 1985; Hamilton and Gallant 1988; Holtzman 1988; Reid 1987). Proponents maintained that late luteal phase dysphoric disorder is a clinically significant condition that is supported by research and clinical literature and that its omission might lead to underdiagnosis, misdiagnosis, failure to give appropriate treatment, and stigmatization by blaming individual women with the problem for their symptoms. Opponents referred to the paucity of clinical and research literature and warned that inclusion might encourage inappropriate diagnosis and treatment and also had the potential to stigmatize women in general. There were concerns about whether there were sufficient data to generate a valid and reliable criteria set for this proposed disorder. Questions were also raised as to whether it was best conceptualized as a mental disorder (rather than an endocrinological or gynecological one) and whether a disorder related to male hormones should be included.

A Late Luteal Phase Work Group was formed and given responsibility for making a recommendation, based on empirical data, as to whether late luteal phase dysphoric disorder should continue to appear in the appendix of DSM-IV, should be included in the main body of the manual, should be included in the section for "Other Clinically Significant Conditions That May Be a Focus of Clinical Attention," or should be left out altogether (American Psychiatric Association 1991). To make a recommendation on this issue, the work group conducted an exhaustive literature review that included clinical and research studies on both premenstrual syndrome and late luteal phase dysphoric disorder. Because late luteal phase dysphoric disorder first appeared in the nomenclature in 1987, published studies using the proposed late luteal phase dysphoric disorder criteria from DSM-III-R were limited, but these increased in number during the period of the review from 1988 to 1992 (Gold et al., in press). The purpose of this literature review was to try to determine "if there is a clinically significant mental disorder associated with the menstrual cycle that can be separated from other mental disorders" (Gold, in press). More than five hundred articles on premenstrual syndrome and late luteal phase dysphoric disorder were reviewed, and information on prevalence, association with preexisting mental disorders, course of illness and prognosis, familial factors, biological and treatment studies, and social, forensic, and occupational issues were examined. The group identified a number of methodological problems in the literature: variable or unclearly specified definitions of premenstrual syndrome, small sample sizes, lack of control groups, prospective daily ratings not used, possibly biased sample selection, failure to delineate timing and duration of symptoms, and failure to collect adequate hormonal samples. Despite these problems, the work group determined that, based on the literature review, a relatively circumscribed group of women (perhaps 3%–5%) suffer from severe and clinically significant dysphoria related to the premenstrual period.

The work group also carried out a reanalysis of previously collected data from more than six hundred subjects from five sites (Hurt et al. 1992; Severino et al., in press). The results of this reanalysis supported the clinical usefulness of the criteria set for late luteal phase dysphoric disorder but suggested some changes in emphasis to reflect that the disturbance is most closely related to mood disorder and to emphasize the dysphoric nature of the symptoms. The revised proposed criteria require severe impairment and minimize physical symptoms.

The literature review and data reanalysis were widely circulated for comments and critique among thirty-six advisers who were selected to represent a range of different perspectives, including individuals who had done research on the disorder and others who were very concerned about its possible misuse. The group attempted to formulate criteria that would be optimal for research purposes and could also be easily and consistently applied by clinicians. They focused on where the disorder should be placed in the classification and what it should be called (Gold, in press). They concluded that the name *late luteal phase dysphoric disorder* was cumbersome and somewhat misleading (because the symptoms may not be related to the endocrinological changes of the late luteal phase) and proposed the name *premenstrual dysphoric disorder* (Gold, in press).

. . . The final decision of the Task Force on DSM-IV was to continue to include the disorder, renamed *premenstrual dysphoric disorder,* in the appendix to the manual, and not to make it part of the official nomenclature. It was decided to refer to premenstrual dysphoric disorder as an example of a depressive disorder not otherwise specified for purposes of differential diagnosis, rather than as an example of a mental disorder not otherwise specified, based on the fact that the data seem to support a strong mood component in the disorder. The appendix in which the criteria set for premenstrual dysphoric disorder is included is titled "Criteria Sets and Axes Provided for Further Study." The introduction to the appendix states that "the task force determined that there was insufficient information to warrant inclusion of these proposals as official categories or axes in DSM-IV"

(American Psychiatric Association 1994, p. 703). It is noted that "the items, thresholds, and durations contained in the research criteria sets are intended to provide a common language for researchers and clinicians who are interested in studying these disorders. It is hoped that such research will help to determine the possible utility of these proposed categories and will result in refinement of the criteria sets" (American Psychiatric Association 1994, p. 703).

The decision to include premenstrual dysphoric disorder in the appendix to DSM-IV received widespread media attention (e.g., Alvardo 1993; Seligman and Gelman 1993; Spam 1993). In some cases, these accounts were fair and balanced accounts of the issues involved (Spam 1993). Unfortunately, many articles reported inaccurate information and contributed to the controversy by fostering the impression that the developers of DSM-IV were attempting to pathologize a large part of the female population. They often stated that premenstrual dysphoric disorder would be included in the main body of the manual as an official diagnosis or claimed that the much more common premenstrual syndrome would be considered a mental disorder in the DSM-IV diagnostic system.

However, the "Differential Diagnosis" section of the text that accompanies the proposed research criteria for premenstrual dysphoric disorder in the DSM-IV appendix states that

> the transient mood changes that many females experience around the time of their period should not be considered a mental disorder. Premenstrual dysphoric disorder should be considered only when the symptoms markedly interfere with work or school or with usual social activities and relationships with others (e.g., avoidance of social activities, decreased productivity and efficiency at work or school). Premenstrual dysphoric disorder can be distinguished from the far more common "premenstrual syndrome" by using prospective daily ratings and the strict criteria listed below. It differs from the "premenstrual syndrome" in its characteristic pattern of symptoms, their severity, and the resulting impairment. (American Psychiatric Association 1994, p. 716)

Although there is a lack of a consistent definition of premenstrual syndrome, the proposed research criteria set for premenstrual dysphoric disorder is an attempt to define a severe dysphoric disorder that causes clinically significant impairment and is not to be confused with the milder premenstrual syndrome. The text for premenstrual dysphoric disorder notes,

> it is estimated that at least 75% of women report minor or isolated premenstrual changes. Limited studies suggest an occurrence of "premenstrual syndrome" (variably defined) of 20%–50%, and that 3%–5% of women experience symptoms that may meet the criteria for this proposed disorder (American Psychiatric Association 1994, p. 716).

It was, in part, because of the tentative nature of the criteria that it was decided to continue to place premenstrual dysphoric disorder in the appendix so that further studies in larger populations could investigate the validity and reliability of the items selected and the ability of the criteria to discriminate these symptoms from milder premenstrual syndrome.

The proposed DSM-IV criteria set for premenstrual dysphoric disorder requires that five or more of the following symptoms (with at least one being one of the first four) be present most of the time during the last week of the luteal phase in most menstrual cycles during the past year (American Psychiatric Association 1994, p. 717):

> 1) feeling sad, hopeless, or self-deprecating; 2) feeling tense, anxious or "on edge"; 3) marked lability of mood interspersed with frequent tearfulness; 4) persistent irritability, anger, and increased interpersonal conflicts; 5) decreased interest in usual activities, which may be associated with withdrawal from social relationships; 6) difficulty concentrating; 7) feeling fatigued, lethargic, or lacking in energy; 8) marked changes in appetite, which may be associated with binge eating or craving certain foods; 9) hypersomnia or insomnia; 10) a subjective feeling of being overwhelmed or out of control; and 11) physical symptoms such as breast tenderness or swelling, headaches, or sensations of "bloating" or weight gain, with tightness of fit of clothing, shoes, or rings. There may also be joint or muscle pain. The symptoms may be accompanied by suicidal thoughts. (American Psychiatric Association 1994, p. 715)

The symptoms must begin to remit within a few days after the onset of the follicular phase and be absent in the week postmenses. The disturbance must markedly interfere with work or school or usual social activities and relationships with others and must not be merely an exacerbation of the symptoms of another mental disorder. The symptoms described in the criteria set must be confirmed by prospective daily ratings during at least two consecutive symptomatic cycles. The criteria set describes a pattern of symptoms that is far more severe and impairing than what is usually called premenstrual syndrome, despite the variations in definitions of premenstrual syndrome. DSM-IV states that the symptoms of premenstrual dysphoric disorder are "typically . . . of comparable severity (but not duration) to those of a major depressive episode" (American Psychiatric Association 1994, p. 715). . . .

Conclusion

For most of the diagnoses in DSM-IV, the emphasis on documentation and empirical data as the foundation for change resulted in remarkably little controversy. However, the gender issues related to diagnosis that have historically been subject to controversy continued to be the subject of disagreement during the development of DSM-IV. In part, this may have resulted from the fact that systematic research efforts on gender differences have begun only recently. However, the larger social questions these issues touch on made it more difficult to settle them on empirical grounds alone or even to reach a shared interpretation of the data that are available. Ultimately it is for others to judge, but we believe that the DSM-IV development process was characterized by serious attempts to base decisions on a fair and balanced interpretation of the available data on gender-related issues in diagnosis. It is hoped that the new section "Culture, Age, and Gender Features" that is included in the texts for many disorders will be helpful in alerting clinicians to gender-related differences in presentation and to possible gender-related pitfalls in making diagnoses. However, perhaps the most important gender-related accomplishment of DSM-IV has been to stimulate and encourage debate on issues related to gender and diagnosis. It is hoped that when possible problems related to gender are noted in the text for specific disorders, this will stimulate studies on those disorders that will inform the next revision of DSM and lead to more accurate diagnostic information.

The major questions concerning the relationship between gender and psychiatric diagnosis remain largely unanswered. It is not at all clear whether and to what extent marked differences in gender prevalence of certain diagnoses reflect true gender differences or are artifacts of ascertainment, definition, or assessment. For those gender differences that do stand up to improved methodological rigor in diagnosis, the next step will be to identify the mechanisms involved in these differences in psychopathology.

References

Alvardo, D. Furor over new diagnosis for PMS. San Jose Mercury News, May 22, 1993, p. 1A.

American Psychiatric Association. DSM-IV Options Book: Work in Progress (9/1/91). Washington, D.C., American Psychiatric Association, 1991.

American Psychiatric Association. Diagnostic and Statistical Manual of Mental Disorders, 3rd Edition, Revised. Washington, D.C., American Psychiatric Association, 1987.

American Psychiatric Association. Diagnostic and Statistical Manual of Mental Disorders, 4th Edition. Washington, D.C., American Psychiatric Association, 1994.

Brown, L. S. Gender-role analysis: A neglected component of psychological assessment. Psychotherapy 23:243–248, 1986.

Caplan, P. The psychiatric association's failure to meet its own standards: The dangers of self-defeating personality disorder as a category. Journal of Personality Disorders 1:178–182, 1987.

Caplan, P. J. How do they decide who is normal? The bizarre, but true, tale of the DSM process. Canadian Psychology 32:162–170, 1991.

Chait, L. R. Premenstrual syndrome and our sisters in crime: A feminist dilemma. Women's Rights Law Reporter 9:267–293, 1986.

Davidson, C. V., Abramovitz, S. I. Sex bias in clinical judgment: Later empirical returns. Psychology of Women Quarterly 4:377–395, 1980.

Deaux, K. Sex and gender. Ann. Rev. Psychol. 36:49–81, 1985.

Eagly, A. H., Crowley, M. Gender and helping behavior: A meta-analytic review of the social psychology literature. Psychol. Bull. 100:283–308, 1986.

Eagly, A. H., Steffen, V. J. Gender and aggressive behavior: A meta-analytic review of the social psychological literature. Psychol. Bull. 100:309–330, 1986.

Earls, F. Sex differences in psychiatric disorders: Origins and developmental influences. Psychiatric Developments 1:1–23, 1987.

Eckholm, E. Premenstrual problems seem to beset baboons. The New York Times, June 4, 1985, p. C2.

Fiester, S. J. Self-defeating personality disorder: A review of data and recommendations for DSM-IV. Journal of Personality Disorders 5:194–209, 1991.

Fiester, S. J. Self-defeating personality disorder, in DSM-IV Sourcebook, Vol 2. Edited by Widiger, T. A., Frances, A. J., Pincus, H. A., et al. Washington, D.C., American Psychiatric Association, 1996.

Fiester, S. J., Gay, M. Sadistic personality disorder: A review of data and recommendations for DSM-IV. Journal of Personality Disorders 5:376–385, 1991.

Fiester, S. J., Gay, M. Sadistic personality disorder, in DSM-IV Sourcebook, Vol 2. Edited by Widiger, T. A., Frances, A. J., Pincus, H. A., et al. Washington, D.C., American Psychiatric Association, 1996.

Ford, M., Widiger, T. Sex bias in the diagnosis of histrionic and antisocial personality disorders. J. Consult. Clin. Psychol. 57:301–305, 1989.

Gallant, S. J. A., Hamilton, J. A. On a premenstrual psychiatric diagnosis: What's in a name? Professional Psychology: Research and Practice 19:271–278, 1988.

Gay, M. Sadistic personality disorder in a child abusing population. Child Abuse Negl. (in press).

Gold, J. H. Late luteal phase dysphoric disorder and the DSM-IV, in DSM-IV Sourcebook, Vol. 4. Edited by Widiger, T. A., Frances, A. J., Pincus, H. A., et al. Washington, D.C., American Psychiatric Association (1996).

Gold, J. H., Endicott, J., Parry, B. L., et al. Late luteal phase dysphoric disorder, in DSM-IV Sourcebook, Vol 2. Edited by Widiger, T. A., Frances, A. J., Pincus, H. A., et al. Washington, D.C., American Psychiatric Association (in press).

Hamilton, S., Rothbart, M., Dawes, R. M. Sex bias, diagnosis, and DSM-III. Sex Roles 15:269–274, 1986.

Hirschfeld, R. M. A., Shea, M. T., Weise, R. Dependent personality disorder: Perspectives for DSM-IV. Journal of Personality Disorders 5:135–149, 1991.

Hirschfeld, R. M. A., Shea, M. T., Talbot, K. M. Dependent personality disorder, in DSM-IV Sourcebook, Vol 2. Edited by Widiger, T. A., Frances, A. J., Pincus, H. A., et al. Washington, D.C., American Psychiatric Association, 1996.

Holtzman, E. Premenstrual syndrome as a legal defense, in The Premenstrual Syndromes. Edited by Gise, L. H., Kose, N. G., Berkowitz, R. L. New York, Churchill Livingstone, 1988, pp. 137–143.

Hurt, S. W., Schnurr, P. P., Severino, S. K., et al. Late luteal phase dysphoric disorder in 670 women evaluated for premenstrual complaints. Am. J. Psychiatry 149:525–530, 1992.

Kaplan, M. A woman's view of DSM-III. Am. Psychol. 38:786–792, 1983.

Lewine, R., Burbach, D., Meltzer, H. Y. Effect of diagnostic criteria on the ratio of male to female schizophrenic patients. Am. J. Psychiatry 141:84–87, 1984.

Loring, M., Powell, B. Gender, race, and DSM-III: A study of the objectivity of psychiatric diagnostic behavior. J. Health Soc. Behav. 29:1–22, 1988.

Pfohl, B. Histrionic personality disorder, in DSM-IV Sourcebook, Vol 2. Edited by Widiger, T. A., Frances, A. J., Pincus, H. A., et al. Washington, D.C., American Psychiatric Association, 1996.

Reid, R. L. Premenstrual syndrome. AACC ENDO 5:1–12, 1987.

Rosewater, L. B. A critical analysis of the proposed self-defeating personality disorder. Journal of Personality Disorders 1:190–195, 1987.

Russell, D. Psychiatric diagnosis and the oppression of women. Int. J. Soc. Psychiatry 31:298–305, 1985.

Seligman, J., Gelman, D. Is it sadness or madness? Psychiatrists clash over how to classify PMS. Newsweek, March 15, 1993, p. 66.

Severino, S. K. et al. Database reanalysis in DSM-IV Sourcebook, Vol 4. Edited by Widiger, T. A., Frances, A. J., Pincus, H. A., et al. Washington, D.C., American Psychiatric Association (in press).

Sherman, J. A. Therapist attitudes and sex-role stereotyping, in Women and Psychotherapy. Edited by Brodsky, A. M., Hare-Mustin, R. T. New York, Guilford Press, 1980, pp. 34–66.

Smith, M. L. Sex bias in counseling and psychotherapy. Psychol. Bull. 187:392–407, 1980.

Snyder, S., Goodpaster, W. A., Pitts, W. M., et al. Demography of psychiatric patients with borderline personality traits. Psychopathology 18:38–49, 1985.

Spam, P. Vicious cycle: The politics of periods. Washington Post, July 8, 1993, pp. C1–C2.

Spitzer, R. L., Williams, J. B. W., Kass, F., et al. National field trial of the DSM-III-R diagnostic criteria for self-defeating personality disorder. Am. J. Psychiatry 146:1561–1567, 1989.

Spitzer, R. L., Fiester, S. J., Gay, M., et al. Results of a survey of forensic psychiatrists on the validity of the sadistic personality disorder diagnosis. Am. J. Psychiatry 148:875–879, 1991.

Sprock, J., Blashfield, R. K., Smith, B. Gender weighting of DSM-III-R personality disorder criteria. Am. J. Psychiatry 147:586–590, 1990.

Walker, L. E. A. The Battered Woman Syndrome. New York, Springer, 1984.

Walker, L. E. A. Inadequacies of the masochistic personality disorder diagnosis for women. Journal of Personality Disorders 1:183–189, 1987.

Walker, L. E. A. Are personality disorders gender biased? in Controversial Issues in Mental Health. Edited by Kirk, S. A., Einbinder, S. D. Boston, Allyn & Bacon, 1994, pp. 22–30.

Widiger, T. A. Deletion of self-defeating and sadistic personality disorders, in DSM-IV Personality Disorders. Edited by Livesley, W. J. New York, Guilford, 1995.

Widiger, T. A., Frances, A. J. Controversies concerning the self-defeating personality disorder, in Self-Defeating Behaviors: Experimental Research, Clinical Impressions, and Practical Implications. Edited by Curtis, R. C. New York, Plenum, 1989, pp. 289–309.

Widiger, T., Nietzel, M. Kaplan's view of DSM-III: The data revisited. Am Psychol. 39:1319–1320, 1984.

Widiger, T., Settle, S. Broverman et al. revisited: An artifactual sex bias. J. Pers. Soc. Psychol. 53:463–469, 1987.

Widiger, T. A., Spitzer, R. L. Sex bias in the diagnosis of personality disorders: Conceptual and methodological issues. Clinical Psychology Review 11:1–22, 1991.

Widiger, T. A., Corbitt, E., Funtowicz, M. Rejoinder to Dr. Walker, in Controversial Issues in Mental Health. Edited by Kirk, S. A., Einbinder, S. D. Boston, Allyn & Bacon, 1994b, pp. 30–38.

Widom, C. S. Sex roles and psychopathology, in Sex Roles and Psychopathology. Edited by Widom, C. S. New York, Plenum, 1984, pp. 3–17.

Williams, J. B. W., Spitzer, R. L. The issue of sex bias in DSM-III: A critique of "A woman's view of DSM-III" by Marcie Kaplan. Am. Psychol. 38:793–798, 1983.

Zeldow, P. B. Sex roles, psychological assessment, and patient management, in Sex Roles and Psychopathology. Edited by Widom, C. S. New York, Plenum, 1984, pp. 355–374.

CHALLENGE QUESTIONS

Is There Gender Bias in the *DSM-IV*?

1. What recommendations with regard to gender would you make to the task force working on *DSM-V*?
2. Should each *DSM* diagnosis have a separate list of gender-related diagnostic criteria?
3. What are some of the social issues that influence the differential assignment of certain diagnoses, such as eating disorders, personality disorders, and depression?
4. What are some of the social issues that make women more likely than men to seek professional help for emotional problems?

Suggested Readings

Becker, D. (1997). *Through the looking glass: Women and borderline personality disorder.* Boulder, CO: Westview Press, A Division of HarperCollins Publishers, Inc.

Glickauf-Hughs, C., & Wells, M. (1998). Self-defeating personality disorder: A re-examination. *Psychotherapy Bulletin, 33*(4), 32–35.

Huprich, S. K., & Fine, M. A. (1997). Diagnoses under consideration—self-defeating and depressive personality disorders: Current status and clinical issues. *Journal of Contemporary Psychotherapy, 27*(4), 303–322.

Livesley, J. W. (Ed.) (1995). *The DSM-IV personality disorders.* New York, NY: The Guilford Press.

Widiger, T. A. (1998). Sex biases in the diagnoses of personality disorders. *Journal of Personality Disorders, 12*(2), 95–118.

The International Society for the Study of Dissociation

This is the Web site of the International Society for the Study of Dissociation (ISSD), a nonprofit group whose efforts focus on research and training for dissociative disorders.

`http://www.issd.org`

Children and Adults With Attention-Deficit/Hyperactivity Disorder

This is the Web site for Children and Adults With Attention-Deficit/Hyperactivity Disorder (CHADD), a nonprofit organization that supports people with ADHD through advocacy and education.

`http://www.chadd.org`

The National Institute on Drug Abuse (NIDA)

This organization supports and conducts research on drug abuse and uses this information to help improve addiction prevention efforts, treatment, and policy.

`http://www.nida.nih.gov`

Pro-Choice Forum

This Web site provides links to articles and comments about legal, ethical, social, and psychological issues related to abortion.

`http://www.prochoiceforum.org.uk/`

Questions and Answers About Memories of Childhood Abuse

This site offers questions and answers from the American Psychological Association concerning the nature, prevalence, current research, and issues in recovered memory.

`http://www.apa.org/pubinfo/mem.html`

Alcoholics Anonymous

This Web site provides information to the public and professionals about Alcoholics Anonymous.

`http://www.alcoholics-anonymous.org`

PART 2

Psychological Conditions

*A*t the heart of abnormal psychology are the psychological conditions and mental disorders for which people seek professional treatment. Although many conditions involve fairly clear sets of symptoms that can be recognized and treated by clinicians, other conditions are vaguer. In fact, some critics contend that there are conditions that are manufactured in the minds of some clients and reinforced by clinicians who are too eager to pathologize people. Particular controversy has emerged about the validity of conditions such as multiple personality disorder, attention deficit disorder, post-abortion syndrome, and the phenomenon of repressed memories. Questions have also arisen about the use of drugs such as MDMA (Ecstasy) and whether or not cognitive deficits may result from their use. Finally, the most appropriate intervention for treating people with alcoholism has been debated for decades; some argue that complete abstinence is the only option, while others believe that controlled drinking is possible.

- Is Multiple Personality Disorder a Valid Diagnosis?

- Does Attention Deficit Disorder Exist?

- Should All Uses of MDMA (Ecstasy) Be Prohibited?

- Does Post-Abortion Syndrome Exist?

- Are Repressed Memories Valid?

- Should Abstinence Be the Goal for Treating People with Alcohol Problems?

ISSUE 3

Is Multiple Personality Disorder a Valid Diagnosis?

YES: Frank W. Putnam, from "Response to Article by Paul R. McHugh," *Journal of the American Academy of Child and Adolescent Psychiatry* (July 1995)

NO: Paul R. McHugh, from "Resolved: Multiple Personality Disorder Is an Individually and Socially Created Artifact," *Journal of the American Academy of Child and Adolescent Psychiatry* (July 1995)

ISSUE SUMMARY

YES: Psychiatrist Frank W. Putnam contends that the diagnosis of multiple personality disorder meets the standards for the three basic forms of validity: content validity, construct validity, and criterion-related validity.

NO: Psychiatrist Paul R. McHugh denies the validity of multiple personality disorder, asserting that this condition is a socially created behavioral disorder induced by psychotherapists.

Mental health experts have been fascinated for many years by the possibility that a person can develop seemingly independent personalities that are characterized by unique attributes and behaviors. For most of the past century, mental health experts used the label "multiple personality disorder" (MPD) to describe this kind of condition. During the past decade the official diagnostic term was changed to "dissociative identity disorder." Regardless of which term is used, the essence of the condition is that an individual possesses two or more distinct personality states, each with an enduring pattern of perceiving, relating to, and thinking about the environment and the self. At least two of these identities recurrently take control of the person's behavior, and the individual is unable to recall important personal information.

Relatively few cases of MPD were reported for most of the twentieth century, but that changed in 1980, when the authors of the *Diagnostic and Statistical Manual of Mental Disorders*, 3rd ed. (*DSM-III*) included this condition in the list of mental disorders. The disorder was characterized as a condition in which a person experiences a disorganization of the self that results in the experience of discrepant individuals residing within one's overall being. Along with this broadening of the diagnosis came a proliferation of cases of MPD. Interestingly, prior to 1970 only a handful of cases had been reported, but in recent decades many thousands of cases have been documented.

With the astronomical increase in the number of diagnosed cases of MPD, clinicians and researchers began to wonder if the increase was due to the increased incidence of the disorder or to an artificial phenomenon due to the broadening of the definition of the disorder. Some skeptics raised the worrisome possibility that the condition is iatrogenic—that it can be generated in a client by a psychotherapist, often through the use of hypnosis. Although presumably well meaning, the psychotherapist might suggest to a client that long-standing psychological problems are the result of a fragmentation of personality, thus leading the client to act and think in ways reflective of seemingly independent identities.

In the following selection, Frank W. Putnam contends that MPD is indeed a valid diagnosis, and he asserts that there are no documented cases in which the full syndrome of MPD was induced by fascination or by hypnosis. Further, he contends that MPD—and its core pathological process, dissociation—can be detected and measured by reliable and valid structured interviews and scales.

In the second selection, Paul R. McHugh contends that many individuals who develop the characteristics of MPD are responding to the crude suggestion of therapists that they harbor some "alter" personalities. Responding to the therapist's suggestion, he concludes, the patient gets caught up in feeling pressured to act in ways that are consistent with the role of having several personalities.

POINT	COUNTERPOINT
• MPD is a valid diagnosis that meets the standards of the three basic forms of validity.	• MPD is little more than a modern-day form of hysteria.
• The notion that MPD is iatrogenic is based on research with role-playing students in staged situations, which has little bearing on real-life clinical work.	• MPD is a condition that is induced by therapists.
• The clinical phenomenology of MPD has been delineated and replicated in numerous studies of more than 1,000 cases.	• Much of the expansion in the diagnosis of MPD is due to the fact that the condition is included in the *DSM*, which leads some practitioners to believe that MPD must exist because there are operational criteria available for making the diagnosis.
• MPD and its core pathological process, dissociation, can be detected and measured by reliable and valid structured interviews and scales.	• Therapists elicit the expression of other personalities by presenting leading questions to the patient that reinforce the idea that the individual possesses separate personalities.

Frank W. Putnam

 **YES**

Response to Article by Paul R. McHugh

For more than a century, the existence of multiple personality disorder (MPD) has provoked heated debate. That both the diagnosis and the controversy are still with us says something about the resiliency of both sides of the question. The similarities between the charges leveled in the current debate and those in the historical record suggest that things, unfortunately, have not changed very much in 100 years. It is unlikely that this exchange will resolve the matter, but perhaps we can move the question along to a higher level. The criticisms leveled at MPD are not credible when examined in the light of what we know about the etiologies of mental illness. Debate can be advanced by critiquing the validity of MPD in the same manner in which the validity of other psychiatric diagnoses are assessed.

What are the criticisms of MPD? There are three basic criticisms made against this diagnosis. The first is that MPD is an iatrogenic disorder produced in patients by their psychiatrists. The second is that MPD is produced by its portrayal in the popular media. The third is that the numbers of MPD cases are increasing exponentially. The first and second charges are often lumped together and viewed as being responsible for the third.

The first accusation is historically the oldest and the most serious because it alleges therapeutic misconduct of the gravest nature. The psychiatrist's fascination with the patient's symptoms supposedly reinforces the behavior and produces the syndrome. A variation of this accusation charges that the condition is produced by the improper use of hypnosis. In either instance, the fact is that there are no cases reported in which the full clinical syndrome of MPD was induced either by fascination or by hypnosis. Experiments by Nicholas Spanos are sometimes cited as examples of the creation of MPD by role-playing students (Spanos, 1986). The reader is invited to compare the verbal responses of undergraduates responding to a staged situation with the psychiatric symptoms of MPD patients reported in the clinical literature. Two clinical studies examined the effects of using hypnosis on the symptoms and behaviors of MPD patients (Putnam et al., 1986; Ross, 1989). There were no significant differences between MPD cases diagnosed and treated with or without hypnosis. Since MPD appears in

From *Journal of the American Academy of Child and Adolescent Psychiatry*, vol. 34, no. 7, July 1995. Copyright © 1995 by Lippincott, Williams & Wilkins. Reprinted by permission.

many patients with no history of hypnotic interventions, the misuse of hypnosis apparently is not responsible for the syndrome.

The second allegation, that MPD is induced by media portrayals, ignores extensive research on the effects of the media on behavior. More than 30 years of research on the relation of television viewing to violence informs us of just how difficult it is to find clear-cut effects produced by exposure to specific media imagery. Certainly there are media effects, but these effects are not simple and direct identifications. Rather they are indirect, cumulative, and heavily confounded by individual and situational variables (Friedlander, 1993). The depiction of violence in the media is vastly more common (perhaps it is even the norm for movies and television) than the portrayal of MPD. Yet, the critics of MPD would have us believe that the minuscule percentage of media time devoted to MPD is directly responsible for the increase in diagnosed cases. This would be an extraordinarily specific and powerful effect—far, far beyond anything found by the thousands of studies on violence conducted by media researchers.

The first and second accusations beg an important question. Why this disorder? If these individuals are so suggestible, why don't they develop other disorders? Why should suggestion effects be unique to MPD? Psychiatrists inquire about and exhibit interest in other symptoms. We do not believe that asking about hallucinations produces them in a patient. Why should asking about the existence of "other parts" of the self produce alter personalities? What is so *magical* about this question? With respect to media portrayals of mental illness, a random channel-walk through the soap opera and talk show circuits will convince one that many other symptoms and disorders fill the airwaves. Eating disorders, obsessive-compulsive disorder, bipolar illness, assorted phobias, sexual dysfunctions, autism, chronic fatigue syndrome, etc., etc., are discussed in graphic detail and glamorized after their own fashion. Why don't suggestible individuals identify with these conditions? Truly, if there is such a high degree of suggestive specificity to MPD, it is worthy of intensive investigation.

The third accusation, that cases of MPD are increasing "exponentially" or "logarithmically," shows little understanding of basic mathematics. Critics often cite inflated numbers of cases without any support for their figures. I have plotted the numbers of published cases year by year, and while it is true that they have increased significantly compared to prior decades, the rise in the slope is not nearly as dramatic as the critics' hyperbole suggests. Over the same period, other disorders, e.g., Lyme disease, obsessive-compulsive disorder, and chronic fatigue syndrome, have shown equal or faster rises in the numbers of published cases. This reflects a basic process in medicine associated with the compilation and dissemination of syndromal profiles. When symptoms that were once viewed as unrelated are organized into a coherent syndromal presentation and that information is widely disseminated, physicians begin to identify the condition more frequently. The rapid rise in the number of cases of "battered child syndrome" following the classic paper by Kempe and his colleagues is a very relevant example of this process in action. A related criticism is that a few clinicians are responsible for most of the diagnosed MPD cases. Again, a review of the MPD literature demonstrates a healthy diversity of authorship comparable with that found for other conditions.

The crucial question raised by this debate is: How should the validity of a psychiatric diagnosis be judged? Considerable thought has gone into this question. (For a more complete discussion, see *The Validity of Psychiatric Diagnosis* by Robins and Barrett, 1989.) Many psychiatrists endorse the model of diagnostic validity put forth by Robins and Guze in 1970 and subsequently amplified by others (Robins and Barrett, 1989). This model requires that psychiatric diagnoses satisfy aspects of three basic forms of validity: content validity, criterion-related validity, and construct validity. Content validity is probably the most fundamental form of validity for psychiatric diagnosis. It requires that the diagnostician be able to give a specific and detailed clinical description of the disorder. Criterion-related validity requires that laboratory tests, e.g., chemical, physiological, radiological, or reliable psychological tests, are consistent with the defined clinical picture. Construct validity requires that the disorder be delimited from other disorders (discriminant validity).

The clinical phenomenology of MPD has been delineated and repeatedly replicated in a series of studies of more than 1,000 cases. A review of the best of these studies demonstrates striking similarities in the symptoms of MPD patients across different sites and investigational methodologies (Coons et al., 1988; Putnam et al., 1986; Ross et al., 1990). They should convince the interested reader that a specific, unique, and reproducible clinical syndrome is being described. A small but growing body of literature on childhood and adolescent MPD links the adult syndrome with childhood precursors, establishing a developmental continuity of symptoms and pathology (Dell and Eisenhower, 1990; Hornstein and Putnam, 1992). The well-delineated, well-replicated set of dissociative symptoms that constitute the core clinical syndrome of MPD satisfies the requirements for content validity.

MPD and its core pathological process, dissociation, can be detected and measured by reliable and valid structured interviews and scales (Carlson et al., 1993; Steinberg et al., 1991). Published data on validity compare very favorably with accepted psychological instruments and satisfy the reliability requirement imposed by Robins and Guze for the inclusion of psychological tests as measures of criterion validity. These instruments have been translated into other languages and proven to discriminate MPD in other cultures. Discriminant validity studies have been conducted for the Dissociative Experiences Scale and the Structured Clinical Interview for DSM-III-R-Dissociative Module, both of which show good receiver operating characteristic curves, a standard method for evaluating the validity of a diagnostic test (Carlson et al., 1993; Steinberg et al., 1991). MPD is well discriminated from other disorders by reliable and valid tests and thus has good criterion-related and construct validates.

Multiple personality disorder has been with us from the beginnings of psychiatry (Ellenberger, 1970). At present we conceptualize this condition as a complex form of posttraumatic dissociative disorder, highly associated with a history of severe trauma usually beginning at an early age. I believe that research demonstrates that the diagnosis of MPD meets the standards of content validity, criterion-related validity, and construct validity considered necessary for the validity of a psychiatric diagnosis. The simplistic argument that MPD is individually and socially caused "hysteria" evades the much more important question of what is the best approach to helping these patients. Denying its existence or blaming psychiatrists and television for MPD patients' symptoms is not constructive. It is important to move beyond debate about the existence of the condition to more serious discussions of therapeutic issues.

References

Carlson, E. B., Putnam, F. W., Ross, C. A., et al. (1993). *Validity of the Dissociative Experiences Scale* in screening for multiple personality disorder: a multicenter study. *Am J Psychiatry* 150:1030–1036.

Coons, P. M., Bowman, E. S., Milstein, V. (1988). Multiple personality disorder: a clinical investigation of 50 cases. *J Nerv Ment Dis* 176:519–527.

Dell, P. F., Eisenhower, J. W. (1990). Adolescent multiple personality disorder. *J Am Acad Child Adolesc Psychiatry* 29:359–366.

Ellenberger, H. F. (1970). *The Discovery of the Unconscious: The History and Evolution of Dynamic Psychiatry.* New York: Basic Books.

Friedlander, B. Z. (1993). Community violence, children's development, and mass media: in pursuit of new insights, new goals and new strategies. In: *Children and Violence,* Reiss, D., Richters, J. E., Radke–Yarrow. M., Scharff, D., eds. New York: Guilford Press, pp. 66–81.

Hornstein, N. L., Putnam, F. W. (1992). Clinical phenomenology of child and adolescent dissociative disorders. *J Am Acad Child Adolesc Psychiatry* 31:1077–1085.

Putnam, F. W., Guroff, J. J., Silberman, E. K., Barban, L., Post, R. M. (1986). The clinical phenomenology of multiple personality disorder: review of 100 recent cases. *J Clin Psychiatry* 47:285–293.

Robins, L. E., Barrett, J. E., ed. (1989). *The Validity of Psychiatric Diagnosis.* New York: Raven Press.

Ross, C. A. (1989). Effects of hypnosis on the features of multiple personality disorder. *Am J Clin Hypn* 32:99–106.

Ross, C. A., Miller, S. D., Bjornson, L., Reagor, P., Fraser, G., Anderson, G. (1990). Structured interview data on 102 cases of multiple personality disorder from four centers. *Am J Psychiatry* 147:596–601.

Spanos, N. P. (1986). Hypnosis, nonvolutional responding, and multiple personality: a social psychological perspective. *Prog Exp Pers Res* 14:1–62.

Steinberg, M., Rounsaville, B., Cicchetti, D. (1991). Detection of dissociative disorders in psychiatric patients by a screening instrument and a structured diagnostic interview. *Am J Psychiatry* 149:1050–1054.

Paul R. McHugh

 **NO**

Resolved: Multiple Personality Disorder Is an Individually and Socially Created Artifact

Where's hysteria now that we need it? With *DSM-IV* [*Diagnostic and Statistical Manual of Mental Disorders*, 4th ed.], psychiatrists have developed a common language and a common approach to diagnosis. But in the process of operationalizing diagnoses, we may have lost some concepts about patient behavior. The term "hysteria" disappeared when *DSM-III* was published; without it, psychiatrists have been deprived of a scientific concept essential to the development of new ideas: the null hypothesis. This loss hits home with the epidemic of multiple personality disorder (MPD).

The work of Talcott Parsons (1964), David Mechanic (1978), and Isidore Pilowsky (1969) taught psychiatrists to appreciate that phenomena such as hysterical paralyses, blindness, and pseudoseizures were actually behaviors with a goal: achieving the "sick role." Inspired by Parsons, Mechanic and Pilowsky used the term "abnormal illness behavior" in lieu of hysteria. Their approach eliminated the stigma of malingering that had been implied in hysteria and indicated that patients could take on such behavior without fraudulent intent. They were describing an old reality of medical experience.

Some people—experiencing emotional distress in the face of a variety of life circumstances and conflicts—complain to doctors about physical or psychological symptoms that they claim are signs of illness. Sometimes they display gross impairments of movement or consciousness; sometimes the features are subtle and changing. These complaints prompt doctors to launch investigations in laboratories, to conduct elaborate and sometimes dangerous studies of the brain or body, and to consult with experts, who examine the patient for esoteric disease. As the investigation proceeds, the patient may become still more persuaded that an illness is at work and begin to model the signs of disorder on the subtle suggestions of the physician's inquiry. For example, a patient with complaints of occasional lapses in alertness might—in the course of investigations that include visits to the epilepsy clinic and to the EEG laboratory for sleep studies, photic stimulation, and nasopharyngeal leads—gradually

From *Journal of the American Academy of Child and Adolescent Psychiatry*, vol. 34, no. 7, July 1995.
Copyright © 1995 by Lippincott, Williams & Wilkins. Reprinted by permission.

develop the frenzied thrashing movements of the limbs that require the protective attention of several nurses and hospital aides.

Eventually, with the patient no better and the investigations proving fruitless, a psychiatric consultant alert to the concept of hysteria and its contemporary link to the "sick role" might recognize that the patient's disorder is not an epileptic but a behavioral one. The patient is displaying movements that attract medical attention and provide the privileges of patienthood.

Talcott Parsons, the Harvard sociologist, pointed out in the 1950s that medicine was an organized component of our society intended to aid, through professional knowledge, the sick and the impaired. To accomplish this, certain individuals—physicians—are licensed by society to decide not only how to manage the sick, but to choose and distinguish the sick from other impaired people. Such an identification can provide these "sick" individuals with certain social privileges, i.e., rest, freedom from employment, and support from others during the reign of the condition. The person given the appellation "sick" by the social spokesman—the physician—was assumed by the society to respond to these privileges with other actions, i.e., cooperating with the intrusions of investigators of the illness and making every effort at rehabilitation so as to return to health. The hidden assumption is that the burdens and pains of illness act to drive the patient toward these cooperative actions with the physicians and thus to be happy to relinquish the few small pleasures that can be found in being treated as a victim of sickness.

However, because there are advantages to the sick role, there are some situations in which a person might seek this role without a "ticket of admission," a disease. This is hardly a remarkable idea as almost anyone has noticed the temptation to "call in sick" when troubles are afoot. But in some patients—those with emotional conflicts, weakened self-criticism, and high suggestibility—this temptation can be transformed, usually with some prompting, into the conviction that they are infirm. This kind of patient may, in fact, use more and more information from the medical profession's activities to amplify the expression of the infirmity.

Psychiatrists have known about these matters of social and psychological dynamics for more than 100 years. They were brought vividly to attention by the distinguished pupil of Jean-Martin Charcot, Joseph Babinski (he of the plantar response). Like Sigmund Freud and Pierre Janet, Babinski had observed Charcot manage patients with, what Charcot called, "hysteroepilepsy." But Babinski was convinced that hysteroepilepsy was not a new disorder. He believed that the women at Charcot's clinic were being persuaded—and not so subtly—to take on the features of epilepsy by the interest Charcot and his assistants expressed (Babinski and Froment, 1918). Babinski also believed that these women were vulnerable to this persuasion because of distressing states of mind provoked in their life circumstances and their roles as intriguing patients and the subject of attention from many distinguished physicians who offered them a haven of care.

Babinski was bringing the null hypothesis to Charcot and with it, not a rejection of these women as legitimate victims of some problem, but an appreciation that behaving as if epileptic obscured reality and made helping their actual problem difficult. Babinski wrote that just as hyste-roepilepsy rested on persuasion, so a form of counterpersuasion could correct it. He demonstrated that these patients improved when they were taken from the wards and clinics where other afflicted women—epileptic and pseudoepileptic—were housed and when the attention of the staff was turned away from their seizures and onto their lives. These measures—isolation and countersuggestion—had the advantage of limiting the rewards for the behavior and of prompting a search for and treatment of the troubles in the personal life.

All this became embedded in the concept of hysteria and needs to be reapplied in the understanding of MPD. The patients I have seen have been referred to the Johns Hopkins Health System because elsewhere they have become stuck in the process of therapy. The histories are similar. They were mostly women who in the course of some distress sought psychiatric assistance. In the course of this assistance—and often early in the process—a therapist offered them a fairly crude suggestion that they might harbor some "alter" personalities. As an example of the crudity of the suggestions to the patient, I offer this published direction of how to both make the diagnosis and elicit "alters":

> The sine qua non of MPD is a second personality who at some time comes out and takes executive control of the patient's behavior. It may happen that an alter personality will reveal itself to you during this [assessment] process, but more likely it will not. So you may have to elicit an alter personality. . . . To begin the process of eliciting an alter, you can begin by indirect questioning such as, "Have you ever felt like another part of you does things that you can't control?" If she gives positive or ambiguous responses, ask for specific examples. You are trying to develop a picture of what the alter personality is like. . . . At this point, you might ask the host personality, "Does this set of feelings have a name?" Occasionally you will get a name. Often the host personality will not know. You can then focus on a particular event or set of behaviors and follow up on those. For instance, you can ask, "Can I talk to the part of you who is taking those long drives to the country?" (Buie, 1992, p. 3).

Once the patient permits the therapist to "talk to the part . . . who is taking those long drives," the patient is committed to having MPD and is forced to act in ways consistent with this role. The patient is then placed into care on units or in services—often titled "the dissociative service"—at the institution. She meets other patients with the same compliant responses to therapists' suggestions. She and the staff begin a continuous search for other "alters." With the discovery of the first "alter," the barrier of self-criticism and self-observation is breached. No obstacles to invention remain.

Countless numbers of personalities emerge over time. What began as two or three may develop to 99 or 100. The distressing symptoms continue as long as therapeutic attention is focused on finding more alters and sustaining the view that the problems relate to an "intriguing capacity" to dissociate or fractionate the self.

At Johns Hopkins, we see patients in whom MPD has been diagnosed because symptoms of depression have continued despite therapy elsewhere. Our referrals have been few and our experience, therefore, is only now building, probably because our views—that MPD may be a therapist-induced artifact—have only recently become generally known in our community (McHugh, 1995). We seem to challenge the widely accepted view and to "turn back the clock." The referrals that come to us often arrive with obstacles to our therapeutic plans. Patients and their referring therapists often wish to stay in regular contact (two to three times weekly) and to continue their work on MPD. At the same time, we at Hopkins are expected to treat the depression or some other supposed "side issue." We, however, following the isolation and countersuggestion approach, try to bring about, at least temporarily, a separation of the patient from the staff and the support groups that sustain the focus on "alters." We refuse to talk to "alters" but rather encourage our patients to review their present difficulties, thus applying the concept of "abnormal illness behavior" to their condition.

The advocates for MPD are in the same position as Charcot was when Babinski offered his proposal of the null hypothesis. As in any scientific discussion, it is not the responsibility of the proposers of the null hypothesis to prove its likelihood. That hypothesis simply claims that nothing special has been discovered. I claim the same in this debate. The investigators proposing a new entity must demonstrate that the null hypothesis should be rejected.

In most of the discussions by champions of MPD just the opposite occurs. Not only is the null hypothesis discarded without any compelling reason, but nonrelevant information is presented to justify a uniqueness to MPD. Perhaps the most common proposal is that MPD must exist in the way proposed because it is included in *DSM-IV* and operational criteria are available to make the diagnosis. This is a misunderstanding of *DSM-IV*. It provides a way in which a diagnosis can be reliably applied to a patient, but it does not in any way validate the existence of the condition or negate a null hypothesis about it.

Charcot had quite reliable ways of diagnosing hysteroepilepsy. It just did not exist as he thought it did, but rather it was a behavior seeking the sick role. It is my opinion that MPD is another behavioral disorder—a socially created artifact—in distressed people who are looking for help. The diagnosis and subsequent procedures for exploring MPD give them a coherent posture toward themselves and others as a particular kind of patient: "sick" certainly, "victim" possibly. This posture, if sustained, will obscure the real problems in their lives and render psychotherapy long, costly, and pointless. If the customary treatments of hysteria are provided, then we can expect that the multiple personality behaviors will be abandoned and proper rehabilitative attention can be given to the patient.

Hysteria as a concept has been neglected in *DSM-III* and *DSM-IV*, but it offers just what it has always offered: a challenge to proposals of new entities in psychiatry. Some diagnoses survive and others do not. MPD has run away with itself, and its proponents must now deal with this challenge. Charcot took such a challenge from his student. Everyone learned in the process.

References

Babinski, J., Froment, J. (1918). *Hysteria or Pithiatism and Reflex Nervous Disorders in the Neurology of War.* Rolleston, J. D., trans; Buzzard, E. F., ed. London: University of London Press.

Buie, S. E. (1992). Introduction to the diagnosis of multiple personality disorder. *Grand Rounds Rev* (4):1–3.

McHugh, P. R. (1995). Witches, multiple personalities, and other psychiatric artifacts. *Nature Med* 1:110–114.

Mechanic, D. (1978). Effects of psychological distress on perceptions of physical health and use of medical and psychiatric facilities. *J Hum Stress* 4:26–32.

Parsons, T. (1964). *Social Structure and Personality.* New York: Free Press.

Pilowsky, I. (1969). Abnormal illness behaviour. *Br J Med Psychol* 42:347–351.

CHALLENGE QUESTIONS

Is Multiple Personality Disorder a Valid Diagnosis?

1. How might the notion of "iatrogenic disorder" be applied to other psychological conditions, such as anxiety disorders, mood disorders, or even learning disorders?
2. McHugh discusses the concept of hysteria. How did theorists such as Sigmund Freud and Jean Martin Charcot characterize hysterical conditions?
3. What factors might motivate some patients to report the experience of multiple personalities?
4. What factors might motivate some clinicians to reinforce the experience of multiple personalities?
5. What explanations other than multiple personality disorder might be used to explain the reports of some people that they have the experience of multiple personalities?
6. What treatment recommendations would you make to a clinician whose patient reports the experience of several personalities?

Suggested Readings

Kluft, R. P. (1995). Current controversies surrounding dissociative identify disorder. In L. Cohen, J. Berzoff, & M. Elin (Eds.), *Dissociative identity disorder: Theoretical and treatment controversies* (pp. 347–377). Northvale, NJ: Jason Aronson.

Piper, A. J. (1997). *Hoax and reality: The bizarre world of multiple personality disorder*. Northvale, NJ: Jason Aronson.

Piper, A. J. (1998). Multiple personality disorder: Witchcraft survives in the twentieth century. *The Skeptical Inquirer*, 22(3), 44–50.

Ross, C. A. (1997). *Dissociative identity disorder: Diagnosis, clinical features, and treatment of multiple personality*. New York, NY: John Wiley & Sons, Inc.

Spanos, N. P. (1996). *Multiple identities and false memories: A sociocognitive perspective*. Washington, DC: American Psychological Association.

ISSUE 4

Does Attention Deficit
Disorder Exist?

YES: Edward M. Hallowell, from "What I've Learned From ADD," *Psychology Today* (May–June 1997)

NO: Thomas Armstrong, from "ADD: Does It Really Exist?" *Phi Delta Kappan* (February 1996)

ISSUE SUMMARY

YES: Psychiatrist Edward M. Hallowell asserts that an appreciation for the complexity of attention deficit disorder (ADD) can provide valuable understanding about the workings of the brain and how this disorder affects the lives of millions of people.

NO: Educational consultant and former special education teacher Thomas Armstrong contends that the diagnosis of ADD has been blown out of proportion by the public and the professional community and is, in fact, a questionable diagnosis.

$\mathbf{A}$nyone who has set foot in an American classroom has observed a range of children whose behaviors and compliance span a relatively wide continuum. At one end are well-behaved children who listen attentively to their teachers, cooperate pleasantly with their peers, and follow instructions with patience and a sense of calm. At the other end are children who seem to be completely out of control. These children are both disturbed and disturbing. They show a constellation of behaviors characterized by inattention and hyperactivity. These children are referred to by teachers and special educators as having attention deficit disorder (ADD) or by the *Diagnostic and Statistical Manual of Mental Disorders,* 4th ed. (*DSM-IV*) label "attention deficit hyperactivity disorder" (ADHD). Their inattention is evidenced by a range of behaviors, including carelessness, distractibility, forgetfulness, and difficulty following through on tasks or organizing themselves. Their hyperactivity is characterized by restlessness, running around, difficulty playing with others, excessive talk, and other behaviors suggesting that they are "on the go."

A few decades ago these hyperactive and impulsive children might have been labeled as having "minimal brain dysfunction," a label that suggested that an underlying neurological problem was the basis for their disruptive behavior. As times have changed, so also have the labels, such that the terms *attention deficit disorder* and *attention deficit hyperactivity disorder* have become commonplace in describing children in every school in America. The numbers of children carrying diagnostic labels involving inattention have grown so rapidly that some critics have questioned whether or not many in our society have come to view this diagnosis as a simple label for a very complex problem. Questions have arisen about whether the symptoms of children identified as having ADD reflect neurological problems or social ills that stem from deficient parenting and problem-laden educational systems.

In the following selection, Edward M. Hallowell speaks from his personal experience as a person who was diagnosed with attention deficit disorder in 1981, when he suddenly was able to make sense of his impatience, distractibility, restlessness, proneness to procrastination, disturbingly brief attention span, and intense bursts of energy. Hallowell's personal experiences brought him to the conclusion that advances in understanding the workings of the brain could help researchers develop more compelling explanations for the seemingly out-of-control behaviors of millions of American children, as well as develop interventions to help the many people who are tormented by this extreme form of restless inattentiveness.

In the second selection, Thomas Armstrong asserts that conditions such as attention deficit disorder are part of a national phenomenon in which there has been a proliferation of relevant books, special assessments, learning programs, residential schools, parent advocacy groups, clinical services, and medications. He points out that prevalence estimates range widely, and he calls into question the nature of the assessments (such as behavior-rating scales) that are used to derive this diagnosis, scales that Armstrong views as too dependent on opinion. He asserts that careful scrutiny will demonstrate that there really is not much difference between children labeled ADD and "normal" children.

POINT

- Proper diagnosis and treatment of ADD allows sufferers to take responsibility more effectively and to become more productive and patient.
- ADD has a biological basis, and millions of individuals with ADD have benefited spectacularly from medications that have relieved many disturbing symptoms.
- The scientifically based prevalence rate of ADD is 5 percent of the population.
- ADD occurs along a spectrum, ranging from severe cases involving rampant disorganization and uncontrollable impulsivity to mild cases in which the symptoms are barely noticeable.

COUNTERPOINT

- ADD has become a diagnosed psychiatric disorder, and millions of children and adults run the risk of stigmatization from the application of this label.
- The evidence for ADD being a medical disorder is unclear, particularly in light of the variable nature of this condition.
- Prevalence estimates of ADD range from 1 percent to 20 percent of the population.
- Under rigorous scientific scrutiny, few if any differences are evident between children who are labeled ADD and those who are considered "normal."

Edward M. Hallowell

 **YES**

What I've Learned From ADD

When I discovered, in 1981, that I had attention deficit disorder (ADD), it was one of the great "Aha!" experiences of my life. Suddenly so many seemingly disparate parts of my personality made sense—the impatience, distractibility, restlessness, amazing ability to procrastinate, and extraordinarily brief attention span (here-one-moment-gone-the-next), not to mention the high bursts of energy and creativity and an indefinable, zany sense of life.

It was a pivotal moment for me, but the repercussions have been more powerful and wide-ranging than I could have imagined 16 years ago. Coming to understand ADD has been like stepping through a port-hole into a wider world, expanding my view of my patients, friends, and family. I now know that many personality traits and psychological problems have a genuine basis in biology—not just ADD, but also depression, learning disorders, anxiety, panic attacks, and even shyness.

That insight has been tremendously freeing, for myself and my patients, and it has also led the mental health field to novel, effective treatments for brain disorders. I use the word "brain" intentionally, to emphasize that in many ways our personality is hardwired. Yet just as important is the fact that biology is only part of the story. We're all born with a set of genes, but how those genes get expressed depends largely on life experience and the way our environment interacts with our biology. If we understand this, we can "manage" our brains more deftly, using methods that range from medicine to lifestyle changes. Diagnosing and treating ADD—in my own life and those of hundreds of patients—has shown me just how remarkable these interventions can be. I have seen more than a few teetering marriages right themselves when the couple understood it was ADD, not bad character, causing their troubles. I have also seen many careers that had been languishing in the bin labeled "underachiever" suddenly take off after diagnosis and treatment of ADD. Scores of students have been able to rescue their academic careers after diagnosis and treatment. It is a powerful diagnosis: powerfully destructive when missed and powerfully constructive when correctly picked up.

ADD has taught me to look at people differently. These days, when I meet someone I often ask myself the question, "What kind of brain does he have?" as a way of trying to understand the person. I've learned that brains

Reprinted with permission from *Psychology Today* Magazine, vol. 3, no. 3, June 1997. Copyright © 1997 Sussex Publishers, Inc.

differ tremendously from person to person, and that some of the most interesting and productive people around have "funny" (i.e., highly idiosyncratic) brains. There is no normal, standard brain, any more than there is a normal, standard automobile, dress, or human face. Our old distinctions of "smart" and "stupid" don't even begin to describe the variety of differences in human brains; indeed, these distinctions trample over those differences.

Today we know more than ever about the brain—but in learning more we have realized how little we actually know. With sophisticated brain scans that map the activity of networks of neurons we can peer inside the once impenetrable armor of our skulls and learn just how brains act when they are seeing, thinking, remembering, and even malfunctioning. And yet the vast territory of the brain still stretches out before us uncharted, like the sixteenth-century maps of the New World we used to see in our fifth-grade history books. Although we are coining new terms all the time (like emotional intelligence or post-traumatic stress disorder or even attention deficit disorder), although we are discovering new neurotransmitters and brain peptides that reveal new connections and networks within the brain, and although we are revising or throwing out old theories as new ones leap into our screens, any honest discussion of mental life must begin with the confession, "There's so much we still don't know."

Disorder and Metaphor?

What do these philosophical flights of fancy have to do with ADD and me? A few years ago ADD burst upon the American scene the way psychiatric disorders sometimes do, emerging as a riveting new metaphor for our cultural milieu. In the 1930s we embraced neurasthenia; in the '50s W. H. Auden coined the term "the age of anxiety"; in the '70s Christopher Lasch dubbed us the "culture of narcissism." Now, in the '90s, ADD has emerged as a symbol of American life. . . . This may explain why *Driven to Distraction* and *Answers to Distraction,* two books I wrote a few years ago with Harvard psychiatrist John Ratey, M.D., found a surprisingly wide and vocal audience.

At the same time, there has been some misunderstanding because of the sudden popularity of ADD. Scientists rightly get upset when they see extravagant claims being made that studies cannot justify—claims, for instance, that up to 25 percent of our population suffers from ADD. (The true number is probably around 5 percent.) And ordinary people are annoyed because they feel this diagnosis has become a catchall excuse—clothed in neurological, scientific language—for any inappropriate behavior. ADD can seem to undercut our country's deep belief in the work ethic. "Why didn't you do your homework?" *"Because I have ADD."* "Why are you late?" *"Because I have ADD."* "Why haven't you paid your income tax in five years?" *"Because I have ADD."* "Why are you so obnoxious?" *"Because I have ADD."* But, in fact, once ADD is properly diagnosed and treated, the opposite happens: The sufferer is able to take responsibility more effectively and becomes more productive and patient. The student who always forgot his homework and was constantly penalized for doing so is able to remember his homework—after his ADD is treated. The same is true for the adult in the workplace, who, once his ADD is treated, is finally able to finish the project he has so "irresponsibly" neglected, or the academician who is at last able to complete her Ph.D. dissertation.

So what is this condition, and where has it been all these centuries? Is it just another fad, or is there some scientific basis to ADD?

ADD is not a new disorder, although it has not been clearly understood until recent years, and its definition will become even more refined as we learn more about it. Right now, we are like blind men describing an elephant. The elephant is there—this vast collection of people with varying attentional strengths and vulnerabilities. However, generating a definitive description, diagnostic workup, and treatment plan with replicable research findings still poses a challenge. As long ago as the 1940s, the term "minimal brain damage syndrome" was used to describe symptoms similar to what we now call ADD. Today, the standard manual of the mental health field, the DSM-IV, defines ADD as a syndrome of involuntary distractibility—a restless, constant wandering of the crucial beam of energy we call attention. That trait is the hallmark of this disorder. More specifically, the syndrome must include six or more symptoms of either inattention or hyperactivity and impulsivity—the latter variant is known as attention deficit disorder with hyperactivity, or ADHD. . . .

To define a disorder solely in terms of attention is a true leap forward, since for centuries nobody paid any attention to attention. Attention was viewed as a choice, and if your mind wandered, you were simply allowing it to do so. Symptoms of ADD—not unlike those of depression, mania, or anxiety disorders—were considered deep and moral flaws.

When people ask me where ADD has been all these years, I respond that it has been in classrooms and offices and homes all over the world, right under our noses all along, only it has been called by different names: laziness, stupidity, rottenness, and worthlessness. For decades children with ADD have been shamed, beaten, punished, and humiliated. They have been told they suffered from a deficit not of attention but of motivation and effort. That approach fails as miserably as trying to beat near-sightedness out of a child—and the damage carries over into adulthood.

It's All in Your Head

The evidence that ADD has a biological basis has mounted over the last 20 years. First, and most moving, there is the clinical evidence from the records of millions of patients who have met the diagnostic criteria and who have benefited spectacularly from standard treatment. These are human stories of salvaged lives. The fact that certain medications predictably relieve target symptoms of ADD means that these symptoms have roots in the physical world.

I recall watching an eighth grader named Noah receive a reward for "Most Improved" at graduation. This boy's mother had been told by an expert that Noah was so severely "disturbed" that she should look into residential placement. He was often in trouble at school. From my first meeting with Noah I was struck by his kindness and tenacity; no expert had understood that he suffered from ADD, as well as mild cerebral palsy. Like many ADDers he was intuitive, warm, and empathic. After coaching, teacher involvement, extra structure, and the medication Ritalin, Noah improved steadily, from the moment of diagnosis in sixth grade until graduation from eighth. As I watched him walk up to receive his award, awkward but proud, shake the hand of the principal, then turn and flash us all a grin, I felt inside a gigantic, "YES!" *Yes* for the triumph of this boy, *yes* for the triumph of knowledge and determination over misunderstanding, *yes* for all the children who in the future will not have to suffer. Standing in the back of the gym, leaning against the wall, I cried some of the happiest tears I've ever shed.

There is also intriguing biological evidence for the existence of ADD. One seems to inherit a susceptibility to this disorder, which appears to cluster in families just as manic-depression and other mental illnesses do. Though no scientist has been able to isolate a single causative gene in any mental disorder—and, in fact, we are coming to understand that a complex interaction of genes, neurotransmitters, hormones, and the environment comes into play in mental illness—there is solid evidence that vulnerability can be passed down through generations. One particularly careful, recent review in *The Journal of The American Academy of Child and Adolescent Psychiatry* supported the heritability of ADD based upon family and twin-adoption studies and analysis of gene inheritance.

Evidence of ADD may even show up in specific areas of the brain. In 1990, Alan Zametkin, M.D., a psychiatrist at the National Institute of Mental Health (NIMH), reported startling findings about the ADD brain in the *New England Journal of Medicine*. Zametkin measured sugar metabolism—a major indicator of brain activity—in the brains of 30 adults who had a childhood history of ADD, along with 30 normal individuals. PET scans (positron emission tomography) allowed Zametkin to determine just how much sugar each participant's brain was absorbing, and in what regions. Sufferers of ADD absorbed less sugar in the areas of the brain that regulate impulse control, attention, and mood. Another study, by NIMH researcher David Hauser, M.D., linked ADD to a rare thyroid condition called generalized resistance to thyroid hormone (GRTH). Seventy percent of individuals with GRTH suffer from ADD—an extraordinarily high correlation. Finally, recent brain scan studies have revealed both anatomical and functional differences in the brains of individuals with ADD—slight but real differences in the size of the corpus callosum (which serves as the switchboard that connects the two hemispheres of the brain), as well as differences in the size of the caudate nucleus, another switching station deep within the brain. These breakthrough studies lay the foundation for promising research, but much more work needs to be done before we may be able to use these findings to actually help us diagnose ADD. They simply point us in the direction of biology—and that pointer is powerful.

The Pivotal Movement

Nothing matters more in ADD than proper diagnosis. Even today this condition is so misunderstood that it is both missed and overdiagnosed. As the public's awareness of the disorder grows, more and more people represent themselves as experts in ADD. As one of my patients said to me, "ADD has become a growth industry." Not every self-proclaimed expert knows ADD from ABC. For instance, depression can cause someone to be distracted and inattentive (and in many cases depression and ADD even occur together). However, a constant pattern of ADD symptoms usually extends back to early childhood, while depression is usually episodic. Thyroid disease can also look very much like ADD, and only testing by a physician can rule this out. High IQ can also mask or delay the diagnosis of ADD.

If the proper care is taken, a diagnosis of ADD can be made with confidence and accuracy, even though there is no single proof-positive test. Like most disorders, ADD occurs on a wide spectrum. In severe cases an individual can barely function due to rampant disorganization or uncontrollable impulsivity, not to mention secondary symptoms such as low self-esteem or depression. Yet very mild cases of ADD can be barely noticeable, especially in a bright individual who has adapted well.

To me, the life history is the one, absolutely convincing "test," which is then supported by the criteria of the DSM-IV and by psychological testing. When someone tells me they've been called "space-shot," "daydreamer," and "out in left field" all their lives, I suspect they might have ADD. At our clinic in Concord, Massachusetts, we use an abbreviated neuropsychological battery that helps us confirm a diagnosis. The battery includes standard written tests that measure memory and logic, impulsivity, and ability to organize complex tasks. Score alone does not tell the whole story; the tester needs to watch the client to determine whether he or she becomes easily frustrated and distracted. We even include a simple motor test that measures how quickly a person can tap their finger. (Patients with ADD are very good at this; depressed patients are not.) Though these tests are helpful, they are by no means definitive. A very smart person without ADD may find these tests boring, and become distracted. On the other hand, one of the great ironies of this kind of testing is that three of the best non-medication treatments available for ADD—structure, motivation, and novelty—are actually built into the testing situation, and can temporarily camouflage ADD.

A diagnosis by itself can change a life. My own father suffered from manicdepression, and I used to wonder if I had inherited the same disorder. When I learned I had ADD, that fact alone made a huge difference to my life. Instead of thinking of myself as having a character flaw, a family legacy, or some potentially ominous "difference" between me and other people, I could see myself in terms of having a unique brain biology. This understanding freed me emotionally. In fact, I would much rather have ADD than not have it, since I love the positive qualities that go along with it—creativity, energy, and unpredictability. I have found tremendous support and goodwill in response to my acknowledging my own

ADD and dyslexia. The only time talking about this diagnosis will get you in trouble is when you offer it as an excuse.

After a diagnosis of ADD, an individual and his or her family can understand and change behavior patterns that may have been a problem for many years. Treatment must be multifaceted, and includes:

- **Educating the individual** and his or her family, friends, and colleagues or schoolteachers about the disorder. Two of the largest national organizations providing this information are CHADD (Children and Adults with Attention Deficit Disorder; call (954) 587-3700) and ADDA (Attention Deficit Disorder Association; call (216) 350-9595).
- **Making lifestyle changes**, such as incorporating structure, exercise, mediation, and prayer into one's daily life. Structural approaches include using practical tools like lists, reminders, simple filing systems, appointment books, and strategically placed bulletin boards. These can help manage the inner chaos of the ADD life, but the structure should be simple. One patient of mine got so excited about the concept of structure he impulsively went out to Staples and spent several thousand dollars on complex organizing materials that he never used. An example of simple structure: I put my car keys in a basket next to my front door so that I do not have to start each day with a frantic search for them.

  Exercise can help drain off anxiety and excess aggression. Regular meditation or prayer can help focus and relax the mind.
- **Coaching, therapy, and social training.** Often ADD sufferers complain that structure is boring. "If I could be structured, I wouldn't have ADD!" moaned one patient. A coach can be invaluable in helping people with ADD organize their life, and encouraging them to stay on track. If a psychotherapist is the coach, he or she needs to be actively involved in advising specific behavioral changes.

  Therapy itself can help resolve old patterns of self-sabotage or low self-esteem, and may help couples address long-standing problems. For example, setting up a simple division of labor between partners can prevent numerous arguments. Social training can help those with ADD learn how to avoid social gaffes. And merely understanding the condition can promote more successful interactions.
- **Medication.** The medications used to treat ADD constitute one of the miracles of modern medicine. Drugs are beneficial in about 80 percent of ADDers, working like a pair of eyeglasses for the brain, enhancing and sharpening mental focus. Medications prescribed include stimulants like Ritalin or Dexedrine, tricyclic antidepressants like Tofranil and Elavil, and even some high-blood pressure medicines like Catapres.

  All of these medications work by influencing levels of key neurotransmitters, particularly dopamine, epinephrine, and norepinephrine. It seems that the resulting change in neurotransmitter availability helps the brain inhibit extraneous stimuli—both internal and external. That allows the mind to focus more effectively. There is no standard dose; dosages can vary widely from person to person, independent of body size.

Ritalin, by far the most popular drug for the treatment of ADD, is safe and effective. Of course, Ritalin and other stimulants can be dangerous if used improperly. But Ritalin is not addictive. Nor is it a euphoric substance—people use drugs to get high, not to focus their minds. For example, you would not cite, "I took Ritalin last night and read three books" as an example of getting high. Using stimulants to cram before exams, however, is as inadvisable as overdosing on coffee. Students do it, but they should be warned against it. Ritalin should only be taken under medical supervision and of course should not be sold, given away, or otherwise misused.

The diagnosis and treatment of ADD represent a triumph of science over human suffering—just one example of the many syndromes of the brain we are at last learning to address without scorn or hidden moral judgment. As we begin to bring mental suffering out of the stigmatized darkness it has inhabited for centuries and into the light of scientific understanding and effective treatment, we all have reason to rejoice.

ADD: Does It Really Exist?

Several years ago I worked for an organization that assisted teachers in using the arts in their classrooms. We were located in a large warehouse in Cambridge, Massachusetts, and several children from the surrounding lower-working-class neighborhood volunteered to help with routine jobs. I recall one child, Eddie, a 9-year-old African American youngster possessed of great vitality and energy, who was particularly valuable in helping out with many tasks. These jobs included going around the city with an adult supervisor, finding recycled materials that could be used by teachers in developing arts programs, and then organizing them and even field-testing them back at the headquarters. In the context of this arts organization, Eddie was a definite asset.

A few months after this experience, I became involved in a special program through Lesley College in Cambridge, where I was getting my master's degree in special education. This project involved studying special education programs designed to help students who were having problems learning or behaving in regular classrooms in several Boston-area school districts. During one visit to a Cambridge resource room, I unexpectedly ran into Eddie. Eddie was a real problem in this classroom. He couldn't stay in his seat, wandered around the room, talked out of turn, and basically made the teacher's life miserable. Eddie seemed like a fish out of water. In the context of this school's special education program, Eddie was anything but an asset. In retrospect, he appeared to fit the definition of a child with attention deficit disorder (ADD).[1]

Over the past 15 years, ADD has grown from a malady known only to a few cognitive researchers and special educators into a national phenomenon. Books on the subject have flooded the marketplace, as have special assessments, learning programs, residential schools, parent advocacy groups, clinical services, and medications to treat the "disorder." (The production of Ritalin or methylphenidate hydrochloride— the most common medication used to treat ADD—has increased 450% in the past four years, according to the Drug Enforcement Agency.[2]) The disorder has solid support as a discrete medical problem from the Department of Education, the American Psychiatric Association, and many other agencies.

From Thomas Armstrong, "ADD: Does It Really Exist?" *Phi Delta Kappan*, vol. 77, no. 6 (February 1996). Copyright © 1996 by Thomas Armstrong. Reprinted by permission of the author.

I'm troubled by the speed with which both the public and the professional community have embraced ADD. Thinking back to my experience with Eddie and the disparity that existed between Eddie in the arts organization and Eddie in the special education classroom, I wonder whether this "disorder" really exists *in* the child at all, or whether, more properly, it exists in the relationships that are present between the child and his or her environment. Unlike other medical disorders, such as diabetes or pneumonia, this is a disorder that pops up in one setting only to disappear in another. A physician mother of a child labeled ADD wrote to me not long ago about her frustration with this protean diagnosis: "I began pointing out to people that my child is capable of long periods of concentration when he is watching his favorite sci-fi video or examining the inner workings of a pin-tumbler lock. I notice that the next year's definition states that some kids with ADD are capable of normal attention in certain specific circumstances. Poof. A few thousand more kids instantly fall into the definition."

There is in fact substantial evidence to suggest that children labeled ADD do not show symptoms of this disorder in several different real-life contexts. First, up to 80% of them don't appear to be ADD when in the physician's office.[3] They also seem to behave normally in other unfamiliar settings where there is a one-to-one interaction with an adult (and this is especially true when the adult happens to be their father).[4] Second, they appear to be indistinguishable from so-called normals when they are in classrooms or other learning environments where children can choose their own learning activities and pace themselves through those experiences.[5] Third, they seem to perform quite normally when they are *paid* to do specific activities designed to assess attention.[6] Fourth, and perhaps most significant, children labeled ADD behave and attend quite normally when they are involved in activities that *interest* them, that are *novel* in some way, or that involve high levels of *stimulation*.[7] Finally, as many as 70% of these children reach adulthood only to discover that the ADD has apparently just gone away.[8]

It's understandable, then, that prevalence figures for ADD vary widely—far more widely than the 3% to 5% figure that popular books and articles use as a standard. As Russell Barkley points out in his classic work on attention deficits, *Attention Deficit Hyperactivity Disorder: A Handbook for Diagnosis and Treatment,* the 3% to 5% figure "hinges on how one chooses to define ADHD, the population studied, the geographic locale of the survey, and even the degree of agreement required among parents, teachers and professionals. . . . Estimates vary between 1[% and] 20%."[9]

In fact, estimates fluctuate even more than Barkley suggests. In one epidemiological survey conducted in England, only two children out of 2,199 were diagnosed as hyperactive (.09%).[10] Conversely, in Israel, 28% of children were rated by teachers as hyperactive.[11] And in an earlier study conducted in the U.S., teachers rated 49.7% of boys as restless, 43.5% of boys as having a "short attention span," and 43.5% of boys as "inattentive to what others say."[12]

The Rating Game

These wildly divergent statistics call into question the assessments used to decide who is diagnosed as having ADD and who is not. Among the most frequently used tools for this purpose are behavior rating scales. These are typically checklists consisting of items that relate to the child's attention and behavior at home or at school. In one widely used assessment, teachers are asked to rate the child on a scale from 1 (almost never) to 5 (almost always) with regard to behavioral statements such as: "Fidgety (hands always busy)," "Restless (squirms in seat)," and "Follows a sequence of instructions." The problem with these scales is that they depend on *subjective judgments* by teachers and parents who may have a deep, and often subconscious, emotional investment in the outcome. After all, a diagnosis of ADD may lead to medication to keep a child compliant at home or may result in special education placement in the school to relieve a regular classroom teacher of having to teach a troublesome child.

Moreover, since these behavior rating scales depend on opinion rather than fact, there are no objective criteria through which to decide *how much* a child is demonstrating symptoms of ADD. What is the difference in terms of hard data, for example, between a child who scores a 5 on being fidgety and a child who scores a 4? Do the scores mean that the first child is one point more fidgety than the second? Of course not. The idea of assigning a number to a behavior trait raises the additional problem, addressed above, of context. The child may be a 5 on "fidgetiness" in some contexts (during worksheet time, for example) and a 1 at other times (during recess, during motivating activities, and at other highly stimulating times of the day). Who is to decide what the final number should be based on? If a teacher places more importance on workbook learning than on hands-on activities, such as building with blocks, the rating may be biased toward academic tasks, yet such an assessment would hardly paint an accurate picture of the child's total experience in school, let alone in life.

It's not surprising, then, to discover that there is often disagreement among parents, teachers, and professionals using these behavior rating scales as to who exactly is hyperactive or ADD. In one study, parent, teacher, and physician groups were asked to identify hyperactive children in a sample of 5,000 elementary school children. Approximately 5% were considered hyperactive by at least one of the groups, while only 1% were considered hyperactive by all three groups.[13] In another study using a well-known behavior rating scale, mothers and fathers agreed that their children were hyperactive only about 32% of the time, and the correspondence between parent and teacher ratings was even worse: they agreed only about 13% of the time.[14]

These behavior rating scales implicitly ask parents and teachers to compare a potential ADD child's attention and behavior to those of a "normal" child. But this raises the question, What is normal behavior? Do normal children fidget? Of course they do. Do normal children have trouble paying attention? Yes, under certain circumstances. Then exactly when does normal fidgeting turn into ADD fidgeting, and when does normal difficulty paying attention become ADD difficulty?

These questions have not been adequately addressed by professionals in the field, yet they remain pressing issues that seriously undermine the legitimacy of these behavior rating scales. Curiously, with all the focus being placed on children who score at the high end of the hyperactivity and distractibility continuum, virtually no one in the field talks about children who must statistically exist at the opposite end of the spectrum: children who are too focused, too compliant, too still, or too *hypo*active. Why don't we have special classes, medications, and treatments for these children as well?

A Brave New World of Soulless Tests

Another ADD diagnostic tool is a test that assigns children special "continuous performance tasks" (CPTs). These tasks usually involve repetitious actions that require the examinee to remain alert and attentive throughout the test. The earliest versions of these tasks were developed to select candidates for radar operations during World War II. Their use with children in today's world is highly questionable. One of the most popular of the current CPT instruments is the Gordon Diagnostic System (GDS). This Orwellian device consists of a plastic box with a large button on the front and an electronic display above it that flashes a series of random digits. The child is told to press the button every time a "1" is followed by a "9." The box then records the number of "hits" and "misses" made by the child. More complex versions involving multiple digits are used with older children and adults.

Quite apart from the fact that this task bears no resemblance to anything else that children will ever do in their lives, the GDS creates an "objective" score that is taken as an important measure of a child's ability to attend. In reality, it tells us only how a child will perform when attending to a repetitive series of meaningless numbers on a soulless task. Yet ADD expert Russell Barkley writes, "[The GDS] is the only CPT that has enough available evidence . . . to be adopted for clinical practice."[15] As a result, the GDS is used not only to diagnose ADD but also to determine and adjust medication doses in children with the label.

There is a broader difficulty with the use of *any* standardized assessment to identify children as having ADD. Most of the tests used (including behavior rating scales and continuous performance tasks) have attempted to be validated as indicators of ADD through a process that involves testing groups of children who have previously been labeled ADD and comparing their test results with those of groups of children who have been judged to be "normal." If the assessment shows that it can discriminate between these two groups to a significant degree, it is then touted as a valid indicator of ADD. However, one must ask how the initial group of ADD children originally came to be identified as ADD. The answer would have to be through an earlier test. And how do we know that the earlier test was a valid indicator of ADD? Because it was validated using two groups: ADD and normal.

How do we know that *this* group of ADD children was in fact ADD? Through an even earlier test . . . and so on, ad infinitum. There is no Prime Mover in this chain of tests; no First Test for ADD that has been declared self-referential and infallible. Consequently, the validity of these tests must always remain in doubt.

In Search of a Deficit

Even if we admit that such tests *could* tell the difference between children labeled ADD and "normal" children, recent evidence suggests that there really aren't any significant differences between these two groups. Researchers at the Hospital for Sick Children in Toronto, for example, discovered that the performance of children who had been labeled ADD did not deteriorate over time on a continuous performance task any more than did that of a group of so-called normal children. They concluded that these "ADD children" did not appear to have a unique sustained attention deficit.[16]

In another study, conducted at the University of Groningen in the Netherlands, children were presented with irrelevant information on a task to see if they would become distracted from their central focus, which involved identifying groups of dots (focusing on groups of four dots and ignoring groups of three or five dots) on a piece of paper. So-called hyperactive children did not become distracted any more than so-called normal children, leading the researchers to conclude that there did not seem to be a focused attention deficit in these children.[17] Other studies have suggested that "ADD children" don't appear to have problems with short-term memory or with other factors that are important in paying attention.[18] Where, then, is the attention deficit?

A Model of Machines and Disease

The ADD myth is essentially a *paradigm* or world view that has certain assumptions about human beings at its core.[19] Unfortunately, the beliefs about human capacity addressed in the ADD paradigm are not terribly positive ones. It appears as if the ADD myth tacitly endorses the view that human beings function very much like machines.[20] From this perspective, ADD represents something very much like a mechanical breakdown. This underlying belief shows up most clearly in the kinds of explanations that parents, teachers, and professionals give to children labeled ADD about their problems. In one book for children titled *Otto Learns About His Medicine,* a red car named Otto goes to a mechanic after experiencing difficulties in car school. The mechanic says to Otto, "Your motor does go too fast," and he recommends a special car medicine.[21]

While attending a national conference on ADD, I heard experts share similar ways of explaining ADD to children, including comparisons to planes ("Your mind is like a big jet plane . . . you're having trouble in the cockpit"), a car radio ("You have trouble filtering out noise"), and television ("You're experiencing difficulty with the channel selector"). These simplistic metaphors seem to imply that human beings really aren't very complex organisms and that one simply needs to find the right wrench, use the proper gas, or tinker with the appropriate circuit box—and all will be well. They are also just a short hop away from more insulting mechanical metaphors ("Your elevator doesn't go all the way to the top floor").

The other feature that strikes me as being at the heart of the ADD myth is the focus on *disease* and *disability*. I was particularly struck by this mindset while attending a workshop with a leading authority on ADD who started out his lecture by saying that he would treat ADD as a medical disorder with its own etiology (causes), pathogenesis (development), clinical features (symptoms), and epidemiology (prevalence). Proponents of this view talk about the fact that there is "no cure" for ADD and that parents need to go through a "grieving process" once they receive a "diagnosis."[22] ADD guru Russell Barkley commented in a recent address: "Although these children do not look physically disabled, they are neurologically handicapped nonetheless. . . . Remember, this is a disabled child."[23] Absent from this perspective is any mention of a child's potential or other manifestations of health—traits that are crucial in helping a child achieve success in life. In fact, the literature on the strengths, talents, and abilities of children labeled ADD is almost nonexistent.[24]

In Search of the ADD Brain

Naturally, in order to make the claim that ADD is a disease, there must be a medical or biological cause for it. Yet, as with everything else about ADD, no one is exactly sure what causes it. Possible biological causes that have been proposed include genetic factors, biochemical abnormalities (imbalances of such brain chemicals as serotonin, dopamine, and norepinephrine), neurological damage, lead poisoning, thyroid problems, prenatal exposure to various chemical agents, and delayed myelinization of the nerve pathways in the brain.[25]

In its search for a physical cause, the ADD movement reached a milestone with the 1990 publication in the *New England Journal of Medicine* of a study by Alan Zametkin and his colleagues at the National Institute of Mental Health.[26] This study appeared to link hyperactivity in adults with reduced metabolism of glucose (a prime energy source) in the premotor cortex and the superior prefrontal cortex—areas of the brain that are involved in the control of attention, planning, and motor activity. In other words, these areas of the brain were not working as hard as they should have been, according to Zametkin.

The media picked up on Zametkin's research and reported it nationally.[27] ADD proponents latched on to this study as "proof" of the medical basis for ADD. Pictures depicting the spread of glucose through a "normal" brain compared to a "hyperactive" brain began showing up in CH.A.D.D. (Children and Adults with Attention Deficit Disorder) literature and at the organization's conventions and meetings. One ADD advocate seemed to speak for many in the ADD movement when she wrote: "In November

1990, parents of children with ADD heaved a collective sigh of relief when Dr. Alan Zametkin released a report that hyperactivity (which is closely linked to ADD) results from an insufficient rate of glucose metabolism in the brain. Finally, commented a supporter, we have an answer to skeptics who pass this off as bratty behavior caused by poor parenting."[28]

What was *not* reported by the media or cheered by the ADD community was the study by Zametkin and others that came out three years later in the *Archives of General Psychiatry*. In an attempt to repeat the 1990 study with adolescents, the researchers found no significant differences between the brains of so-called hyperactive subjects and those of so-called normal subjects.[29] And in retrospect, the results of the first study didn't look so good either. When the original 1990 study was controlled for sex (there were more men in the hyperactive group than in the control group), there was no significant difference between groups.

A recent critique of Zametkin's research by faculty members at the University of Nebraska also pointed out that the study did not make clear whether the lower glucose rates found in "hyperactive brains" were a cause or a result of attention problems.[30] The critics pointed out that, if subjects were startled and then had their levels of adrenalin monitored, adrenalin levels would probably be quite high. We would not say, however, that these individuals had an adrenalin disorder. Rather, we'd look at the underlying conditions that led to abnormal adrenalin levels. Similarly, even if biochemical differences did exist in the so-called hyperactive brain, we ought to be looking at the nonbiological factors that could account for some of these differences, including stress, learning style, and temperament.

The Stigma of ADD

Unfortunately, there seems to be little desire in the professional community to engage in dialogue about the reality of attention deficit disorder; its presence on the American educational scene seems to be a fait accompli. This is regrettable, since ADD is a psychiatric disorder, and millions of children and adults run the risk of stigmatization from the application of this label.

In 1991, when such major educational organizations as the National Education Association (NEA), the National Association of School Psychologists (NASP), and the National Association for the Advancement of Colored People (NAACP) successfully opposed the authorization by Congress of ADD as a legally handicapping condition, NEA spokesperson Debra DeLee wrote, "Establishing a new category [ADD] based on behavioral characteristics alone, such as overactivity, impulsiveness, and inattentiveness, increases the likelihood of inappropriate labeling for racial, ethnic, and linguistic minority students."[31] And Peg Dawson, former NASP president, pointed out, "We don't think that a proliferation of labels is the best way to address the ADD issue. It's in the best interest of all children that we stop creating categories of exclusion and start responding to the needs of individual children."[32] ADD nevertheless continues to gain ground as the label du jour in American education. It's time to stop and take stock of this "disorder" and decide whether it really exists or is instead more a manifestation of society's need to *have* such a disorder.

Notes

1. In this article, I've used the generic term "attention deficit disorder" (ADD) rather than the American Psychiatric Association's current diagnostic category of "attention deficit hyperactivity disorder" (ADHD) because of its wider use in popular culture.

2. Ritalin production figures were provided in a personal communication from the Drug Enforcement Agency's public relations department.

3. Esther K. Sleator and Rina L. Ullmann, "Can the Physician Diagnose Hyperactivity in the Office?," *Pediatrics,* vol. 67, 1981, pp. 13–17.

4. Russell A. Barkley, *Attention Deficit Hyperactivity Disorder: A Handbook for Diagnosis and Treatment* (New York: Guilford, 1990), pp. 56–57.

5. R. G. Jacob, K. D. O'Leary, and C. Rosenblad, "Formal and Informal Classroom Settings: Effects on Hyperactivity," *Journal of Abnormal Child Psychology,* vol. 6, 1978, pp. 47–59; and Donald H. Sykes, Virginia J. Douglas, and Gert Morgenstern, "Sustained Attention in Hyperactive Children," *Journal of Child Psychology and Psychiatry,* vol. 14, 1973, pp. 213–20.

6. Diane McGuinness, *When Children Don't Learn* (New York: Basic Books, 1985), p. 205.

7. Sydney S. Zentall, "Behavioral Comparisons of Hyperactive and Normally Active Children in Natural Settings," *Journal of Abnormal Child Psychology,* vol. 8, 1980, pp. 93–109; and Sydney S. Zentall and Thomas R. Zentall, "Optimal Stimulation: A Model of Disordered Activity and Performance in Normal and Deviant Children," *Psychological Bulletin,* vol. 94, 1983, pp. 446–71.

8. Gabrielle Weiss et al., "Hyperactives as Young Adults," *Archives of General Psychiatry,* June 1979, pp. 675–81.

9. Barkley, p. 61.

10. Eric Taylor and Seija Sandberg, "Hyperactive Behavior in English Schoolchildren: A Questionnaire Survey," *Journal of Abnormal Child Psychology,* vol. 12, 1984, pp. 143–55.

11. Malka Margalit, "Diagnostic Application of the Conners Abbreviated Symptom Questionnaire," *Journal of Clinical Child Psychology,* vol. 12, 1983, pp. 355–57.

12. John S. Werry and Herbert C. Quay, "The Prevalence of Behavior Symptoms in Younger Elementary School Children," *American Journal of Orthopsychiatry,* vol. 41, 1971, pp. 136–43.

13. Nadine M. Lambert, Jonathan Sandoval, and Dana Sassone, "Prevalence of Hyperactivity in Elementary School Children as a Function of Social System Definers," *American Journal of Orthopsychiatry,* vol. 48, 1978, pp. 446–63.

14. McGuinness, pp. 188–89.

15. Barkley, p. 329.

16. Russell Schachar et al., "Attaining and Maintaining Preparation: A Comparison of Attention in Hyperactive, Normal, and Disturbed Control Children," *Journal of Abnormal Child Psychology,* vol. 16, 1988, pp. 361–78.

17. Jaab van der Meere and Joseph Sergeant, "Focused Attention in Pervasively Hyperactive Children," *Journal of Abnormal Child Psychology,* vol. 16, 1988, pp. 627–39.

18. See Esther Benezra and Virginia I. Douglas, "Short-Term Serial Recall in ADDH, Normal, and Reading-Disabled Boys," *Journal of Abnormal Child Psychology,* vol. 16, 1988, pp. 511–25; and Robert A. Rubinstein and Ronald T. Brown, "An Evaluation of the Validity of the Diagnostic Category of Attention Deficit Disorder," *American Journal of Orthopsychiatry,* vol. 54, 1984, pp. 398–414.

19. For an overview of the function of paradigms in scientific development, see Thomas Kuhn, *The Structure of Scientific Revolutions* (Chicago: University of Chicago Press, 1962).

20. For a look at the image of the machine as it affects special education perspectives in general, see Lois Heshusius, "At the Heart of the Advocacy Dilemma: A Mechanistic World View," *Exceptional Children,* vol. 49, 1982, pp. 6–11.

21. Matthew Galvin, *Otto Learns About His Medicine: A Story About Medication for Hyperactive Children* (New York: Magination Press, 1988).

22. See, for example, Lisa J. Bain, *A Parent's Guide to Attention Deficit Disorders* (New York: Delta, 1991), pp. 150–51.

23. Russell Barkley was quoted in a keynote address titled "Help Me, I'm Losing My Child!," included in the *Proceedings of CH.A.D.D. Fourth Annual Conference* (1992), available from Caset Associates Ltd., 3927 Old Lee Highway, Fairfax, VA 22030.

24. Most of the articles I've located in this area center on children labeled both "gifted" and "ADD." See, for example, James T. Webb and Diane Latimer, "ADHD and Children Who Are Gifted," *Exceptional Children,* vol. 60, 1993, pp. 183–84; and James Delisle, "ADD Gifted: How Many Labels Can One Child Take?," *The Gifted Child Today,* March/April 1995, pp. 42–43. One exception was Sydney Zentall, "Production Deficiencies in Elicited Language but Not in the Spontaneous Verbalizations of Hyperactive Children," *Journal of Abnormal Child Psychology,* vol. 16, 1988, pp. 657–73.

25. See Dorothea M. Ross and Sheila A. Ross, *Hyperactivity: Current Issues, Research, and Theory* (New York: John Wiley, 1982); and Cynthia A. Riccio et al., "Neurological Basis of Attention Deficit Hyperactivity Disorder," *Exceptional Children,* vol. 60, pp. 118–24.

26. A. J. Zametkin et al., "Cerebral Glucose Metabolism in Adults with Hyperactivity of Childhood Onset," *New England Journal of Medicine,* vol. 323, 1990, pp. 1361–66.

27. Some of the national media articles highlighting the Zametkin study include Philip Elmer-DeWitt, "Why Junior Won't Sit Still," *Time,* 26 November 1990, p. 59; Gina Kolata, "Hyperactivity Is Linked to Brain Abnormality," *New York Times,* 15 November 1990, p. A-1; and Sally Squires, "Brain Function Yields Physical Clue That Could Help Pinpoint Hyperactivity," *Washington Post,* 15 November 1990, p. A-18.

28. Jeanne Gehret, *Eagle Eyes: A Child's Guide to Paying Attention* (Fairport, N.Y.: Verbal Images Press, 1991).

29. Alan Zametkin et al., "Brain Metabolism in Teenagers with Attention-Deficit Hyperactivity Disorder," *Archives of General Psychiatry,* vol. 50, 1993, pp. 333–40.

30. Robert Reid, John W. Maag, and Stanley F. Vasa, "Attention Deficit Hyperactivity Disorder as a Disability Category: A Critique," *Exceptional Children,* vol. 60, 1993, p. 203.

31. Debra DeLee is quoted in a 29 March 1991 letter from the National Education Association to the Office of Special Education Programs, written in response to the federal government's Notice of Inquiry regarding ADD.

32. Peg Dawson is quoted in the *APA Monitor* (a publication of the American Psychological Association), November 1990.

CHALLENGE QUESTIONS

Does Attention Deficit Disorder Exist?

1. To what extent should conditions involving inattention and hyperactivity be regarded as medical, as opposed to emotional, disorders?
2. What are the minimum behavioral criteria that should be met before recommending that an inattentive or hyperactive individual be given a prescription of a medication such as Ritalin?
3. What might motivate some parents to urge educators and psychologists to diagnose their children with ADD?
4. What interventions other than medication should be instituted in the home and in the classroom to help the hyperactive child?
5. To what extent, if any, can the media be held responsible for cultivating hyperactivity and short attention spans among young people?

Suggested Readings

Armstrong, T. (1997). *The myth of the A.D.D. child: Fifty ways to improve your child's behavior and attention span without drugs, labels, or coercion.* New York, NY: Plume.

Barkley, R. A. (1998). *Attention-deficit hyperactivity disorder: A handbook for diagnosis and treatment.* New York, NY: The Guilford Press.

Barkley, R. A. (1999). Theories of attention-deficit/hyperactivity disorder. In H. C. Quay & A. E. Hogan (Eds.), *Handbook of disruptive disorders* (pp. 295–313). New York, NY: Kluwer Academic Plenum Publishers.

Hallowell, E., & Ratey, J. (1995). *Driven to distraction: Recognizing and coping with attention deficit disorder from childhood through adulthood.* New York, NY: Pantheon Books.

ISSUE 5

Should All Uses of MDMA (Ecstasy) Be Prohibited?

YES: Robert Mathias and Patrick Zickler, from "NIDA Conference Highlights Scientific Findings on MDMA/Ecstasy," *NIDA Notes* (December 2001)

NO: June Riedlinger and Michael Montagne, from "Using MDMA in the Treatment of Depression," in Julie Holland, ed., *Ecstasy: The Complete Guide* (Park Street Press, 2001)

ISSUE SUMMARY

YES: Science writers Robert Mathias and Patrick Zickler argue that MDMA has skyrocketed in popularity and that insufficient attention has been paid to the physical and psychological risks associated with its use.

NO: June Riedlinger, an assistant professor of clinical pharmacy, and Michael Montagne, a professor of pharmacy, contend that the risks associated with MDMA use have been exaggerated and that there are legitimate therapeutic uses for this substance.

$\mathbf{M}$DMA, popularly known as "Ecstasy," was first synthesized at the beginning of the twentieth century when a pharmaceutical company was trying to develop a medication to stop bleeding. However, this product was abandoned because of its dramatic psychoactive properties. MDMA resurfaced in the 1980s when some psychotherapists proposed that it be used to enhance communication in patients. The drug also began appearing on college campuses and in nightclubs, where users were enthralled by its euphoria-inducing effects. Although the Drug Enforcement Agency outlawed MDMA in 1985, the use of this substance continued to grow dramatically throughout the 1990s, as partygoers attending dance marathons known as raves craved MDMA as their recreational drug of choice.

By the late 1990s the rave party scene had caught the attention of the media and law enforcement authorities because of the increasing number of medical emergencies associated with the uncontrolled use of substances such as MDMA. For example, in 1994 there were 253 MDMA-related emergency room incidents, but by the year 2000 the number had risen to 4,511 individuals being rushed to hospitals because they were suffering from dehydration, hyperthermia, and seizures caused by MDMA. As Robert Mathias and Patrick Zickler assert in the following selection, in addition to the immediate physical risks associated with MDMA, there are long-term emotional and cognitive costs. For instance, chronic users of MDMA show evidence of impairment in learning and memory as well as an increased likelihood of developing serious psychological conditions later in life.

In the second selection, June Riedlinger and Michael Montagne acknowledge the potential for adverse effects and neurotoxicity associated with MDMA, but they urge more thoughtful attention to the haphazard ways in which MDMA has been taken by recreational users. They also argue that there are some potentially useful ways in which this substance might be prescribed to treat certain psychological problems, such as depression, for which traditional medications have considerable limitations and side effects. In responding to harsh criticisms of MDMA, Riedlinger and Montagne contend that the problems are attributable to the lack of pharmaceutical regulation; if MDMA were professionally manufactured such that samples of known purity were distributed, most adverse reactions would be avoidable.

POINT

- Even small doses of MDMA can greatly reduce the body's ability to metabolize the drug. Increased toxic effects can lead to harmful reactions, such as dehydration, hyperthermia, and seizures.

- In clinical studies, MDMA users have shown massive impairment on tests of learning, memory, and general intelligence when compared to nonusers.

- Exposure to MDMA is associated with damage to brain cells that release serotonin.

- Compared with nonusers, current and former users of MDMA have drastically higher measures of psychopathology, such as impulsivity, anxiety, and depression.

- Many Ecstasy-related emergencies occur because tablets are frequently laced with other drugs.

COUNTERPOINT

- Reports of adverse reactions have been sensationalized. Most adverse reactions and neurotoxicity can be avoided if the lowest effective therapeutic doses are used.

- Most clinical studies that allege neurotoxicity have recruited volunteers with histories of excessive and prolonged use. No study has been published that assesses individuals with histories of infrequent oral dosing.

- MDMA works to enhance serotonergic function and increase mood in a matter of hours.

- MDMA is, in fact, effective at treating psychopathology. It facilitates psychotherapy and helps to alleviate feelings of hopelessness.

- If MDMA were regulated and samples of known purity were used, most adverse reactions would be avoidable.

**Robert Mathias
and Patrick Zickler**

 **YES**

NIDA Conference Highlights Scientific Findings on MDMA/Ecstasy

In the face of worldwide increases in the use of MDMA, or ecstasy, particularly among teens and young adults, NIDA convened an international array of scientists at the National Institutes of Health in Bethesda, Maryland, in July [2001] for a conference on "MDMA/Ecstasy Research: Advances, Challenges, Future Directions." MDMA researchers from Australia, Europe, and all regions of the United States detailed the latest findings on patterns and trends of MDMA abuse, its complex acute effects on the brain and behavior, and the possible long-term consequences of its use.

In opening remarks, Dr. Glen Hanson, director of NIDA's Division of Neuroscience and Behavioral Research, noted the tremendous interest of the scientific community and the general public in MDMA and its effects. The soldout conference drew an audience of 565 people with a broad range of interests and perspectives. They included scientists, drug abuse prevention and treatment practitioners, clinicians, educators, high school counselors, and representatives from Federal and local public health departments and agencies.

A public health perspective on MDMA by James N. Hall, of the Up Front Drug Information Center in Miami, Florida, provided a sharp contrast to the prevailing public view of MDMA as an innocuous drug. MDMA use began to expand rapidly in the United States in 1996 with "more pills going to younger populations," Mr. Hall said. This upsurge in use led to an increase in drug-related problems. For example, MDMA-related hospital emergency room incidents increased from 253 in 1994 to 4,511 in 2000, according to recent data from the Substance Abuse and Mental Health Services Administration's Drug Abuse Warning Network. "Most of these emergency room mentions are multiple-drug cases," Mr. Hall said, "as polydrug use has become the norm."

The common practice of using MDMA in conjunction with other drugs was just one of several recurring themes sounded during a conference session on current trends and patterns of MDMA use. Other significant

From Robert Mathias and Patrick Zickler, "NIDA Conference Highlights Scientific Findings on MDMA/Ecstasy," *NIDA Notes*, vol. 16, no. 5 (December 2001). Washington, DC: U.S. Government Printing Office, 2001. NIH Publication No. 02-3478.

themes were:

- MDMA now is being used in urban, suburban, and rural areas throughout the country;
- MDMA continues to be used in its traditional settings of all-night dance parties, called "raves," and nightclubs; use also is common now on college campuses and at small group gatherings, such as house parties;
- MDMA is used by all ages but still mainly by adolescents and young adults; use has increased sharply in this population in recent years;
- MDMA users are predominantly white, but ethnically and racially diverse groups of people are now using the drug; and
- MDMA's euphoric effects can lead to unplanned or unwanted sexual contact that increases the risk of transmitting HIV/AIDS and other infectious diseases.

Figure 1

MDMA-Related Hospital Emergency Room Incidents   1994 2000

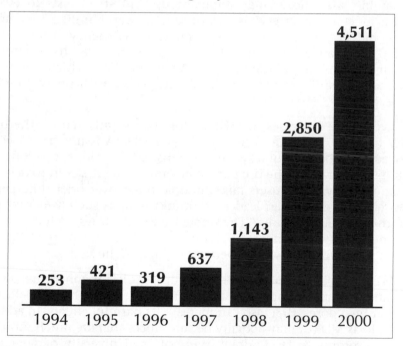

Acute Effects of MDMA

A session on MDMA's acute effects presented the latest findings on how the drug works in the brain and body to produce its perceptual and physiological impact. The session explored the interaction of underlying biological and behavioral factors and mechanisms that may contribute to the possibly harmful effects of MDMA use.

Animal studies have indicated that MDMA increases extracellular levels of the chemical messengers serotonin and dopamine. In laboratory studies to understand how these increases affect humans, Dr. Manuel Tancer of Wayne State University in Detroit asked participants to compare MDMA's effects to those produced by compounds that stimulate serotonin alone and dopamine alone. MDMA's effects were reported to resemble some features of both compounds, noted Dr. Tancer. This indicates that both the dopamine and serotonin systems play a role in producing MDMA's subjective effects in humans.

MDMA also has powerful acute physiological effects in humans that increase with larger doses, according to several presentations. MDMA's cardiovascular effects include large increases in blood pressure, heart rate, and myocardial oxygen consumption, noted Dr. John Mendelson of the University of California, San Francisco. MDMA's elevations of heart rate and blood pressure were comparable to those produced by a maximal dose of dobutamine, a cardiovascular stimulant used in stress tests to evaluate patients for coronary artery disease, he said. However, unlike dobutamine, MDMA did not increase the heart's pumping efficiency. Thus, MDMA-induced heart rate and blood pressure increases may lead to an unexpectedly large increase in myocardial oxygen consumption, which can increase the risk for a cardiovascular catastrophe in people with preexisting heart disease, he said.

Even small increases in MDMA dose can greatly reduce the body's ability to metabolize the drug. This means MDMA is not processed and removed from the body quickly and remains active for longer periods. "As a result, plasma levels of the drug and concomitant increases in toxicity may rise dramatically when users take multiple doses over brief time periods. Increased toxic effects can lead to harmful reactions such as dehydration, hyperthermia, and seizures," Dr. Mendelson said. Drugs such as methamphetamine that are commonly abused in conjunction with MDMA also may increase the cardiovascular effects of MDMA, he said.

MDMA tablets often contain other drugs, such as ephedrine, a stimulant, and dextromethorphan, a cough suppressant that has PCP-like effects at high doses, that also can increase its harmful effects. In addition, drugs sold as MDMA may actually be substances that are much more dangerous, according to Dr. Rodney Irvine of the University of Adelaide in Australia. For example, the hallucinogen PMA (4-methoxyamphetamine), which is similar in some respects to MDMA, has even more severe toxic effects on the cardiovascular system, particularly as dosage increases. The drug has been sold as MDMA in Australia and has been associated with a number of deaths. PMA is now being distributed in the United States and has been linked to deaths in Chicago and Central Florida, according to the Federal Drug Enforcement Administration.

Long-Term Effects of MDMA

During the second day of the conference, researchers from the United States and other countries described current investigations of ecstasy's long-term effects. Introducing the day's program, Dr. Hanson summarized the mechanisms thought to be responsible for MDMA's toxic effects on the brain's serotonin system. In tests of learning and memory, he noted, MDMA users perform more poorly than nonusers on tasks associated with brain regions affected by MDMA. Higher doses of MDMA appear to be associated with more profound effects, and the consequences may be long-lasting.

Dr. Charles Vorhees of Children's Hospital Medical Center in Cincinnati, Ohio, has found that, in rats, exposure to MDMA during a period of brain development that corresponds to human brain development during the trimester before birth is associated with learning deficits that last into adulthood. "The impairment, which affects the rate at which the animals learn new tasks, increases in severity as the dose of MDMA increases and is more pronounced as the tasks become more complex," Dr. Vorhees said.

These findings of MDMA's effects on brain development are limited to studies involving rats, but there is a growing body of research suggesting that—in adult primates—MDMA can cause long-lasting damage. At the Johns Hopkins University School of Medicine in Baltimore, Drs. Una McCann, George Ricaurte, and other investigators have found that exposure to MDMA is associated with damage to brain cells that release serotonin; this damage persists for at least 7 years in nonhuman primates. In humans, the researchers have found that MDMA use is associated with verbal and visual memory problems in individuals who have not used the drug for at least 2 weeks. "We see a relationship between the dose of MDMA and the severity of the effects. In animals, MDMA-induced damage is extensive and long-lasting and we do not yet know if it is reversible," Dr. Ricaurte said. "A person who takes enough of the drug to feel its effects is taking enough to be at serious risk of similar damage to the brain and to memory and learning."

Dr. Linda Chang, a scientist at the Brookhaven National Laboratory in Upton, New York, reported on research using brain imaging techniques to evaluate the effects of occasional use of MDMA. She and her colleagues Dr. Charles Grob and Dr. Russell Poland at the University of California, Los Angeles, used single photon emission computed tomography to evaluate blood flow to the brain—which is regulated in part by serotonin—in 21 MDMA users who had taken the drug at least 6 times per year for more than 1 year (on average, a total of 75 times), but had not used the drug in at least 2 weeks (4 months average abstinence). The participants then were given MDMA in two sessions over the course of a week. Two weeks later, brain images showed decreased blood flow compared to the earlier images. The decrease was greater in those individuals who had higher total use of the drug.

Figure 2

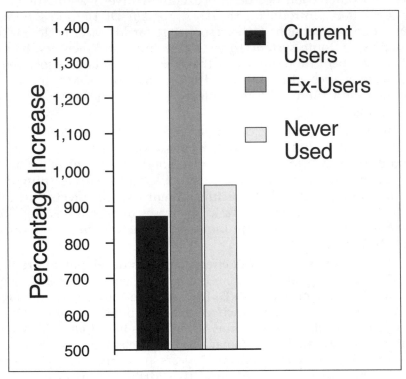

Effects of MDMA Use on Tryptophan Utilization

Note: MDMA disrupts brain processes that use the amino acid tryptophan to make the neurotransmitter serotonin, which affects memory and mood. Five hours after drinking a tryptophan supplement, ex-users of MDMA showed greater elevations of their blood tryptophan levels than did current users or non-users, indicating that less of the amino acid had been converted to serotonin.

MDMA Research in Europe

The popularity of MDMA as a "club drug" began in Europe in the late 1980s—roughly 5 years earlier than in the United States—and researchers there have studied the drug's effects in populations with a longer history of drug use. In Great Britain and Germany researchers have found that MDMA users—and even former users who have not taken the drug for at least 6 months—perform more poorly on some tests of memory and learning than do nonusers. MDMA also is associated with psychological problems such as anxiety and depression, this research suggests.

The learning and memory functions that appear to be impaired by MDMA in animal and human studies are associated with the brain's serotonin system. The specific effects of MDMA can be evaluated directly in animal studies, but in humans nearly all MDMA users also use other drugs such as marijuana, cocaine, and alcohol. In an effort to more fully understand

Figure 3

Effect of MDMA Use on Impulsivity

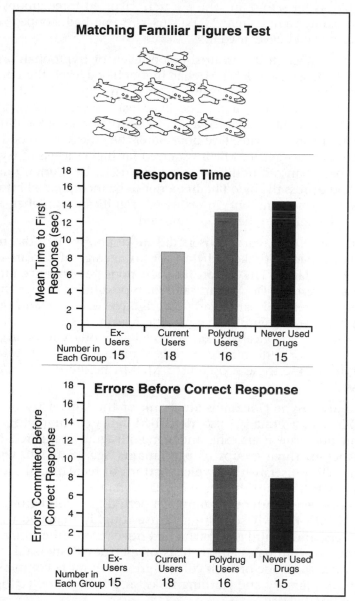

Note: The airplane figure at top is exactly matched by only one of six similar figures below. When asked to find the correct match, current and ex-users of MDMA made quicker choices and made more wrong choices before identifying the correct match than participants who used drugs other than MDMA or who used no drugs at all.

how MDMA affects polydrug users, Dr. Valerie Curran and her colleagues at University College London investigated the effect of MDMA use on the body's ability to use tryptophan, an amino acid that is one of the chemical building blocks for serotonin. The research involved three groups of polydrug users: some were current MDMA users, some had stopped using the drug, and some had never used it.

The researchers first measured blood levels of tryptophan and found that current and ex-users of MDMA had higher blood levels than did nonusers and that the levels were elevated in proportion to the total amount of drug the participants had used. The investigators then gave participants drinks that contained augmented amounts of tryptophan in addition to all other necessary amino acids. Five hours later they measured blood levels of the amino acid. Ex-users of MDMA showed far higher levels of tryptophan in their blood than did nonusers or current users, Dr. Curran said. "Tryptophan should cross the blood-brain barrier to be incorporated into the biosynthesis of serotonin, but in ex-users, significantly higher levels of tryptophan remained in the blood," she said.

In memory tests, current users did more poorly than did nonusers; exusers—who had not taken MDMA for an average of 2 years—had the poorest performance. The reason for such poor performance among the ex-users is uncertain, Dr. Curran said. One possibility is that these were people who developed particularly severe adverse effects and quit using the drug because of them. "Whatever the reason, there is a clear correlation between a biological marker (blood levels of tryptophan), a functional deficit (poor performance on tests of memory), and the total dosage and length of time these people used MDMA before they stopped," Dr. Curran said.

Dr. Euphrosyne Gouzoulis-Mayfrank of the University of Technology in Aachen, Germany, also described research involving MDMA's effects on polydrug users. She and her colleagues compared cognitive performance in three groups of participants age 18 to 30. One group included MDMA users with a typical pattern of recreational use (at least twice per month within the preceding 2 years) who also used marijuana (at least once per month over a 6-month period), a second group who did not use MDMA but whose marijuana use roughly matched that of the MDMA users, and a third group who had never used either drug. "Ecstasy users showed no impairment in tests of alertness," she said, "but performed worse than one or both control groups in more complex tasks of attention, in memory and learning tasks, and in tasks reflecting aspects of general intelligence."

Dr. Michael Morgan of the University of Sussex in Great Britain described research that suggests a relationship between marijuana use, MDMA use, and psychological problems and memory deficits. Dr. Morgan and his colleagues studied the effects among groups of current MDMA users, ex-users, polydrug users who did not use MDMA, and participants who had never used drugs.

The researchers found that the psychological measures were more closely associated in the polydrug population with current marijuana use than with past MDMA use. "Overall, however, current and ex-users of MDMA have dramatically higher measures of psychopathology such as impulsivity than nonusers," Dr. Morgan said. Like Dr. Curran, Dr. Morgan

Figure 4

Long-Term Effects of MDMA Use on Memory

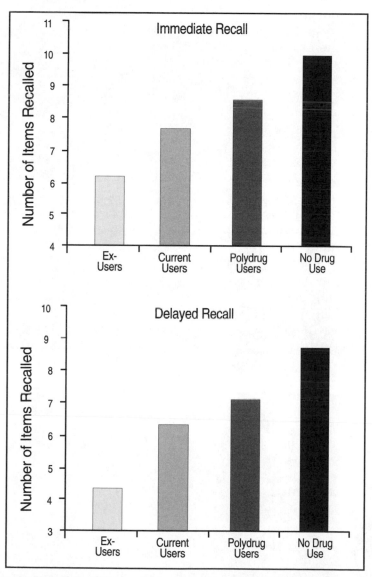

Note: In tests of MDMA effects on memory, ex-users and current users performed worse than participants who used drugs other than MDMA or used no drugs. Ex-users, in particular, showed greatly impaired memory.

found cognitive deficits associated with rates of past MDMA use. In tests of memory, both current and ex-users performed more poorly than non-users. He also found that on some tests ex-users performed worse than did current users, although he noted that the reasons for poorer performance by ex-users could not clearly be linked exclusively to MDMA use. "Nonetheless, as a practical matter, ex-users show massively impaired memory. Not only had they not recovered, they were actually worse than current users," Dr. Morgan said.

NO  June Riedlinger and Michael Montagne

Using MDMA in the Treatment of Depression

Introduction

In this [selection] we discuss the use of the substance MDMA [ecstasy] for the treatment of depression. The first author's personal experience and work as a clinical pharmacist in psychiatry was the foundation for the hypothesis that MDMA could be a healing agent for the life-threatening illness of depression. Before discussing how MDMA may be beneficial in treating depression, a brief review of the medical criteria for the condition is warranted. . . .

Biochemical Basis of Depression

The possibility that some forms of human depression are based on central nervous system deficiencies of the neurotransmitter serotonin (5-hydroxytryptamine, or 5-HT), was first suggested by van Praag (1962) and then reinforced by the findings of other researchers (Coppen 1967; Lapin and Oxenburg 1969). Based on his later research, van Praag (1982) concluded that serotonin disorders are implicated most clearly in a subgroup of approximately 40 percent of patients afflicted with depression. He also emphasized that serotonin disorders probably play a causative, rather than a secondary, role in depression. This is suggested by the fact that serotonin-potentiating compounds, such as the precursors 5-hydroxytryptophan (5-HTP) and L-tryptophan, an essential amino acid, can have a therapeutic effect in depression (van Praag 1981).

It is significant that many of the drugs prescribed for treatment of depression have serotonergic activity. The newest class of antidepressants, the serotonin reuptake inhibitors (Prozac, Zoloft, Paxil, Celexa, and others) and, to varying degrees, the tricyclic antidepressants prevent the recycling of serotonin back into presynaptic nerve endings. Monoamine oxidase (MAO) inhibitors prevent the breakdown of serotonin by the enzyme MAO. In either case, more serotonin is available for binding to receptors (Spiegel and Aebi 1983). The specific mechanism of action of these drugs, however, is still not clear.

From *Park Street Press*, 2001. Copyright © 2001 by Park Street Press. Reprinted by permission.

There is an entire class of psychoactive drugs that almost certainly derives its main effect from serotonin mediation (Freedman et al. 1970; Haigler and Aghajanian 1973; Anden et al. 1974; Winter 1975; Meltzer et al. 1978). These drugs, the psychedelics, are reported to have positive effects in the treatment of various psychological disorders, including depression. We present and discuss the value of psychedelic agents, with a focus on clinical reports and theoretical explanations for one specific drug, MDMA, that may become an efficacious treatment for depression in the future.

Psychedelic Psychotherapy

The possibility that psychedelic drugs could help facilitate the modern psychotherapeutic process was virtually ignored in the United States and Europe until about 1950. Between then and the mid-1960s, more than one thousand clinical papers describing forty thousand patients who had taken part in psychedelic therapy or other research trials were published, as well as several dozen related books; six international conferences on psychedelic drug therapy were held (Grinspoon and Bakalar 1983). Two different types of psychedelic psychotherapy were described (Grinspoon and Bakalar 1979). One emphasized a mystical or conversion experience and its after-effects (psychedelic therapy); using high doses of LSD (more than 200 mcg) was thought to be especially effective in reforming alcoholics and criminals. The other type explored the unconscious in the manner of psychoanalysis (psycholytic therapy); it focused on the treatment of neuroses and psychosomatic disorders using low doses of LSD (100–150 mcg) as well as other psychedelic drugs.

By the mid-1950s, it was recognized that psychedelics function as nonspecific amplifiers, drugs that project into consciousness (amplify) memories, fears, and other subjectively varying (nonspecific) psychological material that had been repressed, or was unconscious. Among the first announcements of this highly significant finding was a report entitled "Ataractic and Hallucinogenic Drugs in Psychiatry," written by a team of international experts convened by the World Health Organization. This report challenged the prevailing idea that psychedelic drugs are psychotomimetic, that is, capable of inducing a model of temporary psychosis. Instead, the team concluded, "It may be a gross oversimplification to speak of drug-specific reactivity patterns. On the contrary, experience suggests that the same drug, in the same dose, in the same subject may produce very different effects according to the precise interpersonal and motivational situation in which it was given" (World Health Organization 1958). Thus, it was made clear that the issues of set (the users' expectations) and setting (the environment for the drug experience) . . . must be taken into account when using psychedelics.

Another important issue to consider in a discussion of drug-assisted psychotherapy is this: at present, psychiatrists prescribe doses of mood elevators or stabilizers with which patients must comply on a daily basis. There is no currently accepted model of one-time or infrequent dosing of medications to alleviate psychic suffering. Thus, Grinspoon and Bakalar

(1986) have emphasized: "It is a misunderstanding to consider psyche-delic drug therapy as a form of chemotherapy, which must be regarded in the same way as prescribing lithium or phenothiazines." Instead, it is more like "a hybrid between pharmacotherapy and psychotherapy" (Grinspoon and Bakalar 1990) that incorporates features of both. . . .

MDMA's Role in the Treatment of Depression

That MDMA is apparently serotonergic was first noted by Nichols and asso-ciates (1982), who introduced it in vitro to homogenized rat brains and then measured the release of serotonin from the synaptosomes (vesicles in the synapses that store neurotransmitters). Elevated levels were detected, suggesting that serotonin release may play a role in MDMA's pharmacologi-cal activity. Subsequent research described in Peroutka (1990) appears to confirm the drug's serotongenicity. As with serotonergic antidepressant drugs, however, the specific mode of action is uncertain. . . .

In any case, MDMA's use in psychotherapy to stimulate positive feel-ings, such as openness and empathy, would seem to recommend it for a possible clinical role in treating depression. Riedlinger (1985) first proposed this in a discussion of MDMA's positive isomer activity and consequent release of serotonin in the brain. Because it is a potent releaser of serotonin into the synapse, and because of its short duration of effect, MDMA seems to be both effective and efficient as a drug for the medical treatment of depression. It works to enhance serotonergic function and mood in a mat-ter of hours instead of weeks (as is the case for most prescription antidepres-sants), and it is effective when administered infrequently, perhaps in weekly or monthly dosing intervals. This compares favorably to the multi-ple daily dosing required for most of the currently available drugs that can be prescribed for treating depression (such as tricyclic antidepressants, MAO inhibitors, serotonin reuptake inhibitors). The other drugs often take sev-eral days or even weeks to produce antidepressant effects and frequently cause lasting troublesome side effects (appetite and sleep changes, sexual dysfunction, sweating, nausea, and headaches). Compassion for the victims of depression, in addition to the evidence of MDMA's serotoninreleasing effect, should compel further research to establish clearly whether MDMA is indeed an alternative antidepressant.

Treating Suicidal Depression With MDMA

The notion that MDMA might be useful in treating suicidal depression is based on a comparison of psychological patterns in suicidal people and MDMA's psycoactive effects. Psychological characteristics of suicidal people tend to vary between different age groups, cultures, economic classes, and gender (Hendin 1982; American Psychiatric Association 1994). Many cases seem to be manifestations of alienation. The anguish of the suicidal person is frequently that of a person in exile. He or she feels totally isolated, singled out by fate to suffer hardships and endless frustrations alone. Such people often find it hard to deal with the conflicts and demands of interpersonal relationships. They withdraw into a private, lonely world. Their justification might be that they feel unworthy of love or that others have abandoned them unfairly. In either case, the isolation typically starts to feel irreversible. There seems to be no possibility of ever establishing meaningful contact with other human beings.

According to the *Harvard Medical School Mental Health Letter* ("Suicide," 1986), "Among the immediate motives for suicide, not surprisingly, despair is most common. In one long-term study, hopelessness alone accounted for most of the association between depression and suicide, and a high level of hopelessness was the strongest signal that a person who had attempted suicide would try again. Intense guilt, psychotic delusions, and even the severity of the depression were much less adequate indicators." The study referred to in the *Mental Health Letter,* by Beck and colleagues (1985), reported that high ratings on the Beck Hopelessness Scale successfully predicted 90.9 percent of eventual cases of suicide in a sample of 165 hospitalized suicide ideators (people who initially went to the doctor with thoughts of suicide) who were followed for five to ten years after taking the test. A subsequent report regarding the study affirmed that "because hopelessness can be reduced fairly rapidly by specific therapeutic interventions . . . the assessment of hopelessness can potentially improve the prevention as well as the prediction of suicide" (Beck et al. 1989). Hopelessness itself might mediate the relationship between dysfunctional attitudes and psychopathology, especially depression.

Interpersonal attitudes related to depression, not hopelessness per se, also may be the root cause of suicide. To that extent, suicide might be considered an act of interpersonal frustration that seeks to communicate misery and break out of isolation ("Suicide," 1986). This goal may be reached, alternatively and more safely, by means of guided psychotherapy. The recalcitrance of suicidal people, however, is a problem for conventional psychotherapy. For therapy to work, a positive, dynamic interaction must take place between the patient and the therapist (Henry et al. 1990; Talley et al. 1990; Strupp 1993). The patient must be willing to communicate what is going on inside. Someone who is consumed by strong feelings of alienation and hopelessness is likely to resist interpersonal contact and open discussion. Of course, it is frequently true that patients hesitate to talk about personal problems at the start of psychotherapy and need several sessions before they warm up to the therapist. Time is often a luxury that suicidal patients cannot afford, however. They may be treatable over the long term with conventional psychotherapy, but first they must be stabilized or otherwise prevented from taking their own lives. Usually this means hospitalization, keeping a suicide watch on such patients, and even actively restraining them if necessary.

Here is where MDMA can perhaps play a viable role, based on certain effects and ramifications for guided psychotherapy succinctly described in an issue of the *Harvard Medical School Mental Health Letter* (Grinspoon and Bakalar 1985): Although MDMA has no officially approved medical or psychiatric application, a few psychiatrists and other therapists had been using it as an aid to psychotherapy for more than fifteen years, in the 1970s and '80s. It has now been taken in a therapeutic setting by hundreds, if not thousands, of people with few reported complications. It is said to fortify the therapeutic alliance by inviting self-disclosure and enhancing trust. Some patients also report changes that last several days to several weeks or longer—improved mood, greater relaxation, heightened self-esteem, and enhanced relations with others. Psychiatrists who have used MDMA with patients suggest that it might be helpful, for example, in marital counseling, in diagnostic interviews, or as a catalyst for insight in psychotherapy. Reports of therapeutic results are so far unpublished and anecdotal and cannot be properly evaluated without more systematic study.

Anecdotal reports by the hundreds of people who have taken MDMA in therapeutic settings are not irrelevant. Their testimonies indicate that certain psychological effects occur consistently across a broad spectrum of usage. This is evident in Adamson's (1985) collection of about fifty such testimonies. The forward, by Ralph Metzner, observes that these firsthand accounts include such words as "ecstasy, empathy, openness, acceptance, forgiveness, and emotional bonding" in reference to MDMA's effects. These are the opposite terms often used to describe the psychological distress of suicidal people: anguish, alienation, recalcitrance, rejection, blame, guilt, and emotional withdrawal. Eisner (1989) also describes several cases of MDMA-assisted psychotherapy in which depression is mentioned specifically as one of the symptoms that is alleviated.

The value of MDMA is that it does not make its users feel better by transporting them into a naive state of bliss. They are aware of the fact that their lives have been burdened by negative thinking, have been based on fears and anxieties. MDMA seems to lend them a different perspective for several hours by minimizing their defensiveness and fear of emotional injury (Greer 1985; Greer and Tolbert 1986, 1990). It stimulates a process by which they are able to look at their problems more objectively and thus transcend a feeling of hopeless entrapment. At the same time, they feel more in touch with their positive emotions. This sustains them as the therapeutic process takes its course. The drug gives them the courage to confront their emotional problems and the strength to work them out, often by enhancing their desire to communicate constructively. Numerous examples of this process are described in Adamson's book (1985).

The particular value of MDMA for suicidal patients and, by extension, for patients with less severe forms of depression is twofold. First, it might be useful as an interventional medicine. By providing the relief from overwhelmingly dark emotions, MDMA likely can help forestall the act of suicide or otherwise alleviate the patient's sense of hopelessness. This buys time for the drug's second major effect, facilitating psychotherapy by helping to enhance the patient's trust and by inviting self-analysis and disclosure. As previously noted, the result is a fortifying of the therapeutic alliance between patient and therapist. Furthermore, MDMA does so in a relatively short time. According to Metzner in Adamson's book (1985): "One therapist has estimated that in five hours of one Adam [MDMA] session clients could activate and process psychic material that would normally require five months of weekly sessions."

Needless to say, such accelerated therapeutic healing can mean the difference between life and death for people in imminent danger of suicide.

Risks of MDMA Use

There has been concern about neurotoxicity and other possible health risks from MDMA use. Most of these adverse reactions appear to be avoidable, if samples of known purity are administered in the lowest effective therapeutic dose range and frequency, after carefully screening patients for risk factors. This is consistent with the view of Grob and colleagues (1990) that fears of MDMA neurotoxicity may have been exaggerated and that rigorous clinical trials of the drug in psychotherapy should be resumed.*

Animal research with MDMA seems to indicate that even its high-dose neurotoxic effects can be minimized by the concurrent administration of fluoxetine (Schmidt 1987; Schmidt et al. 1987). One report by McCann and Ricaurte (1993) suggested that fluoxetine pretreatment, at doses of 20 to 40 mg, does not compromise MDMA's therapeutic effects and, furthermore, decreases postsession insomnia and fatigue. A cautionary editorial by Price and colleagues (1990) maintains that it is premature to pursue clinical trials of MDMA in conditions that are not life-threatening. Both sides would be served by exploring the possible use of MDMA as an intervention drug for the stabilization and subsequent treatment of patients afflicted with severe and perhaps suicidal depression.

Conclusions

Central nervous system deficiency of 5-hydroxytryptamine (serotonin) has been implicated as a biochemical basis of at least some forms of depression. Existing drug treatments for depression include some with serotonergic effects. Studies suggest that psychedelic drugs are also serotonergic, which may indicate that there is a role for psychedelics in the treatment of depression. Such treatment has been attempted using psychedelic drugs in both the indoleamine and phelylalkylamine categories. Encouraging results recommend further research, with special emphasis on drugs in the group called entactogens or empathogens, which cause substantially less distortion of normative consciousness than classic psychedelics, such as LSD or mescaline. They could be assimilated more easily into existing psychotherapy approaches, where their function would be to accelerate and enhance the normal psychotherapeutic process rather than to serve as a maintenance medication. Their usefulness in such an application would be mainly at the start of psychotherapy. The goals would be to reduce the client's fear response, which often inhibits the ability to deal with repressed traumatic material; to facilitate the client's interpersonal communications with the therapist, spouse, or significant others; and to accelerate the formation of a therapeutic alliance between client and therapist.

* [Most articles that allege neurotoxicity have recruited volunteers with histories of excessive and prolonged use. No study has been published that examines infrequent, single oral dosing.—Ed.]

CHALLENGE QUESTIONS

Should All Uses of MDMA (Ecstasy) Be Prohibited?

1. As spokespersons for the federal government, Mathias and Zickler present compelling arguments against the use of MDMA based on extensive research. What are some of the social issues associated with the government's aggressive efforts to reduce MDMA use?
2. Riedlinger and Montagne object to anti-MDMA arguments, which they view as biased and exaggerated. How could one justify the regulated production of MDMA by pharmaceutical companies?
3. Concerns about the detrimental side effects of MDMA use have been downplayed by those who say that such problems are found only in chronic heavy users, rather than occasional recreational users. How could researchers investigate the validity of this argument?
4. Some social critics assert that it is the right of the individual to make choices about substance use and that such choices should not be the concern of the government. What are your thoughts about this viewpoint?
5. Much controversy has emerged in recent years about the medical use of substances such as marijuana to alleviate chronic pain. What are some arguments for and against the use of MDMA for the alleviation of psychological distress such as depression?

Suggested Readings

Cohen, R. S. (1998). *The love drug: Marching to the beat of Ecstasy.* New York: Haworth Medical Press.

Collin, M., and Godfrey, J. (1998). *Altered state: The story of Ecstasy culture and acid house.* New York: Serpent's Tail.

Eisner, B. (1994). *Ecstasy: The MDMA story.* Berkeley, CA: Ronin Publishing.

Parrott, A. C. (Ed.). (2000). *MDMA (Methylenedioxymethamphetamine).* Farmington, CT: S. Karger Publishing.

ISSUE 6

Does Post-Abortion Syndrome Exist?

YES: E. Joanne Angelo, from "Post-Abortion Grief," *The Human Life Review* (Fall 1996)

NO: Joyce Arthur, from "Psychological Aftereffects of Abortion: The Rest of the Story," *The Humanist* (March/April 1997)

ISSUE SUMMARY

YES: Psychiatrist E. Joanne Angelo contends that women who have abortions are at risk of developing a lasting, serious syndrome consisting of several emotional and behavioral problems.

NO: Social activist Joyce Arthur asserts that a general consensus has been reached in the medical and scientific communities that most women who have abortions experience little or no psychological harm.

Perhaps no issue in the twentieth century has engendered more debate and acrimony than the issue of abortion. Since the Supreme Court case *Roe v. Wade* (1973), the debate has moved from the courthouse to the streets of America, in many instances reaching a boiling point in which activists have engaged in violent crimes, including murder, to advance a politically charged cause. On one side of the debate are those who insist that a woman's body is her own and that any decision she makes, including the choice of abortion, is extremely personal and beyond the scope of societal restriction. On the other side are those who insist that society has a right and a responsibility to influence certain personal decisions, such as abortion, when these choices relate to morality. For three decades abortion debates have consisted of powerfully charged tirades rooted in politics, religion, philosophy, and psychology. Arguments on each side of the discussion are often extreme, as spokespersons use every possible source of data to support their positions. Within the realm of mental health, the debate has centered around the question of whether or not women who have abortions suffer lasting emotional problems as a result.

In the following selection, E. Joanne Angelo contends that the choice to have an abortion has profound and lasting psychological effects not unlike the emotional experiences of a mother who suffers the death of her own child. She sees a significant difference, however, in that a woman who has undergone an abortion typically hides her grief as she struggles to deal with the emotions associated with the realization that she has lost a child she will never know. According to Angelo, some women rely on the defense of denial of such emotional reactions, thus leading to the conclusions drawn by some researchers that psychological problems are rarely evoked by the experience of abortion. Angelo maintains that in time, however, many women develop debilitating psychological problems that affect them for years.

In the second selection, Joyce Arthur argues that the research findings are clear on the issue of post-abortion psychological problems—most women who have abortions experience little or no psychological harm. She asserts that some antiabortion spokespersons cite research conducted between 1950 and 1975 to support the notion of post-abortion syndrome, but she maintains that because these studies were conducted at a time when abortion was illegal or highly restricted, the conclusions were biased. According to Arthur, more recent studies have been biased or methodologically flawed, and many writings on this topic have been penned by anti-choice advocates who rely on incorrect or out-of-date pop psychology. Arthur states that not only are serious abortion-related psychological problems rare but the emotions experienced by most women following abortion involve feelings of relief, improved self-esteem, and inner strength.

POINT

- The medical literature has increasingly acknowledged that women who have abortions experience many of the same emotional reactions as mothers who suffer the death of a child.

- Following abortion, many women develop a constellation of psychological symptoms, including feelings of sadness and guilt, with some turning to alcohol, drugs, and maladaptive behaviors in their attempts to cope.

- The research that denies post-abortion syndrome is based on assessments of reactions shortly after abortion; insufficient attention is given to long-term negative experiences.

- The symptoms that many women experience as a result of the abortion experience are often characterized by clinicians under the diagnosis "pathological grief reaction."

COUNTERPOINT

- A general consensus has been reached in the medical and scientific communities that most women who have had abortions experience little or no psychological harm.

- The most frequently reported emotions felt by women following abortion are relief and happiness, with many women experiencing improved self-esteem, inner strength, and a motivation to refocus their lives in a meaningful way.

- Reliable studies have pointed to the conclusion that serious and persistent psychological problems are rare and are usually related to circumstances surrounding the abortion rather than the abortion itself.

- There is little need to posit the notion of a psychological disorder in women who have abortions since abortion is not significantly different from any other stressful life experience.

E. Joanne Angelo

 **YES**

Post-Abortion Grief

Every woman who subjects herself to an induced abortion suffers the death of her own child. She is at risk not only for the surgical and medical complications of abortion—uterine rupture, sepsis, infertility, increased incidence of cancer. She is also at high risk for pathological grief which often brings with it severe and long-lasting negative sequelae for herself, her partner, her surviving children and the whole of society. Grief following a death in the family is a universally accepted experience. A period of mourning following the loss of a loved one is a normal expectation in every culture. It is also generally understood that if this mourning process is blocked or impacted, there will be negative consequences. Shakespeare, in his tragedy *Macbeth*, says, "Give sorrow words, the grief that does not speak knits up the o'erwrought heart and bids it break" (Act IV, scene 3). Yet a mother's grief after an induced abortion has heretofore seldom been acknowledged.

The death of a child is perhaps the most difficult loss to mourn—even the death of a premature baby, a stillborn child, or a miscarriage. The medical literature in recent years has increasingly acknowledged the significance of perinatal loss for parents. Obstetrical journals describe "perinatal grief teams" consisting of nurses, doctors, social workers, clergy and volunteers who help parents cope with the loss of children who die in neonatal intensive care units. Parents are encouraged to name and hold their dead baby, and to take photographs. Religious services assist them in their mourning, and they are encouraged to bury the child with their loved ones in a family grave which they can visit as often as they wish.(1)

Abortion, whether spontaneous or induced, is part of the same continuum of perinatal grief. However, grief after elective abortion is uniquely poignant because it is largely hidden. There are no provisions made to assist the post-abortion woman in her grieving—she has no child to hold, no photographs, no wake or funeral, and no grave to visit. After an elective abortion, a woman typically finds herself alone to cope not only with the loss of the child she will never know, but also with her personal responsibility in the child's death with its ensuing guilt and shame. She may have difficulty understanding her ambivalent feelings—on the one hand, relief (often very temporary) that she is no longer pregnant, and, on the other hand, a profound sense of loss and emptiness. In her

From E. Joanne Angelo, "Post-Abortion Grief," *The Human Life Review*, vol. 22, no. 4 (Fall 1996). Copyright © 1996 by E. Joanne Angelo. Reprinted by permission of the author.

book, *Anatomy of Bereavement,* Beverley Raphael explains, "A woman may have required a high level of defensive denial of her tender feelings for the baby to allow her to make the decision for termination. This denial often carries her through the procedure and hours afterward, so that she seems cheerful, accepting but unwilling to talk at the time when supportive counseling may be offered by the clinic."(2) This may explain why research into psychiatric sequelae of abortion in the immediate post-abortion period often yields negative results.

The Emotional Effects

In the weeks and months after the abortion, feelings of sadness and guilt often threaten to overwhelm the post-abortion woman, yet society offers her no assistance in mourning—she is expected to be grateful that "her problem is solved" and to "get on with her life" as though nothing significant had happened. At the same time, pain and bleeding remind her of the assault on her body, the sudden endocrine changes cause her to become emotionally labile or unstable. She is poignantly aware of the date her child would have been born. Reminders threaten her defensive denial and repression all too frequently: anniversaries of her abortion, other children of the age her child would have been, Mother's Day, the omni-present abortion debate in the media, a visit to the gynecologist, the sound of the suction machine at the dentist's office, or the sound of a vacuum cleaner at home, a baby in a television ad, a new pregnancy, a death in the family, a film depicting prenatal development or abortion, or a pro-life homily. Any of these may trigger a sudden flood of grief, guilt, anger and even despair, which in turn, calls forth even more intense defensive responses.

The post-abortion woman's attempts to comply with society's expectations that she proceed with her life as though she had undergone an innocuous procedure are bought at great personal expense. She may turn to alcohol or drugs to get to sleep at night or to deaden the pain of the intrusive thoughts which haunt her day and night, "I killed my baby! I killed my baby! I don't deserve to live!" Flashbacks to the abortion procedure may occur at any time. She may throw herself into intense activity—work, study, or recreation, or attempt to deal with her feelings of loneliness and emptiness by binge eating alternating with purging or anorexia, or by intense efforts to repair intimate relationships or develop new ones inappropriately, becoming sexually promiscuous, risking sexually transmitted diseases, and repeating pregnancy and abortion. Complaints of vague abdominal pain or pain on sexual intercourse may cause her to seek medical treatment from one physician after another unsuccessfully, and the very examinations to which she is subjected may cause flashbacks to the abortion experience. Her life spirals downward as her general health, personal relationships and job performance become more and more impaired. Discouragement, despair, clinical depression and suicide attempts often follow.(3) Typically, in presenting symptoms over a period of many years, she is treated by numerous physicians and mental health professionals without ever receiving help for the root cause of her problems, her abortion or abortions. Psychiatric textbooks subsume all of the above symptoms under the diagnosis of a Pathological Grief Reaction.

Effects on Marriage and Subsequent Children

Short-term research into the psychiatric sequelae of abortion fails to document its devastating long-term negative effects on women and on their forming and sustaining stable spousal relationships, and of caring appropriately for subsequent children. They may have difficulty bonding with a new baby, or, conversely, become overprotective and inappropriately attached to the next child who bears the burden of replacing the aborted baby. These children are often referred to child psychiatrists because of separation anxiety, or because they are judged to be at risk for physical abuse. Couples may be treated for infertility or dysfunctional marriages which stem from a previous abortion or abortions. Substance abuse, "burnout" on the job, psycho-somatic symptoms, eating disorders, chronic depression and suicide attempts which routinely bring women into psychiatric care can often be traced to an abortion experience several years before through a careful and complete history.

In addition to immediate intervention for the presenting problem, successful treatment of women who have suffered the tragedy of abortion requires that the underlying traumatic loss be acknowledged and appropriately grieved. Psychotherapy involves facilitating the work of mourning which has been so long delayed. Within a therapeutic relationship, the woman is encouraged to share her traumatic loss and to acknowledge her role in it. She is helped to share the mental image she has formed of her child—often one of a baby being torn to pieces or crying out in pain. As the grief work proceeds, her image is transformed into a less disturbing picture of her child at peace. She may name the child and arrange for a religious service to be performed for him or her. She accepts God's forgiveness and may be able to forgive herself and ask forgiveness of her child. Eventually she is able to put the child to rest in her mind. Only then is she free to resume her life productively—to make new relationships or repair old ones, to work, to play, and to be creative once again.(4)

With 30 million abortions in this country since *Roe v. Wade,* and the continuing rate of 1.5 million abortions per year, we can no longer deny the public health significance of their psychological and psychophysical sequelae. Epidemiological studies are urgently needed which are statistically sound and which follow women and men for at least ten years post-abortion. However, it is axiomatic that the best treatment for any epidemic is primary prevention. Abortion is an elective surgical procedure performed on healthy women (pregnancy is not a disease). The immediate abolition of elective abortion would eradicate the iatrogenic epidemic of post-abortion pathology and would serve the best interests of women and society. In

Evangelium Vitae (no. 99) John Paul II spells out the pastoral approach of the church:

> The wound in your heart may not yet have healed. Certainly what happened was and remains terribly wrong. But do not give in to discouragement and do not lose hope. Try rather to understand what happened and face it honestly. If you have not already done so, give yourself over with humility and trust to repentance. The Father of mercies is ready to give you his forgiveness and his peace in the Sacrament of Reconciliation. You will come to understand that nothing is definitely lost and you will also be able to ask forgiveness from your child, who is now living in the Lord. With the friendly and expert help and advice of other people, and as a result of your own painful experience, you can be among the most eloquent defenders of everyone's right to life.

Notes

1. Wathen, N. C. "Perinatal Bereavement," *British Journal of Obstetrics and Gynecology* 97 [1990]: 759–760.
2. Basic Books: New York, 1983.
3. Speckhard, A., & Rue, V. "Complicated Mourning: Dynamics of Impacted Post-Abortion Grief," *Journal of Pre- and Perinatal Psychology* 8 [1993]: 6–12.
4. Angelo, E. J. "The Negative Impact of Abortion on Women and Families," in *Post-Abortion Aftermath,* Mannion, M., ed. [Sheed and Ward: Kansas City, MO, 1994].

Joyce Arthur

Psychological Aftereffects of Abortion: The Rest of the Story

Over the last decade, a consensus has been reached in the medical and scientific communities that most women who have an abortion experience little or no psychological harm. Yet, a woman's ability to cope psychologically after an abortion continues to be the subject of heated debates. Vocal antiabortion advocates claim that most women who have abortions will suffer to some degree from a variant of post-traumatic-stress disorder called *post-abortion syndrome,* characterized by severe and long-lasting guilt, depression, rage, and social and sexual dysfunction. Why is there such a major discrepancy between the scientific consensus and anti-abortion beliefs?

Conflicting studies done over the last thirty years have contributed to this atmosphere of confusion and misinformation. A 1989 review article that evaluated the methodology of seventy-six studies on the psychological aftereffects of abortion noted that both opponents and advocates of abortion could easily prove their case by picking and choosing from a wide range of contradictory evidence. For example, many studies—especially those done between 1950 and 1975—purport to have found significant negative psychological responses to abortion. Such studies, though, often suffer from serious methodological flaws. Some were done when abortion was still illegal or highly restricted, thereby biasing the conclusions in favor of considerable (and understandable) psychological distress. In some cases, research was based on women who were forced to prove a psychiatric disorder in order to obtain the abortion. Further, a large number of studies, both early and recent, consist simply of anecdotal reports of a few women who sought psychiatric help after their abortion. In short, many studies which favor anti-abortion beliefs are flawed because of very small samples, unrepresentative samples, poor data analysis, lack of control groups, and unreliable or invalid research questions.

Researcher bias on the part of scientists and physicians has also been a serious problem. In earlier times, society's views on how women "should" feel after an abortion were heavily skewed toward the traditional model of women as nurturing mothers. In one study done in 1973, post-doctoral psychology students taking psychoanalytic training predicted

From Joyce Arthur, "Psychological Aftereffects of Abortion: The Rest of the Story," *The Humanist,* vol. 57, no. 2 (March/April 1997). Copyright © 1997 by Joyce Arthur. Reprinted by permission.

psychological effects far more severe than those predicted by women themselves before undergoing an abortion. This might be because traditional Freudian theory teaches that a desire to avoid childbearing represents a woman's denial of her basic feminine nature.

Some psychiatric studies, along with much of today's anti-abortion literature, tend to cast women who have abortions into one of two roles: victim or deviant (although these terms are not necessarily used). Victims are coerced into abortion by others around them, in spite of their confusion and ambivalence, and against their basic maternal instincts. Deviants have little difficulty with the abortion decision, which is made casually for convenience sake. Such women have no maternal instinct and are often characterized in a derogatory or pitying fashion as selfish, callous, unfeminine, emotionally stunted, and neurotic.

Books written by anti-abortion advocates that deal with post-abortion effects are, by and large, heavily infected with bias. Not only is contrary evidence unrefuted, it is rarely even mentioned. Incorrect and out-of-date "facts" abound. The authors' pop psychology often seems to be based on little more than their own wishful projections about the nature of women and how they should feel. Here are two typical examples from essays in the anti-abortion book The *Psychological Aspects of Abortion* (1977):

> It is interesting that women who need self-punishment do not abort themselves more often. . . . Abortion is done "to" the woman, with her as only a passive participant. This is further indication of masochism.
>
> — (Howard W. Fisher, "Abortion: Pain or Pleasure")

> . . . sooner or later [after the abortion], the truth will make itself known and felt, and the bitter realization that she was not even unselfish enough to share her life with another human being will take its toll. If she had ever entertained a doubt as to whether her parents and others really considered her unlovable and worthless, she will now be certain that she was indeed never any good in their eyes or her own. A deep depression will be inevitable and her preoccupation with thoughts of suicide that much greater.
>
> — (Conrad W. Baars, "Psychic Causes and Consequences
> of the Abortion Mentality")

With the advent of safe, legal, routinely performed abortions, a wealth of good evidence has come to light that is quite contrary to common antiabortion assertions. The typical abortion patient is a normal, mentally stable woman who makes a strongly resolved decision for abortion within a few days after discovery of the pregnancy and comes through the procedure virtually unscathed. Several scientific review articles—published from 1990 to 1992 in highly respected journals such as *Science* and *American Journal of Psychiatry*—support this conclusion. The reviews evaluated hundreds of studies done over the last thirty years, noting the unusually high number of seriously flawed studies and pointing out common methodological problems. Based upon the more reliable studies, all the reviews concluded that, although psychological disturbances do occur after abortion, they are uncommon and generally mild and short-lived. In many cases, these disturbances are simply a continuation of negative feelings caused by the pregnancy itself. Serious or persistent problems are rare and are frequently related to the circumstances surrounding the abortion rather than the abortion itself.

Further, many women who were denied an abortion showed ongoing, long-term resentment, and their resulting children were more likely to have increased emotional, psychological, and social problems in comparison with control groups of wanted children. These differences between children widened throughout adolescence and early adulthood. Finally, many studies show that giving birth is much more likely than abortion to be associated with severe emotional aftereffects, such as postpartum depression.

The review articles largely concluded that the most frequently reported emotions felt by women immediately following an abortion (experienced by about 75 percent of women) are relief or happiness. Feelings of regret, anxiety, guilt, depression, and other negative emotions are reported by about 5 percent to 30 percent of women. These feelings are usually mild and fade rapidly, within a few weeks. Months or years after an abortion, the majority of women do not regret their decision. In fact, for many women, abortion appears to improve their self-esteem, provide inner strength, and motivate them to refocus their lives in a meaningful way.

Studies on abortion are done primarily through self-report measures, however, and it is possible that some women may be reluctant to admit negative feelings after their abortion. To help quantify this, consider these figures: every year since 1977, 1.3 million to 1.6 million abortions are performed in the United States; about 21 percent of all American women between the ages of fifteen and forty-four have had an abortion. These are very large numbers indeed. The American Psychological Association has pointed out that, even if only 10 percent of the millions of women who have had abortions experienced problems, there would be a significant mental health epidemic, clearly evident by large numbers of dysfunctional women requesting help. There is no evidence of any such epidemic, thereby supporting the general reliability of self-report measures.

Some women who are disturbed or unhappy with their abortion decision belong to support groups like Women Exploited by Abortion and Victims of Choice. Several anti-abortion studies and books purporting to demonstrate the overall harmfulness of abortion limit their samples to the membership of such groups. Not only does this introduce an immediate and fatal flaw to their argument, it shows deliberate obfuscation on the part of the authors. This does not mean, however, that post-abortion support groups are valueless to women. The very existence of such groups points to the strong need for health professionals to identify and provide extra help to women who are most at risk for developing psychological problems related to abortion. Many studies have shown that women at greater risk tend to include:

- emotionally immature teenagers
- women with previous psychiatric problems
- women aborting a wanted pregnancy for medical or genetic reasons
- women who encounter opposition from their partner or parents for their abortion decision
- women who have strong philosophical or religious objection to abortion
- women who are highly ambivalent or confused about their abortion decision and had great difficulty making it
- women who are coerced by others into having an abortion
- women undergoing second-trimester abortions

In spite of psychological problems suffered by a few women after abortion, the existence of post-abortion syndrome is doubted by most experts. There is little need to posit a unique disorder in this case, since abortion is not significantly different from any other stressful life experience that might cause trauma in certain people. Former Surgeon General C. Everett Koop, himself anti-abortion, noted this in 1988. Unfortunately, facts, evidence, and common sense rarely get in the way of anti-abortion advocates who are determined to prove that women suffer terribly from post-abortion syndrome. Certainly, if this syndrome were real it would be a lethal weapon in the fight to reverse *Roe v. Wade*. This was, in fact, the motivation behind a 1989 surgeon general's report on the health effects of abortion on women, which was called for by former President Ronald Reagan on behalf of anti-abortion leaders. Although the report was duly prepared, the surgeon general chose not to release it, apparently because it did not support the anti-abortion position. Meanwhile, anti-abortion literature continues to churn out the myth that women are severely harmed by abortion.

Because abortion is such a volatile issue, it is probably unrealistic to expect this aspect of the controversy to die down soon, if at all. However, by recognizing that a small subset of women may require increased counseling and support during their abortion decision and afterward, the women's community and health professionals can do much to minimize the damage wrought by the anti-abortion movement's dangerous and irresponsible campaign of misinformation.

CHALLENGE QUESTIONS

Does Post-Abortion Syndrome Exist?

1. Considering the fact that the abortion debate is so politically and emotionally charged, what advice would you give to researchers studying the validity of post-abortion reactions to help them avoid bias in their methods and conclusions?
2. To what extent do you believe that women who experience psychological problems following abortion are affected by the intensity of the national debate on this topic?
3. Arthur acknowledges that the women who experience abortion-related psychological problems are those who were at risk because of factors such as immaturity, religious pressures, interpersonal pressures, and medical problems. To what extent should health professionals assess women for such risk factors and provide specialized mental health interventions designed to reduce the extent of their difficulties?
4. The views of Angelo are based on a religious perspective, in that she suggests that women who have had abortions seek God's forgiveness for their life-ending decisions. How should clinicians formulate interventions for religiously committed post-abortion women?
5. Consider your own stand on abortion, and imagine yourself as a clinician trying to help a woman in therapy whose viewpoint is diametrically opposed to yours. How would you approach your treatment of this client?

Suggested Readings

Adler, N. E., David, H. P., Major, B. N., Roth, S. H., Russo, N. F., & Wyatt, G. E. (1992). Psychological factors in abortion: A review. *American Psychologist, 47*(10), 1194–1204.

Beckman, L. J., & Harvey, S. M. (Eds.) (1998). *The new civil war: The psychology, culture and politics of abortion.*Washington, DC: American Psychological Association.

Lewis, W. J. (1997). Factors associated with post-abortion adjustment problems: Implications for triage. *The Canadian Journal of Human Sexuality, 6*(1), 9–16.

Russo, N. F., & Dabul, A. J. (1997). The relationship of abortion to well-being: Do race and religion make a difference? *Professional Psychology: Research and Practice, 28*(1), 23–31.

Stotland, N. (1992). The myth of the abortion trauma syndrome. *Journal of the American Medical Association, 268*(15), 2078–2079.

ISSUE 7

Are Repressed Memories Valid?

YES: Richard P. Kluft, from "The Argument for the Reality of Delayed Recall of Trauma," in Paul S. Appelbaum, Lisa A. Uyehara, and Mark R. Elin, eds., *Trauma and Memory: Clinical and Legal Controversies* (Oxford University Press, 1997)

NO: Elizabeth F. Loftus, from "Creating False Memories," *Scientific American* (September 1997)

ISSUE SUMMARY

YES: Psychiatrist Richard P. Kluft supports the notion that people can recover memories that have been long unavailable, and he cites verified examples in which psychotherapy patients recalled previously inaccessible memories of traumatic events.

NO: Psychologist Elizabeth F. Loftus cites extensive laboratory research to support her conclusion that suggestion and imagination can create "memories" of events that never actually occurred.

Many psychotherapy patients find it difficult to discuss emotionally charged experiences. For some discussion of upsetting life events seems too disturbing, so they intentionally avoid it. For others, however, memories seem to spontaneously arise with regard to events that the patients have not thought about in years. Astute clinicians recognize the importance of responding to such recollections with empathy, as well as caution, particularly when the events cannot be verified and might have explosive consequences in the patient's life. During the past two decades numerous stories have appeared in the media about individuals who suddenly retrieved disturbing memories, often within the context of psychotherapy. Some of the well-publicized cases involved individuals accusing parents or grandparents of having engaged in sexual, physical, or ritualistic abuse very early in the person's life. Various lawsuits and court cases captured public attention and in some instances resulted in large financial settlements and even imprisonment. Although many Americans, including prominent clinicians, accepted the validity of the repressed memory phenomenon, skeptics raised the possibility that these cases might actually have resulted from the persuasive power of suggestion.

Based on extensive clinical experience, Richard P. Kluft describes several clinical cases in which patients recalled past traumatic events that they had pushed out of conscious memory and that were subsequently verified as having actually occurred. He takes issue with those who contest the notion of repressed memories, asserting that these skeptics are basing their conclusions on laboratory exercises that do not adequately mirror the real-life experiences of people who have been traumatized. Kluft asserts that much of this research is a study of social persuasion rather than memory functioning.

Elizabeth F. Loftus cites cases in which psychotherapy patients became convinced that they had been the victims of horrendous early life abuse but subsequently disavowed these experiences and attributed the "memories" to the suggestions of their therapists. Loftus cites extensive research that supports the notion that, under the right circumstances, false memories can be instilled rather easily in some people. Many people are especially suggestible and can be led to "remember" events that never actually occurred, she concludes.

POINT

- Kluft, through clinical experience, summarizes several cases involving patients who recalled traumatic events that they had repressed.
- The phenomenon in which people recover memories of traumatic experiences differs markedly from research phenomena such as the "lost-in-the-mall" research conducted by Loftus.
- Clinicians who attempt to rigidly conform clinical practice to scientific findings are likely to rely on laboratory science, which is not anchored in common sense.
- Some people who retract their stories about having been traumatized do so in response to strong interpersonal pressures.

- A careful scrutiny of the Loftus research shows that only a small minority of subjects who received misdirection cues actually took the indicated misdirection.

COUNTERPOINT

- Some mental health professionals encourage patients to imagine childhood events as a way of recovering supposedly hidden memories.
- More than 200 experiments indicate that people can be led to remember their past in different ways and can even be coaxed into "remembering" entire events that never happened.

- Mental health professionals must be aware of how greatly they can influence the recollection of events in which imagination is used as an aid in recovering presumably lost memories.
- There are several well-publicized cases in which psychotherapy patients came to realize that their psychotherapists encouraged them to "remember" traumatic events that never occurred.
- Misinformation can invade memories when people talk to other people, are suggestively interrogated, or when they read or view media coverage about some event that they may have experienced.

Richard P. Kluft

 **YES**

The Argument for the Reality of Delayed Recall of Trauma

In any debate over the reality of recovered memory, it is useful to clarify the grounds of the debate, that is, to specify the issue that is being debated. If arguments are being proposed to the effect that there is no such thing as recovered memory, so that any apparently recovered memory can be discounted a priori, the premise of the debate can be formulated: resolved, that there is no demonstrable instance in which accurate, once unavailable memories have been recovered. I have avoided the use of the terms *recovered memory* and *repressed memory* in the resolution itself because these terms not only have become politicized, but the former term has no correlation to traditional clinical literature, and the latter represents an overgeneralized use of the term *repression,* which is only one of the processes by which the defensive exclusion of autobiographical experience from available and routinely retrievable memory may occur.

If the affirmative case is proven, then there is no such thing as a recovered memory. Should the negative prevail, such a phenomenon exists. The debate concerns whether there are demonstrable instances of the recovery of repressed, dissociated, or otherwise unavailable memory. Circumspect authorities would observe that since it is impossible to prove a negative, the debate can only be won by the affirmative side's discounting of any and all evidence that repressed and recovered memories exist. This is why vigorous attacks have been launched against virtually every article that appears to document this phenomenon, and efforts have been made to overextend implications that memory not only can be but will be distorted by various forms of suggestion and influence. Another consideration in this debate is that the affirmative side must make its case by advancing falsifiable arguments. Opinions cannot be stated as if they were facts. All recovered memories must be demonstrated to be false by objective data, and by unimpeachable corroborations of their falseness, not simply by allegations or statements of belief. Pope[1] has explored this dilemma very thoughtfully. That is, advancing lines of reasoning that cannot be tested, but permit the infinite, defensive rationalization of one's point of view from a lofty retreat remote from all threat of disconfirmation, falls short of scientific acceptability. . . .

"The argument for the reality of delayed recall of trauma" by Richard P. Kluft, from TRAUMA AND MEMORY, edited by Paul Applebaum, et. al., copyright © 1997 by Oxford University Press. Used by permission of Oxford University Press, Inc.

Clinical Experiences Supporting the Recovery of Long-Unavailable Memories

For many years, in addition to conducting a psychiatric practice in Philadelphia, I had the privilege of treating patients in a small city surrounded by farmlands and semirural areas. During that period, that city's population base was stable, with relatively little mobility. For most of that time the area was underserved by mental health professionals and there was relatively little therapist-switching. I had the opportunity to observe the life cycles of many families over a period of 18 years. It was predominantly in this setting that I followed 210 patients with dissociative identity disorder (DID; formerly multiple personality disorder [MPD]) and was able to sketch out the natural history of this disorder.[2] I came to know many patients and their families in a manner that I rarely experienced in my urban practice, and I remained in contact with them over a prolonged period of time. Often information that was unavailable during my patients' treatments came my way a decade later. In this setting I learned that many of the allegations of abuse that were made by my patients (whether always in conscious awareness or recovered in therapy) were in fact true, even allegations that were vehemently denied by their families at the time when I first treated the patients. I also learned that some of the accusations were lies, and that some were based on misperceptions or distorted recall. In 1984 I cautioned that the therapist "must remain aware . . . that material influenced by intrusive inquiry or iatrogenic dissociation may be subject to distortion. In a given patient, one may find episodes of photographic recall, confabulation, screen phenomena, confusion between dreams or fantasies and reality, irregular recollection, and willful misrepresentation. One awaits a goodness of fit among several forms of data, and often must be satisfied to remain uncertain."[3] I did not encounter instances in which false accusations were triggered in therapy, but I must acknowledge that the possibility exists.

Here I will focus on several examples of confirmed recovered memories. My files contain hundreds of such confirmations.

In the mid-1970s I was treating a female colleague who seemed unable to sort out her relationships with men. A bright and attractive woman, she had distanced herself from her alcoholic family only after winning her own battles with addiction. As her psychoanalytically oriented psychotherapy proceeded, which was supported by her participation in Alcoholics Anonymous, we both appreciated that she became unable to express herself whenever transference feelings toward me came under exploration. After several months of mutual confusion, we decided to use hypnosis to explore her block. She was an excellent hypnotic subject. While in trance she recovered memories of her first therapy, which was conducted by an addiction counselor. He had encouraged the development of an extremely positive transference and then exploited it to seduce her. Once out of trance she was mortified, but she steeled herself to report that, although she had completely forgotten that particular experience, she had reenacted the same pattern with the leader of a therapy group. She had not felt comfortable enough to admit her growing fears that the same might happen with me. Now her shutting down whenever she began to experience feelings toward me made sense to both of us. Her therapy continued to a successful conclusion, and her relationships with men became satisfactory to her.

A decade later, her former alcoholism counselor came to me for psychotherapy. After several sessions, he revealed what he considered the two worst things he had ever done. While an active alcoholic, he had molested his own daughter. When he became a recovering alcoholic and respected therapist, he had become infatuated with a beautiful young patient and had manipulated her idealization of him to seduce her. "You know her. You treated her. You must think I'm a real bastard." He spoke briefly about his relationship with my other patient, confirming her hypnotically retrieved account in detail. The next day, he left me a message which said that he was too embarrassed to return. He transferred to a therapist who had never known his victim.

In another case, two sisters, who were long estranged, were reunited after twenty years as they attended their dying mother. One sister, who was my patient, had always been aware of sexual abuse by her father and had recovered memories of abuse by a baby-sitter in the course of her therapy. She asked her sister if the sister had any knowledge of such an incident. Her sister not only recalled the event but supplied details that confirmed additional circumstances which my patient had recovered in the course of her treatment but which she had not yet shared with her sister. Each confirmed the other's recollection of father-daughter incest, with reference to several specific instances. Furthermore, their dying mother apologized to my patient for her harsh treatment of her, which my patient had recovered in psychotherapy but had doubted to be true.

Another example of confirmed recovered memories concerns a man who had served in Vietnam as a Marine who maintained in therapy that he and his unit had seen no combat over a particular period. However, also in therapy, he recovered memories of an attack on his base and of his killing several armed Vietnamese attackers. After recovering these memories, he disbelieved them. At a Washington, D.C. commemoration for Vietnam veterans he became irritated when a wartime buddy reminded him of his role in this firefight. He told the friend that he must be wrong, that he had never fired his weapon in combat. The man was shocked, and shook his head, uncomprehending. "You were a . . . hero, man!" The patient's military records reveal that his unit had indeed been in combat and had maintained a defensive perimeter around a supply base that was frequently under attack throughout the period during which the patient maintained that his unit had seen no action. For reasons unrelated to this account, this man had joined the Marines, hoping to be killed. He had repeatedly volunteered for hazardous duty in the effort to bring about his own death. Although he eagerly placed himself at risk, he was passionately opposed to taking another human life. Ultimately, he was able to confront the fact that despite his beliefs and apparent wish to die, when faced with a genuine life-and-death decision, he had methodically and efficiently dispatched several enemy combatants at close range, an act that was witnessed by his buddy. His repugnance and conflict over this action apparently drove it from his memory. It took months to work through his guilt over his having taken the lives of the Vietcong attackers.

A woman with multiple personality disorder underwent hypnosis to access personalities and to explore missing periods of time in her life. During her assessment and treatment, she had denied that she had ever been mistreated by a previous therapist. Fourteen months later, a personality that was contacted through hypnosis indicated that the patient's prior psychiatrist had exploited her sexually. Against my advice, she revealed this information to her prior psychiatrist. When he learned that his former patient was revealing his boundary violations, he telephoned me. He asked me to treat him, he admitted his indiscretions, and he insisted that since he was now my patient, I could not reveal what I knew, due to my duty of confidentiality! He was not pleased when I reminded him that I had never agreed to treat him, and that I was not disposed to accept the constraints he tried to impose. This case was one of several in which alleged therapist abuses, which were often not in patients' conscious awareness at the beginning of the patients' therapy with the author, were later confirmed.[4, 5]

A married woman in her late 20s who had been adopted at birth came for a consultation to discuss the pluses and minuses of tracing her birth parents. Now the mother of two toddlers, she was increasingly curious about her own origins. After she located her birth parents, she returned to discuss her reactions. During this interview she spoke at length about the mental illness of her adoptive mother, who ultimately had been institutionalized as a paranoid schizophrenic. While discussing her adoptive mother's suspiciousness and unusual behavior (such as shooting a rifle at aircraft flying over the family farm), she dissociated into an alter personality and began to talk about a psychotic ritual of her mother's, a practice that was repeated over and over again. In it, her mother and she undressed. Her mother made her lie under a blanket on her abdomen and crawl out between her legs to be "born." Then her mother would express delight at her daughter's birth. When the patient switched back to her previous personality, she was amnestic for the above revelations. However, within minutes, she had a flashback of bizarre enematization experiences at her mother's hands.

She decided to enter treatment to explore these phenomena and to better understand herself. Much abuse material emerged under hypnosis. After the third hypnotic session the patient was sure that the recollections were inaccurate, but she appreciated that her long-standing depression was fading. We discussed how to approach the resolution of her uncertainty. Her adoptive parents were deceased. They had raised her on an isolated farm in a wooded rural area with no close neighbors. No close relatives of her parents were available as resources. I asked her to bring in any school and medical records, and any family materials or photo albums in her possession for us to review. I really had no hopes that anything would emerge, but wanted to leave no stone unturned. The next day she called me in tears. Not only had she found albums, she had found her mother's diaries, which described her mother's "experiments on the girl." They included detailed accounts of every abuse the patient had shared with me. Unable to tolerate having this material in her home, she presented me with a box of her mother's diaries and with yearly school pictures of herself, on the backs of which were written her mother's comments and planned experiments (i.e., abuses). When I asked her what she thought I should do with these materials, she paused thoughtfully and replied: "Someday you may find people don't believe child abuse happens, and that people can forget their abuse. If you ever need to prove it happens, you have this box." That conversation occurred in 1978. Upon an 18-year follow-up, she is integrated, symptom-free, and well. Several years after the conclusion of her therapy she went to graduate school in psychology. She currently is a practicing mental health professional. . . .

Perspectives on Discrediting the Possible Recovery of Repressed Memory

Limitations of space preclude the possibility of my making a detailed critique of the arguments against the possibility of the recovery of repressed or otherwise unavailable memory. However, I will comment briefly on a small number of the issues that have been raised in that connection.

Often the argument is made that there are no data to sustain the notion of repression, so that any material alleged to have been repressed and then recovered is a priori suspect. Concepts such as repression and the unconscious mind have proven very elusive subjects of study in the experimental setting. Many laboratory models that have been advanced are far from convincing as paradigms.

The work of Holmes[6] is frequently cited in arguments opposing the existence of repression. It is of historical note that this work appears in an important book[7] containing 18 contributions, 17 of which come to different conclusions than that of Holmes. In this publication, Holmes demonstrates that several experimental constructs of repression were subject to plausible alternative explanations. Unfortunately, he uses motivated skepticism[8] adroitly. His dismissal of the possible relevance of criticism of his paradigms and his disregard of anecdotal clinical information is glib and cavalier.

In his 1970 study he tested the hypothesis that the recall of experiences is determined by the intensity of affect associated with the experiences at the time of recall; that the intensity of the affect associated with given experiences declines over time; and that the affect associated with displeasure will decline more rapidly than that associated with pleasant experiences. He had college students keep a diary of their pleasant and unpleasant experiences for a week. They were to score each experience for pleasantness and unpleasantness on a nine-point scale. A week later they were asked unexpectedly to write down the experiences from their diary cards and to score them again. The results indicated that unpleasant experiences showed greater declines than did pleasant ones and were less likely to be recalled. Holmes concluded that recall of unpleasant experiences was due to reduced affective intensity rather than to repression. He speculated that intensity was reduced because unpleasant experiences, such as failing a French test, were found not to matter that much, or remediative actions could alter the nature of the experience. He also proposed that, with further thought, the attitudes toward the events might become more positive, and therefore the intensity of the negativity would be reduced.

I would like to raise the possibility that the nature of the phenomena that Holmes studied is somewhat different from the materials encountered by clinicians working with traumatized populations. An incestuous experience or a gang-rape might be more traumatic than failing a French test. I do not quarrel with Dr. Holmes' experiment per se, but I do think that trauma-related problems of memory may be managed in a different manner and that this different manner may involve repression and dissociation. I do not think his experimental universe was sufficiently diverse to support his conclusions. Although I consider Holmes's work thought-provoking and ingenious, I seriously doubt that his arguments against the possibility of the recovery of memories[9] deal with the phenomena in question.

When we turn to the famous lost-in-the-mall scenario . . . of Elizabeth Loftus, who is often regarded as a very influential participant in the debate over recovered memory, we encounter another family of difficulties. In her study, 5 young subjects, "all friends and relatives of our research group"[10, 11] were taken through a reflection on early life experiences, most of which were accurate, but one of which—the experimentally suggested one—was not. The subjects were led by siblings and others to believe that they had been lost in a mall, when this had not occurred. Not only was it possible to cause the subjects to report this, but they often confabulated additional details as their stories took on lives of their own. On this basis she argued that it is possible for therapists to implant false memories that will be elaborated further and regarded as credible.[10, 11]

I wonder about the generalizability of this experiment, and am troubled by its ethics. Young children were exposed to deliberately mendacious behavior by their siblings and concerned others, and were then told they were duped. I question whether the possible deleterious long-term effects on the relationship of those involved is acceptable. I wonder about the appropriateness of the strategy of teaching children to become involved in systematic deception. I also wonder about the message conveyed about authority figures and the nature of truth that is given to the young subjects. Were I on a human subjects review committee, I would not have passed on this one. When Dr. Loftus has been asked about this, she dismisses such concerns by stating there have been no adverse effects. She offers as proof that when the children understood what had occurred, some of her own subjects took to doing similar deceptions with their friends.[11] To me this is chilling. Perhaps these subjects are only engaging in a benign attempt to achieve mastery, but I would like to raise the possibility that adult authority figures have taught them to think that truth is a malleable commodity that can be distorted at one's convenience or whimsy. These children may be demonstrating the mechanism of identification with the aggressor, a severely pathological defensive adaptation.

I also think the design leaves much to be desired, because it does not narrow the variables in a manner that allows the results to mean anything. It becomes a Rorschach to confirm one's bias. We see a study not of memory but of social persuasion. Whether the implantation of the so-called memory by an older sibling who says he was there as an eye-witness and who has a powerful affective relationship with and position of authority over the child mirrors the position of the therapist is questionable. The therapist was not a first-hand witness to a patient's past, and the therapist is not lying, or trying consciously to systematically direct the patient's perception of the truth, or using techniques verging on the interrogatory. In addition, children are accustomed to the idea of getting lost.[12] It is a normal fear, it is the plot of innumerable fairy tales, and it is the subject of myriad maternal warnings. Children likely have a preexisting schema in mind with regard to getting lost, which can be tapped readily by suggestion because it is already present.[12] With regard to incest, however, the incest fantasies described as universal by Freud are not traumatic in nature, like the ones reported by incest victims. We cannot assume that there is a schema for abrupt anal or oral rape, for example, that is lying dormant and ready to be brought to immediate fruition by a therapist who asks a bland question about whether the patient has had any unwanted sexual experiences.

As a study on social persuasion, however, the lost-in-the-mall scenario demonstrates that when a family has a story about how an event happened, it may drive out the autobiographical memory of those involved. This need not be an instance in which a child is convinced that an event has occurred when it has not. It could just as easily explain how a child is persuaded that an event that did occur has not occurred, a possibility Loftus herself has acknowledged.[11] It is a curious irony that in 1983, a syndrome was described in which the family conspires to deny the reality of a traumatic event, and finally the victim endorses the alternate reality. This, of course, is the child sexual abuse accommodation syndrome, which was explored by Roland Summit—one of the experts frequently attacked by those who believe that recovered memories of childhood sexual abuse should be discredited. Loftus's lost-in-the-mall scenario offers confirmation of Summit's earlier observations: a family determined to distort a child's sense of reality has a good chance of achieving its objectives.

It is possible that insights gained from Loftus's lost-in-the-mall scenario and Summit's child sexual abuse accommodation syndrome may cast some light on a phenomenon that is of great interest in the current false memory controversy. Retractors are individuals who at one time believed that they were abused, but who have come to believe that their memories of abuse are inaccurate. Some retractors change their minds in the context of strong interpersonal pressures that have features in common with those exerted upon individuals in the lost-in-the-mall scenario and the child sexual abuse accommodation syndrome. Could it be that retractors rather than therapy patients demonstrate the forces that Dr. Loftus has studied? This could prove an interesting subject for future research.

Another aspect of the Loftus research that has received little attention is that only a small minority of the subjects who received misdirection cues took the indicated misdirections. Most did not. This research might be cited as evidence that most persons, even those subjected to an intense campaign to distort their memories and induce confabulations, will reject such suggestions.

Since the reader of this [selection] may have heard many an attack on the gullibility and ineptitude of clinicians by speakers representing themselves as guardians of science, it may be useful to consider an analysis from the perspective of a clinician who worries that the perfect can be the enemy of the good, and that taking too literally the warnings of researchers can destroy the capacity to render good therapy.

The progress of science is a parade of paradigms[13] that strut their arrogant hour upon the stage, expressing themselves in allegories called experiments, depreciating, belittling, and berating everything the paradigm of choice does not embrace. Paradigms collapse by virtue of their exclusion of or failure to address data they had deemed unimportant within the worldview of that particular paradigm. In the language of Greek tragedy, every paradigm has a tragic flaw, overstates its applicability (overweening pride), and is humiliated by fate (retribution).

By disregarding information, paradigms embrace the same mechanisms that we find in the more familiar processes of dissociation, repression, denial, splitting, and even more primitive mechanisms. Perhaps the excesses of such uses of science so fascinate me as a clinician because it helps me to appreciate that laboratory science that is unanchored in common sense is a primitive character disorder verging on decompensation into psychosis, a term that indicates that there is a major failure to appreciate reality. We mock the mad scientist in a grade-B movie and enjoy his or her downfall precisely because, like an incestuous Greek king or a Shakespearean regicide, the order of the universe is destroyed by his or her arrogance and false attempts to impose his or her self-deceived facsimile of natural order upon reality, and his or her defeat is necessary in order to preserve the true order of the world. It follows that the attempt to conform clinical practice rigidly to scientific findings is doomed to defeat, because it will introduce borderline and/or psychotic features into the thinking of the clinician.

Additional Remarks on the Recollection and the Nonrecollection of Trauma

. . . Elizabeth Loftus, Ph.D., is a brilliant researcher and scholar. She has described her own experiences of abuse and reflected upon her incomplete recollection of it. Her words are captured in a deposition cited by

Whitfield.[14] She both denies she repressed the memory of the abuse, and speaks of her uncertainty about the number of occurrences, and of her memory having taken and destroyed her recollections of her abuser. In the same account we find both recollection and the absence of recollection. This might be understood as either confusing, or expectable. As Whitfield notes, trauma dissociates and confuses memory, and trying to block traumata out with guilt, shame, and/or threats of harm can drive its mental representation out of awareness.

Loftus's experience can be understood as capturing the essence of the intimately intertwined nature of both the memory and the banishing from memory of traumatization. Rather than polarized opposites, they may be understood by analogy with the intrusive and numbing aspects of the posttraumatic response. While there are some instances in which clear and striking memory is retained, and some in which its abolition is virtually complete, more often, the two processes proceed side by side. An example of this may be that often only the central aspect of a traumatic event is recalled. The details may neither be registered not retrieved.

References

1. Pope, K. S. Memory, abuse, and science: questioning claims about the false memory epidemic. Am Psychol 1996; 51:957–974.

2. Kluft, R. P. The natural history of multiple personality disorder. *In* RP Kluft (Ed.), Childhood Antecedents of Multiple Personality. Washington, DC: American Psychiatric Press, 1985, pp. 197–238.

3. Kluft, R. P. Treatment of multiple personality disorders. Psychiatr Clin North Am 1984; 7:121–134a.

4. Kluft, R. P. Dissociation and subsequent vulnerability: a preliminary study. Dissociation 1990; 3:167–173.

5. Kluft, R. P. Incest and subsequent revictimization: the case of therapist-patient sexual exploitation, with a description of the sitting duck syndrome. *In* RP Kluft (Ed.), Incest-related Syndromes of Adult Psychopathology. Washington, DC: American Psychiatric Press, 1990, pp. 263–287.

6. Holmes, D. S. The evidence for repression. *In* JL Singer (Ed.), Repression and Dissociation. Chicago: University of Chicago Press, 1990, pp. 85–102.

7. Singer, J. L. (Ed.) Repression and Dissociation. Chicago: University of Chicago Press, 1990.

8. Ditto, P. H., Lopez, D. F. Motivated skepticism: use of differential decision criteria for preferred and non-preferred conclusions. J Pers Soc Psychol 1992; 63:568–584.

9. Holmes, D. L. Repression: theory versus evidence. Paper presented at the University of Kansas Medical Center's Conference on Childhood Sexual Abuse and Memories: Current Controversies. Kansas City, Kansas, April 1995.

10. Loftus, E. The nature of memory: what we know. Paper presented at the University of Kansas Medical Center's Conference on Childhood Sexual Abuse and Memories: Current Controversies. Kansas City, Kansas, April 1995.

11. Loftus, E. Eyewitness memory: implications for the dissociative disorders field. Paper presented at the meeting of the International Society for

the Study of Dissociation, International Fall Conference. Orlando, FL, September 1995.

12.   Pedzek, K., Roe, C. Memory for childhood events: how suggestible is it? Consciousness Cogn 1994; 3:374–387.

13.   Kuhn, T. S. The Structure of Scientific Revolutions (2nd ed., enlarged). Chicago: University of Chicago Press, 1971.

14.   Whitfield, C. L. Memory and Abuse: Remembering and Healing the Effects of Trauma. Deerfield Beach FL: Heath Communications, Inc., 1995.

Elizabeth F. Loftus

 **NO**

Creating False Memories

In 1986 Nadean Cool, a nurse's aide in Wisconsin, sought therapy from a psychiatrist to help her cope with her reaction to a traumatic event experienced by her daughter. During therapy, the psychiatrist used hypnosis and other suggestive techniques to dig out buried memories of abuse that Cool herself had allegedly experienced. In the process, Cool became convinced that she had repressed memories of having been in a satanic cult, of eating babies, of being raped, of having sex with animals and of being forced to watch the murder of her eight-year-old friend. She came to believe that she had more than 120 personalities—children, adults, angels and even a duck— all because, Cool was told, she had experienced severe childhood sexual and physical abuse. The psychiatrist also performed exorcisms on her, one of which lasted for five hours and included the sprinkling of holy water and screams for Satan to leave Cool's body.

When Cool finally realized that false memories had been planted, she sued the psychiatrist for malpractice. In March 1997, after five weeks of trial, her case was settled out of court for $2.4 million.

Nadean Cool is not the only patient to develop false memories as a result of questionable therapy. In Missouri in 1992 a church counselor helped Beth Rutherford to remember during therapy that her father, a clergyman, had regularly raped her between the ages of seven and 14 and that her mother sometimes helped him by holding her down. Under her therapist's guidance, Rutherford developed memories of her father twice impregnating her and forcing her to abort the fetus herself with a coat hanger. The father had to resign from his post as a clergyman when the allegations were made public. Later medical examination of the daughter revealed, however, that she was still a virgin at age 22 and had never been pregnant. The daughter sued the therapist and received a $1-million settlement in 1996.

About a year earlier two juries returned verdicts against a Minnesota psychiatrist accused of planting false memories by former patients Vynnette Hamanne and Elizabeth Carlson, who under hypnosis and sodium amytal, and after being fed misinformation about the workings of memory, had come to remember horrific abuse by family members. The juries awarded Hammane $2.67 million and Carlson $2.5 million for their ordeals.

From *Scientific American*, September 1997, pp. 71–75. Reprinted with permission. Copyright © 1997 by Scientific American, Inc. All Rights reserved.

In all four cases, the women developed memories about childhood abuse in therapy and then later denied their authenticity. How can we determine if memories of childhood abuse are true or false? Without corroboration, it is very difficult to differentiate between false memories and true ones. Also, in these cases, some memories were contrary to physical evidence, such as explicit and detailed recollections of rape and abortion when medical examination confirmed virginity. How is it possible for people to acquire elaborate and confident false memories? A growing number of investigations demonstrate that under the right circumstances false memories can be instilled rather easily in some people.

My own research into memory distortion goes back to the early 1970s, when I began studies of the "misinformation effect." These studies show that when people who witness an event are later exposed to new and misleading information about it, their recollections often become distorted. In one example, participants viewed a simulated automobile accident at an intersection with a stop sign. After the viewing, half the participants received a suggestion that the traffic sign was a yield sign. When asked later what traffic sign they remembered seeing at the intersection, those who had been given the suggestion tended to claim that they had seen a yield sign. Those who had not received the phony information were much more accurate in their recollection of the traffic sign.

My students and I have now conducted more than 200 experiments involving over 20,000 individuals that document how exposure to misinformation induces memory distortion. In these studies, people "recalled" a conspicuous barn in a bucolic scene that contained no buildings at all, broken glass and tape recorders that were not in the scenes they viewed, a white instead of a blue vehicle in a crime scene, and Minnie Mouse when they actually saw Mickey Mouse. Taken together, these studies show that misinformation can change an individual's recollection in predictable and sometimes very powerful ways.

Misinformation has the potential for invading our memories when we talk to other people, when we are suggestively interrogated or when we read or view media coverage about some event that we may have experienced ourselves. After more than two decades of exploring the power of misinformation, researchers have learned a great deal about the conditions that make people susceptible to memory modification. Memories are more easily modified, for instance, when the passage of time allows the original memory to fade.

False Childhood Memories

It is one thing to change a detail or two in an otherwise intact memory but quite another to plant a false memory of an event that never happened. To study false memory, my students and I first had to find a way to plant a pseudomemory that would not cause our subjects undue emotional stress, either in the process of creating the false memory or when we revealed that they had been intentionally deceived. Yet we wanted to try to plant a memory that would be at least mildly traumatic, had the experience actually happened.

My research associate, Jacqueline E. Pickrell, and I settled on trying to plant a specific memory of being lost in a shopping mall or large department store at about the age of five. Here's how we did it. We asked our subjects, 24 individuals ranging in age from 18 to 53, to try to remember childhood events that had been recounted to us by a parent, an older sibling or another close relative. We prepared a booklet for each participant containing one-paragraph stories about three events that had actually happened to him or her and one that had not. We constructed the false event using information about a plausible shopping trip provided by a relative, who also verified that the participant had not in fact been lost at about the age of five. The lost-in-the-mall scenario included the following elements: lost for an extended period, crying, aid and comfort by an elderly woman and, finally, reunion with the family.

After reading each story in the booklet, the participants wrote what they remembered about the event. If they did not remember it, they were instructed to write, "I do not remember this." In two follow-up interviews, we told the participants that we were interested in examining how much detail they could remember and how their memories compared with those of their relative. The event paragraphs were not read to them verbatim, but rather parts were provided as retrieval cues. The participants recalled something about 49 of the 72 true events (68 percent) immediately after the initial reading of the booklet and also in each of the two follow-up interviews. After reading the booklet, seven of the 24 participants (29 percent) remembered either partially or fully the false event constructed for them, and in the two follow-up interviews six participants (25 percent) continued to claim that they remembered the fictitious event. Statistically, there were some differences between the true memories and the false ones: participants used more words to describe the true memories, and they rated the true memories as being somewhat more clear. But if an onlooker were to observe many of our participants describe an event, it would be difficult indeed to tell whether the account was of a true or a false memory.

Of course, being lost, however frightening, is not the same as being abused. But the lost-in-the-mall study is not about real experiences of being lost; it is about planting false memories of being lost. The paradigm shows a way of instilling false memories and takes a step toward allowing us to understand how this might happen in real-world settings. Moreover, the study provides evidence that people can be led to remember their past in different ways, and they can even be coaxed into "remembering" entire events that never happened.

Studies in other laboratories using a similar experimental procedure have produced similar results. For instance, Ira Hyman, Troy H. Husband and F. James Billing of Western Washington University asked college students to recall childhood experiences that had been recounted by their parents. The researchers told the students that the study was about how people remember shared experiences differently. In addition to actual events reported by parents, each participant was given one false event—either an overnight hospitalization for a high fever and a possible ear infection, or a birthday party with pizza and a clown—that supposedly happened at about the age of five. The parents confirmed that neither of these events actually took place.

Hyman found that students fully or partially recalled 84 percent of the true events in the first interview and 88 percent in the second interview. None of the participants recalled the false event during the first interview, but 20 percent said they remembered something about the false event in the second interview. One participant who had been exposed to the emergency hospitalization story later remembered a male doctor, a female nurse and a friend from church who came to visit at the hospital.

In another study, along with true events Hyman presented different false events, such as accidentally spilling a bowl of punch on the parents of the bride at a wedding reception or having to evacuate a grocery store when the overhead sprinkler systems erroneously activated. Again, none of the participants recalled the false event during the first interview, but 18 percent remembered something about it in the second interview and 25 percent in the third interview. For example, during the first interview, one participant, when asked about the fictitious wedding event, stated, "I have no clue. I have never heard that one before." In the second interview, the participant said, "It was an outdoor wedding, and I think we were running around and knocked something over like the punch bowl or something and made a big mess and of course got yelled at for it."

Imagination Inflation

The finding that an external suggestion can lead to the construction of false childhood memories helps us understand the process by which false memories arise. It is natural to wonder whether this research is applicable in real situations such as being interrogated by law officers or in psychotherapy. Although strong suggestion may not routinely occur in police questioning or therapy, suggestion in the form of an imagination exercise sometimes does. For instance, when trying to obtain a confession, law officers may ask a suspect to imagine having participated in a criminal act. Some mental health professionals encourage patients to imagine childhood events as a way of recovering supposedly hidden memories.

Surveys of clinical psychologists reveal that 11 percent instruct their clients to "let the imagination run wild," and 22 percent tell their clients to "give free rein to the imagination." Therapist Wendy Maltz, author of a popular book on childhood sexual abuse, advocates telling the patient: "Spend time imagining that you were sexually abused, without worrying about accuracy, proving anything, or having your ideas make sense. . . . Ask yourself . . . these questions: What time of day is it? Where are you? Indoors or outdoors? What kind of things are happening? Is there one or more person with you?" Maltz further recommends that therapists continue to ask questions such as "Who would have been likely perpetrators? When were you most vulnerable to sexual abuse in your life?"

The increasing use of such imagination exercises led me and several colleagues to wonder about their consequences. What happens when people imagine childhood experiences that did not happen to them? Does imagining a childhood event increase confidence that it occurred? To explore this, we designed a three-stage procedure. We first asked individuals to indicate the likelihood that certain events happened to them during their childhood. The list contains 40 events, each rated on a scale ranging from "definitely did not happen" to "definitely did happen." Two weeks later we asked the participants to imagine that they had experienced some of these events. Different subjects were asked to imagine different events. Sometime later the participants again were asked to respond to the original list of 40 childhood events, indicating how likely it was that these events actually happened to them.

Consider one of the imagination exercises. Participants are told to imagine playing inside at home after school, hearing a strange noise outside, running toward the window, tripping, falling, reaching out and breaking the window with their hand. In addition, we asked participants questions such as "What did you trip on? How did you feel?"

In one study 24 percent of the participants who imagined the broken-window scenario later reported an increase in confidence that the event had occurred, whereas only 12 percent of those who were not asked to imagine the incident reported an increase in the likelihood that it had taken place. We found this "imagination inflation" effect in each of the eight events that participants were asked to imagine. A number of possible explanations come to mind. An obvious one is that an act of imagination simply makes the event seem more familiar and that familiarity is mistakenly related to childhood memories rather than to the act of imagination. Such source confusion—when a person does not remember the source of information—can be especially acute for the distant experiences of childhood.

Studies by Lyn Goff and Henry L. Roediger III of Washington University of recent rather than childhood experiences more directly connect imagined actions to the construction of false memory. During the initial session, the researchers instructed participants to perform the stated action, imagine doing it or just listen to the statement and do nothing else. The actions were simple ones: knock on the table, lift the stapler, break the toothpick, cross your fingers, roll your eyes. During the second session, the participants were asked to imagine some of the actions that they had not previously performed. During the final session, they answered questions about what actions they actually performed during the initial session. The investigators found that the more times participants imagined an unperformed action, the more likely they were to remember having performed it.

Impossible Memories

It is highly unlikely that an adult can recall genuine episodic memories from the first year of life, in part because the hippocampus, which plays a key role in the creation of memories, has not matured enough to form and store long-lasting memories that can be retrieved in adulthood. A procedure for planting "impossible" memories about experiences that occur shortly after birth has been developed by the late Nicholas Spanos and his collaborators at Carleton University. Individuals are led to believe that they have well-coordinated eye movements and visual exploration skills probably because they were born in hospitals that hung swinging, colored mobiles over infant cribs. To confirm whether they had such an experience, half the participants are hypnotized, age-regressed to the day after birth and asked what they remembered. The other half of the group participates in a "guided mnemonic restructuring" procedure that uses age regression as well as active encouragement to re-create the infant experiences by imagining them.

Spanos and his co-workers found that the vast majority of their subjects were susceptible to these memory-planting procedures. Both the hypnotic and guided participants reported infant memories. Surprisingly, the guided group did so somewhat more (95 versus 70 percent). Both groups remembered the colored mobile at a relatively high rate (56 percent of the guided group and 46 percent of the hypnotic subjects). Many participants who did not remember the mobile did recall other things, such as doctors, nurses, bright lights, cribs and masks. Also, in both groups, of those who reported memories of infancy, 49 percent felt that they were real memories, as opposed to 16 percent who claimed that they were merely fantasies. These findings confirm earlier studies that many individuals can be led to construct complex, vivid and detailed false memories via a rather simple procedure. Hypnosis clearly is not necessary.

How False Memories Form

In the lost-in-the-mall study, implantation of false memory occurred when another person, usually a family member, claimed that the incident happened. Corroboration of an event by another person can be a powerful technique for instilling a false memory. In fact, merely claiming to have seen a person do something can lead that person to make a false confession of wrongdoing.

This effect was demonstrated in a study by Saul M. Kassin and his colleagues at Williams College, who investigated the reactions of individuals falsely accused of damaging a computer by pressing the wrong key. The innocent participants initially denied the charge, but when a confederate said that she had seen them perform the action, many participants signed a confession, internalized guilt for the act and went on to confabulate details that were consistent with that belief. These findings show that false incriminating evidence can induce people to accept guilt for a crime they did not commit and even to develop memories to support their guilty feelings.

Research is beginning to give us an understanding of how false memories of complete, emotional and self-participatory experiences are created in adults. First, there are social demands on individuals to remember; for instance, researchers exert some pressure on participants in a study to come up with memories. Second, memory construction by imagining events can be explicitly encouraged when people are having trouble remembering.

And, finally, individuals can be encouraged not to think about whether their constructions are real or not. Creation of false memories is most likely to occur when these external factors are present, whether in an experimental setting, in a therapeutic setting or during everyday activities.

False memories are constructed by combining actual memories with the content of suggestions received from others. During the process, individuals may forget the source of the information. This is a classic example of source confusion, in which the content and the source become dissociated.

Of course, because we can implant false childhood memories in some individuals in no way implies that all memories that arise after suggestion are necessarily false. Put another way, although experimental work on the creation of false memories may raise doubt about the validity of long-buried memories, such as repeated trauma, it in no way disproves them. Without corroboration, there is little that can be done to help even the most experienced evaluator to differentiate true memories from ones that were suggestively planted.

The precise mechanisms by which such false memories are constructed await further research. We still have much to learn about the degree of confidence and the characteristics of false memories created in these ways, and we need to discover what types of individuals are particularly susceptible to these forms of suggestion and who is resistant.

As we continue this work, it is important to heed the cautionary tale in the data we have already obtained: mental health professionals and others must be aware of how greatly they can influence the recollection of events and of the urgent need for maintaining restraint in situations in which imagination is used as an aid in recovering presumably lost memories.

CHALLENGE QUESTIONS

Are Repressed Memories Valid?

1. Kluft suggests that Loftus's research in the laboratory bears little resemblance to the work of the clinician in the context of psychotherapy. What kind of research design could be used to assess the validity of memories that are recovered within the real-life context of psychotherapy?
2. The debate between Loftus and Kluft mirrors many debates between scientists and clinicians. What other issues can you identify in which scientists have been at odds with clinical practitioners?
3. Kluft raises some serious ethical objections with regard to the "lost-in-the-mall" research conducted by Loftus. What arguments can you enumerate on both sides of the debate about the legitimacy of research that involves deception?
4. Imagine that you are a clinician conducting psychotherapy with a woman who seems to remember "out of the blue" some disturbing images involving sexual abuse by her parents when she was three years old. How would you go about dealing with this issue in the therapy?
5. Imagine that you are a member of an ethics committee with the task of writing a set of guidelines for practitioners on the topic of repressed memories. Specify three or four guidelines that you would recommend for clinicians to follow.

Suggested Readings

Baker, R. A. (Ed.) (1998). *Child sexual abuse and false memory syndrome*. Amherst, NY: Prometheus Books.

Loftus, E. F. (1997). Memory for a past that never was. *Current Directions in Psychological Science*, 6(3), 60–65.

Pope, K. S., & Brown, L. S. (Eds.) (1996). *Recovered memories of abuse: Assessment, therapy, forensics*. Washington, DC: American Psychological Association.

Reisner, A. D. (1996). Repressed memories: True and false. *Psychological Record*, 46(4), 563–580.

Williams, L. M., & Banyard, V. L. (Eds.) (1999). *Trauma and memory*. Thousand Oaks, CA: Sage Publications, Inc.

ISSUE 8

Should Abstinence Be the Goal for Treating People with Alcohol Problems?

YES: Patricia Owen, from "Should Abstinence Be the Goal for Alcohol Treatment," *The American Journal of Addictions, 10,* 289–295 (Fall, 2001)

NO: Anne M. Fletcher, from *Sober for Good: New Solutions for Drinking Problems—Advice from Those Who Have Succeeded* (Houghton Mifflin Company, 2001)

ISSUE SUMMARY

YES: Psychologist Patricia Owen asserts that abstinence is the safest and most honest treatment goal for most people who are dependent on alcohol.

NO: Health and medical writer Anne Fletcher contends that many people with alcohol problems can be successful in their efforts to control their drinking, particularly if they are given professional guidance and support.

Each year countless millions of dollars are spent on alcohol, a substance that alters human behavior, cognition, and emotion. The costs to society associated with alcohol abuse are inestimable in terms of health expenses, lost productivity, accidents, and violence. The costs on the intrapsychic and interpersonal level are similarly tremendous. Lives are destroyed, and families are disrupted as a result of the profound addiction with which millions of people struggle. Despite the potential for it to be so destructive, alcohol is a legal substance that most people regard as an acceptable agent for easing tension, facilitating social interaction, and inducing pleasant feelings. The conflictual view of alcohol as being either an acceptable beverage or a harmful toxin is reflected in the debate about whether people with alcohol problems are capable of using this substance in a controlled manner. For decades, Alcoholics Anonymous (AA) has been regarded as one of the most effective interventions for people struggling with alcohol problems.

According to the AA philosophy, abstinence is essential. In contrast, however, others have proposed that abstinence is not necessarily the goal for all problem drinkers.

Psychologist Patricia Owen, who has conducted extensive research on alcoholism, believes that abstinence is indeed the safest and the most honest goal for people with alcohol dependence problems. She also asserts that it is much easier for alcohol-dependent people to abstain than to moderate their drinking.

Health writer Anne Fletcher takes issue with the assertion that abstinence is the only path for people with alcohol problems. She points out drinking problems vary considerably in degree; consequently, it makes sense that interventions should be responsive to the varying levels of maladaptive behavior. Fletcher notes that many problem drinkers can be taught to drink in moderation, and in fact will fare better than they would in their attempts to abstain completely from alcohol use.

POINT

- Abstinence is logical as a treatment goal for problem drinkers because it is the most direct approach.

- Many studies have shown that about half of individuals presenting for treatment are able to achieve abstinence.

- People who are dependent on alcohol find that their attempts at controlled drinking are extremely difficult and typically unsuccessful.

- Experts cannot precisely determine what kinds of people are capable of moderating their alcohol use.

- As is the case in the treatment of medical problems such as diabetes and hypertension, it is the professional's role to state the treatment goal (i.e., abstinence) even if it is at odds with the patient's own ideas about the best course of treatment.

COUNTERPOINT

- Pressuring all people with drinking problems to abstain ignores the fact that drinking problems exist on a continuum, from mild to life-threatening.

- Some studies have shown that people who are offered controlled-drinking approaches at the outset may fare better than those offered abstinence approaches (page 184).

- People can achieve some success in controlling their drinking if they are given professional guidance and help establishing safeguards to monitor their progress.

- Experts have defined a set of characteristics of people who succeed with moderate drinking (e.g., being psychologically stable, well-educated, steadily employed).

- Experts believe that more people would do something about their drinking problem at an earlier point if they were offered a choice between abstinence and a moderated drinking program.

Patricia Owen

 **YES**

Should Abstinence Be the Goal for Alcohol Treatment?

For most people who are dependent on alcohol, abstinence is the safest course and most honest treatment goal. For this subset of drinkers, a goal of abstinence is logical, possible, and, in the end, easier than sustaining moderation. I will take each of these points in turn.

First, abstinence as a treatment goal is logical. If a person presents with problems related to alcohol, the most direct approach is to eliminate the offending behavior, ie, drinking alcohol. By the time they have reached treatment, most people have tried in numerous ways to change their drinking behavior: they've changed the time of day they drink, the setting, the type of beverage, or have made an entire geographical relocation. By simply discontinuing the common source of the problems (ie, alcohol), a person has laid the foundation for change. It should be noted that abstinence is the goal of treatment for models other than Twelve Step approaches. In community reinforcement or voucher programs, cumulative abstinence is reinforced as much or more than daily abstinence. One reason for this approach is that researchers using these strategies have found that in cocaine dependent outpatients, early continuous abstinence predicts longer-term abstinence.[1]

Second, abstinence is possible. Many studies have shown that about half of individuals presenting for treatment are able to achieve abstinence.[e.g., 2] Although results vary with setting and sample, there is no question that individuals can succeed in achieving abstinence. Further, abstinence does not produce a life of sad deprivation. Quality of life indicators (emotional health, relationship with spouse and friends, higher power, performance on the job, legal and health status) generally improve with abstinence. Because of the relapsing nature of alcoholism, several treatments may be needed to achieve abstinence; however, this phenomenon is more an indication of its similarity to other chronic illnesses rather than a reason to abandon the treatment goal itself.[3]

Third, and perhaps most critical to the argument for abstinence as the preferred goal for alcohol treatment, is the issue of control over drinking. If a person is dependent on alcohol, attempts at control are extremely difficult

From *The American Journal of Addiction*, Fall 2001, pp. 289–295. Copyright © 2001 by Taylor & Francis Journals. Reprinted with permission.

and generally unsuccessful. In the end, it may take individuals as much emotional time and energy (often referred to as obsession or preoccupation) *not* to use as they once expended in planning to use. "Loss of control" in this context refers specifically to the inability for an individual to not drink or reliably quit drinking once the first drink is taken.[4] Recent research on neuroadaptation, the brain's adjustment to the effect of repeated alcohol intake, is providing a scientific understanding of the phenomenon of loss of control.[5(p112)] Robinson and Berridge[6] provide a compelling model of loss of control. Repeated use of alcohol can lead to neuronal sensitization to future exposure to alcohol. This sensitization occurs in the very structures of the brain most powerfully associated with what these researchers refer to as incentive salience, or "wanting" rather than "liking." In other words, the alcohol-dependent individual relapses not simply because of the rewarding properties of the substance but because of an intense compulsion, often against all reason. The effect of the ethanol occurs in the mesolimbic structure of the brain, in the dopaminergic systems. Robinson and Berridge note that "the persistence of neural sensitization is hypothesized to leave addicts susceptible to relapse even long after the discontinuation of drug use"[6(pS94)] and that this susceptibility, in animal studies, has been shown to last "months or years."[6(pS96)] Leshner[7] has also observed that "prolonged drug use causes pervasive changes in brain function that persist long after the individual stops taking the drug."[7(p46)] From their review of over 200 studies on the effect of ethanol on the brain, Robinson and Berridge conclude that "Sadly, the persistence of neural sensitization may mean, to paraphrase Alcoholics Anonymous, that in a neurobiological sense once an addict always an addict."[6(pS109)] In fact, they point out that until medication development targets neuroadaptation (of which sensitization is a manifestation), even these approaches will have limited success when compared with abstinence.

There are other compelling reasons for abstinence as a treatment goal beyond those stated above. For example, for people who are dependent on both alcohol and cocaine, drinking after treatment increases the probability of relapsing into cocaine.[8]

Some people incorrectly assume that disease model or Twelve-Step model programs dogmatically insist that all problem drinkers must abstain from alcohol. Nothing is farther from the truth. In fact, in the source book for Alcoholics Anonymous,[9] the writers assert several times that some people are able to moderate or control their use:

> Moderate drinkers have little trouble in giving up liquor entirely if they have good reason for it. They can take it or leave it alone. Then we have a certain type of hard drinker. He may have the habit badly enough to gradually impair him physically and mentally. It may cause him to die a few years before his time. If a sufficiently strong reason, ill health, falling in love, change of environment, or the warning of a doctor becomes operative, this man can also stop or moderate, although he may find it difficult and troublesome and may even need medical attention.[9(p20, 21)]

In other words, the authors and founders of AA repeatedly acknowledge that moderation or relatively easy cessation is possible for some types of drinkers.

The crux of the issue then is two-fold: (1) who is capable of moderating his or her alcohol use? and (2) for those people who cannot, what is the best treatment goal? In terms of the first question, the diagnostic criteria for alcohol abuse and dependence are far from perfect.[10] Someday, using biological or other indicators, we may be able to identify prospectively those heavy drinkers who can moderate their drinking. However, until we can make that distinction or have a biological method to reverse neuroadaptation, abstinence is the best treatment goal. . . .

. . . Periods of use preceding abstinence do not make the ultimate goal of abstinence any less important or achievable. Abstinence-based models generally accept the fact that some people may need to "collect more experience" about their use before attaining abstinence.

Individuals are free to make their own choice about how to deal with problematic use of alcohol. But when they seek help from a professional, it is the professional's role to make an accurate diagnosis and clearly state the treatment goal and plan, even though that plan may be at odds with the patient's own ideas about the best course of treatment. This is not so different from approaches used to treat other chronic diseases. If an out-of-control diabetic comes to a physician's office and says, "my insulin is a little off, but I really want to have a chocolate milkshake and two candy bars every day," the physician doesn't say, "I'm happy to work with you whatever your goals." If a hypertensive says "I won't change my diet, I refuse to take my meds, but I will take a walk around the block once a day for exercise," the physician doesn't say, "well that's a place to start; let me know how it goes and come back in a month." Rather, in both these cases, the physician explains the diagnosis and treatment plan and goal, offers ancillary help, and may bring in the family for reinforcement. Although not all patients will immediately comply,[11] the physician does not use this as a cue to abandon the goal.

We can be respectful, realistic, and compassionate, and cheer people on as they slip and slide their way to abstinence. But, at this point in our understanding about alcohol dependence, we need to be clear about the goal of abstinence and help people obtain it as soon and as successfully as they can.

References

1. Higgins, S. T., Badger, G. J., and Budney, A. J. Initial abstinence and success in achieving longer term cocaine abstinence. *Exp Clin Psychoparmacol.* 2000; 8:377–386.

2. Stinchfield, R., and Owen, P. Hazelden's model of treatment and its outcome. *Addict Behav.* 1998; 23:669–683.

3. McLellan, A. T., Lewis, D. C., O'Brien, C. P., and Kleber, H. D. Drug dependence, a chronic medical illness. *JAMA.* 2000; 284:1689–1695.

4. Erickson, C. K. Voices of the Afflicted [commentary]. *Alcohol Clin Exp Res.* 1998; 22:132–133.

5. National Institute on Alcohol Abuse and Alcoholism. *Tenth Special Report to Congress on Alcohol and Health: Highlights from Current Research.* Bethesda, Md.: U.S. Dept of Health and Human Services; 2000.

6. Robinson, T. E., and Berridge, K. C. The psychology and neurobiology of addiction: an incentive-sensitization view. *Addiction.* 2000; 95:S91–S117.

7. Leshner, A. I. Addiction is a brain disease, and it matters. *Science,* 1997; 278:45–47.

8. McKay, J. R., Alterman, A. I., Rutherford, M. J., Cacciola, J. S., and McLellan, A. T. The relationship of alcohol use to cocaine relapse in cocaine dependent patients in an aftercare study. *J Stud Alcohol.* 1999; 60:176–180.

9. Alcoholics Anonymous World Services. *Alcoholics Anonymous.* New York, NY: Alcoholics Anonymous World Services; 1976.

10. Dawson, D. H. Drinking patterns among individuals with and without DSM-IV alcohol use disorders. *J Stud Alcohol.* 1998; 61:111–120.

11. McLellan, A. T., Lewis, D. C., O'Brien, C. P., and Kleber, H. D. Drug dependence, a chronic medical illness: implications for treatment, insurance, and outcomes evaluation. *JAMA.* 2000; 284(13):1689–1695.

One Drink Does Not a Drunk Make: How the Masters Determined Whether They Could Ever Drink Again

One drink for a recovered "alcoholic" and she'll pick up drinking right where she left off—isn't that a fact? While it is true that the vast majority of the masters feel they cannot have any alcohol, a handful have found that they are able to drink moderately. Another dozen or so have a small amount of alcohol on rare occasions without getting into any trouble. I am not suggesting that moderate or even occasional drinking is a workable goal for most people with serious drinking problems. But this select group of masters is living proof that at least for some people, one drink does not necessarily a drunk make. . . .

Nolan H.'s Story

Always the kind of guy who liked to walk on the wild side, Nolan H. was addicted to both alcohol and cocaine by the time he was in his mid-twenties. Now a churchgoing forty-six-year-old father and responsible married man, he still rides a motorcycle and jetskis at speeds of more than sixty miles per hour—new highs that have taken the place of drugs and alcohol in his life. His alcohol problem has been resolved for twelve years now, but not in the stereotypical way. He's one of the small number of masters who have been able to return to nonproblematic drinking.

More than a decade ago, after the birth of his second child, Nolan knew he was in trouble when he stayed out partying with the boys until the morning's wee hours. "At two A.M., high on cocaine and beer, I was pacing in my living room, with my heart racing—still going one hundred miles an hour. I realized that what I was doing wasn't normal," he says. Not prone to expressing his emotions openly, Nolan slipped his wife a note that morning announcing that he was going to go into treatment and making it clear that he didn't want to back out. After taking about a month to get his business

From SOBER FOR GOOD by Anne M. Fletcher. Copyright © 2001 by Anne Fletcher. Reprinted by permission of Houghton Mifflin Co. All rights reserved.

affairs in order (and having a few final flings with drugs and alcohol), he checked in for a one-month stay at a residential treatment center. Aside from attending AA meetings for the first six months after treatment, he has maintained sobriety on his own since then.

At first it wasn't easy to stay away from his drug-using friends and from bars, but the six-foot-one-inch Nolan soon discovered the joy of running. "When I quit drinking, my weight was up to 237. So I started running, lost weight, and began to feel good." He adds, "The up side of not drinking began far to outweigh the down side. The down side was giving up a couple of hours pleasure, if that. The up side was that I would get up in the morning and feel so good about myself, my body, and my family. I felt good about abstaining." And abstain he did—for eight years.

"I Don't Let Situations Control Whether I Have a Drink"

Then, four years ago, Nolan started wondering whether he could have a glass of wine or a beer now and then and proceeded to try it. Since that time he has been able to drink moderately, but does so only in social situations, never at home. He might have two to three beers twice in one week, then go several weeks with no alcoholic beverages at all. Nolan has no desire to drink unless he's in a restaurant or out with the guys, such as after a sporting event. He admits that he has gotten intoxicated—which for him means having a blood alcohol level above the legal limit for driving—but rarely, maybe once in an entire summer. He adds, "If I know I'm getting a little looped, I usually quit. I just don't want to get drunk."

How does he keep himself from going overboard? Nolan explains, "I've been labeled an alcoholic, and all the men on my father's side were alcoholics. So I always keep an awareness in the back of my mind. If enough people tell you you have a tail, sooner or later you'd better turn around and take a look. I don't take it lightly. I'll say to myself, 'Gee, buddy, you've had some drinks twice this week—that's pushing it.' He adds, "Sometimes when I have an urge to drink, I think of my wife and kids and ask myself, 'Is this the right thing to do?'" Nolan also mentioned that he never allows a circumstance, like being angry, attending a party, or having someone push a drink on him, dictate whether he drinks. "I don't use excuses for having a drink—if I want one, I have it. But I don't let situations control whether I have a drink," he explains.

For those who might doubt that a former alcohol abuser can return to moderate drinking, I spoke to Nolan's wife (with his permission) to confirm that he is now able to manage his alcohol intake. She is not usually with him when he drinks, but her estimation of how much alcohol he consumes is consistent with his description. Although it worries her that he drinks at all because of his history, his current drinking habits have had no negative consequences and no impact on their family.

When I asked Nolan how he is able to exert control over his drinking, he replied, "I never want to go back to feeling that way again—that terrible

WHO CAN DRINK MODERATELY AFTER HAVING A DRINKING PROBLEM?

Experts are virtually unanimous in agreeing that moderate or controlled drinking is not apt to work for the vast majority of people with very serious drinking problems. So what kind of person is most likely to succeed with being able to drink moderately? Studies involving both people who have quit drinking on their own and those who have been through treatment indicate that most alcohol abusers who are able to return to controlled drinking have relatively less serious drinking problems or are people (like college binge drinkers) who "mature out" of heavy alcohol abuse as they become responsible adults. In general, research suggests that successful controlled drinkers tend to be women and people under forty. Also, they typically have alcohol problems of shorter duration (fewer than ten years).

Finally, individuals who are successful with moderate drinking tend to have the following characteristics:

Are psychologically stable

Are well educated

Are steadily employed

Don't regard themselves as "alcoholic" or "problem drinkers"

Don't subscribe to the disease concept of alcohol problems

Believe controlled drinking is possible

Develop alternatives to drinking as a means of coping with stress

---

feeling of regularly coming home drunk and high on drugs, the way I felt the next morning, the guilt." He added, "Tell me I can't do something, and I'll show you that I can. If you want success in life, you don't want alcohol and drugs to control you.". . .

The Problem with Abstinence for All

Pressuring all people with drinking problems to abstain ignores the fact that drinking problems exist on a continuum, from mild to life-threatening. Consider the case of Enrico J., a three-time drunk driving offender who was required to take part in a several-month abstinence-oriented treatment program, followed by weekly AA attendance for a year, when he was a young adult. When he protested that he was not an "alcoholic" but instead was part of a carousing crowd that abused alcohol, he was told he was in denial. He says, "I wasn't ready to quit drinking, and didn't really need to—I needed to learn to be more responsible with my drinking." Now, ten years later, he can take or leave alcohol. He occasionally has a beer or two, but he enjoys it as a beverage rather than using it to get high. In fact, according to the alcohol expert and attorney Stanton Peele, "Most drunk driving offenders are not 'alcoholics,' yet they represent one of the largest groups of people coerced into abstinence-based programs in the United States."

Indeed, a number of experts at the forefront of alcohol research believe that more people would do something about their alcohol problem at an earlier point if at the outset they were offered a choice between abstinence and a moderate drinking approach. Heather F. admits that although she knew that she would probably be better off electing abstinence, she was not ready to make a permanent commitment to it when she first tackled her drinking problem. "If the therapists who allowed me to try drinking moderately had required abstinence from the start, I would have walked right out the door. Because I was able to experiment and make my own decision, I eventually came to see that abstinence is the best option for me."

Dr. Alan Marlatt points out that Canada, Australia, and some European countries routinely offer formal controlled drinking programs, which are likely to attract problem drinkers uninterested in abstinence. As a *U.S. News & World Report* feature stated, "By calling abstinence the only cure, we ensure that the nation's $100 billion alcohol problem won't be solved." If someone elects moderate drinking and it doesn't work out, then he or she can step up to an abstinence-based approach.

Some studies suggest that people who are offered controlled drinking approaches at the outset may actually fare better than those who are offered abstinence-oriented approaches. Perhaps the most famous of these studies was conducted by the psychologists Mark and Linda Sobell in the 1970s. It involved chronic male "alcoholics" who were randomly assigned to either controlled drinking treatment or a traditional abstinence-oriented program. According to Dr. Mark Sobell, "Three years after treatment, it was found that those who received the moderation approach did much better all around. Surprisingly, they even had more abstinent days than those who had been told to be abstinent."

Moderate drinking can also be part of a plan for recovery that starts out with a period of abstinence, goes on to a moderation trial, and involves a return to abstinence if moderate drinking doesn't work. Heather F. recalls, "My first chemical dependency counselor had me start out with three months of abstinence, followed by a trial of moderate drinking. When my drinking crept back up again, I realized that someday I would probably have to give up alcohol completely."

If people *are* allowed to choose whether they want to try moderate drinking or abstinence, won't they all flock to the option that still allows them to drink? Interestingly, studies suggest that even when they are trained in controlled drinking, many alcohol-dependent people wind up choosing abstinence. The psychologist Marc Kern says that a number of participants in the Moderation Management group he directs do just that after following a recommended thirty-day break from alcohol. "Some people find that after a month of no alcohol, it's just easier that way, and they stay with abstinence," he notes.

Dr. Sobell concurs: "Most people whose problems are serious will say, 'I want to stop drinking altogether,' because they just don't want to risk further consequences." He adds, "Occasionally someone will opt for a goal that is clearly not in his best interest, but the frequency of this occurring is far less than one would expect." Dr. Kern's and Dr. Sobell's remarks are echoed by other experts who conclude that when given a choice, people tend to elect goals that are right for their situations.

How the Masters of Moderate Drinking Set Limits

The masters who choose to drink from time to time use various strategies to make sure their drinking doesn't get out of hand: Their experiences support the observation of experts that former problem drinkers who achieve stable moderation not only drink less but make changes in their drinking practices. For instance, they switch to an alcoholic beverage that is not their favorite, they no longer hang around with a drinking crowd, and they drink in different locations or under different circumstances. Nolan H. changed his circle of friends and leisure activities so he was less influenced by the bar and drug culture. He also keeps careful mental track of how often he drinks within a given time period. Bill L., who in the past "abused alcohol in private," states, "Now I drink only in public, where I am very careful about my appearance and behavior. But my most important strategy is planning ahead. Being older and more aware, I now actively plan on not drinking much or at all. I set limits both on time spent drinking and the number and type of drinks I have. I also visualize how I appear to others when I am drinking."

Ed Shaw, a moderate drinker and master who is the cohost and producer of the worldwide radio program *The Ruth and Ed Shaw Show*, has a number of set conditions for drinking. He explains, "I plan when I will drink; it's conscious, not accidental. I normally don't drink any more than once a week, and I never have beer, because for me, 'just one' is bullshit. Also, I try to avoid big drunks who need company, as well as stay away from St. Patrick's Day parties where all they do is drink."

Not only do the masters who drink moderately rely on certain strategies to limit the amount of alcohol they consume, but they also take care of their emotional well-being in order to prevent themselves from going back to their old ways. For instance, Nolan H. has vowed not to drink because of "circumstances" such as being angry. He has found new ways of feeling good through exercising, coaching his sons' athletic teams, enjoying leisure activities, and pursuing his career. More than a decade into sobriety, four years of which he has spent drinking moderately, Nolan still takes stock of the pluses and minuses of drinking. He explains, "Just recently I passed up a day out with the guys because I knew it would be a whole day of drinking. I really didn't want to feel bad the next morning. The joy of drinking in a situation like this just doesn't outweigh the down side for me anymore."

Moderate drinker Pat A. not only attends Moderation Management meetings and keeps alcohol out of her home, but she's involved in professional counseling to resolve problems that initially led her to drink too much. She tries to deal with anger by exercising rather than drinking and has learned to speak up for herself. "I don't let a drink take care of something that does not sit well with me," she declares.

Finally, it's quite clear that even though they are not abstinent, these masters *have* made a long-term commitment to changing their relationship with alcohol—just as other masters have made a commitment to abstinence. Fifteen years into resolving his drinking problem, Jack B., who now has a beer or glass of wine each day, revisited the bar culture with its "various characters," which he sorely missed in the beginning of sobriety. He says, "After I returned to bars in a much more limited way, I came to see the people I had once viewed as fascinating as damaged, broken, beaten-down persons—a painful revelation, yet one that reinforced my commitment *not* to go down that road again."

Getting Help with Moderate Drinking

"The problem," Dr. Marlatt points out, "is that most people who try moderate drinking attempt it on their own, without any tools. If they were offered some professional guidance and had safeguards in place for monitoring their progress, then moderate drinking wouldn't have to end in disaster." Indeed, few masters indicated that they had had any formal help when they tried to drink moderately. That kind of help may be difficult to find in the United States. A study in the mid-1990s found that more than three quarters of two hundred randomly selected treatment programs saw controlled drinking as an unacceptable goal. Outpatient programs were less likely to object to this option than residential programs, according to the same study, but still, about half of them found controlled drinking unacceptable. In describing this study, the U.S. government publication *Alcohol and Health* says, "In general, program respondents indicated an unwillingness to negotiate treatment goals with their clients."

If you want to try moderate drinking, you would be advised to do so as part of a recognized program like Moderation Management or another [similar program] and/or under the guidance of a professional who has experience in assessing the severity of alcohol problems as well as in moderation approaches. That way, you can get some sense of whether you are a candidate for moderate drinking, have access to helpful tools, and receive guidance if moderate drinking fails. . . .

CHALLENGE QUESTIONS

Should Abstinence Be the Goal for Treating People with Alcohol Problems?

1. Owen concurs with the notion that abstinence is indeed the most appropriate goal for people with alcohol dependence, a viewpoint that is promoted by Alcoholics Anonymous (AA). Based on what you know about the approach of AA, discuss whether there are certain personality characteristics that respond especially well with the AA philosophy.
2. Fletcher contends that controlled drinking may work better than abstinence for some people. Consider some of the characteristics (e.g., personality, education, socioeconomic level, emotional stability) that would contribute to effectiveness of a controlled-drinking strategy.
3. Some social critics express alarm about the fact that our society recognizes the extraordinary costs associated with alcohol abuse yet permits and reinforces the omnipresent marketing of alcohol. Discuss the reasons for this seeming contradiction.
4. Imagine that you are a clinician who is treating a man who has been mandated by the court to seek professional help because of his history of legal problems associated with alcohol abuse. He states that he now understands the seriousness of his problem, but insists that he will control his drinking rather than abstain. What approach would you take in treating such an individual?
5. Imagine that you are a researcher who has been given a grant to compare different interventions for college students who have been arrested for alcohol-related problems on campus. What research design would you use to compare the relative effectiveness of abstinence and controlled drinking in this group?

Suggested Readings

Alcoholics Anonymous: The Story of How Many Thousands of Men and Women Have Recovered from Alcoholism (4th edition). (2001). New York: Alcoholics Anonymous World Services, Inc.

Ellis, Albert, and Emmett Velten. (1992). *When AA Doesn't Work for You: Rational Steps to Quitting Alcohol*. Fort Lee, NJ: Barricade Books.

Marlatt, G. Alan, Linda A. Dimeff, John S. Baer, and Daniel R. Kivlahan. (1999). *Brief Alcohol Screening and Intervention for College Students*

(BASICS): A Harm Reduction Approach. New York: The Guilford Press.

Newhouse, Eric. (2001). *Alcohol: Cradle to Grave.* Center City, MN: Hazelden Information and Educational Services, 2001.

Tatarsky, Andrew. (2002). *Harm Reduction Psychotherapy: A New Treatment for Drug and Alcohol Problems.* Northvale, NJ: Jason Aronson.

Internet Mental Health

This Web site provides extensive coverage of topics in the field of mental health, including consideration of various issues pertaining to medication.

http://www.mentalhealth.com

The Treatment Advocacy Center

This Web site focuses on the problems associated with the failure of treatments for people with schizophrenia and other mental illnesses.

http://www.psychlaws.org

Attention Deficit Disorder Association

This is the Web site of ADDA, a nonprofit organization dedicated to education, research, and public advocacy concerning AD/HD.

http://add.org/

Psychosurgery

In this paper, G. Rees Cosgrove and Scott L. Rauch, physicians in the Departments of Neurosurgery and Psychiatry, respectively, of the Massachusetts General Hospital, review the history of the physiological basis for and current perspectives on the practice of psychosurgery.

http://neurosurgery.mgh.harvard.edu/Functional/
Psychosurgery2001.htm

The Mental Health Forum: Archive of Electroconvulsive Therapy Questions

This Web site contains various forums including mental health forums discussing topics such as electroconvulsive therapy.

http://www.medhelp.org

American Psychological Association's *APA-Monitor*

This site contains an article entitled "A History of Prescription Privileges."

http://www.apa.org/monitor/sep98/prescrip.html

PART 3

The Trend Toward Biological Interventions

*A*lthough *the medical model has been prominent in the field of mental health for the past century, in recent years the trend toward biological explanations and interventions for psychological problems has been more evident. The field of psychopharmacology has mushroomed to such an extent that billions of dollars are spent each year on medications for a wide array of emotional and behavioral problems. In addition to recommending medications, some mental health professionals have advocated more extreme medical interventions such as electroconvulsive treatment or psychosurgery. Many psychologists have expressed interest in becoming more central players in the medical sphere by pursuing the right to prescribe medications, an option regarded as objectionable by many physicians and of questionable wisdom by many psychologists.*

- Are Prozac and Similar Antidepressants Safe and Effective?

- Are Antipsychotic Medications the Treatment of Choice for People with Psychosis?

- Is Ritalin Overprescribed?

- Should Psychosurgery Be Used to Treat Certain Psychological Conditions?

- Should Psychologists Prescribe Medication?

- Is Electroconvulsive Therapy Ethical?

ISSUE 9

Are Prozac and Similar Antidepressants Safe and Effective?

YES: William S. Appleton, from *Prozac and the New Antidepressants: What You Need to Know About Prozac, Zoloft, Paxil, Luvox, Wellbutrin, Effexor, Serzone, Vestra, Celexa, St. John's Wort, and Others,* rev. ed. (Plume, 2000)

NO: Joseph Glenmullen, from *Prozac Backlash: Overcoming the Dangers of Prozac, Zoloft, Paxil, and Other Antidepressants With Safe, Effective Alternatives* (Simon & Schuster, 2000)

ISSUE SUMMARY

YES: Psychiatrist William S. Appleton asserts that Prozac and other drugs in the class of selective serotonin reuptake inhibitors can provide effective relief for depression as well as other mental health problems and concerns, with minimal side effects.

NO: Psychiatrist Joseph Glenmullen argues that Prozac and other drugs in the class of selective serotonin reuptake inhibitors are neither as effective nor as safe as pharmaceutical companies have led people to believe.

$\mathbf{A}$fter Prozac was first publicly released in the late 1980s, it took very little time for this medication to soar in sales and become one of the most widely prescribed drugs in history. In a very brief period of time Prozac was being touted as a wonder drug. Not only were Prozac and other selective serotonin reuptake inhibitors (SSRIs) promoted as effective in treating depression, but these drugs were also recommended for other psychiatric disorders, most notably obsessive compulsive disorder. The proliferation of prescriptions for SSRIs continued, as reports spread that these medications were also helpful to people with problems of life functioning that are not quite so serious as to be diagnosed mental disorders.

As the 1990s progressed, the miracle drugs in the SSRI class began to lose some of their luster, as reports of worrisome side effects emerged in the media. Of greatest concern were anecdotal reports that some individuals taking SSRIs experienced uncontrollable suicidal or assaultive impulses. The pharmaceutical companies and many mental health professionals initially downplayed these reports, insisting that these behaviors were symptoms of severe depression rather than attributable to the medications. As these troubling reports accumulated, some cautions were offered about the possibility that a very small percentage of patients might have idiosyncratic reactions involving impulsivity.

The current state of affairs calls for a balanced consideration of the costs and benefits associated with SSRIs. There is ample documentation that millions of people feel that they have benefited immeasurably from taking these medications. At the same time, it would be naive to conclude that SSRIs are panaceas for all that ails the emotional lives of human beings.

In the following selection, William S. Appleton speaks with considerable enthusiasm about the ways in which Prozac and similar medications can benefit people afflicted by a range of psychological problems, particularly depression. He contends that with adequate education about the striking benefits of SSRIs, more people can alleviate their painful emotional symptoms than currently do. He maintains that the psychological benefits of these medications are dramatic and that the side effects are minimal.

In the second selection, Joseph Glenmullen expresses alarm about the side effects of Prozac and the other SSRI medications, some of which he says will not become evident until people have taken the drug for years or even decades. He argues that the pharmaceutical companies underreport these side effects and suppress facts that might deter people from beginning such treatment. Glenmullen warns that future generations may look back on the era of these drugs as a "frightening human experiment."

POINT

- Prozac is a drug in a group of antidepressants whose development has been based on neuroscience rather than chance. These cleaner drugs affect only serotonin and produce fewer side effects than older antidepressants.

- Because antidepressants such as Prozac are well tolerated, have fairly low lethal potential (associated with accidental or intentional overdose), and have been proven to be effective, they can be prescribed by family doctors rather than expert psychopharmacologists.

- Although there are side effects associated with Prozac and similar drugs, many go away, especially nausea and headache. Also, some symptoms, such as anxiety, loss of sex drive, and abdominal distress, are due to the depression itself, not the drugs.

COUNTERPOINT

- Dramatic changes in one neurotransmitter, like boosting serotonin, can trigger compensatory changes in others, such as a dramatic drop in dopamine, producing dangerous side effects.

- Despite their lack of sophisticated information about antidepressants, family doctors are being pressured by managed care insurance companies to prescribe drugs like Prozac rather than make costly referrals to specialists who might be able to treat patients with more effective, safer alternatives.

- There have been reports that the longterm side effects of Prozac and similar drugs include neurological disorders, debilitating withdrawal syndromes, sexual dysfunction, and suicidal and violent behavior.

William S. Appleton  **YES**

Prozac and the New Antidepressants

What Are Antidepressants?

Antidepressants are drugs that are used to treat depression. They are often prescribed by general practitioners, psychiatrists, and by psychopharmacologists; the latter are medical psychiatrists who specialize in the study of the effects on behavior of drugs, as well as naturally occurring substances within the body, such as serotonin. Psychopharmacologists are keenly interested in the design and development of safer and more effective antidepressants. It is through their cooperation with research scientists at drug companies that the new, improved antidepressants were, and continue to be, developed. . . .

In the last twenty years, antidepressants have begun to be designed based on neuroscience, rather than discovered by chance. Thus, cleaner drugs affecting only serotonin have been developed, producing many fewer side effects than the older antidepressants, which affected a variety of neurotransmitters, some of which were irrelevant to their clinical effect. Progress in designing new antidepressants is slow, because the brain contains about 10 billion cells, and more than fifty known neurotransmitters along with many unknown others, which influence many targets and produce varying effects on cell genes. In spite of this extraordinary complexity, progress is being made. Once the drug is designed, the gradual process of careful testing begins. It was fifteen years from the development of Prozac in 1972 by the scientists of Eli Lilly to its release by the U.S. Food and Drug Administration [FDA] for public use in 1987. . . .

It is my belief that the new antidepressants do substantially better than the old ones in outpatient depressives. The reason for this is partly that they are better drugs, but mainly that they are being used more effectively. A doctor does not have to be an expert psychopharmacologist to use Prozac better than he used Elavil. Often when he prescribed Elavil he was afraid the patient would overdose, so very small doses were given in case the person took all of them at once. Since the typical family doctor did not see the depressed individual very often, he or she was in no position to trust the patient with a large supply of Elavil. The family doctor typically prescribed

From PROZAC AND THE NEW ANTIDEPRESSANTS (Revised Edition) by William S. Appleton, copyright © 1997, 2000 by William S. Appleton. Used by permission of Plume, an imprint of Penguin Group (USA) Inc.

too little of the drug, and the patient did not recover. In the relatively rare case where the dosage was adequate, the general practitioner did not see the patient often enough to cope with the side effects, and the patient was likely to stop taking the medication. Only the psychiatrist or psychopharmacologist, who saw the patient more frequently, could encourage the acceptance of dry mouth, dizziness, blurred vision, constipation, and other unpleasant side effects while the dose was being raised to a point where it would be effective. The older antidepressants had dose ranges from one to twelve tablets and required careful increases, from a modest beginning to all twelve tablets in cases where the full amount was required. This rarely happened. Either the patient received too little of the drug or stopped taking the drug because of a side effect. In either case, he or she did not get better.

With many of the new antidepressants, patients require only one tablet a day. The family doctor does not have to carefully raise the dose until an effective level is reached. The drugs have a fairly low lethal potential so that the physician does not fear giving a month's supply at a time. [In contrast] one week's supply of Elavil could kill a patient.

Finally, the new antidepressants do not make patients faint or cause severe constipation, hand tremors, dry mouth, weight gain, or blurred vision. Because they are tolerated much better, patients do not stop taking them as often before they are successful at reducing symptoms. More patients are completing a full dose for an adequate period of time, are not discontinuing use of the drug against the doctor's advice, and are benefiting. The new drugs are thus doing a substantially better job in outpatient depressives, the majority of whom are being treated not by expert psychopharmacologists but by family doctors. The reason the new antidepressants have made such an impression is that they are easy to prescribe, are safe, can be given in full dose, and produce few side effects. . . .

The Selective Serotonin Reuptake Inhibitors (SSRIs): Prozac, Zoloft, Paxil, Luvox, and Celexa

Serotonin

Serotonin is one of the chemicals in the brain that transmits messages from one brain cell to another. It would be nice if the serotonin story were as simple as this: too little causes depression; too much, mania. But in fact, brain activities are controlled by the coming together of many different chemicals (also known as neurotransmitters), which serve as messengers from one cell to the next. Brain cells are excited not only by serotonin but also by norepinephrine, histamine, GABA, and acetylcholine, to name just a few. The interactions of the fifty-odd neurotransmitters with serotonin, therefore, involve serotonin in many brain activities that are disturbed in psychiatric symptoms and disorders, such as depression, anxiety, irritability, confused thinking, abnormal appetite, and disturbance of the sleep cycle. Furthermore, the neurotransmitters affect one another, and that may be why serotonin and nonserotonin antidepressants work equally well—when you give a drug affecting one neurotransmitter, you automatically affect the other neurotransmitters. . . .

Side Effects of the SSRIs

Nausea without vomiting, loose stools and diarrhea, nervousness and anxiety, loss of appetite, insomnia, headache, and sexual dysfunction are all potential side effects of the SSRIs. As treatment continues, many of the side effects go away, especially nausea and headache. Some of the symptoms, such as anxiety, headache, loss of sex drive, and abdominal distress, are due to the depression itself, and not to the drug. In general, the higher the dose of the drug, the more side effects. It therefore makes sense to start at as low a dosage as possible and move up gradually. Antidepressants work slowly, taking days to weeks, and the tendency to increase the dosage instead of waiting for the therapeutic effect causes more side effects than are necessary. When side effects do occur, the dose can be reduced or divided or taken at a different time of day, another antidepressant can be tried, or the side effects can be treated. . . .

Prozac (Fluoxetine)

Making the Prozac Decision

As Prozac has become overwhelmingly popular, the matter of who should take it has become muddled. Originally released for the treatment of major depression, its use has spread to many other conditions. Not only are people with eating, sexual, and anxiety disorders, depressives, schizophrenics, obsessive-compulsives, and post-traumatic stress disorder patients candidates for Prozac, but also those who are subsyndromal: the timid; those with low energy and low self-esteem; those who are irritable, perfectionist, inflexible, or suffering from a general malaise or unhappiness, and those who are too aggressive or abusive. In short, anyone—sick or not—may benefit from the civilizing effects of Prozac. . . .

The Benefits of Prozac

Large, controlled studies of Prozac have established its effectiveness in major depression to be equal to that of the tricyclic antidepressants (e.g., Elavil and Tofranil), with fewer side effects. There are studies of its use in other well-defined conditions which support its prescription in obsessive-compulsive disorder, bulimia, premenstrual dysphoric disorder, and other diagnostic types . . . concerning SSRIs in general. With respect to its use in the timid, irritable, overly sensitive, insecure, and fatigued, and those lacking self-confidence, Prozac's success has been established by anecdote rather than controlled study. Anecdotal evidence can be as reliable as the reports of miracles, but that does not make either of them untrue. There are many people who believe Prozac has restored them to full functioning, and I am convinced from my own observation that they are right in their belief. But a large group feel only somewhat better, and others have been hurt by the drug. It is the physician's duty to know what can go wrong and watch for it carefully over time, even if the decision to take Prozac has been handed over to the patient out of the doctor's ignorance, as opposed to carelessness. If a person says to me that he is suffering and I think there is a reasonable chance Prozac will relieve him, I feel obliged to prescribe it. I consider this no more irresponsible than if a postsurgical patient complained of pain and I issued a narcotic. However, I would not prescribe morphine for someone with chronic low-grade back pain, because it is dangerous to do so. The question is, how dangerous is it to prescribe Prozac for more vague, nondisease conditions, ones that are either subsyndromal or perhaps matters of temperament and character rather than syndromes or even subsyndromes?

How Does Prozac Work?

Because the serotonin story remains a mystery, and because no one has proven that depressives have too little of it, it seems more useful to think of Prozac's actions in terms used by those who take it.

In major depression, the reduction in anxiety, bodily aches and pains, trouble thinking and concentrating, sleep disturbance, motor retardation, and depressed mood has been measured both on the basis of patients' and physicians' accounts of their overall impressions and by means of specialized depression scales administered by trained raters who did not know if the patient was on a drug or a placebo. The way Prozac works in the large variety of other psychiatric disorders it has been used to treat is, I think, as follows:

As an Anti-Rage Drug On Prozac, the physically abusive strike out less or not at all, the formerly irritable no longer scream in frustration, and the overly aggressive become less abrasive. Prozac can be thought of as a calming and civilizing drug.

The obvious bad side effect of this is that one can become tranquil in situations in which it would be more appropriate to cry out. One of my patients entered into an abusive intimate relationship while on Prozac. When he went off the drug, he realized the relationship had been a terrible mistake. The doctor and the person considering Prozac must not only identify the presence of anger, rage, and aggression, but evaluate these emotions in the context of the person's life. Are they signals that should be attended to and used as data upon which to form judgments, or are they pathologic aberrations requiring Prozac for their removal?

Improved Effectiveness Whether the source of feeling strong and in control comes from the mind actually working better or from improved morale and self-esteem, which bring the expectation of success, the person on Prozac has a sense of being more effective and therefore likely to overcome obstacles. Thus, the person with a history of social phobia is able to give a speech or enter a room of strangers, and someone who never spoke up at sales meetings will begin to do so.

The relationship of anxiety and depression to self-esteem is well known. If your heart is racing with fear and dread of the future, or if you feel stupid and inept because of depression, then you will not expect to overcome the novel and difficult situations you encounter at work or in your social life. Whether your mind functions better, your self-esteem is improved, your anxiety or depression relieved, or your hopes raised—whatever the reason—you feel more in control and effective, and thus your performance improves.

The Pleasure Center Is Turned on   Prozac is not a euphoriant giving people a high like marijuana or cocaine, but like other antidepressants, it turns on the pleasure center that depression extinguishes. A main reason why people feel depressed, lose interest in previously enjoyed activities, stop eating, have no energy, and are unable to concentrate and make decisions is that they anticipate no pleasure from these activities. When Prozac activates the pleasure center, normal appetites and interests return. The depressive's social withdrawal ends; friends are called in the anticipation of a good time. Desire for food and sex returns because they promise enjoyment, and life seems worth sustaining. The pain and misery gone, pleasure once again rewards and motivates activities.

Decreased Sensitivity   Many depressives are thin-skinned and easily hurt by a snub or an unintended slight. They may agonize for hours after a social gathering about why someone did not speak to or dance with them or what a particular remark meant that seemed to wound them. Some of these sufferers actively seek one social event after another, motivated by a feeling of emptiness and sadness and a desire for relief through human contact, but often they are disappointed by snubs and rejections that less sensitive people would not even have noticed. Like many symptoms of depression, this one is connected to many of the others. If you feel worthless and have low self-esteem, you are much more easily hurt than if you are sure of yourself. If your pleasure center is turned off and you are already in pain, a snub hurts more than if you feel well. The same goes for criticism, which shakes the fragile equilibrium of the depressive, and therefore can be tolerated less well than by the nondepressed.

Prozac makes the depressed person less sensitive to slights and criticisms, and more able to consider the suggestions of a boss or family member without overreacting with hurt or rage.

Increased Hope   Depressed people are negative about their abilities, and about the past and the future. Feeling without hope, they are unable to plan their lives, from the smallest social event to the largest project, and are plagued by passivity and indecision. If you ask them to the movies on a Saturday night, they cannot give a straight answer, since they do not know whether they will feel well enough to go. Once again, the symptoms of depression are related to one another. Without the ability to experience pleasure, it is hard to hope that future action will be fruitful. If you feel ineffective and worthless, it is impossible to believe that your efforts will be rewarded, so that you are filled with hopeful anticipation. Without hope, people sit still and alone, unable to motivate themselves to act. Once Prozac restores hope, the person begins to plan social activities, and at work is able to take the many small steps leading to the completion of a big project or sale.

What Is Unique About How Prozac Works?

The five things I have just discussed—decreased rage, increased self-esteem, activation of the pleasure center, diminished sensitivity, and the restoration of hope—are not unique to Prozac. The other SSRIs are all equally capable of producing these results. The older antidepressants certainly could turn on the pleasure center, restore hope, and increase self-esteem, but because of their tricky dose schedules (from one to twelve pills) and their annoying side effects (dry mouth, constipation, blood pressure drop, racing pulse, weight gain, blurred vision), their use was reserved for more severe depressions, and given in ineffective, inadequate dosages by nonspecialists. Thus, the large group of nonmajor depressives—the shy, the overly sensitive, the obsessed, the impulsive, the insecure, the irritable, and the aggressive—were rarely if ever medicated using the older antidepressants, and almost never in adequate dosages because the side effects would have made them intolerable.

In the general population, rage, along with physical and verbal abuse, nasty impatience, and a hostile confrontational attitude, are diminished by the SSRIs, as they never were before by the older antidepressants. Hypersensitivity to rejection and criticism, fearfulness, timidity, shyness, rigidity, perfectionism, and impulsivity are all affected by Prozac and the other SSRIs.

Prozac is not different from the other SSRIs, it was simply there first, used most, and has been the focus of the largest mythology. Zoloft, Paxil, Luvox, and Celexa have never appeared on the covers of popular magazines, or been singled out for attack by the Scientologists. Prozac is the name everybody knows, the one appearing on book titles. It is the drug people are likely to ask for.

The Prozac Phenomenon

Anne consulted with me during her first month at the Harvard Graduate School of Design. She had just moved to Cambridge from Chicago, where she had worked as an assistant in an architectural firm. Now Anne was embarking on becoming an architect herself.

"I'm on Zoloft. I came to see you because I'm running out of medication and need a new doctor here in Cambridge," she explained, with a straightforward, friendly smile.

Every fall, I see droves of new students like Anne on one of the popular Prozac-type antidepressants that boost the brain chemical serotonin: Prozac, Zoloft, Paxil, Luvox, and others. Instead of just renewing the serotonin booster, I first inquire about the patient's history: Why is she on the drug? What other treatment has she had? How long has she been on the medication? Has she tried going off it? As in Anne's case, the answers are often unsettling.

Anne had been on 150 milligrams a day of Zoloft for three years. Her primary-care doctor put her on a serotonin booster to give her a lift because Anne was "upset" over her boyfriend's breaking up with her. At the time she had relatively mild symptoms that would not qualify for a diagnosis of depression. She had been weepy and a little distracted for a week when her doctor gave her the initial prescription. Anne had not seen a psychiatrist, psychologist, or social worker for a psychological evaluation. Her primary-care doctor at her HMO simply prescribed Zoloft.

"Why 150 milligrams a day?" I inquired.

"Is that a high dose?" Anne asked, surprised.

I explained that in my experience most people only need 50 milligrams or 100 at most. The maximum dose is 200. Anything above 150 is usually reserved for people with severe symptoms, which she clearly had not had. Anne had no idea why she had been put on such a high dose.

"What happened with your ex-boyfriend?" I asked.

"We got back together a few months later. We've been married now for two years, quite happily."

"Did your doctor make any effort to see if you still needed the drug once the crisis had passed?"

"No."

Reprinted with the permission of Simon & Schuster Adult Publishing Group, from PROZAC BACKLASH: Overcoming the Dangers of Prozac, Zoloft, Paxil, and Other Antidepressants with Safe, Effective Alternatives by Joseph Glenmullen, M.D. Copyright © 2000 by Joseph Glenmullen. All rights reserved.

"How often did you check in with him?"

"I didn't."

"You never saw him again?"

"No."

"How did you get more medication?"

"He gave me a prescription for a year. At the end of the year, I just telephoned his office and they called in another year's supply to the pharmacy."

I shook my head, unable to suppress my dismay at such cursory treatment. Unfortunately, stories like Anne's are quite common nowadays.

"You're not sure I need the Zoloft?"

I told Anne that at the time of the breakup, many doctors, including myself, would have recommended psychotherapy, which might well have seen her through the crisis given how mild her symptoms were and how quickly the crisis passed. I was especially concerned that no effort had been made to periodically reassess whether or not she needed the medication. Now Anne had had three years' exposure to a high dose of Zoloft.

"Three years' exposure . . . is that cause for concern?"

In recent years, the danger of long-term side effects has emerged in association with Prozac-type drugs, making it imperative to minimize one's exposure to them. Neurological disorders including disfiguring facial and whole body tics, indicating potential brain damage, are an increasing concern with patients on the drugs. Withdrawal syndromes—which can be debilitating—are estimated to affect up to 50% of patients, depending on the particular drug. Sexual dysfunction affects 60% of people. Increasing reports are being made of people becoming dependent on the medications after chronic use. With related drugs targeting serotonin, there is evidence that they may effect a "chemical lobotomy" by destroying the nerve endings that they target in the brain. Prozactype drugs are now wearing off in some 34% of patients who can suddenly find themselves with a return of dread symptoms. And startling new information on Prozac's precipitating suicidal and violent behavior has come to light.

"What do you recommend I do?" asked Anne as I described these dangers.

"I suggest we gradually lower your Zoloft dose to see if you can go off the medication. I suspect you don't need it."

"But I've just started this demanding degree program," Anne responded anxiously.

"We would reduce your dose slowly to see if you had a return of any symptoms."

Anne shook her head. "I'm afraid to make any changes right now. I just left my job and made this big move. Being in graduate school is a huge adjustment. My husband is just starting a new job in Boston. I feel there is too much at stake."

Many patients stay on their medication because they fear rocking the boat. In Anne's case, she was making a reasonable point; this was not the best time to experiment. Almost any other time in the three years she had been on it would have been better. Unfortunately, these earlier opportunities had been lost. Now she was faced with the difficult decision of lowering the dose at an inopportune time or extending her exposure to the drug another six months to a year.

After we discussed her situation at length, Anne's position remained unchanged. Before we ended the meeting, I gave her a month's prescription for Zoloft. It is a reflection of how seriously I take patients being on these drugs that I do not give people a year's supply. Instead, Anne and I made another appointment for the following month. Meeting with her monthly, I would get to know her better, hear about her progress in graduate school, and be better able to re-evaluate her medication needs by the end of her semester.

I have mixed feelings about writing prescriptions for people like Anne. Basing my judgment on experience with many patients, I thought she would have no trouble substantially reducing her dose. Once a Prozac-type drug is working, much lower doses are often sufficient to maintain its effects. In fact, I felt fairly confident that Anne could have stopped the medication altogether based on the trivial symptoms for which it was prescribed to her in the first place. Still, so long as patients are making informed choices, their wishes should be respected.

Two weeks later, Anne appeared in my office far sooner than expected. She looked exhausted and irritable. Tears welling in her eyes she said, "I went down to 100 milligrams of Zoloft and my symptoms have returned. In fact, I feel worse than when I went on the medication. I can't sleep. I can't concentrate."

"I thought you weren't going to reduce the dose."

"I had no idea Zoloft is so expensive."

"What do you mean?"

"The prescription you gave me cost over one hundred fifty dollars for a month!"

"How could you not have known? You've been on it for three years."

"My HMO gave it to me. I only made a ten-dollar copayment a month."

I suddenly remembered Anne had been working before she returned to school. Like most people with medical insurance through an employer, Anne's health care included medication coverage. By contrast, many student health plans, like Harvard's, do not cover medication.

"I can't afford this," said Anne. "I'm living on a student budget. Frankly, I couldn't have afforded it on my old job. But look at me. I desperately need it."

"When did you lower the dose?"

"Two days ago."

"Have you had any dizziness?"

"Not when I'm sitting still like this, but if I got up and moved around I would."

"What if you just turn your head?"

Anne turned slowly from left to right. "Yes," she said, surprised. "It feels like I have water sloshing around in my head. What does that mean?"

"This isn't a return of your symptoms. It's withdrawal from the Zoloft."

"It is?" said Anne incredulous.

"The dizziness is the giveaway. And the fact that the symptoms appeared so quickly. Some people, after lowering their doses of these types of drugs, are unable to walk and have to take to bed because they are so unsteady. Others have electric shock–like sensations in their brains or visual hallucinations of flashing lights."

Anne winced at the prospect. Nevertheless, she decided to "tough it out," hoping she had already made it through the worst of the withdrawal.

Fortunately, Anne's withdrawal symptoms cleared within days. She felt completely back to normal, confirming that what she experienced was withdrawal and not a return of her original symptoms, which, in fact, had been far milder.

Now motivated not only by the cost but also by her distaste for a drug causing clear-cut withdrawal symptoms, Anne proceeded to taper off the Zoloft. Each time she reduced the dose, she again had a few days of mild withdrawal symptoms.

Although Anne did not develop tics on Zoloft, others of my patients have developed tics and twitches on Prozac-type antidepressants that persisted for months after the drug was stopped. The tics may be facial, like fly-catcher tongue darting or chewing-the-cud jawing, or involve the whole body, like involuntary pelvic thrusting. The tics are *the* dread side effect in psychiatry. With earlier classes of drugs that cause these kinds of tics, they are disfiguring, untreatable, and permanent in up to 50% of cases.

These side effects raise concerns that patients may sustain silent brain damage that we have no way of assessing. Such damage could be compounded in the future by other medications, viruses, and toxins, which injure the involuntary motor system, and by the normal aging process, which causes a progressive loss of brain cells. It could predispose patients later in life to prematurely develop senile tics, gait disturbances, and other neurological conditions that normally affect only the elderly.

After stopping Zoloft, Anne continued to check in with me periodically and did fine without medication. What if she hadn't come to Harvard and gotten a second opinion about being on the drug? Anne was unnecessarily exposed to the potential risks of Zoloft. In my experience, as many as 75% of patients are needlessly on these drugs for mild, even trivial, conditions.

The dangerous side effects . . . have been the subject of intense research and discussion within psychiatry in recent years. Still, many doctors outside of academic medical centers are not adequately informed about them. Most patients are still unaware of the dangers.

In the December 1997 issue of the *Journal of Clinical Psychopharmacology,* Dr. Ronald Pies wrote an alert on the long-term risks of these serotonergic drugs. Pies is on the faculty of both Harvard and Tufts Medical Schools. Commenting on the neurological side effects, including tic disorders, Pies wrote that "we simply do not know how many cases are being overlooked. Neither do we know how many cases will develop in patients taking these agents for 5, 10, 15, or more years." Because of the risks, Pies argued that Prozac-type drugs should not "be prescribed for the 'worried well' or for patients with mild depression, who respond favorably to psychotherapy alone."

For patients whose symptoms are more severe, the risk-benefit ratio of taking the drugs can be quite different. In these circumstances, I still recommend medication to patients. The risks of severe psychiatric syndromes can be worse than the risks of short-term use of the medication. Many patients with moderate to severe symptoms feel desperate for something to jump-start them back to normal life. By combining drugs with psychotherapy and other alternatives, one can usually minimize exposure to the drugs, keeping the dosage low and weaning off medication within six months to a year.

The 10-20-30-Year Pattern

Unfortunately, the dangerous side effects emerging with Prozac, Zoloft, Paxil, and other serotonin boosters are right on schedule, appearing like clockwork in a 10-20-30-year pattern characteristic of popular psychiatric drugs. The first potent antidepressants of the modern era were cocaine elixirs, introduced in the late 1800s. At the turn of the century cocaine elixirs were the most popular prescription medications, prescribed for everything from depression to shyness, just as the Prozac group are today. Freud wrote three famous "cocaine papers" advocating the drug's use. Since cocaine elixirs, we have had numerous amphetamines, bromides, barbiturates, narcotics, and tranquilizers, all hailed as miracle cures until their dangerous side effects emerged.

Reviewing the history of these drugs, one finds a strikingly similar pattern: Initially, the drugs are aggressively marketed with claims that they are revolutionary breakthroughs, remarkable scientific advances over their predecessors. Early on, a few doctors champion their cause, becoming celebrities along with the drugs. Often, a handful of celebrities step forward to endorse the miracle cure. As they gain momentum, use of the drugs spreads beyond the confines of psychiatry and they are prescribed by general practitioners for everyday maladies. Indeed, the burgeoning list of "conditions" they are used to treat, including everyday life, is often one of the first clues that one is looking at a general mood brightener that provides a quick fix.

In the typical life span of the drugs, the earliest signs of problems appear about ten years after introduction. Pharmaceutical companies and drug proponents deny the problems, adopting the strategy of defending the medication to the last. As we lack serious long-term monitoring of drug side effects and rely almost entirely on spontaneous, voluntary reporting by doctors, it is typically only at the twenty-year mark that enough data has accrued for the problems to be undeniable and for a significant number of physicians to be sounding the alarm. Still another ten years or more elapse before professional organizations and regulatory agencies actively take steps to curtail overprescribing. Thus, the cycle from miracle to disaster typically takes thirty years or more. By then, even the most popular drugs are no longer covered by their patent and even their manufacturers have an incentive to abandon medications that have become passé and disreputable. Typically their energies are then focused on the next breakthrough: newly patented, more profitable agents, which can be promoted as "safer" because their hazards are not yet known.

The Prozac Group

Prozac and the other serotonin boosters—Zoloft, Paxil, and Luvox—have been the panaceas of the past decade. The pharmaceutical giant Eli Lilly marketed Prozac in the late 1980s as a dramatic new type of mood-altering drug, a designer medical bullet targeting serotonin. Lilly's sophisticated marketing made the new drug an instant success: In less than two years, Prozac was outselling all other antidepressants. In March 1990, the green-and-white Prozac capsule appeared on the cover of *Newsweek* under the banner "The Promise of Prozac." The glowing cover story described Prozac as a medical "breakthrough" already being prescribed for so many conditions in addition to depression that "even healthy people have started asking for it." *New York* magazine called the novel pill a "wonder drug." The *National Enquirer* described it as a miracle diet pill.

In 1993, psychiatrist Peter Kramer's enormously influential book *Listening to Prozac* made sensational claims that these new serotonergic agents not only treated serious depression but also cured a host of everyday maladies like timidity, shyness, sensitivity, lack of confidence, perfectionism, fastidiousness, fear of rejection, low self-esteem, competitiveness, jealousy, and fear of intimacy.

Couched in a barrage of almost senseless data, which unfortunately looked like impregnable science to the lay reader, Kramer's endorsement of the drugs was so sweeping he even described them as making people feel "better than well." His most astonishing claim was that the Prozac group could "transform" people by fundamentally altering their personalities. Coining the phrase "cosmetic psychopharmacology," Kramer proclaimed, "Some people might prefer pharmacologic to psychologic self-actualization. Psychic steroids for mental gymnastics, medicinal attacks on the humors, antiwallflower compound. . . . Since you only live once, why not do it as a blonde? Why not as a peppy blond?"

The general media had a feeding frenzy over Kramer's notion that these drugs could change personality, treating it as a historic breakthrough. The cover of *Newsweek* announced, "Beyond Prozac: How Science Will Let You Change Your Personality with a Pill." Inside, the feature article was a minds-made-to-order scientific thriller asserting we would soon have many personalities-in-a-bottle to choose from. This was not the "one pill makes you larger, one pill makes you smaller" ode of the sixties counterculture but, seemingly, the voice of the scientific establishment.

As with earlier panaceas, celebrities came forward to endorse them. Television personality Mike Wallace testified, "I will take Zoloft every day for the rest of my life. And I'm quite content to do it." "Serotonin boosters are extraordinary" was the impression given to the general public.

Indeed, the publicity made serotonin a household word. Droves of patients came into doctors' offices demanding one of the new pills. Coincidentally, it was at this time that managed care insurers began to exert increasing influence over doctors in their treatment plans for patients. In the area of mental health, this took the form of pressuring primary-care doctors to prescribe drugs rather than refer patients to specialists who might be able to treat them with more effective, safer alternatives. In the early 1990s, serotonin boosters became managed care's answer to the "problem" of more costly alternatives, with little thought given to the consequences for patients. This is why patients like Anne are prescribed one of the Prozac-type drugs for mild, often trivial conditions.

Soon primary-care doctors were writing 70% of prescriptions for Prozac, Zoloft, Paxil, and Luvox. To the already long list of conditions treated with the drugs were added anxiety, obsessions, compulsions, eating disorders, headaches, back pain, impulsivity, drug and alcohol abuse, hair pulling, nail biting, upset stomach, irritability, sexual addictions, premature ejaculation, attention deficit disorder, and premenstrual syndrome. Diet centers began prescribing the Prozac group for weight loss. Employee assistance programs began using them to prop up exhausted factory workers putting in grueling overtime shifts as a result of corporate downsizing. Serotonin boosters are all-purpose psychoanalgesics, not just "antidepressants," which was merely the first application for which they were approved.

Early on, a few reasoned voices tried to introduce some skepticism and caution about the new drugs. *The New Yorker* described *Listening to Prozac* as "a love letter to the drug" and for months ran a series of satirical cartoons. Among these was an illustration of three books with the titles *Listening to Tylenol, Listening to Tums,* and *Listening to Tic-Tacs.* Its caption read, "Life's daily aches and pains need no longer be endured. Don't miss out." Another cartoon depicted Karl Marx, Dostoevsky, and Edgar Allan Poe gleefully on Prozac. Proclaimed Marx, "Sure! Capitalism can work out its kinks!" Said Poe to a raven, "Hello, birdie!" Still another piece was entitled "Listening to Bourbon."

The *New York Times Book Review* called Kramer's speculations "in the realm of science fiction." The cover of *The New Republic* depicted a sporty, all-American couple smiling and waving under the headline "That Prozac Moment!" Below was a surgeon general–style warning: "This drug may offer pseudo solutions to real problems." In the accompanying article, entitled "Shiny Happy People," David Rothman, a professor of social medicine and history at Columbia University, wrote a scathing critique of cosmetic psychopharmacology.

One of the most articulate critics of the hype surrounding serotonin boosters was Sherwin Nuland, a professor of surgery and historian of medicine at the Yale University School of Medicine, and the author of the acclaimed *How We Die.* Writing in *The New York Review of Books,* Nuland decried the public's being "subjected to the arguments of seemingly authoritative physicians and scientists who propose views that don't stand up to the scrutiny of trained professional eyes." He called the pop psychopharmacology swirling around the serotonin boosters "preposterous," "unsubstantiated," and a "psychopharmacological fantasy." Noting that "it remains anything but certain that clinical depression is, in fact, caused by a decrease in serotonin," he denounced the junk science of serotonin deficiencies and biochemical imbalances as "uncertain gropings for proof of a fanciful theory."

Unfortunately, the din in the general media drowned out the few reasoned voices. As Prozac rocketed up the charts, it became the number-two best-selling drug in America. Zoloft and Paxil rank almost as high. More than 60 million prescriptions for the drugs were written in 1998. Annual sales of the three exceed $4 billion a year. Tens of millions of people, perhaps as many as 10% of the American population, have been exposed to serotonin boosters. Half a million children are prescribed the drugs, with pediatric use one of the fastest-growing "markets." This in spite of the fact that repeated studies have shown antidepressant drugs are no more effective in children than placebos.

A particularly important element in the success of these medications has been the perception that they are safe and have virtually no side effects. Prescribed for everything from headaches to premenstrual syndrome, they may seem as safe as aspirin. Minimizing the drugs' risks, in *Listening to Prozac,* Peter Kramer declared, "There is no unhappy ending to this story. . . . the patient recovers and pays no price for the recovery." Given the history of earlier miracle cures, one wonders at the wisdom of conveying this impression to the public.

Prozac Backlash

To understand the side effects of these drugs, one needs to know a few basic facts of brain chemistry. Brain chemicals are called neurotransmitters. Of the more than a hundred neurotransmitters now known, three are important for our purposes: serotonin, adrenaline, and dopamine, popularly referred to as the brain's "feel good" neurotransmitters. Whereas earlier mood brighteners like cocaine and amphetamines boost all three of these neurotransmitters, the Prozac group were hailed as a breakthrough because they are "selective" for serotonin. This selectivity gives the impression that serotonin is localized in a depression center in the brain. If a depressed person's serotonin is low, the impression given is that the drugs top it up in a safe, targeted manner.

This impression does not match reality, however. Serotonin is one of the oldest neurotransmitters in the evolution of life forms. In humans only about 5% of serotonin is found in the brain. The other 95% is distributed throughout the rest of the body. The majority is in the gastrointestinal tract, where serotonin modulates the rhythmic movements kneading food through the stomach. In the cardiovascular system, serotonin helps regulate blood vessels to control the flow of blood. Serotonin is also found in blood cells and plays an important role in clotting. In the reproductive system, serotonin's influence on the genitals accounts for its sexual effects. Serotonin plays a significant role in controlling a host of hormones that regulate a panoply of physiologic processes.

In the human brain, serotonin is one of the chemicals by which brain cells signal, or communicate with, one another. Serotonin nerves originate in the deepest, oldest part of the brain, called the brain stem. But while serotonin nerves originate here, they radiate diffusely, penetrating virtually every part of the brain. Efrain Azmitia, a professor of biology and psychiatry at New York University and one of the world's leading authorities on serotonin, says, "The brain serotonin system is the single largest brain system known and can be characterized as a 'giant' neuronal system."

During gestation, this giant system orchestrates some of the development of the brain, regulating the maturation of the brain's architecture. No wonder this vast network then has global modulatory effects throughout the nervous system. Says Azmitia, "Serotonin has been implicated in sleep, aggression, sexual activity, appetite, learning, and memory to name but a few behaviors altered by serotonin drugs or damage to the 5-HT [serotonin nerve] fibers. . . . The broad range of functions complements the extensive anatomy of the serotonin neurons [brain cells]."

So while pharmaceutical companies have marketed Prozac, Zoloft, Paxil, and Luvox as "selective" for serotonin, serotonin is anything but selective in its widespread effects. There is, in fact, no known depression center in the brain. Rather, the drugs have global effects owing to serotonin's vast influence. . . .

In the most cutting-edge research, the current and formerly popular antidepressants—including cocaine, amphetamines, and the Prozac group—appear to boost neurotransmitters beyond levels achieved under ordinary circumstances. Barry Jacobs, a professor of neuroscience at Princeton University, wrote in the December 1991 issue of the *Journal of Clinical Psychiatry* that most "external manipulation" of the system by drugs creates serotonin levels "beyond the physiological range achieved under [normal] environmental/biological conditions." Boosting serotonin to this degree "might more appropriately be considered *pathologic,* rather than reflective of the normal biological role of 5-HT [serotonin] [italics added]."

Similarly, psychiatrist Steven Hyman, director of the National Institute of Mental Health, wrote in 1996, "Chronic administration of psychotropic drugs [i.e., drugs with psychological effects] creates perturbations [imbalances] in neurotransmitter function that likely exceed the strength and time course of almost any natural stimulus." This "hyperstimulation" triggers "compensatory" reactions in the brain in its efforts to achieve "a new adapted state which may be qualitatively as well as quantitatively different from the normal state."

Most recently, neuroscientists have learned not only that the effects of a single neurotransmitter like serotonin are extremely widespread but that different neurotransmitters do not function independently of one another. Critical systems like serotonin, adrenaline, and dopamine are linked through complex circuitry. Dramatic changes in one, like boosting serotonin, can trigger compensatory changes in the others.

Chief among the brain's reactions to artificially elevated serotonin levels is a compensatory drop in dopamine. Drugs producing a dopamine drop are well known to cause the dangerous side effects that are now appearing with Prozac and other drugs in its class. We simply did not know that serotonin boosters had these powerful secondary effects on other neurotransmitters when they were introduced. At the time they were an utterly new class of medications whose long-term dangers were unknown. Doctors and scientists are just beginning to understand the connections between the serotonin and dopamine systems in the brain that are thought to be responsible for the drugs' severe effects. But with earlier classes of drugs, the brain damage that can result is slowly progressive and often silent, and only manifests itself once it is severe. A critical variable determining the degree of damage appears to be total cumulative exposure to the drugs.

Thus, even the highly touted "selectivity" of the Prozac group is an illusion. In fact, the extreme emphasis these drugs place on serotonin may be a liability, because changes in serotonin levels can trigger secondary, or indirect, changes in dopamine. I call the compensatory reactions of the brain to these serotonergic drugs "Prozac backlash." . . . Experts believe this backlash is responsible for the severe side effects emerging with the drugs.

The Lack of Systematic Monitoring of Long-Term Side Effects

In light of the emergence of such serious side effects, one might ask why the public has not been made more aware. The answer lies in the lack of an adequate public health policy for monitoring long-term side effects of prescription drugs. The FDA does have an approval process for new drugs coming to market, but this approval is only assurance of *short-term* safety. Pharmaceutical companies are required to perform clinical studies of new psychiatric drugs in patients, but the tests typically last for only six to eight weeks, whereas the most serious, long-term side effects of drugs take years, sometimes decades, to emerge. Under these circumstances, prescribing an entirely new class of agents to millions of people is nothing short of an ongoing human experiment.

"Man is becoming the primary guinea pig," says Ross Baldessarini, a professor of psychiatry and neuroscience at Harvard Medical School and one of the country's leading psychopharmacologists. Psychopharmacology is the relatively new subspecialty of psychiatrists who only prescribe drugs and do not practice psychotherapy. Baldessarini made the sober comment at a Harvard conference on psychiatric drugs in the fall of 1998. "You really don't know what to expect," he said, when drugs are designed on the computer to target specific brain cells and receive only limited testing in laboratory animals before being prescribed to people.

But the even greater shortcoming in our public health monitoring system is what happens after new drugs have been introduced. A meager 4% of the FDA's budget is allocated to monitoring side effects after drugs are approved and being prescribed to millions of people. . . . Because long-term monitoring is virtually nonexistent, in a 1993 article in the *Journal of the American Medical Association,* the then commissioner of the FDA, David Kessler, revealed that "only about 1% of serious events [side effects] are reported to the FDA." The FDA itself is not responsible for this state of affairs, says Thomas Moore, a leading authority on drug side effects at the George Washington University Medical Center. The FDA's budget is set by Congress. In his 1998 book *Prescription for Disaster,* Moore details the intense pressure Congress is under from lobbyists for the pharmaceutical industry to weaken rather than strengthen drug testing and monitoring.

In the absence of thorough follow-up, long-term drug effects only slowly come to light through random, spontaneous reports in obscure medical journals, which even most doctors do not read. This loose, word-of-mouth system takes years, often decades, to gain momentum around even common, dangerous effects. In *Prescription for Disaster,* Moore says that "initial drug testing is essential but incomplete." Our "flawed monitoring system" gives people an "illusion of safety" when, in fact, serious drug problems "tend to be slow, insidious, and difficult to see."

A final reason why it can take so long for dangerous effects to come to public attention is that as problems do emerge, pharmaceutical companies and drug proponents typically adopt the strategy of defending the drug to the last. This has been the repeated pattern in the 150 years since potent synthetic drugs targeting the brain were first invented. And we are already seeing this happen in the case of serotonin boosters.

While systematic studies have shown that 60% of patients on serotonin boosters suffer often severe sexual side effects, Eli Lilly's official figure is just 2–5%. The manufacturers of Zoloft, Paxil, and Luvox also provide misleadingly low figures in their official information on the medications.

When people try to withdraw from serotonin boosters—especially Zoloft, Paxil, and Luvox—they may experience debilitating withdrawal syndromes. Mistaking withdrawal for a return of their original symptoms, many patients restart the medication, needlessly prolonging their exposure to the drug. Pharmaceutical companies are so concerned about withdrawal syndromes that Eli Lilly recently funded a panel of drug advocates, prominent academic psychiatrists, who wrote a series of professional papers suggesting the euphemism "antidepressant discontinuation syndrome" as an alternative to "withdrawal," avoiding the latter's negative connotations.

In the case of suicidality and violence, Eli Lilly has adamantly denied this side effect. But new information has come to light that the pharmaceutical giant has paid millions of dollars to victims and survivors of Prozac-related suicides and murders. . . .

In spite of . . . efforts at spin control, in the most recent edition of the *Diagnostic and Statistical Manual (DSM IV),* the American Psychiatric Association added a specific diagnostic category recognizing the neurological side effects being seen with Prozac-type medications, including the untreatable tics that first alerted me to the downside of these drugs.

Having talked with hundreds of patients in my private practice and at the Harvard University Health Services, I know the biggest concern of people on these drugs is the possibility of long-term consequences. Many patients ask, "Will I eventually get some kind of brain damage after years of being on Paxil?" "Will my liver be injured after metabolizing so much Zoloft?" "Will the memory problems I'm having go away when I stop Prozac?"

Numerous authors who have written of their experience with serotonin boosters echo these concerns. Writing in the *Boston Phoenix* in April 1998 about her dependence on prescription antidepressants, in an article entitled "Hooked," Deborah Abramson worries that "research five or ten years down the road might reveal that one of the drugs I take greatly increases the likelihood of some kind of cancer."

In her best-selling memoir *Prozac Nation*, Elizabeth Wurtzel writes, "I can't help feeling that anything that works so effectively, that's so transformative, has got to be hurting me at another end, maybe sometime down the road. . . . I don't know if there are any statistics on this, but how long is a person who is on psychotropic drugs supposed to live? How long before your brain, not to mention the rest of you, will begin to mush and deteriorate?" Expressing her concerns to her psychiatrist, Wurtzel says, "Come on, level with me, anything that works this well has got to have some unknown downside. . . . He says a bunch of reassuring things, explains over and over again how carefully he is monitoring me—all the while admitting that psychopharmacology is more art than science, that he and his colleagues are all basically shooting in the dark. And he acts as if a million doctors didn't say the same things to women about DES, about the IUD, about silicon breast implants, as if they didn't once claim that Valium was a nonaddictive tranquilizer and that Halcion was a miracle sleeping pill." . . .

As the more dangerous side effects of the Prozac group come into view, perhaps we will be able to see not only the dark side of these latest miracle cures but also the liability of any potent, synthetic drug targeting the brain. Future generations may well look back on the last 150 years of these drugs as a frightening human experiment. If this happens, either they will be banned altogether because they do more harm than good or their use will be strictly limited to only the most severe cases.

CHALLENGE QUESTIONS

Are Prozac and Similar Antidepressants Safe and Effective?

1. To what extent should clinicians first turn to nonmedication interventions in treating people with depression before recommending drugs such as Prozac?
2. What steps can be taken to ensure that pharmaceutical companies are providing the entire story about possible short-term and long-term side effects of medications?
3. To what extent should nonclinical behaviors, such as shyness or a tendency to worry, be treated with medications rather than behavioral interventions?
4. In what ways might the widespread use of Prozac and similar medications change broader social units, such as the family or even society?
5. What are your views on the recent increase in the prescription of Prozac and similar medications to very young children?

Suggested Readings

Breggin, P. (2001). *The anti-depressant fact book: What your doctor won't tell you about Prozac, Zoloft, Paxil, Celexa, and Luvox.* Cambridge, MA: Perseus Books.

Fieve, R. (1996). *Prozac: Questions and answers for patients, family and physicians.* New York: Avon.

Kramer, P. (1997). *Listening to Prozac.* New York: Penguin Books.

Morrisson, A. (1999). *The antidepressant sourcebook: A user's guide for patients and families.* New York: Main Street Books.

Sachs, J., & Smith, L. (1998). *Nature's Prozac: Natural therapies and techniques to rid yourself of anxiety, depression, panic attacks and stress.* Upper Saddle River, NJ: Prentice Hall.

ISSUE 10

Are Antipsychotic Medications the Treatment of Choice for People with Psychosis?

YES: E. Fuller Torrey, from *Surviving Schizophrenia: A Manual for Families, Consumers, and Providers, 4th edition* (Quill, 2001)

NO: Robert Whitaker, from *Mad in America: Bad Science, Bad Medicine, and the Enduring Mistreatment of the Mentally Ill* (Perseus, 2002)

ISSUE SUMMARY

YES: Psychiatrist E. Fuller Torrey, an outspoken advocate for the needs of the mentally ill and their families, contends that antipsychotic medications play a centrally important role in alleviating psychotic symptoms and reducing the likelihood of rehospitalization.

NO: Journalist and social critic Robert Whitaker asserts that antipsychotic medications make people chronically ill, cause serious side effects, and increase the likelihood of rehospitalization; furthermore, reliance on these medical treatments for the mentally ill neglect important questions such as what it means to be human.

When antipsychotic medications were introduced in the 1950s and were popularized in the 1960s, at first, scientists and clinicians alike imagined that these medications would "cure" schizophrenia, or at the very least, help severely disturbed patients regain control. Little attention was given to the downside of powerful psychopharmacological interventions. As the years went by, however, disturbing evidence emerged regarding debilitating side effects such as tardive dyskinesia, a condition in which the individual experiences uncontrollable bodily movements. Pharmacological research continued in earnest as scientists looked for medications with minimal side effects that would treat not only the positive symptoms of psychosis (e.g., hallucinations), but also the negative symptoms (e.g., apathy and affective flattening). In recent years, many people have experienced tremendous improvement in their lives as a result of antipsychotic medications; at the same time, concerns have been raised about their widespread use.

Psychiatrist E. Fuller Torrey has established an international reputation as a professional devoted to educating the public about the nature of schizophrenia and appropriate ways for responding to and treating people. Torrey firmly believes that antipsychotic medications provide a safe method for treating debilitating psychotic symptoms by bringing about therapeutic changes in the brain; furthermore, they reduce the likelihood of rehospitalization.

Author and social critic Robert Whitaker expresses vehement alarm about the proliferation of antipsychotic medications. He contends that these agents make people chronically ill, cause worrisome side effects, and increase the likelihood of rehospitalization. He also criticizes such medical treatments as unfortunate reflections of warped societal and philosophical values.

POINT

- Research shows that taking antipsychotic drugs reduces the likelihood that people with schizophrenia will be rehospitalized.

- Antipsychotic drugs, as a group, are one of the safest groups of drugs in common use and are the greatest advance in the treatment of schizophrenia that has occurred to date.

- Studies show that the incidence of neuroleptic-related tardive dyskinesia has been overestimated, and in fact is a condition that affects less that 20% of those taking these drugs.

- Antipsychotic medication changes the brain in an effective way. Such changes include increased density of glial cells in the frontal cortex, an increase in synapses, and changes in the properties of synapses.

- The data on the effectiveness of drugs are so clear that any physician or psychiatrist who fails to try them on a person with schizophrenia is probably incompetent. It is not that drugs are the only ingredient, but they are the most essential.

COUNTERPOINT

- In the research study that launched the emptying of state hospitals in the 1960s, patients who took neuroleptics were more apt to be rehospitalized than those given a placebo.

- Research over the years has demonstrated that antipsychotic drugs make people chronically ill, a fact that psychiatry has cast aside.

- Antipsychotic drugs cause an increase in dopamine receptors, which is a change associated both with tardive dyskinesia and an increased biological vulnerability to psychosis; long-term outcomes are much better in countries where such medications are less frequently used.

- Antipsychotic drugs do not fix any brain abnormalities, nor do they put brain chemistry back into balance.

- History provides a lesson in understanding what is essential in treating people with psychosis: The Quakers viewed psychotic individuals as suffering "brethren" who needed comfort, and who had a God-given capacity for recovery. Humanitarian and optimistic caregivers could "assist Nature" in helping them heal.

E. Fuller Torrey  **YES**

The Treatment of Schizophrenia: Medications

Once a competent doctor has been located and the intricacies of hospitalization have been mastered, then the treatment of schizophrenia becomes comparatively simple. Drugs are the most important treatment for schizophrenia, just as they are the most important treatment for many physical diseases of the human body. Drugs do not *cure,* but rather *control,* the symptoms of schizophrenia—as they do those of diabetes. The drugs we now have to treat schizophrenia are far from perfect, but they work for most of the people with the disease if they are used correctly.

The main drugs used to treat schizophrenia are usually called antipsychotics. They have also been called neuroleptics and major tranquilizers, but the best term is "antipsychotic" because that is what they are. They frequently do not produce tranquilization, so that term is a misnomer. The antipsychotic drugs were discovered in 1952 by French psychiatrist Pierre Deniker. He had heard about a new tranquilizer that his anesthesiology colleagues were using to sedate patients during surgery and decided to try it on psychiatric patients; the drug was chlorpromazine (Thorazine, Largactil).

Antipsychotics can be divided into two classes: first-generation and second-generation. Those are commonly referred to, respectively, as "typical" and "atypical," based on the previously widespread belief that the effectiveness of "typicals" was related to their ability to block dopamine receptors, whereas the effectiveness of the "atypicals" was related to their action on other neurotransmitter receptors. Associated with the dopamine blockade are certain side effects found commonly in first-generation antipsychotics but rarely in second-generation antipsychotics. These side effects are usually abbreviated EPS (extrapyramidal signs) and consist of Parkinsonian-like symptoms, acute dystonic reactions, and akathisia. Researchers are now less certain that dopamine blockade is the primary reason why the first-generation antipsychotics are effective, and in fact there is considerable overlap in receptor activity of "typical" and "atypical" antipsychotics. It is therefore more accurate simply to classify antipsychotics into first-generation (beginning with the introduction of chlorpromazine

From SURVIVING SCHIZOPHRENIA: A MANUAL FOR FAMILIES, CONSUMERS, AND PROVIDERS 4th Edition, by E. Fuller Torrey, Copyright © 2002 by E. Fuller Torrey. Used by permission of HarperCollins.

in 1952) and second-generation (beginning with the introduction of cloz-apine in the United States in 1990). Such a division is admittedly America-centric, since clozapine was used in some European countries in the 1970s and 1980s. . . .

Do They Work?

The efficacy of antipsychotic drugs is well established. Studies show that approximately 70 percent of patients with schizophrenia clearly improve on these drugs, 25 percent improve minimally or not at all, and 5 percent get worse. This is approximately the same level of effectiveness that penicillin exerts in pneumonia or streptomycin in tuberculosis. Antipsychotic drugs reduce symptoms of the disease, shorten the stay in the hospital, and reduce the chances of rehospitalization dramatically. Whereas persons with schizophrenia entering a psychiatric hospital used to stay for several weeks or months, the average stay with these drugs is now reduced to days. And the data on their preventing rehospitalization are even more impressive. John Davis, for example, reviewed 24 scientifically controlled studies test-ing whether antipsychotic drugs were effective. All 24 studies found that persons with schizophrenia who took antipsychotic drugs were less likely to have to return to the hospital than those who did not take these drugs. The differences between the two groups were highly significant, especially for persons with chronic schizophrenia. On the average, a person who takes the drugs has a 3-out-of-5 chance (60 percent) of not being rehospitalized by the end of one year, whereas the person who does not take the drugs has only a 1-out-of-5 chance (20 percent) of not being rehospitalized.

When studies have been done on the long-acting, injectable form of antipsychotics (where compliance in taking the drug is assured), the results are even more impressive. In one study of chronic patients, only 8 percent of the patients who were taking the drug relapsed within one year, but 68 percent of those not taking the drug relapsed. In another study of patients taking long-acting, injectable antipsychotics, 80 percent relapsed within two years when the drug was stopped. What all this means is that though taking the drugs does not guarantee you will *not* get sick again, and not tak-ing the drugs does not guarantee you *will* get sick again, their use improves the odds toward staying out of the hospital tremendously. The data on the effectiveness of drugs are so clear that any physician or psychiatrist who fails to try them on a person with schizophrenia is probably incompetent. It is not that drugs are the *only* ingredient necessary to treat schizophrenia successfully; they are just the most essential ingredient.

Antipsychotic drugs are not equally effective for all the symptoms of schizophrenia. They are most effective at reducing delusions, hallucina-tions, aggressive or bizarre behavior, thinking disorders, and the symptoms having to do with the overacuteness of the senses—the so-called "positive" symptoms. For example, against auditory hallucinations, one of the most common and disabling symptoms of schizophrenia, antipsychotic drugs are 80 to 90 percent effective in being able to relieve the hallucinations, usually making them disappear altogether. The drugs have less efficacy against symptoms such as apathy, ambivalence, poverty of thought, and flattening of the emotions—the "negative" symptoms.

Do They Change the Brain?

Some opponents of the use of antipsychotics have alleged that because these medications change the brain, that means they are dangerous and should not be used. Antipsychotic medications do, of course, change the brain—that is why they are effective. Medications used to treat epilepsy, Parkinson's disease, and other brain diseases also change the brain. And medications used to treat diseases in other organs, such as the heart and joints, may bring about structural changes to those organs as well.

The brain changes produced by antipsychotic drugs are relatively minor. The main changes that have been claimed to date are an increase in density of glial cells in the frontal cortex, an increase in synapses (connections between neurons), and changes in the properties of the synapses. There is no evidence that antipsychotic drugs cause the loss of neurons. Much research is ongoing in this area, since understanding the nature of these changes may help us understand how these drugs work, why they cause side effects, and who will respond to which drug. . . .

Does Early Treatment Help?

Some studies have suggested that early treatment may lead to a better clinical outcome in schizophrenia and, conversely, that delayed treatment may lead to a worse outcome. Dr. Richard Wyatt of the National Institute of Mental Health reanalyzed 22 studies on the course of schizophrenia and concluded that "early intervention with neuroleptics in first-break schizophrenic patients increases the likelihood of an improved long-term course." An analysis of the [Jeffrey] Lieberman et al. study of individuals undergoing their first episode of schizophrenia similarly concluded that "greater duration of illness [prior to beginning treatment] was found to predict increased time to remission" in younger but not in older patients. An Irish study of untreated patients with schizophrenia also found that "untreated psychosis in schizophrenia appears to have a progressive and, ultimately, a profoundly debilitating effect on long-term outcome." The implication of these studies is that the failure by mental illness professionals to treat individuals with schizophrenia with antipsychotic medications as early in the course of their illness as possible may produce a worse outcome. Other recent studies have not found this to be true, and this is an area of ongoing research. Until it is clarified, it should be assumed that treatment should begin as early in the course of the disease as possible.

Adverse Effects

"The antipsychotic agents," says Dr. Ross J. Baldessarini, "are among the safest drugs available in medicine." As one of the foremost experts on these drugs, Dr. Baldessarini should know, yet his claim is at variance with popular stereotypes of the drugs. It is widely believed that the first-generation antipsychotic drugs have terrible adverse effects, are dangerous, and almost invariably produce tardive dyskinesia (involuntary muscle movements) and other irreversible conditions that may be worse than the original schizophrenia.

Dr. Baldessarini is in fact correct, and the popular stereotype is wrong. Antipsychotic drugs, compared with drugs used to treat other diseases, are relatively safe. It is almost impossible to commit suicide with them by overdosing, and their serious adverse effects are comparatively rare.

Then why is there such a strong misperception and fear of these drugs? Much of the reason can be traced to theories of causation of the disease. As we have noted, it is only in recent years that the evidence for schizophrenia's being a real biological disease has become clear. The resistance to this idea among mental illness professionals trained in the psychogenic belief systems has been impressive. And one of the ways this resistance is shown is by strongly opposing the use of drugs; implicitly, if the drugs are too dangerous to be used, then patients will again have to rely on psychotherapy and other nondrug modes of treatment. For this reason, occasional mental illness professionals—who should be better informed—still warn patients with schizophrenia about all kinds of terrible calamities that will befall them if they take antipsychotic drugs. Additional opposition to antipsychotic drug use comes from the Church of Scientology, whose founder, L. Ron Hubbard, was virulently anti-psychiatry. . . .

This is *not* to say that antipsychotic drugs are perfectly safe and have no adverse effects whatsoever. They do have adverse effects, sometimes so severe that the drug must be stopped. The adverse effects have on occasion even been fatal, but this is very rare. One of the main goals of the current search for second-generation antipsychotic drugs is to find effective compounds that will continue to suppress psychotic symptoms while producing minimal undesirable adverse effects. But it is important to repeat that the point to be remembered is that antipsychotic drugs, as a group, are one of the safest groups of drugs in common use and are the greatest advance in the treatment of schizophrenia that has occurred to date.

The adverse effects of first-generation antipsychotic drugs can be discussed as a group. Some adverse effects are more common with particular drugs, but the differences are not great. And, like adverse effects to all drugs used in medicine, it is not possible to predict with any accuracy which person is likely to get which adverse effect. . . .

Tardive Dyskinesia

Tardive dyskinesia is the single most important adverse effect of first-generation antipsychotic drugs. Much of the fear of using these drugs is in fact linked to this adverse effect, and it has become a banner regularly waved by anti-psychiatry zealots. Tardive dyskinesia is certainly a serious problem, but it is not nearly as common as the apostles of hysteria have claimed.

Tardive dyskinesia consists of involuntary movements of the tongue and mouth, such as chewing movements, sucking movements, pushing the cheek out with the tongue, and smacking of the lips. Occasionally these are accompanied by jerky, purposeless movements of the arms or legs or, rarely, even the whole body. It usually begins while the patient is taking the drug but, rarely, may begin shortly after the drug has been stopped. Occasionally it persists indefinitely, and no effective treatment has been found to date.

The incidence of tardive dyskinesia is difficult to ascertain because it may occur as part of the disease process as well as being a side effect of medication. A study of the records of over 600 patients admitted to an asylum in England between 1845 and 1890 found an "extraordinary prevalence of abnormal movements and postures. . . . Movement disorder, often equivalent to tardive dyskinesia, was noted in nearly one-third of schizophrenics." A recent study of spontaneous dyskinesia in individuals with schizophrenia who had never been treated with antipsychotic medication reported it to be present in 12 percent of individuals below age 30 and in 25 percent of individuals aged 30 to 50. Most estimates of the incidence of tardive dyskinesia have assumed that all such cases are drug-related when in fact a substantial percentage are not. In a study of this problem aptly titled "Not All That Moves Is Tardive Dyskinesia," Khot and Wyatt concluded that the true incidence of drug-related tardive dyskinesia was less than 20 percent. This also falls within the 10 to 20 percent range estimated by the American Psychiatric Association's 1980 task force on the subject.

Much current research is taking place in an attempt to identify which persons with schizophrenia are most likely to get tardive dyskinesia. It is clear that the older the person, the more susceptible he or she is. It is also clearly established that women are more susceptible than men and that patients with more affective symptoms (for example, depression or mania) are more susceptible. Many other risk factors are being investigated including ethnicity (higher in Jews, lower in Asians), dose of medication, duration of medication, use of depot injectable medication, use of anticholinergic drugs, concurrent diabetes, concurrent alcohol or drug abuse, concurrent evidence of organic brain disease, and concurrent Parkinsonian-like symptoms, but none of them has yet been clearly established. There is also no firm evidence that any particular first-generation antipsychotic is more or less likely to cause tardive dyskinesia.

Previously, most people believed that once the symptoms of tardive dyskinesia began they would almost always get worse if the person continued taking the antipsychotic medication. This put many individuals with schizophrenia into a cruel bind, needing the medication to remain well but not wishing to worsen the early symptoms of tardive dyskinesia. A 10-year follow-up of 44 patients with tardive dyskinesia who remained on the same antipsychotic medication found that in 30 percent the tardive dyskinesia got worse, in 50 percent it remained the same, and in 20 percent the tardive dyskinesia actually improved. In another 10-year follow-up study it was reported that approximately 5 percent of existing cases of tardive dyskinesia disappeared each year *even in individuals continuing to take their anipsychotic medications.*

According to Dr. Daniel Casey, a leading researcher on tardive dyskinesia, 20 patients out of every 100 with schizophrenia will get tardive dyskinesia;

among these, five patients will have their tardive dyskinesia completely disappear and five others will have at least a 50 percent improvement. Casey then added: "Of the 10 remaining TD [tardive dyskinesia] patients, almost all of them will have mild to moderate symptoms. Severe TD is a very uncommon syndrome that probably occurs in approximately 1 in 100 to 1 in 1,000 TD patients."

The best treatment for tardive dyskinesia is to switch the person to a second-generation antipsychotic, especially clozapine. All patients taking first-generation antipsychotics should be watched for early signs such as tongue movements. The use of the Abnormal Involuntary Movement Scale (AIMS) is useful for measuring the progression of tardive dyskinesia. For fully developed cases of tardive dyskinesia there is no known effective treatment, although trials of levodopa, vitamin E, oxypertine, sodium valproate, and tiapride have shown some promise. . . .

The Medication-Savvy Consumer and Family

Smart consumers and their families quickly learn what Edward Francell teaches—that medication is "the foundation of recovery." Francell, a social worker who has been diagnosed at various times as having schizophrenia and manic-depressive illness, says that his improvement really began when he shifted from "passive recipiency" of whatever psychiatrists told him to do to active, informed involvement. "Recovery began," said Francell, "when I got off the bench and became an active player in the treatment game," shifting from spectator to player. . . .

Robert Whitaker

Mad in America

My interest in this subject, the history of medical treatments for the mad, began in a simple manner. In the summer of 1998, I stumbled onto an unusual line of psychiatric research, which I reported on for the *Boston Globe*. In order to study the "biology" of schizophrenia, American scientists were giving the mentally ill chemical agents—amphetamines, ketamine, and methylphenidate—expected to heighten their psychosis. That seemed an unusual thing to do, particularly since some of the people recruited into the experiments had come stumbling into emergency rooms seeking help. Equally striking was the response of "ex-patients" to the experiments.

They were outraged, but not particularly *surprised*.

That seemed more than a little curious—why would they not be surprised?—and then I bumped into several studies in the medical literature that really struck me as odd. Over the past twenty-five years, outcomes for people in the United States with schizophrenia have *worsened*. They are now no better than they were in the first decades of the twentieth century, when the therapy of the day was to wrap the insane in wet sheets. Even more perplexing, schizophrenia outcomes in the United States and other developed countries today are much worse than in the poor countries of the world. The World Health Organization [WHO] has looked at this question repeatedly—initially, nobody could believe this disparity in outcomes—and each time it has come back with the same result. Suffer a psychotic break in a poor country like India or Nigeria, and chances are that in a couple of years you will be doing fairly well. But suffer a similar break in the United States or other developed countries, and it is likely that you will become chronically ill. Why should that be so? Why should living in a country with rich resources, and with advanced medical treatments for disorders of every kind, be so toxic to those who are severely mentally ill? Or to put it another way, why should living in countries where the poor struggle every day to find enough to eat and treatment for a mental disorder is likely to be provided by a shaman, whose armamentarium may consist of witch-doctor potions, be so helpful to recovery?

This medical failure is a profound one. More than 2 million Americans suffer from schizophrenia, and their difficult lives bring unimaginable

From MAD IN AMERICA, pp. 287–291. Copyright © 2001 by Robert Whitaker. Reprinted by permission.

heartache to their families, and to others who love them. Too many of the people so diagnosed end up in prison, homeless, or shuttling in and out of psychiatric hospitals. Our society as a whole is affected by this failure as well, and in a way that we don't normally appreciate. We usually think of the financial burden: Schizophrenia, it is said, is a "disease" that costs the United States more than $45 billion annually. But there is a much deeper cost. We, as a society, are *estranged* from the "mad" in our midst. We fear them and their illness. We read of occasional acts of violence committed by those said to be schizophrenic, and we respond by setting up programs that focus on keeping them medicated. But is that the best response? If the medications work so well, then why do "schizophrenics" fare so poorly in the United States?

The search to understand this therapeutic failure necessarily takes one deep into history. The past becomes a foil for understanding the present. It is a journey that begins with the founding of the first hospital in the colonies by Pennsylvania Quakers in 1751, and from there one can trace a path, however winding and twisted, to the poor outcomes of today. It is also a history that contains one surprise after another. For instance, we think of the 1800s as a time when the insane were routinely chained up and neglected, and yet, in the early nineteenth century, there arose a form of humanitarian care that has never been equaled since. Go forward one hundred years, however, and the path detours into one of the darkest chapters in America's history, one that, I believe, we have never dared to fully explore. Yet it is in that dark chapter that one finds the seeds for today's failure.

What one also quickly discovers is that a history of mad medicine reveals very little about what it is like to be "crazy" or "insane," or, as we say today, "ill with schizophrenia." However, it does reveal a great deal about the society that would "cure" these patients. Medical treatments for the severely mentally ill inevitably reflect the societal and philosophical values of the day. What is the nature of man? What does it mean to be human? Where is the line between "normals" and the "mad" to be drawn? What rights do the "mentally ill" have over their own minds? The medical treatments a society employs all arise from its answers to those questions. As such, mad medicine does provide a prism through which to view a society, and that is why the poor outcomes for those diagnosed with schizophrenia raise questions, I would think, for all of us. . . .

This book began with a straightforward goal, and that was to explore why schizophrenia outcomes are so poor in the United States today. It seemed like a simple question, and yet it quickly opened the door to a larger story—the story of how we as a society have historically treated those we call "mad." It clearly is a troubled history, one that begs to be better known. There are, perhaps, many lessons that can be drawn from it, but one seems to stand out above all others. Any hope of reforming our care of those "ill with schizophrenia" will require us to rediscover, in our science, a capacity for humility and candor.

There is one moment in the past where we can find such humility. It can be seen in moral therapy as practiced in its most ideal form, by the

Quakers in York, England, or by Thomas Kirkbride at the Pennsylvania Hospital for the Insane in the mid-nineteenth century. In their writings, the York Quakers regularly confessed that they understood little about any possible physical causes of madness. But what they did see clearly was "brethren" who were suffering and needed comfort. That was the understanding that drove their care, and so they sought to run their asylum in a way that was best for their patients, rather than in a way that was best for them, as managers of the asylum. They put their patients' comforts and needs *first*. They also perceived of their patients as having a God-given capacity for recovery, and thus simply tried to "assist Nature" in helping them heal. It was care that was at once humanitarian and optimistic, and it did help many get well. But equally important, the York Quakers were quite willing to accept that many of their brethren would continue in their crazy ways. That was all right, too. They would provide a refuge for those who could not regain their mental health and at least make sure they had warm shelter and good food.

In the 1960s, as the United States set out to reform its care, it did look back to moral treatment for inspiration. President John Kennedy and the Joint Commission on Mental Illness and Mental Health spoke of the need for American society to see those who were distraught in mind as part of the human family, and deserving of empathy. Eugenics had stirred America to treat the severely mentally ill with scorn and neglect, and it was time to change our ways. We would welcome the mentally ill back into society. Asylums would be replaced with community care. But the design of that reform also rested on a medical notion of the most unusual sort, that neuroleptics "might be described as moral treatment in pill form." The confusion in that perception was profound: Neuroleptics were a medical treatment with roots in frontal lobotomy and the brain-damaging therapeutics of the eugenics era. Our vision for reform and the medical treatment that would be the cornerstone of that reform were hopelessly at odds.

Something had to give, and the moment of choice occurred very early on. The research study that launched the emptying of the state hospitals was the six-week trial conducted by the National Institute of Mental Health in the early 1960s, which concluded that neuroleptics were safe and antischizophrenic. But then, a very short while later, the NIMH found in a follow-up study that the patients who had been treated with neuroleptics were more likely than the placebo patients to have been rehospitalized. Something clearly was amiss. A choice, in essence, was presented to psychiatry. Would it hold to the original vision of reform, which called for the provision of care that would promote *recovery*? If so, it would clearly need to rethink the merits of neuroleptics. The drugs were apparently making people chronically ill, and that was quite apart from whatever other drawbacks they might have. Or would it cast aside questions of recovery and instead defend the drugs?

There can be no doubt today about which choice American psychiatry made. Evidence of the harm caused by the drugs was simply allowed to pile up and up, then pushed away in the corner where it wouldn't be seen. There was Bockoven's study that relapse rates were lower in the pre-neuroleptic era. Rappaport's study. Mosher's. Reports of neuroleptic malignant syndrome and tardive dyskinesia. Van Putten's report of medicated patients in boarding homes spending their days idly looking at television, too numbed in mind and spirit to even have a favorite program. Studies detailing the high incidence of akathisia, Parkinson's, and a myriad of other types of motor dysfunction. Case reports of akathisia driving patients so out of their minds it made them suicidal or even homicidal. Harding's study and then the WHO studies. All of this research told of suffering, and of loss. And where were the studies showing that the drugs were leading people to *recovery*? Researchers studiously avoided this question. In 1998, British investigators reviewed the published results of 2,000 clinical trials of neuroleptics over the previous fifty years and found that only one in twenty-five studies even bothered to assess "daily living activities" or "social functioning." The trials again and again simply looked at whether the drugs knocked down visible symptoms of psychosis and ignored what was really happening to the patients as *people*.

It is not difficult today to put together a wish list for reform. An obvious place to start would be to revisit the work of Emil Kraepelin. Were many of his psychotic patients actually suffering from encephalitis lethargica, and has that led to an overly pessimistic view of schizophrenia? The next step would be to investigate what the poor countries are doing right. How are the "mad" treated in India and Nigeria? What are the secrets of care—beyond not keeping patients regularly medicated—that help so many people in those countries get well? Closer to home, any number of studies would be welcome. A study that compares neuroleptics to sedatives would be helpful. How would conventional treatment stack up against care that provided "delusional" people with a safe place to live, food, and the use of sedatives to help restore their sleep-wake cycles? Or how about an NIMH-funded experiment modeled on the work of Finnish investigators? There, physicians led by Yrjö Alanen at the University of Turku have developed a treatment program that combines social support, family therapy, vocational therapy, and the selective use of antipsychotics. They are picking apart differences in patient types and have found that some patients do better with low doses of antipsychotics, and others with no drugs at all. They are reporting great results—a majority of patients so treated are remaining well for years, and holding jobs—so why not try it here?

At the top of this wish list, though, would be a simple plea for honesty. Stop telling those diagnosed with schizophrenia that they suffer from too much dopamine or serotonin activity and that the drugs put these brain chemicals back into "balance." That whole spiel is a form of medical fraud, and it is impossible to imagine any other group of patients—ill, say, with cancer or cardiovascular disease—being deceived in this way.

In truth, the prevailing view in American psychiatry today is that there are any number of factors—biological and environmental—that can lead to schizophrenia. A person's genetic makeup obviously may play a role. Relatives of people with schizophrenia appear to be at increased risk of developing the disorder, and thus the thought is that they may inherit genes that make them less able to cope with environmental stresses. The genetic factors are said to *predispose* people to schizophrenia, rather than cause it. Another prominent theory is that complications during pregnancy or during delivery may affect the developing brain, and that this trauma leads to deficiencies in brain function once neuronal systems have natured. Yet another thought is that some people with schizophrenia have difficulty filtering incoming sensory data, and that this problem is due to abnormal function in brain cells known as interneurons. A number of investigators are still studying the role that different neurotransmitters may play in the disorder. The biological paths to schizophrenia may be many, but none is yet known for sure. It is also possible that the capacity to go mad, as it were, is in all of us. Extreme emotional trauma can clearly trigger psychosis, and some argue that psychosis is a mechanism for coping with that trauma. That view of the disorder is consistent with the fact that in the absence of neuroleptics, many people who suffer a schizophrenic break recover from it, and never relapse again.

Thus, if we wanted to be candid today in our talk about schizophrenia, we would admit to this: Little is known about what causes schizophrenia. Antipsychotic drugs do not fix any known brain abnormality, nor do they put brain chemistry back into balance. What they do is alter brain function in a manner that diminishes certain characteristic symptoms. We also know that they cause an increase in dopamine receptors, which is a change associated both with tardive dyskinesia and an increased biological vulnerability to psychosis, and that long-term outcomes are much better in countries where such medications are less frequently used. Although such candor might be humbling to our sense of medical prowess, it might also lead us to rethink what we, as a society, should do to help those who struggle with "madness."

But, none of this, I'm afraid, is going to happen. Olanzapine is now Eli Lilly's top-selling drug, surpassing even Prozac. There will be no rethinking of the merits of a form of care that is bringing profits to so many. Indeed, it is hard to be optimistic that the future will bring any break with the past. There is no evidence of any budding humility in American psychiatry that might stir the introspection that would be a necessary first step toward reform. At least in the public arena, all we usually hear about are advancements in knowledge and treatment, as if the march of progress is certain. Eli Lilly and Janssen have even teamed up with leaders of U.S. mental-health advocacy groups to mount "educational" missions to poor countries in East Asia, so that we can export our model of care to them. Hubris is everywhere, and in mad medicine, that has always been a prescription for disaster. In fact, if the past is any guide to the future, today we can be certain of only one thing: The day will come when people will look back at our current medicines for schizophrenia and the stories we tell to patients about their abnormal brain chemistry, and they will shake their heads in utter disbelief.

CHALLENGE QUESTIONS

Are Antipsychotic Medications the Treatment of Choice for People with Psychosis?

1. Psychiatrist E. Fuller Torrey has spent much of his career educating the public, patients, and their families about schizophrenia and its treatments. If you had the opportunity to interview Dr. Torrey, what would be the most challenging question that you would ask him about the treatment of people with schizophrenia?
2. Much has been written in recent years about the rights of patients to refuse medication. What issues should be considered in determining whether psychotic individuals should be forced to take antipsychotic medication against their expressed will?
3. Imagine that you are a clinician who is treating an individual with delusions, hallucinations, and disordered thought. What information would you want to gather in order to make a diagnosis? Assuming that you conclude that the individual has schizophrenia, what issues would you consider in making a recommendation regarding antipsychotic medication?
4. Imagine that you are a researcher who has just received a grant to compare the relative effectiveness of antipsychotic medication and herbal remedies for the treatment of psychotic symptoms. What kind of research design would you recommend?
5. Imagine that you have just been awarded a multi-million dollar grant to develop the most humane intervention for treating people with schizophrenia. Discuss the components that you would include in the treatment program.

Suggested Readings

Amador, Xavier, and Anna-Lisa, Johanson. (2000). *I Am Not Sick: I Don't Need Help!* Peconic, New York: Vida Press.

Boyle, Mary. (2002). *Schizophrenia: A Scientific Delusion?* New York: Routledge.

Nasar, Sylvia. (1999). *A Beautiful Mind: A Biography of John Forbes Nash, Jr., Winner of the Nobel Prize in Economics, 1994.* New York: Simon & Schuster.

Szasz, Thomas. (2002). *Liberation By Oppression: A Comparative Study of Slavery and Psychiatry.* New Brunswick, NJ: Transaction Publishers.

Weiden, Peter J., Patricia L. Scheifler, Ronald J. Diamond, and Ruth, Ross. (1999). *Breakthroughs in Antipsychotic Medications: A Guide for Consumers, Families, and Clinicians.* New York: W.W. Norton & Company.

ISSUE 11

Is Ritalin Overprescribed?

YES: Peter R. Breggin, from *The Ritalin Fact Book: What Your Doctor Won't Tell You about ADHD and Stimulant Drugs* (Perseus, 2002)

NO: Russell A. Barkley, from *Taking Charge of ADHD: The Complete, Authoritative Guide for Parents* (Guilford, 2000)

ISSUE SUMMARY

YES: Physician Peter R. Breggin asserts that Ritalin and similar stimulants are dangerous addictive medications that should not be prescribed to children because they suppress growth and lead to a number of worrisome physical and psychological symptoms.

NO: Psychologist and prominent ADHD researcher Russell A. Barkley objects to criticisms of Ritalin and similar stimulants, maintaining that these medications serve as important parts of interventions aimed at helping children increase their attention and concentration.

Fifteen years ago it would have been unfathomable to imagine a school-aged child entering a school and gunning down classmates; yet such images have become indelibly marked in the minds of Americans. Such alarming events have caused educators, parents, and mental health professionals to increasingly focus their attention on the behavior of young people, look for ways to help underachievers reach their potential, and make sure troubled youth get the help they need. Children with attention deficit hyperactivity disorder (ADHD) have been of particular concern because of the psychological problems they experience and also because of the disruption they cause at school, at home, and in the community.

ADHD is a disorder involving inattentiveness and hyperactivity-impulsivity, and it is a condition that is usually evident early in life. Even during the toddler years, children with this condition show a range of problematic behaviors, including defiance, resistance, and hostility. Many of them are incessant in their hyperactivity, incapable of paying attention even briefly. Their lives usually involve impaired relationships and serious inner distress.

The most common interventions for ADHD involve behavioral techniques and medication, particularly stimulants such as Ritalin (methylphenidate). Proponents of medication express relief about the fact that such an effective intervention is available to help young people who need it; opponents are distressed by the increasing tendency to rely on a chemical for controlling active children rather than on methods that have been used for generations.

Peter Breggin, who is widely known and respected for his critical analysis of trends in psychiatry, is appalled by the extensive use of Ritalin-like medications. Breggin raises serious concerns about the physical dangers and psychological risks associated with these medications, and argues that the literature supporting their effectiveness is limited and biased.

Russell Barkley, who has established an international reputation as a researcher and expert on ADHD, views behavior disorders such as ADHD as serious conditions of brain dysfunction that warrant medical intervention; he asserts that stimulant medication helps ADHD children improve their attention and concentration, and therefore succeed academically.

POINT

- Like amphetamines, stimulants have a high potential for abuse and can cause potentially serious withdrawal symptoms.

- The growth of many children is suppressed or even stunted by stimulants.

- Drug-company propaganda has led the public to believe that psychiatric drugs correct biochemical imbalances; in fact, these drugs disrupt normal brain function.

- There is no evidence that stimulant drugs actually improve academic performance. Drug-induced impairments cannot make children wiser; they can only make children sit down, shut up, and do what they are told.

- There are hundreds of cases documenting Ritalin-induced psychiatric reactions including agitation, hostility, depression, psychosis and other troubling conditions.

COUNTERPOINT

- There are no reported cases of addiction or serious drug dependence on these medications; nor does research support the notion that children taking these drugs are at greater risk of abusing other substances during their teenage years.

- It is a myth to suggest that stimulant medications stunt children's growth; recent studies have shown that this is not as much of a problem as once thought.

- ADHD is largely a genetic disorder associated with deficiencies in brain functioning; stimulant medication helps normalize functioning in most cases.

- Stimulant medication's ability to improve children's attention span, resistance to distraction, and concentration is beneficial to their academic performance.

- Although stimulant medications can produce temporary symptoms of psychosis at very high doses, such reactions are very rare at low doses; such reactions occur in fewer than 1% of cases and last only until the dose wears off.

Peter R. Breggin  **YES**

The Ritalin Fact Book: What Your Doctor Won't Tell You about ADHD and Stimulant Drugs

Of Cages and Creativity—How Stimulants Work

If you are considering the use of stimulant drugs for yourself or your children, you probably want answers to the following questions:

Do stimulants really help children?
How do they work?
Are they dangerous?

In response to these questions, too many doctors tell parents and patients that stimulants work well and have few if any serious risks. They may also explain that the drugs work by "correcting biochemical imbalances" or "improving focus and attention." . . .

Observing Children in the Classroom

The effectiveness of stimulant drugs is often "proven" by asking teachers to rate the behavior of children in a classroom setting. The teachers will be given checklists to fill out for the children containing items that are used in the official diagnostic manual to determine if a child has ADHD. This *Diagnostic and Statistical Manual of Mental Disorders, IV* is published by the American Psychiatric Association (1994). It contains items such as "often fidgets with hands or feet or squirms in seat," "often leaves seat in classroom," "often blurts out answers," "has difficulty awaiting turn," and "often does not seem to listen."

Teachers and parents almost always report a reduction of these kinds of behaviors in children given stimulants. The teachers and parents have not been told that this involves a suppression of spontaneous behavior with enforced submissiveness and so they fail to recognize that the drugs are suppressing or dulling the children.

From *Insight on the News*, August 14, 1995. Copyright © 1995 by Peter R. Breggin M.D. Reprinted by permission of the author.

Teachers are especially likely to find that the children are "improved" because they are asked to rate behaviors such as "blurts out answers" or "leaves seat" that are especially reduced when overall spontaneity is crushed. The reduction in spontaneous behavior, as well as the enforced submissiveness, makes the children less talkative, less likely to leave their seats, and less likely to socialize with their neighbors. These reductions in overall spontaneous behavior make it easier for teachers to run their classrooms without having to pay attention to the individual child.

Exactly as in the animal studies, stimulants also make children more compulsive. For the chimpanzees, this means sitting by themselves while they groom one small spot on the arm or play endlessly with a pebble. For our children, this drug-enforced compulsivity makes them focus on previously unendurable boring tasks such as copying from the board or writing something down ten times. These children often become so compulsive that they bear down too hard on the paper as they write or persist at the task even when asked to stop. Studies describe them as abnormally overfocused. However, teachers and parents are likely to mistake such behavior for a genuine "buckling down" on schoolwork and homework.

Table 1 is entitled "Harmful Stimulant Drug Reactions Commonly Misidentified as 'Therapeutic' or 'Beneficial.'" When children are given Ritalin, Adderall, and other stimulant drugs, they frequently develop these kinds of reactions. Unfortunately, researchers, doctors, teachers, and parents routinely misinterpret these toxic effects as improvements in the children.

Do the children learn better? Are their scholastic abilities improved? Of course not. Drug-induced impairments cannot make a child wiser, more thoughtful, or better informed. They can only make children sit down, shut up, and do what they are told. As we shall see, there is no evidence that

Table 1

Harmful Stimulant Drug Reactions Commonly Misidentified as "Therapeutic" or "Beneficial," Selected from 20 Controlled Clinical Trials Involving Children Diagnosed with ADHD

Obsessive Compulsive Effects	Social Withdrawal Effects	Behaviorally Suppressive Effects
Compulsive persistence at meaningless activities (called stereotypical or perseverative behavior)	Social withdrawal and isolation	Compliant in structured environment; socially inhibited, passive, and submissive
Increased obsessive-compulsive behavior (e.g., repeating chores endlessly and ineffectively)	General dampened social behavior	Somber, subdued, apathetic, lethargic, dopey, dazed, and tired
Mental rigidity (called cognitive perseveration)	Reduced communication and socialization	Bland, emotionally flat, humorless, not smiling, depressed, and sad with frequent crying
Inflexible thinking	Decreased responsiveness to parents and other children	Lacking in initiative, spontaneity, curiosity, surprise, or pleasure
Overly narrow or excessive focusing	Increased solitary play and diminished overall play	

Modified from Breggin (1999b, 1999c). References to the 20 clinical trials provided in Breggin (1999b, 1999c).

stimulant drugs actually improve academic performance. But they do sometimes lead to improved grades because many teachers will reward more submissive, unobtrusive behavior with better grades.

Some of the staunchest advocates of stimulants for children have in effect admitted that the drugs work by enforcing blind obedience. Russell Barkley, one of the most widely published Ritalin/ADHD advocates, uses the term "compliance" to describe this improved behavior. Stimulant drugs do indeed tend to make children more compliant, that is, more manageable and obedient. They do so at the expense of their imaginations, their creativity, their capacity to generate activity, and their overall enthusiasm for life.

"Correcting Biochemical Imbalances"

Recently I gave a lecture to students and professionals at a medical center. Initially, some of them were surprised when I explained that all psychoactive drugs disrupt normal brain function. They, too, had been misled by drug-company propaganda to believe that psychiatric drugs correct biochemical imbalances. However, several were immediately able to see the truth once I reminded them about the facts.

Research on psychoactive drugs almost always begins with animal studies. As a first step, a series of animal brains will be examined to measure the normal activity of a specific function, such as the rate of firing of a particular type of brain cell (neuron). Tiny electrodes may be inserted into the brains to measure the activity of the cells. Or the animal brain may be removed in order to determine the normal amount of a specific chemical in the region.

Next, a new series of animals will be given the stimulant drug, such as Ritalin or Adderall. Then their brains will be examined to determine how the drug changes these normal functions. For example, the brain cells may begin to fire more rapidly than normal for a while and then, later on, more slowly than normal. Or the specific chemical messenger may increase above normal in amount for a while and then decrease below normal later on.

The pharmacological action of any psychoactive drug is demonstrated by how it disrupts the normal function of an animal's brain. That disruption is the basis of the psychoactive effect. The researchers, the drug company, the FDA, and everyone else involved in the field will then assume that the drug disrupts human brain function in exactly the same fashion. When textbooks or reviews discuss the drug's "mode of action," they will simply describe what has been learned from research on how the drug interferes with the functioning of the normal animal brain.

However, when the drug company and its experts get ready to present this information to the medical profession and the public, they will perform remarkable verbal sleights of hand. The known fact that the drug disrupts normal brain function will be ignored and instead the drug will be falsely promoted as correcting biochemical imbalances. The claim about correcting biochemical imbalances is a deliberate deception to make the drugs look positive. Similarly, the known fact that the drug suppresses behavior will be ignored, and in the case of the stimulants, nothing at all will be said about it. How the drug actually works will remain shrouded in mystery. . . .

How Stimulants Cause Psychiatric Disorders

Stimulants are powerful psychoactive substances that impact the brain and mind. We have already seen that their primary or therapeutic impact involves flattening all spontaneous behavior, enforcing submissiveness, and causing obsessive focus on rote activities. Therefore, it should be no surprise that they can cause a variety of other mental abnormalities.

In reviewing adverse drug reaction reports made to the FDA concerning Ritalin, I found hundreds of cases of Ritalin-induced psychiatric reactions. Children taking Ritalin were most commonly reported to develop—in the following order—agitation, hostility, depression and psychotic depression, abnormal thinking, hallucinations, psychosis, and emotional instability (called "lability"). There were many reports of overdose, intentional overdose, and suicide attempts, confirming the risk of depression and potential suicide. . . .

I have taken several approaches to summarizing the overall adverse effects of stimulants. Table 1 . . . uses data from twenty clinical trials to describe adverse psychiatric effects such as apathy, depression, and overfocusing that are commonly mistaken for improvements in children's behavior.

Table 2, "Toxic Reactions to Stimulants: Usually in Overdose and Occasionally at Low Doses," is drawn entirely from the "Overdose" sections of

Table 2

Toxic Reactions to Stimulants: Usually in Overdose and Occasionally at Low Doses

Agitation	Elevated heart rate
Tremors	Palpitations
Increased neurologic reflexes	Cardiac arrhythmias
Muscle twitching	Hypertension
Convulsions	Enlarged pupils
Coma	Dry mouth, nose, and eyes
Euphoria	Increased respiration[a]
Confusion	Nausea, vomiting, diarrhea, and cramps[a]
Hallucinations	
Delirium	Muscle breakdown[a]
Sweating	Hypotension, shock, and circulatory collapse[a]
Flushing	
Headache	Panic states[a]
High fever	Assaultiveness[a]

[a]Indicates the item was taken from the FDA-approved overdose section of the labels for Dexedrine, Adderall, and Adderall XR, but not Ritalin. The remainder was taken from the Ritalin label with some overlap. The Dexedrine and Adderall labels both state that "individual patient response to amphetamines varies widely" and "toxic symptoms occasionally occur as an idiosyncrasy at doses as low as 2 mg." The Adderall XR label also states that patient responses "vary widely" and "toxic symptoms" may occur "at low doses." *Most of the symptoms can occur with any of the stimulants at routine clinical doses.*

the official FDA-approved labels for Ritalin, Dexedrine, Adderall, and Adderall XR. Almost any adverse reaction that occurs in overdose can also occur at lower doses.

For an overview of stimulant effects taken from a broader variety of medical sources other than the drug labels, see Table 3, "Overview of Harmful Reactions to Stimulant Drugs: Ritalin, Dexedrine, Adderall, Concerta, and Metadate."

Tables 1, 2, and 3 cover most of the adverse effects of stimulants that are likely to show up in routine clinical use. They are compiled from standard or mainstream sources that tend to approve or advocate the use of stimulant drugs. There is a great tendency in the medical literature to minimize adverse drug effects in order to support or promote the use of medications in general. Therefore, the individual sources are not as comprehensive as the data that I have compiled in this book from all of the sources. *In addition, few if any*

Table 3

Overview of Harmful Reactions to Stimulant Drugs: Ritalin, Dexedrine, Adderall, Concerta, and Metadate

Brain and Mind Function

Obsessive-compulsive behavior

Zombie-like (robotic) behavior with loss of emotional spontaneity

Drowsiness, "dopey," reduced alertness

Abnormal movements, tics, Tourette's

Nervous habits (picking at skin, pulling hair)

Convulsions

Headache

Stroke

Mania, psychosis

Visual and tactile hallucinations

Agitation, anxiety, nervousness

Insomnia

Irritability, hostility, aggression

Depression, suicide, easy crying, social withdrawal

Confusion, mental impairments (decreased cognition and learning)

Stimulant addiction and abuse

Gastrointestinal Function

Anorexia

Nausea, vomiting, bad taste

Stomachache

Cramps

Dry mouth

Constipation, diarrhea

Liver dysfunction

Withdrawal and Rebound Reactions

Insomnia

Excessive sleep

Evening crash

Depression

Rebound worsening of ADHD-like symptoms

Overactivity and irritability

Endocrine and Metabolic Function

Pituitary dysfunction, including growth hormone and prolactin disruption

Weight loss

Growth suppression

Disturbed sexual function

Cardiovascular Function

Hypertension

Abnormal heartbeat

Heart disease

Cardiac arrest

Other Functions

Blurred vision

Hair loss

Dizziness

Hypersensitivity reaction with rash

Modified from Breggin (1999a, 1999c).

sources fully address the brain damage and dysfunction produced by these drugs, including strong evidence for stimulant-induced brain shrinkage, cell death, and persistent biochemical changes. . . .

Stimulants Commonly Cause Mental Disorders

Stimulants commonly cause a variety of serious emotional disturbances. I am not alone in drawing this conclusion. A handbook frequently used by physicians lists the . . . rates of adverse mental effects caused by stimulants [in Table 4].

Table 4

Rates of Adverse Mental Effects Reported in Stimulant Clinical Trials

Adverse Stimulant Effect	Amphetamines (Dexedrine, Adderall)	Methylphenidate (Ritalin, Concerta, Metadate ER)
Drowsiness, less alert	5.5%	5.7%
Confused, "dopey"	10.3% (8–12%)	3.9% (2–10%)
Depression	39%	8.7%
Agitation, restlessness	More than 10%	6.7% (3.3% to more than 10%)
Irritability, stimulation	25% (17–29%)	17.3% (11–19%)

The data are from Maxmen and Ward (1995, p. 366). The numbers are percentages of patients reported in studies to suffer from the adverse effects. Numbers in parentheses represent the range reported in studies.

The rates in [Table 4] are drawn from clinical studies. Not many parents would expose their children to these drugs if they were aware of the frequency with which the drugs can impair a child's mental life.

The studies are usually conducted by advocates for drugs and tend to minimize adverse drug reactions. Therefore, most of the rates are actually higher than reported in [Table 4]. While the rates for these adverse effects vary widely from study to study, the main point is inescapable: Stimulants frequently harm the brain and mind.

As a part of my scientific presentation at the NIH Consensus Development Conference on the Diagnosis and Treatment of Attention Deficit Hyperactivity Disorder in 1998, I reviewed eight representative controlled clinical trials to estimate the frequency of adverse effects. All of the studies were conducted by advocates of stimulants and aimed at proving that the drugs are safe and effective. I have reviewed them in the scientific literature and in *Talking Back to Ritalin* (rev. ed., 2001a). Based on these studies, I estimate that the reported rate of serious adverse reactions in children was as high as 10–20 percent or more. The real rate in clinical practice would be even higher.

In reviewing Table 4, it is important to realize that symptoms such as "irritability," "agitation," and "confused" are related to each other. They reflect gross underlying brain dysfunctions that then become manifested in varying ways. When brain function is disrupted in such a global or generalized way, almost any mental abnormality or mixture of abnormalities can result. . . .

My clinical experience confirms the data in Table 4: Children taking stimulants frequently become very depressed and even suicidal. Their doctors often fail to recognize the source of the depression. Instead of stopping the stimulant medication, they add an antidepressant, causing even greater emotional disturbances in the child.

How common is stimulant-induced depression? Very common! . . .

How Stimulants Harm the Child's Body

. . . From the heart to the skin, stimulants can also harm a variety of other organs of the body. By interfering with normal growth-hormone production, stimulants impair and even stunt the growth of the entire body.

Some harmful effects on the body result indirectly from the disruption of brain function, some result more directly from toxic effects on the organs themselves, and some result from both. . . .

Stunting Growth

In many cases, the growth of children is obviously suppressed or even stunted by stimulants. Some of the children look skinny and unhealthy as if starving, while others seem normal. Most will rebound with an unbelievably rapid growth in height and weight—if the drugs are stopped while the child is still growing. In one study, Ritalin reduced the expected monthly weight gain by 25 percent. When the drug was stopped, weight gain accelerated far above the normally expected rate.

When children seem to be growing well while taking stimulants, some doctors or parents will observe, "John's very big; the stimulants haven't hurt him." Unfortunately, we don't know how tall or large Johnny might have become without the drug, and the fact that he's achieved an even above-average size says little about the drug's actual effect on his unique genetic endowment for growth.

Too many doctors are misled into believing that growth suppression is a relatively harmless problem that results from a child losing his or her appetite. However, there's more to it than the mere loss of appetite. The stimulants cause marked dysfunction in the production of growth hormone. Specifically, they cause an abnormal increase in growth hormone during the day and then an abnormal compensatory suppression of the hormone at night, when it most significantly affects growth.

The impact on growth hormone is so dramatic that researchers have observed that growth-hormone levels can be used as a marker for whether or not children are taking their medication. If the growth-hormone cycle isn't disrupted, then the children are not taking the medication. Because stimulants always impair growth-hormone production, we should assume that there is always some impairment of growth, even if it remains grossly undetectable.

Some doctors used to tell parents not to worry about growth suppression because there is a compensatory growth spurt when the drugs are stopped. While the body does try to catch up when the stimulant is stopped, the phase of accelerated growth is abnormally rapid and not necessarily altogether healthy. In addition, there's no guarantee that irreversible harm hasn't been done along the way during weeks or months of stimulant treatment. Furthermore, nowadays children are kept on stimulants for months or years at a time, so the body is given no opportunity to go through a growth spurt.

The disruption of growth hormone should be viewed as an ominous finding. It means that all growth processes are being impaired, including the growth of the brain, heart, and lungs. The entire body relies on growth hormone to regulate its developmental processes. Citing many research reports, a respected research team wrote:

> Research reveals that methylphenidate stimulates daytime release of growth hormone, disrupting the usual nocturnal release. This is troublesome since disturbances in the normal release of growth hormone may not only influence height velocity but may also impair other critical aspects of physical development such as sexual maturation.

The researchers should also have emphasized the threat to the growth of the brain and hence the mind.

The authors of a medical textbook suggest that the growth lag caused by stimulants is temporary "in most cases." This assumes that the children are given regular drug vacations in order to catch up. Although these authors are staunch advocates of stimulants for children, they go on to recognize that "the effects on growth that the long-term use of stimulants has on children leads some physicians to believe that this drug should never be prescribed for children." This observation—like many others in this book—should give strength to parents who believe, as I do, that children should never be given these drugs for "ADHD" or the control of behavior.

Despite decades of sophisticated research demonstrating that stimulants disrupt growth hormone, cause growth suppression, and lead to accelerated growth spurts when stopped, some drug advocates have tried to demonstrate that there are no significant effects on growth. In my experience, the doctors who make these claims typically go to extremes in order to convince professionals and parents that it's safe to use these drugs. One such study was published in 1996 in an attempt to undermine a large, consistent body of research demonstrating growth suppression. However, the new study used only one measurement of height and weight for each child and attempted to draw conclusions from it. The researchers did not use consecutive measures on the same child to show the effect of the drug; they took one measure on every child and attempted to compare that one measurement to a similar measure in a control group of children who were not drug treated. Using these dubious methods as well as a badly flawed control group and questionable statistics, the authors leaped from one single measurement to a conclusion about the long-term effect of stimulants on growth. By contrast, many other studies have used multiple measurements to show a definite inhibition of growth.

As a result of disrupting pituitary function, stimulants also interfere with the normal cycles of prolactin production. Prolactin can be found throughout the body, but its functions are poorly understood. It does, however, participate in the regulation of sexual development, yet another fact that should raise caution in regard to giving stimulants to children and adolescents.

Causing Heart Problems

As already noted, stimulants produce a combined assault on the heart, first by overstimulating heart rate and blood pressure, and then by weakening the muscles of the overstressed organ. Palpitations are one signal that the heart is beating irregularly.

What's the result?

My review of spontaneous reports of adverse Ritalin effects made to the FDA disclosed a very large number of Ritalin-induced cases of cardiovascular disease. Many concerned the well-known problem of stimulant-caused hypertension. Most of them involved arrhythmias and conduction problems that sometimes cause sudden cardiac arrest. There were more than a dozen reports of cardiac arrest or heart failure. This was a relatively small portion of the 2,821 reports made during the period of time (1985 through early 1997) but presents an important signal of danger.

I have been consulted in several cases in which stimulant drugs have caused fatal cardiac arrhythmias in children. In one case, the child's heart on autopsy showed a pattern of deterioration that the coroner compared to changes he had observed in chronic cocaine addicts.

A number of animal studies confirm that stimulants such as Ritalin weaken heart muscle and reduce its function. Stimulants also cause high blood pressure, a special concern among African-American boys, who are especially prone to develop severe hypertension as relatively young adults. Weakened heart muscle combined with hypertension is, of course, a hazard for any human being.

Causing Strokes

Ritalin, Adderall, and all stimulants can cause strokes (cerebral vascular accidents). These potentially catastrophic events can result from bleeding or inflammation of the blood vessels in the brain. Hypertension probably plays a key role in many of these disasters. Physicians sometimes seem particularly unaware of stimulant-induced strokes, probably leading to underreporting of the problem.

Bleeding in the brain in association with oral amphetamine use has been reported in the literature since 1970. There are reports of strokes after a "single low dose exposure," but most reports have been made in association with stimulant abuse.

A report in *Lancet* in 1988 described the first published case of stroke involving Ritalin in a boy receiving the drug for hyperactivity. The author observed, "Physicians who prescribe methylphenidate [Ritalin] for long-term use should be aware of this potential complication and specifically question patients regarding symptoms of cerebral ischaemia [reduced blood flow], including headache." Remember that Ritalin and amphetamine both produce gross reductions in blood flow to the brain, thereby creating the conditions for stroke.

A report in 2000 in the *Journal of Child Neurology* describes the case of an eight-year-old boy who developed vasculitis and stroke after taking Ritalin for one and one-half years for hyperactivity. These authors also issue a warning: "We draw your attention to the risk of using methylphenidate [Ritalin] for a long period of time."

Overall, stimulants pose serious cardiovascular hazards. Individuals suffering from or at risk of experiencing hypertension, heart disease, or strokes should especially avoid stimulants. . . .

How Stimulants Cause Withdrawal, Addiction, and Abuse

The following remarkable warning appears in capital letters in a boxed section as the first item to be read in the Adderall and the Dexedrine labels:

> AMPHETAMINES HAVE A HIGH POTENTIAL FOR ABUSE. ADMINISTRATION OF AMPHETAMINES FOR PROLONGED PERIODS OF TIME MAY LEAD TO DRUG DEPENDENCE AND MUST BE AVOIDED.

Although it does not appear with the same strength in the Ritalin label, this statement is equally true for Ritalin and all of the other stimulants commonly used to treat children. It should also be taken as a warning that all of these drugs cause potentially severe withdrawal reactions.

Much of the medical profession acts as if it has never been admonished that stimulant administration for prolonged periods of time "must be avoided." Instead, long-term use of stimulants is often encouraged, and parents are told to keep their children on amphetamines for months and years.

If the medical profession were prescribing rationally, the forewarning to avoid long-term administration, and the lack of evidence for any long-term efficacy, would utterly prevent the prescription of stimulants to children or adults for more than a few weeks' duration.

Withdrawal Reactions and Worsening Behavior

Symptoms of withdrawal can take place a few hours after the last dose of a stimulant, so that children commonly begin to go into withdrawal by the evening or the next morning. If a child's behavior appears to get worse or to deteriorate in any way a few hours or more after taking a stimulant drug, there's a high probability that the child is undergoing a withdrawal reaction.

Teachers often observe, "I can tell when Johnny hasn't taken his medication," meaning that they can see his behavior become more distressed or distressing. They don't realize that this is typically caused by a withdrawal reaction rather than by Johnny's own problems.

Parents and teachers sometimes believe that a child needs stimulants because the child's behavior deteriorates when one or two doses are missed. Such abrupt changes in a child are more likely due to withdrawal symptoms than to a child's inherent need for the drug. If we thought of alcohol or narcotics in the same way, we would think that alcoholics and narcotics addicts "needed" their drugs in order to be normal. In fact, they need to get free of their drugs in order to have a hope of becoming normal or healthy human beings.

The Ritalin label confirms, however inadequately, the danger of serious withdrawal problems. In a boxed section labeled "Drug Dependence," it states, "Careful supervision is required during drug withdrawal, since severe depression as well as the effects of chronic overactivity can be unmasked." The sentence is marred by spin doctoring that suggests that the symptoms are somehow being "unmasked" rather than directly caused by the Ritalin withdrawal. The label then states, "Long-term follow-up may be required because of the patient's basic personality disturbances." Again, this is spin doctoring of the fact that long-term exposure to these drugs, followed by withdrawal, can leave the patient with "basic personality disturbances" that the individual never had before taking stimulants. . . .

NO

**Russell A. Barkley with George
J. DuPaul and Daniel Connor**

The Stimulants

Medication is probably the most widely publicized, most hotly debated treatment for ADHD. As a whole, the hundreds of studies conducted indicate that stimulants, certain antidepressants, and clonidine (a drug used to treat high blood pressure in many adults) can be of great help to those with ADHD. The stimulants, the drugs most commonly used, have been shown to be effective in improving behavior, academic work, and social adjustment in anywhere from 50% to 95% of children with ADHD. How well your child responds may, however, depend on the presence of other problems, and the truth is that medication does not help everyone. For that reason—and because medication is no exception to the rule that misinformation about ADHD abounds—you should gather as much background knowledge as you can before agreeing to a trial of medication for your child. This article gives the most up-to-date information available on the stimulant medications. The brand names of these medications (with generic names in parentheses) include Ritalin (methylphenidate), Dexedrine (*d*-amphetamine), Adderall (*d*- and *l*-amphetamine combination), and Cylert (pemoline). . . .

Stimulant Drugs Are Dangerous and Should Not Be Taken by Any Child

During the 1980s and again in the mid- to late 1990s, an inaccurate and regrettably successful media propaganda campaign against the use of stimulants, particularly Ritalin (methylphenidate), with children was waged by a fringe religious group, causing a dramatic rise in media coverage of this medication. The 1990s campaign was fueled by the release of misleading, alarmist, and biased information about stimulant medication abuse in the United States by the Drug Enforcement Administration as part of an effort to prevent Ritalin from being reclassified as a nonaddictive drug—a change that would have made prescribing this medication more convenient for physicians. As a consequence, the use of these medications for children with ADHD continues to be controversial in the public's mind, although there is absolutely no controversy among the scientific community as to the safety and effectiveness of these medications.

From TAKING CHARGE OF ADHD: The Complete Authorative Guide for Parents, Guilford Press, 2000. Copyright © 2000 by GUILFORD Publications. Reprinted by permission.

Stimulants Just Cover Up the "Real Problem" and Do Not Deal Directly with the Root Causes of the Child's ADHD

Many parents come to us with the concern that stimulants do not treat the "real problems," but it is simply untrue. Critics of these medications mistakenly assume that a child's ADHD symptoms stem from purely social causes, such as poor discipline or lack of love at home. . . . [T]here is no scientific evidence that purely social causes are at the root of a child's ADHD. We now know that ADHD is largely a genetic disorder associated with deficiencies in the functioning of certain regions in the brain related to inhibition, attention, and self-control. The stimulants deal directly with the part of the brain that is underactive and gives rise to the outward symptoms of ADHD, as explained later in this [article]. In this sense, the stimulants are no different from using insulin for a child with diabetes. Unfortunately, like insulin, stimulants have only a temporary effect, which leads some people to believe they're masking the problem rather than helping it. Like a diabetic who needs insulin, your child may have to take stimulant medicine daily for a long time, but these drugs are a way of tackling the problem directly. *Stimulants are the only treatment to date that normalizes the inattentive, impulsive, and restless behavior in children with ADHD.* However, even though the stimulants do *improve* the behavior of 70–90% of all children with ADHD, the stimulants do not *normalize* the behavioral problems of all of these children who respond positively to medication. For approximately 30–45% of children with ADHD, their behavior will be significantly improved but not normalized by this medication.

Stimulants Make Children "High," as Other Drugs Do, and Are Addictive

You may have heard that adults who take stimulants often have a sense of elevated mood, euphoria, or excessive well-being. While this does happen, it is not common, and in children it is rare. Some children do describe feeling "funny," "different," or dizzy. Others actually become a little bland in their mood, and a few even report feelings of sadness. These mood changes occur a few hours after the medicine is taken and occur more often among children treated with higher doses. In most children, these changes are very minor.

Parents are often also quite concerned about the risk of addiction to stimulants and about an increased risk of abusing other drugs when the children become teenagers. There are no reported cases of addiction or serious drug dependence to date with these medications, and the several studies that have examined whether children on these drugs are more likely than those not taking them to abuse other substances as teenagers suggest that they are not. Indeed, several recent studies conducted by Dr. Timothy E. Wilens and colleagues at Massachusetts General Hospital

(Harvard Medical School), and by Drs. Howard Chilcoat and Naomi Breslau at Henry Ford Hospital in Detroit, found that taking stimulants during childhood did not predipose children with ADHD to an increased risk of substance use or abuse as teenagers. In fact, Dr. Wilens's study found that adolescents with ADHD who had remained on their medication during the teen years had a significantly lower likelihood of substance use or abuse than did children with ADHD who were not taking medications during adolescence. Thus the scientific literature to date should reassure parents that they are not predisposing their children to the potential for later substance use or abuse by giving stimulants to their children for the management of ADHD. Parents should know that the most important factors in determining a child's risk for adolescent substance use or abuse are (1) early onset of conduct disorder or antisocial behavior in the child, (2) poor monitoring by parents of the child's or teen's whereabouts in the community, (3) the affiliation of the child or teen with other teens who are using or abusing illegal substances, and (4) the degree to which the parents may also be using alcohol or tobacco products or illegal substances.

Stimulant Medications Stunt Children's Growth, and Their Use Is Strictly Limited by Age

Some studies in the early 1970s seemed to suggest that children taking these medicines might be stunted in their height and weight gain. More recent and better studies have shown that this is not as much of a problem as was once thought. Your child's eventual adult height or skeletal size is not going to be affected by taking the medicine, and the effects on your child's weight are also likely to be minimal, resulting in a loss of one or two pounds during the initial year of treatment. Any weight lost should return by the second or later years of treatment. Keep in mind that children respond very differently to these medicines, some experiencing no weight change and others losing more than just a few pounds. Your child should be followed by your physician to make sure that any weight loss is not serious.

The initial belief in the 1970s that stimulants might stunt the growth of children with ADHD led to the common practice by physicians of recommending that children take these medications only for school days and stop taking them on weekends, on school holidays, and during summer vacations. Because we now know that the risk of growth problems arising from these medications is much less than was originally believed, it is not necessary that all children taking stimulants have such drug holidays. Many can continue to take medication throughout the weekends and summers. They will derive benefits from doing so in their relations with peers; their participation in organized clubs, sports, and summer programs; and their general behavior at home. Parents whose children experience significant behavioral problems during these and other weekend and summer activities, and whose children are not having growth problems from the medication, should discuss with the children's physicians the possible value of continuing the children's stimulant medication during these periods. . . .

Stimulants Do Not Result in Lasting Benefits to a Child's Academic Achievement

The argument that stimulants have no lasting positive effects on academic achievement is a misleading one, concocted as part of broader efforts to dissuade parents from considering the use of stimulants for their children with ADHD. If one takes a simplistic view of the term academic achievement and expects stimulants to directly increase the amount of academic knowledge and skill in a school subject matter that a child acquires, then of course the stimulants will disappoint. The pills do not contain any knowledge that is automatically placed in a child's brain when consumed. A child with ADHD who does not know her multiplication tables today, while not taking any medication, will not automatically know them tomorrow after taking a dose of stimulant medication. To expect this kind of change would be silly and demonstrates the flaws in this criticism of stimulants.

What the stimulants do is help the child with ADHD show what she knows during performance of school assignments by improving the child's attention span, concentration, resistance to distraction, and thoughtful, reflective behavior. They also make the child more available to learn what is being taught in school by reducing the child's off-task, disruptive, and otherwise inattentive behavior. Given these gains, several years of medication may very well leave the child with more academic knowledge than she would have had without medication, but unfortunately no studies have examined this issue beyond 14 to 18 months of medication use. We simply don't know about the long-term benefits to academic knowledge or skills from continued use of medication over several years or more of schooling.

If we view the term *academic achievement* more broadly, as how well the child is behaving at school, getting along with peers, following classroom rules and teacher directions, completing assignments, and completing them accurately, the evidence is overwhelming that the stimulant medications produce significant improvements. Even if the stimulants do not increase a child's academic knowledge, the fact that they result in improvements in many other areas of school functioning is sufficient justification for parents to consider the possible use of these medications with their children. Such changes not only can boost self-confidence and self-esteem in the classroom setting, but can make the child more likable to the peer group and therefore give him more opportunities to make or keep classmates as friends. They can also reduce the amount of censure, punishment, and rejection the child experiences at school from both peers and teachers, and may well preclude the child from needing to be retained in grade due to substandard academic achievement. For all of these reasons, the improvements in school adjustment and success that result from the stimulants are frequently the most common reasons for prescribing these medications for children with ADHD. . . .

The Side Effects

There are many side effects that children can experience when taking these medicines, but the vast majority are minor. Again, keep in mind that if any of these are bothersome enough to warrant stopping the medication, they will likely go away once the medicine "washes out" of a child's body— within 24 hours. Most of these side effects are clearly related to the dose of medicine the child is taking: Higher doses produce more side effects. It has been estimated, however, that from 1% to 3% of children with ADHD cannot tolerate *any* dose of *any* stimulant medication.

It's impossible to predict whether your child will have any of the side effects discussed here, but we do have some revealing test findings: Over half of children with ADHD we tested in our clinic showed decreased appetite, insomnia, anxiousness, irritability, or proneness to crying. *However many of these side effects (especially those associated with mood) were present when the children took a fake pill (called a placebo). This means that these side effects may represent problems that are associated with ADHD rather than with the medicine.* In most cases the actual side effects were quite mild. Stomachaches and headaches were reported in about a third of the children, but these were also mild. . . .

All of the stimulants seem to reduce a child's appetite to some degree— temporarily and mainly in the late morning or early afternoon, which explains why over half of all children on these drugs may eat little of their lunch while on the medicine. For many children their appetite comes back (sometimes with a vengeance!) by evening. That is why you should make sure that a child who is on this medicine has a chance to eat adequate types and amounts of food each day to grow well. . . .

Your physician may find that your child's heart rate and blood pressure increase a little while taking these medicines. These changes are minor and do not place most children with ADHD at any risk. However, if your child is one of the rare children who has high blood pressure already, you should make sure your doctor takes this into consideration. Cylert may be less likely to produce these effects on heart rate and blood pressure. . . .

Nearly half of all children placed on medication may notice that it is harder to fall asleep at bedtime after taking these medicines during the day. Most children fall asleep within an hour or so after their typical bedtime. If not, and this is a problem for your child, tell your physician so that the dose can be lowered. . . .

All of the stimulant medications can produce temporary symptoms of psychosis (thought disorganization, rapid speech, skin hallucinations, extreme anxiety, supersensitivity to noises, etc.) at very high doses. In very rare cases this can happen at low doses. Such reactions occur in fewer than 1% of the cases and last only until the dose wears off. . . .

CHALLENGE QUESTIONS

Is Ritalin Overprescribed?

1. Some people argue that parents and teachers play a prominent role in causing and maintaining problematic behaviors in children, because they fail to set limits or follow through with consequences for misbehavior. Taking this viewpoint, enumerate some dysfunctional styles that might contribute to children acting out of control.
2. Breggin contends that stimulants suppress spontaneous behavior with enforced submissiveness, thus dulling children. How would you go about differentiating spontaneous energy from disruptively annoying behaviors?
3. Some social critics have expressed alarm about the extent to which people are managing problems with medications such as Ritalin and Prozac. Discuss the extent to which medication provides a treatment for the basic problem (neurochemical dysfunction) or serves as a temporary method for alleviating symptoms of a more deeply rooted emotional nature.
4. Imagine that you are a psychiatrist being consulted by parents of a five-year-old boy who is reportedly "acting up" in kindergarten. They request a prescription of Ritalin for him. What kind of information would you want to have before making your decision about the prescription, and what kind of preliminary steps would you recommend before going along with the parents' request?
5. Imagine that you are a researcher who has been given research support to study different methods of intervening in a class composed of 20 "hyperactive" boys. What research methods would you use to compare the effectiveness of Ritalin to behavioral methods aimed at reducing the activity level of these boys?

Suggested Readings

DeGrandpre, Richard. (1999). *Ritalin Nation: Rapid-Fire Culture and the Transformation of Human Consciousness*. New York: W.W. Norton & Company.

Fowler, M. C. (1999). *Maybe You Know My Kid: A Parent's Guide to Identifying, Understanding, and Helping Your Child with Attention-Deficit Hyperactivity Disorder* (3rd edition). Secaucus, NJ: Birch Lane Press.

Safer, Daniel, J. (2000). Are Stimulants Overprescribed for Youths with ADHD? *Annals of Clinical Psychiatry*, 12(1), 32–55.

Stein, David, B. (1999). *Ritalin Is Not the Answer: A Drug-Free, Practical Program for Children Diagnosed with ADD or ADHD.* San Francisco: Jossey-Bass.

Taymans, Juliana, M., Lynda, L. West, and Madeline Sullivan (Eds.) (2000). *Unlocking Potential: College and Other Choices for People with LD and AD/HD.* Bethesda, MD: Woodbine House.

ISSUE 12

Should Psychosurgery Be Used to Treat Certain Psychological Conditions?

YES: Fred Ovsiew and Jonathan Bird, from "The Past and Future of Psychosurgery," *Current Opinion in Psychiatry* (January 1997)

NO: Frank T. Vertosick, Jr., from "Lobotomy's Back," *Discover* (October 1997)

ISSUE SUMMARY

YES: Psychiatrists Fred Ovsiew and Jonathan Bird assert that psychosurgery is an invaluable intervention for certain kinds of seriously disordered patients who have not responded to other forms of treatment, and that failure to provide this intervention to those who need it would be ethically questionable.

NO: Neurosurgeon Frank T. Vertosick, Jr., argues that psychosurgical procedures rest on a shaky scientific foundation and involve procedures that cause irreversible injury to the brain.

In the 1930s psychosurgical techniques involved severing the connections between areas of the brain that were thought to be responsible for symptoms of disorders, such as schizophrenia. These relatively primitive surgical techniques did result in the reduction of some problematic symptoms, but they also caused some disturbing personality changes. Much of the barbarism associated with earlier versions of psychosurgery caused this procedure to fall out of favor, although in recent years there has been a minor resurgence of interest.

Some professionals recommend the use of psychosurgery for patients who do not benefit from psychotherapy or medication and whose symptoms seriously impair living. For example, people with severe cases of obsessive-compulsive disorder have been treated with cingulotomy, a procedure that involves the precise lesioning of the cingulate bundle, an area of the brain implicated in anxiety and compulsive behavior. Small holes are drilled into the skull, and electrodes are positioned in each cingulate bundle. Then electric current is used to create lesions, which results in the reduction of obsessions and compulsions. This psychosurgical procedure and others like it have produced some compelling case histories of people who report that their lives improved remarkably as a result. At the same time, the invasive nature of a surgical procedure in such an important part of the human body evokes intense anxiety associated with the potentially devastating effects of the slightest of errors.

Fred Ovsiew and Jonathan Bird write about the benefits of psychosurgery for patients who have not responded to other interventions. Although Ovsiew and Bird acknowledge that the deliberate injuring of the brain seems anathema to many clinicians and scientists, they maintain that it is important to recognize that significant improvements in personality have been reported in individuals who have experienced brain hemorrhages and strokes. Such findings about the beneficial effects resulting from alterations of the brain concur with the generally positive reports about patients who have undergone psychosurgery for various debilitating mental disorders. In addressing ethical questions associated with psychosurgery, Ovsiew and Bird argue that an adequate theoretical justification is not necessary for the ethical use of psychosurgery; rather, they argue that withholding psychosurgery becomes ethically questionable for severely ill, treatment-resistant patients.

Frank T. Vertosick, Jr., on the other hand, is appalled by a procedure that attempts to cure mental disorders by "frying holes" in parts of the brain. Vertosick recalls the debates of the 1950s when the rising use of psychosurgery ignited a national debate over the morality of inflicting irreversible brain injuries in the most emotionally vulnerable patients. Although he acknowledges that there have been major advances in the way in which surgeons approach psychosurgery, Vertosick remains profoundly concerned that procedures such as cingulotomy rest on no firmer scientific foundation than the disdained prefrontal lobotomy of decades past.

POINT

- Advances in neurosurgical equipment and techniques allow for new approaches to treating psychiatric problems.
- Researchers have demonstrated that psychosurgery has helped a considerable number of treatment-resistant patients.
- Withholding psychosurgery becomes ethically questionable for severely ill, treatment-resistant patients.
- A theoretical justification is not necessary for the ethical use of psychosurgery, only adequate demonstrations of safety and efficacy.

COUNTERPOINT

- Neurosurgery remains a crude endeavor in which parts of the brain are destroyed in order to treat mental illness.
- Some forms of contemporary psychosurgery, such as cingulotomy, rest on no firmer scientific foundation than lobotomy.
- Too much of the decision about psychosurgery rests on the recommendation of a psychiatrist rather than on the experiences of the patient.
- Only a few major medical centers can muster the psychiatric, bioethical, and surgical resources to perform and evaluate the procedure correctly.

Fred Ovsiew and Jonathan Bird  **YES**

The Past and Future
of Psychosurgery

The history of neurosurgical treatment for psychiatric disorders is not a happy one. It comprises misunderstanding of brain function, indifference to complications, and resorting to desperate treatments for lack of better ones. Egaz Moniz, a Portuguese neurologist, was fascinated by the improved behavior of Fulton's and Jacobson's chimpanzee Becky after frontal lobectomy but ignored the opposite effects of the surgery on the simultaneously reported Lucie (1). Moniz's frontal lobotomy procedure was taken up worldwide, notably by Freeman and Watts in the USA, and by the advent of the neuroleptic era tens of thousands of surgical procedures had been performed on psychiatric patients (2). Despite efforts consistent with the methods of the day, adequate studies of surgical interventions were not performed (2).

Today, pharmacological and psychological treatments of proven efficacy and relative safety have replaced psychosurgery. Yet treatment-resistant patients remain, although data recording their prevalence are limited. In a comprehensive review, Fava and Davidson (3) found that nonresponsiveness to antidepressant pharmacotherapy occurred in between 19 and 34% of depressed patients. However, treatment resistance is variably defined and the number of patients still disabled by depression after maximum use of all available modalities of treatment over a prolonged period is unknown. The proportion of patients with obsessive-compulsive disorder (OCD) meeting similar criteria is unstudied; Mindus et al. (4) estimated that 10% of OCD patients have 'malignant' refractory illnesses.

Does psychosurgery have a place in the contemporary management of this extreme group of psychiatric patients? Developments in neurosurgical techniques may allow new approaches to psychiatric problems (5).

Stereotaxis is well established and can be guided by contemporary neuroimaging. Electrical stimulation can reversibly shut down gray matter regions and avert destructive lesioning techniques with a possible reduction in cognitive morbidity (6–8). Gamma irradiation (the gamma knife) produces precisely focused lesions without open procedures and may reduce morbidity, although some results have been disappointing (9) and the dosimetry of the procedure is still under investigation (10). Avoiding the

From *Current Opinion in Psychiatry*, vol. 10, no. 1, January 1997. Copyright © 1997 by Lippincott, Williams & Wilkins. Reprinted by permission.

need for burr holes allows the possibility of controlled studies using sham psychosurgical procedures, a desideratum always considered ethically impossible (4). Thalamic and striatal gamma knife lesions have alleviated pain and movement disorders (11,12), even as open procedures continue to be employed successfully for these indications, with electrophysiological recording during open procedures allowing identification of functionally significant areas before lesioning (13–17).

Deliberately injuring the brain is anathema to many clinicians and scientists whose professional activities cannot but lead to nearly religious awe of the complexity and precision of brain function. Yet after subarachnoid hemorrhage, a small group of patients exhibits an improvement in psychiatric state. Storey's careful study of personality change after subarachnoid hemorrhage (18) identified patients who emerged from the neurological catastrophe not just undamaged but better than ever before. Of his 261 patients, 13 (5%) fell into the 'improved personality' group: 'less sarcastic and irritable, less tense and anxious, less fussy and overmeticulous, and more pleasant to live with generally' (p 137) (18). These patients lacked intellectual and, for the most part, motor disability.

Similar findings came from a study by Logue et al. (19). In nine (10%) of 90 patients after subarachnoid hemorrhage, the patient and an informant agreed that the personality had changed for the better. In three, a pre-existing depressive illness had been relieved. A tendency to compulsive checking was reduced in one of the nine; a more severe OCD was relieved in another patient who did not fit into the 'improvement in personality' category. However, eight of the nine patients with improved personality showed memory impairment and for several patients adverse emotional changes were present along with favorable ones.

Improvement in movement disorders after stroke has been reported in at least nine patients (20–26), although for the most part the reports lack information on functional status. The typical patient has parkinsonism and after subthalamic nucleus stroke (a lesion that ordinarily produces hemiballism) experiences contralateral relief of akinesia and rigidity. Indeed, James Parkinson noted relief after a stroke in one of the patients he originally reported (27).

Such curious observations of spontaneously occurring brain lesions notwithstanding, only appropriately controlled studies of psychosurgery patients will answer nagging questions about efficacy and safety. Investigators have recognized this challenge. Hay et al. (28) reported retrospectively 26 Australian OCD patients treated surgically; six had only cingulate lesions, three had only orbitomedial lesions, and 17 had both sets of lesions. 'Obvious' improvement was seen in 10 (38%) and comparison with matched unoperated control individuals confirmed that the improvement was caused by surgery. Four (15%) of these patients had an adverse change in personality traits of initiative and energy (29). Although no general intellectual deterioration was seen, the surgical patients as a group performed more poorly than the control individuals on the Wisconsin Card Sort Test (30). Both personality and cognitive alterations represent just the kind of 'frontal' deterioration feared from psychosurgery. However, the procedures performed in many of these patients were more extensive than is the current practice in other centers.

Hodgkiss et al. (31) reviewed the experience of the Geoffrey Knight National Unit for Affective Disorders, the major psychosurgical program in the UK. Of 249 patients with severe mood disorder or OCD who underwent bilateral lesions of subcaudate white matter, 84 (34%) were judged 'well' at 1-year follow-up. In a prospective study of 23 patients, no adverse cognitive alternations were seen at long-term follow-up, even though 'frontal' tests were transiently impaired in the immediate postoperative period (32). Improvement of depression in these patients, however, was correlated with reduced performance on a number of neuropsychological tasks, including tests of frontal function (33).

Baer et al. (34) in Boston, USA, conducted a prospective but unblinded and uncontrolled study of cingulotomy in OCD. The authors found that five (28%) of 18 patients had responded well; three (17%) others were noted on less solid evidence to have improved. No adverse consequences were seen by careful clinical assessment but neuropsychological data were not available.

Nyman and Mindus (35) studied the effect of anterior capsulotomy on neuropsychological status in Swedish patients treated surgically for anxiety disorders including OCD. One-half of a group of 10 patients showed increased perseverative response on neuropsychological tasks, although the authors commented on the lack of clinical observation of perseveration. They further noted that longer term follow-up of a different group of patients who underwent gamma knife capsulotomy suggested that the abnormalities may be transient. Mindus et al. (4) proposed a controlled trial of gamma knife anterior capsulotomy for OCD. Preliminary data from an open trial by investigators at Brown University and the Massachusetts General Hospital in the USA and the Karolinska Institute in Sweden, meant to establish the safety and optimal size and site of the procedure, showed improvement in about one-third of 25 patients with no adverse acute or longer term consequences for cognition or personality (Rasmussen S, personal communication).

If psychosurgery works, how does it work? An answer to this question presupposes an understanding of the pathophysiology of the disorders for which psychosurgery is performed and such understanding is incomplete to say the least. Increasingly, data implicate a limbic loop involving lateral frontal and orbitofrontal cortex, striatum, cingulate gyrus, and thalamus in depression and OCDs as well as Tourette syndrome (36–40). In particular, cingulate and orbitofrontal hyperactivity have been recognized in OCD and depression. Jeanmonod et al. (41) proposed that spiking in medial thalamic nuclei was the pathophysiological commonality for 'positive symptoms', including central pain, abnormal movements, and certain psychiatric symptoms, and on this basis performed stereotactic thalamotomy with intra-operative electrophysiological recording in 104 patients. Such findings have yet to produce a fully elaborated and confirmed theory. Moreover, abnormal findings, whether by electrophysiology or by functional neuroimaging, may reflect downstream effects of more fundamental disturbances, even compensatory ones, the eradication of which is undesirable. Thus, despite progress, psychosurgical interventions cannot at present be fully rationally grounded on adequate theories of psychiatric disorders.

However, this does not mean that psychosurgery must be held in abeyance. The same reservations could be expressed about many medical treatments, including the pharmacological treatment of psychiatric disorders, which remains largely empirical. Perhaps psychosurgery programs, with careful neuropsychiatric assessment of seriously ill patients including even the possibility of intracranial recording, can yield information helpful in theory formation. An adequate theoretical justification is not necessary for the ethical use of psychosurgery, only adequate demonstrations of safety and efficacy. If such are forthcoming, withholding psychosurgery becomes ethically questionable for the small proportion but substantial number of severely ill, treatment-resistant patients. Depression and OCD are proper indications; aggressive behavior and possible applications, although surgical approaches to Tourette syndrome itself have been disappointing (42). Appropriate evaluation procedures have been outlined for OCD patients (43). At present, no clear choice can be made among the available procedures, although some data suggest that cingulotomy is safest, although least often effective (44,45). Legal and ethical safeguards for informed consent and other issues must be in place (46,47). With such precautions, especially in a research setting, psychosurgical intervention now deserves a respectful hearing.

References

1. Jasper, H. H., Riggio, S., and Goldman-Rakic, P. S. A historical perspective: the rise and fall of prefrontal lobotomy. In Epilepsy and the functional anatomy of the frontal lobe. Edited by Jasper, H. H., Riggio, S., Goldman-Rakic, P. S., New York: Raven Press; 1995: 97–114.

2. Swayze, V. W. Frontal leukotomy and related psychosurgical procedures in the era before antipsychotics (1935–1954): a historical overview. Am J Psychiatry 1995, 152: 505–515.

3. Fava, M., and Davidson, K. G. Definition and epidemiology of treatment-resistant depression. Psychiatr Clin North Am 1996, 19: 179–200.

4. Mindus, P., Rasmussen, S. A., and Lindquist, C. Neurosurgical treatment for refractory obsessive-compulsive disorder: implications for understanding frontal lobe function. J Neuropsychiatry Clin Neurosci 1994, 6: 467–477.

5. Yudofsky, S., and Ovsiew, F. Neurosurgical and related interventions for the treatment of patients with psychiatric disorders. J Neuropsychiatry Clin Neurosci 1990, 2: 253–255.

6. Caparres-Lefebvre, D., Blond, S., Pecheux, N., Pasquier, F., and Petit, H. Neuropsychological evaluation before and after thalamic stimulation in 9 parkinsonian patients [in French]. Rev Neurol (Paris) 1992, 148: 117–122.

7. Benabid, A. L., Pollak, P., Gao, D., Hoffmann, D., Limousin, P., Gay, E., Payen, I., and Benazzouz, A. Chronic electrical stimulation of the ventralis intermedius nucleus of the thalamus as a treatment of movement disorders. J Neurosurg 1996, 84: 203–214.

8. Iacono, R. P., Lonser, R. R., Mandybur, G., and Yamada, S. Stimulation of the globus pallidus in Parkinson's disease. Br J Neurosurg 1995, 9: 505–510.

9. Friedman, J. H., Epstein, M., Sanes, J. N., Lieberman, P., Cullen, K., Lindquist, C., and Daamen, M. Gamma knife pallidotomy in advanced Parkinson's disease. Ann Neurol 1996, 39: 535–538.

10. Kihlstrom, L., Guo, W-L., Lindquist, C., and Mindus, P. Radiobiology of radio-surgery for refractory anxiety disorders. Neurosurgery 1995, 36: 294–302.

11. Friehs, G. M., Ojakangas, C. L., Pachatz, P., Schrottner, O., Ott, E., and Pendl, G. Thalamotomy and caudatotomy with the gamma knife as a treatment for parkinsonism with a comment on lesion sizes. Stereotact Funct Neurosurg 1994, 64 (suppl 1): 209–221.

12. Young, R. F., Vermeulen, S. S., Grimm, P., Posewitz, A. E., Jacques, D. B., Rand, R. W., and Copcut, B. G. Gamma knife thalamotomy for the treatment of persistent pain. Stereotact Funct Neurosurg 1994, 64 (suppl 1): 172–181.

13. Baron, M. S., Vitek, J. L., Bakay, R. A. E., Green, J., Kaneoke, Y., Hashimoto, T., Turner, R. S., Woodard, J. L., Cole, S. A., McDonald, W. M., and DeLong, M. R. Treatment of advanced Parkinson's disease by posterior GPi pallidotomy: 1-year results of a pilot study. Ann Neurol 1996, 40: 355–366.

14. Goetz, C. G., and Diederich, N. J. There is a renaissance of interest in pallidotomy for Parkinson's disease. Nature Med 1996, 2: 510–514.

15. Bergman, H., Wichmann, T., and DeLong, M. R. Reversal of experimental parkinsonism by lesions of the subthalamic nucleus. Science 1990, 249: 1436–1438.

16. Jankovic, J., Cardoso, F., Grossman, R. G., and Hamilton, W. J. Outcome after stereotactic thalamotomy for parkinsonian, essential, and other types of tremor. Neurosurgery 1995, 37: 680–687.

17. Cardoso, F., Jankovic, J., Grossman, R. G., and Hamilton, W. J. Outcome after stereotactic thalamotomy for dystonia and hemiballismus. Neurosurgery 1995, 36: 501–508.

18. Storey, P. B. Brain damage and personality change after subarachnoid hemorrhage. Br J Psychiatry 1970, 117: 129–142.

19. Logue, V., Durward, M., Pratt, R. T. C., Miercy, M., and Nixon, W. L. B. The quality of survival after rupture of an anterior cerebral aneurysm. Br J Psychiatry 1968, 114: 137–160.

20. Dubois, B., Pillon, B., De Saxce, H., Lhermitte, F., and Agid, Y. Disappearance of parkinsonian signs after spontaneous vascular 'thalamotomy'. Arch Neurol 1986, 43: 815–817.

21. Hashimoto, T., Fujita, T., and Yanagisawa, N. Improvement in hemiballism after transient hypoxia in a case of subthalamic hemorrhage [in Japanese]. Rinsho Shinkeigaku (Clin Neurol) 1990, 30: 877–882.

22. Rivest, J., Quinn, N., Gibbs, J., and Marsden, C. D. Unilateral abolition of extra-pyramidal rigidity after ipsilateral cerebellar infarction. Mov Disord 1990, 5: 328–330.

23. Scoditti, U., Rustichelli, P., and Calzetti, S. Spontaneous hemiballism and disappearance of parkinsonism following contralateral lenticular lacunar infarct. Ital J Neurol Sci 1989, 10: 575–577.

24. Sellal, F., Hirsch, E., Lisovoski, F., Mutschler, V., Collard, M., and Marescaux, C. Contralateral disappearance of parkinsonian signs after subthalamic hematoma. Neurology 1992, 42: 255–256.

25. Stephenson, J. W. Disappearance of tremor in a case of paralysis agitans following an attack of hemiplegia with comments on the production of the tremor in paralysis agitans. Arch Neurol Psychiatry 1930, 23: 199–200.

26. Yamada, A., Takeuchi, H., and Miki, H. Unilateral abolition of parkinsonian rigidity after subthalamic nucleus hemorrhage [in Japanese]. Rinsho Shinkeigaku (Clin Neurol) 1992, 32: 887–889.

27. Parkinson, J. An essay on the shaking palsy. London: Sherwood, Neely and Jones; 1817.

28. Hay, P., Sachdev, P., Cumming, S., Smith, J. S., Lee, T., Kitchener, P., and Matheson, J. Treatment of obsessive-compulsive disorder by psychosurgery. Acta Psychiatr Scand 1993, 87: 197–207.

29. Sachdev, P., and Hay, P. Does neurosurgery for obsessive-compulsive disorder produce personality change? J Nerv Ment Dis 1995, 183: 408–413.

30. Cumming, S., Hay, P., Lee, T., and Sachdev, P. Neuropsychological outcome from psychosurgery for obsessive-compulsive disorder. Aust NZ J Psychiatry 1995, 29: 293–298.

31. Hodgkiss, A. D., Malizia, A. L., Bartlett, J. R., and Bridges, P. K. Outcome after the psychosurgical operation of stereotactic subcaudate tractotomy, 1979–1991. J Neuropsychiatry Clin Neurosci 1995, 7: 230–234.

32. Kartsounis, L. D., Poynton, A., Bridges, P. K., and Bartlett, J. R. Neuropsychological correlates of stereotactic subcaudate tractotomy: a prospective study. Brain 1991, 114: 2657–2673.

33. Poynton, A. M., Kartsounis, L. D., and Bridges, P. K. A prospective clinical study of stereotactic subcaudate tractotomy. Psychol Med 1995, 25: 763–770.

34. Baer, L., Rauch, S. L., Ballantine, H. T., Martuza, R., Cosgrove, R., Cassem E., Giriunas, I., Manzo, P. A., Dimino, C., and Jenike, M. A. Cingulotomy for intractable obsessive-compulsive disorder: prospective long-term follow-up of 18 patients. Arch Gen Psychiatry 1995, 52: 384–392.

35. Nyman, H., and Mindus, P. Neuropsychological correlates of intractable anxiety disorder before and after capsulotomy. Acta Psychiatr Scand 1995, 91: 23–31.

36. Ebert, D., and Ebmeier, K. P. The role of the cingulate gyrus in depression: from functional anatomy to neurochemistry. Biol Psychiatry 1996, 39: 1044–1050.

37. Weeks, R. A., Turjanski, N., and Brooks, D. J. Tourette's syndrome: a disorder of cingulate and orbitofrontal function? Quart J Med 1996, 89: 401–408.

38. Zald, D. H., and Kim, S. W. Anatomy and function of the orbital frontal cortex, II: function and relevance to obsessive-compulsive disorder. J Neuropsychiatry Clin Neurosci 1996, 8: 249–261.

39. Zald, D. H., and Kim, S. W. Anatomy and function of the orbital frontal cortex, I: anatomy, neurocircuitry, and obsessive-compulsive disorder. J Neuropsychiatry Clin Neurosci 1996, 8: 125–138.

40. Wolf, S. S., Jones, D. W., Knable, M. B., Gorey, J. G., Lee, K. S., Hyde, T. M., Coppola, R., and Weinberger, D. R. Tourette syndrome: prediction of phenotypic variation in monozygotic twins by caudate nucleus D2 receptor binding. Science 1996, 273: 1225–1227.

41. Jeanmonod, D., Magnin, M., and Morel, A. Low-threshold calcium spike bursts in the human thalamus: common pathophysiology for sensory, motor and limbic positive symptoms. Brain 1996, 119: 363–375.

42. Rauch, S. L., Baer, L., Cosgrove, G. R., and Jenike, M. A. Neurosurgical treatment of Tourette's syndrome: a critical review. Compr Psychiatry 1995, 36: 141–156.

43. Mindus, P., and Jenike, M. A. Neurosurgical treatment of malignant obsessive compulsive disorder. Psychiatr Clin North Am 1992, 15: 921–938.

44. Sachdev, P., and Hay, P. Site and size of lesion and psychosurgical outcome in obsessive-compulsive disorder: a magnetic resonance imaging study. Biol Psychiatry 1996, 39: 739–742.

45. Cosgrove, G. R., and Rauch, S. L. Psychosurgery. Neurosurg Clin North Am 1995, 6: 167–176.

46. Hundert, E. M. Autonomy, informed consent, and psychosurgery. J Clin Ethics 1994, 5: 264–266.

47. Stagno, S. J., Smith, M. L., and Hassenbusch, S. J. Reconsidering 'psychosurgery': issues of informed consent and physician responsibility. J Clin Ethics 1994, 5: 217–223.

Frank T. Vertosick, Jr.

Lobotomy's Back

In 1949 lobotomy was hailed as a medical miracle.

But images of zombielike patients and surgeons with ice picks soon put an end to the practice.

Now, however, the practitioners have refined their tools.

Last year a team of Harvard investigators headed by neurosurgeon G. Rees Cosgrove published a technical report bearing the ponderous title "Magnetic Resonance Image—Guided Stereotactic Cingulotomy for Intractable Psychiatric Disease." Although steeped in medical jargon, the report's central thesis—that psychiatric diseases can be treated by the selective destruction of healthy brain tissue—dates back to a much earlier, less sophisticated age when the search for a surgical cure for mental illness spawned an entire medical specialty known as psychosurgery.

Psychosurgery enjoyed a brief period of global acceptance around the time of World War II but was quickly driven from the medical mainstream with the advent of better, nonsurgical methods of treating the mentally ill. Now, almost half a century after psychosurgery's demise, the Harvard Medical School and a handful of other centers are hoping that new and improved surgical techniques can revive it. Today's neurosurgeons are also trying to rename the field "psychiatric surgery," presumably to avoid the Hitchcockian overtones of the older moniker. But, as rock star Prince discovered, shedding the name that made you famous isn't easy.

In their 1996 paper that appeared in the respected journal *Neurosurgery,* Cosgrove and his co-workers described a brain operation designed to relieve emotional distress and reduce abnormal behavior. Between 1991 and 1995, they performed cingulotomies—which means, essentially, that they burned dime-size holes in the frontal lobes of the brain—on 34 patients suffering from one of the following afflictions: severe depression; bipolar disorder, or manic-depression; obsessive-compulsive disorder (OCD); and generalized anxiety disorder. The target of their operations, the cingulate gyrus, is a thin ribbon of gray matter believed to play a role in human emotional states. The authors used a computer-guided technique known as stereotaxis to advance an electrode into the cingulate gyrus, then cooked the tissue with electric current.

Cingulotomy produced major clinical improvement, as judged by psychiatrists, in a little over a third of the patients; another quarter of

From Frank T. Vertosick, Jr., "Lobotomy's Back," *Discover,* vol. 18, no. 10 (October 1997). Copyright © 1997 by *Discover.* Reprinted by permission.

them had a "possible response" to surgery. Not stellar results to be sure, but the Harvard patients all had severe disease that had proved resistant to all other available therapies. Any good outcomes in this population might be significant, and the investigators believed that their results were good enough to warrant a larger trial of cingulotomy.

Despite its high-tech approach, however, the Harvard paper still looks anachronistic, to say the least. Finding a paper extolling the virtues of psychosurgery in today's medical literature is rather like finding one advocating blood-letting. Modern neurosurgeons destroying normal brain to treat mental illness? To borrow from Samuel Johnson, this is akin to a dog walking on its hind legs—the question is not how well the act can be done but why it's even attempted.

In spite of its elevated reputation, neurosurgery is a crude business, even—or especially—to a neurosurgeon, and I've been in practice for ten years. When confronted with an exposed brain at the operating table, I feel as if I'm about to repair a computer with a chain saw. The living brain has a surreal fragility; its porcelain surface is laced with delicate arteries that begin as thick cords but quickly branch into finer and finer threads. Looking at the surface of the brain is like looking at a satellite photo of a large city—one immediately senses a function far more complex than what is visible.

The idea that a sophisticated derangement in brain function, like OCD, can be cured by frying holes in the frontal lobe looks as patently absurd as recovering a lost file from a floppy disk by burning it with a curling iron. But experience suggests that such lesions can work, if they are done correctly and on the right patients.

Psychosurgery got its start back in 1890 when Gottlieb Burckhart, a Swiss psychiatrist and surgeon, tried removing portions of the cerebral cortex from schizophrenic brains. His victims, previously agitated and tormented by violent hallucinations, became more "peaceful" after the operation. Burckhart's operation didn't impress his colleagues, though, and an angry outcry from the European medical community prevented its further use.

Psychosurgery surfaced again with a vengeance in Portugal, during the mid-1930s; shortly thereafter, neurologist Walter Freeman enthusiastically imported it to the United States. Psychiatrists started to believe Freeman's proselytizing hype, and desperate families of the mentally ill began seeking surgery for their loved ones. During World War II the United States saw an increased demand for mental health care as thousands of combat-fatigued veterans crowded already overburdened hospitals. In this setting, psychosurgery became established as a standard therapy. Over the 20-odd years that psychosurgery held the attention of the medical mainstream, perhaps as many as 35,000 patients underwent psychiatric operations of one form or another.

But as Burckhart had discovered decades earlier, the medical community could not long ignore the ethical quagmire surrounding psychiatric brain operations. In the 1950s the rising use of psychosurgery ignited a national debate over the morality of inflicting irreversible brain injuries on the most emotionally vulnerable patients. While this debate smoldered among academics right up to the 1970s, the introduction of the tranquilizer chlorpromizine in 1954 rendered many of the concerns about psychosurgery moot.

Armed with effective chemical therapies, psychiatrists soon turned to pills instead of the knife and quit referring their patients for surgery. A few centers continued to use modified forms of psychosurgery on very small numbers of patients, both here and in Europe, well into the 1980s, so psychosurgery as a specialty never died—although psychosurgery as an industry did.

Should psychosurgery be brought back from the realm of the experimental and made a mainstream treatment once again? Should we reopen this ethical can of worms? As Cosgrove's report shows, there are those who think we should. Hundreds of severely incapacitated people fail all other treatments, including drugs, electroshock, and psychotherapy, leaving surgery their only option. The illness most helped by cingulotomy—major depression—can be life-threatening. If psychosurgery works, shouldn't it be used?

The successful resurrection of extinct brain operations has a recent precedent: pallidotomy for parkinsonism. In this procedure, parts of the globus pallidus, a clump of tissue in the core of the brain controlling limb coordination, are surgically destroyed. The operation is technically similar to cingulotomy, and in the past few years it has enjoyed a renaissance. Before the discovery of L-dopa—a chemical substitute for the brain chemical dopamine—surgeons carried out pallidotomies and a number of other destructive procedures to ease the tremor and rigidity of Parkinson's disease. After the introduction of L-dopa, the role of the surgeon in the treatment of Parkinson's lessened, and the operations soon fell into relative disuse.

While L-dopa did revolutionize the treatment of Parkinson's, the drug proved ineffective in a small number of patients. Still others responded to medical therapy only to become resistant to it months or years later. As neurologists accumulated more experience with drug treatments for Parkinson's, they realized that medical therapy alone could not keep the disease at bay. A growing demand for alternative treatments renewed interest in pallidotomy, and several medical centers began trying it again. Since today's image-guided pallidotomy can be done with far greater accuracy than was ever possible before, modern surgical results have been excellent, and pallidotomy is currently available nationwide.

But bringing back pallidotomy, an operation with no historical baggage, was a piece of cake. To achieve a similar comeback in their own field, modern neurosurgeons must overcome psychosurgery's dark past—a considerably more difficult task.

Looking back today, psychosurgery is seen as nothing short of a mental health holocaust perpetrated by mind-stealing hacks in the dimly lit clinics of public psychiatric hospitals. It will always be synonymous with the flagship operation of its heyday, the dreaded prefrontal lobotomy.

In the conventional form of the operation, a neurosurgeon poked holes in the patient's skull just above and in front of the ear canals on both sides of the head and plunged a flat knife, called a leucotome, into the frontal lobes to a depth of about two inches. By sweeping the leucotome up and down within the brain, the surgeon amputated the anterior tips of the frontal lobes, the so-called prefrontal areas, from the rest of the brain. In contrast to the half-inch lesions of pallidotomy and cingulotomy, the lobotomist sliced an area of brain equal to the cross section of an orange.

This technique soon gave way to a quicker, albeit somewhat grislier, version of prefrontal lobe destruction. Before World War II, brain surgeons—not exactly a dime a dozen even today—were quite scarce; this lack of surgical expertise hindered the wider use of psychosurgery. To rid himself of the need for a surgeon, Freeman began tinkering with the transorbital approach invented by Amarro Fiamberti in Italy. (At this point, James Watts, Freeman's surgical colleague in conventional lobotomies, ended their collaboration, saying the transorbital procedure was too risky.)

In Freeman's modification of the procedure, the lobotomist inserted an ice pick (yes, an ice pick) under the upper eyelid and drove it upward into the frontal lobe with a few sharp raps of a mallet. The pick was then twisted and jiggled about, thus scrambling the anterior frontal lobes. The ice-pick lobotomy could be done by anyone with a strong stomach, and, even better, it could be done anywhere. Freeman carried his ice pick in his pocket, using it on one occasion to perform a lobotomy in a motel room. A cheap outpatient procedure, the ice-pick lobotomy became a common psychosurgical choice in state hospitals across the country.

In the late 1950s lobotomy's popularity waned, and no one has done a true lobotomy in this country since Freeman performed his last transorbital operation in 1967. (It ended in the patient's death.) But the mythology surrounding lobotomies still permeates our culture. Just last year the operation surfaced on the television show *Chicago Hope*. Few of us have ever met a lobotomized patient, but we all know what to expect—or at least we think we do. Who can forget the vacant stare of the freshly knifed Jack Nicholson in *One Flew Over the Cuckoo's Nest*? At best, according to the popular conception, the luckier victims recovered enough to wander about like incontinent zombies.

Although some patients ended up this way, or worse, the zombie stereotype derives more from Hollywood fiction than from medical reality. Lobotomy peaked in the 1950s, not during the Middle Ages. While we may have been a little more bioethically challenged back then, we weren't Neanderthals either. Lobotomy could never have survived for 20 years if it yielded a lot of cretins. In fact, intelligence, in those cases where it was measured pre- and post-operatively by formal testing, remained unaffected by a competent lobotomy and in some cases it even improved.

Not surprisingly, the operation did have disturbing side effects. Patients often suffered major personality changes and became apathetic, prone to inappropriate social behavior, and infatuated with their own toilet habits. They told pointless jokes and exhibited poor hygiene. Postoperative deaths, although uncommon, occurred and could be gruesome. But all these problems must be put into the context of the era: in the 1940s brain surgery for any disease was very risky.

It's easy for us to forget that the media first hailed psychosurgery as a medical miracle. Lobotomy's reputation once ran so high that the Nobel committee awarded the prize in Medicine and Physiology to its inventor, the Portuguese neurologist Egas Moniz, in 1949. But less than a decade after this endorsement, lobotomy was dead and its memory vilified.

The operation's descent into disgrace had many causes. For one thing, lobotomy never had a scientific basis. Moniz got the idea for it in a flash after hearing a presentation by Fulton and Jacobsen, two Yale physicians, during a 1935 neurological conference in London. The Americans described two chimpanzees, Becky and Lucy, that had become remarkably calm after frontal lobe ablation.

This single, almost casual observation prompted Moniz to return home and begin human trials immediately. Further animal work would not be useful, he argued, since no animal models of mental illness existed. Why he rejected the thought of further animal experimentation while still viewing Fulton and Jakcobsen's tiny report as a virtual epiphany remains a mystery. Moniz, who had just endured a nasty priority fight concerning his invention of cerebral angiography, may have rushed into human trials in order to stake the earliest claim to lobotomy.

The association of the frontal lobes with emotional and intellectual dysfunction was hardly a radical idea, even in 1935. The frontal lobes of lower mammals are vanishingly tiny; even chimps and apes have fairly small ones. In humans, on the other hand, the frontal lobes make up nearly two-thirds of the cerebrum, or higher brain. Since mental illnesses are uniquely human afflictions, a therapeutic surgical assault on the frontal lobes seemed quite plausible.

Moniz subsequently created a fanciful theory of "abnormally stabilized pathways" in the brain to justify his operation. He reasoned that cutting brain fibers might interrupt the abnormal brain circuitry of psychiatric patients, freeing them from a cycle of endless rumination. Since then, no better rationale for lobotomy has been advanced. Nevertheless, a lack of scientific justification doesn't doom an operation as long as the operation works. Many good operations, pallidotomy included, can trace their origins to pseudoscience or serendipity. But was lobotomy ever a good operation? We've had half a century to study it and we're still not sure.

Unfortunately, lobotomists showed no great talent for comprehensive, long-term analysis of their data. The esteemed Moniz often followed his patients for only a few weeks after their surgery. The peripatetic Freeman drove about the country doing hundreds of ice-pick procedures, but only near the end of his life did he find out how the majority of them fared. Even then, his assessments proved vague and unconvincing.

Only a single certain conclusion emerged from the dozens of lobotomy studies that have appeared over the years: schizophrenics don't get better after surgery. This is ironic, given that they were the first to undergo psychosurgery. We now have an inkling as to why the treatment doesn't work. Unlike depression and mania, which are disorders of mood, schizophrenia is a disorder of thought. And what a lobotomy alters is emotional state, not cognitive abilities.

Most lobotomists had vague and paternalistic ideas of what constituted a "good" result. Results were typically judged by psychiatrists, families, or institutional custodians; detailed surveys of what the patients thought rarely appear in the psychosurgery literature. This seems strange, since a cure, as judged by outsiders, may not be viewed that way by the patient. Is the patient, although inwardly miserable, cured because he no longer assaults the nursing staff, or because he can now sit quietly for hours without screaming? A careful reading of Freeman's more detailed case histories shows that a few patients didn't even see themselves as ill in the first place, although they realized that their behavior disturbed others.

Probably the most important factor in lobotomy's demise was its deep physical and metaphysical ugliness. More than one seasoned professional vomited or passed out while watching Freeman crack through a patient's orbital bone with his ice pick. Moreover, prospective patients often had to be dragged to an operating room or clinic. In *Psychosurgery*, the textbook he coauthored with Watts, Freeman frankly describes his unorthodox methods of obtaining "consent" for lobotomy. Occasionally, forcible sedation was needed to keep the patient from backing out at the last minute.

Freeman's landmark treatise also notes that if the patient was "too disturbed" to sign a consent, a close relative could give permission instead. He didn't elaborate on how disturbed a person needed to be to abdicate his right to refuse lobotomy. Freeman never considered the possibility that relatives might have less than honorable motives for agreeing to the dissection of their loved one's frontal lobes. Tennessee Williams, however, had no trouble envisioning such a nasty scenario. In his play *Suddenly Last Summer*, Mrs. Venable orders her young niece, Catharine, to be lobotomized. Catharine knew a little too much about the deviate practices of Mrs. Venable's late son, Sebastian. Who would believe the poor child after she had the appropriate "therapy" at Lion's View asylum?

It's doubtful that many real families ever had such fanciful motives behind their surrogate assents for lobotomy, although even mundane motives can be illegitimate. Was it right to authorize a lobotomy to make an argumentative person a quiet one? Or to stop behaviors repugnant to everyone—everyone, that is, except the patient?

In retrospect, the real question isn't why lobotomy died, but why it survived for so long. The answer is simple: Walter Freeman. Lobotomy became his career, his crusade, and he spread psychosurgery's gospel with boundless enthusiasm. His elegant bearing and Freudian goatee gave him the look of a world-renowned healer of minds. In the end, his force of will could no longer counter lobotomy's growing ethical opposition and pharmaceutical competition. Freeman did his best to carry on, but it was no use.

Modern psychosurgery has no evangelist equal to Freeman to spread its message, and so it must survive only on its merits. Time will tell whether it can.

There are good reasons to think the field can be revived. For starters, modern procedures like magnetic, resonance-guided cingulotomy bear little resemblance to the ugly lobotomies of the past. Computer-guided electrodes the thickness of pencil lead that can inflict minute injuries with millimeter precision have replaced ice picks and leucotomes. Procedures now take place only in sophisticated operating theaters, not in motel rooms or in the back rooms of county hospitals.

Modern neurosurgeons like Cosgrove approach their operations not as true believers but as skeptical scientists. Freeman's arm-twisting consents are also gone; today multidisciplinary committees review each patient on a rigorous case-by-case basis. And no one but the patient can give consent for cingulotomy—there were no Mrs. Venables involved in the Harvard study. Unlike the itinerant lobotomists of Freeman's time, modern psychosurgeons follow their patients closely for years and test them exhaustively.

But two problems remain. First, Cosgrove's report, like earlier psychosurgery studies, makes no mention of the patients' perception of their operations; it details only what their psychiatrists thought. Patients can't even request this surgery on their own; an operation is offered only if the psychiatrist agrees. In other "quality of life" operations—face-lifts, surgical removal of herniated spinal disks, elective joint replacements—the patient approaches the surgeon directly, requests surgery, and then personally decides if the postoperative outcome is satisfactory. An orthopedic surgeon doesn't ask an internist if a knee replacement has alleviated a patient's pain. So why must we rely on psychiatrists to tell us if a patient no longer feels depressed after cingulotomy?

Second, the cingulotomy rests on no firmer scientific foundation than lobotomy did. First performed in 1952 as a modified version of the lobotomy, cingulotomy was based on Freeman's observations that lobotomy patients seemed to have less "psychological tension" when fibers near the cingulate gyrus were severed. This ribbon of brain tissue is thought to be a conduit between the limbic region, a primitive area involved in emotional behavior, and the frontal lobes, the seat of reason and judgment. But we lack any more detailed understanding of how the cingulate gyrus functions. As such, cingulotomy can trace its intellectual heritage right back to the chimps Becky and Lucy.

Psychosurgery will never become as routine as it was in the 1940s and 1950s. The most refractory of the chronically disabling mental illnesses, schizophrenia, can't be treated surgically. Depression, while quite common, usually responds to one of the many excellent medical therapies that must be tried first, leaving few patients as candidates for surgery. And patients with OCD often respond to nonsurgical treatments. Thus, the pool of patients likely to benefit from cingulotomy will always be fairly small. In addition, few major medical centers can muster the psychiatric, bioethical, and surgical resources to perform and evaluate the procedure correctly.

Then there is that sticky public relations problem. No matter how refined their surgeries, modem psychosurgeons will still be perceived as lobotomists. An unfair label, perhaps, but one that will prove difficult to shed.

A greater concern may be that the public won't care at all. In Freeman's day, society paid to house and care for great numbers of the mentally infirm, making psychiatric disease a public health problem of the first order. This may be why no one bothered to ask the patients what they thought of surgery—the lobotomists weren't treating patients, they were treating a national crisis. Since lobotomy did make patients easier to care for, and even got many out of institutions and off the public dole, psychosurgeons served the national interest well. Freeman acknowledged that the lobotomist often put the needs of society over those of the individual, arguing that it was better for a patient "to have a simplified intellect capable of elementary acts than an intellect where reigns disorder of subtle synthesis. Society can accommodate itself to the humble laborer, but it justifiably mistrusts the mad thinker."

The goal of lobotomy wasn't to control disease but to control patients. Some would argue that our present heavy use of psychotropic drugs is just as flawed, in that we don't make the patients better—we just succeed in preventing them from bothering us.

As a nation, we could seriously question all our recent efforts in the mental health arena. During the last three decades, mental illness has been literally cast into the streets. Asylums have vanished and many private health plans now refuse to pay for psychiatric treatment. Before we judge the lobotomists of old too severely, we should go to the nearest street grate and see how we are dealing with our mental health crisis today. High-profile diseases like AIDS and breast cancer dominate the headlines and the federal research budgets, leaving many victims of mental illness to suffer in silent solitude.

Modern psychosurgeons are thus courageous in seeking to address a difficult problem. By trying to bring the best neurosurgical technologies to a group of patients who have run out of hope, they risk the scorn of those who see only what psychosurgery was and not what it can be. I wish them luck. Given the lessons of history, they'll surely need it.

CHALLENGE QUESTIONS

Should Psychosurgery Be Used to Treat Certain Psychological Conditions?

1. Ovsiew and Bird support the use of psychosurgery for seriously impaired patients who do not respond to psychotherapy or medication. What criteria should be used to determine the appropriateness of psychosurgery as an intervention?
2. Vertosick raises ethical concerns about the use of psychosurgery. In what ways is psychosurgery markedly different from other kinds of major elective surgery?
3. A significant concern about extreme interventions such as psychosurgery is the issue of informed consent. What are some of the issues involved for loved ones and clinicians who are trying to make a life-changing surgical decision for an individual who is considered incapable of making the decision?
4. What problems would be involved in designing a research study to compare the efficacy of psychosurgery and medication for the treatment of debilitating obsessive-compulsive disorder?
5. Considering that psychosurgery is still regarded as an experimental procedure, many insurance companies resist reimbursing for this intervention. What are the arguments for and against this?

Suggested Readings

Jenike, M. A. (1998). Neurosurgical treatment of obsessive-compulsive disorder. *British Journal of Psychiatry, 173*(35S), 79–90.

Marino, J. R., & Cosgrove, G. R. (1997). Neurosurgical treatment of neuropsychiatric illness. *Psychiatric Clinics of North America, 20*(4), 933–943.

Pressman, J. D. (1998). *Last resort: Psychosurgery and the limits of medicine.* New York, NY: Cambridge University Press.

Sachdev, P., & Sachdev, J. (1997). Sixty years of psychosurgery: Its present status and its future. *Australian and New Zealand Journal of Psychiatry, 31*(4), 457–464.

Weingarten, S. M. (1999). Psychosurgery. In B. L. Miller, & J. L. Cummings (Eds.), *The human frontal lobes: Functions and disorders. The science and practice of neuropsychology series.* (pp. 446–460). New York, NY: The Guilford Press.

ISSUE 13

Should Psychologists Prescribe Medication?

YES: Robert Resnick, from "To Prescribe or Not To Prescribe—
Is That the Question?" *The Psychologist* (April 2003)

NO: William N. Robiner et al., from "Prescriptive Authority
for Psychologists: A Looming Health Hazard?" *Clinical Psychology:
Science and Practice* (Fall 2002)

ISSUE SUMMARY

Yes: Psychologist Robert Resnick endorses the recommendation
that psychologists be given prescription privileges in order to
expand psychopharmacological availability to people needing
medication.

No: Psychologist William Robiner and his colleagues object to the
notion of granting prescription privileges to psychologists, and
express several concerns pertaining to training and competence.

During the past two decades, tremendous advances have been made in
understanding biologically based causes and treatments for a wide array of
emotional and behavioral disorders. The introduction of selective serotonin
reuptake inhibitors in the 1980s began a revolution in the treatment of
depression and several other serotonin-related conditions such as obsessive-
compulsive disorder. During these past two decades, medications such as
Ritalin and similar stimulants have become increasingly prescribed not only
for children with attention-deficit/hyperactivity disorder, but also for adults
with attentional problems. Psychopharmacological interventions have become
so common and accepted in society that commercials and advertisements are
found in all the media boasting about the effectiveness of these medications.
As mental health professionals have increasingly endorsed the prescription of
medications, questions have arisen about the possibility of permitting non-
physician professionals to prescribe these medications for their patients.

Psychologist Robert Resnick asserts that there is ample justification for
giving prescription privileges to psychologists. He cites the social benefit for
patients in underserved areas of the United States who would be able to

turn to professionals other than physicians for psychopharmacological prescriptions. Resnick contends that well-trained psychologists would be able to provide a comprehensive service in which they offer a range of services including assessment, consultation, therapy, and medication.

Psychologist William Robiner and his colleagues express serious objections to the proposal to give prescription privileges to psychologists. Concern is expressed about the fact that the medically relevant training of psychologists differs markedly from that received by physicians and by other professionals with prescription privileges. Robiner and his colleagues criticize the arguments that have been put forth by those advocating prescription privileges for psychologists, noting that prescribing psychologists are not especially likely to relocate to underserved geographical regions; nor will they necessarily be able to respond to the needs of patients who seem to prefer obtaining their prescriptions from physicians.

POINT

- In many areas of the United States, people have urgent and unmet health needs that can be alleviated by professionals who can provide both psychotherapy, and when needed, medication.
- Prescribing psychologists will offer patients better options and more knowledgeable referrals. Of concern is the fact that 85% of prescriptions used to treat mental problems are written by physicians who have little or no training in psychiatry.

- As evidenced by a program initiated in 1991 by the U.S. Department of Defense, psychologists can be successfully trained to prescribe; after several years and thousands of prescriptions written by this small number of military psychologists, there has not been one inappropriate use, missed physical diagnosis or complication, or one untoward outcome.
- Giving psychologists prescribing privileges would make it easier for patients to obtain quality and accessible mental health care in a timely fashion and at the lowest cost; it is much more efficient to see one professional rather than two.

COUNTERPOINT

- There is little reason to believe that psychologists with prescriptive authority would relocate to areas lacking other prescribers, or would focus their practices to address the needs of underserved populations.
- There are several reasons why non-psychiatric physicians account for the majority of psychotropic prescriptions written including the fact that (1) some patients are more comfortable seeing their primary care physician than a mental health professional; and (2) managed care companies recommend such treatment by primary care physicians over referrals to specialist mental health professionals.
- It is not known how well the successes of these ten military prescribing psychologists, who were trained in a military medical setting, and whose care was confined to a patient population largely screened for health and other factors, would generalize to independently practicing psychologists working in a diversity of settings.
- As an alternative to giving psychologists prescription privileges, efficiency of service delivery in the mental health system can be enhanced by taking steps to improve collaboration between psychologists and medical personnel who prescribe medications.

215

Robert Resnick

To Prescribe or Not To Prescribe— Is That the Question?

A patient is speaking to the doctor, relating several months of sadness, loss of appetite and sleep, irritability and just plain 'feeling lousy'. After further discussion the doctor concludes the patient is experiencing significant depression and decides upon a course of treatment: psychotherapy and the short-term use of an antidepressant. The doctor takes out a pad, writes a prescription for one of the newer antidepressant medications, and arranges to start psychotherapy with the patient next week while monitoring the response to the medication. A psychiatrist? No, a psychologist in the State of New Mexico. In March 2002 New Mexico became the first state in the United States to permit psychologists, with additional training, to prescribe medication for nervous, emotional and mental problems.

While New Mexico is the first of the 50 states to obtain the legal right to prescribe medications used in mental health practices, it is not alone. Eleven other states will be introducing proposed modifications in their state laws to permit psychologists to prescribe medications. An additional 20 states have groups of psychologists laying the groundwork to introduce such legislative change.

Why do psychologists want to prescribe? The answer is a bit complicated. Physicians have historically been the only professionals permitted to prescribe, but in the last 50 years, in addition to dentists and podiatrists (who can prescribe medications but are not medical doctors) many other healthcare professionals have added this service through changes in state law. Nurses and optometrists are permitted to prescribe medications in all states, physician assistants and pharmacists in many. For psychology it is not a case of 'me too' or 'monkey see, monkey do'. It is about quality care, and it is about accessible care.

To illustrate: I am a specialist in attention deficit disorder, and frequently medication is used as part of the overall treatment plan. Recently, a 10-year-old child was referred to me. Jason had significant problems with inattention and hyperactivity, and was failing in school. His parents had tried everything they could to get him to pay attention in school and

From *The Psychologist*, vol. 16, no. 4, April 2003, pp. 184–186. Copyright © 2003 by British Psychological Society. Reprinted by permission.

complete homework. After the evaluation and a diagnosis of attention deficit hyperactivity disorder, I decided upon a four-part plan: work with Jason to develop better coping mechanisms for his behaviour; help his parents develop different ways of parenting and relating to him; establish school-based strategies aimed at reducing classroom distraction and ensuring that homework and classwork was completed; and the use of a medication known to be effective in reducing the impulsivity and hyperactivity. The first three parts of the treatment plan were put in place within the first 24 to 48 hours. However, it took six weeks (with another report card grading period ending) before Jason and his parents were able to get an appointment with their paediatrician who would prescribe the medicine. Then, a four-week wait to see the paediatrician again for follow-up and adjustment of the medication towards the correct dose. If, as a psychologist, I had the right to prescribe medication, as I was seeing Jason and his parents weekly in psychotherapy, this part of the treatment plan would have been 'on board' within 24 hours as well. Lest the reader believe the paediatrician should have been involved earlier, the referral came from the paediatrician! This is not an uncommon experience among psychologists who see, and are referred, patients who need both psychotherapy and medication management. Frequently these referrals come from physicians who are ill equipped or trained to diagnose and treat psychological and mental issues.

There is clear evidence in the US that there are very grave and urgent unmet mental health needs. These needs could be met by professionals who can provide both psychotherapy and, when needed, medication. For example, there are over 450 counties in the United States with no psychiatrists in residence. An additional concern is that only about a third of the psychiatry training positions (residencies) are filled with American medical school graduates, with the majority of the remaining residency position being filled by physicians whose first language is not English. Language problems make it very difficult to work with minorities, inner-city families, Native Americans and rural communities. To illustrate the concern: A foreign-trained psychiatry resident whose English comprehension was passable but not extensive, admitted a man for 'being crazy', 'because he talks to animals'. After I evaluated him the next morning, he was released with apologies. This was a African-American jazz musician who, when speaking about his band members told the resident 'I says to this cat, and the cat says to me'. Talks to animals! Right!

Also of concern is the fact that 85 per cent of prescriptions used to treat mental problems are written by physicians who have little or no training in psychiatry (Zimmerman & Wienckowski, 1991). The average psychiatric training is less than seven weeks and the average number of instructional hours in psychiatric medications is only 99 in the four years of US medical school training (see *www.aamc.org*). Thus another component of the complicated answer would include the ability of families to obtain quality and accessible mental health services in a timely fashion and at the lowest cost. It is much more efficient (in terms of time lost from work or school) and more cost-effective to see one professional rather than two.

Can psychologists be trained to be psychologist prescribers? They already have been! Many psychologists in medical schools and government agencies have either written prescriptions 'under the table' or did everything but sign them, seeking out a physician who would simply add his or her name. This has been going on for decades, though most of the training was self-taught and some by 'osmosis'. In 1991, however, the US Department of Defense began a four-year demonstration programme, to determine if psychologists who were in the military could be trained to prescribe medications. Several years later and thousands of prescriptions written, there has not been one inappropriate use, missed physical diagnosis or complication; nor has there been one untoward outcome. Clearly, psychologists can be trained to provide medication management at a very high level of competence as well as to provide high-quality psychotherapy.

The demonstration project was modified, over time, and evolved into a two-year postdoctoral programme. The first year is didactics, and the second on-the-job clinical experience. How is this training different from medical school? Prescribing psychologists embrace a more integrative or psychological model of prescribing. Psychological training is a health model focusing on strengths first then weaknesses, rather than the disease model of medical school. As a consequence psychologists are less likely to 'knee-jerk' a medication to treat symptoms. Indeed, the experience of the military psychologists has demonstrated this point over and over again.

We in the psychologist prescription movement acknowledge two truths that are—or should be—self-evident: medications are indeed effective for some patients, and current prescription writing practices are inadequate and dangerous, especially for underserved populations. We also recognise a very important 'treatment' given to prescribing psychologists: the authority to discontinue medications that have been prescribed by other professionals. Particularly with mental problems, there has been a tendency to practise 'polypharmacy'—prescribing more and more medications to treat newly created symptoms. In part, this is due to the problems cited earlier in psychiatric and medical training. A quick example: A depressed patient is given an antidepressant then gets the side-effect of sleep problems. Now a sedative is prescribed, but there are side-effects of morning drowsiness and fatigue. When a stimulant is added to provide 'alertness', extrapyramidal symptoms such as severe dry mouth and lip-smacking develop and an anticholenergic drug is added. So the right to prescribe is also the right to *stop* inappropriate medications. You should note that over 7000 people a year die from legally prescribed medications (Kohn *et al.*, 2000: *www.nap.edu/books/0309068371/html*).

For almost a hundred years American psychology has debated the expansion of its competence and scope of practice. While never achieving unanimity, it has matured as a healthcare profession and will continue to do so. Clearly, a larger scope of practice will enable a psychologist to offer comprehensive services, including assessment, consultation, psychotherapy and, yes, when needed, medication. As psychology, like other professions, began the quest for independent prescriptive authority, organised medicine and some psychologists ominously warned of health hazards. In each instance the woeful predictions of wrongly treated patients flocking to hospitals and thousands of deaths never materialised.

Finally, I would argue that the best reason for psychologists having the ability to prescribe medication is not that it is good for psychology, but that it is good for the consumers. Psychologists have not entered this area of practice quickly or impulsively, but did so with deliberation and debate beginning in 1984. As a result, the additional training required for psychologists to prescribe medications has crucial differences from medical school training. Our training model is not disease-based. We include intensive and extensive training in the interaction of psychotherapy and medication, stressing when one is therapeutically superior to the other and when the use of both is in the best interest of the patient. In the final analysis, isn't this what this should be about? Isn't it what is best for the individuals, families and public we serve? It should be.

References

Kohn, L. T., Corrigan, J. M., & Donaldson, M. S. (Eds.) (2000). *To err is human: Building a safer health system*. Washington, DC: National Academy Press.

Zimmerman, M. A., & Wienckowski, L. A. (1991, Winter). Revisiting health and mental health linkages: A policy whose time has come . . . again. *Journal of Public Health Policy*, 510–524.

William N. Robiner, et al. 　　　　　　　　　　　　　　 **NO**

Prescriptive Authority for Psychologists: A Looming Health Hazard?

Advances in neuroscience, the development of safer, efficacious drugs such as the SSRIs, and changing realities in health care economics are transforming the delivery of mental health services. As these unfold, and as the use of psychotropics increases (Pincus et al., 1998), psychologists' interest in obtaining prescriptive authority for psychotropic medication has also increased (Ax, Forbes, & Thompson, 1997; Brentar & McNamara, 1991a, 1991b; Burns, DeLeon, Chemtob, Welch, & Samuels, 1988; Cullen & Newman, 1997; DeLeon, Folen, Jennings, Wilkis, & Wright, 1991; DeLeon, Fox, & Graham, 1991; DeLeon & Wiggins, 1996; Fox, 1988; Sammons, 1994). In this article we address a range of issues related to prescriptive authority for psychologists, including training, accreditation, regulation, and other topics raised by proponents of the prescriptive agenda, and discuss our concerns about it. . . .

Department of Defense Psychopharmacology Project

The controversy surrounding psychologists' prescription privileges was heightened by the Department of Defense (DoD) Psychopharmacology Demonstration Project (PDP). The PDP ultimately trained ten psychologists to prescribe in military health care settings (U.S. General Accounting Office, 1999). The initial PDP participants undertook some preparation in chemistry and biochemistry before completing a majority of first-year medical school courses. During their first full-time year at the Uniformed Services University of the Health Sciences, they worked with the Psychiatry-Liaison service and assumed night call with second-year psychiatry residents. In the second full-time year, they completed core basic science courses and continued psychopharmacology training and clinical work. After 2-day written and oral examinations, they had a third year of supervised clinical work at Walter Reed Army Medical

From *Clinical Psychology: Science and Practice*, vol. 9, no. 3, Fall 2002. pp. 231–248. Copyright © 2002 by Oxford University Press UK. Reprinted with permission.

Center or Malcolm Grow Medical Center. The PDP curriculum underwent subsequent iterations, streamlining training to 1 year of coursework and a year of supervised clinical practice (Sammons & Brown, 1997; Sammons, Sexton, & Meredith, 1996). For example, the didactic hours decreased by 48% in the second iteration. Most PDP graduates have functioned as prescribing psychologists in branches of the military. One graduate went on to medical school.

The PDP was discontinued after the first few years. Advocates of psychologist prescription privileges argue that the successes of the small sample of PDP participants justify extending prescriptive authority to other psychologists who undergo training consistent with the American Psychological Association (APA) (Council of Representatives [COR], 1996) model, even though that training model and the likely resources available for the training differ substantially from the PDP. It is not known how well the successes of the 10 PDP psychologists, who were trained within a military medical school and military hospital settings, and whose care was confined to a patient population largely screened for health and other factors, would generalize to the potentially thousands of psychologists who might wish to obtain psychopharmacology training and to practice independently across the spectrum of clinical or counseling settings with diverse populations (Bieliauskas, 1992a; Kennedy, 1998). If the clinical psychopharmacology training psychologists obtain elsewhere is less rigorous or is based on more limited access to medical populations than the PDP, the outcomes of the PDP potentially would overestimate outcomes of such training.

Additional skepticism seems warranted especially in light of the concerns about certain limitations of the PDP fellows' clinical proficiencies, such as in treating medically complex patients (Kennedy, 1998). The Final Report of the American College of Neuropsychopharmacology (1998) on the PDP assessed graduates as weaker medically and psychiatrically than psychiatrists. The report indicated that graduates only saw patients ages 18–65, some had limited formularies, and some continued to have dependent prescriptive practice (i.e., supervised by a physician). Moreover, the PDP graduates advised against "short-cut" programs and considered that a year of intensive full-time clinical experience, including inpatient care, was essential. Some of the program's psychiatrists, physicians, and graduates expressed doubts about the safety and effectiveness of psychologists prescribing independently outside of the interdisciplinary team of the military context. This latter concern has been echoed in a survey of military psychiatrists, nonpsychiatric physicians, and social workers (Klusman, 1998). Given the likelihood that other programs would lack some of the advantages of the PDP, and would provide less training than some of the PDP graduates received, we question how well the conditions of the PDP would be duplicated. Despite the positive experiences of PDP graduates, these concerns justify wariness about prescribing psychologists relative to other prescribers, especially for populations not included or emphasized in the PDP. We believe that more complete disclosure and consideration of the limitations and problems noted in the PDP are needed, both in the dialogue within the profession as well as in terms of public policy reviews of the prescriptive agenda. . . .

Quality of Care: The Central Concern about Psychologist Prescribing

Our primary concern is the risk of suboptimal care if psychologists undertake prescribing that could arise from their limited breadth and depth of knowledge about human physiology, medicine, and related areas. This risk would be compounded by psychologists' limited supervised physical clinical training experiences. Such knowledge and skills are fundamental to competent prescribing but have been limited or absent in training professional (i.e., clinical, counseling, school) psychologists. In one survey, more than two thirds of psychologists in independent practice described their training related to psychopharmacological issues as poor (APA, 1992b, p. 50). This is not surprising given the limited psychopharmacology training in doctoral programs and psychology internships (APA, 1992b).

Although advocates of prescription privileges readily acknowledge that additional training is needed to prepare psychologists to prescribe, the central questions are these. How much training is needed? Is it possible to attain adequate knowledge and skill through abbreviated training, such as proposed in models by the APA (CoR, 1996) or the California Psychological Association-California School of Professional Psychology Blue Ribbon Panel (1995)? How would psychologists who undergo the proposed training measure up to other prescribers? The concern is that abbreviated "crash courses" are inadequate to make up for psychologists' deficits in medical education (Bieliauskas, 1992a; Bütz, 1994).

At times, advocates for psychologist prescription privileges gloss over the complexity of knowledge sets inherent in competent prescribing (Kennedy, 1998; Kingsbury, 1992; Pies; 1991). For example, Patrick DeLeon, PhD, JD, Past President of the APA, contends that "prescription privileges is no big deal. It's like learning how to use a desk-top computer" (Roan, 1993). Related speculation that technological advances, such as computer-assisted learning (DeLeon & Wiggins, 1996), or prescriptive algorithms, could abbreviate the education necessary to prescribe competently strikes even proponents of prescription privileges as naïve (Pachman, 1996). Similarly, it seems unlikely that relying on more active roles of pharmacists or computerized systems for administration of drugs would compensate adequately for gaps in prescribers' medical knowledge. Ultimately, competence in prescribing demands adequate understanding not just of psychology and psychopharmacology but also of other domains of medical knowledge (e.g., human physiology, pathophysiology, biochemistry, clinical medicine) and clinical proficiencies (e.g., physical examination, interpretation of laboratory data) that historically have been excluded from the education and training of psychologists. More specifically, thorough understanding and proficiency related to two broad medical domains are required: understanding patients' medical status prior to and concurrent with prescribing and their medical status during and after treatment (i.e., their physiological responses to prescribed medications) (Pies, 1991; Robiner, 1999; see Table 1).

Table 1

Knowledge Base and Clinical Proficiencies Required for Prescribing

Psychopathology and Psychological Issues	Medical Status Prior to Prescribing	Response to Treatments
Primary psychiatric conditions	Comorbid medical conditions	Knowledge of adverse reactions 1. Side effects 2. Toxic effects
Comorbid psychiatric conditions	Contraindications	Ability to recognize, diagnose, and treat adverse reactions
Prevalence and course of psychiatric conditions	Medical effects of concurrent treatments 1. Drug interactions 2. Other treatments (e.g., dialysis, plasmaphoresis)	Ability to differentiate between physical and psychiatric effects of psychoactive agents and concurrent medications
Knowledge of nonpharmacologic treatment options	Long-term effects of medications History of medication use	Other issues related to monitoring, titrating, or discontinuing prescribed medications

Note: The education of psychologists typically addresses column 1, but neglects columns 2 and 3.

There are scant data regarding how well prepared psychologists are to prescribe. Anecdotally, psychologists' confidence in diagnosing patients and providing other types of psychological treatment, combined with limited psychopharmacology training and informal exposure to medications, may provide some sense that they have much of the knowledge related to prescribing. Thus far, however, little is known about how well the combination of doctoral training in psychology and relatively brief, focused training in psychopharmacology would develop psychologists' knowledge base and clinical proficiency for managing patients' medications, especially long-term and in diverse settings. Noteworthy differences exist between pharmacotherapy and current aspects of psychologists' clinical practice. As one psychologist turned psychiatrist observes:

> The effects of medications on the kidney, the heart, and so forth is important for the use of many medications. Managing these effects is often crucial and has more to do with biochemistry and physiology than with psychology. I was surprised to discover how little about medication use has to do with psychological principles and how much of it is just medical. (Kingsbury, 1992, p. 5)

Training for Prescribing

Proponents have construed prescriptive authority for psychologists as an "evolutionary" or "logical" step (DeLeon, Folen, et al., 1991; Fox, 1988) or even a "right" (Brentar & McNamara, 1991a) that is consistent with the trend in other health care disciplines towards broadened scopes of professional practice, including prescribing.

The first premise is debatable, especially given its fundamental departure from psychology's historic training paradigms and conceptualizations of psychopathology and intervention. The education and training for a doctoral degree in psychology largely neglects key topics relevant to prescribing (i.e., the biological and physical sciences, physical examination). Also, psychology historically has questioned, de-emphasized, or even eschewed the "medical model" (Matthews, 1998; May & Belsky, 1992). Pursuing prescriptive authority reflects a profound change in the direction toward embracing the medical model. Adding prescribing to psychology's scope of practice might more realistically be characterized as "revolutionary" or "radical," requiring major shifts in focus; marked expansions of training and continuing education in key areas; reformulation of accreditation criteria; modification of regulatory structure, domains, and processes; expanded ethical guidelines; and uniform requirements that at least part of psychologists' training occur within health care settings.

The second premise, that psychologists' scope of practice should broaden because some nonphysicians such as physician assistants (PAs) and advanced practice nurses (APNs) prescribe also is dubious. This seems to be based on the notion that the overall length of doctoral training that psychologists undergo might justify prescribing despite the limited relevance to prescribing of much of their actual training. Disparities in training between psychology and other professions with prescriptive authority challenge the notion that those professions' scopes of practice justify expanding psychologists' scope of practice to incorporate prescription privileges. Other professions' training models are much closer to that of physicians than to that of psychologists, and their clinical practice is more focused on physical functioning, including medication effects. Comparing the boundaries of other professions' scope of practice with psychology's is inappropriate given the differences in training between those other disciplines and psychology. . . .

The comparisons that advocates draw between psychology's and other disciplines' scope of practice compel closer inspection of the entry requirements and training models for psychology and other prescribing disciplines (McCabe & Grover, 1999). As outlined below, the differences in emphasis and structure are noteworthy. Since prescribing psychologists would probably be compared most closely with psychiatrists, our emphasis is on these two groups.

Undergraduate Training

The APA task force (Smyer et al., 1993) noted that other health professions (e.g., nursing, allied health professions) require undergraduate preparation in anatomy, biology, inorganic and organic chemistry, pharmacology, human physiology, (and some require physics); undergraduate psychology degrees and admission to psychology graduate school do not. The biological sciences and related course work is the educational foundation for knowledge and conceptual understanding related to prescribing safely. Hence, the APA task force envisioned that students with strong undergraduate, postbaccalaureate, or early graduate biological backgrounds would be admitted to psychopharmacology training (Smyer et al., 1993). The problem is that such backgrounds are rare. A survey of psychology graduate students revealed that only 27% thought they had the undergraduate preparation to undertake training to prescribe (Tatman et al., 1997). Only 7% had completed the recommended undergraduate biology and chemistry prerequisites (APA, 1992b; Smyer et al., 1993). Robiner et al. (2001) found that psychologists generally had taken fewer than five courses in the biological and physical sciences during their undergraduate and graduate education. . . .

Unlike medical school applicants and medical students, whose mastery of these areas is reflected through a competitive selection process (e.g., based on grades in biological and physical science courses, MCAT scores) and screened again in objective measures (i.e., national board scores such as steps one, two, and three of the United States Medical Licensing Examination [USMLE]; specialty board examinations following residency), entry into proposed psychopharmacology training programs for psychologists would not require standardized, objective indices of applicants' understanding of the biological and physical sciences. It is not known whether competitive performance in biological and physical science courses with laboratory prerequisites would play any role in determining eligibility for psychologists' psychopharmacology training. In summary, the discrepancies between physicians' and psychologists' education in the biological and physical sciences, and objective mechanisms verifying that general scientific knowledge has been acquired (i.e., psychology has none), begin at the undergraduate level.

The APA College of Professional Psychology in conjunction with Professional Examination Services developed an examination for psychologists who have undergone training in clinical psychopharmacology, the Psychopharmacology Examination for Psychologists (PEP). Other groups have developed other tests (e.g., Veritas Assessment Systems). Within the APA (1996) model, psychologists seeking prescription privileges would be expected to pass one of these written tests. Such testing is an important safeguard, but may be limited, especially in an era when commercial courses have been designed to prepare individuals for tests. Whereas proponents would argue that passage of that examination demonstrates adequate knowledge for prescribing, it seems questionable that a single 3-hour, 150-item test on psychopharmacology could assure adequate knowledge of the broad spectrum of medical issues beyond clinical psychopharmacology per se that are relevant to prescribing safely or knowledge and clinical skill sets comparable to that of other prescribers (e.g., physicians, nurse practitioners).

Graduate Training

Educational discrepancies between psychologists and physicians widen at the graduate level. The training of physicians and other doctoral providers (e.g., dentists) entails coursework in anatomy, biochemistry, cell biology, immunology, microbiology, pathology, pharmacology, physiology, as well as laboratory experiences in the biological and physical sciences and physical, clinical training. Doctoral-level psychology education never has (see APA Office of Program Consultation and Accreditation, 1996). Rather, graduate education in psychology has been characterized as comprising "vastly differing models of study and practice" with "no effort to standardize the training of psychologists" (Klein, 1996). Programs vary in how much training is provided in the biological and physical sciences (Sammons et al., 1996), but it is generally quite limited for degrees in professional psychology. Some types of psychology degrees, (e.g., school psychology) have relatively limited exposure to psychopathology and psychological treatments, let alone the physical sciences (DeMers, 1994; Moyer, 1995) or medical environments. . . .

Surveys suggest that only 25% of psychology graduate students had courses in psychopharmacology (Tatman et al., 1997) and 36% of licensed psychologists indicated that their graduate programs offered psychopharmacology courses (Ferguson, 1997). Presumably fewer had courses in pharmacology or pathophysiology, which are intrinsic to prescribing safely (i.e., due to potential interactions and adverse effects). These limitations are of greater concern than the limitations identified in medical students' psychiatric training (Zimmerman & Wienckowski, 1991) or estimates that medical school students receive only approximately 100 hours of pharmacology instruction (Association for Medical School Pharmacology [1990] cited by the APA Task Force [APA, 1992b]); physicians' other didactics are relevant to prescribing and their lengthy supervised training across a continuum of settings and supervisors includes wide exposure to related topics and patient populations.

By the time psychologists obtain doctorates, most have obtained relatively little training that overlaps with that of physicians or other prescribers. Moreover, there are no objective quality assurance processes to ensure that the biological and physical sciences are well understood by entrants to psychology graduate school or by entrants to proposed postdoctoral psychopharmacology training programs. Even the Examination for the Professional Practice of Psychology (EPPP), the written test required for licensure in psychology, minimally queries knowledge of the biological and physical sciences (e.g., biochemistry) (Association of State and Provincial Psychology Boards, 2000).

Proposed Postdoctoral Level Psychopharmacology Training

. . . The APA (CoR, 1996) emphasizes that the proposed training is "unique to the needs of the practicing psychologist, and does not simply follow traditional medical practices." We question whether such condensed training overcomes current shortcomings to achieve knowledge and clinical proficiency equivalent to that of other prescribers, especially psychiatrists, and ensure competent prescribing that the public should reasonably expect of its doctors. Furthermore, it seems incumbent upon proponents of the prescriptive agenda to fully inform legislators and the public precisely how the psychopharmacology training proposed by the APA differs from "traditional medical practices." . . .

Proponents of prescription privileges recognize that the supervised practice in proposed psychopharmacology training "essential for effective, safe, ethical and practical incorporation of drugs into a psychological practice . . . is a substantive matter" (Fox et al., 1992, p. 218). Curiously, despite recognition of this substantiveness, the scope and requirements for supervised pharmacotherapeutic practice are not fully delineated in the APA model, so it is not possible to evaluate how adequate the supervised practice would be. Consistent with the APA model, training programs are designed for trainees to see a series of patients (e.g., ≥ 100) for psychopharmacologic management. The APA model fails to specify minimal criteria for (a) the breadth of patients' mental health conditions; (b) the duration of treatment (i.e., to allow for adequate monitoring and feedback) or requirements for outpatient or inpatient experiences; (c) exposure to adverse medication effects; or (d) exposure to patients with comorbid medical conditions and complex drug regimens. Also, the qualifications for supervisors are vague. Whereas the CPA-CSPP Panel (1995) recommended an 18-month practicum, the APA model does not specify any length. That the didactic and practical training would be abbreviated relative to the PDP, and less likely to occur in organized, academic health care settings with lengthy track records of providing medical or psychiatric training, raises questions about how comparable such programs would be to the PDP.

We doubt that the proposed models of training in psychopharmacology for psychologists (APA, 1996; CPA/CSPP, 1995; Fox et al., 1992) would prepare them to provide care equivalent to that provided by psychiatrists or other health professionals. Not only would they obtain less didactics in relevant areas, but the supervised pharmacologic care of patients would be considerably less comprehensive and less well organized than training within psychiatric residencies. . . .

Regulatory and Legal Issues

. . . A number of legal issues also would arise if psychologists were granted prescriptive authority. This includes the level of independence versus dependence of this authority, potential restrictions on their prescriptive practices (e.g., limited formulary and duration of treatment; specific settings), and the most appropriate standard of care to which psychologists would be held. Would psychologists be compared with other "reasonably prudent" psychologists who have undergone the proposed psychopharmacology training, or with other prescribers, such as psychiatrists, who have greater training and experience related to medication management and who have set the standard for prescribing psychoactive medications thus far? From the consumer's perspective, it seems likely that a standard of care closer to that provided by psychiatrists would promote accountability and afford greater protections and legal remedies than an unknown, less stringent, evolving standard based on psychologists who might gain prescriptive authority based on training that is less intensive than that of other prescribers. In addition, formulation of ethical guidelines relevant to prescribing, which are beyond the current APA (1992a) Ethical Principles of Psychologists and Code of Conduct, would be needed (Buelow & Chafetz, 1996) to address a range of ethical challenges associated with prescribing (Heiby, 1998).

Proponents' Focus on Peripheral Issues

In essentially waging a campaign for prescriptive authority, proponents tend to focus on certain provocative issues to promote their cause and divert attention away from the inadequacies in psychologists' education, knowledge, and skills in areas critical to prescribing. For example, DeLeon and Wiggins (1996) decry problems of current prescribers as if psychologists (who would have less extensive physical science backgrounds and more limited supervised prescriptive practical training) would avoid developing problematic patterns if they prescribe. Alternative strategies, such as enhancing the ability of current prescribers through such means as education and redesign of prescribing systems (Lesar, Briceland, & Stein, 1997), or enhancing psychologists' collaborative practices, as proposed in the APA task force's (Smyer et al., 1993) Level 2 training, might address such problems without requiring that psychologists prescribe.

Similarly, underserved populations (e.g., rural populations, the seriously and persistently mentally ill [SPMI], the elderly) have been invoked to frame prescriptive authority as a policy response to meet pressing societal needs (DeLeon, Sammons, & Sexton, 1995; Hanson et al., 1999). This line of reasoning is flawed in failing to consider the similar access patterns to psychologists and psychiatrists across the urban-rural continuum (Hendryx, Borders, & Johnson, 1995; Holzer, Goldsmith, & Ciarlo, 1998) and the APA task force's expectation that only "a small . . . minority of psychologists" (APA, 1992b, p. 106) would seek Level 3 psychopharmacology training. Such data and predictions, along with the virtual absence of any concrete plan to redistribute prescribing psychologists to meet the actual needs of underserved populations (May & Belsky, 1992), render broadening psychologists' scope of practice to include prescriptive authority an indirect, needlessly risky, and highly inefficient public policy response to rural areas' shortage of psychopharmacologic prescribers. . . .

Ultimately, there is little reason to assume that psychologists with prescriptive authority actually would relocate to areas lacking other prescribers, or would focus their practices to address the needs of other types of underserved populations (Adams & Bieliauskas, 1994; Bieliauskas, 1992a, 1992b). Even some proponents of prescriptive privileges concede that psychologists may not be more inclined than psychiatrists to work with underserved groups (Hanson et al., 1999).

Attempts to garner support for the prescriptive agenda on the basis of underserved populations also ignores efforts by the American Psychiatric Association to enhance psychiatric consultation to primary care providers ("APA board takes action," 1998) and the potential benefits of expanded use of telehealth technology to supplement the expertise of primary care practitioners in areas underserved by psychiatrists. Similarly, it ignores data that psychiatrists see significantly more SPMI and socially disadvantaged patients than do psychologists (Olfson & Pincus, 1996), which brings into question whether prescriptive authority would have a major impact in expanding care to SPMI populations. Pursuing prescriptive authority may distract focus from important opportunities for psychologists to improve their collaborations with primary care providers to collectively address needs as suggested by groups such as the National Depressive and Manic-Depressive Association (Hirschfeld et al., 1977) or the National Alliance for the Mentally Ill (NAMI). . . .

Another rationale of proponents of prescription privileges is that many mental health services, including prescriptions of psychotropic medications, are provided by nonpsychiatric physicians who have little psychiatric training (DeLeon & Wiggins, 1996). Indeed, the general medical sector is an essential component of the mental health system, serving an estimated 40–50% of people with mental disorders according to the utilization data of the Epidemiologic Catchment Area (ECA) study (Narrow, Regier, Rae, Manderscheid, & Locke, 1993). Similarly, data from the National Ambulatory Medicare Care Survey (NAMCS) reveal that outpatient appointments with primary care physicians and medical specialists account respectively for 48% and 19% of all appointments involving psychoactive prescription drugs: More than the appointments with psychiatrists (33%) (Pincus et al., 1998). General physicians provide somewhat more of the nation's outpatient mental health services (35%) than either psychologists (31%) or psychiatrists (27%) (Olfson & Pincus, 1996).

According to DeLeon and Wiggins (1996), an estimated 135.8 million prescriptions for psychoactive medications were written in 1991, of which only 17.3% were by psychiatrists. Such statistics, albeit interesting, do *not* indicate how many of these physician interactions for prescriptions are enhanced by consultations involving psychiatrists, psychologists, or other mental health professionals, or how many truly need mental health consultation. There are no benchmarks for how many prescriptions nonpsychiatric physicians should write or what percentage of them ought to be informed by collaborations with mental health professionals. It is possible that the large number of prescriptions written by nonpsychiatric physicians reflect that consultation with mental health professionals may be necessary only for subgroups of patients, or that adequate consultation already occurs related to many patients who might need medication. Moreover, despite focus on such patterns (DeLeon & Wiggins, 1996), the numbers neither reveal anything about problematic patterns of prescribing by physicians nor do they persuade that psychologists should prescribe. They probably do reflect several factors, such as (1) some people are more comfortable seeing their primary care physician than a mental health professional (Geller & Muus, 1997; Murstein & Fontaine, 1993), and (2) managed care organizations and capitated systems encourage primary care physicians to treat mental disorders rather than refer to specialist mental health professionals (Pincus et al., 1998). Such systems of health care delivery are similar to the service delivery models in other countries (e.g., Great Britain), where lower per capita rates of psychiatrists reflect psychiatrists' roles as specialist consultants to nonpsychiatric physicians who play primary roles in the psychopharmacological management of most patients' care (Scully, 1999).

The widespread prescription of psychoactive agents by nonpsychiatrist physicians reflects the significant opportunities for psychiatrists and psychologists (especially those with Level 2 training) to collaborate and consult about psychopharmacology. The data confirm the importance of continuing the ongoing efforts to enhance psychopharmacology training of nonpsychiatric physicians and other prescribers. Such trends do not, however, indicate a need or justification for psychologists to prescribe.

Medication Adverse Effects and Errors

Prescribers even of limited formularies necessarily assume some responsibility for the broader health status of their patients (Heiby, 1998; Kingsbury, 1992). Psychoactive medications have been described as presenting more complex drug interactions and adverse effects than any other class of drug (Hayes, 1998). Many people who take psychoactive medications also take other medications that complicate their care. Fewer than 30% who take an antidepressant take no other medications, so it is important to understand the comorbid conditions and other medications that patients concurrently experience (Preskorn, 1999). In primary care and psychiatric settings, more than 70% of patients prescribed an antidepressant take at least one other drug and a third take at least three other drugs (Preskorn, 1999). Polypharmacy rates are often higher with the elderly and medically ill, and in more specialized clinics (e.g., HIV). . . .

The timing of the intensification of psychologists' lobbying for prescriptive authority is ironic in light of growing national concern about errors in prescribing medication (Classen, Pestotnik, Evans, Lloyd, & Burke, 1997). Nationally, medication errors are estimated to lead to as many as 7,000 deaths annually (Phillips, Christenfeld, & Glynn, 1998). The Federal Drug Administration currently receives 235,000 reports per year about adverse drug events (Institute of Medicine Committee on Quality of Health Care in America, 1999). This could increase as medication options expand, requiring constant upgrades in knowledge of the entire pharmaceutical spectrum. In 1998, the FDA approved 90 new drugs, 30 new molecular entities, 124 new or expanded use of agents, and 344 generic drugs, not counting over the counter and orphan drugs (FDA, 1999). That nearly half of the drugs currently marketed have become available in the last decade (Shatin, Gardner, & Stergachis, 1999) suggests that the knowledge base for prescribing is becoming even more complex, requiring yet more extensive scientific understanding. Between 1970 and 1997, the annual number of publications on drug-drug interactions increased fivefold (Preskorn, 1999), reflecting factors such as increased use of medications for chronic conditions and an aging society with more medical problems and more complex medication regimens. Such trends underscore the need for strong basic education in medicine and pharmacology to prepare prescribers to understand medical conditions in integrating pharmacologic developments into their practice.

Among the many contributing factors to medication errors are *inadequate knowledge* and use of knowledge regarding drug therapy and *inadequate recognition* of important patient factors (e.g., impaired renal function, drug allergies) (Lesar et al., 1997). The influence of other factors that require more sophisticated scientific understanding, such as genetic variation in drug metabolism and uptake, is increasingly likely to affect prescribing. Along with other recommendations, Lesar et al. (1997) recommended *improved prescriber education.* There have not been calls from outside of psychology to create a new category of prescribers with relatively *less* training (as psychologist prescribers would be).

Given the paucity of education and training directly related to prescribing throughout undergraduate and graduate training in psychology (Robiner et al., 2001), the scant data about psychologists' proficiency in managing medications, which is limited to relatively few individuals, as well as inadequacies in psychologists' knowledge related to psychopharmacology (Robiner et al., 2001), we doubt that abbreviated psychopharmacology training for psychologists would be sufficient to ensure adequate competence in prescribing. Moreover, we are concerned that psychologists would lack the medical expertise to recognize, assess (e.g., all relevant hematological assays), and understand adverse effects and initiate proper medical care.

Short cuts in education seem likely to undermine patient care and contribute to medication errors along the patterns outlined by Lesar et al. (1997). Such training, especially if paired with independent prescriptive authority, risks generating a wave of suboptimal medication management and potentially avoidable adverse drug events. In addition to potentially hazardous consequences for patients, problems associated with psychologist prescribing would present regulatory conundrums, provide a new basis for litigation, and ultimately could detract from the public's esteem of psychologists in general.

Closing Considerations

We appreciate the important roles psychologists play within the delivery of health care broadly and mental health care in particular. Our findings and conclusions in no way belittle psychologists' knowledge or proficiencies in other areas. We agree with the APA task force (APA, 1992b) that it would be beneficial to promote psychologists' psychopharmacology knowledge so as to inform and enhance their collaborations with primary care providers and psychiatrists in providing care to patients who need medications. However, achieving the APA task force's goals for enhancing the care of patients needing medications does not require prescriptive authority for psychologists. Instead, we recommend that the APA refocus its energies to better educate psychologists about psychopharmacology to enhance the psychological services that psychologists provide and their collaborations with prescribers. This is a type of training that most psychology graduate students need and would welcome (Tatman et al., 1997). Also, survey data suggest that most (90%) licensed psychologists feel that psychologists should pursue a minimum of the collaborative practice level of training and most (79%) would be personally willing to pursue it (Ferguson, 1997). Moreover, most (85%) applied psychologists already consult regularly with physicians, so such training would enhance services that already are provided (Barkley, 1991).

Unfortunately, if psychologists prescribe, medically complex patients (e.g., older patients taking multiple medications) would probably be most vulnerable to the adverse consequences that potentially could derive from shortcomings in psychologists' scientific and medical training (Hayes & Heiby, 1996; Klein, 1996). Promoting psychologists' collaborative practices with prescribers rather than psychologists' prescription privileges would preclude new risks to patients associated with a potentially suboptimal level of care. Collaboration would avoid further confusion about psychologists' identities (Ax et al., 1997), skills, scope of practice, and the differentiation between psychology and psychiatry (Murstein & Fontaine, 1993; Wood, Jones, & Benjamin, 1986). . . .

As psychologists, educators of psychologists, and related health professionals, the authors have actively supported psychology's many other advances (e.g., Medicare reimbursement, licensure, provision of nonpharmacologic interventions), including appropriate, innovative roles of psychologists in health care (Schofield, 1969). We caution against framing the debate about prescription privileges as a chapter in the saga of struggles between psychology and psychiatry (DeLeon & Wiggins, 1996). Rather, at its core it is a controversy about the education and training necessary to promote safe and effective treatment that limits unnecessary risks to patients.

We have doubts that the shortcomings in psychologists' education and knowledge related to prescribing can be surmounted through abbreviated training, such as that currently advocated by the APA. Our skepticism that these gaps can be overcome within such a shorter time frame than is involved in the training of other prescribers leads us to urge psychologists to resist the temptation to venture into aspects of health care (i.e., prescribing and its related clinical activities) for which they would not be well-prepared. As legislators and regulators are lobbied about psychologists prescriptive privileges agenda, they need to weigh judiciously any hoped-for benefits against the potential risks associated with the inadequacies in psychologists' preparation to prescribe, even after they may have obtained the psychopharmacology training in accordance with the model recommended by the APA (CoR, 1996).

Acknowledgment

The authors appreciatively acknowledge the editorial guidance and other contributions of William Schofield, PhD, and Irving I. Gottesman, PhD, in the preparation of this article.

References

Adams, K. M., & Bieliauskas, L. A. (1994). On perhaps becoming what you had previously despised: Psychologists as prescribers of medication. *Journal of Clinical Psychology in Medical Settings, 1,* 189–197.

American College of Neuropsychopharmacology. (1998, May). *Final report: DoD prescribing psychologists: External analysis, monitoring, and evaluation of the program and its participants.* Nashville, TN: Author.

American Psychological Association. (1992a). Ethical principles of psychologists and code of conduct. *American Psychologist, 47,* 1597–1611.

American Psychological Association (1992b). *Report of the ad hoc task force on psychopharmacology.* Washington, DC: Author.

American Psychological Association. (1996). *Model legislation for prescriptive authority.* Washington, DC: Author.

APA board takes action to provide consult services in certain areas. (1998, April 17). *Psychiatric News,* 2.

Association for Medical School Pharmacology. (1990, October). *Knowledge objectives in medical pharmacology* (2nd edition). Author.

Association of State and Provincial Psychology Boards. (2000). Psychology Licensure Exam (EPPP). Available online at www.asppb.org/eppp.htm#content.

Ax, R. K., Forbes, M. R., & Thompson, D. D. (1997). Prescription privileges for psychologists: A survey of predoctoral interns and directors of training. *Professional Psychology: Research and Practice, 28,* 509–513.

Barkley, R. A. (1991, Spring). Health Services Committee: Prescribing privileges for health psychologists: Implications from the Clinical Child Psychology Task Force. *Health Psychologist, 13*(1), 2.

Bieliauskas, L. A. (1992a). Prescription privileges for psychologists? Reality orientation for proponents. *Physical Medicine and Rehabilitation: State of the Art Reviews, 6,* 587–595.

Bieliauskas, L. A. (1992b). Rebuttal of Dr. Frank's position. *Physical Medicine and Rehabilitation: State of the Art Reviews, 6,* 584.

Brentar, J., & McNamara, J. R. (1991a). Prescription privileges for psychology: The next step in its evolution as a profession. *Professional Psychology: Research and Practice, 22,* 194–195.

Brentar, J., & McNamara, J. R. (1991b). The right to prescribe medication: Considerations for professional psychology. *Professional Psychology: Research and Practice, 22,* 179–187.

Buelow, G. D., & Chafetz, M. D. (1996). Proposed ethical practice guidelines for clinical pharmacopsychology: Sharpening a new focus in psychology. *Professional Psychology: Research and Practice, 27,* 53–58.

Burns, S. M., DeLeon, P. H., Chemtob, C. M., Welch, B. L., & Samuels, R. M. (1988). Psychotropic medication: A new technique for psychology? *Psychotherapy, 25,* 508–515.

Bütz, M. R. (1994). Psychopharmacology: Psychology's Jurassic Park? *Psychotherapy, 31,* 692–699.

California Psychological Association, Professional Education Task Force, California School of Professional Psychology. (1995, January). *Report of the Blue Ribbon Panel.* Los Angeles: Author.

Classen, D. C., Pestotnik, S. L., Evans, S., Lloyd, J. F., & Burke, J. P. (1997). Adverse drug events in hospitalized patients: Excess length of stay, extra costs, and attributable mortality. *Journal of the American Medical Association, 277,* 301–306.

Council of Representatives, American Psychological Association. (1996). *Recommended postdoctoral training in psychopharmacology for prescription privileges.* Washington, DC: Author.

Cullen, E. A., & Newman, R. (1997). In pursuit of prescription privileges. *Professional Psychology: Research and Practice, 28,* 101–106.

DeLeon, P. H., Folen, R. A., Jennings, F. L., Wilkis, D. J., & Wright, R. H. (1991). The case for prescription privileges: A logical evolution of professional practice. *Journal of Clinical Child Psychology, 20,* 254–267.

DeLeon, P. H., Fox, R. E., & Graham, S. R. (1991). Prescription privileges: Psychology's next frontier? *American Psychologist, 46,* 384–393.

DeLeon, P. H., Sammons, M. T., & Sexton, J. L. (1995). Focusing on society's real needs: Responsibility and prescription privileges? *American Psychologist, 50,* 1022–1032.

DeLeon, P. H., & Wiggins, J. (1996). Prescription privileges for psychologists. *American Psychologist, 51,* 225–229.

DeMers, S. (1994). Legal and ethical issues in school psychologists' participation in psychopharmacological interventions with children. *School Psychology Quarterly, 9,* 41–52.

Ferguson, V. V. (1997). *Prescription privileges for psychologists: A study of rural and urban licensed psychologists' opinions.* Unpublished doctoral dissertation, University of South Dakota, Vermillion, SD.

Food and Drug Administration. (1999, May). *Managing the risks from medical product use, Creating a risk management framework.* Report to the FDA Commissioner from the Task Force on Risk Management, U.S. Department of Health and Human Services. Washington, DC: Author.

Fox, R. E. (1988). Prescription privileges: Their implications for the practice of psychology. *Psychotherapy, 25,* 501–507.

Fox, R. E., Schwelitz, F. D., & Barclay, A. G. (1992). A proposed curriculum for psychopharmacology training for professional psychologists. *Professional Psychology: Research and Practice, 23,* 216–219.

Geller, J. M., & Muus, K. J. (1997). *The role of rural primary care physicians in the provision of mental health services* (Letter to the Field No. 5). Frontier Mental Health Services Resource Network. Available online at www.du.edu/frontier-mh/letter5.html.

Hanson, K. M., Louie, C. E., Van Male, L. M., Pugh, A. O., Karl, C., Muhlenbrook, L., Lilly, R. L., & Hagglund, K. J. (1999). Involving the future: The need to consider the views of psychologists-in-training regarding prescription privileges for psychologists. *Professional Psychology: Research and Practice, 30,* 203–208.

Hayes, G. J. (1998). Diving into the chemical soup. In S. C. Hayes & E. M. Heiby (Eds.), *Prescription privileges for psychologists: A critical appraisal.* Reno, NV: Context Press.

Hayes, S. C., & Heiby, E. (1996). Psychology's drug problem: Do we need a fix or should we just say no? *American Psychologist, 51,* 198–206.

Heiby, E. (1998). The case against prescription privileges for psychologists: An overview. In S. C. Hayes & E. M. Heiby (Eds.), *Prescription privileges for psychologists: A critical appraisal.* Reno, NV: Context Press.

Hendryx, M. S., Borders, T., & Johnson, T. (1995). The distribution of mental health providers in a rural state. *Administration and Policy in Mental Health, 23,* 153–155.

Hirschfeld, R. M., Keller, M. B., Panico, S., Arons, B. S., Barlow, D., Davidoff, F., Endicott, J., Froom, J., Goldstein, M., Gorman, J. M., Guthrie, D., Marek, R. G., Maurer, T. A., Meyer, R., Phillips, K., Ross, J., Schwenk, T. L., Sharfstein, S. S., Thase, M. E., & Wyatt, R. J. (1997): The National Depressive and Manic-Depressive Association consensus statement on the undertreatment of depression. *Journal of the American Medical Association, 277,* 333–340.

Holzer, C. E., III, Goldsmith, H. F., & Ciarlo, J. A. (1998). Effects of rural-urban county type on the availability of health and mental health care providers. In R. W. Manderscheid & M. J. Henderson (Eds.), *Mental health, United States* (pp. 204–213). Rockville, MD: U.S. Department of Health and Human Services.

Institute of Medicine Committee on Quality of Health Care in America. (1999). In L. T. Kohn, J. M. Corrigan, & M. S. Donaldson (Eds.), *To err is human: Building a safer health system*. Washington, DC: National Academy Press.

Kennedy, J. (1998, April 3). Prescription privileges for psychologists: A view from the field. *Psychiatric News, 33*(7), 26.

Kingsbury, S. J. (1992). Some effects of prescribing privileges. *Professional Psychology: Research and Practice, 23*, 3–5.

Klein, R. (1996). Comments on expanding the clinical role of psychologists. *American Psychologist, 5*, 216–218.

Klusman, L. E. (1998). Military health care providers' views on prescribing privileges for psychologists. *Professional Psychology: Research and Practice, 29*, 223–229.

Lesar, T. S., Briceland, L., & Stein, D. S. (1997). Factors related to errors in medication prescribing. *Journal of the American Medical Association, 277*, 312–317.

Matthews, W. J. (1998, March 23). In opposition to prescription privileges for psychologists. GO Inside. Available online at http://goinside.com/98/3/oppose.html.

May, W. T., & Belsky, J. (1992). Response to "Prescription privileges: Psychology's next frontier?" or the siren call: Should psychologists medicate? *American Psychologist, 47*, 427.

Moyer, D. (1995). An opposing view on prescription privileges for psychologists. *Professional Psychology: Research and Practice, 26*, 586–590.

Murstein, B. I., & Fontaine P. A. (1993). The public's knowledge about psychologists and other mental health professionals. *American Psychologist, 7*, 838–845.

Narrow, W. E., Regier, D. A., Rae, D. S., Manderscheid, R. W., & Locke, B. Z. (1993). Use of services by persons with mental and addictive disorders: Findings from the National Institute of Mental Health Epidemiologic Catchment Area Program. *Archives of General Psychiatry, 50*, 95–107.

Office of Program Consultation and Accreditation, American Psychological Association. (1996). *Book 1: Guidelines and principles for accreditation of programs in professional psychology*. Washington, DC: Author.

Olfson, M., & Pincus, H. A. (1996). Outpatient mental health care in nonhospital settings: Distribution of patients across provider groups. *American Journal of Psychiatry, 153*, 1353–1356.

Pachman, J. S. (1996). The dawn of a revolution in mental health. *American Psychologist, 51*, 213–215.

Phillips, D. P., Christenfeld, N., & Glynn, L. M. (1998). Increase in US medication-error deaths between 1983 and 1993. *Lancet, 351*, 643–644.

Pies, R. W. (1991). The "deep structure" of clinical medicine and prescribing privileges for psychologists. *Journal of Clinical Psychiatry, 52*, 4–8.

Pincus, H. A., Tanielian, T. L., Marcus, S. C., Olfson, M., Zarin, D. A., Thompson, J., & Zito, J. M. (1998). Prescribing trends in psychotropic medications: Primary care, psychiatry, and other medical specialties. *Journal of the American Medical Association, 279*, 526–531.

Preskorn, S. H. (1999). *Outpatient management of depression: A guide for the practitioner* (2nd ed.). Caddo, OK: Professional Communications, Inc.

Roan, S. (1993, September 7). Tug-of-war over prescription powers; health: Pharmacists, nurses and other non-doctors want the authority to prescribe drugs. Others insist only physicians have the training to do so safely. *Los Angeles Times*, Part E, 1, 6.

Robiner, W. N. (1999, May). Why psychologists should not pursue prescription privileges. In J. Boyd, M. Chesney, R. Kollmorgen, J. L. Raymond, W. Robiner, & J. Boller, *Prescriptive authority for psychologists: Pros and cons*. Annual Meeting of the Minnesota Psychological Association, Minneapolis.

Robiner, W. N., Bearman, D. L., Berman, M., Grove, W., Colón, E., Armstrong, J., Mareck, S., & Tanenbaum, R. (2001). *Prescriptive authority for psychologists: Despite deficits in education and knowledge?* Manuscript submitted for publication.

Sammons, M. T. (1994). Prescription privileges and psychology: A reply to Adams and Bieliauskas. *Journal of Clinical Psychology in Medical Settings, 1,* 199–207.

Sammons, M. T., & Brown, A. B. (1997). The Department of Defense Psychopharmacology Demonstration Project: An evolving program for postdoctoral education in psychology. *Professional Psychology: Research and Practice, 28,* 107–112.

Sammons, M. T., Sexton, J. L., & Meredith, J. M. (1996). Basic science training in psychopharmacology: How much is enough? *American Psychologist, 51,* 230–234.

Schofield, W. (1969). The role of psychology in the delivery of health services. *American Psychologist, 24,* 565–584.

Scully, J. H., Jr. (1999). The psychiatric workforce. In S. Weissman, M. Sabshin, & H. Eist (Eds.), *Psychiatry in the new millennium* (pp. 273–283). Washington, DC: American Psychiatric Press.

Shatin, D., Gardner, J., & Stergachis, A. (1999). Letter. *Journal of the American Medical Association, 281*(4), 319–320.

Smyer, M. A., Balster, R. L., Egli, D., Johnson, D. L., Kilbey, M. M., Leith, N. J., & Puente, A. E. (1993). Summary of the report of the Ad Hoc Task Force on Psychopharmacology of the American Psychological Association. *Professional Psychology: Research and Practice, 24,* 394–403.

Tatman, S. M., Peters, D. B., Greene, A. L., & Bongar, B. (1997). Graduate students' attitudes toward prescription privileges training. *Professional Psychology: Research and Practice, 28,* 515–517.

U.S. General Accounting Office. (1999). *Prescribing psychologists: DOD demonstration participants perform well but have little effect on readiness or costs: Report to the Chairman and Ranking Minority Member, Committee on Armed Services, U.S. Senate.* Washington, DC: Author.

Wood, W., Jones, M., & Benjamin, L. T., Jr. (1986). Surveying psychology's public image. *American Psychologist, 41,* 947–953.

Zimmerman, M. A., & Wienckowski, L. A. (1991). Revisiting health and mental health linkages: A policy whose time has come . . . again. *Journal of Public Health Policy, 12,* 510–524.

CHALLENGE QUESTIONS

Should Psychologists Prescribe Medication?

1. Imagine that you are suffering from an intense degree of anxiety or depression for which medication has been shown to be an effective intervention. From whom would you want to seek a prescription, and what factors would influence your choice?
2. An argument has been made that giving psychologists the right to prescribe medications would address the fact that there are many regions in which prescribing mental health professionals are not available. Discuss the strengths and weaknesses of this argument.
3. In recent years, increased attention has been given to the aggressive marketing of psychotropic medications. Of particular concern are practices in which physicians are lavishly indulged with gifts or expensive dinners in order to "learn about" a pharmaceutical company's product. Discuss the ethical issues involved in such practices, and consider ways in which objectionable marketing practices could be changed.
4. Imagine that you are a researcher with a grant to evaluate effectiveness and satisfaction associated with psychologists being given prescription privileges. What factors would go into designing a study on this topic?
5. Consider the fact that the majority of prescriptions for mental health conditions are written by nonpsychiatric physicians. Discuss the benefits and problems associated with this practice.

Suggested Readings

Gutierrez, P. M., & Silk, K. R. (1998). Prescription privileges for psychologists: A review of the psychological literature. *Professional Psychology: Research and Practice, 29*, 213–222.

Hayes, S. C., & Heiby, E. M. (eds.). (1998). *Prescription Privileges for Psychologists: A Critical Appraisal*. Reno, NV: Context Press.

Hobson, J. A., & Leonard, J. A. (2001). *Out of Its Mind: Psychiatry in Crisis*. Boston: Perseus.

Johnstone, L. (2003). Back to basics. *The Psychologist, 16*(4), 186–7.

Sternberg, R. J. (2001). Prescription privileges for psychologists: A view from academe. *The California Psychologist, 34*(10), 16–17.

ISSUE 14

Is Electroconvulsive Therapy Ethical?

YES: Max Fink, from *Electroshock: Restoring the Mind* (Oxford University Press, 1999)

NO: Leonard R. Frank, from "Shock Treatment IV: Resistance in the 1990s," in Robert F. Morgan, ed., *Electroshock: The Case Against* (Morgan Foundation, 1999)

ISSUE SUMMARY

YES: Physician Max Fink asserts that electroconvulsive therapy (ECT) is an effective intervention whose use has been limited as a result of social stigma and philosophical bias, which have been reinforced by intimidation from the pharmaceutical and managed care industries.

NO: Leonard R. Frank, editor and cofounder of the Network Against Psychiatric Assault, criticizes the use of ECT because of its disturbing side effects, some of which he personally has suffered, and asserts that its resurgence in popularity is economically based.

For more than six decades some psychiatrists have treated their patients with electroconvulsive therapy (ECT), an extreme intervention involving the administration of an electric shock with the aim of controlling disturbing emotional and behavioral symptoms. Most commonly used in cases of debilitating depression, ECT consists of a treatment in which electric shock is applied through electrodes attached to the head. The premise of ECT is that radical alterations in the brain's chemistry stimulate beneficial changes in neurons, thus reducing certain kinds of symptoms. ECT grew in popularity among American psychiatrists during the 1940s and 1950s, but so did criticisms of this procedure because it was so often abused as a means of disciplining and controlling disruptive patients in psychiatric hospitals. As a result of considerable controversy surrounding ECT, the method became infrequently used by the 1970s. In recent years, however, there has been renewed interest in this intervention, which some experts regard as an effective and efficient option, especially for severely symptomatic individuals who do not respond to medication or psychotherapy.

In the following selection, Max Fink asserts that ECT is an effective intervention whose use has been limited as a result of social stigma and philosophical bias against it. Fink views ECT as a safe treatment that has been demonstrated to be effective with a range of psychiatric disorders, including severe depression, mania, schizophrenia, and catatonia. In trying to explain the reluctance of American psychiatrists to recommend ECT, Fink contends that they are intimidated by the pharmaceutical industry, managed care companies, and political forces that have underfunded psychiatric care and research.

In the second selection, Leonard R. Frank speaks against ECT as a former patient who was given extensive treatments with ECT and its predecessor, insulin-induced coma treatments. Expressing alarm about the resurgence of ECT, he criticizes claims that it is effective and safe, and he contends that its current popularity is economically based. Highlighting a number of disturbing side effects, some of which he personally suffered, Frank speaks about this method as one that destroys "the memories and lives of those subjected to it."

POINT

- ECT is a safe and reliable form of treatment.

- ECT is not as widely used as it should be, because psychiatrists are intimidated by the pharmaceutical industry, managed care companies, and political forces that have underfunded psychiatric care and research.

- The antidepressant effects of ECT occur earlier and are more robust than those of antidepressant drugs.

- It is shameful that many agencies that are licensed to treat the mentally ill lack the facilities to give ECT.

- Many criticisms about ECT are based on references to problems that were associated with ECT when it was first introduced, which are wholly unwarranted today because modern practice has made ECT safe.

COUNTERPOINT

- The serious risks associated with ECT are consistently understated and overlooked.

- The increase in ECT, particularly in the psychiatric wards of general hospitals, has been due in part to the fact that costs are paid for by insurance companies, causing some hospitals to reap considerable financial benefits from their use of ECT.

- After 50 years of research on ECT, no methodologically sound study has shown beneficial effects of ECT lasting as long as four weeks.

- ECT is one of the most controversial treatments in psychiatry, and it has great potential for destroying the memories and lives of those who are subjected to it.

- The side effects associated with ECT are very serious and include amnesia, denial, euphoria, apathy, wide mood swings, helplessness, and submissiveness—effects that offset the problems that supposedly justified the use of ECT in the first place.

239

Max Fink

YES

Electroshock in the 1990s

Within the past decade, clinical and research interest in ECT [electro-convulsive therapy] has revived. The resurgence has been most marked in the United States, where the greatest efforts are under way to improve its safety and its efficacy. Psychiatrists in other countries have sought to reintroduce ECT, but its use varies widely. ECT is an accepted part of psychiatric practice in the Scandinavian countries, Great Britain, Ireland, Australia, and New Zealand, and usage is similar to that in the United States. A stigma attached to ECT limits its use in Germany, Japan, Italy, and the Netherlands to a few academic medical centers. Low reimbursement rates hamper its use in Canada and Japan, and also affect its availability in the United States. The unavailability of modern equipment and the expense of the medicines for anesthesia prevent its use in Africa, Asia, and Eastern Europe, and many patients in these countries who do receive it are subjected to unmodified ECT, such as was delivered in the 1930s and 1940s.

ECT is mainly a treatment for hospitalized patients, although many institutions are developing programs for outpatient ECT. The equipment and trained personnel are, for the most part, in the academic hospitals. Academic leaders recognize the merits of the treatment; some even encourage research and teaching. ECT is ignored by the research scientists at the National Institute of Mental Health. Few of the state, federal, or Veterans Administration hospitals provide ECT, and where it is available its use is infrequent. While 8 percent to 12 percent of adult inpatients at academic hospitals receive ECT, fewer than 0.2 percent of adults at nonacademic centers do. Such a discrepancy reflects the continuing social stigma and philosophical bias against electroshock. Before the federal Medicare and the Hill-Burton legislative acts of the 1960s opened access for all patients to any hospital facility, such discrepancies may have been common. But now that the nation has adopted an open-admission policy to its psychiatric facilities, the discrepancy is unjustified. It is shameful that many agencies licensed to treat the mentally ill lack the facilities to give the treatment.

Effects of Research on Practice

When ECT was revived in the late 1970s, the principal concern was its effects on cognition and memory. Unilateral ECT won favor with many practitioners

From ELECTROSHOCK: RESTORING THE MIND by Max Fink. Copyright © 1999 by Max Fink, M.D. Used by permission of Oxford University Press, Inc.

after demonstrations that it reduced effects on memory. But other practitioners reported that unilateral ECT required more treatments than, and was not as effective as, bilateral ECT. The seizures in unilateral ECT were often brief, with poorly defined EEG seizure patterns. Studies of the interaction of electrode placement, energy dosing, and current form show that unilateral treatments, even with precise energy dosing, are less efficient than bilateral ECT. As a result, bilateral ECT is now preferred. When unilateral ECT is considered, its use includes precise energy dosing. Sinusoidal currents elicited unnecessarily high degrees of EEG and memory effects, compared with brief pulse square-wave currents, so the former have now been discarded.

We have learned that monitoring the motor seizure is not sufficient to measure the adequacy of an individual treatment, so we now look to EEG measures as more reliable indices. By recording and displaying the seizure EEG, we rely on the seizure characteristics as a guide to an effective treatment. Practitioners depend more on these characteristics than on criteria based on the motor convulsion and the change in heart rate as measures of beneficial treatment.

The interseizure EEG has stimulated research interest. Studies in 1957 had shown that a good clinical response in ECT depended on the slowing of the frequencies in the interseizure EEG. The observation was confirmed in 1972 and again in 1996, and the interseizure EEG is once again used as a guide to an effective course of treatment.

The indications for ECT have been broadened. As we have seen, it has gone from being a last resort for unresponsive depressed and suicidal patients to being a treatment option for patients with delusional depression, mania, schizophrenia, and catatonia. ECT can also be useful in patients with parkinsonism and those suffering from neuroleptic drug toxicity. Treatment can be safely given in the presence of complex systemic disorders and mental retardation.

Yet research on ECT is limited. Most of the research is directed at determining which treatment—medication or continuation ECT—can best maintain the benefits of a course of ECT in patients with severe depression. Some scientists still believe that sophisticated brain-imaging methods will find evidence of persistent brain dysfunction after ECT. So far, such studies have yielded no new information about mental illness or about ECT. Others seek the benefits of ECT without a seizure by the use of rapid magnetic pulses instead of electrical ones. The method, called "rapid transcranial magnetic stimulation" (rTMS), has yet to be proven of benefit.

Future of Electroshock

Psychiatric care in the United States is in such turmoil that the problem of restoring the availability of electroshock seems nearly insignificant. American psychiatry lacks the leaders to stand up to the pharmaceutical industry and the managed care executives who are taking ever larger portions of the financial resources allocated to treating mental illness. State legislatures are cutting funds for mental health care, urging their mental hospital administrators to reduce patient admissions and shorten durations of stay. The state mental hospitals, which served as the ultimate haven for the mentally ill, are being closed and patients are being consigned to a motley collection of inadequate substitutions. The nonthreatening and passive homeless are on the streets; those who are more ill go in and out of the revolving doors of community centers and emergency wards or to hospitals equipped only for short-term care. Those who fall between end up in halfway houses and adult homes.

At one time the states supported research centers that were the jewels of the nation's mental health activities. Few institutes are still supported by the states, and even these are forced to compete for larger portions of their budgets from federal resources and private charity.

Academic researchers depend on industry to support increasing portions of their salaries. Industry sponsorship has taken over major aspects of the training of psychiatric residents by providing funds for lectures and seminars at medical schools and hospitals, and for national and international meetings. Industry employees organize carefully crafted symposia, and the ensuing discussions are published as supplements to freely distributed psychiatric journals. The opportunity for independent assessment and open dialogue about the efficacy and safety of psychoactive drugs, and especially comparisons with other treatments such as electroshock, has been virtually eliminated.

The leaders of the lay agencies that speak for the mentally ill are confused, torn between the promises of an industry hawking its products, state mental health agencies seeking to self-destruct, and managed care companies striving to limit expenditures for the care of the mentally ill. The lay agencies are sensitive to the stigma of electroshock and avoid mention of it for fear of losing members and financial support. For that reason, they do not encourage state and municipal legislatures to provide the treatment.

In this turmoil, few psychiatrists speak up in behalf of electroshock for their patients. The two U.S. manufacturers who make modern ECT devices and support educational efforts are too small to do more than survive. Although their new devices have highly sophisticated EEG-recording capabilities that can monitor electroshock treatments with great precision, these manufacturers can do little to ensure that their instruments are properly used.

In the brouhaha over the revival of ECT in the 1970s, the anti-ECT lobby tried to persuade the FDA to limit the sale and use of ECT devices in the United States. Their claim was that the devices were unsafe. In the early 1980s the FDA ruled that the devices in use were safe and reliable. The devices delivered energies with a fixed maximum under standard conditions, a maximum that had been set arbitrarily. Patients' seizure thresholds, however, rise with age, and many of the elderly need higher energies for effective treatment. The device manufacturers developed such devices, but when they applied to the FDA for modification of the standards, they were turned down and could not sell their equipment. The devices now sold in the United States are inadequate for effective treatment of some patients. Since the higher-energy devices are sold in the rest of the world, we have the awkward situation that patients in Canada, Europe, and Australia are being effectively treated while we in this country fail in treating some patients with similar conditions.

There is one opportunity on the economic horizon for a broader recognition of the merits of electroshock. The duration of inpatient treatment for patients receiving electroshock seems to be longer than for those receiving other treatments. But patients come to ECT after drug trials, often many trials, have failed. If the duration of inpatient care of patients given ECT is estimated from the day of the decision to use ECT, it is shorter and the costs are lower than the costs for psychotropic drugs. In one academic general hospital, of 19 depressed patients treated with ECT alone, the average hospital stay averaged 41 days, and for the 55 patients treated with tricyclic antidepressants (TCA) alone, the average stay was 55 days. The longest stay was for patients first treated with TCA and, when those failed, with ECT—an average length of stay of 71 days. The estimated cost of the stay for ECT treatment was $20,000 and for TCA alone it was $26,500, a savings of $6,500 for ECT over TCA. The same financial advantage is found when outpatient ECT is prescribed.

A study of patients discharged from general hospitals with a principal diagnosis of depressive disorder found that the initiation of ECT within five days of admission leads to shorter and less costly inpatient treatment than for those treated with drugs alone or delayed ECT. Other studies found that the antidepresssant effects of ECT occur earlier and are more robust than those of antidepressant drugs.

For the present, few managed care insurers recognize the merits of ECT, either as a relief for their insured ill patients or as a financial benefit to their shareholders. Payment for ECT is rarely approved for a patient with schizophrenia, so that patient must endure one drug trial after another. The most specious arguments are made about patients seen as catatonic, where neuroleptic drug trials are required, despite the evidence that neuroleptic drugs may precipitate the more acute state of neuroleptic malignant syndrome (NMS).

As managed care organizations assume a greater role in medical care, they reduce costs by limiting the conditions for which payments will be made, cutting professional fees and negotiating cheaper hospital costs. Once these measures have squeezed out of the system all the "excess" costs they can, the demand for the most efficient treatments will gain support. The advantages of ECT over medication should promote its greater use. Such an effect is already apparent in the expanding number of institutions seeking to develop qualified ECT facilities, in the interest of practitioners in obtaining education credits for ECT, and in the overt inclusion of electroshock as a valid treatment in algorithms now recommended for depression.

Many object to the revival of ECT by reminding others of the problems with electroshock when it was first introduced; at the time it was virtually the only effective treatment for the mentally ill. Such criticism is wholly unwarranted today; it is no more reasonable than to speak of the excesses in tonsillectomy, hysterectomy, pallidotomy, insulin coma, and labotomy that marked the enthusiastic reception of those procedures in earlier decades. Our appreciation of electroshock must be based on its present practice. We call on it because it is effective, often more so than alternate treatments, and because modern practice has made it safe.

NO

Shock Treatment: Resistance in the 1990s

Electroshock: Death, Brain Damage, Memory Loss, and Brainwashing

Since its introduction in 1938, electroshock, or electroconvulsive therapy (ECT), has been one of psychiatry's most controversial procedures. Approximately 100,000 people in the United States undergo ECT yearly, and recent media reports indicate a resurgence of its use. Proponents claim that changes in the technology of ECT administration have greatly reduced the fears and risks formerly associated with the procedure. I charge, however, that ECT as routinely used today is at least as harmful overall as it was before these changes were instituted. I recount my own experience with combined insulin coma–electroshock during the early 1960s and the story of the first electroshock "treatment." I report on who is now being electroshocked, at what cost, where, and for what reasons. I discuss ECT technique modifications and describe how ECT is currently administered. I examine assertions and evidence concerning ECT's effectiveness. . . .

In October 1962, at the age of 30, I had a run-in with psychiatry and got the worst of it. According to my hospital records (Frank, 1976), the "medical examiners," in recommending that I be committed, wrote the following: "Reportedly has been showing progressive personality changes over past two or so years. Grew withdrawn and asocial, couldn't or wouldn't work, and spent most of his time reading or doing nothing. Grew a beard, ate only vegetarian food, and lived life of a beatnik—to a certain extent" (p. 63). I was labeled "paranoid schizophrenic, severe and chronic," denied my freedom for nine months, and assaulted with a variety of drugs and fifty insulin-coma and thirty-five electroshock "treatments."

Each shock treatment was for me a Hiroshima. The shocking destroyed large parts of my memory, including the two-year period preceding the last shock. Not a day passes that images from that period of confinement do not float into consciousness. Nor does the night provide escape, for my dreams bear them as well. I am back there again in the "treatment room;" coming out of that last insulin coma (the only one I remember); strapped down, a

From Leonard R. Frank, "Shock Treatment IV: Resistance in the 1990s," in Robert F. Morgan, ed., *Electroshock: The Case Against* (Morgan Foundation, 1999). Copyright © 1999 by Dr. Robert F. Morgan. Reprinted by permission.

tube in my nose, a hypodermic needle in my arm; sweating, starving, suffocating, struggling to move; a group of strangers around the bed grabbing at me; thinking—Where am I? What the hell is happening to me?

Well into the shock series, which took place at Twin Pines Hospital in Belmont, California, a few miles south of San Francisco, the treating psychiatrist wrote to my father:

> In evaluating Leonard's progress to date, I think it is important to point out there is some slight improvement, but he still has all the delusional beliefs regarding his beard, dietary regime, and religious observances that he had prior to treatment. We hope that in continuing the treatments we will be able to modify some of these beliefs so that he can make a reasonable adjustment to life. (p. 77)

During the comatose phase of one of my treatments, my beard was removed—as "a therapeutic device to provoke anxiety and make some change in his body image," the consulting psychiatrist had written in his report recommending this procedure. He continued, "Consultation should be obtained from the TP [Twin Pines] attorney as to the civil rights issue—but I doubt that these are crucial. The therapeutic effort is worth it—inasmuch that he can always grow another" (p. 76).

Earlier, several psychiatrists had tried unsuccessfully to persuade me to shave off my beard. "Leonard seems to attach a great deal of religious significance to the beard," the treating psychiatrist had noted at the time. He had even brought in a local rabbi to change my thinking (p. 75), but to no avail. I have no recollection of any of this. It is all from my medical records.

> Genuine religious conversions are also seen after the new modified lobotomy operations. For the mind is freed from its old strait-jacket and new religious beliefs and attitudes can now more easily take the place of the old. (Sargant, 1957, p. 71)
>
> At the "Mental Health Center" [in Albuquerque] where I work, there is a sign on the wall near the inpatient wards that reads: "PATIENTS' RIGHTS: Patients have the right to religious freedom unless clinically contraindicated." (Jones, 1988, p. 2)

One day, about a week after my last treatment, I was sitting in the day room, which was adjacent to the shock-treatment wing of the hospital building. It was just before lunch and near the end of the treatment session (which lasts about five hours) for those being insulin-shocked. The thick metal door separating the two areas had been left slightly ajar. Suddenly, from behind the door, I heard the scream of a young man whom I had recently come to know and who was then starting an insulin course. It was a scream like nothing I had ever heard before, an all-out scream. Hurriedly, one of the nurses closed the door. The screams, now less audible, continued a while longer. I do not remember my own screams; his, I remember.

> [The insulin-coma patient] is prevented from seeing all at once the actions and treatment of those patients further along in their therapy . . .

> As much as possible, he is saved the trauma of sudden introduction to the sight of patients in different stages of coma—a sight which is not very pleasant to an unaccustomed eye. (Gralnick, 1944, p. 184)

During the years since my institutionalization, I have often asked myself how psychiatrists, or anyone else for that matter, could justify shocking a human being. Soon after I began researching my book *The History of Shock Treatment* (1978), I discovered Gordon's (1948) review of the literature, in which he compiled fifty theories purporting to explain the "healing" mechanism of the various forms of shock therapy then in use, including insulin, Metrazol, and electroshock. Here are some excerpts:

> Because prefontal lobotomy improves the mentally ill by destruction, the improvement obtained by all the shock therapies must also involve some destructive processes.
> They help by way of a circulatory shake up . . .
> It decreases cerebral function.
> The treatments bring the patient and physician in closer contact. Helpless and dependent, the patient sees in the physician a mother.
> Threat of death mobilizes all the vital instincts and forces a reestablishment of contacts with reality. . . .
> The treatment is considered by patients as punishment for sins and gives feelings of relief.
> Victory over death and joy of rebirth produce the results.
> The resulting amnesia is healing.
> Erotization is the therapeutic factor.
> The personality is brought down to a lower level and adjustment is obtained more easily in a primitive vegetative existence than in a highly developed personality. Imbecility replaces insanity. (pp. 399–401)

One of the more interesting explanations I found was proposed by Manfred Sakel, the Austrian psychiatrist who, in 1933, introduced insulin coma as a treatment for schizophrenia. According to Sakel (cited in Ray, 1942, p. 250):

> [W]ith chronic schizophrenics, as with confirmed criminals, we can't hope for reform. Here the faulty pattern of functioning is irrevocably entrenched. Hence we must use more drastic measures to silence the dysfunctioning cells and so liberate the activity of the normal cells. This time we must *kill* the too vocal dysfunctioning cells. But can we do this without killing normal cells also? Can we *select* the cells we wish to destroy? I think we can. [italics in original]

Electroshock may be considered one of the most controversial treatments in psychiatry. As I document below, the last decade has witnessed a resurgence of ECT's popularity, accompanied by assertions from proponents concerning its effectiveness and safety—assertions which deny or obscure basic facts about the historical origins of ECT, the economic reasons behind its current popularity, as well as its potential for destroying the memories and lives of those subjected to it. . . .

Electroshock Facts and Figures

Since 1938, between ten and fifteen million people worldwide have undergone electroshock. While no precise figure is available, it is estimated that about 100,000 people in the United States are electroshocked annually (Fink, cited in Rymer, 1989, p. 68). Moreover, the numbers appear to be increasing. Recent media accounts report a resurgence of ECT interest and use. One reason for this is the well-publicized enthusiasm of such proponents as Max Fink, editor-in-chief of *Convulsive Therapy,* the leading journal in the field. Fink was recently cited as saying that "[ECT should be given to] all patients whose condition is severe enough to require hospitalization" (Edelson, 1988. p. 3).

A survey of the American Psychiatric Association (APA) membership focusing on ECT (APA, 1978) showed that 22% fell into the "User" category. Users were defined as psychiatrists who had "personally treated patients with ECT" or "recommended to residents under their supervision that ECT be used on patients" during the last six months (p. 5). If valid today, this figure indicates that approximately 7,700 APA members are electroshock Users.

A survey of all 184 member hospitals of the National Association of Private Psychiatric Hospitals (Levy and Albrecht, 1985) elicited the following information on electroshock practices from the 153 respondents (83%) who answered a nineteen-item questionnaire sent to them in 1982. Fifty-eight percent of the respondents used electroshock (3% did not use electroshock because they considered it to be "inappropriate treatment for any illness").

The hospitals using ECT found it appropriate for a variety of diagnoses: 100% for "major depressive disorder," 58% for "schizophrenia," and 13% for "obsessive-compulsive disorder." Twenty-six percent of the ECT-using hospitals reported no contraindications in the use of the procedure.

Darnton (1989) reported that the number of private free-standing psychiatric hospitals grew from 184 in 1980 to 450 in 1988. In addition, nearly 2,000 general hospitals offer inpatient psychiatric service (p. 67). While the use of ECT in state hospitals has fallen off sharply over the last twenty years, the psychiatric wards of general hospitals have increased their reliance on ECT in the treatment of their adult inpatients (Thompson, 1986).

In cases of depression, an ECT series ranges from six to twelve seizures—in those of schizophrenia, from fifteen to thirty-five seizures— given three times a week, and usually entails four weeks of hospitalization. In 72% of the cases, according to the APA (1978, p. 8) survey cited above, electroshock costs are paid for by insurance companies. This fact led one psychiatrist to comment, "Finding that the patient has insurance seemed like the most common indication for giving electroshock" (Viscott, 1972, p. 356). The overall cost for a series of electroshock in a private hospital ranges from $10,000 to $25,000. With room rates averaging $500 to $600 a day, and bed occupancy generally falling, some hospitals have obtained considerable financial advantage from their use of ECT. A regular ECT User can expect yearly earnings of at least $200,000, about twice the median income of other psychiatrists. *Electroshock is a $2–3 billion-a-year industry.*

More than two-thirds of electroshock subjects are women, and a growing number are elderly. In California, one of the states that requires Users to report quarterly the number and age categories of electroshock subjects, "the percentage 65 and over" being electroshocked increased gradually from 29% to 43% between 1977 and 1983 (Warren, 1986, p. 51). More recently, Drop and Welch (1989) reported that 60% of the ECT subjects in a recent two-year period at the Massachusetts General Hospital in Boston were over 60 years and 10% were in their eighties (p. 88).

There are published reports of persons over 100 years old (Alexopoulos, Young, and Abrams, 1989) and as young as $34^{1}/_{2}$ months (Bender, 1955) who have been electroshocked. In the latter case, the child had been referred in 1947 to the children's ward of New York's Bellevue Hospital "because of distressing anxiety that frequently reached a state of panic. . . . The child was mute and autistic." The morning after admission he received the first of a series of twenty electroshocks and was discharged one month later. "The discharge note indicated a 'moderate improvement' since he was eating and sleeping better, was more friendly with the other children, and he was toilet trained" (pp. 418–419).

Children continue to be electroshocked. Black, Wilcox, and Stewart (1985) reported on "the successful use of ECT in a prepubertal boy with severe depression." Sandy, 11 years old, received twelve unilateral ECTs at the University of Iowa Hospitals and Clinics in Iowa City. He "improved remarkably" and "was discharged in good condition. Follow-up over the next eight years revealed five more hospitalizations for depression" (p. 98).

Some of the better known people who have undergone shock treatment include: Antonin Artaud, Thomas Eagleton, Claude Eatherly, Frances Farmer, Zelda Fitzgerald, James Forrestal, Janet Frame, Ernest Hemingway, Vladimir Horowitz, Bob Kaufman, Seymour Krim, Vivien Leigh, Oscar Levant, Robert Lowell, Vaslav Nijinsky, Jimmy Pearsall, Robert Pirsig, Sylvia Plath, Paul Robeson, Gene Tierney, and Frank Wisner.

In the early 1970s electroshock survivors—together with other former psychiatric inmates/"patients"—began forming organizations aimed at regulating or abolishing electroshock and other psychiatric practices which they believed were harmful. In 1975, one group, the Network Against Psychiatric Assault (San Francisco/Berkeley), was instrumental in the passage of legislation that regulated the use of electroshock in California. Since then, more than thirty states have passed similar legislation.

In 1982, the Coalition to Stop Electroshock led a successful referendum campaign to outlaw ECT in Berkeley, California. Although the courts overturned the ban six weeks after it went into effect, this was the first time in American history that the use of any established medical procedure had been prohibited by popular vote.

The Committee for Truth in Psychiatry (CTIP), all of whose members are electroshock survivors, was formed in 1984 to support the Food and Drug Administration (FDA) in its original (1979) classification of the ECT device in the high risk category of medical devices, Class III, which earmarks a device of its related procedure for a safety investigation. To prevent an investigation of ECT, the APA had petitioned the FDA in 1982 for reclassification of the ECT device to Class II, which signifies low risk. After many years of indecision, the FDA proposed in 1990 to make this reclassification—but has not yet done so. . . .

Claims of Electroshock Effectiveness

Virtually all the psychiatrists who evaluate, write about, and do research on electroshock are themselves Users. This partially explains why claims regarding ECT's effectiveness abound in the professional literature—while the risks associated with the procedure are consistently understated or overlooked. User estimates of ECT's effectiveness in the treatment of the affective disorders (i.e., depression, mania, and manic-depression) usually range from 75% to 90%. Two important questions, however, need to be addressed: What is meant by effectiveness, and how long does it last?

Breggin (1979, p. 135; 1981, pp. 252–253) has proposed a "brain-disabling hypothesis" to explain the workings of electroshock. The hypothesis suggests that ECT "effectiveness" stems from the brain damage ECT causes. As happens in cases of serious head injury, ECT produces amnesia, denial, euphoria, apathy, wide and unpredictable mood swings, helplessness and submissiveness. Each one of these effects may appear to offset the problems which justified the use of ECT in the first place.

Amnesia victims, having forgotten their problems, tend to complain less. Denial serves a similar purpose. Because of their embarrassment, ECT subjects tend to discount or deny unresolved personal problems, as well as ECT-caused intellectual deficits. With euphoria, the subject's depression seems to lift. With apathy, the subject's "agitation" (if that had been perceived as part of the original problem) seems to diminish. Dependency and submissiveness tend to make what may have been a resistive, hostile subject more cooperative and friendly. In hailing the wonders of electroshock, psychiatrists often simply redefine the symptoms of psychiatrogenic brain damage as signs of improvement and/or recovery.

Electroshock advocates themselves unwittingly provide support for the brain-disabling hypothesis. Fink, Kahn, and Green (1958) offered a good example of this when describing a set of criteria for rating improvement in ECT subjects: "When a depressed patient, who had been withdrawn, crying, and had expressed suicidal thoughts, no longer is seclusive, and is jovial, friendly and euphoric, denies his problems and sees his previous thoughts of suicide as 'silly' a rating of 'much improved' is made" (p. 117). Two additional illustrations are given below; see Cleckley (cited in Thigpen, 1976) and Hoch (1948).

On the question of duration of benefit from ECT, Weiner (1984)—in one of the most important review articles on ECT published during the last decade—was unable to cite a single study purporting to show long-term, or even medium-term, benefits from ECT. Opton (1985) drew this conclusion from the Weiner review: "In this comprehensive review of the literature, after fifty years of research on ECT, no methodologically sound study was found that reported beneficial effects of ECT lasting as long as four weeks" (p. 2). Pinel (1984), in his peer commentary on the Weiner article, accepted Weiner's conclusion that "the risks of ECT-related brain damage are slight" and then added, "it is difficult to justify any risks at all until ECT has been shown unambiguously to produce significant long-term therapeutic benefits" (p. 31).

The following excerpt from an article in *Clinical Psychiatry News* reveals the short-range outlook of many ECT Users:

> The relapse rate after successful treatment for affective disorders is very high, from 20% to 50% within six months after a *successful* course of ECT, according to Dr. Richard Abrams [a well-known ECT proponent]. "I think it is reasonable and appropriate to always initiate maintenance in the form of a tricyclic [an antidepressant drug] or lithium" he said. For patients who relapse despite adequate drug therapy, maintenance ECT [periodic single electroshocks, spaced several weeks or months apart] has been used successfully. (Klug, 1984, p. 16) [italics added]

The underlying assumption of this approach is that affective disorders are for the most part chronic and irreversible. There is a popular saying among psychiatrists, "Once a schizophrenic, always a schizophrenic." While not a maxim, "Once a depressive, always a depressive" is nevertheless a core belief among many ECT Users. It "explains" so much for them. From this perspective, there are hardly any ECT failures, only patients with recurring depressive episodes who require ongoing psychiatric treatment, intensive and maintenance by turns.

Proponents also claim, but cannot demonstrate, that ECT is effective in cases of depression where there is a risk of suicide. They often cite a study by Avery and Winokur (1976) to support their position. But this study makes no such claim, as we can see from the authors' own conclusion: "In the present study, treatment [ECT and antidepressants] was not shown to affect the suicide rate" (p. 1033). Nevertheless, Allen (1978), in the very first paragraph of his article on ECT observed, "Avery and Winokur showed that suicide mortality in patients afflicted with psychotic depression was lower in patients treated with ECT than in those who were not" (p. 47). . . .

Electroshock Modifications

In recent years, to allay growing public fears concerning the use of electroshock, proponents have launched a media campaign claiming, among other things, that with the introduction of certain modifications in the administration of ECT, the problems once associated with the procedure have been solved, or at least substantially reduced. These techniques center around the use of anesthetics and muscle relaxants, changes in electrode placement, and the use of brief-pulse electrical stimulation.

However, investigation and common sense indicate that while these modifications may offer some advantages—for example, muscle relaxants prevent the subject's thrashing about, thereby greatly reducing the risk of bone and spinal fractures, and making the procedure less frightening to watch—the basic facts underlying the administration of electroshock have not changed at all. The nature of the human brain and that of electricity are the same today as they were more than fifty years ago when ECT was introduced. Whatever may be the ameliorating factors of the newer delivery techniques, when a convulsogenic dose of electricity is applied to the brain, there is going to be a certain amount of brain damage, some of which will be permanent.

There is even evidence that the drug modifications make ECT more destructive than ever because the central nervous system depressants, anesthetics and muscle relaxants raise the subject's convulsive threshold which, in turn, makes it necessary to apply a larger dose of electricity to set off the convulsion. And, the more current applied, the more amnesia and brain damage. As Reed (1988) noted, "The amnesia directly relating to ECT depends on the amount of current used to trigger the generalized convulsion" (p. 29).

Other problems are associated with the use of premedications in ECT. In his study of 254 ECT deaths, Impastato (1957) reported that thirteen of sixty-six persons from the "cerebral death" group had received muscle relaxants and that these "appear to play a major role in the death of some of these patients" (p. 42). There were also five other patients who died immediately after receiving muscle relaxants but before being given the electric shock. These figures are from a period when muscle relaxants were not widely used. More recently, Ulett (1972) concurred with Impastato on the danger of muscle relaxants in ECT: "The objection to the use of muscle relaxants is that, although decreasing the rate of fracture complication, they unquestionably increase the chance of fatal accident" (p. 284). Given the paucity of ECT-death studies in recent years, it is difficult to gauge the extent of this problem in current practice.

Another modification, unilateral ECT, has received much attention since its introduction in the late 1950s but has not replaced—and is not likely to replace—bilateral ECT as the standard technique. According to the APA survey on ECT (1978, p. 6), 75% of the Users reported using bilateral electrode placement exclusively. In bilateral ECT, the electrodes are placed on the subject's temples so that the current passes through the brain's frontal lobe area. In unilateral ECT, one electrode is placed on a temple and the other just above the back of the neck on the same (usually the nondominant) side of the head. Unilateral placement, proponents claim, results in less memory loss. But proponents of bilateral ECT assert that unilateral ECT is less effective and therefore requires more treatments (Gregory, Shawcross, and Gill, 1985).

Cleckley (cited in Thigpen, 1976) offered this explanation for the ineffectiveness of unilateral ECT: "My thought about unilateral stimulation is that it fails to cure. I think this failure to cure is in direct proportion to the avoidance of memory loss" (p. 40). During his interview with Abrams (1988b), Kalinowsky made this comment about unilateral ECT: "My experience is completely negative and if patients improve at all, it's probably due to the repeated anesthesia induction with methohexital" (p. 38).

Given the need for "somewhat more current to produce a seizure" in each treatment session (Fink, 1978, p. 79) and for more treatment sessions per series, unilateral ECT may be more brain damaging in some cases than bilateral ECT.

The problems associated with brief-pulse stimulation, another innovation in ECT administration, are similar to those associated with unilateral ECT. While brief-pulse stimulation may cause less amnesia than the routinely used sine-wave stimulation, the newer technique "may be insufficient to induce an adequate generalized seizure" (Reed, 1988, p. 29).

What Ulett (1972) wrote about unidirectional current stimulation—a supposed advance in ECT technology introduced by Liberson (1948)—may also apply to brief-pulse stimulation, and to unilateral ECT as well: "[I]t is often necessary to give a greater number of these milder treatments to achieve the desired therapeutic result" (p. 287). . . .

Conclusion

Mystification and conditioning have undoubtedly played an important role in shaping the public's tolerant attitude toward electroshock. But it is not only the uniformed and misinformed public that has stood by silently during the electroshock era. There has hardly been a voice of protest from the informed elite—even when one of its own has been victimized.

While undergoing a series of involuntary electroshocks at the famed Mayo Clinic in 1961, Ernest Hemingway told visitor A. E. Hotchner, "Well, what is the sense of ruining my head and erasing my memory, which is my capital, and putting me out of business? It was a brilliant cure but we lost the patient. It's a bum turn, Hotch, terrible." (cited in Hotchner, 1967, p. 308).

A few days after his release from the Mayo Clinic following a second course of ECT, Hemingway killed himself with a shotgun. With all that has been written about him since his death, no recognized figure from the world of literature, academia, law religion or science has spoken out against those responsible for this tragedy. As might have been expected, the psychiatric professional has also been silent. Not only did the psychiatrist who electroshocked Hemingway escape the censure of his colleagues, but a few years later they elected him president of the American Psychiatric Association.

Since ancient times, physicians have been trying to cure epilepsy. One might therefore think that they would object to the use of artificially-induced seizures as a method of treatment. But no such objection has been forthcoming. On the contrary, the medical profession's passive acquiescence to the use of electroshock has recently turned to active support:

The AMA [American Medical Association] has endorsed the use of electroconvulsive therapy (ECT) as an effective treatment modality in selected patients, as outlined by the American Psychiatric Association. . . . [The AMA] recognized ECT as a safe procedure in proper hands. (ECT, Animal Rights, 1989, p. 9)

ECT User Robert Peck titled his book *The Miracle of Shock Treatment* (1974). Antonin Artaud (cited in Sontag, 1976), the French actor and playwright, who was electroshocked in the early 1940s, wrote afterwards: "Anyone who has gone through the electric shock never again rises out of its darkness and his life has been lowered a notch" (p. 530). In which perspective—or at what point between these two perspectives—is the truth to be found? This is no trivia question. For some, it will be the gravest question they will ever have to answer.

References

Abrams, R. (1988b). Interview with Lothar Kalinowsky, M.D. *Convulsive Therapy, 4,* 25–39.

Alexopoulos, C. S., Young, R. C., and Abrams, R. C. (1989). ECT in the high-risk geriatric patient. *Convulsive Therapy, 5,* 75–87.

Allen, M. R. (1978). Electroconvulsive therapy: An old question, new answers, *Psychiatric Annals, 8,* 47–65.

American Psychiatric Association. (1978). *Electroconvulsive Therapy.* Task Force Report 14. Washington, D.C.: American Psychiatric Association.

Avery, D., and Winokur, O. (1976). Mortality in depressed patients treated with electroconvulsive therapy and antidepressants. *Archives of General Psychiatry, 33,* 1029–1037.

Bender, L. (1955). The development of a schizophrenic child treated with electric convulsions at three years of age. In C. Caplan (Ed.), *Emotional Problems of Early Childhood* (pp. 407–425). New York: Basic Books.

Black, D. W., Wilcox, J. A., and Stewart, M. (1985). The use of ECT in children: Case report. *Journal of Clinical Psychiatry, 46,* 98–99.

Breggin, P. R. (1979). *Electroshock: Its Brain-Disabling Effects.* New York: Springer.

Darnton, N. (1989, July 31). Committed youth. *Newsweek,* pp. 66–72.

Drop, L. J., and Welch, C. A. (1989). Anesthesia for electroconvulsive therapy in patients with major cardiovascular risk factors. *Convulsive Therapy, 5,* 88–101.

ECT, animal rights among topics discussed at AMA's Dallas meeting. (1989, January 20). *Psychiatric News,* p. 9; 23.

Edelson, E. (1988, December 28). ECT elicits controversy—and results. *Houston Chronicle,* p. 3.

Fink, M. (1978). Electroshock therapy: Myths and realities. *Hospital Practice, 13,* 77–82.

Fink, M., Kahn, R. L., and Green, M. (1958). Experimental studies of electroshock process. *Diseases of the Nervous System, 19,* 113–118.

Frank, L. R. (1976). The Frank papers. In J. Friedberg, *Shock Treatment is not Good for Your Brain* (pp. 62–81). San Francisco: Glide Publications.

Frank, L. R. (1978). *The History of Shock Treatment.* San Francisco: Frank.

Gordon, H. L. (1948). Fifty shock therapy theories. *Military Surgeon, 103,* 397–401.

Gralnick, A. (1944). Psychotherapeutic and interpersonal aspects of insulin treatment. *Psychiatric Quarterly, 18,* 177–196.

Gregory, S., Shawcross, C. R., and Gill, D. (1985). The Nottingham ECT study: A double-blind comparison of bilateral, unilateral and simulated ECT in depressive illness. *British Journal of Psychiatry, 146,* 520–524.

Hoch, P. H. (1948). Discussion and concluding remarks. *Journal of Personality, 17,* 48–51.

Hotchner, A. E. (1967). *Papa Hemingway.* New York: Bantam.

Impastato, D. (1957). Prevention of fatalities in electroshock therapy. *Diseases of the Nervous System, 18* (supplement), 34–75.

Jones, T. (1988, June). Letter. *Dendron* (Eugene, Oregon), p. 2.

Klug, J. (1984, June). Benefits of ECT outweigh risks in most patients. *Clinical Psychiatry News,* p. 16.

Levy, S. D., and Albrecht, E. (1985). Electroconvulsive therapy: A survey of use in the private psychiatric hospital. *Journal of Clinical Psychiatry, 46*, 125–127.

Liberson, W. T. (1948). Brief stimuli therapy: Physiological and clinical observations. *American Journal of Psychiatry, 105*, 28–39.

Opton, E. M., Jr. (1985, June 4). Letter to the members of the panel. National Institute of Health Consensus Development Conference on Electroconvulsive Therapy.

Peck, R. E. (1974). *The Miracle of Shock Treatment.* Jericho, New York: Exposition Press. Philadelphia Psychiatric Society. (1943). Symposium: Complications of and contraindications to electric shock therapy. *Archives of Neurology and Psychiatry, 49*, 786–791.

Pinel, J. PJ. (1984). After forty-five years ECT is still controversial. *Behavioral and Brain Sciences, 7*, 30–31.

Ray, M. B. (1942). *Doctors of the Mind: The Story of Psychiatry.* Indianapolis and New York: Bobbs-Merrill.

Reed, K. (1988). Electroconvulsive therapy: A clinical discussion. *Psychiatric Medicine, 6*, 23–33.

Rymer, R. (1989, March-April). Electroshock. *Hippocrates*, pp. 65–72.

Sargant, W. (1957). *Battle for the Mind: A Physiology of Conversion and Brainwashing.* Baltimore: Penguin.

Thigpen, C. H. (1976). Letter. *Convulsive Therapy Bulletin, 1*, 40.

Thompson, J. W. (1986). Utilization of ECT in U.S. psychiatric facilities, 1975 to 1980. *Psychopharmacology Bulletin, 22*, 463–465.

Ulett, G. A. (1972). *A Synopsis of Contemporary Psychiatry.* St. Louis: C. V. Mosby.

Viscott, D. (1972). *The Making of a Psychiatrist.* Greenwich, Connecticut: Faucett.

Warren, C. A. B. (1986). Electroconvulsive therapy: "new" treatment of the 1980s. *Research in Law, Deviance and Social Control, 8*, 41–55.

Weiner, R. D. (1984). Does electroconvulsive therapy cause brain damage? *Behavioral and Brain Sciences, 7*, 1–22 (peer commentary section, pp. 22–54).

CHALLENGE QUESTIONS

Is Electroconvulsive Therapy Ethical?

1. Fink views ECT as a safe intervention that has been underutilized partly because of ideological and financial pressures to use drugs instead. What kind of research study could be designed to compare the therapeutic effectiveness of ECT with the benefits of medication?
2. Frank criticizes ECT as an intervention that involves very serious and lasting side effects. Given the fact that this intervention is typically recommended for seriously impaired individuals, what steps should be taken to ensure that patients are protected from being given a treatment that involves considerable risk?
3. Imagine that you are a clinician treating a suicidal woman who is incapable of eating and for whom antidepressant medications have had no therapeutic effect. What arguments for and against ECT could be made with regard to the treatment of this client?
4. Psychopharmacological medications work by bringing about changes in brain chemistry. Consider the assumptions about what makes ECT effective. In what ways are the two interventions similar and different?
5. Fink contends that much of the negativity associated with ECT stems from its misuse in earlier decades and from the unfavorable presentation of ECT in the movie *One Flew Over the Cuckoo's Nest*. What aspects of these historical issues may account for the continuing negativity about ECT, even decades later?

Suggested Readings

Breggin, P. R. (1997). *Brain disabling treatments in psychiatry: Drugs, electroshock, and the role of the FDA.* New York, NY: Springer Publishing Company.

Fink, M. (1997). The decision to use ECT: For whom? When? In A. J. Rush (Ed.), *Mood disorders: Systematic medication management. Modern problems of pharmacopsychiatry, vol. 25* (pp. 203–214). Basel, Switzerland: Karger.

Fink, M. (1997). Prejudice against ECT: Competition with psychological philosophies as a contribution to its stigma. *Convulsive Therapy, 13*(4), 253–265.

Salzman, C. (1998). ECT, research, and professional ambivalence. *American Journal of Psychiatry, 155*(1), 1–2.

Media Psychology: Division 46 of the American Psychological Association

The American Psychological Association's Division of Media Psychology provides information on the impacts and importance of the media.

http://www.apa.org/divisions/div46

Feminists Against Censorship

This is the Web site of Feminists Against Censorship (FAC), a group of feminists from academia and elsewhere promoting free speech and fighting censorship from a feminist perspective.

http://www.fiawol.demon.co.uk/FAC

DivorceInfo.com

This Web site provides information so that people can make informed decisions about divorce. It also discusses the strengths and limitations of research on divorce.

http://www.divorceinfo.com/judithwallerstein.htm

Men Can Stop Rape

This Web site addresses issues on the topics of rape and violence, with the goal of promoting gender equity and the building of men's capacity to be strong without being violent.

http://www.mencanstoprape.org/

Oregon's Death With Dignity Act

This site of the Oregon Health Division of the Oregon Department of Human Resources contains an overview of the 1997 Oregon Death With Dignity Act, which allows physician-assisted suicide for the terminally ill.

http://www.dhs.state.or.us/publichealth/chs/pas/pas.cfm

Society for the Psychological Study of Lesbian, Gay, and Bisexual Issues: Division 44 of the American Psychological Association

This division of the American Psychological Association focuses on gaining an understanding for and promoting the education of gay, lesbian, and bisexual issues in psychology.

http://www.apa.org/divisions/div44

PART 4

Social Issues

*M*any issues in the field of abnormal psychology interface with social issues, with heated debates emerging about topics with societal impact. Some of the controversies pertain to questions about the extent to which societal forces cause psychological disturbance; for example, some critics have raised concerns about the impact of exposure to media violence or pornography on behavior. Other issues pertain to the role and function of mental health professionals, particularly in situations in which their work touches upon complex ethical issues such as consulting in cases of physician-assisted suicide or providing therapy to clients wanting to change their sexual orientation.

- Does Media Violence Promote Violent Behavior in Young People?

- Is Pornography Harmful?

- Is Divorce Always Detrimental to Children?

- Does Evolution Explain Why Men Rape?

- Should Mental Health Professionals Serve as Gatekeepers for Physician-Assisted Suicide?

- Is Sexual Orientation Conversion Therapy Ethical?

ISSUE 15

Does Media Violence Promote Violent Behavior in Young People?

YES: L. Rowell Huesmann and Jessica Moise, from "Media Violence: A Demonstrated Public Health Threat to Children," *Harvard Mental Health Letter* (June 1996)

NO: Jonathan L. Freedman, from "Violence in the Mass Media and Violence in Society: The Link Is Unproven," *Harvard Mental Health Letter* (May 1996)

ISSUE SUMMARY

YES: Psychology and communication researchers L. Rowell Huesmann and Jessica Moise assert that there is a clear relationship between aggression and children's viewing of media violence, and they point to several theoretical explanations for this connection.

NO: Psychology professor Jonathan L. Freedman disagrees with the conclusion of researchers that there is a relationship between aggression and children's viewing of media violence, and he argues that many conclusions in this area are based on methodologically flawed studies.

In recent years the attention of American society has been drawn to a number of profoundly troubling events in which young children have engaged in unthinkable forms of violence. Following the massacre at Columbine High School in Littleton, Colorado, in the spring of 1999, Americans were bewildered in their efforts to understand why teenagers would carefully plan out the murder of their classmates and then turn the guns on themselves. In looking for answers, many commentators turned to the proliferation of violent images on television, in the movies, and in video games. To explain why young Americans have turned from traditional pursuits of youth to aggression and violence, critics of media violence have pointed to the explosion of graphic imagery in every medium.

Social learning theorists have provided ample experimental support for the notion that exposure to media violence can significantly influence the behavior of young people. According to social learning theory, people acquire many new responses by imitating the behavior of other people. Social learning theorist Albert Bandura proposed that people receive vicarious reinforcement when they identify with a person whom they observe being reinforced. Thus, if a boy watches a violent man in a movie receive attention and admiration from others, he might be drawn to engage in similar behaviors on the premise that such adulation can also come his way.

In the following selection, L. Rowell Huesmann and Jessica Moise contend that there is a clear relationship between aggression and children's viewing of media violence. They specify five well-validated theoretical explanations for this connection: (1) children imitate what they observe; (2) media violence stimulates aggression by desensitizing children; (3) children watch violent media portrayals in an attempt to justify their own aggression; (4) the observation of aggression results in cognitive priming, or the activation of existing aggressive thoughts; and (5) children become physiologically aroused in response to observing violence.

Jonathan L. Freedman, in the second selection, asserts that research on the relationship between exposure to media violence and aggression has yielded inconsistent results. He points to methodological problems inherent in much of the research; for example, demand characteristics within research studies cause children to respond in ways that they know the experimenter expects. Furthermore, Freedman says, a corresponding set of expectations influences researchers who become involved in such research with the anticipation that they will find a connection between exposure to violence and aggressive behavior.

POINT

- The relationship between aggression and exposure to media violence has been supported by a wide variety of experiments conducted in different countries by researchers with different points of view.

- Despite Freedman's insistence that the correlation between aggression and exposure to violence is statistically small, its impact has real social significance.

- Because media heroes are admired and have special authority, children are likely to imitate their behavior and learn that aggression is an acceptable solution to conflict.

- Children younger than 11 do not make the distinction between fiction and reality very well.

COUNTERPOINT

- Most of the studies of the relationship between aggression and exposure to media violence have serious methodological flaws and have yielded inconsistent results.

- The correlations between aggression and violence exposure are quite small, accounting for only 1 to 10 percent of individual differences in the aggressiveness of children.

- If children are learning anything from the media, it is that the forces of good will overcome evil assailants, who are the first to use violence.

- Children are able to recognize fiction as early as the age of 5; those watching retaliatory violence do not believe they could act successfully by engaging in such behaviors.

L. Rowell Huesmann
and Jessica Moise

 **YES**

Media Violence: A Demonstrated Public Health Threat to Children

Imagine that the Surgeon General is presented with a series of studies on a widely distributed product. For 30 years well-controlled experiments have been showing that use of the product causes symptoms of a particular affliction. Many field surveys have shown that this affliction is always more common among people who use the product regularly. A smaller number of studies have examined the long-term effects of the product in different environments, and most have shown at least some evidence of harm, although it is difficult to disentangle effects of the product itself from the effects of factors that lead people to use it. Over all, the studies suggest that if a person with a 50% risk for the affliction uses the product, the risk rises to 60% or 70%. Furthermore, we have a fairly good understanding of how use of the product contributes to the affliction, which is persistent, difficult to cure, and sometimes lethal. The product is economically important, and its manufacturers spend large sums trying to disparage the scientific research. A few scientists who have never done any empirical work in the field regularly point out supposed flaws in the research and belittle its conclusions. The incidence of the affliction has increased dramatically since the product was first introduced. What should the Surgeon General do?

This description applies to the relationship between lung cancer and cigarettes. It also applies to the relationship between aggression and children's viewing of mass media violence. The Surgeon General has rightly come to the same conclusion in both cases and has issued similar warnings.

Cause and Effect

Dr. Freedman's highly selective reading of the research minimizes overwhelming evidence. First, there are the carefully controlled laboratory studies in which children are exposed to violent film clips and short-term changes in their behavior are observed. More than 100 such studies over

From L. Rowell Huesmann and Jessica Moise, "Media Violence: A Demonstrated Public Health Threat to Children," *Harvard Mental Health Letter*, vol. 12, no. 12 (June 1996). Copyright © 1996 by The President and Fellows of Harvard College. Reprinted by permission of The Harvard Medical School Health Publications Group.

the last 40 years have shown that at least some children exposed to visual depictions of dramatic violence behave more aggressively afterward both toward inanimate objects and toward other children. These results have been found in many countries among boys and girls of all social classes, races, ages, and levels of intelligence.

Freedman claims that these studies use dubious measures of aggression. He cites only one example: asking children whether they would want the researcher to prick a balloon. But this measure is not at all representative. Most studies have used such evidence as physical attacks on other children and dolls. In one typical study Kaj Bjorkqvist exposed five- and six-year-old Finnish children to either violent or non-violent films. Observers who did not know which kind of film each child had seen then watched them play together. Children who had just seen a violent film were more likely to hit other children, scream at them, threaten them, and intentionally destroy their toys.

Freedman claims that these experiments confuse the effects of arousal with the effects of violence. He argues that "anyone who is aroused will display more of almost any behavior." But most studies have shown that pro-social behavior decreases after children view an aggressive film. Finally, Freedman says the experiments are contaminated by demand characteristics. In other words, the children are only doing what they think the researchers want them to do. That conclusion is extremely implausible, considering the wide variety of experiments conducted in different countries by researchers with different points of view.

Large Body of Evidence

More than 50 field studies over the last 20 years have also shown that children who habitually watch more media violence behave more aggressively and accept aggression more readily as a way to solve problems. The relationship usually persists when researchers control for age, sex, social class, and previous level of aggression. Disbelievers often suggest that the correlation is statistically small. According to Freedman, it accounts for "only 1% to 10% of individual differences in children's aggressiveness." But an increase of that size (a more accurate figure would be 2% to 16%) has real social significance. No single factor has been found to explain more than 16% of individual differences in aggression.

Of course, correlations do not prove causality. That is the purpose of laboratory experiments. The two approaches are complementary. Experiments establish causal relationship, and field studies show that the relationship holds in a wide variety of real-world situations. The causal relationship is further confirmed by the finding that children who view TV violence at an early age are more likely to commit aggressive acts at a later age. In 1982 Eron and Huesmann found that boys who spent the most time viewing violent television shows at age eight were most likely to have criminal convictions at age 30. Most other long-term studies have come to similar conclusions, even after controlling for children's initial aggressiveness, social class, and education. A few studies have found no effect on some measures of violence, but almost all have found a significant effect on some measures.

Freedman singles out for criticism a study by Huesmann and his colleagues that was concluded in the late 1970s. He says we found "no statistically significant effect for either sex in Australia, Finland, the Netherlands, Poland, or kibbutz children in Israel." That is not true. We found that the television viewing habits of children as young as six or seven predicted subsequent increases in childhood aggression among boys in Finland and among both sexes in the United States, in Poland, and in Israeli cities. In Australia and on Israeli kibbutzim, television viewing habits were correlated with simultaneous aggression. Freedman also suggests that another study conducted in the Netherlands came to conclusions so different from ours that we banned it from a book we were writing. In fact, the results of that study were remarkably similar to our own, and we did not refuse to publish it. The Dutch researchers themselves chose to publish separately in a different format.

Cultural Differences

Freedman argues that the strongest results reported in the study, such as those for Israeli city children, are so incongruous that they arouse suspicion. He is wrong. Given the influence of culture and social learning on aggressive behavior, different results in different cultures are to be expected. In fact, the similarity of the findings in different countries is remarkable here. One reason we found no connection between television violence viewing and aggression among children on kibbutzim is the strong cultural prohibition against intragroup aggression in those communities. Another reason is that kibbutz children usually watched television in a group and discussed the shows with an adult caretaker afterward.

Two recently published meta-analyses summarize the findings of many studies conducted over the past 30 years. In an analysis of 217 experiments and field studies, Paik and Comstock concluded that the association between exposure to television violence and aggressive behavior is extremely strong, especially in the data accumulated over the last 15 years. In the other meta-analysis, Wood, Wong, and Chachere came to the same conclusion after combined analysis of 23 studies of unstructured social interaction.

We now have well-validated theoretical explanations of these results. Exposure to media violence leads to aggression at least five ways. The first is imitation, or observational learning. Children imitate the actions of their parents, other children, and media heroes, especially when the action is rewarded and the child admires and identifies with the model. When generalized, this process creates what are sometimes called cognitive scripts for complex social problem-solving: internalized programs that guide everyday social behavior in an automatic way and are highly resistant to change.

Turning Off

Second, media violence stimulates aggression by desensitizing children to the effects of violence. The more televised violence a child watches, the more acceptable aggressive behavior becomes for that child. Furthermore, children who watch violent television become suspicious and expect others to act violently—an attributional bias that promotes aggressive behavior.

Justification is a third process by which media violence stimulates aggression. A child who has behaved aggressively watches violent television shows to relieve guilt and justify the aggression. The child then feels less inhibited about aggressing again.

A fourth process is cognitive priming or cueing—the activation of existing aggressive thoughts, feelings, and behavior. This explains why children observe one kind of aggression on television and commit another kind of aggressive act afterward. Even an innocuous object that has been associated with aggression may later stimulate violence. Josephson demonstrated this . . . in a study of schoolboy hockey players. She subjected the boys to frustration and then showed them either a violent or a nonviolent television program. The aggressor in the violent program carried a walkie-talkie. Later, when the referee in a hockey game carried a similar walkie-talkie, the boys who had seen the violent film were more likely to start fights during the game.

A Numbing Effect

The fifth process by which media violence induces aggression is physiological arousal and desensitization. Boys who are heavy television watchers show lower than average physiological arousal in response to new scenes of violence. Similar short-term effects are found in laboratory studies. The arousal stimulated by viewing violence is unpleasant at first, but children who constantly watch violent television become habituated, and their emotional and physiological responses decline. Meanwhile the propensity to aggression is heightened by any pleasurable arousal, such as sexual feeling, that is associated with media violence.

Freedman argues that in violent TV shows, villains "start the fight and are punished" and the heroes "almost always have special legal or moral authority." Therefore, he concludes, children are learning from these programs that the forces of good will overcome evil assailants. On the contrary, it is precisely because media heroes are admired and have special authority that children are likely to imitate their behavior and learn that aggression is an acceptable solution to conflict. Freedman also claims that media violence has little effect because children can distinguish real life from fiction. But children under 11 do not make this distinction very well. Studies have shown that many of them think cartoons and other fantasy shows depict life as it really is.

The studies are conclusive. The evidence leaves no room for doubt that exposure to media violence stimulates aggression. It is time to move on and consider how best to inoculate our children against this insidious threat.

Jonathan L. Freedman

 NO

Violence in the Mass Media and Violence in Society

Imagine that the Food and Drug Administration (FDA) is presented with a series of studies testing the effectiveness of a new drug. There are some laboratory tests that produce fairly consistent positive effects, but the drug does not always work as expected and no attempt has been made to discover why. Most of the clinical tests are negative; there are also a few weak positive results and a few results suggesting that the drug is less effective than a placebo. Obviously the FDA would reject this application, yet the widely accepted evidence that watching television violence causes aggression is no more adequate.

In laboratory tests of this thesis, some children are shown violent programs, others are shown nonviolent programs, and their aggressiveness is measured immediately afterward. The results, although far from consistent, generally show some increase in aggression after a child watches a violent program. Like most laboratory studies of real-world conditions, however, these findings have limited value. In the first place, most of the studies have used dubious measures of aggression. In one experiment, for example, children were asked, "If I had a balloon, would you want me to prick it?" Other measures have been more plausible, but none is unimpeachable. Second, there is the problem of distinguishing effects of violence from effects of interest and excitement. In general, the violent films in these experiments are more arousing than the neutral films. Anyone who is aroused will display more of almost any behavior; there is nothing special about aggression in this respect. Finally and most important, these experiments are seriously contaminated by what psychologists call demand characteristics of the situation: the familiar fact that people try to do what the experimenter wants. Since the children know the experimenter has chosen the violent film, they may assume that they are being given permission to be aggressive.

Putting It to the Test

The simplest way to conduct a real-world study is to find out whether children who watch more violent television are also more aggressive.

From Jonathan L. Freedman, "Violence in the Mass Media and Violence in Society: The Link Is Unproven," *Harvard Mental Health Letter*, vol. 12, no. 11 (May 1996). Copyright © 1996 by The President and Fellows of Harvard College. Reprinted by permission of The Harvard Medical School Health Publications Group.

They are, but the correlations are small, accounting for only 1% to 10% of individual differences in children's aggressiveness. In any case, correlations do not prove causality. Boys watch more TV football than girls, and they play more football than girls, but no one, so far as I know, believes that television is what makes boys more interested in football. Probably personality characteristics that make children more aggressive also make them prefer violent television programs.

To control for the child's initial aggressiveness, some studies have measured children's TV viewing and their aggression at intervals of several years, using statistical techniques to judge the effect of early television viewing on later aggression. One such study found evidence of an effect, but most have found none.

For practical reasons, there have been only a few truly controlled experiments in which some children in a real-world environment are assigned to watch violent programs for a certain period of time and others are assigned to watch non-violent programs. Two or three of these experiments indicated slight, short-lived effects of TV violence on aggression; one found a strong effect in the opposite of the expected direction, and most found no effect. All the positive results were obtained by a single research group, which conducted studies with very small numbers of children and used inappropriate statistics.

Scrutinizing the Evidence

An account of two studies will give some idea of how weak the research results are and how seriously they have been misinterpreted.

A study published by Lynette Friedrichs and Aletha Stein is often described (for example, in reports by the National Institute of Mental Health and the American Psychological Association) as having found that children who watched violent programs became more aggressive. What the study actually showed was quite different. In a first analysis the authors found that TV violence had no effect on physical aggression, verbal aggression, aggressive fantasy, or object aggression (competition for a toy or other object). Next they computed indexes statistically combining various kinds of aggression, a technique that greatly increases the likelihood of connections appearing purely by chance. Still they found nothing.

They then divided the children into two groups—those who were already aggressive and those who were not. They found that children originally lower in aggression seemed to become more aggressive and children originally higher in aggression seemed to become less aggressive no matter which type of program they watched. This is a well-known statistical artifact called regression toward the mean, and it has no substantive significance. Furthermore, the less aggressive children actually became more aggressive after watching the neutral program than after watching the violent program. The only comfort for the experimenters was that the level of aggression in highly aggressive children fell more when they watched a neutral program than when they watched a violent program.

Somehow that was sufficient for the study to be widely cited as strong evidence that TV violence causes aggression.

An ambitious cross-national study was conducted by a team led by Rowell Huesmann and Leonard Eron and reported in 1986. In this widely cited research the effect of watching violent television on aggressiveness at a later age was observed in seven groups of boys and seven groups of girls in six countries. After controlling for initial aggressiveness, the researchers found no statistically significant effect for either sex in Australia, Finland, the Netherlands, Poland, or kibbutz children in Israel. The effect sought by the investigators was found only in the United States and among urban Israeli children, and the latter effect was so large, so far beyond the normal range for this kind of research and so incongruous with the results in other countries, that it must be regarded with suspicion. Nevertheless, the senior authors concluded that the pattern of results supported their position. The Netherlands researchers disagreed; they acknowledged that they had not been able to link TV violence to aggression, and they criticized the methods used by some of the other groups. The senior authors refused to include their chapter in the book that came out of the study, and they had to publish a separate report.

A Second Look

If the evidence is so inadequate, why have so many committees evaluating it concluded that the link exists? In the first place, these committees have been composed largely of people chosen with the expectation of reaching that conclusion. Furthermore, committee members who were not already familiar with the research could not possibly have read it all themselves, and must have relied on what they were told by experts who were often biased. The reports of these committees are often seriously inadequate. The National Institute of Mental Health, for example, conducted a huge study but solicited only one review of the literature, from a strong advocate of the view that television violence causes aggression. The review was sketchy—it left out many important studies—and deeply flawed.

The belief that TV violence causes aggression has seemed plausible because it is intuitively obvious that this powerful medium has effects on children. After all, children imitate and learn from what they see. The question, however, is what they see on television and what they learn. We know that children tend to imitate actions that are rewarded and avoid actions that are punished. In most violent television programs villains start the fight and are punished. The programs also show heroes using violence to fight violence, but the heroes almost always have special legal or moral authority; they are police, other government agents, or protectors of society like Batman and the Power Rangers. If children are learning anything from these programs, it is that the forces of good will overcome evil assailants who are the first to use violence. That may be overoptimistic, but it hardly encourages the children themselves to initiate aggression.

Telling the Difference

Furthermore, these programs are fiction, and children know it as early as the age of five. Children watching Power Rangers do not think they can beam up to the command center, and children watching "Aladdin" do not believe in flying carpets. Similarly, children watching the retaliatory violence of the heroes in these programs do not come to believe they themselves could successfully act in the same way. (Researchers concerned about mass media violence should be more interested in the fights that occur during hockey and football games, which are real and therefore may be imitated by children who play those sports).

Recently I testified before a Senate committee, and one Senator told me he knew TV made children aggressive because his own son had met him at the door with a karate kick after watching the Power Rangers. The Senator was confusing aggression with rough play, and imitation of specific actions with learning to be aggressive. Children do imitate what they see on television; this has strong effects on the way they play, and it may also influence the forms their real-life aggression takes. Children who watch the Ninja Turtles or Power Rangers may practice martial arts, just as years ago they might have been wielding toy guns, and long before that, wrestling or dueling with wooden swords. If there had been no television, the Senator's son might have butted him in the stomach or poked him in the ribs with a gun. The question is not whether the boy learned his karate kick from TV, but whether TV has made him more aggressive than he would have been otherwise.

Television is an easy target for the concern about violence in our society but a misleading one. We should no longer waste time worrying about this subject. Instead let us turn our attention to the obvious major causes of violence, which include poverty, racial conflict, drug abuse, and poor parenting.

CHALLENGE QUESTIONS

Does Media Violence Promote Violent Behavior in Young People?

1. Huesmann and Moise make strong statements to support their argument that children who watch media violence are likely to act aggressively. Assuming that their conclusion is correct, how might parents and educators counteract the negative effects of this kind of exposure?
2. Freedman contends that some misleading conclusions have been drawn from studies involving flawed methodology. If cost were not a concern, what might be the most effective method for studying the relationship between media violence and aggression?
3. What factors influence media executives to produce violent programming?
4. Some might argue that media violence provides a safe outlet for biologically determined fantasies and urges. What arguments can be made for and against this premise?
5. Imagine that you are a clinician who is being asked to consult with a 10-year-old boy whose behavior is excessively aggressive. How would you evaluate the role of media violence? What recommendations would you make if there seemed to be a relationship between the boy's aggressive behavior and his watching violent programs?

Suggested Readings

Freedman, J. L. (1988). Television violence and aggression: What the evidence shows. In S. Oskamp (Ed.), *Television as a social issue. Applied social psychology annual, vol. 8* (pp. 144–162). Beverly Hills, CA: Sage Publications, Inc.

Freedman, J. L. (1992). Television violence and aggression: What psychologists should tell the public. In P. Suedfeld & P. E. Tetlock (Eds.), *Psychology and social policy* (pp. 179–189). New York, NY: Hemisphere Publishing Corp.

Hepburn, M. A. (1997). T.V. violence! A medium's effect under scrutiny. *Social Education, 61*(5), 244–249.

Huesmann, L. R., Moise, J. F., & Podolski, C. (1997). The effects of media violence on the development of antisocial behavior. In D. M. Stoff & J. Breiling (Eds.), *Handbook of antisocial behavior* (pp. 181–193). New York, NY: John Wiley & Sons, Inc.

Smith, S. L., & Donnerstein, E. (1998). Harmful effects of exposure to media violence: Learning of aggression, emotional desensitization, and fear. In R. G. Green & E. Donnerstein (Eds.), *Human aggression: Theories, research, and implications for social policy* (pp. 167–202). San Diego, CA: Academic Press, Inc.

ISSUE 16

Is Pornography Harmful?

YES: Diana E. H. Russell, from *Dangerous Relationships: Pornography, Misogyny, and Rape* (Sage Publications, 1998)

NO: Nadine Strossen, from *Defending Pornography: Free Speech, Sex, and the Fight for Women's Rights* (Scribner, 1995)

ISSUE SUMMARY

YES: Sociology professor Diana E. H. Russell considers pornography profoundly harmful because it predisposes men to want to rape women and undermines internal and social inhibitions against acting out rape fantasies.

NO: Law professor Nadine Strossen contends that there is no credible research to support the claim that sexist, violent imagery leads to harmful behavior against women.

Social learning theorists have long held that people are prone to engage in behaviors that other people seem to find pleasurable. As exposure to graphic sexual imagery has become mainstream in American society, increasing numbers of people of all ages and both sexes have been stimulated by images that provoke intense, pleasurable biological responses. As the limits in social definitions of what is acceptable have been pushed further and further, the appetites of many people have turned toward images that are increasingly novel and unfamiliar. In the realm of pornography, images that were once unspeakable have become common ingredients on X-rated Internet sites and in adult videos. Debates over pornography have been based on a variety of arguments, including political, religious, psychological, and social. On one side are those who see pornography as an insidious force that undermines individual psychological functioning, interpersonal relationships, and social mores. On the other side are those who view pornography in political terms as involving a very personal choice about what people choose to read or watch.

Diana E. H. Russell considers pornography in the most negative of terms and as the basis for much of the violence that men perpetrate against women. In the following selection, she contends that pornography predisposes some males to want to rape women and undermines some males' internal and social inhibitions against acting out their desire to rape. According to Russell, pornography objectifies and dehumanizes women, perpetuates myths that women enjoy rape, and desensitizes males to rape.

In the second selection, Nadine Strossen contends that there is no credible evidence to support the contention that exposure to sexist, violent imagery leads to sexist, violent behavior. Furthermore, she states that experiments have failed to establish a link between women's exposure to such materials and their development of negative self-images, an assertion that some have made. Strossen argues that the alleged causal relationship is conclusively refuted by the fact that levels of violence and discrimination against women are often inversely related to the availability of sexually explicit materials, including violent sexually explicit materials.

POINT

- Pornography predisposes some males to want to rape women.

- Viewers of pornography can develop arousal patterns to depictions of rape, murder, child sexual abuse, or other assaultive behavior.

- Exposure to pornography is associated with a marked increase in males' acceptance of male dominance in intimate relationships.

- Exposure to pornography increases men's self-reported likelihood of committing rape.
- Exposure to pornography leads to a desensitization, which results in increased violence and sexual exploitation of women.

COUNTERPOINT

- There is no credible evidence to substantiate a clear connection between any type of sexually explicit material and any sexist or violent behavior.

- Levels of violence and discrimination against women are often inversely related to the availability of sexually explicit materials, including violent sexually explicit materials.

- Violence and discrimination against women is common in countries where sexually oriented material is almost completely unavailable (e.g., Saudi Arabia, Iran, and China), yet violence is uncommon in countries where such material is readily available (e.g., Denmark, Germany, and Japan).

- There are no consistent correlations between exposure to pornography and violence against women.

- Research shows that sex offenders had less exposure to sexually explicit materials than most men, that they first saw such materials at a later age than nonoffenders, that they were overwhelmingly more likely to have been punished for looking at these materials as teenagers, and that they often find sexual images more distressing than arousing.

Diana E. H. Russell  **YES**

Pornography as a Cause of Rape

Sociologist David Finkelhor has developed a very useful multicausal theory to explain the occurrence of child sexual abuse. According to Finkelhor's (1984) model, in order for child sexual abuse to occur, four conditions have to be met. First, someone has to *want* to abuse a child sexually. Second, this person's internal inhibitions against acting out this desire have to be undermined. Third, this person's social inhibitions against acting out this desire (e.g., fear of being caught and punished) have to be undermined. Fourth, the would-be perpetrator has to undermine or overcome his or her chosen victim's capacity to avoid or resist the sexual abuse.

According to my theory, these four conditions also have to be met in order for rape, battery, and other forms of sexual assault on adult women to occur (Russell, 1984). Although my theory can be applied to other forms of sexual abuse and violence against women besides rape, this formulation of it will focus on rape because most of the research relevant to my theory has been limited to this form of sexual assault.

In *Sexual Exploitation* (1984), I suggest many factors that may predispose a large number of males in the United States to want to rape or assault women sexually. Some examples discussed in that book are (a) biological factors, (b) childhood experiences of sexual abuse, (c) male sex-role socialization, (d) exposure to mass media that encourage rape, and (e) exposure to pornography. Here I will discuss only the role of pornography.

Although women have been known to rape both males and females, males are by far the predominant perpetrators of sexual assault as well as the biggest consumers of pornography. Hence, my theory will focus on male perpetrators.

. . . As previously noted, in order for rape to occur, a man must not only be predisposed to rape, but his internal and social inhibitions against acting out his rape desires must be undermined. My theory, in a nutshell, is that pornography (a) predisposes some males to want to rape women and intensifies the predisposition in other males already so predisposed; (b) undermines some males' internal inhibitions against acting out their desire to rape; and (c) undermines some males' social inhibitions against acting out their desire to rape.

From Diana E. H. Russell, *Dangerous Relationships: Pornography, Misogyny, and Rape* (Sage Publications, 1998). Copyright © 1998 by Sage Publications, Inc. Reprinted by permission. Notes and references omitted.

The Meaning of "Cause"

Given the intense debate about whether or not pornography plays a causal role in rape, it is surprising that so few of those engaged in it ever state what they mean by "cause." . . .

[P]ornography clearly does not cause rape, as it seems safe to assume that some pornography consumers do not rape women and that many rapes are unrelated to pornography. However, the concept of *multiple causation* (defined below) *is* applicable to the relationship between pornography and rape.

> With the conception of MULTIPLE CAUSATION, various possible causes may be seen for a given event, any one of which may be a sufficient but not necessary condition for the occurrence of the effect, or a necessary but not sufficient condition. . . .

This section will provide the evidence for the four different ways in which pornography can induce this predisposition.

1. Predisposes by pairing of sexually arousing stimuli with portrayals of rape   The laws of social learning (e.g., classical conditioning, instrumental conditioning, and social modeling), about which there is now considerable consensus among psychologists, apply to all the mass media, including pornography. As Donnerstein (1983) testified at the hearings in Minneapolis: "If you assume that your child can learn from Sesame Street how to count one, two, three, four, five, believe me, they can learn how to pick up a gun" (p. 11). Presumably, males can learn equally well how to rape, beat, sexually abuse, and degrade females.

A simple application of the laws of social learning suggests that viewers of pornography can develop arousal responses to depictions of rape, murder, child sexual abuse, or other assaultive behavior. Researcher S. Rachman of the Institute of Psychiatry, Maudsley Hospital, London, has demonstrated that male subjects can learn to become sexually aroused by seeing a picture of a woman's boot after repeatedly seeing women's boots in association with sexually arousing slides of nude females (Rachman & Hodgson, 1968). The laws of learning that operated in the acquisition of the boot fetish can also teach males who were not previously aroused by depictions of rape to become so. All it may take is the repeated association of rape with arousing portrayals of female nudity (or clothed females in provocative poses).

Even for males who are not sexually excited during movie portrayals of rape, masturbation following the movie reinforces the association between rape and sexual gratification. This constitutes what R. J. McGuire, J. M. Carlisle, and B. G. Young refer to as "masturbatory conditioning" (Cline, 1974, p. 210). The pleasurable experience of orgasm—an expected and planned-for activity in many pornography parlors—is an exceptionally potent reinforcer. The fact that pornography is widely used by males as ejaculation material is a major factor that differentiates it from other mass media, intensifying the lessons that male consumers learn from it.

2. Predisposes by generating rape fantasies   Further evidence that exposure to pornography can create in males a predisposition to rape where none existed before is provided by an experiment conducted by Malamuth. Malamuth (1981a) classified 29 male students as sexually force-oriented or non-force-oriented on the basis of their responses to a questionnaire. These students were then randomly assigned to view either a rape version of a slide-audio presentation or a mutually consenting version. The account of rape and the pictures illustrating it were based on a story in a popular pornographic magazine, which Malamuth describes as follows:

> The man in this story finds an attractive woman on a deserted road. When he approaches her, she faints with fear. In the rape version, the man ties her up and forcibly undresses her. The accompanying narrative is as follows: "You take her into the car. Though this experience is new to you, there is a temptation too powerful to resist. When she awakens, you tell her she had better do exactly as you say or she'll be sorry. With terrified eyes she agrees. She is undressed and she is willing to succumb to whatever you want. You kiss her and she returns the kiss." Portrayal of the man and woman in sexual acts follows; intercourse is implied rather than explicit. (p. 38)

In the mutually consenting version of the story the victim was not tied up or threatened. Instead, on her awakening in the car, the man told her that she was safe and "that no one will do her any harm. She seems to like you and you begin to kiss." The rest of the story is identical to the rape version (Malamuth, 1981a, p. 38).

All subjects were then exposed to the same audio description of a rape read by a female. This rape involved threats with a knife, beatings, and physical restraint. The victim was portrayed as pleading, crying, screaming, and fighting against the rapist (Abel, Barlow, Blanchard, & Guild, 1977, p. 898). Malamuth (1981a) reports that measures of penile tumescence as well as self-reported arousal "indicated that relatively high levels of sexual arousal were generated by all the experimental stimuli" (p. 33).

After the 29 male students had been exposed to the rape audio tape, they were asked to try to reach as high a level of sexual arousal as possible by fantasizing about whatever they wanted but without any direct stimulation of the penis (Malamuth, 1981a, p. 40). Self-reported sexual arousal during the fantasy period indicated that those students who had been exposed to the rape version of the first slide-audio presentation created more violent sexual fantasies than those exposed to the mutually consenting version *irrespective of whether they had been [previously] classified as force-oriented or non-force oriented* (p. 33).

As the rape version of the slide-audio presentation is typical of what is seen in pornography, the results of this experiment suggest that similar pornographic depictions are likely to generate rape fantasies even in previously non-force-oriented male consumers. As Edna Einsiedel (1986) points out,

> Current evidence suggests a high correlation between deviant fantasies and deviant behaviors. . . . Some treatment methods are also predicated on the link between fantasies and behavior by attempting to alter fantasy patterns in order to change the deviant behaviors. (1986, p. 60)

Because so many people resist the idea that a desire to rape may develop as a result of viewing pornography, let us focus for a moment on behavior other than rape. There is abundant testimonial evidence that at least some males decide they would like to perform certain sex acts on women after seeing pornography portraying such sex acts. For example, one of the men who answered Shere Hite's (1981) question on pornography wrote: "It's great for me. *It gives me new ideas to try and see,* and it's always sexually exciting" (p. 780; emphasis added). Of course, there's nothing wrong with getting new ideas from pornography or anywhere else, nor with trying them out, as long as they are not actions that subordinate or violate others. Unfortunately, many of the behaviors modeled in pornography *do* subordinate and violate women, sometimes viciously.

The following statements about men imitating abusive sexual acts that they had seen in pornography were made by women testifying at the pornography hearings in Minneapolis, Minnesota, in 1983 (Russell, Part 1, 1993b). Ms. M testified that

> I agreed to act out in private a lot of the scenarios that my husband read to me. These depicted bondage and different sexual acts that I found very humiliating to do. . . . He read the pornography like a textbook, like a journal. When he finally convinced me to be bound, he read in the magazine how to tie the knots and bind me in a way that I couldn't escape. Most of the scenes where I had to dress up or go through different fantasies were the exact same scenes that he had read in the magazines.

Ms. O described a case in which a man

> brought pornographic magazines, books, and paraphernalia into the bedroom with him and told her that if she did not perform the sexual acts in the "dirty" books and magazines, he would beat her and kill her.

Ms. S testified about the experiences of a group of women prostitutes who, she said,

> were forced constantly to enact specific scenes that men had witnessed in pornography. . . . These men . . . would set up scenarios, usually with more than one woman, to copy scenes that they had seen portrayed in magazines and books.

For example, Ms. S quoted a woman in her group as saying,

> He held up a porn magazine with a picture of a beaten woman and said, "I want you to look like that. I want you to hurt." He then began

beating me. When I did not cry fast enough, he lit a cigarette and held it right above my breast for a long time before he burned me.

Ms. S also described what three men did to a nude woman prostitute. They first tied her up while she was seated on a chair, then,

They burned her with cigarettes and attached nipple clips to her breasts. They had many S and M magazines with them and showed her many pictures of women appearing to consent, enjoy, and encourage this abuse. She was held for twelve hours while she was continuously raped and beaten.

Ms. S also cited the following example of men imitating pornography:

They [several johns] forced the women to act simultaneously with the movie. In the movie at this point, a group of men were urinating on a naked woman. All the men in the room were able to perform this task, so they all started urinating on the woman who was now naked.

When someone engages in a particularly unusual act previously encountered in pornography, it suggests that the decision to do so was inspired by the pornography. One woman, for example, testified to the *Attorney General's Commission on Pornography* (1986) about the pornography-related death of her son:

My son, Troy Daniel Dunaway, was murdered on August 6, 1981, by the greed and avarice of the publishers of *Hustler* magazine. My son read the article "Orgasm of Death," set up the sexual experiment depicted therein, followed the explicit instructions of the article, and ended up dead. He would still be alive today were he not enticed and incited into this action by *Hustler* magazine's "How to Do" August 1981 article, an article which was found at his feet and which directly caused his death. (p. 797) . . .

3. Predisposes by sexualizing dominance and submission The first two ways in which pornography can predispose some males to desire rape, or intensify this desire . . . , both relate to the viewing of *violent* pornography. However, both violent *and* nonviolent pornography sexualizes dominance and submission. Hence, nonviolent pornography can also predispose some males to want to rape women.

. . . Check and Guloien conducted an experiment in which they exposed 436 male Toronto residents and college students to one of the three types of sexual material [sexually violent pornography, nonviolent dehumanizing pornography, and erotica] over three viewing sessions, or to no sexual material. Subjects in the no-exposure condition (the control group) participated in only one session in which they viewed and evaluated a videotape that was devoid of sexual material.

These researchers investigated the impact of exposure to pornography and erotica on many variables, including the subjects' self-reported likelihood of raping and their self-reported sexually aggressive behavior. The latter behavior ranged from having coerced "a woman to engage in sexual intercourse by 'threatening to end the relationship otherwise,'" to actually holding a woman down and physically forcing her to have intercourse" (Check & Guloien, 1989, pp. 165–166). Significantly, in an earlier study by Check and his colleagues, convicted rapists had scored three times higher on sexually aggressive behavior than had a control group of violent non-sex offenders (p. 166).

Following are some of the significant findings that Check and Guloien (1989) reported:

- "More than twice as many men who had been exposed to sexually violent or to nonviolent dehumanizing pornography reported that there was at least some likelihood that they would rape, compared to the men in the no-exposure condition" (p. 177).
- "High-frequency consumers who had been exposed to the nonviolent, dehumanizing pornography subsequently reported a greater likelihood of raping, [and] were more sexually callous . . . than high-frequency pornography consumers in the no-exposure condition" (p. 176).
- "Exposure to the nonviolent, erotica materials did not have any demonstrated antisocial impact" (p. 178).

. . . [M]en's self-reported likelihood of raping is not the best measure of *desire* to rape because this variable combines desire with the self-reported probability of acting out that desire. Nevertheless, since rape is clearly an act of dominance that forces submission, as are other coerced sex acts, Check and Guloien's finding that exposure to pornography increases men's self-reported likelihood of rape does offer tentative support for my theoretical model's claim that pornography predisposes some males to desire rape or intensifies this desire by sexualizing dominance and submission. Furthermore, this effect is not confined to violent pornography. It also makes sense theoretically that the sexualizing of dominance and submission would include the eroticization of rape and/or other abusive sexual behavior for some males. . . .

4. Predisposes by creating an appetite for increasingly stronger material Dolf Zillmann and Jennings Bryant (1984) have studied the effects of what they refer to as "massive exposure" to pornography. (In fact, it was not particularly massive: 4 hours and 48 minutes per week over a period of 6 weeks. In later publications, Zillmann and Bryant use the term "prolonged exposure" instead of "massive" exposure.) These researchers, unlike Malamuth and Donnerstein, are interested in ascertaining the effects of nonviolent pornography and, in the study to be described, their sample was drawn from an adult nonstudent population.

Male subjects in the so-called *massive exposure* condition saw 36 nonviolent pornographic films, six per session per week; male subjects in the *intermediate* condition saw 18 such movies, three per session per week.

Male subjects in the control group saw 36 nonpornographic movies. Various measures were taken after 1 week, 2 weeks, and 3 weeks of exposure. Information was also obtained about the kind of materials that the subjects were most interested in viewing.

Zillmann and Bryant (1984) report that as a result of massive exposure to pornography, "consumers graduate from common to less common forms" (p. 127), including pornography portraying "some degree of pseudoviolence or violence" (p. 154). These researchers suggest that this change may be "because familiar material becomes unexciting as a result of habituation" (p. 127).

According to Zillmann and Bryant's research, then, pornography can transform a male who was not previously interested in the more abusive types of pornography into one who *is* turned on by such material. This is consistent with Malamuth's findings . . . that males who did not previously find rape sexually arousing generate such fantasies after being exposed to a typical example of violent pornography.

The Role of Pornography in Undermining Some Males' *Internal* Inhibitions Against Acting Out Their Desire to Rape

. . . Evidence has [shown] that 25% to 30% of males admit that there is some likelihood that they would rape a woman if they could be assured that they would get away with it. It is reasonable to assume that a substantially higher percentage of males would *like* to rape a woman but would refrain from doing so because of their internal inhibitions against these coercive acts. Presumably, the strength of these males' motivation to rape as well as their internal inhibitions against raping range from very weak to very strong, and also fluctuate in the same individual over time.

[There are] seven ways in which pornography can undermine some males' internal inhibitions against acting out rape desires. . . .

1. Objectifying women   Feminists have been emphasizing the role of objectification (treating females as sex objects) in the occurrence of rape for many years (e.g., Medea & Thompson, 1974; Russell, 1975). Males' tendency to objectify females makes it easier for them to rape girls and women. Check and Guloien (1989) note that other psychologists (e.g., Philip Zimbardo, H. C. Kelman) have observed that "dehumanization of victims is an important disinhibitor of cruelty toward others" (p. 161). The rapists quoted in the following passages demonstrate the link between objectification and rape behavior.

> It was difficult for me to admit that I was dealing with a human being when I was talking to a woman, because, if you read men's magazines, you hear about your stereo, your car, your chick. (Russell, 1975, pp. 249–250)

After this rapist had hit his victim several times in the face, she stopped resisting and begged him not to hurt her.

> When she said that, all of a sudden it came into my head, "My God, this is a human being!" I came to my senses and saw that I was hurting this person. (p. 249)

Another rapist said of his victim, "I wanted this beautiful fine *thing* and I got it" (Russell, 1975, p. 245; emphasis added).

Dehumanizing oppressed groups or enemy nations in times of war is an important mechanism for facilitating brutal behavior toward members of those groups. Ms. U, for example, testified that

> A society that sells books, movies, and video games like "Custer's Last Stand [Revenge]" on its street corners, gives white men permission to do what they did to me. Like they [her rapists] said, I'm scum. It is a game to track me down, rape and torture me. (Russell, 1993b)

The dehumanization of women that occurs in pornography is often not recognized because of its sexual guise and its pervasiveness. It is also important to note that the objectification of women is as common in nonviolent pornography as it is in violent pornography.

Doug McKenzie-Mohr and Mark Zanna (1990) conducted an experiment to test whether certain types of males would be more likely to objectify a woman sexually after viewing 15 minutes of nonviolent pornography. They selected 60 male students whom they classified into one of two categories: masculine sex-typed or gender schematic individuals who "encode all cross-sex interactions in sexual terms and all members of the opposite sex in terms of sexual attractiveness" (Bem, 1991, p. 361); and androgynous or gender aschematic males who do not encode cross sex interactions and women in these ways (McKenzie-Mohr & Zanna, 1990, pp. 297, 299).

McKenzie-Mohr and Zanna (1990) found that after exposure to nonviolent pornography, the masculine sex-typed males "treated our female experimenter who was interacting with them in a professional setting, in a manner that was both cognitively and behaviorally sexist" (p. 305). In comparison with the androgynous males, for example, the masculine sex-typed males positioned themselves closer to the female experimenter and had "greater recall for information about her physical appearance" and less about the survey she was conducting (p. 305). The experimenter also rated these males as more sexually motivated based on her answers to questions such as, "How much did you feel he was looking at your body?" "How sexually motivated did you find the subject?" (p. 301).

This experiment confirmed McKenzie-Mohr and Zanna's hypothesis that exposure to nonviolent pornography causes masculine sex-typed males, in contrast to androgynous males, to view and treat a woman as a sex object.

2. Rape myths   If males believe that women enjoy rape and find it sexually exciting, this belief is likely to undermine the inhibitions of some of those who would like to rape women. Sociologists Diana Scully (1985) and Martha Burt (1980) have reported that rapists are particularly apt to believe rape myths. Scully, for example, found that 65% of the rapists in her study believed that "women cause their own rape by the way they act and the clothes they wear"; and 69% agreed that "most men accused of rape are really innocent." However, as Scully points out, it is not possible to know if their beliefs preceded their behavior or constitute an attempt to rationalize it. Hence, findings from the experimental data are more telling for our purposes than these interviews with rapists.

Since the myth that women enjoy rape is widely held, the argument that consumers of pornography realize that such portrayals are false is totally unconvincing (Brownmiller, 1975; Burt, 1980; Russell, 1975). Indeed, several studies have shown that portrayals of women enjoying rape and other kinds of sexual violence can lead to increased acceptance of rape myths in both males and females. In an experiment conducted by Neil Malamuth and James Check (1985), for example, one group of college students saw a pornographic depiction in which a woman was portrayed as sexually aroused by sexual violence, and a second group was exposed to control materials. Subsequently, all subjects were shown a second rape portrayal. The students who had been exposed to the pornographic depiction of rape were significantly more likely than the students in the control group:

1. to perceive the second rape victim as suffering less trauma;
2. to believe that she actually enjoyed being raped; and
3. to believe that women in general enjoy rape and forced sexual acts. (Check & Malamuth, 1985, p. 419)

Other examples of the rape myths that male subjects in these studies are more apt to believe after viewing pornography are as follows:

• A woman who goes to the home or the apartment of a man on their first date implies that she is willing to have sex;
• Any healthy woman can successfully resist a rapist if she really wants to;
• Many women have an unconscious wish to be raped, and may then unconsciously set up a situation in which they are likely to be attacked;
• If a girl engages in necking or petting and she lets things get out of hand, it is her own fault if her partner forces sex on her. (Briere, Malamuth, & Check, 1985, p. 400)

In Maxwell and Check's 1992 study of 247 high school students (described above), they found very high rates of what they called "rape supportive beliefs," that is, acceptance of rape myths and violence against women. The boys who were the most frequent consumers of pornography, who reported learning a lot from it, or both, were more accepting of rape supportive beliefs than their peers who were less frequent consumers of pornography and/or who said they had not learned as much from it.

A quarter of girls and 57% of boys expressed the belief that it was at least "maybe okay" for a boy to hold a girl down and force her to have intercourse in one or more of the situations described by the researchers. In addition, only 21% of the boys and 57% of the girls believed that forced intercourse was "definitely not okay" in any of the situations. The situation in which forced intercourse was most accepted was when the girl had sexually excited her date. In this case, 43% of the boys and 16% of the girls stated that it was at least "maybe okay" for the boy to force intercourse on her (Maxwell & Check, 1992).

According to Donnerstein (1983), "After only 10 minutes of exposure to aggressive pornography, particularly material in which women are shown being aggressed against, you find male subjects are much more willing to accept these particular [rape] myths" (p. 6). These males are also more inclined to believe that 25% of the women they know would enjoy being raped (p. 6).

3. Acceptance of interpersonal violence   Males' internal inhibitions against acting out their desire to rape can also be undermined if they consider male violence against women to be acceptable behavior. Studies have shown that when male subjects view portrayals of sexual violence that have positive consequences—as they often do in pornography—it increases their acceptance of violence against women. Examples of some of the beliefs used to measure acceptance of interpersonal violence include the following:

- Being roughed up is sexually stimulating to many women;
- Sometimes the only way a man can get a cold woman turned on is to use force;
- Many times a woman will pretend she doesn't want to have intercourse because she doesn't want to seem loose, but she's really hoping the man will force her. (Briere et al., 1985, p. 401)

Malamuth and Check (1981) conducted an experiment of particular interest because the movies shown were part of the regular campus film program. Students were randomly assigned to view either a feature-length film that portrayed violence against women as being justifiable and having positive consequences (*Swept Away* or *The Getaway*) or a film without sexual violence. Malamuth and Check found that exposure to the sexually violent movies increased the male subjects' acceptance of interpersonal violence against women, but not the female subjects' acceptance of this variable. These effects were measured several days after the films had been seen.

Malamuth (1986) suggests several processes by which sexual violence in the media "might lead to attitudes that are more accepting of violence against women" (p. 4). Some of these processes also probably facilitate the undermining of pornography consumers' internal inhibitions against acting out rape desires.

1. Labeling sexual violence more as a sexual rather than a violent act.
2. Adding to perceptions that sexual aggression is normative and culturally acceptable.

3. Changing attributions of responsibility to place more blame on the victim.
4. Elevating the positive value of sexual aggression by associating it with sexual pleasure and a sense of conquest.
5. Reducing negative emotional reactions to sexually aggressive acts. (Malamuth, 1986, p. 5)

4. Trivializing rape According to Donnerstein (1985), in most studies on the effects of pornography, "subjects have been exposed to only a few minutes of pornographic material" (p. 341). In contrast, Zillmann and Bryant (1984) examined the impact on male subjects of what they refer to as "massive exposure" to nonviolent pornography (4 hours and 48 minutes per week over a period of 6 weeks . . .). After 3 weeks the subjects were told that they were participating in an American Bar Association study that required them to evaluate a trial in which a man was prosecuted for the rape of a female hitchhiker. At the end of this mock trial, various measures were taken of the subjects' opinions about the trial and about rape in general. For example, they were asked to recommend the prison term they thought most fair.

Zillmann and Bryant (1984) found that the male subjects who had been exposed to the massive amounts of pornography considered rape a less serious crime than they had before they were exposed to it; they thought that prison sentences for rape should be shorter; and they perceived sexual aggression and abuse as causing less suffering for the victims, even in the case of an adult male having sexual intercourse with a 12-year-old girl (p. 132). The researchers concluded that "heavy exposure to common nonviolent pornography trivialized rape as a criminal offense" (p. 117).

The more trivialized rape is in the perceptions of males who would like to rape women or girls, the more likely they are to act out their desires. Since the research cited above shows that exposure to pornography increases males' trivialization of rape, it is reasonable to infer that this process contributes to undermining some male consumers' internal inhibitions against acting out their desires to rape.

5. Sex callousness toward females In the same experiment on massive exposure, Zillmann and Bryant (1984) found that "males' sex callousness toward women was significantly enhanced" by prolonged exposure to pornography (p. 117). These male subjects, for example, became increasingly accepting of statements such as, "A woman doesn't mean 'no' until she slaps you"; "A man should find them, fool them, fuck them, and forget them"; and "If they are old enough to bleed, they are old enough to butcher." However, judging by these statements, it is difficult to distinguish sex callousness from a general hostility toward women.

Check and Guloien (1989) divided their sample of 436 male subjects into high-frequency pornography consumers (once per month or more often) and low-frequency pornography consumers (less than once per month). They found that the high-frequency pornography consumers scored significantly higher than the low-frequency consumers on sex callousness toward women (pp. 175–176). In addition, after high-frequency consumers had been exposed to the nonviolent, dehumanizing pornography, they became significantly more sexually callous toward women than the high-frequency consumers in the control group who had not been exposed to any sexual materials. The low-frequency consumers, on the other hand, were unaffected by exposure to the nonviolent dehumanizing pornography (p. 176).

Rapists as a group score higher than nonrapists on sex callousness and hostility toward women. Since the research cited above shows that exposure to pornography increases males' sex calloused attitudes toward women, it is reasonable to infer that this process contributes to undermining some male consumers' internal inhibitions against acting out their desires to rape.

6. Acceptance of male dominance in intimate relationships A marked increase in males' acceptance of male dominance in intimate relationships was yet another result of the massive exposure to pornography (Zillmann & Bryant, 1984, p. 121). The notion that women are, or ought to be, equal in intimate relationships was more likely to be abandoned by these male subjects (p. 122). Finally, their support of the women's liberation movement also declined sharply (p. 134).

These findings demonstrate that pornography increases the acceptability of sexism. As Van White (1984) points out, "by using pornography, by looking at other human beings as a lower form of life, they [the pornographers] are perpetuating the same kind of hatred that brings racism to society" (p. 186).

For example, Ms. O testified about the ex-husband of a woman friend and next-door neighbor: "When he looked at the magazines, he made hateful, obscene, violent remarks about women in general and about me. He told me that because I am female I am here to be used and abused by him, and that because he is a male he is the master and I am his slave" (Russell, 1993b, p. 51).

Rapists as a group reveal a higher acceptance of male dominance in intimate relationships than nonrapists. Since Zillman and Bryant's research shows that exposure to pornography increases males' acceptance of male dominance in intimate relationships, it is reasonable to infer that this process contributes to undermining some male consumers' internal inhibitions against acting out their desires to rape.

7. Desensitizing males to rape In an experiment specifically designed to study desensitization, Donnerstein and Linz showed 10 hours of R-rated or X-rated movies over a period of 5 days to male subjects (Donnerstein & Linz, 1985, p. 34A). Some students saw X-rated movies depicting sexual assault; others saw X-rated movies depicting only consenting sex; and a third group saw R-rated sexually violent movies. . . .

Donnerstein and Linz (1985) described the impact of the R-rated movies on their subjects as follows:

> Initially, after the first day of viewing, the men rated themselves as significantly above the norm for depression, anxiety, and annoyance on a mood adjective checklist. After each subsequent day of viewing, these scores dropped until, on the fourth day of viewing, the males' levels of anxiety, depression, and annoyance were indistinguishable from baseline norms. (p. 34F)

By the fifth day, the subjects rated the movies as less graphic and less gory and estimated fewer violent or offensive scenes than after the first day of viewing. They also rated the films as significantly less debasing and degrading to women, more humorous, and more enjoyable, and reported a greater willingness to see this type of film again (Donnerstein & Linz, 1985, p. 34F). Their sexual arousal to this material, however, did not decrease over this 5-day period (Donnerstein, 1983, p. 10).

On the last day, the subjects went to a law school, where they saw a documentary reenactment of a real rape trial. A control group of subjects who had never seen the films also participated in this part of the experiment. Subjects who had seen the R-rated movies: (a) rated the rape victim as significantly more worthless, (b) rated her injury as significantly less severe, and (c) assigned greater blame to her for being raped than did the subjects who had not seen the films. In contrast, these effects were not observed for the X-rated nonviolent films. However, the results were much the same for the violent X-rated films, despite the fact that the R-rated material was "much more graphically violent" (Donnerstein, 1985, pp. 12–13).

Donnerstein and Linz (1985) point out that critics of media violence research believe "that only those who are *already* predisposed toward violence are influenced by exposure to media violence" (p. 34F). This view is contradicted by the fact that Donnerstein and Linz actually preselected their subjects to ensure that they were not psychotic, hostile, or anxious; that is, they were not predisposed toward violence prior to the research.

Donnerstein and Linz's research shows that exposure to woman-slashing films (soft-core snuff pornography) increases males' desensitization to extreme portrayals of violence against women. It seems reasonable to infer that desensitization contributes to undermining some male viewers' internal inhibitions against acting out their desires to rape.

In summary: I have presented only a small portion of the research evidence for seven different effects of pornography, all of which probably contribute to the undermining of some males' internal inhibitions against acting out their rape desires. This list is not intended to be comprehensive.

Why Censoring Pornography Would Not Reduce Discrimination or Violence Against Women

The only thing pornography is known to cause directly is the solitary act of masturbation. As for corruption, the only immediate victim is English prose.

—Gore Vidal, writer

[I have] aimed to illuminate the legal flaws and misconceptions of MacKinnon-Dworkin–style antipornography laws, to show how such law undermines rather than advances important women's rights and human rights causes, and to paint a picture of the suppressed society that this type of law would produce when put in practice. Especially given recently renewed interest in MacDworkinite laws, they—and their chilling consequences—are my immediate concern. I have accordingly exposed the overwhelming problems that are inherent in all such laws. But, for the sake of argument, let's make the purely hypothetical assumption that we could fix those problems: let's pretend we could wave a magic wand that would miraculously make the laws do what they are supposed to without trampling on rights that are vital to everyone, and without stifling speech that serves women.

Even in this "Never-Never Land," where we could neutralize its negative side effects, would censorship "cure"—or at least reduce—the discrimination and violence against women allegedly caused by pornography? That is the assumption that underlies the feminist procensorship position, fueling the argument that we should trade in our free speech rights to promote women's safety and equality rights. In fact, though, the hoped-for benefits of censorship are as hypothetical as our exercise in wishing away the evils of censorship. I will show this by examining the largely unexamined assumption that censorship would reduce sexism and violence against women. This assumption rests, in turn, on three others:

- that exposure to sexist, violent imagery leads to sexist, violent behavior;

From DEFENDING PORNOGRAPHY: Free Speech, Sex, and the Fight for Women's Rights, Scribner, 1995. Copyright © 1995 by Carol Mann Agency. Reprinted by permission.

- that the effective suppression of pornography would significantly reduce exposure to sexist, violent imagery; and
- that censorship would effectively suppress pornography.

To justify censoring pornography on the rationale that it would reduce violence or discrimination against women, one would have to provide actual support for all three of these assumptions. Each presupposes the others. Yet the only one of them that has received substantial attention is the first—that exposure to sexist, violent imagery leads to sexist, violent behavior—and, as I show later . . . there is no credible evidence to bear it out. Even feminist advocates of censoring pornography have acknowledged that this asserted causal connection cannot be proven, and therefore fall back on the argument that it should be accepted "on faith." Catharine MacKinnon has well captured this fallback position through her defensive double negative . . . : "There is no evidence that pornography does no harm."

Of course, given the impossibility of proving that there is *no* evidence of *no* harm, we would have no free speech, and indeed no freedom of any kind, were such a burden of proof actually to be imposed on those seeking to enjoy their liberties. To appreciate this, just substitute for the word "pornography" in MacKinnon's pronouncement any other type of expression or any other human right. We would have to acknowledge that "there is no evidence" that television does no harm, or that editorials criticizing government officials do no harm, or that religious sermons do no harm, and so forth. There certainly is no evidence that feminist writing in general, or MacKinnon's in particular, does no harm.

In its 1992 *Butler* decision, accepting the antipornography feminist position, the Canadian Supreme Court also accepted this dangerous intuitive approach to limiting sexual expression, stating:

> It might be suggested that proof of actual harm should be required. . . .
> [I]t is sufficient . . . for Parliament to have a reasonable basis for concluding that harm will result and this requirement does not demand actual proof of harm.

Even if we were willing to follow the Canadian Supreme Court and procensorship feminists in believing, without evidence, that exposure to sexist, violent imagery does lead to sexist, violent behavior, we still should not accept their calls for censorship. Even if we assumed that *seeing* pornography leads to committing sexist and violent actions, it still would not follow that *censoring* pornography would reduce sexism or violence, due to flaws in the remaining two assumptions: we still would have to prove that pornography has a corner on the sexism and violence market, and that pornography is in fact entirely suppressible.

Even if pornography could be completely suppressed, the sexist, violent imagery that pervades the mainstream media would remain untouched. Therefore, if exposure to such materials caused violence and sexism, these problems would still remain with us. But no censorship regime could completely suppress pornography. It would continue to exist underground. In this respect, censorship would bring us the worst of both worlds. On one hand, as we have just seen from examining the Canadian situation, suppressive laws make it difficult to obtain a wide range of sexually oriented materials, so that most people would not have access to those materials. On the other hand, though, some such materials would continue to be produced and consumed no matter what. Every governmental effort to prohibit any allegedly harmful material has always caused this kind of "double trouble." Witness the infamous "Prohibition" of alcohol earlier in this century, for example.

Let's now examine in more detail the fallacies in each of the three assumptions underlying the feminist procensorship stance. And let's start with the single assumption that has been the focus of discussion—the alleged causal relationship between exposure to sexist, violent imagery and sexist, violent behavior.

Monkey See, Monkey Do?

Aside from the mere fear that sexual expression might cause discrimination or violence against women, advocates of censorship attempt to rely on four types of evidence concerning this alleged causal link: laboratory research data concerning the attitudinal effects of showing various types of sexually explicit materials to volunteer subjects, who are usually male college students; correlational data concerning availability of sexually oriented materials and anti-female discrimination or violence; anecdotal data consisting of accounts by sex offenders and their victims concerning any role that pornography may have played in the offenses; and studies of sex offenders, assessing factors that may have led to their crimes.

As even some leading procensorship feminists have acknowledged, along with the Canadian Supreme Court in *Butler*, none of these types of "evidence" prove that pornography harms women. Rather than retracing the previous works that have reviewed this evidence and reaffirmed its failure to substantiate the alleged causal connection, I will simply summarize their conclusions.

Laboratory Experiments

The most comprehensive recent review of the social science data is contained in Marcia Pally's 1994 book *Sex and Sensibility: Reflections on Forbidden Mirrors and the Will to Censor*. It exhaustively canvasses laboratory studies that have evaluated the impact of exposing experimental subjects to sexually explicit expression of many varieties, and concludes that no credible evidence substantiates a clear causal connection between any type of sexually explicit material and any sexist or violent behavior. The book also draws the same conclusion from its thorough review of field and correlation studies, as well as sociological surveys, in the U.S., Canada, Europe, and Asia.

Numerous academic and governmental surveys of the social science studies have similarly rejected the purported link between sexual expression and aggression. The National Research Council's Panel on Understanding and Preventing Violence concluded, in 1993: "Demonstrated empirical links between pornography and sex crimes in general are weak or absent."

Given the overwhelming consensus that laboratory studies do not demonstrate a causal tie between exposure to sexually explicit imagery and violent behavior, the Meese Pornography Commission Report's contrary conclusion, not surprisingly, has been the subject of heated criticism, including criticism by dissenting commissioners and by the very social scientists on whose research the report purportedly relied.

The many grounds on which the Commission's report was widely repudiated include that: six of the Commission's eleven members already were committed antipornography crusaders when they were appointed to it; the Commission was poorly funded and undertook no research; its hearings were slanted toward preconceived antipornography conclusions in terms of the witnesses invited to testify and the questions they were asked; and, in assessing the alleged harmful effects of pornography, the Commission's report relied essentially upon morality, expressly noting at several points that its conclusions were based on "common sense," "personal insight," and "intuition."

Two of the Meese Commission's harshest critics were, interestingly, two female members of that very Commission, Judith Becker and Ellen Levine. Becker is a psychiatrist and psychologist whose entire extensive career has been devoted to studying sexual violence and abuse, from both research and clinical perspectives. Levine is a journalist who has focused on women's issues, and who edits a popular women's magazine. In their formal dissent from the Commission's report, they concluded:

> [T]he social science research has not been designed to evaluate the relationship between exposure to pornography and the commission of sexual crimes; therefore efforts to tease the current data into proof of a casual [sic] link between these acts simply cannot be accepted.

Three of the foremost researchers concerned with the alleged causal relationship between sexually explicit materials and sexual violence, Edward Donnerstein, Daniel Linz, and Steven Penrod, also have sharply disputed the Meese Commission's findings about a purported causal relationship.

Since the feminist censorship proposals aim at sexually explicit material that allegedly is "degrading" to women, it is especially noteworthy that research data show no link between exposure to "degrading" sexually explicit material and sexual aggression.

Even two research literature surveys that were conducted for the Meese Commission, one by University of Calgary professor Edna Einseidel and the other by then–Surgeon General C. Everett Koop, also failed to find any link between "degrading" pornography and sex crimes or aggression. Surgeon General Koop's survey concluded that only two reliable generalizations could be made about the impact of exposure to "degrading" sexual material on its viewers: it caused them to think that a variety of sexual practices were more common than they had previously believed, and it caused them to more accurately estimate the prevalence of varied sexual practices.

Experiments also fail to establish any link between women's exposure to such materials and their development of negative self-images. Carol Krafka found that, in comparison with other women, women who were exposed to sexually "degrading" materials did not engage in more sex-role stereotyping; nor did they experience lower self-esteem, have less satisfaction with their body image, accept more anti-woman myths about rape, or show greater acceptance of violence against women. Similar conclusions have been reached by Donnerstein, Linz, and Penrod.

Correlational Data

Both the Meese Commission and procensorship feminists have attempted to rely on studies that allegedly show a correlation between the availability of sexually explicit materials and sexual offense rates. Of course, though, a positive correlation between two phenomena does not prove that one causes the other. Accordingly, even if the studies did consistently show a positive correlation between the prevalence of sexual materials and sexual offenses—which they do not—they still would not establish that exposure to the materials *caused* the rise in offenses. The same correlation could also reflect the opposite causal chain—if, for example, rapists relived their violent acts by purchasing sexually violent magazines or videotapes.

Any correlation between the availability of sexual materials and the rate of sex offenses could also reflect an independent factor that causes increases in both. Cynthia Gentry's correlational studies have identified just such an independent variable in geographical areas that have high rates of both the circulation of sexually explicit magazines and sexual violence: namely, a high population of men between the ages of eighteen and thirty-four. Similarly, Larry Baron and Murray Straus have noted that areas where both sexual materials and sexual aggression are prevalent are characterized by a "hypermasculated or macho culture pattern," which may well be the underlying causal agent. Accordingly, Joseph Scott and Loretta Schwalm found that communities with higher rape rates experienced stronger sales not only of porn magazines, but also of *all* male-oriented magazines, including *Field and Stream*.

Even more damning to the attempt to rest the "porn-causes-rape-or-discrimination" theory on alleged correlations is that there simply are no consistent correlations. While the asserted correlation would not be *sufficient* to prove the claimed causal connection, it is *necessary* to prove that connection. Therefore, the existence of the alleged causal relationship is conclusively refuted by the fact that levels of violence and discrimination against women are often *inversely* related to the availability of sexually explicit materials, including violent sexually explicit materials. This inverse relationship appears in various kinds of comparisons: between different states within the United States; between different countries; and between different periods within the same country.

Within the United States, the Baron and Straus research has shown no consistent pattern between the availability of sexual materials and the number of rapes from state to state. Utah is the lowest-ranking state in the availability of sexual materials but twenty-fifth in the number of rapes, whereas New Hampshire ranks ninth highest in the availability of sexual materials but only forty-fourth in the number of rapes.

The lack of a consistent correlation between pornography consumption and violence against women is underscored by one claim of the pro-censorship feminists themselves: they maintain that the availability and consumption of pornography, including violent pornography, have been increasing throughout the United States. At the same time, though, the rates of sex crimes have been decreasing or remaining steady. The Bureau of Justice Statistics reports that between 1973 and 1987, the national rape rate remained steady and the attempted rape rate decreased. Since these data were gathered from household surveys rather than from police records, they are considered to be the most accurate measures of the incidence of crimes. These data also cover the period during which feminists helped to create a social, political, and legal climate that should have encouraged higher percentages of rape victims to report their assaults. Thus, the fact that rapes reported to the Bureau of Justice Statistics have not increased provokes serious questions about the procensorship feminists' theories of pornography-induced harm. Similar questions are raised by data showing a decrease in wife battery between 1975 and 1985, again despite changes that should have encouraged the increased reporting of this chronically underreported crime.

Noting that "[t]he mass-market pornography . . . industr[y] took off after World War II," Marcia Pally has commented:

> In the decades since the 1950s, with the marketing of sexual material . . . , the country has seen the greatest advances in sensitivity to violence against women and children. Before the . . . mass publication of sexual images, no rape or incest hot lines and battered women's shelters existed; date and marital rape were not yet phrases in the language. Should one conclude that the presence of pornography . . . has inspired public outrage at sexual crimes?

Pally's rhetorical question underscores the illogicality of presuming that just because two phenomena happen to coexist, they therefore are causally linked. I have already shown that any correlation that might exist between the increased availability of pornography and *increased* misogynistic discrimination or violence could well be explained by other factors. The same is true for any correlation that might exist between the increased availability of pornography and *decreased* misogynistic discrimination or violence.

In a comparative state-by-state analysis, Larry Baron and Murray Straus have found a positive correlation between the circulation of pornographic magazines and the state's "index of gender equality," a composite of twenty-four indicators of economic, political, and legal equality. As the researchers have observed, these findings may suggest that both sexually explicit material and gender equality flourish in tolerant climates with fewer restrictions on speech.

The absence of any consistent correlation between the availability of sexual materials and sexual violence is also clear in international comparisons. On the one hand, violence and discrimination against women are common in countries where sexually oriented material is almost completely unavailable, including Saudi Arabia, Iran, and China (where the sale and distribution of erotica is now a capital offense). On the other hand, violence against women is uncommon in countries where such material is readily available, including Denmark, Germany, and Japan.

Furthermore, patterns in other countries over time show no correlation between the increased availability of sexually explicit materials and increased violence against women. The 1991 analysis by University of Copenhagen professor Berl Kutchinsky revealed that, while nonsexual violent crime had increased up to 300 percent in Denmark, Sweden, and West Germany from 1964 to 1984, all three countries' rape rates either declined or remained constant during this same period, despite their lifting of restrictions on sexual materials. Kutchinsky's studies further show that sex crimes against girls dropped from 30 per 100,000 to 5 per 100,000 between 1965, when Denmark liberalized its obscenity laws, and 1982.

In the decade 1964–1974, there was a much greater increase in rape rates in Singapore, which tightly restricts sexually oriented expression, than in Sweden, which had liberalized its obscenity laws during that period. In Japan, where sexually explicit materials are easily accessible and stress themes of bondage, rape, and violence, rape rates decreased 45 percent during the same decade. Moreover, Japan reports a rape rate of 2.4 per 100,000 people, compared with 34.5 in the United States, although violent erotica is more prevalent in Japan.

Anecdotes and Suspicions

As Seventh Circuit Court of Appeals Judge Richard Posner observed about MacKinnon's book *Only Words*:

> MacKinnon's treatment of the central issue of pornography as she herself poses it—the harm that pornography does to women—is shockingly casual. Much of her evidence is anecdotal, and in a nation of 260 million people, anecdotes are a weak form of evidence.

Many procensorship advocates attempt to rest their case on self-serving "porn-made-me-do-it" claims by sexual offenders, as well as on statements by victims or police officers that sexual offenders had sexually explicit materials in their possession at the time they committed their crimes.

The logical fallacy of relying on anecdotes to establish a general causal connection between exposure to sexual materials and violence against women was aptly noted by journalist Ellen Willis: "Anti-porn activists cite cases of sexual killers who were also users of pornography, but this is no more logical than arguing that marriage causes rape because some rapists are married."

Even assuming that sexual materials really were the triggering factors behind some specific crimes, that could not justify restrictions on such materials. As former Supreme Court justice William O. Douglas wrote: "The First Amendment demands more than a horrible example or two of the perpetrator of a crime of sexual violence, in whose pocket is found a pornographic book, before it allows the Nation to be saddled with a regime of censorship." If we attempted to ban all words or images that had ever been blamed for inspiring or instigating particular crimes by some aberrant or antisocial individual, we would end up with little left to read or view. Throughout history and around the world, criminals have regularly blamed their conduct on a sweeping array of words and images in books, movies, and television.

As noted by the 1979 report of the British Committee on Obscenity and Film Censorship, "For those who are susceptible to them, the stimuli to aggressive behavior are all around us." To illustrate the innumerable crimes that have been incited by words or images, the Committee cited a young man who attempted to kill his parents with a meat cleaver after watching a dramatized version of Dostoyevsky's *The Brothers Karamazov*, and a Jamaican man of African descent in London who raped a white woman, saying that the televised showing of Alex Haley's *Roots* had "inspired" him to treat her as white men had treated black women. Additional examples cited by Ohio State University law professor Earl Finbar Murphy underscore that word blaming and image blaming extend to many religious works, too:

> Heinrich Pommerenke, who was a rapist, abuser, and mass slayer of women in Germany, was prompted to his series of ghastly deeds by Cecil B. De-Mille's *The Ten Commandments*. During the scene of the Jewish women dancing about the Golden Calf, all the doubts of his life became clear: Women were the source of the world's troubles and it was his mission to both punish them for this and to execute them. Leaving the theater, he slew the first victim in a park nearby. John George Haigh, the British vampire who sucked his victims' blood through soda straws and dissolved their drained bodies in acid baths, first had his murder-inciting dreams and vampire longings from watching the "voluptuous" procedure of—an Anglican High Church Service.

Were we to ban words or images on the grounds that they had incited some susceptible individuals to commit crimes, the Bible would be in great jeopardy. No other work has more often been blamed for more heinous crimes by the perpetrators of such crimes. The Bible has been named as the instigating or justifying factor for many individual and mass crimes, ranging from the religious wars, inquisitions, witch burnings, and pogroms of earlier eras to systematic child abuse and ritual murders today.

Marcia Pally's *Sex and Sensibility* contains a lengthy litany of some of the multitudinous, horrific bad acts that have been blamed on the "Good Book." She also cites some of the many passages depicting the "graphic, sexually explicit subordination of women" that would allow the entire Bible to be banned under the procensorship feminists' antipornography law. Pally writes:

> [T]he Bible has unbeatable worldwide sales and includes detailed justification of child abuse, wife battery, rape, and the daily humiliation of women. Short stories running through the text serve as models for sexual assault and the mauling of children. The entire set of books is available to children, who are encouraged or required to read it. It is printed and distributed by some of the world's most powerful organizations. . . .
>
> With refreshing frankness, the Bible tells men it is their rightful place to rule women. . . . [It] specifies exactly how many shekels less than men women are worth. Genesis 19:1–8 tells one of many tales about fathers setting up their daughters to be gang raped. Even more prevalent are . . . glamorized war stories in which the fruits of victory are the local girls. . . . [P]erhaps most gruesome is the snuff story about the guy who set his maid up to be gang raped and, after her death from the assault, cut her body up into little pieces. . . . Unlike movies and television programs, these tales are generally taken to be true, not simulated, accounts.

In 1992, Gene Kasmar petitioned the Brooklyn Center, Minnesota, school board to ban the Bible from school classrooms and libraries on the ground that it is lewd, indecent, obscene, offensive, violent, and dangerous to women and children. He specifically complained about biblical references to concubines, explicit sex, child abuse, incest, nakedness, and mistreatment of women—all subjects, significantly, that would trigger the feminist-style antipornography laws.

In response, the chief counsel of Pat Robertson's American Center for Law and Justice in Virginia, Jay Sekulow, flew to Minnesota and argued that the Bible "is worthy of study for its literary and historic qualities." While the Brooklyn Center School Board apparently agreed with this assessment, voting unanimously to reject Kasmar's petition, it must be recalled that Sekulow's argument would be unavailing under Dworkin-MacKinnon-type antipornography laws. Under the MacDworkin model law, any work could be banned on the basis of even one isolated passage that meets the definition of pornography, and the work could not be saved by any serious literary, historic, or other value it might offer. Consequently, the feminist antipornography law could be used by Kasmar and others to ban the Bible not only from public schools, but also from public libraries, bookstores, and all other venues.

The countless expressive works that have been blamed for crimes include many that convey profeminist messages. Therefore, an anecdotal, image-blaming rationale for censorship would condemn many feminist works. For example, the television movie *The Burning Bed*, which told the true story of a battered wife who set fire to her sleeping husband, was blamed for some "copycat" crimes, as well as for some acts of violence by men against women. The argument that such incidents would justify suppression would mark the end of any films or other works depicting—and deploring—the real violence that plagues the lives of too many actual women.

Under a censorship regime that permits anecdotal, book-blaming "evidence," all other feminist materials would be equally endangered, not "just" works that depict the violence that has been inflicted on women. That is because, as feminist writings themselves have observed, some sexual assaults are committed by men who feel threatened by the women's movement. Should feminist works therefore be banned on the theory that they might well motivate a man to act out his misogynistic aggression?

Studies of Sex Offenders

The scientists who have investigated the impact of exposure to sexual materials in real life have not found that either sexual materials or attitudes toward women play any significant role in prompting actual violence. In general, these studies show that sex offenders had less exposure to sexually explicit materials than most men, that they first saw such materials at a later age than nonoffenders, that they were overwhelmingly more likely to have been punished for looking at them as teenagers, and that they often find sexual images more distressing than arousing.

While no evidence substantiates that viewing pornography leads to violence and discrimination against women, some evidence indicates that, if anything, there may well be an inverse causal relationship between exposure to sexually explicit materials and misogynistic violence or discrimination. One of the leading researchers in this area, Edward Donnerstein of the University of California at Santa Barbara, has written: "A good amount of research strongly supports the position that exposure to erotica can reduce aggressive responses in people who are predisposed to aggress." Similarly, John Money, of Johns Hopkins Medical School, a leading expert on sexual violence, has noted that most people with criminal sexualities were raised with strict, antisexual, repressive attitudes. He predicts that the "current repressive attitudes toward sex will breed an ever-widening epidemic of aberrant sexual behavior."

In one 1989 experiment, males who had been exposed to pornography were more willing to come to the aid of a female subject who appeared to be hurt than were men who had been exposed to other stimuli. Laboratory studies further indicate that there may well be an inverse causal relationship between exposure to violent sexually explicit material and sexual arousal. For example, in 1991, Howard Barbaree and William Marshall, of Queen's College in Ontario, found:

> For most men, hearing a description of an encounter where the man is forcing the woman to have sex, and the woman is in distress or pain, dampens the arousal by about 50 percent compared to arousal levels using a scene of consenting lovemaking. . . . Ordinarily violence inhibits

sexual arousal in men. A blood flow loss of 50 percent means a man would not be able to penetrate a woman.

The foregoing research findings are certainly more consistent with what feminist scholars have been writing about rape than is the procensorship feminists' pornocentric analysis: namely, rape is not a crime about sex, but rather, about violence.

See No Pornography, See No Sexist and Violent Imagery?

Pornography constitutes only a small subset of the sexist or violent imagery that pervades our culture and media. New York Law School professor Carlin Meyer recently conducted a comprehensive survey of the views of women's sexuality, status, and gender roles that are purveyed in nonpornographic media:

> Today, mainstream television, film, advertising, music, art, and popular (including religious) literature are the primary propagators of Western views of sexuality and sex roles. Not only do we read, see and experience their language and imagery more often and at earlier ages than we do most explicit sexual representation, but precisely because mainstream imagery is ordinary and everyday, it more powerfully convinces us that it depicts the world as it is or ought to be.

Other cultural and media analysts have likewise concluded that more-damaging sexist imagery is more broadly purveyed through mainstream, nonsexual representations. Thelma McCormack, director of York University's Feminist Studies Centre, has concluded that "the enemy of women's equality is our mainstream culture with its images of women as family-centered," rather than imagery of women as sexual. According to McCormack:

> Surveys and public opinion studies confirm the connection between gender-role traditionalism and an acceptance or belief in the normality of a stratified social system. The more traditional a person's views are about women, the more likely he or she is to accept inequality as inevitable, functional, natural, desirable and immutable. In short, if any image of woman can be said to influence our thinking about gender equality, it is the domestic woman not the Dionysian one.

Social science researchers have found that acceptance of the rape myth and other misogynistic attitudes concerning women and violence are just as likely to result from exposure to many types of mass media—from soap operas to popular commercial films—as from even intense exposure to violent, misogynistic sexually explicit materials. Accordingly, if we really wanted to purge all sexist, violent representations from our culture, we would have to cast the net far beyond pornography, notwithstanding how comprehensive and elastic that category is. Would even procensorship feminists want to deal such a deathblow to First Amendment freedoms?

Censor Pornography, See No Pornography?

Procensorship feminists themselves have acknowledged that censorship would probably just drive pornography underground. Indeed, as recently as 1987, Catharine MacKinnon recognized that "pornography cannot be reformed or suppressed or banned."

The assumption that censorship would substantially reduce the availability or impact of pornography also overlooks evidence that censorship makes some viewers more desirous of pornography and more receptive to its imagery. This "forbidden fruits" effect has been corroborated by historical experience and social science research. All recent studies of the suppression of sexual expression, including Walter Kendrick's 1987 book *The Secret Museum: Pornography in Modern Culture* and Edward de Grazia's 1992 book *Girls Lean Back Everywhere: The Law of Obscenity and the Assault on Genius*, demonstrate that any censorship effort simply increases the attention that a targeted work receives. Social scientific studies that were included in the report of the 1970 President's Commission on Obscenity and Pornography suggested that censorship of sexually explicit materials may increase their desirability and impact, and also that a viewer's awareness that sexually oriented parts of a film have been censored may lead to frustration and subsequent aggressive behavior.

The foregoing data about the impact of censoring pornography are consistent with broader research findings: the evidence suggests that censorship of *any* material increases an audience's desire to obtain the material and disposes the audience to be more receptive to it. Critical viewing skills, and the ability to regard media images skeptically and analytically, atrophy under a censorial regime. A public that learns to question everything it sees or hears is better equipped to reject culturally propagated values than is one that assumes the media have been purged of all "incorrect" perspectives.

Even assuming for the sake of argument that there were a causal link between pornography and anti-female discrimination and violence, the insignificant contribution that censorship might make to reducing them would not outweigh the substantial damage that censorship would do to feminist goals. From the lack of actual evidence to substantiate the alleged causal link, the conclusion follows even more inescapably: *Censoring pornography would do women more harm than good.*

CHALLENGE QUESTIONS

Is Pornography Harmful?

1. Readers of Russell's vehement criticism of pornography might conclude that pornography should be banned. Assuming that this position is correct, how would you determine what constitutes pornography?
2. Although many people would concur with Strossen's stand against censorship, most would recognize the importance of prohibiting certain images, such as those involving sexual acts with children. Explain why such images are considered unacceptable in our society.
3. Since the advent of the Internet, there has been increasing concern about the ease with which children can access pornography. Why is the viewing of pornography by children or adolescents worrisome?
4. Imagine that you are a researcher studying the relationship between sexual aggression and exposure to violent pornography. What ethical challenges would you face in conducting this kind of research?
5. Imagine that you are a clinician treating a couple in psychotherapy who are seeking help because the man insists that his wife participate in the sexual activities he has watched in sexually explicit videos. How would you go about treating this couple?

Suggested Readings

Carse, A. L. (1995). Pornography: An uncivil liberty? *Hypatia*, 10(1), 155–182.

Concepcion, C. M. (1999). On pornography, representation and sexual agency. *Hypatia*, 14(1), 97–100.

Donnerstein, E., & Malamuth, N. (1997). Pornography: Its consequences on the observer. In L. B. Schlesinger & E. Revitch (Eds.), *Sexual dynamics of anti-social behavior* (pp. 30–49). Springfield, IL: Charles C. Thomas Publisher.

Stock, W. E. (1997). Sex as commodity: Men and the sex industry. In R. F. Levant & G. R. Brooks (Eds.), *Men and sex: New psychological perspectives* (pp. 100–132). New York, NY: John Wiley & Sons, Inc.

Strossen, N. (1995). The perils of pornophobia. *The Humanist*, 55(3), 7–10.

ISSUE 17

Is Divorce Always Detrimental to Children?

YES: Judith Wallerstein, Julia Lewis, and Sandra Blakeslee, from *The Unexpected Legacy of Divorce: A Twenty-Five Year Landmark Study* (Hyperion, 2000)

NO: E. Mavis Hetherington and John Kelly, from *For Better or For Worse: Divorce Reconsidered* (W. W. Norton, 2002)

ISSUE SUMMARY

YES: Psychology professors Judith Wallerstein and Julia Lewis, and Sandra Blakeslee, a science and medicine correspondent for the *New York Times,* assert that children of divorced parents suffer emotional damage that impedes normal growth and functioning and permanently alters their lives.

NO: Professor of psychology E. Mavis Hetheringon and writer John Kelly dismiss some of what they view as myths of the divorce culture, stating that divorce is not necessarily detrimental to all children but can, in fact, provide opportunities for growth for the children as well as the parents involved in the divorce.

During the past several decades societal attitudes about divorce have changed tremendously. In the 1950s and 1960s people who divorced were commonly stereotyped as weak and flawed individuals. The sense of social stigma that they experienced was compounded by the judgmental response of several organized religions in which divorce was considered absolutely unacceptable. Society changed dramatically in the late 1960s and 1970s, as did attitudes about divorce. The highly publicized divorces of celebrities brought the topic into mainstream discussions as well as into the realm of possibility for many unhappily married people looking to alter the course of their lives. Other attitudes were also changing, as Americans became increasingly accepting of new forms of commitment and as women were accorded more respect and autonomy in society. Legal experts proposed laws that would facilitate the process by which married people could untie their marital knot.

As the number of divorces has escalated, some experts have grown concerned about the impact of divorce on children whose parents choose to go their separate ways. Judith Wallerstein has become one of the most prominent critics of what she calls a "divorce culture." In the following selection, Wallerstein, Julia Lewis, and Sandra Blakeslee harshly attack arguments implying that divorce is really not so bad for children or that, in some cases, it is actually beneficial to their well-being. They assert that children in postdivorce families are not happier, healthier, or better adjusted, even if their separated parents are happier. Furthermore, the authors contend that these offspring experience long-lasting problems with self-esteem, relationships, and trust.

E. Mavis Hetherington and John Kelly argue in the second selection that the negative effects of divorce have been grossly exaggerated. They also contend that the ardent critics of divorce have failed to acknowledge the positive effects experienced by many postdivorce children. Hetherington and Kelly acknowledge that divorce can be brutally painful for children, but they worry that these children's problems are sometimes associated with self-fulfilling prophecies, in that since they expect to experience negative consequences from their parents' divorce, they do. These authors maintain that insufficient attention has been given to the cases in which divorce has rescued adults and children from the horror of domestic abuse and has provided countless numbers of people with opportunities for life-transforming personal growth.

POINT

- Children of divorce experience more than a singular trauma as the result of divorce. In fact, the instability and turmoil that accompany their parents' search for new partners and lovers has a cumulative effect on the children.

- Divorce permanently alters the lives of children.

- Children of divorce live in fear that they will repeat the mistakes of their parents.

- Children of divorce develop more slowly because they are trying to process so many changes and emotions at once. They fall prey to the dangers of adolescence, such as sex, drugs, and alcohol, at an earlier age than children from intact families.

- It is a myth of the divorce culture that divorce automatically saves children from an unhappy marriage. Most of the children from moderately unhappy marriages that ended in divorce stated that they were not happier after the divorce.

COUNTERPOINT

- The potential negative effects of divorce on children can be moderated in cases in which a parent is stable and engages in competent parenting following the divorce.

- The effects of divorce are not irreversible; a negative experience at one point in time can be countered by a positive experience at another.

- After divorce, the direction of change is not decided; individuals greatly influence their own future.

- Some children emerge from divorce resilient, mature, and responsible because of the experiences associated with the divorce.

- Some individuals, particularly some women and girls, contend that their lives are better following divorce and that they experienced opportunities for life-changing personal exploration and growth.

Judith Wallerstein, Julia Lewis,
and Sandra Blakeslee

YES

Growing Up Is Harder

One of the many myths of our divorce culture is that divorce automatically rescues children from an unhappy marriage. Indeed, many parents cling to this belief as a way of making themselves feel less guilty. No one wants to hurt his or her child, and thinking that divorce is a solution to everyone's pain genuinely helps. Moreover, it's true that divorce delivers a child from a violent or cruel marriage. . . . However, when one looks at the thousands of children that my colleagues and I have interviewed at our center since 1980, most of whom were from moderately unhappy marriages that ended in divorce, one message is clear: the children do not say they are happier. Rather, they say flatly, "The day my parents divorced is the day my childhood ended."

What do they mean? Typically parent and child relationships change radically after divorce—temporarily or, as in Karen's family, permanently. Ten years after the breakup only one-half of the mothers and one-quarter of the fathers in our study were able to provide the kind of nurturant care that had distinguished their parenting before the divorce. To [cite an individual who] said . . . his parents [were] "offstage" while he grew up, after a divorce one or both parents often move onto center stage and refuse to budge. The child becomes the backstage prop manager making sure the show goes on.

What most parents don't realize is that their children can be reasonably content despite the failing marriage. Kids are not necessarily overwhelmed with distress because Mommy and Daddy are arguing. In fact, children and adults can cope pretty well in protecting one another during the stress of a failing marriage or unhappy intact marriage. Mothers and fathers often make every effort to shield their marital troubles from their children. It's only after one or both have decided to divorce that they fight in full view. Children who sense tension at home turn their attention outside, spending more time with friends and participating in school activities. . . . Children learn at an early age to turn a deaf ear to their parents' quarrels. The notion that all or even most parents who divorce are locked into screaming conflict that their children witness is plainly wrong. In many unhappy marriages, one or both people suffer for many years in total silence—feeling lonely, sexually deprived, and profoundly disappointed. Most of the children of divorce say that they had no idea their parents' marriage was teetering on the brink. Although some had secretly thought about

From THE UNEXPECTED LEGACY OF DIVORCE by Judith Wallerstein. Copyright © 2000 Judith Wallerstein. Reprinted by permission of Hyperion.

divorce or discussed it with their siblings, they had no inkling that their parents were planning to break up. Nor did they understand the reality of what divorce would entail for them.

For children, divorce is a watershed that permanently alters their lives. The world is newly perceived as a far less reliable, more dangerous place because the closest relationships in their lives can no longer be expected to hold firm. More than anything else, this new anxiety represents the end of childhood.

Karen confirmed this change in several of our follow-up interviews. Ten years after her parents' divorce, I learned that she was attending the University of California at Santa Cruz so that she could run home on weekends and be available for crises. And there were plenty of those, mostly involving both her younger brother and sister. When she was twenty, she told me angrily, "Since their divorce I've been responsible for both my parents. My dad became a pathetically needy man who always wants a woman to take care of him. I'm the backup when his girlfriends leave him. My mom is still a mess, always involved with the wrong kind of men. I've had to take care of them as well as my brother and sister."

Many Losses

When most people hear the word "divorce," they think it means one failed marriage. The child of divorce is thought to experience one huge loss of the intact family after which stability and a second, happier marriage comes along. But this is not what happens to most children of divorce. They experience not one, not two, but many more losses as their parents go in search of new lovers or partners. Each of these "transitions" (as demographers call them) throws the child's life into turmoil and brings back painful reminders of the first loss. National studies show that the more transitions there are, the more the child is harmed because the impact of repeated loss is cumulative. The prevalence of this instability in the lives of these children hasn't been properly weighed or even recognized by most people. While we do have legal records of second, third, and fourth remarriages and divorces, we have no reliable count of how many live-in or long-term lovers a child of divorce will typically encounter. Children observe each of their parents' courtships with a mixture of excitement and anxiety. For adolescents, the erotic stimulation of seeing their parents with changing partners can be difficult to contain. Several young teenage girls in the study began their own sexual activity when they observed a parent's involvement in a passionate affair. Children and adolescents watch their parents' lovers, with everything from love to resentment, hoping for some clue about the future. They participate actively as helper, critic, and audience and are not afraid to intervene. One mother returning home from a date found her schoolage children asleep in her bed. Since they'd told her earlier that they didn't like her boyfriend, she took the hint. Many new lovers are attentive to the children, regularly bringing little gifts. But even the most charming lovers can disappear overnight. Second marriages with children are much more likely to end in divorce than first marriages. Thus the child's typical experience is not one marriage followed by one divorce, but several or sometimes many relationships for both their mother and father followed by loss or by eventual stability.

Karen's experience is typical of many that I have seen. Her father's second wife, who was nice to the children, left without warning three years into the marriage. After she was gone, her father had four more girlfriends who caused him a great deal of suffering when they also left. Karen's mother had three unhappy love affairs prior to her remarriage, which ended after five years. Obviously Karen and her siblings experienced more than "one divorce." Their childhoods were filled with a history of new attachments followed by losses and consequent distress for both parents. Karen's brother, at age thirty, told me: "What is marriage? Only a piece of paper and a piece of metal. If you love someone, it breaks your heart."

In this study, only 7 of the original 131 children experienced stable second marriages in which they had good relationships with a stepparent and stepsiblings on both sides of the divorced family. Two-thirds of the children grew up in families where they experienced multiple divorces and remarriages of one or both of their parents. Such figures don't capture the many cohabitations and brief love affairs that never become legal relationships. Given this experience, can we be surprised that so many children of divorce conclude that love is fleeting?

Ghosts of Childhood

When I turned to the notes of my interview with Karen fifteen years after her parents' divorce, the image of a young woman crying inconsolably entered my mind. Karen was sitting on the sofa in my old office, with her chin in her hands and elbows on her knees, telling me about her live-in relationship with her boyfriend Nick.

"I've made a terrible mistake," she said, twisting a damp tissue into the shape of a rope. "I can't believe I've gotten myself into this. I never should have done it. It's like my worst nightmare come to life. It's what I grew up dreading most and look what happened." Karen gripped her fingers tightly until her knuckles shone like moons.

"What's wrong?" I asked, as gently as I could.

"Everything," she moaned. "He drinks beer. He has no ambition, no life goals, no education, no regular job. He's going nowhere. When I come home after work, he's just sitting there in front of the TV and that's where he's been all day." Then Karen's voice dropped. "But he loves me," she said in anguish. "He would be devastated if I ever left him." Even in her great distress and anger she was intensely cognizant of her boyfriend's suffering. I thought to myself, this epitomizes Karen—she's always aware of other people's hurts and suffering.

"But then why did you move in with him?"

"I'm not sure. I knew I didn't love him. But I was scared of marriage. I was scared of divorce, and I'm terrified of being alone. Look, you can hope for love but you can't expect it! When Nick asked me to live with him, I was afraid that I'd get older and that I wouldn't have another chance. I kept thinking that I'd end up lonely like my dad. And Mom."

I looked at this beautiful young woman and shook my head in disbelief. Could she really think that shacking up with a man she didn't love was all she could hope for? Karen must have read my mind because she quickly said, "I know. People have been telling me how pretty I am since I was a child. But I don't believe it. And I don't care. Looks were always important to my mother. She wears tons of makeup and dresses like a model. I thought she was silly and still do. I don't want to look like her or live my life that way."

"How did you meet Nick?"

She sighed as she answered, "Well, we hardly knew each other in high school. We were never lovers or even friends. I think that he had a crush on me from afar. Then in my junior year I broke my ankle and during the six weeks that I was hobbling around, he was very kind to me, carrying my stuff and visiting me. He was the only one who took any care of me. He also comes from a divorced family with lots of troubles. When he dropped out of school, I felt very sorry for him."

"Then how did he come back into your life?"

"I was having a real bad time. My brother was getting into serious trouble with the law and my dad wouldn't do anything to help. I pleaded with him but he was totally indifferent. I was frantic and beginning to realize that all my efforts to hold my family together were wasted. So when Nick asked me to move in with him, I said yes. Anything to get away, even though I knew from the outset he had no plans for the future, no training, no formal education. After the first day, I said to myself, 'Oh, my God, what did I do?' But at least I know he won't betray me. At least I'm safe from that."

"Karen, this fear of betrayal is pretty central to you. You keep mentioning it."

"It's been central to my life," she agreed. "Both my parents played around. I saw it all around me. They felt that if you are not getting what you want, you just look elsewhere." (I've never heard anyone put the alternative morality of our divorce culture so succinctly.)

Karen took her hands away from her face and silently ripped the tissue in half. "There's another reason I moved in with him," she whispered. "It will probably distress you." Karen spoke hesitantly, clasped her hands in her lap, and elaborated slowly, as if every word were painful and she had to extract them one by one. "I figured that this is one man who will never leave me." Silence. "Because he has no ambitions, he will always have fewer choices than me. So if I stay with him and even marry him someday, I won't ever have to worry about his walking out."

Karen was right about my being distressed. Her statement was chilling. How utterly tragic that this lovely woman would begin her adult journey so burdened down with fears. What kind of life could she build on such fragile foundations?

Like a good caregiver child, Karen reinstalled her troubled relationships with her mother and father into her early relationships with men. As rescuers, most young women like Karen are used to giving priority to the needs of others. Indeed, they are usually not aware of their own needs or desires. Karen confessed that she had never in her life thought about what would make her happy. "That would be like asking for the moon," she said. "I was always too worried about my family to ask for me." As a result, these young women are often trapped into rescuing a troubled man. How can they reject a pitiful man who clings to them? The guilt would be unbearable. Others find troubled men more exciting. One young woman who had frequent contact with both parents during her growing up years explained: "I think I subconsciously pick men who are not going to work out. Men who are nice and considerate bore me. My latest is irresponsible. I don't trust him. I'm sure he cheats. But he's the one I want."

⋘◉⋙

What prompts so many children of divorce to rush into a cohabitation or early marriage with as much forethought as buying a new pair of shoes? Answers lie in the ghosts that rise to haunt them as they enter adulthood. Men and women from divorced families live in fear that they will repeat their parents' history, hardly daring to hope that they can do better. These fears, which were present but less commanding during adolescence, become overpowering in young adulthood, more so if one or both of their parents failed to achieve a lasting relationship after a first or second divorce. Dating and courtship raise their hopes of being loved sky-high—but also their fears of being hurt and rejected. Being alone raises memories of lonely years in the postdivorce family and feels like the abandonment they dread. They're trapped between the wish for love and the fear of loss.

This amalgam of fear and loneliness can lead to multiple affairs, hasty marriages, early divorce, and—if no take-home lessons are gleaned from it all—a second and third round of the same. Or they can stay trapped in bad relationships for many years. Here's how it works: at the threshold of young adulthood, relationships move center stage. But for many that stage is barren of good memories for how an adult man and woman can live together in a loving relationship. This is the central impediment blocking the developmental journey for children of divorce. The psychological scaffolding that they need to construct a happy marriage has been badly damaged by the two people they depended on while growing up.

Let's look closely at the process of growing up. Children learn all kinds of lessons at their parents' knees, from the time they are born to the time they leave home. There is no landscape more fascinating to the baby than the mother's face. There is no more exciting image to the child than the frame that includes Mom and Dad kissing, fighting, conferring, frowning, crying, yelling, or hugging in the adjoining room. These thousand and one images are internalized and they form the template for the child's view of how men and women treat each other, how parents and children communicate, how brothers and sisters get along. From day one, children watch their parents and absorb the minutiae of human interaction. They observe their parents as private persons (when the adult thinks no one is paying attention) and as public persons onstage outside the home. They listen carefully to what the parents say (although they often pretend not to hear) and they ponder what the parents fail to say. No scientist ever looked through a microscope more intently than the average child who observes her family day in and night out. And they make judgments from early on. Children as young as four years old tell me, "I want to be a daddy like my dad" or "I won't be a mommy like my mommy." They have powerful feelings of love, hate, envy, admiration, pity, respect, and disdain. This is the theater of our lives—our first and most important school for learning about ourselves and all others. From this we extrapolate the interactions of human society. The images of each family are imprinted on each child's heart and mind, becoming the inner theater that shapes expectations, hopes, and fears.

But over and beyond the child's view of mother and father as individuals is the child's view of the relationship between them—the nature of the relationship *as a couple.* Our scholarly literature is full of mother–child and, more recently, father–child experiments, but as every child could tell the professors, the child sees her parents as a twosome. She is intensely and passionately aware of their interaction. What could be more important or more enthralling? These complex images of parental interaction are central to the family theater and are of lasting importance to children of divorce and to children from intact families.

All the young people in the intact families described the relationship between their parents as if they had followed them around day and night. They described their parents' laughter, their teasing, how they knew how to push each other's buttons and how they comforted one another. They even speculated in detail about their parents' sex life. They told me whether Dad kissed Mom when he returned home or whether he pinched her bottom or whether the parents were reserved. Others wondered what their parents had in common or why they stayed married. Along with these observations, they made moral judgments and they reached conclusions that had direct implications for their future lives.

How is the inner template of the child of divorce different from that of the young adult in the intact family—especially if the child of divorce, in accord with the current advice of mediators and court personnel, has access to both parents and the parents refrain from fighting during the postdivorce years?

As every child of divorce told me, no matter how often they see their parents, the image of them together as a loving couple is forever lost. A father in one home and a mother in another home does not represent a marriage, however well they communicate. Separate may be equal but it is not together. As children grow up and choose partners of their own, they lack this central image of the intact marriage. In its place they confront a void that threatens to swallow them whole. Unlike children from intact families, children of divorce in our study spoke very little about their parents' interaction. They hardly ever referred to their parents' behavior at the breakup. By and large their central complaint is that no one had explained the divorce to them and that the reasons were shrouded in mystery. When reasons were offered, they sounded to them like platitudes designed to avoid telling what really happened. Their parents said, we were different people, we had nothing in common. Children of divorce hardly mentioned their parents together except to express their disdain when the parents continued to fight or behave badly with each other at the birthdays of grandchildren and the like. Indeed, the parents' interaction was a black hole—as if the couple had vanished from memory and the children's conscious inner life.

This need for a good internal image of the parents as a couple is important to the child's development throughout her growing up years, but at adolescence, the significance of this internal template of man–woman relationships rises. Memories and images from past and present come together and crescendo in a mighty chorus of voices at entry into young adulthood when the young person confronts for real the issues of choice in love and commitment. In the old Yiddish folk song, the marriage broker asks the maiden, "Whom will you marry?" and her first words echo the contemporary theme of Karen and her millions of sisters and brothers. She replies, "Who will be true to me? Will he take care of me? Will he leave at the crack of dawn when we have our first fight? Will he love me?"

But children of divorce have one more strike against them. Unlike children who lose a parent due to illness, accident, or war, children of divorce lose the template they need because of their parents' *failure*. Parents who divorce may think of their decision to end the marriage as wise, courageous, and the best remedy for their unhappiness—indeed, it may be so—but for the child the divorce carries one meaning: the parents have failed at one of the central tasks of adulthood. Together and separately, they failed to maintain the marriage. Even if the young person decides as an adult that the divorce was necessary, that in fact the parents had little in common to begin with, the divorce still represents failure—failure to keep the man or the woman, failure to maintain the relationship, failure to be faithful, or failure to stick around. This failure in turn shapes the child's inner template of self and family. If they failed, I can fail, too. And if, as happens so frequently, the child observes more failed relationships in the years after divorce, the conclusion is simple. *I have never seen a man and a woman together on the same beam. Failure is inevitable.*

Courtship is always fraught with excitement, yearning, and anxiety. Every adult is aware that this is the most important decision of one's life. Fear of making the wrong choice and of being rejected and betrayed is certainly not confined to children of divorce. But the differences between the children of divorce and those from intact marriages were striking beyond my expectations. The young men and women from intact families, along with their fears, brought a confidence that they had seen it work, that they had some very clear ideas about how to do it. They said so in very convincing terms.

No single adult in the divorced group spoke this way. Their memories and internal images were by contrast impoverished or frightening because they lacked guidelines to use in muting their fears. Indeed, they were helpless in the face of their fears.

Gina, a forty-year-old successful executive in an international company, told me, "I grew up feeling that men are unreliable, just flaky, that like my dad they only really want to play with toys. I know that I've gone out with men who seemed reliable and wonderful, but still, putting all my eggs in one basket with one man is totally frightening. I'm better off relying on me."

Growing Up Takes Longer

When Karen came to see me in 1994 on the eve of her marriage, she was bursting to tell me everything that had happened since our last visit. I remembered her crying her eyes out, complaining about Nick, and here she was, glowing with happiness and optimism. What happened to her between the ages of twenty-five and thirty-four?

First, she described her decision to leave Nick, a journey that took her to a new life in Washington, D.C., where she stayed with a close friend from college and examined her options. "I realized that I wanted to help children but to make a difference I'd need a degree, I'd need some expertise," she said. Working her contacts, Karen soon heard about a masters of public health program at Johns Hopkins that would allow her to combine her interest in child welfare and community organization. Drawing on student loans and what remained from her grandmother's inheritance, she applied and was accepted into the three-year program, moved to Baltimore, and worked part-time in a pediatric outreach program while attending school. Karen, at last following her own desires, was an outstanding student who soon caught the attention of senior professors who mentored her as she negotiated career opportunities. "I have the best job," Karen informed me. "I work with severely handicapped children in five southern states where I run a rural outreach program. We're based in Chapel Hill. I love my work, Judy. I make it my business to spend a lot of time out in the community working with the children. People ask how I can stand it but I don't find it depressing because I get a lot of gifts from the children. They open up and share things with me, their hopes, their dreams, the things they want to do, and the many things they fear. I realize from being with them how precious life is and how you only have this day."

"Karen, you've been helping other people ever since I met you, when you were ten years old. But now it looks like you decided to take a chance on what you want. Maybe the dice will fall your way."

"That's right. I decided to take a chance and I discovered what I want. And I finally figured out what I don't want. I don't want another edition of my relationships with my mom or dad. I don't want a man who is dependent on me."

"And you do want?"

"I want a lover and a husband. I'm no longer frantic to find just anybody because if I have to, I can live alone. I can stand on my own two feet. I'm no longer afraid." And then the sadness around her eyes returned. "But it's not really all behind me. Like I told you, part of me is always waiting for disaster to strike. I keep reminding myself that I'm doing this to myself, but the truth is that I live in dread that something bad will happen to me. Some terrible loss that will change my life. It gets worse as things get better for me. Maybe that's the permanent result of their divorce." She leaned forward so that she was almost doubled at the waist, as if holding herself in one piece. "Gavin teases me all the time about being afraid of change. But I think I've learned how to contain it. I no longer wake up in terror when I go to sleep happy." She paused to think about what she meant. "But it never really goes away, never."

On hearing her story, I realized that Karen's journey into full adulthood required several more steps. Leaving her first serious relationship was only an overture. The Karen who graduated in public health and who had helped establish a successful regional program to help crippled children was a different person altogether. She had acquired a new identity as a competent and proud young woman who could if necessary manage by herself. Over and beyond her professional achievements, Karen was finally able to relinquish her role as the person responsible for her parents and siblings. This was a slow and painful process. The turning point was her realization that her brother and sister were adults who were exploiting her generosity. "I had to move on," she said. "I'd done enough." With that she closed the door, a free woman. Having achieved intellectual and emotional growth, she was ready to be the partner of an adult man who wanted a lover and a wife, not a caregiver. In loving a man who loved her and treated her as an equal, she felt safe for the first time in her life and was able to vanquish her fears. Although residues of her early fears did not disappear, they faded into the background. Within this relationship, Karen completed her struggle to reach adulthood.

In hearing story after story like Karen's about how difficult life was during their twenties, I realized that compared to children from intact families, children of divorce follow a different trajectory for growing up. *It takes them longer.* Their adolescence is protracted and their entry into adulthood is delayed.

Children of divorce need more time to grow up because they have to accomplish more: they must simultaneously let go of the past and create mental models for where they are headed, carving their own way. Those who succeed deserve gold medals for integrity and perseverance. Having rejected their parents as role models, they have to invent who they want to be and what they want to achieve in adult life. This is far and beyond what most adolescents are expected to achieve. Given the normal challenges of growing up—which they had to accomplish on their own—it's no surprise that children of divorce get waylaid by ill-fated love affairs and similar derailments. Most are well into their late twenties and thirties before they graduate into adulthood.

My analysis may not seem to match the pseudomaturity exhibited by many children of divorce who often appear on a fast track to adulthood. Compared with youngsters from more protected families, they get into the trappings of adolescent culture at an earlier age. Sex, drugs, and alcohol are rites of passage into being accepted by an older crowd. At the same time, they're independent and justifiably proud of their ability to make their own decisions and to advise their parents.

But let's not be fooled by the swagger. The developmental path from adolescence into adulthood is thrown out of sync after divorce. Many children of divorce can't get past adolescence because they cannot bring closure to the normal process of separating from their parents. In the normal course of adolescence, children spend several years in a kind of push and pull pas de deux with their parents, slowly weaning themselves from home. But Karen hardly experienced this separation process. By the time she left for college at age eighteen, she was still tied to her parents by her needs and theirs.

And she was not alone. By late adolescence most children of divorce are more tied to their parents and paradoxically more eager to let go than their peers in intact families. Like the folk story of Brer Rabbit and the Tar Baby, the divorce is as sticky as the tar that held the rabbit. The young people want out but can't move on because of unfinished business at home.

Children of divorce are held back from adulthood because the vision of it is so frightening. From the outset, they are more anxious and uncomfortable with the opposite sex and it's harder for them to build a relationship and gradually give it time to develop. Feeling vulnerable, bewildered, and terribly alone, and driven by biology and social pressures, these young men and women throw themselves into a shadow play of the real thing involving sex without love, passion without commitment, togetherness without a future. . . .

The fact that Karen and others were able to turn their lives around is very good news for all of us who have been worried about the long-term effects of divorce on children. It sometimes took many years and several failed relationships, but close to half of the women and over a third of the men in our study were finally able to create a new template with themselves in starring roles. They did it the hard way—by learning from their own experience. They got hurt, kept going, and tried again. Some had relatives, especially grandparents, who loved them and provided close-up role models for what was possible. Some had childhood memories from before the divorce that gave them hope and self-confidence when they felt like giving up. Only a few had mentors, but when they came along they were greatly appreciated. One young man told me, "My boss has been like a father to me, the father that I always wanted and never had." Men and women alike were especially grateful to lovers who stood by them and insisted that they stick around for the long haul. Karen's husband undoubtedly played a major part in her recovery. Finally, a third of the men and women in our study sought professional help from therapists and found, in individual sessions, that they could establish a trusting relationship with another person and use it to get at the roots of their difficulties. It helped that they were young because it meant they had the energy and determination to really change their lives. Clearly people enter adulthood "unfinished," which means the decade of the twenties lends itself to personal development and change.

**E. Mavis Hetherington
and John Kelly**

 **NO**

A New Story about Divorce

Neighbors, friends, even some of the women in Liddy Pennybaker's[1] book group knew about James's infidelities, so when word spread that Liddy had asked for a divorce, everyone thought they knew why.

James frequently went to social events alone, and just as frequently left with an attractive female on his arm. But to Liddy, James's affairs were more in the nature of a last straw than anything else. By the time receipts from out-of-town hotels began appearing in the Pennybakers' American Express bills, Liddy was already halfway out of the marriage. She resented James not spending more time with the children. She had grown tired of his scowls when she ate anything with more than a hundred calories in it. She was sick of his aloofness and condescension when she had friends from her church group to the house. She hated James's social climbing and phony laugh when he was around powerful people.

In truth, Liddy felt almost grateful for the affairs—not that she liked being hurt and humiliated, but the affairs finally focused her, forced her to face a truth she had been resisting for two years. The marriage was over!

Before, when Liddy thought about divorce, she thought about it the way a child thinks about being a grown-up—as a kind of fantasy game. Liddy would spend hours trying on new lives, imagining what it would be like to have a career or to be married to someone else. But whenever she sat down and actually analyzed the costs of divorce, the price always seemed too high.

The thought of telling the children was especially frightening. And leaving would mean ignoring, trashing everything she, the minister's daughter, had been brought up to believe. Oddly enough, the marriage itself also made Liddy hesitate. It still had its good moments and so did James, despite all his lies and deceptions. Walking out on her marriage would make Liddy feel as if she were tearing down a home she had built with her own hands, a home a part of her still loved and felt safe in. Besides, what would she be walking out to? She hadn't worked since her marriage and she didn't have a degree. She had dropped out of college to marry James.

❧◉☙

Chapter One: A New Story About Divorce from FOR BETTER OR FOR WORSE: DIVORCE RECONSIDERED by E. Mavis Hetherington & John Kelly. Copyright © 2002 by E. Mavis Hetherington and John Kelly. Used by permission of W. W. Norton & Company, Inc.

The ambivalence, the weighing of hopes against fears, of past happiness against current dissatisfactions that Liddy Pennybaker wrestled with in deciding to divorce occurs in most marital breakups.

Every divorce is a unique tragedy because every divorce brings an end to a unique civilization—one built on thousands of shared experiences, memories, hopes, and dreams. That wonderful Two-for-the-Road summer in Europe, the first day in the new house, the heart-stopping trip to the emergency room—only the people who shared those moments know what it means to lose them forever. So divorce takes a uniquely personal toll on the divorced. But the experience of divorce also has many commonalities. The end of a marriage always, or almost always, produces heartache, fear, self-doubt, confusion, and of course many anxious questions.

What happens to me and my children now? What should I expect, fear, hope for? What kinds of challenges and pitfalls do I face? And how do I go about building a better life?

Like other books on divorce, *For Better or For Worse* offers answers to these questions. But the answers you will find here are different. *For Better or For Worse* has a new story to tell about divorce, and it is an important story because it is based on the most comprehensive examination of divorce ever conducted: an in-depth examination of nearly 1,400 families and over 2,500 children, many followed for more than three decades. When I finished my research, the adults I had met as young men and women were now in middle age and most had been remarried for a decade or more, and the children I had met as preschoolers were now teachers, accountants, computer scientists, and engineers; many were married; a few had already gone through a divorce of their own.

The unparalleled scope of my research has produced new and surprising findings about divorce and its immediate aftermath, findings that will make us better able to anticipate the consequences of marital failure for ourselves, our children, and for future partners and marriages.

Among the most important findings to emerge are:

- How divorce changes people's behavior, feelings, friendships, health, and, in the case of adults, their work and sex lives
- Why even people who are eager to leave a marriage often question the decision later
- Why the end of the first year is usually the most painful point in the entire postdivorce period
- Why casual postdivorce sex is more emotionally risky for women than men
- Why divorce heightens vulnerability to psychological problems and physical illness
- Why preadolescent girls usually adjust more easily to divorce than boys
- Why men and women rarely marry the person they leave a marriage for
- Why a familial history of divorce is a greater divorce risk to a woman than a man.

For Better or For Worse also has a second, even more important story to tell. This one is about a new kind of experience created by divorce. Traditionally, marital failure has been viewed as a single event, one that produces temporarily intense but limited effects. People suffer, they heal, and then go on with their lives. What happens to them later, as single parents, in a new romantic relationship, or in a second marriage, is dependent on the conditions they encounter later. Or so the traditional view holds.

But as I followed my families over the years and, in many cases, over the decades, I found this view to be insufficient. Marital failure cannot be understood as a single event; it is part of a series of interconnected transitions on a pathway of life experiences that lead to and issue from divorce. The quality of life in a first marriage influences adults' and children's responses to divorce and experiences in a single-parent family, and these in turn cast a shadow across new romantic relationships, a second marriage, and life in a stepfamily.

Sometimes I saw happy second marriages heal painful, divorce-induced emotional scars. But reactions work the other way around as well. Unhappy second marriages and unhappy stepfamilies can reopen old divorce wounds, and a legacy of fear and mistrust from a first marriage can erode happiness in a remarriage.

As I studied nearly fourteen hundred families across time, I realized that the divorce revolution begun in the 1960s had created entirely new patterns of intimate relations, with less stability and fewer certainties but more options. People were not just marrying and staying with the same partner, the traditional pattern for married life. Half of this new generation were divorcing, and they were taking diverse pathways from marital breakup. Some were opting to cohabit or remain single or to have multiple romantic partners. Others were forming relationships with partners of the same sex. Others again were remarrying, often several times.

On one level, *For Better or For Worse* is a portrait of the new ways Americans have learned to live and love and parent in a divorce-prone society. On another level, the book serves as a primer on what might be called the postnuclear family experience. *For Better or For Worse* explains the options that have become available to the newly divorced over the past few decades. Based on the experiences of my study families, it explains which options are most likely to lead to postmarital success or failure, and why.

At the center of the primer is a new and, I think, more balanced view of divorce and its consequences. After forty years of research, I harbor no doubts about the ability of divorce to devastate. It can and does ruin lives. I've seen it happen more times than I like to think about. But that said, I also think much current writing on divorce—both popular and academic—has exaggerated its negative effects and ignored its sometimes considerable positive effects. Divorce has undoubtedly rescued many adults and children from the horror of domestic abuse, but it is not just a preventative measure. I have seen divorce provide many women and girls, in particular, with a remarkable opportunity for life-transforming personal growth, as we shall see later.

The reason our current view of marital failure is so unremittingly negative is that it is based on studies that have only examined people for a year or two after their divorce, and a year or two is not enough time to distinguish between short- and long-term effects. Additionally, many divorce studies do not employ a comparison group of married couples, and thus are unable to distinguish between problems common to all families and problems unique to divorced families.

Once you remove these distortions by doing what I did, examining men, women, and children for over twenty years and including a comparison group of non-divorced married couples, many of our current beliefs about marital failure turn out to be myths. Six examples of the most common myths follow.

Myth One: Divorce Only Has Two Outcomes: Win or Lose

Divorce is too complex a process to produce just winners and losers. People adjust in many different ways, and these patterns of adjusting change over time. The most common include:

- *Enhanced.* Two decades after divorce, the 20 percent of individuals who were classified as Enhanced came closest to looking like traditional postdivorce winners. Successful at work, Enhancers also succeeded socially, as parents, and often in new marriages, though in one key aspect the group did depart from the conventional picture of postdivorce winners. The Enhanced flourished because of the things that had happened to them during and after divorce, not despite them. Competencies that would have remained latent if they had stayed in a marriage were fostered by the urgent need to overcome the challenges of divorce and single parenthood.
- *Competent Loners.* Men and women who do not remarry are often considered divorce losers. But the 10 percent of men and women in my research who were classified as Competent Loners looked a lot like Enhancers; the only major difference was that they were more emotionally self-sustaining. A Competent Loner did not need—or, in many cases, want—a partner; he or she was fully capable of building a meaningful and happy life without a marriage or a longtime companion.
- *Good Enoughs.* For the people in this category, divorce was like a speed bump in the road. It caused a lot of tumult while the person was going over it, but failed to leave a lasting impression—either positive or negative. Two decades later, Good Enoughs (who represented 40 percent of my study sample and were my largest post-divorce group) had different partners and different marriages, but usually the same problems.
- *Seekers.* Seekers were distinguished by a desire to remarry quickly. Alone, the average Seeker, who was usually a man, felt rootless and insecure. He needed a spouse and a marriage to give his life structure, meaning, and a secure base. Unmarried Seekers often became desperately unhappy and clinically depressed; they also had more drinking problems than other divorced adults.
- *Libertines.* The polar opposites of Seekers, Libertines wanted freedom, not a new set of restrictions. They came out of marriage, as one member of the group said, "ready to live life in the fast lane."

Plunging necklines, trendy clothing, tight-fitting jeans, and sports cars were the symbols of their intention. Libertines had the highest rates of casual sex and singles bar patronage in the study.

However, by the end of the first year after divorce many Libertines felt that their life was empty, pointless, a dead end, and they began to seek more stable, committed relationships. As one Libertine said, "After awhile even a sexual smorgasbord gets to be a bit of a bore."

- *The Defeated.* The men and women in this group succumbed to depression, to substance abuse, to a sense of purposelessness. Some of the people in this category lost everything—jobs, homes, second spouses, children, self-esteem; others managed to rebuild a halfway functional new life, but it was joyless. The Defeated often remained embittered over the life they had lost.

Myth Two: Children Always Lose Out After a Divorce

This is another article of faith in popular wisdom and it contains an undeniable truth. In the short run, divorce usually is brutally painful to a child. But its negative long-term effects have been exaggerated to the point where we now have created a self-fulfilling prophecy. At the end of my study, a fair number of my adult children of divorce described themselves as permanently "scarred." But objective assessments of these "victims" told a different story. Twenty-five percent of youths from divorced families in comparison to 10 percent from non-divorced families did have serious social, emotional, or psychological problems. But most of the young men and women from my divorced families looked a lot like their contemporaries from non-divorced homes. Although they looked back on their parents' breakup as a painful experience, most were successfully going about the chief tasks of young adulthood: establishing careers, creating intimate relationships, building meaningful lives for themselves.

Most unexpectedly—since it has seldom been reported before—a minority of my young adults emerged from divorce and postnuclear family life enhanced. Uncommonly resilient, mature, responsible, and focused, these children of divorce blossomed, not despite the things that had happened to them during divorce and after, but, like Enhanced adults, because of them.

Myth Three: The Pathways Following Divorce Are Fixed and Unchanging

The effects of divorce are not irrevocable; they do not lock a person into a particular pattern of adjustment. A negative experience at one major transition point, such as divorce, can be offset by a positive experience at another point, transforming a Defeated individual into a Good Enough or a Good Enough individual into Enhanced. But the opposite can happen, too. A person can go from Good Enough to Defeated.

Also, the direction of change is never predetermined. After a divorce, to a great extent individuals influence their own destiny. . . . [A] single mother's decision to go back to school to upgrade her work skills, or a divorced man's hurried remarriage, or an adolescent's decision to terminate a pregnancy can close or open the gates to a new life path.

Myth Four: Men Are the Big Winners in Divorce

In the tabloid press, men always seem to be leaving their wives for younger, slimmer, and prettier women, so-called trophy wives. But in real life, it is usually the women who do the leaving. Indeed, men-as-divorce-winners may be the biggest myth about divorce. In my research, two out of every three marriages ended because the wife walked out.

Furthermore, women did better emotionally after divorce than men did. They were less likely to mope and feel sorry for themselves and also less likely to continue to pine for a former spouse. Women were better at building a new social network of friends and at finding ways to assuage their pain. And while the economic disparity between men and women following divorce continues to be great, with the woman's economic resources declining by about 30 percent and the man's by 10 percent, this difference is beginning to close, thanks to better education of women and stricter enforcement of child support laws. Still, many women, even middle-class women, fall into poverty after divorce.

Myth Five: The Absence of a Father—and Consequent Poverty—Are the Two Greatest Postdivorce Risks to Children

Fathers do contribute vitally to the financial, social, and emotional well-being of a child. But the contribution is not made through a man's sheer physical presence. A child does not automatically become psychologically well adjusted or a competent student just because he or she lives with Dad. Qualities like stability and competency in children have to be nurtured carefully and patiently by active, engaged fathering.

In fact, we found that if a man was psychologically absent before the divorce and a custodial mother is reasonably well adjusted and parents competently following divorce, single-family life often has little enduring negative developmental impact on a child, particularly if that child is a girl. An involved, supportive, firm custodial mother often is able to counter adverse effects of both the lack of a father and poverty.

Myth Six: Death and Divorce Produce Similar Outcomes

Both death of a father and divorce are associated with the lack of a father in the household, yet children from widowed families show fewer problems than those in divorced, mother-headed families. Why? The conflict associated with the end of a marriage is one reason. Another are the experiences and attitudes of divorced mothers. Widows get more support from families, friends, and inlaws; to some extent there is a "well, you brought it on yourself" attitude to the divorced. Widows also communicate idealized images of their dead husband to their children, whereas divorced women are likely to put down and belittle their ex-spouses, much to the confusion and pain of their children.

However, the death of a marriage, like the death of a loved one, often does produce a mourninglike sadness and grieving. But unlike death, divorce does not provide a sense of closure, of a chapter ending. The unresolved issues of divorce can retain their emotional sting because their source comes by every Saturday morning to pick up the children. Moreover, divorce breeds complicating factors of continued conflict and guilt. Questions like "Was I too selfish?" "Did I try hard enough?" "Could I have done more?" can grate like sandpaper on a guilty conscience.

ം🔊ം

Although our work uncovered many myths about divorce, on one critical point my research does confirm, resoundingly, the conventional wisdom about divorce:

The end of a marriage is usually brutally painful.

In their worst nightmares, few if any of the middle-class women in my study imagined that they would ever find themselves in a welfare office filling out application forms, or moving back in with a parent; but after divorce a surprisingly large number had to do one or both. Similarly, I don't think that many of the divorced men in my studies ever imagined sitting up night after night watching reruns of *Star Trek* and *M*A*S*H* to avoid an empty bed in a half-furnished apartment. And I know none of them ever thought that talking to their children would become almost as difficult as talking to a stranger.

To the boys and girls in my research, divorce seemed cataclysmic and inexplicable. How could a child feel safe in a world where adults had suddenly become untrustworthy? Marital failure was so outside a child's normal range of experience that the only way many youngsters could make sense of it was to blame themselves. Small wonder, then, that one four-year-old confided to me: "My daddy left my mommy and me because he doesn't like me anymore."

From the Pain of Divorce to the Satisfaction of the Postnuclear Family

One of our newly divorced men, a geography professor, started worrying about his sanity when he began looking up at birds in the branches of the trees and shouting, "Get off that branch, you God-damned bird!" However, once the confusion of divorce had passed, the man realized that his bizarre behavior had a purpose. "Somehow it gave me something to vent my anger on," he said to me one day. "It gave me a sense of power when everything was so out of control."

Another, a very buttoned-down young banker, was appalled when he found himself crouched behind a boxwood in his old front yard, peering through a window, watching his former wife and a strange man making love on the living-room floor. "I don't know what's happening to me," he told me later. "I've never done anything like that before. I've never even thought of doing anything like that before."

It was easy to understand their concern. Behaviors like Peeping Tomism and harassing birds are worrisome, but they are also fairly normal in the first year after a divorce, as are erratic mood swings, vulnerability to psychological disorders and physical illness, and doubts about the decision to leave.

But very few of the millions of men and women who get divorced each year anticipate these reactions or know that they are usually temporary and self-correcting. The newly divorced also tend to be blind to the long shadow that the past casts over their new lives. Although *For Better or For Worse* is not a self-help book in the conventional sense of the word, it does explain what to expect and when to expect it. It describes what happens to men, women, and children at one and two years after divorce and at five, ten, fifteen, and twenty years.

To guide you through the challenges and options confronted in postdivorce life, I will describe some of the pathways taken by families I studied over the years. Through their experience, you will be introduced to strategies that can ease adjustment to a marital breakup and produce success in a new single family or a second marriage. I think you will be surprised at how commonsensical some of the strategies are and how novel others are. For example:

- Selecting the right kind of school can measurably increase a child's chances of successfully navigating life after divorce.
- Parental monitoring and supervision are particularly critical with adolescents because children from divorced and remarried families are more vulnerable to peer influence.
- Timing is often key to succeeding in a second marriage. Remarriages that occur prior to a child's adolescence succeed more often than those that occur when a youngster is in his or her early teens.
- Marrying a person from an intact family significantly reduces the higher risk of marital instability carried by adult children of divorce.

How the Virginia Longitudinal Study Changed the Way Divorce Is Studied

My interest in divorce grew out of my work in another area of family life. I think I have always had a special interest in the role fathers play in girls' lives because I had the good fortune to have a father who promoted female achievement and independence at a time when fathers rarely encouraged either.

In the late 1960s, my interest in fathers and daughters led to a startling research finding. At the time, informed opinion held that a mother shaped a daughter's gender identity, a father a son's. But a series of studies I did in the 1960s showed that fathers play the more important role in the gender identity of both boys and girls. The finding raised an interesting and important question: What happens to a girl when a father is absent due to death or divorce?

In my first study of families without fathers, I found that peers and especially mothers step in and assume the gender-shaping role men play in two-parent families. But the new study also raised a new question. Why did girls from divorced families have more social and psychological problems than girls from widowed families? Was there a unique developmental dynamic—perhaps even a uniquely harmful dynamic—in divorced families?

The Virginia Longitudinal Study (VLS), the most comprehensive study of divorce ever conducted, was intended to answer this question.

Most earlier research had relied only on the report of a single family member, usually a mother, to study the effects of divorce. The VLS expanded the study base to include not only the mother, father, and one focal child and a sibling in the family, but also people around the family. I also used a vast array of study tools, including interviews, questionnaires, standardized tests, and observations. Some of these instruments had never been used before, though they are now common in family studies. For example, I devised detailed methods of observing family interactions and activities; I and my team of investigators studied families in the home as they solved problems, as they chatted over dinner, and in the hours between the child's arrival at home and bedtime. We had a very personal look at how our families behaved when they disagreed, fought, relaxed, played, and soothed each other.

The VLS also was the first study to employ a structured diary in studying divorce. In order to assess each adult's mood fluctuations and activities, I had them keep diaries. Three days a week at half-hour intervals, parents had to note where they were, who they were with, what they were doing, and how they were feeling. If a person was having sex, she had to note that in the diary; the same was true if she were out on a date, having a fight at work, sitting in a singles bar, arguing with her mother, or trying to soothe an upset child.

The diaries yielded a great deal of unique and very fine-grained detail. For example, I found that a woman's feelings of anger and helplessness usually lasted longer after a fight with a son than a daughter. I also found that casual sex produced extreme depression and feelings of being unloved in many women and sent a few to the edge. Though suicide attempts were rare in the VLS, the seven that did occur were all attempts by women, and all were triggered by casual sex.

The children in the study—who were age four at the start of the VLS—received even more intense scrutiny. They were observed alone and with parents, peers, and siblings. We observed them at home, in school, on the playground, and also at the Hetherington Laboratory at the University of Virginia. Parents, teachers, and study observers were asked to assess each "target child." As the child grew older, the list of assessors grew to include peers, brothers and sisters, and the child himself, who was periodically asked to make self-assessments.

One of the most important aspects of the VLS was the use of a non-divorced comparison group. With its help, we were able to distinguish between the normal changes all families and family members undergo and changes that were linked directly to the impact of divorce and remarriage.

Initially, the Virginia Longitudinal Study of Divorce, which was launched in 1972, was intended to study how seventy-two preschool children and their families adapted to divorce at two months, one year, and two years. To provide a yardstick of comparison, seventy-two non-divorced families were also included in the study. The study's two-year time limit reflected then current thinking that most families had restabilized by two years after divorce.

But then something unexpected happened. The seventy-two men and women in my divorced group began to remarry and form stepfamilies, and the seventy-two couples in my married comparison group began to divorce. I seemed to be studying a moving target!

At first, I was frustrated. Didn't these folks have any respect for science? But then I realized I had been given a golden opportunity. Women's liberation and employment, no-fault divorce, the sexual revolution, self-actualization, the movements of the sixties and seventies, all were dramatically changing American mating habits. In the blink of an eye, the entire country seemed to jump from the paternal certainties of *Father Knows Best* to the postmodern chaos of *The Brady Bunch*.

Politicians, religious leaders, newspapers, magazines, and television documentaries decried the "breakdown of the nuclear family"; my fellow academics hailed the "emergence of the non-traditional family." But whatever phrase people chose, everyone agreed: America was in the midst of an unprecedented social change—one that would be played out for decades to come in the nation's living rooms, bedrooms, courtrooms, and legislatures.

But was the change positive or negative or a little bit of both?

Would casualties of the divorce revolution begin to inflate the statistics on domestic violence, welfare, school dropouts, unmarried mothers, out-of-wedlock children, juvenile crime, and substance abuse? Or was the revolution simply a reasonable, even a healthy adjustment to a world where female needs were considered the equal of male needs, and where longer life spans made monogamy seem more burdensome than it had when people died at younger ages? As society changes, shouldn't social institutions such as marriage and family also change in response?

I decided my preschooler study would be a good vehicle to explore these questions. I already had a large body of data on divorce and I had a study sample that was coupling and uncoupling and recoupling as energetically as any group in the country. However, if I wanted to use the study as a vehicle to explore not merely divorce but postnuclear family pathways, I would have to expand the time frame and enlarge the number of participants. At six years after divorce, I raised the number of families from 144 to 180—equally balanced between divorced, non-divorced, and stepfamilies, with two children in each family. The original target child and the sibling closest in age were studied throughout the remainder of the study. At eleven years after divorce, when VLS target children were fifteen, I increased the sample to 300 families and 600 children; and at twenty years, when the children were twenty-four, to 450 families and 900 children. Whenever one of the offspring cohabited for more than six months, married, or had a child, an additional full wave of assessment was done of the new family. Thus, we are currently continuing to study our families. It should be noted that at the end of the VLS, 122 of my original 144 families were still participating, a remarkable retention rate for a two-decade-long study.

However, in order to complete my picture of postnuclear family life, I also had to draw on data from two other longitudinal studies done concurrently with the VLS. Indeed, a VLS finding inspired one of them. I noticed that early adolescents had more difficulty adapting to a parent's remarriage than younger children and older adolescents. So in the early 1990s, in conjunction with Glen Clingempeel, a clinical psychologist, I organized the 202-family Philadelphia Divorce and Remarriage (D&R) Study to explore why. The second study, the Nonshared Environment Study (NSES), done in collaboration with David Reiss, a psychiatrist, and Robert Plomin, a behavior geneticist, involved 720 families and 1,440 children. Designed to examine how heredity and environment contribute to differences in development among adolescent siblings in the same household, the NSES, which intensively examined more different kinds of stepfamilies than any previous research project, gave me an opportunity to explore a second question: How do different types of stepfamilies affect the well-being of remarried parents and their children? . . .

While I have drawn heavily on all three studies, particularly the VLS, in a very real sense the new story *For Better or For Worse* tells about divorce and about the new life experience that has grown out of it is based on a superstudy of the nearly fourteen hundred families who participated in the Virginia Longitudinal, NSE, and D&R studies.

My approach to the study of divorce was that of scholar. But I knew from the outset that my work would have important practical implications—how could I not, when nearly every day of my research I was being asked: "What should I do? What does this mean? Should I stay or go?"

For Better or For Worse is many things—the summation of a life's work, a portrait of how America lives and loves now, and a practical guide to a new kind of life experience. But most of all, it is a response to my study participants' cries for help.

My work has given me a very unusual opportunity. For the last thirty years, I've had a chance to watch the marital and relationship mores of a society change, and I want to pass on what I have seen and learned to the millions of men and women who embark on the uncertain adventure of divorce each year. Though *For Better or For Worse* might be seen as a book about why marriages fail, even more it is a book about options and opportunities, about the choices to be made that can lead to fulfillment or to dissatisfaction and despair.

Note

1.   All names and recognizable details have been changed to protect the privacy of the participants.

CHALLENGE QUESTIONS

Is Divorce Always Detrimental to Children?

1. If you were conducting research on the impact of divorce on children, what kind of measures would you use?
2. Hetherington and Kelly assert that the effects of divorce are not irreversible and that a negative-experience at one point can be countered by a positive experience at another point. If you were counseling adults who were in the process of divorce, what recommendations would you provide about the best way to give their children positive experiences to compensate for the more negative experiences?
3. Wallerstein, Lewis, and Blakeslee state that children of divorce live in fear that they will repeat the mistakes of their parents. What specific concerns do you imagine that children of divorce might have when they marry?
4. Hetherington and Kelly argue that some children of divorce emerge from divorce resilient, mature, and responsible because of their experiences. In what ways might the experience of parental divorce benefit children who have gone through this?
5. To what extent should we be concerned that those who downplay the detrimental impact of divorce are engaging in self-serving rationalization? Alternatively, to what extent should we be concerned that those who emphasize the negative impact of divorce are espousing a political or religious agenda?

Suggested Readings

Booth, A., & Amato, P. R. (2001, February). Parental predivorce relations and offspring postdivorce well-being. *Journal of Marriage and the Family,* 197–212.

Coontz, S. (1997). *The way we really are: Coming to terms with America's changing families.* New York: BasicBooks.

Coontz, S. (2000). *The way we never were: American families and the nostalgia trap.* New York: BasicBooks.

Whitehead, B. D. (1998). *The divorce culture: Rethinking our commitments to marriage and family.* New York: Random House.

Hetherington, E. M. (1999). *Coping with divorce, single parenting and remarriage: A risk and resiliency perspective.* Mahwah, NJ: Lawrence Erlbaum Associates.

ISSUE 18

Does Evolution Explain
Why Men Rape?

YES: Randy Thornhill and Craig T. Palmer, from "Why Men Rape," *The Sciences* (January/February 2000)

NO: Susan Brownmiller, from *Against Our Will: Men, Women and Rape* (Simon & Schuster, 1975)

ISSUE SUMMARY

YES: Evolutionary biologist Randy Thornhill and evolutionary anthropologist Craig T. Palmer assert that the reasons why men rape are misunderstood. They contend that, rather than an act of gratuitous violence, rape can be understood as a biologically determined behavior in which socially disenfranchised men resort to this extreme act in order to gain access to women.

NO: Journalist Susan Brownmiller argues that rape is an exemplification of the male-female struggle in which men humiliate and degrade women in a blunt and ugly expression of physical power.

Rape is one of the most troubling and traumatizing of social problems, which is reflected in statistics that are almost unbelievable. It is estimated that in a given year, more than a quarter of a million individuals are the victims of rape, attempted rape, or sexual assault, and that the vast majority of these victims are females. More than one-third of all such cases involve completed rape. In addition to the horrendous physical harm associated with sexual assault, the psychological consequences are usually devastating, causing emotional havoc in the life of the rape victim for years or decades following the trauma. Despite the fact that increased attention has been given to the social problem of rape, controversy regarding explanations about why men commit this act continues.

In 1975 Susan Brownmiller caught the attention of the world with her harsh social commentary on rape. In *Against Our Will: Men, Women and Rape* (Simon & Schuster), Brownmiller assertively attacked widely held misconceptions about rape, such as the notion that victims of rape are somehow responsible for being assaulted or, worse yet, actually wanted to be attacked.

In a compelling and straightforward presentation, Brownmiller discussed rape in such blunt terms that she sparked a dialogue that has lasted for decades.

In 2000 Randy Thornhill and Craig T. Palmer took a social and scholarly risk by discussing rape from a vantage point that they knew would be politically unpopular. Rather than viewing rape as representing a vicious, demeaning, and violent act against women, they argued that this behavior can be understood in evolutionary terms as representing the act of socially disenfranchised men who are desperate to gain access to women. Highlighting the fact that rape takes place among many species, Thornhill and Palmer asserted that this behavior is probably biologically rather than socially determined. Thornhill and Palmer further argued that society can only prevent rape by understanding male and female sexuality. Since publishing their theory, which is reprinted in the following selection, Thornhill and Palmer have been bombarded with criticism for what many view as flawed methodology and thinking. Nevertheless, they sparked a level of discussion that is heated and intense.

In the second selection, an excerpt from *Against Our Will,* Brownmiller asserts that rape is a process of intimidation by which women are kept in a state of fear by men who are motivated by a desire to exert control over women. She views rape as an act of violence committed by men who are socialized to devalue women. In explaining why rape continues to be so prevalent, Brownmiller acknowledges that most men do not rape but that they do benefit indirectly from the "rape system," a hierarchy that separates the genders, with men being on top. This chapter, first published in 1975 and reprinted almost two decades later, is considered one of the most important publications on the topic of rape.

POINT

- Females have evolved to carefully select mates who best support their offspring. That is why we understand that sex is "something females have that males want."

- Rape takes place not only among human beings but also among various other animal species.

- Men might resort to rape when they are socially disenfranchised and, thus, unable to gain access to women.

- The fact that men are able to maintain sexual arousal and copulate with unwilling women suggests that men have evolved psychological mechanisms that enable them to engage in forced copulation. This ability may reflect a "rape adaptation."

COUNTERPOINT

- The intent of rape is not merely to take but to humiliate and to degrade. Thus, men have always viewed sex as the "female treasure."

- Rape is a brief expression of physical power that exemplifies the male-female struggle.

- Access to women does not deter men from rape, as evidenced by the existence of officially sanctioned brothels for American soldiers during the Vietnam War.

- Rape is not a crime of irrational, impulsive, uncontrollable lust; it is a deliberate, hostile, violent act of degradation and possession on the part of a would-be conqueror, designed to intimidate and inspire fear.

Why Men Rape

A friend of ours once told us about her rape. The details hardly matter, but in outline her story is numbingly familiar. After a movie she returned with her date to his car, which had been left in an isolated parking lot. She was expecting him to drive her home. Instead, the man locked the car doors and physically forced her to have sex with him.

Our friend was emotionally scarred by her experience: she became anxious about dating, and even about going out in public. She had trouble sleeping, eating and concentrating on her work. Indeed, like some war veterans, rape victims often suffer from post-traumatic stress disorder, in which symptoms such as anxiety, memory loss, obsessive thoughts and emotional numbness linger after a deeply disturbing experience. Yet gruesome ordeals like that of our friend are all too common: in a 1992 survey of American women aged eighteen and older, 13 percent of the respondents reported having been the victim of at least one rape, where rape was defined as unwelcome oral, anal or vaginal penetration achieved through the use or threat of force. Surely, eradicating sexual violence is an issue that modern society should make a top priority. But first a perplexing question must be confronted and answered: Why do men rape?

The quest for the answer to that question has occupied the two of us collectively for more than forty years. As a purely scientific puzzle, the problem is hard enough. But it is further roiled by strong ideological currents. Many social theorists view rape not only as an ugly crime but as a symptom of an unhealthy society, in which men fear and disrespect women. In 1975 the feminist writer Susan Brownmiller asserted that rape is motivated not by lust but by the urge to control and dominate. In the twenty-five years since, Brownmiller's view has become mainstream. All men feel sexual desire, the theory goes, but not all men rape. Rape is viewed as an unnatural behavior that has nothing to do with sex, and one that has no corollary in the animal world.

Undoubtedly, individual rapists may have a variety of motivations. A man may rape because, for instance, he wants to impress his friends by losing his virginity, or because he wants to avenge himself against a woman who has spurned him. But social scientists have not convincingly demonstrated that rapists are not at least partly motivated by sexual desire as well. Indeed,

From Randy Thornhill and Craig T. Palmer, "Why Men Rape," *The Sciences* (January/February 2000). Adapted from Randy Thornhill and Craig T. Palmer, *A Natural History of Rape: Biological Bases of Sexual Coercion* (MIT Press, 2000). Copyright © 2000 by Randy Thornhill and Craig T. Palmer. Reprinted by permission of MIT Press.

how could a rape take place at all without sexual motivation on the part of the rapist? Isn't sexual arousal of the rapist the one common factor in all rapes, including date rapes, rapes of children, rapes of women under anesthetic and even gang rapes committed by soldiers during war?

&

We want to challenge the dearly held idea that rape is not about sex. We realize that our approach and our frankness will rankle some social scientists, including some serious and well-intentioned rape investigators. But many facts point to the conclusion that rape is, in its very essence, a sexual act. Furthermore, we argue, rape has evolved over millennia of human history, along with courtship, sexual attraction and other behaviors related to the production of offspring.

Consider the following facts:

- Most rape victims are women of childbearing age.
- In many cultures rape is treated as a crime against the victim's *husband*.
- Rape victims suffer *less* emotional distress when they are subjected to *more* violence.
- Rape takes place not only among human beings but also in a variety of other animal species.
- Married women and women of childbearing age experience more psychological distress after a rape than do girls, single women or women who are past menopause.

As bizarre as some of those facts may seem, they all make sense when rape is viewed as a natural, biological phenomenon that is a product of the human evolutionary heritage.

Here we must hasten to emphasize that by categorizing a behavior as "natural" and "biological" we do not in any way mean to imply that the behavior is justified or even inevitable. *Biological* means "of or pertaining to life," so the word applies to every human feature and behavior. But to infer from that—as many of our critics assert that we do—that what is biological is somehow right or good, would be to fall into the so-called naturalistic fallacy. That mistake is obvious enough when one considers such natural disasters as epidemics, floods and tornadoes. In those cases it is clear that what is natural is not always desirable. And of course much can be, and is, done to protect people against natural threats—from administering antibiotics to drawing up emergency evacuation plans. In other words, the fact that rape is an ancient part of human nature in no way excuses the rapist.

&

Why, then, have the editors of scholarly journals refused to publish papers that treat rape from a Darwinian perspective? Why have pickets and audience protesters caused public lectures on the evolutionary basis of rape to be canceled or terminated? Why have investigators working to discover the evolutionary causes of rape been denied positions at universities?

The reason is the deep schism between many social scientists and investigators such as ourselves who are proponents of what is variously called
sociobiology or evolutionary psychology. Social scientists regard culture—
everything from eating habits to language—as an entirely human invention,
one that develops arbitrarily. According to that view, the desires of men and
women are learned behaviors. Rape takes place only when men learn to rape,
and it can be eradicated simply by substituting new lessons. Sociobiologists,
by contrast, emphasize that learned behavior, and indeed all culture, is the
result of psychological adaptations that have evolved over long periods of
time. Those adaptations, like all traits of individual human beings, have both
genetic and environmental components. We fervently believe that, just as
the leopard's spots and the giraffe's elongated neck are the result of aeons of
past Darwinian selection, so also is rape.

That conclusion has profound and immediate practical consequences.
The rape-prevention measures that are being taught to police officers, lawyers, parents, college students and potential rapists are based on the prevailing social-science view, and are therefore doomed to fail. The Darwinian
theory of evolution by natural selection is the most powerful scientific
theory that applies to living things. As long as efforts to prevent rape remain
uninformed by that theory, they will continue to be handicapped by ideas
about human nature that are fundamentally inadequate. We believe that
only by acknowledging the evolutionary roots of rape can prevention tactics
be devised that really work.

⋅◈⋅

From a Darwinian perspective, every kind of animal—whether grasshopper
or gorilla, German or Ghanaian—has evolved to produce healthy children
that will survive to pass along their parents' genetic legacy. The mechanics of
the phenomenon are simple: animals born without traits that led to reproduction died out, whereas the ones that reproduced the most succeeded in
conveying their genes to posterity. Crudely speaking, sex feels good because
over evolutionary time the animals that liked having sex created more offspring than the animals that didn't.

As everyone knows all too well, however, sex and the social behaviors
that go with it are endlessly complicated. Their mysterious and tangled per-
mutations have inspired flights of literary genius throughout the ages, from
Oedipus Rex to *Portnoy's Complaint*. And a quick perusal of the personal-
growth section of any bookstore—past such titles as *Men Are from Mars,
Women Are from Venus* and *You Just Don't Understand*—is enough to show
that one reason sex is so complicated is that men and women perceive it so
differently. Is that the case only because boys and girls receive different
messages during their upbringing? Or, as we believe, do those differences
between the sexes go deeper?

Over vast periods of evolutionary time, men and women have confronted quite different reproductive challenges. Whereas fathers can share
the responsibilities of child rearing, they do not have to. Like most of their

male counterparts in the rest of the animal kingdom, human males can reproduce successfully with a minimal expenditure of time and energy; once the brief act of sexual intercourse is completed, their contribution can cease. By contrast, the minimum effort required for a woman to reproduce successfully includes nine months of pregnancy and a painful childbirth. Typically, ancestral females also had to devote themselves to prolonged breast-feeding and many years of child care if they were to ensure the survival of their genes. In short, a man can have many children, with little inconvenience to himself; a woman can have only a few, and with great effort.

That difference is the key to understanding the origins of certain important adaptations—features that persist because they were favored by natural selection in the past. Given the low cost in time and energy that mating entails for the male, selection favored males who mated frequently. By contrast, selection favored females who gave careful consideration to their choice of a mate; that way, the high costs of mating for the female would be undertaken under circumstances that were most likely to produce healthy offspring. The result is that men show greater interest than women do in having a variety of sexual partners and in having casual sex without investment or commitment. That commonplace observation has been confirmed by many empirical studies. The evolutionary psychologist David M. Buss of the University of Texas at Austin, for instance, has found that women around the world use wealth, status and earning potential as major criteria in selecting a mate, and that they value those attributes in mates more than men do.

Remember, none of the foregoing behavioral manifestations of evolution need be conscious. People do not necessarily have sex because they want children, and they certainly do not conduct thorough cost-benefit analyses before taking a partner to bed. As Darwin made clear, individual organisms merely serve as the instruments of evolution. Men today find young women attractive because during human evolutionary history the males who preferred prepubescent girls or women too old to conceive were outreproduced by the males who were drawn to females of high reproductive potential. And women today prefer successful men because the females who passed on the most genes, and thereby became our ancestors, were the ones who carefully selected partners who could best support their offspring. That is why, as the anthropologist Donald Symons of the University of California, Santa Barbara, has observed, people everywhere understand sex as "something females have that males want."

A dozen roses, romantic dinners by candlelight, a Tiffany engagement ring: the classic courtship ritual requires lots of time, energy and careful attention to detail. But people are far from unique in that regard: the males of most animal species spend much of their energies attracting, wooing and securing sexual partners. The male woodcock, for instance, performs a dramatic display each spring at mating time, soaring high into the air and then tumbling to the ground. Male fireflies are even flashier, blinking like neon signs. The male bowerbird builds a veritable honeymoon cottage: an intricate, sculpted nest that he decorates with flowers and other colorful bric-a-brac. Male deer and antelope lock antlers in a display of brute strength to compete for females.

Once a female's interest is piqued, the male behaves in various ways to make her more sexually receptive. Depending on the species, he dances, fans his feathers or offers gifts of food. In the nursery web spider, the food gift is an attempt to distract the female, who otherwise might literally devour her partner during the sex act. The common thread that binds nearly all animal species seems to be that males are willing to abandon all sense and decorum, even to risk their lives, in the frantic quest for sex.

But though most male animals expend a great deal of time and energy enticing females, forced copulation—rape—also occurs, at least occasionally, in a variety of insects, birds, fishes, reptiles, amphibians, marine mammals and nonhuman primates. In some animal species, moreover, rape is commonplace. In many scorpionfly species, for instance—insects that one of us (Thornhill) has studied in depth—males have two well-formulated strategies for mating. Either they offer the female a nuptial gift (a mass of hardened saliva they have produced, or a dead insect) or they chase a female and take her by force.

A remarkable feature of these scorpionflies is an appendage that seems specially designed for rape. Called the notal organ, it is a clamp on the top of the male's abdomen with which he can grab on to one of the female's forewings during mating, to prevent her escape. Besides rape, the notal organ does not appear to have any other function. For example, when the notal organs of males are experimentally covered with beeswax, to keep them from functioning, the males cannot rape. Such males still mate successfully, however, when they are allowed to present nuptial gifts to females. And other experiments have shown that the notal organ is not an adaptation for transferring sperm: in unforced mating, the organ contributes nothing to insemination.

Not surprisingly, females prefer voluntary mating to mating by force: they will approach a male bearing a nuptial gift and flee a male that does not have one. Intriguingly, however, the males, too, seem to prefer a consensual arrangement: they rape only when they cannot obtain a nuptial gift. Experiments have shown that when male scorpionflies possessing nuptial gifts are removed from an area, giftless males—typically, the wimpier ones that had failed in male-male competitions over prey—quickly shift from attempting rape to guarding a gift that has been left untended. That preference for consensual sex makes sense in evolutionary terms, because when females are willing, males are much more likely to achieve penetration and sperm transfer.

Human males obviously have no external organ specifically designed for rape. One must therefore look to the male psyche—to a potential mental rape organ—to discover any special-purpose adaptation of the human male to rape.

Since women are choosy, men have been selected for finding a way to be chosen. One way to do that is to possess traits that women prefer: men with symmetrical body features are attractive to women, presumably because such features are a sign of health. A second way that men can gain access to women is by defeating other men in fights or other kinds of competitions— thereby gaining power, resources and social status, other qualities that women find attractive.

Rape can be understood as a third kind of sexual strategy: one more way to gain access to females. There are several mechanisms by which such a strategy could function. For example, men might resort to rape when they are socially disenfranchised, and thus unable to gain access to women through looks, wealth or status. Alternatively, men could have evolved to practice rape when the costs seem low—when, for instance, a woman is alone and unprotected (and thus retaliation seems unlikely), or when they have physical control over a woman (and so cannot be injured by her). Over evolutionary time, some men may have succeeded in passing on their genes through rape, thus perpetuating the behavior. It is also possible, however, that rape evolved not as a reproductive strategy in itself but merely as a side effect of other adaptations, such as the strong male sex drive and the male desire to mate with a variety of women.

Take, for instance, the fact that men are able to maintain sexual arousal and copulate with unwilling women. That ability invites inquiry, according to the psychologist Margo Wilson of McMaster University in Hamilton, Ontario, and her coworkers, because it is not a trait that is common to the males of all animal species. Its existence in human males could signal that they have evolved psychological mechanisms that specifically enable them to engage in forced copulation—in short, it could be a rape adaptation. But that is not the only plausible explanation. The psychologist Neil M. Malamuth of the University of California, Los Angeles, points out that the ability to copulate with unwilling women may be simply a by-product of men's "greater capacity for impersonal sex."

More research is needed to decide the question of whether rape is an adaptation or merely a by-product of other sexual adaptations. Both hypotheses are plausible: one of us (Thornhill) supports the former, whereas the other (Palmer) endorses the latter. Regardless of which hypothesis prevails, however, there is no doubt that rape has evolutionary—and thus genetic— origins. All traits and behaviors stem from a complex interplay between genes and the environment. If rape is an adaptation, men must possess genes that exist specifically because rape increased reproductive success. If rape turns out to be merely a side effect of other adaptations, then the genes involved exist for reasons that have nothing to do with rape. Either way, however, the evolutionary perspective explains a number of otherwise puzzling facts about the persistence of rape among human males.

For example, if rape is evolutionary in origin, it should be a threat mostly to women of childbearing age. And, in fact, young adult women are vastly overrepresented among rape victims in the female population as a whole, and female children and post-reproductive-age women are greatly underrepresented.

By the same token, if rape has persisted in the human population through the action of sexual selection, rapists should not seriously injure their victims—the rapist's reproductive success would be hampered, after all, if he killed his victim or inflicted so much harm that the potential pregnancy was compromised. Once again, the evolutionary logic seems to predict reality. Rapists seldom engage in gratuitous violence; instead, they usually limit themselves to the force required to subdue or control their victims. A survey by one of us (Palmer), of volunteers at rape crisis centers, found that only 15 percent of the victims whom the volunteers had encountered reported having been beaten in excess of what was needed to accomplish the rape. And in a 1979 study of 1,401 rape victims, a team led by the sociologist Thomas W. McCahill found that most of the victims reported being pushed or held, but that acts of gratuitous violence, such as beating, slapping or choking, were reported in only a minority of the rapes—22 percent or less. A very small number of rape victims are murdered: about .01 percent (that figure includes unreported as well as reported rapes). Even in those few cases, it may be that the murder takes place not because the rapist is motivated by a desire to kill, but because by removing the only witness to the crime he greatly increases his chance of escaping punishment.

Rape is more distressing for women than are other violent crimes, and evolutionary theory can help explain that as well. In recent years research on human unhappiness informed by evolutionary theory has developed substantial evidence about the functional role of psychological pain. Such pain is thought to be an adaptation that helps people guard against circumstances that reduce their reproductive success; it does so by spurring behavioral changes aimed at preventing future pain [see "What Good Is Feeling Bad?" by Randolph M. Nesse, *The Sciences*, November/December 1991]. Thus one would expect the greatest psychological pain to be associated with events that lower one's reproductive success, and, indeed, emotionally traumatic events such as the death of a relative, the loss of social status, desertion by one's mate and the trauma of being raped can all be interpreted as having that effect.

Rape reduces female reproductive success in several ways. For one thing, the victim may be injured. Moreover, if she becomes pregnant, she is deprived of her chance to choose the best father for her children. A rape may also cause a woman to lose the investment of her long-term partner, because it calls into question whether the child she later bears is really his. A variety of studies have shown that both men and women care more for their genetic offspring than for stepchildren.

One of us (Thornhill), in association with the anthropologist Nancy W. Thornhill, has conducted a series of studies on the factors that contribute to the emotional pain that women experience after a rape. Those studies confirmed that the more the rape interfered with the women's reproductive interests, the more pain they felt. The data, obtained from the Joseph J. Peters Institute in Philadelphia, came from interviews with 790 girls and women who had reported a sexual assault and who were subsequently examined at Philadelphia General Hospital between 1973 and 1975. The subjects, who ranged in age from two months to eighty-eight years, were asked a variety of questions designed to evaluate their psychological responses to the rape. Among other things, they were asked about changes in their sleeping habits, in their feelings toward known and unknown men, in their sexual relations with their partners (children were not asked about sexual matters), and in their eating habits and social activities.

Analysis of the data showed that young women suffered greater distress after a rape than did children or women who were past reproductive age. That finding makes evolutionary sense, because it is young women who were at risk of being impregnated by an undesirable mate. Married women, moreover, were more traumatized than unmarried women, and they were more likely to feel that their future had been harmed by the rape. That, too, makes evolutionary sense, because the doubt a rape sows about paternity can lead a long-term mate to withdraw his support.

Among the women in the study, psychological pain rose inversely to the violence of the attack. In other words, when the rapist exerted less force, the victim was more upset afterward. Those findings, surprising at first, make sense in the evolutionary context: a victim who exhibits physical evidence that sexual access was forced may have less difficulty convincing her husband or boyfriend that what took place was rape rather than consensual sex. In evolutionary terms, such evidence would be reassuring to a pair-bonded male, because rape is a one-time event, whereas consensual sex with other partners is likely to be frequent, and thus more threatening to paternity.

Finally, women of reproductive age reported more emotional distress when the assault involved sexual intercourse than when it involved other kinds of sexual behavior. Among young girls and older women, however, penilevaginal intercourse was no more upsetting than other kinds of assaults. Again, the possibility of an unwanted pregnancy may be a key factor in the degree of trauma the victim experiences.

For all those reasons, the psychological pain that rape victims suffer appears to be an evolved defense against rape. The human females who outreproduced others—and thus became our ancestors—were people who were highly distressed about rape. Their distress presumably served their interests by motivating them to identify the circumstances that resulted in the rape, assess the problems the rape caused, and act to avoid rapes in the future.

◆

If women today are to protect themselves from rape, and men are to desist from it, people must be given advice that is based on knowledge. Insisting

that rape is not about sex misinforms both men and women about the motivations behind rape—a dangerous error that not only hinders prevention
efforts but may actually *increase* the incidence of rape.

What we envision is an evolutionarily informed program for young
men that teaches them to restrain their sexual behavior. Completion of
such a course might be required, say, before a young man is granted a
driver's license. The program might start by inducing the young men to
acknowledge the power of their sexual impulses, and then explaining why
human males have evolved in that way. The young men should learn that
past Darwinian selection is the reason that a man can get an erection just
by looking at a photo of a naked woman, why he may be tempted to
demand sex even if he knows that his date truly doesn't want it, and why
he may mistake a woman's friendly comment or tight blouse as an invitation to sex. Most of all, the program should stress that a man's evolved sexual desires offer him no excuse whatsoever for raping a woman, and that if
he understands and resists those desires, he may be able to prevent their
manifestation in sexually coercive behavior. The criminal penalties for rape
should also be discussed in detail.

Young women also need a new kind of education. For example, in
today's rape-prevention handbooks, women are often told that sexual
attractiveness does not influence rapists. That is emphatically not true.
Because a woman is considered most attractive when her fertility is at its
peak, from her midteens through her twenties, tactics that focus on protecting women in those age groups will be most effective in reducing the overall
frequency of rape.

Young women should be informed that, during the evolution of
human sexuality, the existence of female choice has favored men who are
quickly aroused by signals of a female's willingness to grant sexual access.
Furthermore, women need to realize that, because selection favored males
who had many mates, men tend to read signals of acceptance into a
woman's actions even when no such signals are intended.

In spite of protestations to the contrary, women should also be advised that
the way they dress can put them at risk. In the past, most discussions of
female appearance in the context of rape have, entirely unfairly, asserted
that a victim's dress and behavior should affect the degree of punishment
meted out to the rapist: thus if the victim was dressed provocatively, she
"had it coming to her"—and the rapist would get off lightly. But current
attempts to avoid blaming the victim have led to false propaganda that
dress and behavior have little or no influence on a woman's chances of
being raped. As a consequence, important knowledge about how to avoid
dangerous circumstances is often suppressed. Surely the point that no
woman's behavior gives a man the right to rape her can be made without
encouraging women to overlook the role they themselves may be playing
in compromising their safety.

Until relatively recently in Europe and the United States, strict social taboos kept young men and women from spending unsupervised time together, and in many other countries young women are still kept cloistered away from men. Such physical barriers are understandably abhorrent to many people, since they greatly limit the freedom of women. But the toppling of those barriers in modern Western countries raises problems of its own. The common practice of unsupervised dating in cars and private homes, which is often accompanied by the consumption of alcohol, has placed young women in environments that are conducive to rape to an extent that is probably unparalleled in history. After studying the data on the risk factors for rape, the sex investigators Elizabeth R. Allgeier and Albert R. Allgeier, both of Bowling Green State University in Ohio, recommended that men and women interact only in public places during the early stages of their relationships—or, at least, that women exert more control than they generally do over the circumstances in which they consent to be alone with men.

◄◉►

An evolutionary perspective on rape might not only help prevent rapes but also lead to more effective counseling for rape victims. A therapy program explaining that men rape because they collectively want to dominate women will not help a victim understand why her attacker appeared to be sexually motivated, why she can no longer concentrate enough to conduct her life effectively, or why her husband or boyfriend may view the attack as an instance of infidelity. In addition, men who are made aware of the evolutionary reasons for their suspicions about their wives' or girlfriends' claims of rape should be in a better position to change their reactions to such claims.

Unlike many other contentious social issues, such as abortion and homosexual rights, everyone has the same goal regarding rape: to end it. Evolutionary biology provides clear information that society can use to achieve that goal. Social science, by contrast, promotes erroneous solutions, because it fails to recognize that Darwinian selection has shaped not only human bodies but human psychology, learning patterns and behavior as well. The fact is that men, relative to women, are more aggressive, sexually assertive and eager to copulate, and less discriminating about mates—traits that contribute to the existence of rape. When social scientists mistakenly assert that socialization alone causes those gender differences, they ignore the fact that the same differences also exist in all the other animal species in which males offer less parental investment than females and compete for access to females.

In addressing the question of rape, the choice between the politically constructed answers of social science and the evidentiary answers of evolutionary biology is essentially a choice between ideology and knowledge. As scientists who would like to see rape eradicated from human life, we sincerely hope that truth will prevail.

Women Fight Back

To a woman the definition of rape is fairly simple. A sexual invasion of the body by force, an incursion into the private, personal inner space without consent—in short, an internal assault from one of several avenues and by one of several methods—constitutes a deliberate violation of emotional, physical and rational integrity and is a hostile, degrading act of violence that deserves the name of rape.

Yet by tracing man's concept of rape as he defined it in his earliest laws, we now know with certainty that the criminal act he viewed with horror, and the deadly punishments he saw fit to apply, had little to do with an actual act of sexual violence that a woman's body might sustain. . . .

Man's historic desire to maintain sole, total and complete access to woman's vagina, as codified by his earliest laws of marriage, sprang from his need to be the sole physical instrument governing impregnation, progeny and inheritance rights. As man understood his male reality, it was perfectly lawful to capture and rape some other tribe's women, for what better way for his own tribe to increase? But it was unlawful, he felt, for the insult to be returned. The criminal act he viewed with horror and punished as rape was not sexual assault *per se,* but an act of unlawful possession, a trespass against his tribal right to control vaginal access to all women who belonged to him and his kin.

Since marriage, by law, was consummated in one manner only, by defloration of virginity with attendant ceremonial tokens, the act man came to construe as criminal rape was the illegal destruction of virginity outside a marriage contract of his making. Later, when he came to see his own definition as too narrow for the times, he broadened his criminal concept to cover the ruination of his wife's chastity as well, thus extending the law's concern to nonvirgins too. Although these legal origins have been buried in the morass of forgotten history, as the laws of rape continued to evolve they never shook free of their initial concept—that the violation was first and foremost a violation of *male* rights of possession, based on *male* requirements of virginity, chastity and consent to private access as the female bargain in the marriage contract (the underpinnings, as he enforced them, of man's economic estate).

To our modern way of thinking, these theoretical origins are peculiar and difficult to fully grasp. A huge disparity in thought—male logic versus

From "Women Fight Back." Abridged with permission of Simon & Schuster Adult Publishing Group from AGAINST OUR WILL: Men, Women and Rape by Susan Brownmiller. Copyright © 1975 by Susan Brownmiller.

female logic—affects perception of rape to this very day, confounding the analytic processes of some of the best legal minds. Today's young rapist has no thought of capturing a wife or securing an inheritance or estate. His is an act of impermanent conquest, not a practical approach to ownership and control. The economic advantage of rape is a forgotten concept. What remains is the basic male-female struggle, a hit-and-run attack, a brief expression of physical power, a conscious process of intimidation, a blunt, ugly sexual invasion with possible lasting psychological effects on all women.

When rape is placed where it truly belongs, within the context of modern criminal violence and not within the purview of ancient masculine codes, the crime retains its unique dimensions, falling midway between robbery and assault. It is, in one act, both a blow to the body and a blow to the mind, and a "taking" of sex through the use or threat of force. Yet the differences between rape and an assault or a robbery are as distinctive as the obvious similarities. In a prosecutable case of assault, bodily damage to the victim is clearly evident. In a case of rape, the threat of force does not secure a tangible commodity as we understand the term, although sex traditionally has been viewed by men as "the female treasure"; more precisely, in rape the threat of force obtains a highly valued sexual service through temporary access to the victim's intimate parts, and the intent is not merely to "take," but to humiliate and degrade.

This, then, is the modern reality of rape as it is defined by twentieth-century practice. It is not, however, the reality of rape as it is defined by twentieth-century law. . . .

Since the beginning of written history, criminal rape has been bound up with the common law of consent in marriage, and it is time, once and for all, to make a clean break. A sexual assault is an invasion of bodily integrity and a violation of freedom and self-determination wherever it happens to take place, in or out of the marriage bed. I recognize that it is easier to write these words than to draw up a workable legal provision, and I recognize the difficulties that juries will have in their deliberations when faced with a wife who accuses her husband of forcing her into copulation against her will, but the principle of bodily self-determination must be established without qualification, I think, if it is to become an inviolable principle on any level. . . .

In a sexual assault physical harm is much more than a threat; it is a reality because violence is an integral part of the act. Body contact and physical intrusion are the purpose of the crime, not appropriation of a physically detached and removable item like money. Yet the nature of the crime as it is practiced does bear robbery a close resemblance, because the sexual goal for the rapist resembles the monetary goal of the robber (often both goals are accomplished during the course of one confrontation if the victim is a woman), and so, in a sex crime, a bargain between offender and victim may also be struck. In this respect, a sexual assault is closer in victim response to a robbery than it is to a simple case of assault, for an assaultive event may not have a specific goal beyond the physical contest, and furthermore, people who find themselves in an assaultive situation usually defend themselves by fighting back.

Under the rules of law, victims of robbery and assault are not required to prove they resisted, or that they didn't consent, or that the act was accomplished with sufficient force, or sufficient threat of force, to overcome their will, because the law presumes it highly unlikely that a person willingly gives away money, except to a charity or to a favorite cause, and the law presumes that no person willingly submits to a brutal beating and the infliction of bodily harm and permanent damage. But victims of rape and other forms of sexual assault do need to prove these evidentiary requirements—that they resisted, that they didn't consent, that their will was overcome by overwhelming force and fear—because the law has never been able to satisfactorily distinguish an act of mutually desired sexual union from an act of forced, criminal sexual aggression.

Admittedly, part of the law's confusion springs from the normal, biologic, male procedural activity in an act of *unforced* copulation, but insertion of the penis (a descriptive phrase less semantically loaded than penetration, I think) is not in itself, despite what many men think, an act of male dominance. The real reason for the law's everlasting confusion as to what constitutes an act of rape and what constitutes an act of mutual intercourse is the underlying cultural assumption that it is the natural masculine role to proceed aggressively toward the stated goal, while the natural feminine role is to "resist" or "submit." And so to protect male interests, the law seeks to gauge the victim's behavior during the offending act in the belief that force or the threat of force is not conclusive *in and of itself.*

According to Menachem Amir's study, the assailant actually displays a dangerous weapon in no more than one-fifth of all police-founded cases of rape. Clearly, these are the cases a jury would most likely believe. But most rapes are not accomplished by means of a knife, a gun, a lead pipe or whatever. The force that is employed more often consists of an initial stranglehold, manhandling, beating, shoving, tearing at clothes, a verbal threat of death or disfigurement, the sheer physical presence of two, three, four, five assailants, etc. Without doubt, any of these circumstances can and does produce immobilizing terror in a victim, terror sufficient to render her incapable of resistance or to make her believe that resistance would be futile. . . .

The theory of aggressive male domination over women as a natural right is so deeply embedded in our cultural value system that all recent attempts to expose it—in movies, television commercials or even in children's textbooks—have barely managed to scratch the surface. As I see it, the problem is not that polarized role playing (man as doer; woman as bystander) and exaggerated portrayals of the female body as passive sex object are simply "demeaning" to women's dignity and self-conception, or that such portrayals fail to provide positive role models for young girls, but that cultural sexism is a conscious form of female degradation designed to boost the male ego by offering "proof" of his native superiority (and of female inferiority) everywhere he looks. . . .

Once we accept as basic truth that rape is not a crime of irrational, impulsive, uncontrollable lust, but is a deliberate, hostile, violent act of degradation and possession on the part of a would-be conqueror, designed to intimidate and inspire fear, we must look toward those elements in our culture that promote and propagandize these attitudes, which offer men, and in particular, impressionable, adolescent males, who form the potential raping population, the ideology and psychologic encouragement to commit their acts of aggression *without awareness, for the most part, that they have committed a punishable crime*, let alone a moral wrong. The myth of the heroic rapist that permeates false notions of masculinity, from the successful seducer to the man who "takes what he wants when he wants it," is inculcated in young boys from the time they first become aware that being a male means access to certain mysterious rites and privileges, including the right to buy a woman's body. When young men learn that females may be bought for a price, and that acts of sex command set prices, then how should they not also conclude that that which may be bought may also be taken without the civility of a monetary exchange?

That there *might* be a connection between prostitution and rape is certainly not a new idea. Operating from the old (and discredited) lust, drive and relief theory, men have occasionally put forward the notion that the way to control criminal rape is to ensure the ready accessibility of female bodies at a reasonable price through the legalization of prostitution, so that the male impulse might be satisfied with ease, efficiency and a minimum of bother. . . . To my mind the experience of the American military in Vietnam, where brothels for GI's were officially sanctioned, even incorporated into the base-camp recreation areas, should prove conclusively that the availability of sex for a small price is no deterrent to the decision to rape, any more than the availability of a base-camp shooting range is a deterrent to the killing of unarmed civilians and children.

But my horror at the idea of legalized prostitution is not that it doesn't work as a rape deterrent, but that it institutionalizes the concept that it is man's monetary right, if not his divine right, to gain access to the female body, and that sex is a female service that should not be denied the civilized male. Perpetuation of the concept that the "powerful male impulse" must be satisfied with immediacy by a cooperative class of women, set aside and expressly licensed for this purpose, is part and parcel of the mass psychology of rape. Indeed, until the day is reached when prostitution is totally eliminated (a millennium that will not arrive until men, who create the demand, and not women who supply it, are fully prosecuted under the law), the false perception of sexual access as an adjunct of male power and privilege will continue to fuel the rapist mentality.

Pornography has been so thickly glossed over with the patina of chic these days in the name of verbal freedom and sophistication that important distinctions between freedom of political expression (a democratic necessity), honest sex education for children (a societal good) and ugly smut (the deliberate devaluation of the role of women through obscene, distorted depictions) have been hopelessly confused. . . .

[H]ard-core pornography is not a celebration of sexual freedom; it is a cynical exploitation of female sexual activity through the device of making all such activity, and consequently all females, "dirty." . . .

The gut distaste that a majority of women feel when we look at pornography, a distaste that, incredibly, it is no longer fashionable to admit, comes, I think, from the gut knowledge that we and our bodies are being stripped, exposed and contorted for the purpose of ridicule to bolster that "masculine esteem" which gets its kick and sense of power from viewing females as anonymous, panting playthings, adult toys, dehumanized objects to be used, abused, broken and discarded. . . .

There can be no "equality" in porn, no female equivalent, no turning of the tables in the name of bawdy fun. Pornography, like rape, is a male invention, designed to dehumanize women, to reduce the female to an object of sexual access, not to free sensuality from moralistic or parental inhibition. The staple of porn will always be the naked female body, breasts and genitals exposed, because as man devised it, her naked body is the female's "shame," her private parts the private property of man, while his are the ancient, holy, universal, patriarchal instrument of his power, his rule by force over *her*.

Pornography is the undiluted essence of anti-female propaganda. Yet the very same liberals who were so quick to understand the method and purpose behind the mighty propaganda machine of Hitler's Third Reich, the consciously spewed-out anti-Semitic caricatures and obscenities that gave an ideological base to the Holocaust and the Final Solution, the very same liberals who, enlightened by blacks, searched their own conscience and came to understand that their tolerance of "nigger" jokes and portrayals of shuffling, rolling-eyed servants in movies perpetuated the degrading myths of black inferiority and gave an ideological base to the continuation of black oppression—these very same liberals now fervidly maintain that the hatred and contempt for women that find expression in four-letter words used as expletives and in what are quaintly called "adult" or "erotic" books and movies are a valid extension of freedom of speech that must be preserved as a Constitutional right.

. . . The majority report of the President's Commission on Obscenity and Pornography tried to pooh-pooh the opinion of law enforcement agencies around the country that claimed their own concrete experience with offenders who were caught with the stuff led them to conclude that pornographic material is a causative factor in crimes of sexual violence. The commission maintained that it was not possible at this time to scientifically prove or disprove such a connection.

But does one need scientific methodology in order to conclude that the anti-female propaganda that permeates our nation's cultural output promotes a climate in which acts of sexual hostility directed against women are not only tolerated but ideologically encouraged? A similar debate has raged for many years over whether or not the extensive glorification of violence (the gangster as hero; the loving treatment accorded bloody shoot-'em-ups in movies, books and on TV) has a causal effect, a direct relationship to the rising rate of crime, particularly among youth. Interestingly enough, in this area—nonsexual and not specifically related to abuses against women—public opinion seems to be swinging to the position that explicit violence in the entertainment media does have a deleterious effect; it makes violence commonplace, numbingly routine and no longer morally shocking. . . .

Men are not unmindful of the rape problem. To the contrary, their paternalistic codes reserved the harshest penalties for a violation of their property. But given an approach to rape that saw the crime as an illegal encroachment by an unlicensed intruder, a stranger come into their midst, the advice they gave (and still try to give) was all of one piece: a set of rules and regulations designed to keep their property penned in, much as a sheep-herder might try to keep his flock protected from an outlaw rustler by taking precautions against their straying too far from the fold. By seeing the rapist always as a stranger, never as one of their own, and by viewing the female as a careless, dumb creature with an unfortunate tendency to stray, they exhorted, admonished and warned the female to hide herself from male eyes as much as possible. In short, they told her not to claim the privileges they reserved for themselves. Such advice—well intentioned, solicitous and genuinely concerned—succeeded only in further aggravating the problem, for the message they gave was to live a life of fear, and to it they appended the dire warning that the woman who did not follow the rules must be held responsible for her own violation.

Clinton Duffy, the famous warden of San Quentin, couldn't understand why women didn't imprison themselves under maximum security conditions for their own protection. He wrote, "Many break the most elementary rules of caution every day. The particularly flagrant violators, those who go to barrooms alone, or accept pickups from strangers, or wear unusually tight sweaters and skirts, or make a habit of teasing, become rape bait by their actions alone. When it happens they have nobody to blame but themselves." . . .

A fairly decent article on rape in the March, 1974, issue of *The Reader's Digest* was written by two men who felt obliged to warn,

> Don't broadcast the fact that you live alone or with another woman. List only your last name and initial on the mailbox and in the phone book. Before entering your car, check to see if anyone is hiding on the rear seat or on the rear floor. If you're alone in a car, keep the doors locked and the windows rolled up. If you think someone is following you . . . do not go directly home if there is no adult male there. Possible weapons are a hatpin, corkscrew, pen, keys, umbrella. If no weapons are available, fight back physically only if you feel you can do so with telling effect.

What immediately pops into mind after reading the advice of Warden Duffy and *The Reader's Digest* is the old-time stand-up comedian's favorite figure of ridicule, the hysterical old maid armed with hatpin and umbrella who looks under the bed each night before retiring. Long a laughable stereotype of sexual repression, it now appears that the crazy old lady was a pioneer of sound mind after all.

But the negative value of this sort of advice, I'm afraid, far outweighs the positive. What it tells us, implicitly and explicitly, is:

1. A woman alone probably won't be able to defend herself. Another woman who might possibly come to her aid will be of no use whatsoever.
2. Despite the fact that it is men who are the rapists, a woman's ultimate security lies in being accompanied by men at all times.
3. A woman who claims to value her sexual integrity cannot expect the same amount of freedom and independence that men routinely enjoy. Even a small pleasure like taking a spin in an automobile with the windows open is dangerous, reckless behavior.
4. In the exercise of rational caution, a woman should engage in an amazing amount of pretense. She should pretend she has a male protector even if she hasn't. She should deny or obscure her personal identity, life-style and independence, and function on a sustained level of suspicion that approaches a clinical definition of paranoia.

Of course I think all people, female and male, child and adult, must be alert and on guard against the warning signs of criminal violence and should take care in potentially hazardous situations, such as a dark, unfamiliar street at night, or an unexpected knock on the door, but to impose a special burden of caution on women is no solution at all. There can be no private solutions to the problem of rape. A woman who follows this sort of special cautionary advice to the letter and thinks she is acting in society's interest—or even in her own personal interest—is deluding herself rather sadly. While the risk to one potential victim might be slightly diminished (and I even doubt this, since I have known of nuns who were raped within walled convents), not only does the number of potential rapists on the loose remain constant, but the ultimate effect of rape upon the woman's mental and emotional health has been accomplished *even without the act.* For to accept a special burden of self-protection is to reinforce the concept that women must live and move about in fear and can never expect to achieve the personal freedom, independence and self-assurance of men.

That's what rape is all about, isn't it? And a possible deep-down reason why even the best of our concerned, well-meaning men run to stereotypic warnings when they seek to grapple with the problem of rape deterrence is that they *prefer* to see rape as a woman's problem, rather than a societal problem resulting from a distorted masculine philosophy of aggression. For when men raise the spectre of the unknown rapist, they refuse to take psychologic responsibility for the nature of his act. . . .

Unthinkingly cruel, because it is deceptive, is the confidential advice given from men to women (it appears in *The Reader's Digest* article), or even from women to women in some feminist literature, that a sharp kick to the groin or a thumb in the eye will work miracles. Such advice is often accompanied by a diagram in which the vulnerable points of the human anatomy are clearly marked—as if the mere knowledge of these pressure spots can translate itself into devastating action. It is true that this knowledge has been deliberately obscured or withheld from us in the past, but mere knowledge is not enough. What women need is systematic training in self-defense that begins in childhood, so that the inhibition resulting from the prohibition may be overcome.

It would be decidedly less than honest if at this juncture I did not admit that my researches for [my] book included a three-month training program in jujitsu and karate, three nights a week, two and a half hours a night. . . . I learned I had natural weapons that I didn't know I possessed, like elbows and knees. I learned how to kick backward as well as forward. I learned how to fight dirty, and I learned that I loved it.

Most surprising to me, I think, was the recognition that these basic aggressive movements, the sudden twists, jabs and punches that were so foreign to my experience and ladylike existence, were the stuff that all little boys grow up learning, that boy kids are applauded for mastering while girl kids are put in fresh white pinafores and patent-leather. Mary Janes and told not to muss them up. And did that early difference in rearing ever raise its draconic head! At the start of our lessons our Japanese instructor freely invited all the women in the class, one by one, to punch him in the chest. It was not a foolhardy invitation, for we discovered that the inhibition against hitting was so strong in each of us that on the first try none of us could make physical contact. Indeed, the inhibition against striking out proved to be a greater hindrance to our becoming fighting women than our pathetic underdeveloped muscles. (Improvement in both departments was amazingly swift.)

Not surprisingly, the men in our class did not share our inhibitions in the slightest. Aggressive physical grappling was part of their heritage, not ours. And yet, and yet . . . we women discovered in wonderment that as we learned to place our kicks and jabs with precision we were actually able to inspire fear in the men. We *could* hurt them, we learned to our astonishment, and hurt them hard at the core of their sexual being—if we broke that Biblical injunction.

Is it possible that there is some sort of metaphysical justice in the anatomical fact that the male sex organ, which has been misused from time immemorial as a weapon of terror against women, should have at its root an awkward place of painful vulnerability? Acutely conscious of their susceptibility to damage, men have protected their testicles throughout history with armor, supports and forbidding codes of "clean," above-the-belt fighting. A gentleman's agreement is understandable—among gentlemen. When women are threatened, as I learned in my self-defense class, "Kick him in the balls, it's your best maneuver." How strange it was to hear for the first time in my life that women could fight back, *should* fight back and make full use of a natural advantage; that it is *in our interest* to know how to do it. How strange it was to understand with the full force of unexpected revelation that male allusions to psychological defeat, particularly at the hands of a woman, were couched in phrases like emasculation, castration and ball-breaking because of that very special physical vulnerability.

Fighting back. On a multiplicity of levels, that is the activity we must engage in, together, if we—women—are to redress the imbalance and rid ourselves and men of the ideology of rape.

Rape can be eradicated, not merely controlled or avoided on an individual basis, but the approach must be long-range and cooperative, and must have the understanding and good will of many men as well as women.

CHALLENGE QUESTIONS

Does Evolution Explain
Why Men Rape?

1. Some view the arguments of Thornhill and Palmer as steps toward excusing men who rape by explaining their behavior as biologically determined. What are some of the social costs and benefits of such dialogue?
2. The theory proposed by Thornhill and Palmer is quite speculative. How might a researcher go about studying the validity of their argument?
3. For three decades Brownmiller has kept rape in the consciousness of society. What impact has the work of Brownmiller and other feminist theorists had on societal attitudes about rape?
4. The phenomenon of "acquaintance rape" has been surrounded by legal controversy in recent years. How would Thornhill and Palmer view the behavior of men who initiate unwanted sexual activity with women in a casual or dating context? How would Brownmiller view such behavior?
5. Imagine that you are a clinician treating a man who has raped women. Based on the arguments of Thornhill/Palmer and Brownmiller, how would you go about trying to understand this man's behavior and treating him psychotherapeutically?

Suggested Readings

Koss, M. P. (2000, April). Evolutionary models of why men rape: Acknowledging the complexities. *Trauma, Violence, and Abuse: A Review Journal.*

Koss, M. P., Goodman, L., Browne, A., Fitzgerald, L., Keita, G. P., & Russo, N. F. (1994). *No safe haven: Violence against women at home, work, and in the community.* Washington, DC: American Psychological Association Press.

Low, B. (1999). *Why sex matters: A Darwinian look at human behavior.* Princeton, NJ: Princeton University Press.

Raine, N. V. (1998). *After silence: Rape and my journey back.* New York: Crown Publishers.

Russell, D. (1994). *Against pornography: The evidence of harm.* Berkeley, CA: Russell Publications.

Thornhill, R., & Palmer, C. T. (2000). *A natural history of rape: Biological bases of sexual coercion.* Cambridge, MA: MIT Press.

ISSUE 19

Should Mental Health Professionals Serve as Gatekeepers for Physician-Assisted Suicide?

YES: Rhea K. Farberman, from "Terminal Illness and Hastened Death Requests: The Important Role of the Mental Health Professional," *Professional Psychology: Research and Practice* (vol. 28, no. 6, 1997)

NO: Mark D. Sullivan, Linda Ganzini, and Stuart J. Youngner, from "Should Psychiatrists Serve as Gatekeepers for Physician-Assisted Suicide?" *The Hastings Center Report* (July–August 1998)

ISSUE SUMMARY

YES: Rhea K. Farberman, director of public communications for the American Psychological Association, makes the case that mental health professionals should be called upon to assess terminally ill people who request hastened death in order to ensure that decision making is rational and free of coercion.

NO: Psychiatrists Mark D. Sullivan, Linda Ganzini, and Stuart J. Youngner argue that the reliance on mental health professionals to be suicide gatekeepers involves an inappropriate use of clinical procedures to disguise society's ambivalence about suicide itself.

Most mental health professionals are drawn to their careers out of a desire to help people live happier and healthier lives. Few ever give a thought to the possibility that they might be called upon to help people take their own lives. In recent decades, however, increasing attention has been given to the legal and ethical right of an individual to choose suicide, particularly in cases in which the person has a terminal disease. Michigan physician Jack Kevorkian brought the issue into public awareness because he facilitated the deaths of dozens of seriously ill individuals throughout the 1990s.

The professional assessment of seriously ill individuals wanting to commit suicide is complex primarily because it is difficult to determine the extent to which profound depression about being sick propels these individuals to make impulsive decisions. As Americans have grown increasingly accepting of the right of seriously ill people to take their own lives, they have also turned more and more to mental health professionals to play a role in this process. Mental health professionals have been called upon to help protect the sick person's rights, provide support to loved ones, and evaluate whether or not the sick person has the capacity to make a rational decision.

In the following selection, Rhea K. Farberman argues that a mental health assessment by a qualified mental health professional is imperative for any ill person requesting a hastened death. She contends that the professional should first work to separate clinical depression from the patient's grief, fear of dying, fear of the unknown, and fear of pain. Farberman urges professionals to put aside their personal beliefs on the issue and to strive to ensure that the patient's decision-making process is rational, well reasoned, and free of coercion.

Taking a much more cautious stand on the issue, Mark D. Sullivan, Linda Ganzini, and Stuart J. Youngner argue in the second selection that the reliance on mental health professionals to be suicide gatekeepers is associated with an inappropriate use of clinical procedures to disguise society's ambivalence about suicide itself. They assert that society is shifting responsibility for a troubling moral decision to an outside specialist, rather than relying on shared decision making involving the patient, family, and physician. Sullivan, Ganzini, and Youngner offer several points of caution about using mental health professionals in this context.

POINT

- A mental health assessment by a qualified mental health professional is imperative for any ill person requesting a hastened death.
- A mental health professional helps to evaluate if the patient has the capacity to make a rational decision about dying.
- In light of extensive clinical and research experience, psychologists and other mental health professionals are an underused resource when patients and their significant others are forced to deal with end-of-life care issues.
- Competent mental health professionals recognize the importance of basing recommendations on data derived from several sources, including the involvement of significant others and family members.

COUNTERPOINT

- Mental health professionals should not have the social authority to use themselves as the measure of when it is the right time for a person to die.
- The determination of adequate decision-making capacity is difficult because competence is a complex social, rather than scientific, construct.
- The relevant expertise in this area is limited in light of the fact that so few mental health professionals regularly work with seriously ill and dying patients in hospital, nursing home, and hospice settings.
- There is a risk that, in the absence of robust independent standards, mental health professionals may resolve the ethical dilemmas concerning physician-assisted suicide in an ad hoc fashion, using themselves as the "reasonable person" standard by which to judge the patient's decision to die.

Rhea K. Farberman

 **YES**

Terminal Illness and Hastened Death Requests

Do terminally ill individuals have the right to decide the timing of their death and to have assistance in a hastened death? This article is based on an American Psychological Association briefing paper prepared for the media regarding the June 1997 Supreme Court decision on physician-assisted suicide. The Court's decision clarified the role medical doctors can play in caring for the terminally ill, but the role of mental health professionals is still evolving. It is clear, however, that on the basis of behavioral research and clinical experience, a mental health assessment by a qualified mental health professional is imperative for any ill person requesting a hastened death.

Becoming ill is unfortunately a part of living. The number of terminally ill persons who decide to hasten their death is difficult to define and estimate, but several recent studies have found a fairly large number of requests for assistance in dying as well as a high rate of acquiescence to these requests by physicians. In addition, public opinion polls consistently show that at least 60% of those surveyed are in favor of physician-assisted suicide for terminally ill patients.

New technologies have given health care professionals more effective ways to treat and retard serious illness and therefore sustain life. We can all agree that this medical progress has lengthened life and changed the end-of-life process. However, there is disagreement as to whether this progress is beneficial for the patient. Has the end-of-life process been changed in a way that is harmful to human dignity and self-determination? Or, is every day worth living regardless of the quality of that existence? These are complex questions that involve our fundamental values about life and liberty. They elude easy answers.

In June 1997, the U.S. Supreme Court ruled that terminally ill people do *not* have a constitutional right to doctor-assisted suicide, but the Court gave states the option of enacting their own assistance-in-dying statutes (*Vacco v. Quill*, 96-10, 1997; *Washington v. Glucksberg*, 95-1858, 1997). The Court's decision lent some greater clarity to the role that medical doctors can play in providing care and comfort to the terminally ill; still evolving, however, is the

From *Professional Psychology: Research and Practice*, vol. 28, no. 6, pp. 544–547. Copyright © 1997 by American Psychological Association. Reprinted with permission.

role of the mental health professional in working with terminally ill people. What is clear is that there is still much controversy and difference of opinion about the end-of-life process and, therefore, end-of-life care. Further court challenges about the right of dying people are likely. Because of this uncertainty, it is altogether likely that medical teams and families will still have to deal with hastened death requests from dying patients.

There are several concerns about such a request for a hastened death from a terminally ill person. One such concern is that depression and suicidal thoughts in seriously ill people are common. A 1994 study found that the prevalence rates for both major and minor depression among terminally ill cancer patients receiving palliative (relief of pain and discomfort) care ranged from 13% to 26%. At the same time, the capacity of physicians untrained in psychiatry to diagnose depression is alarmingly low. On the basis of numerous studies, it is estimated that depression is correctly diagnosed by physicians in only 20% to 60% of the cases presented. It is important to remember that the reasoning on which a terminally ill person (whose judgments are not impaired by mental disorders) bases a decision to end his or her life is fundamentally different from the reasoning a clinically depressed person uses to justify suicide.

Depression in Seriously Ill People

Although many people consider depression normal in a seriously ill person, depression is a diagnoseable illness and is highly treatable. The first task of a mental health professional when dealing with a terminally ill person is to separate the patient's prospective grief, fear of dying, fear of the unknown, and fear of pain from clinical depression.

It is often assumed, but not correctly so, that the most pain-ridden, physically distressed terminally ill patients are more likely to become depressed or suicidal when compared to other less afflicted patients. In reality, a person's lifelong values, temperament, and behavior are often better indicators of who is at risk for suicide thoughts when ill. In fact, the importance of terminal illness, physical decline, or chronic pain as a reason for suicide has been seriously questioned by the behavioral science research on end-of-life decisions.

Ill people and elderly people are often concerned about becoming a burden to their families. Some research has in fact shown that control, quality of life, and loss of independence are weightier issues for terminally ill patients than is actual pain. However, pain lessens the patient's ability to do things for him or herself, which in turn adds to the patient's concern about the loss of independence and about burdening loved ones.

In short, there is no simple formula explaining what motivates an ill person to want to end his or her life. Most research points to multiple causes, including anxiety, fear, desire for control and dignity, a lack of information or an inability to get questions answered, depression, and cognitive losses. Although pain management is at times a problem for terminally ill patients (research shows that terminal cancer patients are particularly at risk for insufficient pain control), pain, in and of itself, is not the single most important factor in suicide ideation. Much of this research suggests that what is needed for the terminally ill patient is improved palliative care and more psychosocial support at the end of his or her life.

The Role of Mental Health Professionals in End-of-Life Decisions

In the absence of mental illness, a terminally ill person can be capable of rational thinking and an informed choice. However, separating sadness brought on by the loss of ability and the loss of the persona the patient once was from clinical depression brought on by a mental disorder is a complex clinical judgment. One critical factor is the patient's self-esteem. The self-esteem of a person who is grieving or is terminally ill is not affected by the illness; however, the self-esteem of a clinically depressed person is.

Attempting to determine to what degree, if any, a terminally ill person is experiencing depression or other cognitive impairments is extremely difficult. The mental health professional who is called on to make such an evaluation should have specific training and clinical experience working with that population group, be it elderly persons, cancer patients, AIDS patients, and so forth.

Today, psychologists and other mental health professionals are an underused resource when patients and their significant others are forced to deal with end-of-life care issues. Psychologists not only have clinical experience on this issue, but also have conducted much of the research from which we have learned a great deal about depression, the diagnosis of depressive illness, patients' coping with end of life, and support of significant others during the end-of-life process.

Some health professionals who work in hospitals and hospice settings say that in reality, hastened death is already a relatively common occurrence—the opening of the morphine drip to allow for a lethal dose of the pain killer, for example. The role of the psychologist working with a terminally ill patient who wishes to end his or her life is not to control the patient's decision but to attempt to ensure that the patient's decision-making process is rational, well-reasoned, and free of coercion.

Mental health professionals who work in this area must approach their work in a neutral manner. Their personal beliefs on the issue should not influence the process. The role of the mental health professional is (a) to attempt to ensure that the end-of-life decision-making process includes a complete assessment of the patient's ability to make a rational judgment and (b) to help protect the patient's right to self-determination. The mental health professional attempts to bring the pertinent issues to the patient and his or her family and significant others and to assist the patient and significant others in understanding and working through those issues.

The American Psychological Association (APA) does not advocate for or against assisted suicide. What psychologists do support is high-quality end-of-life care and informed end-of-life decisions that are based on the correct assessment of the patient's mental capacity, social support systems, and degree of self-determination.

Surveys of mental health professionals have found that most (as high as 81% in the case of a survey of members of APA's Division of Psychotherapy) believe that assisted suicide *can be* a rational choice within the following parameters: (a) The patient is acting under his or her own free will, (b) the patient is competent to make an informed and reasonable judgment, (c) the patient's physical condition is hopeless, and (d) the patient is under no outside pressure (financial pressure, pressure from family, and so forth) to make the choice.

The Psychologist's Role

In helping terminally ill patients make end-of-life decisions, psychologists should do the following:

1. Protect the client's rights.
2. Support the family.
3. Don't allow physicians to affix a mental illness diagnosis if it is inappropriate.
4. Help evaluate if the patient has the capacity to make a rational decision, that is, does not have a mental disorder that significantly impairs his or her ability to reason, is fully informed of all treatment options, understands all treatment options, is not being coerced, and is using a rational, reasoned process to reach his or her decision.

Early referral of a terminally ill patient to a mental health professional can help prevent premature deterioration in the quality of life for the patient and allows for the teaching of coping skills to both the patient and his or her family. In addition, research has shown that psychological interventions with both cardiac and cancer patients can help in the recovery process by strengthening medical compliance and by helping the patient make healthful lifestyle choices. Another reason for having a mental health professional available to a person who has been diagnosed with a serious illness is that research has shown that a person with such an illness is at greatest risk for suicide when he or she first learns of the diagnosis.

The analysis of end-of-life care by a psychologist or other competent mental health professional would typically include the assessment of data from multiple interviews with the patient as well as multiple contacts with the family or significant others, a full review of the patient history, and a full cognitive and depression assessment. The psychologist should bring to this work a thorough understanding of the pertinent psychological literature and data on end-of-life issues.

Furthermore, because end-of-life decisions have family and social consequences, significant others and family members should be involved in the decision-making process if at all possible. In fact, there is research that shows that survivors who are involved in end-of-life decisions do better after the death than those who were not part of the decision-making process.

In determining whether a person is competent to make a reasoned end-of-life decision, most psychologists like to see convergent validity across a number of different measures of the patient's mental health and capacity (i.e., multiple assessments that point to the same conclusion). If significant symptoms of a mood disorder or depression are present, treatment should be attempted before any request for assistance in dying is considered. With resolution of the depression, the patient's capacity to weigh the available options may improve and his or her attitude toward death may change.

The Dilemma for Physicians

Adequate pain control is critical for terminally ill patients, but it is often problematic for physicians. Fear of the patient's addiction affects the physician's willingness to prescribe the strong pain drugs required and also interferes with the patient's willingness to take the prescribed medications. Physicians also worry about how state and federal regulatory agencies will interpret their writing such prescriptions.

In addition, as discussed before, most primary care and internal medicine doctors are not trained in the assessment and treatment of psychiatric illness. They cannot be expected to accurately diagnose a depressive disorder.

Public Policy Questions

Additional public discourse and legislative action on the question of end-of-life care are expected. Already some state legislatures are looking at proposed legislation that would mandate certain pain control procedures for terminally ill people.

What continues to be critical for the courts, legislatures, and the public to recognize is the importance of ensuring that an appropriately trained and licensed mental health professional is involved in the end-of-life decision process. Having a terminal illness is a stressful, sad, and painful experience for any human being. However, terminal illness, in and of itself, is not typically the cause of suicide ideation. The important clinical assessment is whether the patient is fearful, is not receiving the correct treatment for pain, and is concerned about the emotional or financial stress he or she feels is being inflicted on the family or whether the patient is suffering from a clinical depression or a cognitive deficit.

Concern does exist within the psychological community that if some states do move to legalize assisted suicide, this could present a slippery slope equation for our society. That is, if hastened death becomes an option for the terminally ill, will society's attitude toward those people with other types of health or physical challenges be affected? How will legalized assisted suicide affect the position within our society of elderly people, people with chronic debilitating illness, or people with disabilities? In short, every American has a stake in whatever course this country takes vis-à-vis end-of-life issues, because the direction taken will affect whole communities. Psychological research has proven without question that behavior is often modeled.

An added caution: At a time when the population is aging (elderly people are disproportionately represented in the national suicide statistics), where there exist extreme financial pressures on the provision of medical care, and when the social safety net is at risk, many mental health professionals worry that physician-assisted suicide may become legal *without* the added requirement of a mental health assessment by a qualified mental health professional.

More Research Needed

Suicidal thoughts are complex and difficult to study. More research about what motivates a person with a terminal illness to want to hasten his or her death is needed. For example, answers are needed to the following questions:

1. What effect do improved social–psychological supports have on the hastened death ideation of terminally ill patients?
2. What effect does improved palliative care have on the hastened death ideation of terminally ill patients?
3. How do the issues of race, age, ageism, disabilities, religious beliefs, and gender play into the risk factors of an individual for end-of-life decisions?

Complicating the issue is the fact that no definitive data exist on the prevalence (with terminally ill patients) of suicide ideation caused by a depressive illness. Studies have shown that about 5% of the total U.S. population will at any one time suffer from a major depression with some level of suicidal thinking. From this figure, it may be assumed that some fraction of terminally ill patients will suffer from clinical depression that coincides with their illness but did not arise from it.

Conclusion

Any discussion about the ending of a life is controversial and highly charged because it involves our most personal value systems. In the final analysis, we may be called on, both individually and as a society, to balance the important and yet competing interests of preserving human life versus the desire to die peacefully and with dignity. This is a vexing equation for all health care professionals, for the ill and their families, for religious institutions, and for society as a whole. What the state-of-the-art behavioral research and clinical experience of mental health professionals can tell us to date is that a mental health assessment of any ill person who is requesting assistance in hastening his or her death is imperative.

Mark D. Sullivan, Linda Ganzini, and Stuart J. Youngner

Should Psychiatrists Serve as Gatekeepers for Physician-Assisted Suicide?

$\mathbf{A}$s our society debates the legalization of physician-assisted suicide for terminally ill persons, mandatory psychiatric evaluation has been suggested as a safeguard against abuse. This is to guarantee that the patient choosing physician-assisted death is mentally competent to do so. As psychiatrists who have provided both psychiatric and ethics consultation for dying patients, we believe there are serious unacknowledged problems with this "safeguard."

Our arguments do not depend on a moral position for or against physician-assisted suicide. Nor do we deny that psychiatry has a great deal to offer in the evaluation and treatment of patients who request assistance in dying. Rather, we argue that due to the lack of applicable objective standards of decisionmaking capacity and the inevitable distortion of the mental health professional's role as a clinician, we should think carefully before requiring psychiatric certification of competence in every case. We are concerned that this "safeguard" inappropriately uses a technical clinical procedure to disguise our society's ambivalence about suicide itself. By making every patient who requests physician-assisted suicide jump the hurdle of psychiatric evaluation, we shift responsibility for a troubling moral decision from the therapeutically directed and socially embedded context of shared decisionmaking of patient, family, and primary physician to an outside specialist. As this specialist, the consultant psychiatrist becomes a secular priest dressed in the clothes of a medical expert.

The Question of Safeguards

Health professionals who believe assisted suicide may sometimes be appropriate have called for safeguards to ensure that suffering patients who are assisted to die are choosing suicide freely and autonomously. To address these concerns, recent initiatives for the legalization of assisted suicide have incorporated specific restrictions to assure autonomous decisionmaking. Some initiatives have included the requirement that the request be expressed

From Mark D. Sullivan, Linda Ganzini, and Stuart J. Youngner, "Should Psychiatrists Serve as Gatekeepers for Physician-Assisted Suicide?" *The Hastings Center Report*, vol. 28, no. 4 (July–August 1998). Copyright © 1998 by The Hastings Center. Reprinted by permission of The Hastings Center and the authors.

consistently over a specified period of time in order to prevent impulsive decisions and allow time for ambivalence to be manifested. A delay of fifteen days in Oregon and nine days in Northern Australia (the only other region in which physician-assisted suicide was legal, until overturned by the Australian Parliament in March 1997) is required between a request for assisted suicide and its implementation.[1]

The most important safeguard of autonomous choice is the restriction of access to physician-assisted suicide to those whose decisionmaking capacity is above a threshold that qualifies them as "competent" to make the choice of suicide. Expert discussion of safeguards in the implementation of physician-assisted suicide frequently includes a call for mandatory psychiatric consultation.[2] The Oregon initiative requires that a psychiatric consultation be completed in just those cases where the primary physician believes that the patient has a mental disorder affecting his or her judgment, but the injunction mentioned this safeguard as inadequate.[3] The Northern Australia statute required psychiatric consultation in all cases, and a "Model State Act to Authorize and Regulate Physician-Assisted Suicide" recently published in the United States mandates that "a professional mental health provider (psychiatrist, psychologist, or psychiatric social worker) evaluate the patient to determine that his or her decision is fully informed, free of undue influence, and not distorted by depression or any other form of mental illness."[4] There is thus widespread support for mandatory psychiatric evaluation to verify the competence of all those who request physician-assisted suicide.

How Our Society Understands and Copes With Suicide

Psychiatrists who have cared for suicidal patients can describe how deeply ambivalent these patients can be about suicide. What is not as apparent from the clinical perspective is the ambivalence of psychiatrists and our culture about the morality of suicide. Talcott Parsons described how societies inevitably institutionalize expectations for their members and how "deviance" from these roles is considered a threat to the social fabric.[5] Suicide is a wonderful object for Parsonian analysis because societies have employed a variety of models, sometimes conflicting and sometimes complementary, to understand and manage suicide. Traditionally, suicide has been viewed as a choice. Reflecting this, for many years our society used the legal model to manage suicide. Suicide was a crime, punishable by the criminal justice system. It was considered not simply an assault on the self, but an assault on the community as well. While suicide is no longer a criminal offense in any state, assisting the suicide of another is in many. The religious/moral model also viewed suicide as a choice, but emphasized an individual's violation of core human values rather than laws that protect the social fabric. The Catholic Church and Orthodox Judaism, for example, are adamantly opposed to all suicide, even if it appears rationally chosen.[6] While Protestant fundamentalists are generally opposed to suicide, some Protestant denominations take a more tolerant stance.[7] Many nonreligious persons also find suicide immoral.

The modern medical model considers suicide to be, not the choice of a rational agent, but a symptom of mental illness. Epidemiological studies have overwhelmingly linked suicide to treatable psychiatric disorders. "Psychological autopsy" studies have documented that up to 90 percent of completed suicides had some psychiatric disorder at the time of death.[8] Treatment studies have shown that identification and treatment of psychiatric disorders can result in a substantial decrease in risk of suicide. Depression, and to a lesser extent medical illness, have been identified as the primary risk factors for suicide in the elderly.[9] This fact has been codified into diagnostic systems (e.g., DSM-IV, ICD-10) that consider suicidal ideas as one of the diagnostic criteria of mental disorder. It has also been codified into law, where danger to self is justification for involuntary mental health treatment.

On balance, this medicalization of suicide has substantially benefited the mentally ill by removing legal and moral sanctions and promoting effective treatment. Over the past few years, however, the hegemony of this medical/psychiatric view has been challenged. Many in our society now see some suicides among those who are terminally ill as the product of rational choice while continuing to see most suicides in other contexts as the product of mental illness.[10] However, a valid method for determining which suicides are rational and which are not has never been developed by psychiatrists, psychologists, or any other profession.

In summary, our society currently uses all three models—legal, religious/ moral, and medical—to cope with physician-assisted suicide. Different jurisdictions, communities, institutions, and individuals may rely on different models. Acceptance of the conclusions of one model does not necessarily imply agreement with the conclusions of another. One person might believe that suicide is rational in some situations, but always morally unacceptable. Another might believe truly rational suicide would be morally acceptable, but that suicide is nearly always the irrational product of a diagnosable and treatable psychiatric condition. It is likely that many persons, including psychiatrists and other mental health professionals, are not always aware of which model they are employing to analyze a particular case. For example, a recent survey of Oregon psychologists revealed that those who objected to physician-assisted suicide for religious reasons were also more concerned about the mental health and social consequences of the legalization of physician-assisted suicide.[11] Although the concept of competence is intended to sort out rational from irrational decisions, it may blur the lines between the moral and medical models for a highly contentious issue such as assisted suicide.

Competence in the Clinical Setting

Clinical assessment of decisionmaking capacity is ethically important because of the central role that "adequate decisionmaking capacity" or competence plays in valid consent, the cornerstone in the protection of patient autonomy. This makes it inevitable that adequate decisionmaking capacity becomes a key issue in evaluating patients' requests for physician-assisted death. However, requiring that a psychiatrist control access to physician-assisted suicide is problematic for the following reasons. First, competence is a complex social, rather than scientific construct. In fact, psychiatrists use a sliding scale to determine when decisionmaking capacity is adequate, and the scale slides according to the values of the psychiatrists themselves. Second, the relationship of mental illness and decisionmaking capacity in dying patients is not as clear as is implied by some initiatives, statutes, and court decisions. Third, although psychiatrists have a great deal to offer in the assessment and enhancement of patient decisionmaking, casting them in the role of gatekeeper poses risks for patients, society, and the psychiatric profession itself. These risks should not be overlooked in shaping public policy.

Competence as a Social Construct   A "scientific" or purely objective definition of competence is unattainable because thresholds for adequate decisionmaking capacity are in fact socially established. Indeed, competence is not well measured by standardized instruments, but "is a malleable entity that is inevitably molded to fit the particular interpersonal, emotional, clinical, and cultural context."[12] "Competence" is used clinically to resolve situations in which two extremely important social goals come into conflict—that is, the promotion of self-determination (autonomy) and the promotion of patient welfare (beneficence or nonmaleficence).[13] As the consequences of physician-patient disagreement grow more serious, the tension between the principles of autonomy and beneficence also grows. It is important to recognize that this tension originates beyond the bounds of the physician-patient relationship. The growing visibility of patient requests for physician-assisted suicide has inspired calls for mandatory psychiatric evaluations of competence precisely because many citizens believe that suicide and assisting suicide are often great harms.

Tests of decisionmaking capacity have been traditionally ranked on a continuum of increasing stringency, with more stringent standards used for treatment refusals with more serious consequences. Simply making a choice or agreeing with the physician's recommendation are examples of more lenient standards. More stringent standards demand an examination of the process of reasoning underlying the patient's decision, such as the ability to understand, appreciate, or reason about one's clinical situation.[14] For example, when a patient refuses an invasive intervention with little chance of success, the physician rarely challenges his or her reasoning process. However, when the patient makes a choice that appears to be harmful, more rigorous tests of decisionmaking capacity are brought to bear. By employing this sliding scale, physicians gain flexibility to balance concerns about patient autonomy and patient welfare.

The malleability of competence is a two-edged sword. It allows competence to be used as a socially viable compromise between the conflicting values of respect for autonomy and prevention of harm, but it vests tremendous power in the expert who assesses decisionmaking capacity. The employment of a sliding scale for the determination of adequate decisionmaking capacity blurs the line between the process and product of decisionmaking. Without a truly independent standard for decisionmaking capacity, psychiatrists may apply standards derived from their own opinion of the harms associated with decisions such as requests for assisted suicide.

In the absence of robust independent standards, psychiatrists may resolve the ethical dilemmas concerning physician-assisted suicide in an ad hoc fashion, using themselves as the "reasonable person" standard by which to judge the patient's decision. Do I agree that this patient has an intolerable quality of life? Would I consider such a quality of life intolerable for myself? Would I consider suicide morally acceptable in this situation? Too often, to ask what a competent person would do in such a dire situation comes down to asking ourselves what we would do. In one survey psychiatrists' support for legalized physician-assisted suicide was highly correlated to desire for physician-assisted suicide for themselves in the case of terminal illness.[15] A survey of Oregon psychologists revealed that the conditions under which respondents would consider assisted suicide for themselves are highly correlated to conditions under which they believe it should be allowed for other people.[16]

While psychiatrists have skills relevant to the understanding and evaluation of patients' decisions, they should not have the social authority to use themselves as the measure of when it is right to die. In a society that is as confused and conflicted about physician-assisted death as ours is, allowing such individual discretion will result in arbitrary and unfair practices. Society is unsure about how to honor patients' choices to die, as are individual physicians. Deep disagreement exists about what constitutes an intolerable quality of life and whether suicide is ever an acceptable alternative to suffering. We question whether the clinical apparatus of competence assessment can resolve this tension.

Competence and Psychiatric Disorders   One reason psychiatrists have been selected to perform competence evaluations in the terminally ill is that the prevalence of psychiatric disorders in this population is high, and diagnosing these disorders is difficult. While there is validity to these concerns, we do not believe they justify universal psychiatric verification of competence in patients requesting assisted suicide.

Psychiatric disorders are common in the terminally ill. Delirium has been noted in 25 to 40 percent of hospitalized cancer patients; in the final stages, up to 85 percent of cancer patients may suffer from delirium.[17] Depression has also been diagnosed in approximately 5 to 58 percent of hospitalized cancer patients, with up to 77 percent of advanced cancer patients having severe depressive symptoms.[18] High rates of psychiatric disorders and interest in physician-assisted suicide have been noted in patients with HIV infection and AIDS.[19] Although the rates of psychiatric disorder climb as medical severity increases, accuracy of diagnosis by primary care physicians diminishes.[20] Not only is depression often missed, but delirium is often misdiagnosed as depression.[21] Psychiatrists may thus offer expertise in diagnosing a mental disorder that primary care physicians lack.

Psychiatric disorders are the commonest cause of impaired capacity to make medical decisions. Yet even the most serious mental disorders may not critically disrupt decisionmaking capacity. It is now widely accepted, for example, that some psychotic patients can provide valid consent to participate in research from which they personally derive no benefit. Meeting criteria for commitment to involuntary treatment no longer implies incompetence to refuse antipsychoticmedication.[22] Clinical and legal consensus now demands that a mental disorder be demonstrated to seriously disrupt the relevant decisionmaking capacity before a patient is declared incompetent and forfeits the right to make those specific decisions him- or herself. Making a psychiatric diagnosis may assist in directing the clinician's attention to where decision-making might be impaired, but does not itself prove that decisionmaking capacity has been compromised.

Psychiatrists have raised concerns that depression may cause medically ill persons to choose to hasten their deaths, but the available data indicate variable effects of depression on treatment preference. In one study using hypothetical illness scenarios, elderly depressed patients did choose aggressive medical treatment less often than nondepressed patients in the good prognosis scenarios. However, among these mildly to moderately depressed patients, current depression severity was not as strongly linked to treatment preference as were their estimates of their quality of life in these hypothetical situations.[23] Except in a minority who were severely depressed, successful treatment of depression did not significantly alter treatment preferences.[24] Another study of twenty-two depressed elderly patients revealed that moderate to severe major depression was associated with a high rate of treatment refusal in good prognosis hypothetical scenarios, which showed reversal with depression treatment.[25] A study of 2,536 elderly patients found that scoring in the depressed range on a depression scale predicted a desire for more, rather than less life-saving treatment.[26] Therefore, depression may or may not alter decisions about end-of-life treatment by elderly patients. We have argued elsewhere that depression diagnosis and clinical assessment of the capacity to make medical decisions are distinct tasks.[27]

Studies that examine the psychiatric correlates of terminally ill persons' desire for hastened death are few. For example, James Henderson Brown and colleagues queried patients on an inpatient hospital palliative care service regarding their desire for hastened death.[28] Patients were eligible to participate in the study if they had a terminal illness and either pain or severe disfigurement and severe disability, but were not too sick to consent. Of 331 potential participants, only forty-four were eligible using these inclusion criteria. Ten of forty-four (24 percent) patients desired to die, and all were found to have a "clinical depression." The authors concluded that the desire for death in terminally ill persons does not occur in the absence of psychopathology. However, the criteria for participation, which excluded 287 hospice patients, may have limited the generalizability of their findings. Harvey Max Chochinov and colleagues interviewed cancer patients on a hospice inpatient service and found that 8.5 percent acknowledged a desire for death that was serious and pervasive. Although these patients had higher depression scores than patients who did not persistently desire death, 41 percent did not meet criteria for major depressive disorder.[29]

Studies led by William Breitbart[30] and Ezekiel Emanuel[31] also demonstrate that terminally ill persons who express an interest in physician-assisted suicide have higher depression scores, but these researchers did not measure the percentage who met criteria for major depression. Nor did major depression indicate those who would and those who would not be interested in assisted suicide in a future state of severe pain among forty-eight patients with painful metastatic cancer.[32] In total, these studies suggest that though depression is common among persons desiring assisted suicide, it clearly does not account for all of the variance in decisionmaking.

Moreover, many psychiatrists do not regularly work with seriously ill and dying patients in hospital, nursing home, and hospice settings. In a survey of over 700 Oregon psychiatrists and psychologists, only three respondents reported working with hospice patients in the past year. Only 6 percent of psychiatrists were very confident that they could, within the context of a single evaluation, assess whether a psychiatric disorder was impairing the judgment of a patient desiring assisted suicide.[33]

Psychiatrists' treatment options for the terminally ill are limited by the limited time available for the treatment to be effective and by the severity of the patient's medical illness. Data suggest that psychiatric treatment may or may not affect treatment preferences. Some patients asking for assisted suicide will be willing to try psychiatric treatment and some will not. Even for patients who actively participate in treatment, it will be difficult to determine when enough treatment has been administered—psychiatrists' values as well as their clinical expertise will inevitably determine when the point of "enough" treatment has been reached. For example, how many trials of antidepressant medication are needed before the psychiatrist concludes that the depression is intractable or that the patient is not really depressed?

These observations point to a useful and important role for trained and experienced psychiatrists in the assessment and treatment of seriously ill patients who wish to hasten their deaths. They also argue for more research and better training for psychiatrists in this critical area. They do not, however, make a convincing case for mandatory involvement and a gatekeeping role for the psychiatrist in all cases. . . .

Counterarguments

There are two remaining arguments for psychiatry's role in determining competence to participate in physician-assisted suicide to which we would like to respond. First, some might argue that the problems in assessing competence for suicide are no different from other situations in which competence is addressed. Why do we specifically object to competence evaluation for those requesting physician-assisted suicide? What makes it different from the psychiatrist's role in evaluating competence to stand trial, to make a will, or even more relevant here, to refuse life-sustaining medical treatment? Do not the same problems of subjectivity and potential for bias exist?

There are a couple of critical differences. The evaluation of competence to stand trial, make a will, or refuse medical treatment is not mandatory for every person who is about to undertake these acts. In each of these cases, patient competence is assumed. The psychiatrist is called in only when competence is challenged or questioned by one of the persons naturally involved in the process, such as a lawyer, judge, or relative. We know of no other clinical situation in which psychiatric evaluation for competence is universally required; the presumption for persons standing trial or making medical decisions (even patients who refuse life-sustaining treatment) is that they are competent. Mandating a mental health evaluation for all patients requesting assisted suicide implies a presumption of incompetence. It makes the request for assisted suicide, although legal, adequate grounds for challenging the competence of the person making the request.

In addition, these other decisions or acts for which competence may be called into question are not in themselves morally controversial. No one argues that standing trial or making a will is morally wrong. Quite the contrary, both are viewed as necessary social functions. Thus, it is highly unlikely that a psychiatrist's opinion about competence will be influenced by his view that standing trial or making a will is harmful per se. Refusal of life-sustaining treatment may be considered to be a harm by a minority of our citizens. However, the legal system clearly recognizes this right and the vast majority of health professionals (including psychiatrists) and citizens accept it as a moral right as well. To argue that because psychiatrists are called in to evaluate competence in some cases of treatment refusal, they should be called in on all requests for physician-assisted suicide is illogical. The view that death through assisted suicide is a greater harm to patients than death through treatment refusal reflects social ambivalence about suicide rather than clearly distinct clinical situations. Since the same psychosocial factors—for example, depression, delirium, and anxiety—that affect requests for physician-assisted suicide also affect treatment refusal, a more consistent argument for those advocating the gatekeeper role would be that psychiatrists should be the gatekeepers for all refusals of life-saving treatment as well.

A second counterargument to our position asserts that psychiatrists, despite their shortcomings, are the professionals best qualified to evaluate decisionmaking capacity and no more biased than other physicians. We do not deny that involvement of psychiatrists in the evaluation and treatment of persons who request physician-assisted suicide can be extremely helpful. The psychiatrist can assist the patient in exploring the often multiple meanings of the request to die. Susan Block and Andrew Billings write, "Most patients, in saying that they want to die are asking for assistance in living—for help in dealing with depression, anxiety about the future, grief, lack of control, dependence, and spiritual despair."[34] The efficacy of psychiatric treatment in the medically ill elderly has been repeatedly demonstrated in recent years.[35] Suffering may be diminished with both psychotherapy and psychotropic medications. The psychiatrist may intervene to improve the patient's relationships with physician and family. Indeed, there are many cases in which psychiatric involvement is absolutely essential.

However, institutionalizing or bureaucratizing such involvement could be problematic. This would imply a greater expertise than is warranted and would shift responsibility from the traditional seat of shared decisionmaking—the patient, the family, and the physician or health care team—to an outside expert who may not have a primary commitment to patient welfare. A required evaluation of competence puts the patient in a "one down" position in which his or her sanity is judged by an outside expert. This intrinsically adversarial position is likely to prevent the development of a therapeutic alliance necessary for the psychiatrist to function in the traditional role as healer. Forcing evaluations in cases where they are neither wanted nor necessary could trivialize the process or turn it into an activity that serves neither patients, society, nor our profession. By making psychiatric involvement optional, a complicated social decision can be kept woven as deeply as possible into the social fabric, allowing society to appreciate rather than avoid its own ambivalence about death, dying, and suicide.

Healers, Not Gatekeepers

We believe that psychiatrists' primary involvement with patients requesting assisted suicide should be in the role of healer rather than gatekeeper. Psychiatric evaluation of the dying patient should always be done for the benefit of the patient. If psychiatric diagnosis is done primarily for social control rather than individual welfare, psychiatrists function as priests or police rather than as physicians. The primary duty of psychiatrists to the dying is not to man the gate to assisted dying, but to nurture autonomous choice and diminish the anguish of the dying process.

We encourage our medical colleagues to involve psychiatrists in the evaluation and care of the dying. Psychotropic medication, supportive therapy, and family intervention can ease suffering and promote autonomous choice. Psychiatric consultation to assess and promote autonomous decisionmaking should be an option initiated by patient, family, or primary physician, not mandated by law. Psychiatrists, on the other hand, must improve their expertise in caring for dying patients and make themselves more available to patients and medical colleagues. An emphasis must be placed on improving the research basis for carrying out psychiatric assessments of dying patients who desire physician-assisted suicide. Legal mandates that require psychiatric certification of competence prior to all cases of euthanasia or physician-assisted suicide hold risks for both the psychiatric profession and the patients it should serve. This practice could distort the role of the psychiatrist as a physician whose first responsibility is the welfare of her patient. It runs the risk of overselling the independence and impartiality of the clinical procedure by which decisionmaking capacity is assessed. It shifts the accountability for value judgments from the traditional context of patient-family-physician.

There is a price to be paid for not making psychiatric consultation mandatory. Some treatable psychiatric disorders will be missed in those opting for assisted suicide. But the benefit for these individuals must be balanced against the serious problems, the arbitrary evaluations and social obfuscation, that would accompany universal mandatory psychiatric consultation. And it may be more difficult politically to endorse or legalize physician-assisted suicide without the psychiatric safeguard. But the societal debate about assisted suicide will be more honest and revealing.

In our culture's current state of ambivalence and confusion about suicide, the moral and medical models run hopelessly together. Using a technical clinical determination of competence to judge the moral acceptability of suicide obscures important value judgments we are making about when life is worth living and when it is not. To foster the most honest debate possible about assisted suicide and to promote truly patient-centered end-of-life care, we should avoid making psychiatrists gatekeepers for assisted suicide.

References

1. Christopher J. Ryan and Miranda Kaye, "Euthanasia in Australia: the Northern Territory Rights of the Terminally Ill Act," *NEJM* 334 (1996): 326–28.

2. W. F. Baile, J. R. Dimaggio, D. V. Schapira, and J. S. Janofsky, "The Request for Assistance in Dying: The Need for Psychiatric Consultation," *Cancer* 72 (1993): 2786–91; Guy I. Benrubi, "Euthanasia: The Need for Procedural Safeguards," *NEJM* 326 (1992): 197–98.

3. Ballot Measure 16. In Oregon voters' pamphlet. Portland, Ore.: Multnomah County Elections Division, 1994.

4. Charles H. Baron, Clyde Bergstresser, Dan W. Brock, Gabrielle F. Cole et al., "A Model State Act to Authorize and Regulate Physician-Assisted Suicide," *Harvard Journal on Legislation* 33 (1996): 1–34.

5. Talcott Parsons, "Definitions of Health and Disease in Light of American Values and Social Structures." In *Patients, Physicians, and Illness,* ed. E. Gartly Jaco (New York: Free Press, 1979), pp. 120–44.

6. Fred Rosner, "Suicide in Biblical, Talmudic, and Rabbinic Writings," *Tradition: A Journal of Orthodox Thought* 11 (1970): 25–40.

7. Presbyterian Senior Services, The Presbytery of New York, "Pastoral Letter on Euthanasia and Suicide," 9 March 1976, p. 3.

8. Gabrielle A. Carlson, Charles L. Rich, Patricia Grayson, and Richard C. Fowler, "Secular Trends in Psychiatric Diagnoses of Suicide Victims," *Journal of Affective Disorders* 21 (1991): 127–32.

9. Robert L. Frierson, "Suicide Attempts by the Old and the Very Old," *Archives of Internal Medicine* 151 (1991): 141–44; Thomas B. Mackenzie and Michael K. Popkin, "Medical Illness and Suicide." In *Suicide Over the Life Cycle: Risk Factors, Assessment, and Treatment of Suicidal Patients,* ed. Susan J. Blumenthal and David J. Kupfer (Washington D.C.: American Psychiatric Press, 1990), pp. 205–32.

10. Robert J. Blendon, Ulrike S. Szalay, Richard A. Knox, "Should Physicians Aid Their Patients in Dying? The Public Perspective," *JAMA* 269 (1993): 590–91.

11. Darien S. Fenn and Linda Ganzini, personal communication.

12. Stuart J. Youngner, "Competency to Refuse Life-Sustaining Treatment." In *End-of-Life Decisions: A Psychosocial Perspective,* ed. Maurice D. Steinberg and Stuart J. Youngner (Washington, D.C.: *American Psychiatric Press,* 1998).

13. Loren H. Roth, Alan Meisel, and Charles W. Lidz, "Tests of Competency to Consent to Treatment," *American Journal of Psychiatry* 134 (1977): 279–84; Allen E. Buchanan and Dan W. Brock, *Deciding for Others* (Cambridge: Cambridge University Press, 1989), p. 77.

14. Youngner, "Competency to Refuse Life-Sustaining Treatment."

15. Linda Ganzini, Darien S. Fenn, Melinda A. Lee et al., "Attitudes of Oregon Psychiatrists Toward Physician Assisted Suicide," *American Journal of Psychiatry* 153 (1996): 1469–75.

16. Fenn and Ganzini, personal communication.

17. Mary Jane Massie, Jimmie Holland, and Ellen Glass, "Delirium in Terminal Cancer Patients," *American Journal of Psychiatry* 140 (1983): 1048–50.

18. Judith B. Bukberg, Doris T. Penman, and Jimmie C. Holland, "Depression in Hospitalized Cancer Patients," *Psychosomatic Medicine* 46 (1984): 199–212.

19. William Breitbart, Barry D. Rosenfeld, and Steven D. Passik, "Interest in Physician-Assisted Suicide among Ambulatory HIV-Infected Patients," *American Journal of Psychiatry* 153 (1996): 238–42.

20. H. C. Schulberg, M. Saul, and M. N. McClelland, "Assessing Depression in Primary Medical and Psychiatric Practices," *Archives of General Psychiatry* 42 (1985): 1164–70.

21. Kathleen R. Farrell and Linda Ganzini, "Misdiagnosing Delirium as Depression in Medically Ill Elderly Patients," *Archives of Internal Medicine* 155 (1995): 2459–64.

22. *Rogers v. Okin,* 478 F Supp 1342 (D Mass, 1979).

23. Melinda A. Lee and Linda Ganzini, "Depression in the Elderly: Effect on Patient Attitudes toward Life-Sustaining Therapy," *Journal of the American Geriatric Society* 40 (1992): 983–88.

24. Linda Ganzini, Melinda A. Lee, Ronald T. Heintz et al., "The Effect of Depression Treatment on Elderly Patients' Preferences for Life-Sustaining Medical Therapy," *American Journal of Psychiatry* 151 (1994): 1631–36.

25. S. C. Hooper, K. J. Vaughan, C. C. Tennant, and J. M. Perz, "Major Depression and Refusal of Life-Sustaining Treatment in the Elderly," *Medical Journal of Australia* 165 (1996): 416–19.

26. Joanne M. Garrett, Russell P. Harris, Jean K. Norburn et al., "Life-Sustaining Treatments During Terminal Illness: Who Wants What?" *Journal of General Internal Medicine* 9 (1993): 361–68.

27. Mark D. Sullivan and Stuart J. Youngner, "Depression, Competence, and the Right to Refuse Life-Saving Medical Treatment," *American Journal of Psychiatry* 151 (1994): 971–78.

28. James Henderson Brown, Paul Henteleff, Samia Barakat, and Cheryl June Rowe, "Is It Normal for Terminally Ill Patients to Desire Death?" *American Journal of Psychiatry* 143 (1986): 208–11.

29. Harvey Max Chochinov, Keith G. Wilson, Murray Enns et al., "Desire for Death in the Terminally Ill," *American Journal of Psychiatry* 152 (1995): 1185–91.

30. Mark D. Sullivan, Suzanne A. Rapp, Dermot Fitzgibbon, and C. Richard Chapman, "Pain and the Choice to Hasten Death Among Patients with Painful Metastatic Cancer," *Journal of Palliative Care,* in press.

31. Ezekiel J. Emanuel, "Empirical Studies on Euthanasia and Assisted Suicide," *Journal of Clinical Ethics* 6 (1995): 158–60.

32. Sullivan et al., "Pain and the Choice to Hasten Death."

33. Ganzini et al., "Attitudes of Oregon Psychiatrists."

34. Susan D. Block and J. Andrew Billings, "Patient Requests for Euthanasia and Assisted Suicide: The Role of the Psychiatrist," *Psychosomatics* 36 (1995): 445–57.

35. J. Stephen McDaniel, Dominque L. Musselman, Maryfrances R. Porter et al., "Depression in Patients with Cancer: Diagnosis, Biology, and Treatment," *Archives of General Psychiatry* 52 (1995): 89–99.

CHALLENGE QUESTIONS

Should Mental Health Professionals Serve as Gatekeepers for Physician-Assisted Suicide?

1. Farberman makes some strong arguments with regard to the importance of involving mental health professionals in cases of physician-assisted suicide. What criteria should be specified in order to determine the competence of the mental health professional to play this role?
2. Sullivan, Ganzini, and Youngner do not believe that there is a convincing case for mandatory involvement of mental health professionals in cases of physician-assisted suicide in general. For what kinds of specific cases could a strong argument be made for requiring such involvement?
3. In 1997 the U.S. Supreme Court ruled that terminally ill people do not have a constitutional right to doctor-assisted suicide, but it also declared that states have the option of enacting assistance-in-dying statutes. What arguments can be made for and against the constitutionality of the right to physician-assisted suicide?
4. What kinds of emotional burdens might be experienced by mental health professionals who become involved in the assessment of terminally ill patients?

Suggested Readings

Block, S. D., & Billings, J. A. (1998). Evaluating patient requests for euthanasia and assisted suicide in terminal illness: The role of the psychiatrist. In M. D. Steinberg & S. J. Youngner (Eds.), *End-of-life decisions: A psychosocial perspective* (pp. 205–233). Washington, DC: American Psychiatric Press, Inc.

Ganzini, L., Fenn, D. S., Lee, M. A., Heintz, R. T., & Bloom, J. D. (1996). Attitudes of Oregon psychiatrists toward physician-assisted suicide. *American Journal of Psychiatry, 153,* 1469–1475.

Peruzzi, N., Canapary, A., & Bongar, B. (1996). Physician-assisted suicide: The role of mental health professionals. *Ethics & Behavior, 6(4),* 353–366.

ISSUE 20

Is Sexual Orientation Conversion Therapy Ethical?

YES: Mark A. Yarhouse, from "When Clients Seek Treatment for Same-Sex Attraction: Ethical Issues in the 'Right to Choose' Debate," *Psychotherapy: Theory/Research/Practice/Training* (Summer 1998)

NO: Douglas C. Haldeman, from "The Practice and Ethics of Sexual Orientation Conversion Therapy," *Journal of Consulting and Clinical Psychology* (April 1994)

ISSUE SUMMARY

YES: Psychologist Mark A. Yarhouse asserts that mental health professionals have an ethical responsibility to allow individuals to pursue treatment aimed at curbing same-sex attraction, stating that doing so affirms the client's dignity and autonomy.

NO: Psychologist Douglas C. Haldeman criticizes therapy involving sexual reorientation, insisting that there is no evidence that such treatments are effective and that they run the risk of further stigmatizing homosexuality.

It has only been in the last few decades that the American Psychiatric Association (APA) has come to terms with the notion that it was inappropriate to include "homosexuality" in its official listing of mental disorders. This decision followed years of debate, which culminated in the realization that pathologizing people because of sexual orientation is unwarranted. Letting go of homosexuality as a diagnosable mental disorder did not come easily for psychiatry; in fact, for several years the official list of diagnoses included the label "ego-dystonic homosexuality" to refer to individuals who suffered a range of emotional symptoms associated with being gay or lesbian. Eventually, even this diagnostic label was deleted in response to criticisms that it perpetuated the tendency of the mental health establishment to pathologize homosexuality.

Even though homosexuality was removed from the list of diagnostic labels, troubling experiences with discrimination, social exclusion, and inner turmoil continue to haunt millions of men and women in the process of coming to terms with their homosexual orientation. As these individuals have turned to mental health professionals for help through critical times, they have found a range of responses. Many mental health professionals strive to help these clients develop healthy ways of thinking about themselves in which they accept their sexuality and their capacity for living happy and fulfilling lives in intimate and loving relationships with same-sex partners. Other mental health professionals view sexual orientation as a malleable characteristic that can be changed in those who wish to reorient themselves. Rather than focusing on self-acceptance, these clinicians work with the client to change sexual orientation. Debates between these two camps have been intense.

In the following selection, Mark A. Yarhouse contends that psychologists—and, by extension, other mental health professionals—have an ethical responsibility to allow individuals to pursue treatment aimed at curbing experiences of same-sex attraction. He asserts that in this approach to treatment, the clinician affirms the client's rights to dignity and autonomy and respects the client as an individual who is capable of choosing among available treatment modalities. Yarhouse contends that, rather than being discriminatory, this approach to clients actually demonstrates respect for diversity.

In the second selection, Douglas C. Haldeman criticizes therapy approaches that involve sexual reorientation and insists that there is no evidence that such treatments are effective. Asserting that conversion therapies are unethical because they are predicated on a devaluation of homosexual identity and behavior, Haldeman maintains that the appropriate focus of the profession should be on what reverses prejudice, not what reverses sexual orientation.

POINT

- When clients feel distressed about their experiences of same-sex attraction and express interest in treatment based on personal, religious, or moral grounds, clinicians have an ethical responsibility to direct them to appropriate services.

- Clients should be seen as having the right to choose treatment for their experiences of same-sex attraction.

- Clinicians should presume that people are autonomous agents, particularly with respect to their decisions concerning their work in therapy.

- Some clients may choose to pursue change of sexual orientation due to religious and cultural values concerning the purpose and design of human sexuality and sexual behavior.

COUNTERPOINT

- It is unethical for clinicians to recommend treatments that are not empirically supported; furthermore, conversion therapies are unethical because they are predicated on a devaluation of homosexual identity and behavior.

- Given the extensive societal devaluation of homosexuality, it is not surprising that many gay people seek to become heterosexual; clinicians should be combating stigma with a vigorous avowal of empirical truth.

- The concept that individuals seek to change their sexual orientation of their own free will is fallacious.

- Many gay males and lesbians consider sexual orientation conversion because of the severe conflict they experience between their homoerotic feelings and their need for acceptance by a homophobic religious community.

Mark A. Yarhouse  **YES**

When Clients Seek Treatment for Same-Sex Attraction

The focus of this article is the examination of ethical issues related to psychologists providing treatment to clients who experience same-sex attraction and seek change. Of particular concern are the ethical issues of psychologists who work with clients who are distressed as a result of the conflict they experience between same-sex attraction and behavior and their own valuative framework. Obviously, many gay and lesbian clients enter therapy and do not have as their goal a change of orientation or behavior. Rather, they enter therapy for concerns related to mood disorders, anxiety disorders, sexual dysfunctions, relationship problems, and so on. Still others enter therapy concerned about their sexual orientation and want to integrate their impulses into a gay identity and are pursuing "gay-affirmative" therapy. The question of the psychologist's responsibility to assist homosexual persons in these areas is beyond the scope of this article and has been addressed elsewhere (Browning, Reynolds, & Dworkin, 1991; Shannon & Woods, 1991).

There are a number of ethical considerations for psychologists who provide treatment to clients who experience same-sex attraction and are seeking change of behavior or orientation. The purpose of this article is to develop and elaborate on an ethical principle of particular importance in the treatment care of homosexual persons: *Ethical Principle D: Respect for Rights and Dignity* (APA, 1992). Ethical Principle D, which is an aspirational ethical principle for psychologists, provides a foundation for the ethical care of those who report distress concerning their experience of same-sex attraction. This care receives further support from several Ethical Standards that are enforceable standards for the professional conduct of psychologists.

Respect for People's Rights and Dignity

. . . According to Ethical Principle D, psychologists are to "accord appropriate respect to the fundamental rights, dignity, and worth of all people" (APA, 1992, p. 1599). Perhaps what is most relevant to this discussion of same-sex attraction is that psychologists are called to respect their clients' rights to

From Mark A. Yarhouse, "When Clients Seek Treatment for Same-Sex Attraction: Ethical Issues in the 'Right to Choose' Debate," *Psychotherapy: Theory/Research/Practice/Training,* vol. 35, no. 2 (Summer 1998), pp. 248–259. Copyright © 1998 by The Division of Psychotherapy (29) of The American Psychological Association. Reprinted by permission.

"privacy, confidentiality, self-determination, and autonomy" (p. 1600), and they are to be aware of difference, including differences related to sexual orientation and religion.

In the space that follows, two points will be developed related to this ethical principle. First, clients should be seen as having the right to choose treatment for their experience of same-sex attraction. It will be argued that this right to choose is grounded in (a) the autonomy and self-respect of persons, and (b) the multicultural dimension of the work of psychologists, which includes respect for normative religious values and cultural differences. Second, in light of a respectful stance toward those who report distress concerning their experience of same-sex attraction, psychologists should provide a form of advanced informed consent to treatment, so that their clients have as much information as possible concerning the state of scientific research pertaining to this controversial topic.

Autonomy and Self-Determination

Psychologists view people as agents capable of comprehending principles related to behavior that they should engage in, as well as behaviors from which they should refrain. The capacity to choose between alternatives is referred to as "agency," which has been defined as "the capacity for an organism to behave in compliance with, in addition to, in opposition to, or without regard for biological or sociological stimulations" (Rychlak, 1988, p. 84). Agency and *autonomy* are related concepts. Sobocinski (1990) discusses what it means to respect a person's autonomy. He argues that "respecting others as autonomous individuals involves recognizing them as essentially self-governing agents, capable of exercising competent, self-determination in the selection of choices and actions" (p. 241). In fact, the Ethics Code of the APA (1992) presupposes that under most circumstances clients have the right to choose treatment and to be informed of various treatment modalities and alternatives to treatment. "Psychologists obtain appropriate informed consent to therapy or related procedures, using language that is reasonably understandable to participants" (APA, 1992, p. 1605). In other words, psychologists are ethically obligated to use informed consent precisely because people are capable of agency.

Psychologists generally agree that clients are self-determining agents insofar as they have the ability and right to make decisions regarding therapy. At the same time, some psychologists argue that homosexual clients are unique in that their ability to choose freely between alternatives is diminished (and sometimes eradicated) by negative societal messages about same-sex attraction and behavior. Initial attempts to validate both the existence of negative social stigma and the autonomy and self-determination of the individual were relatively balanced. For example, Pillard (1982, p. 94) quotes Silverstein (1972, p. 4) as arguing that various environmental stressors constrain a person's ability to choose freely: "To suggest that a person comes voluntarily to change his sexual orientation is to ignore the powerful environmental stress, oppression if you will, that has been telling him for years that he should change." Silverstein goes on in his address to argue that after processing the guilt and shame associated with their experience of same-sex attraction (as well as ways in which they have been injured by various social structures), therapists can have a discussion with clients about their desire to pursue change: "After [dissolving the shame about their desires], let them choose, but not before. I don't know any more than you what would happen, but I think their choice would be more voluntary and free than it is at present" (p. 4).

This approach is balanced insofar as psychologists are called upon to recognize powerful societal forces and the impact of those forces on their clients, yet protect the autonomy and self-determination of individuals pursuing treatment. Unfortunately, this approach has been challenged in recent years by a perspective that seems to view any desire to change as a result of internalized homophobia. Some argue that homosexuals never freely make the choice to change their orientation (Davison, 1982; Halderman, 1991, 1994; Murphy, 1992). They argue that people do not have the "right to choose" such treatment, and some appear to favor gay-affirmative therapy to the exclusion of any other kind of treatment. . . .

Psychologists must be cautious about this kind of claim. The perspective that keeps in balance the influences of societal messages, while at the same time respects the autonomy of the individual, is at risk of being replaced by a view based upon a generalization lacking any empirical support. Psychologists cannot verify that homosexuals who choose treatment "almost always" do so because of internalized familial hostility and societal intolerance. Certainly many homosexual clients seek treatment because of the pressure they feel in a predominantly heterosexual society (and psychologists should be sensitive to this as a very real concern for many gay men and lesbians). However, the decision to pursue change of behavior, desires, and even orientation is a complicated one. A more accurate representation is that some homosexuals pursue change because of societal pressure, and so on, while others pursue change for a variety of reasons, including values they hold concerning purpose and design of sexual behavior. These values come from a number of sources, including family, culture, and religion. And while some of these sources may at times reject same-sex behavior or attraction based on prejudices or stereotypes, these sources may also hold normative beliefs or values that are legitimate points of disagreement in a diverse and pluralistic society.

A related argument is whether or not treatment should be provided to a "nondisorder." Some who oppose providing professional services to clients who experience same-sex attraction and seek change note that in 1974 the American Psychiatric Association removed homosexuality as a pathological condition per se from the *Diagnostic and Statistical Manual (DSM)*. However, what often goes unnoticed is that the *DSM* contains relevant diagnostic codes which are appropriate, for example, "when the focus of clinical attention is uncertainty about multiple issues related to identity such as . . . sexual orientation and behavior, moral values," and so on (diagnostic code 313.82; American Psychiatric Association, 1994, p. 300). The *DSM* certainly presumes a rationale for providing services when concerns arise surrounding sexual identity and behavior. . . .

Religious Belief and Multiculturalism

In the past 20 years perhaps no change in psychology has been as dramatic as the shift away from treating homosexual clients for their experience of same-sex attraction towards helping them to accept and integrate these impulses as part of a gay or lesbian identity (Browning et al., 1991; Coleman, 1982; Morin, 1991; Shannon & Woods, 1991). As was mentioned above, this new approach is referred to as "gay-affirmative therapy," and can include emphasis on identity development and management, interpersonal concerns, and specific issues such as antigay violence and AIDS (Shannon & Wood, 1991, pp. 197–210), as well as substance abuse, sexual abuse, and domestic violence, which Browning et al. (1991, pp. 189–191) identify as specific concerns for lesbian clients.

An additional concern in gay-affirmative therapy, according to Shannon and Woods (1991) and Browning et al. (1991), is that therapists discuss spiritual and existential issues in their work with homosexual clients. Shannon and Woods argue that "psychotherapy that does not address the existential/spiritual dimension is seriously lacking" (p. 211). Unfortunately, these authors limit their discussion of religious and spiritual themes to the harm religion may cause someone who experiences same-sex attraction, arguing that religion can lead to feelings of "isolation and alienation" (p. 212). Similarly, Browning et al. argue that "traditionally, people have met their spiritual needs through caring for others and through religion. The Western Judeo-Christian tradition has not been kind to lesbian women, with scriptural interpretations, customs, and religious doctrines used to create shame" (p. 192). They suggest that therapists help homosexuals "recognize and validate needs for spiritual community and discover ways to fulfill them" through "alternatives to traditional religion" (p. 192). Shannon and Woods offer a similar solution: they encourage therapists to distinguish between spirituality and religiosity, so that their clients can "find meaning in life without participating in an organized religion that is antithetical to the individual's personhood" (p. 212).

From an organized religious perspective, this understanding of religion is truncated and myopic. Despite efforts in recent years within the APA to incorporate an understanding of genuine religious experience into the clinical practice of psychology (Jones, 1994; Shafranske, 1996), recent literature on the relationship between homosexuality and religion completely ignores the normative or prescriptive dimension of religious experience in many faith communities and erroneously assumes that one view of those who experience same-sex attraction is exhaustive and complete (i.e., to integrate same-sex impulses into a gay identity). One important exception to this prescription of the homosexual community is the silenced minority of those who experience same-sex attraction and seek to change their behavior, impulses, or orientation, or who seek to live rich and fulfilling lives and remain celibate. Those who desire change may have personal convictions informed by religious or cultural values concerning the purpose and design of human sexuality and sexual expression.[1] People may appeal to religious, moral, or cultural values and convictions that serve as valuative frameworks within which they aspire to live. Clearly psychologists must be sensitive to the fact that many homosexual persons disagree with the perspective on human sexuality articulated in the Jewish faith, various Protestant denominations, and the Roman Catholic Church, for example; many homosexuals report anger and frustration in response to the official teachings of these religious communities. At the same time, many homosexual persons are committed to these institutions, agree with the historical teachings concerning the moral status of same-sex behavior, and seek to live in conformity with the teachings of their religious community. This is clearly evidenced in the formation of Courage, a support group for Catholics who experience same-sex attraction and are attempting to live celibate lives in accord with the official teachings of the Roman Catholic Church. Others who report distress concerning their experience of same-sex attraction become involved in various support groups and 12-step groups (some of which have as their goal changing sexual orientation); still others come to psychologists for help.

Multicultural diversity, which is valued in various APA publications, challenges psychologists to respect the cultural, moral, and religious values and convictions of their clients: "In their work-related activities, psychologists respect the rights of others to hold values, attitudes, and opinions that differ from their own" (Ethical Standard 1.09; APA, 1992, p. 1601). Principle D clearly states that psychologists are to be "aware of cultural, individual, and role differences, including those due to . . . religion" (p. 1600). If psychologists override the values of their clients, are they saying that psychologists can respect and be tolerant of religious diversity so long as clients do not make choices that actually reflect the normative teaching of their religion? Or does one way of understanding diversity (related to sexual orientation) take precedence over other expressions of diversity (religious or cultural diversity)? From an ethical standpoint, when clients present for therapy distressed about their experience of same-sex attraction and express interest in pursuing treatment for their inclinations on personal religious, or moral grounds, psychologists have an ethical responsibility to assess this expressed interest and do all they can to provide and direct them to appropriate services in a responsible manner. . . .

Advanced Informed Consent

Informed consent helps psychologists insure a client's sense of autonomy and self-determination. Informed consent will vary from case to case, but it generally includes an assessment of the capacity of the person to consent, adequate knowledge of the intervention in question, and some written documentation of consent (APA, 1992, p. 1605; Corey, Corey, & Callahan, 1993; Keith-Spiegel & Koocher, 1985).

Clients who enter therapy reporting distress about their experience of same-sex attraction should be in an informed position as to the benefits and drawbacks of pursuing treatment. Considering the present state of knowledge in the areas of human sexuality and same-sex attraction, and in light of the degree of controversy surrounding this research, a comprehensive presentation is important for clients to make a truly informed decision. This raises the topic of *advanced informed consent*. In the case of clients who report distress concerning their experience of same-sex attraction, advanced informed consent to treatment should include the following content areas:

1. Hypotheses as to what is causing their problems (including etiology of same-sex attraction and the subjective experience of distress reported by a particular client)
2. Professional treatments available, including success rates and definitions and methodologies used to report "success"
3. Alternatives to professional treatment, including reported success rates and the relative lack of empirical support for claims of success
4. Possible benefits and risks of pursuing treatment at this time
5. Possible outcomes with or without treatment (and alternative explanations for possible outcomes)

Cause of Difficulties

Psychologists have an ethical obligation to discuss with clients hypotheses as to what may be causing their difficulties. In the case of persons distressed by their experience of same-sex attraction, this can be understood in at least three ways: (a) whether sexual orientation is a stable, enduring, universal reality or whether it is a social construction; (b) the etiology of same-sex attraction; and (c) what makes a particular person feel distress in relation to his or her experience of same-sex attraction. The following subsections provide an introduction only to the kinds of issues that may come up when persons seek treatment for their experience of same-sex attraction.

What Is Homosexuality?   There is significant debate today as to what homosexuality actually is. This debate is generally characterized as being between essentialists and constructivists. Essentialists argue that homosexuality and sexual orientation more generally is a stable, enduring, universal reality, which is accurately described by the taxonomy of our contemporary understanding. Proponents of this view often reference research implicating physiological antecedents related to the experience of same-sex attraction. Some (but not all) essentialists argue that this essence is tied to the core of one's self as a human being, and because this real essence is a part of what properly defines the core of the person, homosexual behavior is naturally occurring, morally blameless behavior that should find expression (Sullivan, 1995).

Constructivists, in contrast, view homosexuality as a social construct, so that the term "homosexuality" does not refer to something real but is a linguistic construct fashioned by a society for discussing sexual preferences. In support of this position, constructivists note that sexual conduct and attitudes toward it vary throughout history and across cultures, and that human homosexual orientation per se has no true parallel in subhuman species (Carrier, 1980; Greenberg, 1988). There are a variety of expressions of constructivism, some of which implicate early childhood development in the construction of a homosexual identity (Troiden, 1993). In any case, what unites the various schools of constructivism is the contention that it is shared cultural meanings and understandings of the organization of sexual behavior that determine the forms through which people experience their sexuality, rather than that experience being determined by an enduring, stable, universal reality.

Etiology   Researchers also disagree about what causes experiences of same-sex attraction. Psychologists should discuss with clients various competing theories as to the etiology of same-sex attraction. Proponents of gay-affirmative therapy tend to view same-sex behavior as an expression of sexual diversity and often see homosexuality as following a specific developmental course. Troiden (1993), for example, views the development of a homosexual identity as occurring in four stages: (a) sensitization (a person is sensitized by feeling marginalized), (b) identity confusion (often during adolescence, when feeling "different" is associated with same-sex attraction), (c) identity assumption (acceptance of a homosexual identity and association with others who identify themselves as gay), and (d) commitment (marked by increased commitment to and disclosure of homosexual identity).

In contrast, several psychoanalytic and psychodynamic theorists have discussed the etiology of homosexuality from a depth psychology perspective (Bieber et al., 1962; Moberly, 1983; Nicolosi, 1991, 1993; van den Aardweg, 1986). For example, van den Aardweg (1986) draws upon insights from Adler, who stressed the inferiority complex as well as the interpersonal and social dimensions of the person. According to van den Aardweg, homosexuality is symptomatic of a self-pitying neurosis that centers on feeling inferior with respect to one's masculinity. His therapy is referred to "anticomplaining" therapy, in which he develops the concept of the inner child in the adult who experiences same-sex attraction. In contrast, Moberly (1983) developed her theory for the etiology of homosexuality from a psychodynamic perspective. She views homosexuality as signaling a relational deficit with the same-sex parent: "Needs for love from, dependency on, and identification with, the parent of the same sex are met through the child's attachment to the parent" (p. 5). Failure to meet these legitimate developmental needs leads to a "defensive detachment" and a relational "ambivalence," which "marks the abiding defect in the person's actual relational capacity" (p. 6).

Proponents of this view reference empirical studies to support the hypothesis that problems in the parent–child relationship may be in some way related to some experiences of same-sex attraction. These include reports of distant relationships with the same-sex parent, including loss of a father or mother through divorce or death (Saghir & Robins, 1973), as well as studies reporting higher incidence rates of childhood sexual abuse among homosexuals as compared to their heterosexual peers (Doll et al., 1992; Laumann, Gagnon, Michael, & Michaels, 1994; Peters & Cantrell, 1991).

Psychological theories for the etiology of same-sex attraction have been criticized but not refuted. Most recently, researchers have focused on biological explanations for the etiology of homosexuality. These studies have included research on differences in brain structure and function (LeVay, 1991; Swaab & Hofman, 1990), prenatal hormonal mechanisms (Ellis & Ames, 1987), and genetic factors, as evidenced by twin studies (Bailey & Pillard, 1991) and markers on chromosomes that may be associated with homosexuality (Hamer, Hu, Magnuson, Hu, & Pattatucci, 1993; Hu et al., 1995; for a detailed review of this literature, see Byne & Parsons, 1993).

Psychologists should discuss with clients the various theories for the etiology of same-sex attraction and acknowledge that most experts in the field agree that there is no one explanation of homosexuality that accounts for every person's experience of same-sex attraction. Rather, the etiology of homosexuality may be related to a host of interrelated factors—shifting ratios of antecedents to same-sex attraction that vary from person to person and across cultures—some of which may be biological in origin and may provide a "push" in the direction of homosexuality. Other influences may take the form of psychosocial and environmental factors (e.g., parent-child relational deficits or experiences of childhood sexual abuse), as well as decisions made at key times in an individual's life.

Distress Psychologists should also seek to understand why a particular client is reporting distress with respect to his or her experience of same-sex attraction. A number of concerns may bring a homosexual client into treatment. For example, clients may come into therapy distressed about the social stigma attached to homosexuality. They may feel completely content with their experience of same-sex attraction but may struggle with whether or not to identify themselves as "gay" in a culture that is heterosexual in majority. A related concern has to do with internalized homophobia, which many proponents of gay-affirmative therapy view as the root cause of most concerns among distressed homosexuals (Halderman, 1991; cf., O'Donohue & Caselles, 1993). Along these lines, McConaghy notes that it is important "to establish that [clients] are in their customary state of mental health and are not suffering a psychiatric disorder . . . any decision about treatment in relation to their sexual orientation should be postponed until they have returned to their normal emotional state" (1993, p. 134).

Other clients may not know what they think about their experiences of same-sex attraction, but they may be asking for a safe place to articulate—perhaps for the first time—their ambivalent feelings toward their impulses and inclinations. Still others may report that their difficulties stem from genuine religious convictions about the proper intention for sexual expression and may be combined to some extent with cultural/ethnic values concerning human sexuality, gender roles, and the propagation of one's race (Greene, 1994). Psychologists should be prepared to respect the values of clients even if they differ from their own, and they should be prepared to discuss a range of options in light of the current research on homosexuality.

Professional Treatments Available

A discussion of available treatments should follow a thorough discussion of the client's goals. Some clients seek change of orientation; others report interest in reducing anxiety about heterosexual behavior or decreasing homosexual thoughts or behavior; still others seek help in living a celibate life.

Change of orientation techniques have included behavioral sex therapy (Masters & Johnson, 1979), individual psychoanalytic therapy (Bieber et al., 1962), individual reparative therapy based on psychodynamic theory (Nicolosi, 1993) and group therapies offered from a psychoanalytic perspective (Hadden, 1958), psychodynamic/reparative therapy perspective (Nicolosi, 1991, 1993), social learning perspective (Birk, 1974, 1980), and a variety of other theoretical perspectives (Beukenkamp, 1960; Mintz, 1966). Success rates have ranged from between 25–50% at best, although success was often measured by self-report and therapist-report, which are susceptible to over reporting of positive outcomes and under reporting of negative outcomes. Only a few studies utilized control groups. It should be noted, however, that the dearth of controlled outcome studies and more stringent methodologies does not disprove the success of treatment. Sometimes it is presumed that improved methodologies would automatically discredit reports of success.

Unfortunately, few researchers today publish studies on therapy for homosexuals who seek change. Those who do report on such interventions are often criticized. For example, a controversial intervention is reparative therapy, which is based on dynamic theory and assumes that some homosexuals experience a same-sex relational deficit. Nicolosi (1991, 1993) offers a detailed description of reparative therapy, which he states "proceeds from the assumption that some childhood developmental tasks were not completed" (p. 211). . . . Because of the assumption that people "eroticize" what they "are not identified with," therapy focuses on "the full development of the client's masculine gender identity" (1993, pp. 199, 211–212).

In any case, those who are asking to change orientation should be informed that a variety of interventions exist. They should also be told that definitions of "success" vary significantly. Early studies defined a "heterosexual shift" as choosing "to change and to give up homosexual contacts" (Pittman & DeYoung, 1971, p. 66). Similar definitions of success have been criticized as superficial. At the other extreme, critics of reorientation programs often define success so strictly as to negate the value of any change whatsoever. For example, Haldeman (1991) argues that any lustful thoughts or same-sex impulses experienced by clients refute the claim of a "cure." At issue here is how to interpret continuing experiences of same-sex attraction and arousal. This may indicate that treatment was ineffective. However, continued struggles with same-sex arousal may be expected residual effects from years of homosexual fantasy and behavior. Psychologists certainly refrain from decrying chemical dependency programs simply because someone experiences cravings following treatment. In any case, this is certainly an area where clarity of definitions and expectations is needed.

Those who seek to change behavior rather than orientation should be aware of research that utilizes rigorous methodology and supports efforts to change, including the use of imaginal desensitization/alternative behavioral completion, covert modeling, behavioral rehearsal, assertiveness training, and aversion therapy. For example, McConaghy (1969, 1970, 1976) reports on the use of behavioral and aversion therapies and the use of penile plethysmograph responses as means of measuring change of homosexual impulses. In one study McConaghy (1970) notes that of 35 patients contracted at one-year follow-up (of a total of 40 in the original study), 7 reported change of orientation from predominantly homosexual to predominantly heterosexual (although McConaghy is conservative in his interpretation of their reported change of orientation). A total of 10 patients showed marked improvement and 15 additional patients showed some improvement. Of these, many reported greater emotional stability and decreased preoccupation with homosexual thoughts; still others were reportedly able to control compulsions to anonymous homosexual encounters. Elsewhere McConaghy (1993, pp. 134–138) discusses a range of cognitive and behavioral interventions for those who seek change and reports that homosexual clients can learn "to control homosexual feelings or behaviors they experience as compulsive and to reduce anxiety concerning heterosexual activity" (1990, p. 576).

Murphy (1992) offers a critical review of a number of other professional interventions to diminish sexual desire, including surgery (which Murphy states have been abandoned as of the early 1980s) and drug and hormone therapy. McConaghy also reviews the use of medroxyprogesterone acetate "to cease unacceptable sexual behaviors while not altering their enjoyment of acceptable behaviors" (1993, p. 134; cf., Silverstein, 1991). Both Murphy and McConaghy also note that interventions are often combined so that, for example, drug treatments are provided in conjunction with behavior therapy.

Alternatives to Professional Treatment

In addition to the professional interventions mentioned above, increasing numbers of paraprofessional religious groups are offering services to persons distressed by their experience of same-sex attraction. A plausible hypothesis is that these groups have emerged in part because of the decrease in professional services provided to homosexuals who seek change. However, while most of these groups do make claims for change of orientation, there are no published controlled outcome studies to support the numerous anecdotal reports of change. Although these groups receive appropriate criticism for not providing empirical support for claims of success, it should be noted that the lack of empirical support does not disprove the effectiveness of these groups. As with professional interventions, it is often presumed that more stringent methodology would automatically discredit these groups. Paraprofessional groups remain attractive to some psychologists and clients because they offer services at little or no charge and are often used as an adjunct to professional therapy, similar to how therapists encourage alcoholics to attend Alcoholics Anonymous (AA) meetings while they continue to receive professional care.

There are several examples of religion-based support groups, including Exodus International-affiliated ministries and Homosexuals Anonymous. These organizations tend to view homosexuality as a learned behavior that can be changed, and proponents give the impression that change of orientation can be expected (Consiglio, 1989, 1993; Dallas, 1991). Other religion-based support groups, such as Courage, emphasize celibacy and behavior change (Harvey, 1987). Although Courage does not discourage those who have the desire and the financial resources to attempt change of orientation from doing so. Courage does take a more conservative approach in general as it cautions people to not be disheartened if, after attempts at change, they are unable to experience a heterosexual orientation. Unfortunately, as with most of the other religion-based groups, Courage publishes no outcome data on those who attend group meetings. . . .

Benefits and Risks of Treatment

Clients should also be made aware of the benefits and risks of treatment. Risks of treatment include the financial and emotional investment for those who pursue change. Professional interventions such as reparative therapy can last for 2 or more years (with no guarantee of "success"), and the financial cost can be tremendous. The financial investment may pale in comparison to the emotional investment, especially depending upon the expectations of the client. For example, those who have as their goal complete change of sexual orientation and who view failure to achieve a "complete heterosexual shift" as evidence of lack of faith, lack of spiritual maturity, or as a sign of moral degradation may be in a far worse state than those who attempt change but recognize the potential limitations of change techniques. A related concern is that lack of success in treatment may lead to anger and resentment. These feelings may be directed inward (taking the form of depression or suicidality), or they may be directed at the therapist, family members, society, God, the church, support groups, and so on. One arguable but plausible hypothesis is that some of those who are truly disillusioned by attempts to change may become the most ardent supporters of gay-affirmative therapy, in part because they held such high hopes for treatment, and the dichotomy between the psychological sense of "success" and "failure" may have been too great a strain to bear. Clearly the risk of failure and what that means to a client is an important part of informed consent.

In addition, some have criticized the use of aversion therapy and some behavioral therapies as potentially harmful to the person seeking change (i.e., may cause depression, anxiety, or decreased self-esteem). Critics of these interventions question their ethical status (Coleman, 1982; Wilson & Davison, 1974) and some note that change away from treating homosexuality as a pathology toward treating it as a moral concern (Murphy, 1992). Moral concerns, however, can still direct the focus of treatment, and psychologists have an ethical responsibility to respect the moral values of clients (Ethical Standards 1.09, APA, 1992).

The benefits of treatment my include change of sexual orientation, although this claim is precisely what is debated among mental health professionals. Some of those who report change of sexual orientation also report satisfying heterosexual relationships, including marriage (although most mental health professionals agree that heterosexual marriage should not be held out as the goal of treatment as such). Other benefits of treatment appear to be greater emotional stability, decreased preoccupation with homosexual thoughts, and decreased compulsive sexual behavior (McConaghy, 1970, reports these gains among several clients at one-year follow up).

Possible Outcomes With and Without Treatment

Possible outcome with treatment has been discussed. Some may experience change of behavior or impulses. It is possible that some may experience change of orientation. Others will not experience change that is satisfying in light of their goals for treatment. Outcome without treatment may be difficult to predict. Some may choose to live a celibate life, having had as their goal change of orientation. Others may choose to limit their sexual relationships to an exclusive or monogamous sexual relationship, having had anonymous sexual encounters or having engaged in compulsive sexual activities in the past. However, the research on rates of nonmonogamy among homosexuals as compared to heterosexuals suggests this may be unlikely. For example, Laumann et al. (1994) published findings that homosexual males on average reported 42.8 lifetime sexual partners as compared to 16.5 lifetime sexual partners among heterosexual males, 9.4 lifetime sexual partners among lesbians, and 4.6 lifetime sexual partners among heterosexual females.

It should be noted, however, that some researchers argue that it is difficult to compare rates of nonmonogamy between homosexuals and heterosexuals. For example, McWhirter and Mattison (1984) contend that homosexual partners may not make promises to each other that they intend to remain monogamous. At least one study has attempted to account for this possibility. Blumstein and Schwartz (1990) created a category for "close-coupled" homosexual partners to distinguish committed male homosexual relationships. Blumstein and Schwartz (1990) found that 79% of close-coupled male homosexuals reported at least one experience of nonmonogamy in the previous year, as compared to 19% of lesbians, 10% of married heterosexuals, and 23% of cohabiting heterosexuals. Even in this study, question remain concerning the relationship between emotional fidelity and sexual exclusivity, as 36% of gay men and 71% of lesbians surveyed valued sexual monogamy.

In any case, those who seek treatment for their experience of same-sex attraction may also choose to integrate their experience of same-sex attraction into a gay identity. These individuals should be aware of concerns identified as relevant to clinical work with gay men and lesbians. This is actually an area where there is some agreement even between otherwise polarized gay-affirmative therapists and reparative therapists, for example. These concerns include increased rates of depressive symptomatology, alcohol and drug use, and suicidal ideation, as well as common sexual practices that increase the risk of physical harm and disease (Laumann et al., 1994;

McWhirter & Mattison, 1984). Of course, numerous contradictory theories have been advanced to account for the differences reported in these studies. Some researchers argue that coming out of the closet (as measured by degree of communication about sexual preference and degree of comfort with being gay) and relationship involvement correlate with lower scores on measures of anxiety and depression as compared to those who remain distressed by their experience of same-sex attraction (Schmitt & Kurdek, 1987). For others, being out of the closet may not guarantee lower levels of depression, anxiety, and so on, especially if they experience discrimination (McKirman & Peterson, 1988; Mosbacher, 1993). What complicates our understanding is that most of the major national surveys do not make the distinction between "closeted" and "out" homosexuals, so there is less information from nationally representative samples than is desirable. The largest nationally representative samples include relatively small subpopulations of homosexual individuals, and the survey protocols are often designed for a generic (usually heterosexual) sample rather than a homosexual population (Laumann et al., 1994). The smaller and more famous surveys of homosexual individuals have much smaller sample sizes and tend to be of convenience samples (Bell & Weinberg, 1978).

In any case, clients should have the opportunity to make informed decisions about their treatment, and these findings, though difficult to interpret, may be deemed important by clients making decisions about their health and well-being. Obviously, many people who choose not to pursue treatment do not report these concerns, and there is retrospective research that supports the claim that those who identify themselves as homosexual may feel better about themselves than they did prior to that decision (Bell & Weinberg, 1978). The professional ethical issue here is that, as suggested by Ethical Principle D and in light of the benefit of advanced informed consent to treatment, those who come to therapy reporting distress concerning their experience of same-sex attraction should at some point in treatment have a frank discussion of possible outcomes with or without treatment.

Conclusion

Psychologists take seriously autonomy and agency of the individual. The human capacity to choose is relevant to therapeutic conceptualizations and interventions, and some clients choose to make moral concerns a focus of treatment, or they seek to change their behavior precisely because of an overarching moral evaluative framework. Individuals have the right to seek treatment aimed at curbing homosexual inclinations or modifying homosexual behaviors, not only because it affirms their right to dignity, autonomy, and agency, as persons presumed capable of freely choosing among treatment modalities and behavior, but also because it demonstrates a high regard for cultural and religious differences.

Psychologists who work with clients distressed by their experience of same-sex attraction should only do so with advanced informed consent. A comprehensive presentation of relevant findings should precede any decision for or against treatment, as the use of informed consent respects the autonomy and agency of clients and demonstrates multicultural sensitivity to normative religious values.

Note

1. Beverly Greene (1994) reports on the relationship between cultural and sexual identity among ethnic minority groups. Interestingly, according to Greene, in contrast to other minorities, "African American gay men and lesbians claim a strong attachment to their cultural heritage and to their communities and cite their identities as African American as primary" (p. 246).

References

American Psychiatric Association. (1994). *Diagnostic and statistical manual of mental disorders* (4th ed.). Washington, DC: Author.
American Psychological Association. (1992). Ethical principles of psychologists and code of conduct. *American Psychologist, 47*(12), 1597–1611.
Bailey, J. M., & Pillard, R. C. (1991). A genetic study of male sexual orientation. *Archives of General Psychiatry, 48,* 1089–1096.
Beukenkamp, C. (1960). Phantom patricide. *Archives of General Psychiatry, 3,* 282–288.
Bell, A. P., & Weinberg, M. S. (1978). *Homosexualities: A study of diversity among men and women.* New York: Simon and Schuster.
Bieber, I., Dain, H. J., Dince, P. R., Drellich, M. G., Grand, H. G., Gundlach, R. H., Kremer, M. W., Rifkin, A. H., Wilbur, C. B., & Bieber, T. B. (1962). *Homosexuality: A psychoanalytic study of male homosexuality.* New York: Basic.
Birk, L. (1974). Group psychotherapy for men who are homosexual. *Journal of Sex and Marital Therapy, 1,* 29–52.
Birk, L. (1980). The myth of classical homosexuality: Views of a behavioral psychotherapist. In J. Marmor (Ed.), *Homosexual behavior: A modern reappraisal* (pp. 376–390). New York Basic.
Blumstein, P., & Schwartz, P. (1990). Intimate relationships and the creation of sexuality. In S. A. Sanders & J. M. Reinisch (Eds.), *Homosexuality/heterosexuality: Concepts of sexual orientation* (pp. 307–320). New York: Oxford University Press.
Browning, C., Reynolds, A. L., & Dworkin, S. H. (1991). Affirmative psychotherapy for lesbian women. *The Counseling Psychologist, 19*(2), 177–196.
Byne, W., & Parsons, B. (1993). Human sexual orientation: The biologic theories reappraised. *Archives of General Psychiatry, 50,* 228–239.
Carrier, J. (1980). Homosexual behavior in cross-cultural perspective. In J. Marmor (Ed.), *Homosexual behavior: A modern reappraisal* (pp. 100–122). New York: Basic.
Coleman, E. (1982). Changing approaches to the treatment of homosexuality. In W. Paul, J. D. Weinrich, J. C. Gonsiorek, & M. E. Hotvedt (Eds.), *Homosexuality: Social, psychological, and biological issues* (pp. 81–88). Beverly Hills: Sage.
Consiglio, W. (1989). *Homosexual no more: Practical strategies for Christians overcoming homosexuality.* Wheaton, IL: Victor.
Consiglio, W. (1993). Doing therapy in an alien culture with Christians overcoming homosexuality. *Journal of Pastoral Counseling, 28,* 66–95.
Corey, G., Corey, M. S., & Callahan, P. (1993). *Issues and ethics in the helping professions* (4th ed.). Pacific Grove, CA: Brooks/Cole.
Dallas, J. (1991). *Desires in conflict: Answering the struggle for sexual identity.* Eugene, OR: Harvest House.

Davison, G. C. (1982). Politics, ethics, and therapy for homosexuality. In W. Paul, J. D. Weinrich, J. C. Gonsiorek, & M. E. Hotvedt (Eds.), *Homosexuality: Social, psychological, and biological issues* (pp. 89–98). Beverly Hills: Sage.

Doll, L. S., Joy, D., Bartholow, B. N., Harrison, J. S., Bolan, G., Douglas, J. M., Saltzman, L. E., Moss, P. M., & Delgado, W. (1992). Self-reported childhood and adolescent sexual abuse among adult homosexual and bisexual men. *Child Abuse and Neglect, 16,* 855–864.

Ellis, L., & Ames, A. (1987). Neurohormonal functioning and sexual orientation: A theory of homosexuality-heterosexuality. *Psychological Bulletin, 101,* 233–258.

Greenberg, D. (1988). *The construction of homosexuality.* Chicago: University of Chicago Press.

Greene, B. (1994). Ethnic-minority lesbians and gay men: Mental health and treatment issues. *Journal of Consulting and Clinical Psychology, 62*(2), 243–251.

Hadden, S. B. (1958). Treatment of homosexuality in individual and group psychotherapy. *American Journal of Psychiatry, 114,* 810–815.

Haldeman, D. C. (1991). Sexual orientation conversion therapy: A scientific examination. In J. Gonsiorek & J. Weinrich (Eds.), *Homosexuality: Research implications for public policy* (pp. 149–160). Newbury Park, CA: Sage.

Haldeman, D. C. (1994). The practice and ethics of sexual orientation conversion therapy. *Journal of Consulting and Clinical Psychology, 62*(2), 221–227.

Hamer, D. H., Hu, S., Magnuson, V. L., Hu, N., & Pattatuci, A. M. (1993). A linkage between DNA markers on the X chromosome and male sexual orientation, *Science, 261,* 321–327.

Harvey, J. F. (1987). *The homosexual person: New thinking in pastoral care.* San Francisco: Ignatius.

Hu, S., Pattatucci, A. M., Patterson, C., Li, L., Fulker, D. W., Cherny, S. S., Kruglyak, L., & Hamer, D. H. (1995). Linkage between sexual orientation and chromosome Xq28 in males but not in females. *Nature Genetics, 11,* 248–256.

Jones, S. L. (1994). A constructive relationship for religion with the science and profession of psychology: Perhaps the boldest model yet. *American Psychologist, 49*(3), 184–199.

Keith-Spiegel, P., & Koocher, G. P. (1985). *Ethics in psychology: Professional standards and cases.* New York: Random House.

Laumann, E. O., Gagnon, J. H., Michael, R. T., & Michaels, S. (1994). *The Social organization of sexuality.* Chicago: University of Chicago Press.

LeVay, S. (1991). A difference in the hypothalamic structure between heterosexual and homosexual men. *Science, 253,* 1034–1037.

Masters, W., & Johnson, V. (1979). *Homosexuality in perspective.* Boston: Little, Brown, & Co.

McConaghy, N. (1969). Subjective and penile plethysmograph responses following aversion-relief and apomorphine aversion therapy for homosexual impulses. *British Journal of Psychiatry, 115,* 723–730.

McConaghy, N. (1970). Subjective and penile plethysmograph responses to aversion therapy for homosexuality: A follow-up study. *British Journal of Psychiatry, 117,* 555–560.

McConaghy, N. (1976). Is a homosexual orientation irreversible? *British Journal of Psychiatry, 129,* 556–563.

McConaghy, N. (1990). Sexual deviation. In A. S. Bellack, M. Hersen, & A. E. Kazdin (Eds.), *International handbook of behavior modification and therapy* (2nd ed., pp. 565–580). New York: Plenum.

McConaghy, N. (1993). *Sexual behavior: Problems and management.* New York: Plenum.

McKirman, D. J., & Peterson, P. L. (1988). Stress, expectancies, and vulnerability to substance abuse: A test of a model among homosexual men. *Journal of Abnormal Psychology, 97*(4), 461–466.

McWhirter, D. P., & Mattison, A. M. (1984). *The male couple.* New York: Prentice-Hall.

Mintz, E. E. (1966). Overt male homosexuals in combined group and individual treatment. *Journal of Consulting Psychology, 30*(3), 193–198.

Moberly, E. (1983). *Homosexuality: A new Christian ethic.* Cambridge: James Clarke & Co.

Morin, S. F. (1991). Removing the stigma: Lesbian and gay affirmative counseling. *The Counseling Psychologist, 19*(2), 245–247.

Mosbacher, D. (1993). Alcohol and other drug use in female medical students: A comparison of lesbians and heterosexuals. *Journal of Gay & Lesbian Psychotherapy, 2,* 37–48.

Murphy, T. F. (1992). Redirecting sexual orientation: Techniques and justifications. *The Journal of Sex Research, 29*(4), 501–523.

Nicolosi, J. (1991). *Reparative therapy of male homosexuality: A new clinical approach.* Northvale, NJ: Jason Aronson.

Nicolosi, J. (1993). *Healing homosexuality: Case stories of reparative therapy,* Northvale, NJ: Jason Aronson.

O'Donohue, W., & Caselles, C. E. (1993). Homophobia: Conceptual, definitional, and value issues. *Journal of Psychopathology and Behavioral Assessment, 15*(3), 177–195.

Peters, D. K., & Cantrell, P. J. (1991). Factors distinguishing samples of lesbian and heterosexual women. *Journal of Homosexuality, 21*(4), 1–15.

Pillard, R. C. (1982). Psychotherapeutic treatment for the invisible minority. In W. Paul, J. D. Weinrich, J. C. Gonsiorek, & M. E. Hotvedt (Eds.), *Homosexuality: Social, psychological, and biological issues* (pp. 99–114). Beverly Hills: Sage.

Pittman, F. S., & DeYoung, C. D. (1971). The treatment of homosexuals in heterogeneous groups. *International Journal of Group Psychotherapy, 21,* 62–73.

Rychlak, J. F. (1988). Explaining helping relationships through learning theories and the question of human agency. *Counseling and Values, 32,* 83–92.

Saghir, M. T., & Robins, E. (1973). *Male and female homosexuality: A comprehensive investigation.* Baltimore, MD: Williams and Wilkins.

Schmitt, J. P., & Kurdek, L. A. (1987). Personality correlates of positive identity and relationship involvement in gay men. *Journal of Homosexuality, 13*(4), 101–109.

Shafranske, E. P. (Ed.). (1996). *Religion and the clinical practice of psychology.* Washington, DC: American Psychological Association.

Shannon, J. W., & Woods, W. J. (1991). Affirmative psychotherapy for gay men. *The Counseling Psychologist, 19*(2), 197–215.

Silverstein, C. (1972, October). *Behavior modification and the gay community.* Paper presented at the annual convention of the Association for Advancement of Behavioral Therapy. New York, NY.

Silverstein, C. (1991). Psychological and medical treatments of homosexuality. In J. C. Gonsiorek & J. D. Weinrich (Eds.), *Homosexuality: Research implications for public policy* (pp. 101–114). Newbury Park, CA: Sage.

Sobocinski, M. R. (1990). Ethical principles in the counseling of gay and lesbian adolescents: Issues of autonomy, competence, and confidentiality. *Professional Psychology: Research and Practice, 21*(4), 240–247.

Sullivan, A. (1995). *Virtually normal: An argument about homosexuality.* New York: Alfred A. Knopf.

Swaab, D. F., & Hofman, M. A. (1990). An enlarged suprachiasmatic nucleus in homosexual men. *Brain Research, 537,* 141–148.

Troiden, R. (1993). The formation of homosexual identities. In L. D. Garnets & D. C. Kimmel (Eds.), *Psychological perspectives on lesbian and gay male experiences* (pp. 191–217). NY: Columbia University Press.

Van Den Aardweg, G. J. M. (1986). *On the origins and treatment of homosexuality.* New York: Prager.

Wilson, G. T., & Davison, G. C. (1974). Behavior therapy and homosexuality: A critical perspective. *Behavior Therapy, 5,* 16–28.

Douglas C. Haldeman  **NO**

The Practice and Ethics of Sexual Orientation Conversion Therapy

The question of how to change sexual orientation has been discussed as long as homoeroticism itself has been described in the literature. For over a century, medical, psychotherapeutic, and religious practitioners have sought to reverse unwanted homosexual orientation through variousmethods: These include psychoanalytic therapy, prayer and spiritual interventions, electric shock, nauseainducing drugs, hormone therapy, surgery, and various adjunctive behavioral treatments, including masturbatory reconditioning, rest, visits to prostitutes, and excessive bicycle riding (Murphy, 1992). Early attempts to reverse sexual orientation were founded on the unquestioned assumption that homosexuality is an unwanted, unhealthy condition. Although homosexuality has long been absent from the taxonomy of mental disorders, efforts to reorient gay men and lesbians persist. Recently, for example, a coalition of mental health practitioners formed an organization dedicated to the "rehabilitation" of gay men and lesbians. Many practitioners still adhere to the officially debunked "illness" model of homosexuality, and many base their treatments on religious proscriptions against homosexual behavior. Still others defend sexual reorientation therapy as a matter of free choice for the unhappy client, claiming that their treatments do not imply a negative judgment on homosexuality per se. They seek to provide what they describe as a treatment alternative for men and women whose homosexuality is somehow incongruent with their values, life goals, or psychological structures.

Of the articles to be examined in this review, few have addressed the question of how sexual orientation is defined. Such a definition seems necessary before one can describe how sexual orientation is changed. However, most research in this area offers a dichotomous view of human sexuality in which undesired homoerotic impulses can be eradicated through a program that replaces them with heterosexual competence. Few studies even rely on the relatively simplistic Kinsey scale (Kinsey, Pomeroy, & Martin, 1948) to make an attempt at assessing a subject's sexual orientation. Although a comprehensive discussion is well beyond the scope of this article, I began

From *Journal of Consulting and Clinical Psychology*, vol. 62, no. 2, pp. 221–227. Copyright © 1994 by American Psychological Association. Reprinted with permission.

with a passing reference to what is meant by the terms *homosexuality* and *heterosexuality*.

The data of Kinsey et al. (1948) suggested that as many as 10% of American men considered themselves to be primarily or exclusively homosexual for at least 3 years of their adult lives. His assessment was based on the subject's actual behavior as well as the content of the subject's fantasy life. Subsequent efforts to quantify sexual orientation have incorporated gender-based, social, and affectional variables (Coleman, 1987). Several complex questions involved in the defining of sexual orientation have been either reduced or overlooked in the literature on conversion therapy. For instance, those conversion therapy programs that claim the greatest success included more subjects whose behavioral histories and fantasy lives appeared to have significant heteroerotic components (Haldeman, 1991). Instructing a "homosexual" subject with a priori heteroerotic responsiveness in heterosexual behavior appears to be easier than replacing the cognitive sociosexual schema and redirecting the behavior of the "homosexual" subject with no reported heteroerotic inclinations. Nevertheless, both types of "homosexual" subjects are often included in the same treatment group.

Any definition of sexuality based solely on behavior is bound to be deficient and misleading. Sense of identity, internalized sociocultural expectations, and importance of social and political affiliations all help define an individual's sexual orientation, and these variables may change over time. The content of an individual's fantasy life may provide information that is not influenced by the individual's need for social acceptance, but even these are subject, in some women and men, to variations in gender of object choice, based on environmental or political factors. Social demand variables also figure in describing sexual orientation, given the frequency with which gay men and lesbians marry (Bell & Weinberg, 1978). . . .

The categories homosexual, heterosexual, and bisexual, conceived by many researchers as fixed and dichotomous, are in reality very fluid for many. Therefore, in addition to how sexual orientation is defined, one must also consider how it is experienced by the individual. For many gay men, the process of "coming out" may be likened to an internal evolution of sorts, a conscious recognition of what has always been. On the other hand, many lesbians describe "coming out" as a process tied to choices or social and political constructions. In this regard, many lesbians may have more in common with heterosexual women than with gay men, suggesting a gender-based distinction relative to the development of homosexual identity.

Questions about the complex nature of sexual orientation and its development in the individual must be addressed before change in sexual orientation is assessed. Many previously heterosexually identified individuals "come out" as lesbian or gay later in life, and some people who identify themselves as gay or lesbian engage in heterosexual behavior and relationships for a variety of personal and social reasons. How, then, are spontaneously occurring shifts in sexual orientation over the life span to be differentiated from behavior resulting from the interventions of a conversion therapist? Essentially, the fixed, behavior-based model of sexual orientation assumed by almost all conversion therapists may be invalid. For many individuals, sexual orientation is a variable construct subject to changes in erotic and affectional preference, as well as changes in social values and political philosophy that may ebb and flow throughout life. For some, "coming out" may be a process with no true endpoint. Practitioners assessing change in sexual orientation have ignored the complex variations in an individual's erotic responses and shifts in the sociocultural landscape.

Psychological Conversion Programs

The case for conversion therapy rests on its ability to understand who is being converted and its ability to describe the nature of the conversion taking place. Acknowledging the theoretical complexities and ambiguities left unaddressed by most conversion therapists, the first question is "Are these treatments effective?" In assessing the efficacy of conversion therapy, psychotherapeutic and religious programs will be reviewed. Those interested in reviews of medical therapies (drug or hormonal and surgical interventions) are referred to Silverstein (1991) and Murphy (1992).

Psychotherapeutic approaches to sexual reorientation have been based on the a priori assumption that homoeroticism is an undesirable condition. Two basic hypotheses serve as the foundation for most therapies designed to reverse sexual orientation. The first is that homosexuality results from an arrest in normal development or from pathological attachment patterns in early life. The second is that homosexuality stems from faulty learning. Therapies most closely associated with the first perspective are of the psychoanalytic and neo-analytic orientations.

Psychoanalytic tradition posited that homosexual orientation represented an arrest in normal psychosexual development, most often in the context of a particular dysfunctional family constellation. Such a family typically featured a close-binding mother and an absent or distant father. Despite the relative renown of this therapy, it is based solely on clinical speculation and has never been empirically validated. Subsequent studies have indicated that etiologic factors in the development of sexual orientation are unclear but that the traditional psychoanalytic formulations concerning family dynamics are not viable (Bell, Weinberg, & Hammersmith, 1981).

Psychoanalytic treatment of homosexuality is exemplified by the work of Bieber et al. (1962), who advocate intensive, long-term therapy aimed at resolving the unconscious anxiety stemming from childhood conflicts that supposedly cause homosexuality. Bieber et al. saw homosexuality as always pathological and incompatible with a happy life. Their methodology has been criticized for use of an entirely clinical sample and for basing outcomes on subjective therapist impression, not externally validated data or even self-report. Follow-up data have been poorly presented and not empirical in nature. Bieber et al. (1962) reported a 27% success rate in heterosexual shift after long-term therapy; of these, however, only 18% were exclusively homosexual in the first place. Fifty percent of the successfully treated subjects were more appropriately labeled bisexual. This blending of "apples and oranges" returns us to the original question: Who is being converted, and what is the nature of the conversion?

Another analytically based study reported virtually no increase in heterosexual behavior in a group of homosexual men (Curran & Parr, 1957). Other studies report greater success rates: For instance, Mayerson and Lief (1965) indicate that, of 19 subjects, half reported engaging in exclusive heterosexual behavior 4.5 years posttreatment. However, as in Bieber et al.'s study, those subjects had heteroerotic traits to begin with; exclusively homosexual subjects reported little change, and outcomes were based on patient self-report. As in other studies, an expansion of the sexual repertoire toward heterosexual behavior is viewed as equivalent to a shift of sexual orientation.

California psychologist Joseph Nicolosi has developed a program of reparative therapy for "non-gay" homosexuals, individuals who reported being uncomfortable with their same-sex orientation. Nicolosi stated, "I do not believe that the gay life-style can ever be healthy, nor that the homosexual identity can ever be completely ego-syntonic" (1991, p. 13). This belief erroneously presupposes a unitary gay lifestyle, a concept more reductionist than that of sexual orientation. It also prejudicially and without empirical justification assumes that homosexually oriented people can never be normal or happy, a point refuted numerous times in the literature. Nonetheless, this statement is the foundation for his theoretical approach, which cites numerous studies that suggest that gay men have greater frequencies of disrupted bonds with their fathers, as well as a host of psychological concerns, such as assertion problems. These observations are used to justify a pathological assessment of homosexuality. The error in such reasoning is that the conclusion has preceded the data. There may be cause to examine the potentially harmful impact of a detached father and his effect on the individual's self-concept or capacity for intimacy, but why should a detached father be selected as the key player in causing homosexuality, unless an a priori decision about the pathological nature of homosexuality has been made and unless he is being investigated as the cause? This perspective is not consistent with available data, nor does it explain the millions of heterosexual men who come from backgrounds similar to those of gay men, or for that matter, those gay men with strong father–son relationships. Nicolosi does not support his hypothesis or his treatment methods with any empirical data.

Group treatments have also been used in sexual reorientation. One study of 32 subjects reports a 37% shift to heterosexuality (Hadden, 1966), but the results must be viewed with some skepticism, because of the entirely self-report nature of the outcome measures. Individuals involved in such group treatments are especially susceptible to the influence of social demand in their own reporting of treatment success. Similarly, a study of 10 gay men resulted in the therapist's impressionistic claims that homosexual patients were able to "increase contact" with heterosexuals (Mintz, 1966). Birk (1980) described a combination insight-oriented-social-learning-group format for treating homosexuality. He claimed that overall,

38% of his patients achieved "solid heterosexual shifts." Nonetheless, he acknowledges that these shifts represent "an adaptation to life, not a meta-morphosis," and that homosexual fantasies and activity are ongoing, even for the "happily married" individual (Birk, 1980, p. 387). If a solid hetero-sexual shift is defined as one in which a happily married person may engage in more than occasional homosexual encounters, perhaps this method is best described as a laboratory for heterosexual behavior, rather than a change of sexual orientation. A minority of subjects, likely with pre-existing heteroerotic tendencies, may be taught proficiency in heterosexual activities. Eager to equate heterosexual competence with orientation change, these researchers have ignored the complex questions associated with the assessment of sexual orientation. Behavior alone is a misleading barometer of sexual orientation, which includes biological, gender-based, social, and affectional variables. No researchers who conducted conversion studies have displayed any such thoughtfulness in their assessment or categorization of subjects.

Behavioral programs designed to reverse homosexual orientation are based on the premise that homoerotic impulses arise from faulty learning. These studies seek to countercondition the "learned" homoerotic response with aversive stimuli, replacing it with the reinforced, desired heteroerotic response. The aversive stimulus, typically consisting of electric shock or convulsion- or nausea-inducing drugs, is administered during presentation of same-sex erotic visual material. The cessation of the aversive stimulus is accompanied by the presentation of heteroerotic visual material, suppos-edly to replace homoeroticism in the sexual response hierarchy. These methods have been reviewed by Sansweet (1975). Some programs attempted to augment aversive conditioning techniques with a social learning compo-nent (assertiveness training, how to ask women out on dates, etc.; Feldman & McCullogh, 1965). Later, the same investigators modified their approach, calling it "anticipatory avoidance conditioning," which enabled subjects to avoid electrical shock when viewing slides of same-sex nudes (Feldman, 1966). Such a stressful situation could likely inhibit feelings of sexual responsiveness in any direction; nevertheless, a 58% cure rate was claimed, with outcome criteria defined as the suppression of homoerotic response. Cautela (1967) reported on single subjects who were taught to imagine such aversive stimuli rather than undergo them directly. His later work focuses on structured aversive fantasy, in which subjects are asked to visualize repulsive homoerotic encounters in stressful circumstances (Cautela & Kearney, 1986). The investigators deny a homophobic bias to this therapeutic approach.

Other studies suggest that aversive interventions may extinguish homosexual responsiveness but do little to promote alternative orientation. One investigator suggests that the poor outcomes of conversion treatments are due to the fact that they "disregard the complex learned repertoire and topography of homosexual behavior" (Faustman, 1976). Other studies echo the finding that aversive therapies in homosexuality do not alter subjects' sexual orientation (McConaghy, 1981). Another study similarly suggests that behavioral conditioning decreases homosexual orientation but does not elevate heterosexual interest (Rangaswami, 1982). Methodologically, the near-exclusive use of self-report outcome measures is problematic, particularly in an area where social demand factors may strongly influence subjects' reports. The few studies that do attempt to externally validate sexual reorientation through behavioral measures show no change after treatment (Conrad & Wincze, 1976).

Masters and Johnson (1979) reported on the treatment of 54 "dissatisfied" homosexual men. This was unprecedented for the authors, as their previous works on heterosexual dysfunction did not include treatment for dissatisfied heterosexual people. The authors hypothesized homosexuality to be the result of failed or ridiculed attempts at heterosexuality, neglecting the obvious: that heterosexual "failures" among homosexual people are to be expected because the behavior in question is outside the individual's normal sexual response pattern. Despite their comments to the contrary, the study is founded on heterosexist bias. Gonsiorek (1981) raises a variety of concerns with the Masters and Johnson study. Of the numerous methodological problems with this study, perhaps most significant is the composition of the sample itself. Of 54 subjects, only 9 (17%) identified themselves as Kinsey 5 or 6 (exclusively homosexual). The other 45 subjects (83%) ranged from 2 to 4 on the Kinsey scale (predominantly heterosexual to bisexual). Furthermore, because 30% of the sample was lost to follow-up, it is conceivable that the outcome sample does not include any homosexual men. Perhaps this is why such a high success rate is reported after 2 weeks of treatment. It is likely that, rather than converting or reverting homosexual people to heterosexuality, this program enhances heterosexual responsiveness in people with already established heteroerotic sexual maps.

Evidence for the efficacy of sexual conversion programs is less than compelling. All research in this area has evolved from unproven hypothetical formulations about the pathological nature of homosexuality. The illness model has never been empirically validated; to the contrary, a broad literature validates the nonpathological view of homosexuality, leading to its declassification as a mental disorder (Gonsiorek, 1991). Thus, treatments in both analytic and behavioral modes are designed to cure something that has never been demonstrated to be an illness. From a methodological standpoint, the studies reviewed here reveal inadequacies in the selection criteria and the classification of subjects and poorly designed and administered outcome measures. In short, no consistency emerges from the extant database, which suggests that sexual orientation is amenable to redirection or significant influence from psychological intervention.

Religion-Based Conversion Programs

In a recent symposium on Christian approaches to the treatment of lesbians and gay men, one panelist said of his numerous unsuccessful attempts at sexual reorientation: "I felt it was what I had to do in order to gain a right to live on the planet." Such is the experience of many gay men and lesbians, who experience severe conflict between their homoerotic feelings and their need for acceptance by a homophobic religious community. This conflict causes such individuals to seek the guidance of pastoral care providers or Christian support groups whose aim is to reorient gay men and lesbians. Such programs seek to divest the individual of his or her "sinful" feelings or at least to make the pursuit of a heterosexual or celibate lifestyle possible. Their theoretical base is founded on interpretations of scripture that condemn homosexual behavior, their often unspecified treatment methods rely on prayer, and their outcomes are generally limited to testimonials. Nonetheless, these programs bear some passing examination because of the tremendous psychological impact they have on the many unhappy gay men and lesbians who seek their services and because of some psychologists' willingness to refer to them. Lastly, many such programs have been associated with significant ethical problems.

Gay men who are most likely to be inclined toward doctrinaire religious practice are also likely to have lower self-concepts, to see homosexuality as more sinful, feel a greater sense of apprehension about negative responses from others, and are more depressed in general (Weinberg & Williams, 1974). Such individuals make vulnerable targets for the "ex-gay" ministries, as they are known. Fundamentalist Christian groups, such as Homosexuals Anonymous, Metanoia Ministries, Love In Action, Exodus International, and EXIT of Melodyland are the most visible purveyors of conversion therapy. The workings of these groups are well documented by Blair (1982), who states that, although many of these practitioners publicly promise change, they privately acknowledge that celibacy is the realistic goal to which gay men and lesbians must aspire. He further characterizes many religious conversionists as individuals deeply troubled about their own sexual orientation, or whose own sexual conversion is incomplete. Blair reports a host of problems with such counselors, including the sexual abuse of clients.

The most notable of such ministers is Colin Cook. Cook's counseling program, Quest, led to the development of Homosexuals Anonymous, the largest antigay fundamentalist counseling organization in the world. The work of Cook, his ultimate demise, and the subsequent cover-up by the Seventh Day Adventist Church, are described by sociologist Ronald Lawson (1987). Over the course of 7 years, approximately 200 people received reorientation counseling from Cook, his wife, and an associate. From this ministry sprang Homosexuals Anonymous, a 14-step program modeled after Alcoholics Anonymous, which has become the largest fundamentalist organization in the world with a unitary antigay focus. Lawson, in attempting to research the efficacy of Cook's program, was denied access to counselees on the basis of confidentiality. Nonetheless, he managed to interview 14 clients, none of whom reported any change in sexual orientation. All but two reported that Cook had had sex with them during treatment. According to Blair, another homosexual pastor who used his ministry to gain sexual access to vulnerable gay people was Guy Charles, founder of Liberation in Jesus Christ. Charles was a homosexual man who had claimed a heterosexual conversion subsequent to his acceptance to Christ. Like Cook, Charles was ultimately disavowed by the Christian organization that sponsored him after charges of sexual misconduct were raised.

To date, the only spiritually based sexual orientation conversion program to appear in the literature has been a study by Pattison and Pattison (1980). These authors describe a supernatural healing approach in treating 30 individuals culled from a group of 300 who sought sexual reorientation counseling at EXIT of Melodyland, a charismatic ex-gay ministry affiliated with a Christian amusement park. The Pattisons do not explain their sampling criteria, nor do they explain why 19 of their 30 subjects refused follow-up interviews. Their data indicate that only 3 of the 11 (of 300) subjects report no current homosexual desires, fantasies, or impulses, and that 1 of the 3 subjects is listed as still being "incidentally homosexual." Of the other 8 subjects, several indicated ongoing neurotic conflict about their homosexual impulses. Although 6 of these men have married heterosexually, 2 admit to more than incidental homosexual ideation as an ongoing issue.

Recently, founders of another prominent ex-gay ministry, Exodus International, denounced their conversion therapy procedures as ineffective. Michael Busse and Gary Cooper, co-founders of Exodus and lovers for 13 years, were involved with the organization from 1976 to 1979. The program was described by these men as "ineffective . . . not one person was healed." They stated that the program often exacerbated already prominent feelings of guilt and personal failure among the counselees; many were driven to suicidal thoughts as a result of the failed reparative therapy ("*Newsbriefs,*" 1990, p. 43).

The fundamentalist Christian conversion programs hold enormous symbolic power over many people. Possibly exacerbating the harm to naive, shameridden counselees, these programs operate under the formidable auspices of the Christian church, and outside the jurisdiction of any professional organizations that may impose ethical standards of practice and accountability on them. A closer look at such programs is warranted, given the frequency with which spiritual conversion programs seek to legitimize themselves with psychologists as affiliates.

An examination of psychotherapeutic and spiritual approaches to conversion therapy reveal a wide range of scientific concerns, from theoretical weaknesses to methodological problems and poor outcomes. This literature does not suggest a bright future in studying ways to reorient people sexually. Individuals undergoing conversion treatment are not likely to emerge as heterosexually inclined, but they often do become shamed, conflicted, and fearful about their homerotic feelings. It is not uncommon for gay men and lesbians who have undergone aversion treatments to notice a temporary sharp decline in their sexual dysfunction. Similarly, subjects who have undergone failed attempts at conversion therapy often report increased guilt, anxiety, and low self-esteem. Some flee into heterosexual marriages that are doomed to problems inevitably involving spouses, and often children as well. Not one investigator has ever raised the possibility that conversion treatments may harm some participants, even in a field where a 30% success rate is seen as high. The research question, "What is being accomplished by conversion treatments?" may well be replaced by, "What harm has been done in the name of sexual reorientation?" At present, no data are extant.

Ethical Considerations

We have considered the question of whether sexual orientations are amenable to change or modification by means of therapeutic interventions. Of equal, if not greater, import is the question of whether psychology should provide or endorse such "cures." Ethicists object to conversion therapy on two grounds: first, that it constitutes a cure for a condition that has been judged not to be an illness, and second, that it reinforces a prejudicial and unjustified devaluation of homosexuality.

The American Psychiatric Association's 1973 decision to remove homosexuality from its *Diagnostic and Statistical Manual of Mental Disorders* marked the official passing of the illness model of homosexuality. The American Psychological Association (APA) followed suit with a resolution affirming this anti-illness perspective, stating, in part, ". . . the APA urges all mental health professionals to take the lead in removing the stigma of mental illness that has long been associated with homosexual orientations" (APA, 1975). Homosexuality was replaced with the confusing "ego-dystonic homosexuality" diagnosis, which was dropped altogether in 1987. . . .

Proponents of conversion therapy continue to insist, in the absence of any evidence, that homosexuality is pathological. This model was rejected because of a lack of such evidence, and its demise has been described by Gonsiorek (1991). This review underscores the faulty logic inherent in classic psychoanalytic theories of family dysfunction as etiologic of homosexuality. Researcher bias, as well as methodological inadequacies, characterize studies supporting the illness model. Psychological test data, from Hooker's (1975) study to present-day studies, have been reviewed and show no substantive differences between homosexual and heterosexual subjects.

Were there properties intrinsic to homosexuality that make it a pathological condition, we would be able to observe and measure them directly. In reality, however, there exists a wide literature indicating just the opposite: that gay men and lesbians do not differ significantly from heterosexual men and women on measures of psychological stability, social or vocational adjustment, or capacity for decision making. In fact, psychological adjustment among gay men and lesbians seems to be directly correlated to the degree that they have accepted their sexual orientation (Weinberg & Williams, 1974). In light of such evidence, the number of studies examining the pathogensis of homosexuality has diminished in recent years.

Davison (1976, 1978, 1991) has detailed many of the ethical objections to conversion therapies. A behavior therapist once well known for his program to change sexual orientation, Davison believes that a disservice is done to the gay or lesbian individual by offering sexual orientation change as a therapeutic option. In Davison's view, conversion therapy reinforces antigay prejudice. He asks, "how can therapists honestly speak of nonprejudice when they participate in therapy regimens that by their very existence—and regardless of their efficacy—would seem to condone the current societal prejudice and perhaps also impede social change?" (1991, p. 141).

In his paraphrase of Halleck (1971), Davison states that therapeutic neutrality is a myth and that therapists, by the nature of their role, cannot help but influence patients with respect to values. Davison suggests that the question of whether sexual orientation can be changed is secondary to the consideration that it should not be changed, because of the devaluation and pathologizing of homosexuality implicit in offering a "cure" for it. Because therapists operate from positions of power, to affirm the viability of homosexuality and then engage in therapeutic efforts to change it sends a mixed message: If a cure is offered, then there must be an illness. This point is echoed by Begelman, who stated that "(conversion therapies) by their very existence, constitute a significant causal element in reinforcing the social doctrine that homosexuality is bad; therapists . . . further strengthen the prejudice that homosexuality is a 'problem behavior', since treatment may be offered for it" (1975, p. 180). Charles Silverstein (1977), points to social factors (e.g., rejecting families, hostile peer interactions, and disapproving society) as being responsible for people seeking sexual orientation change. These authors indicate that what were historically viewed as "ego-dystonic" responses to homosexuality are really internalized reactions to a hostile society.

Proponents of conversion therapy often deny any coercive intent, claiming that theirs is a valuable service for distressed lesbians and gay men who freely seek their services. However, the concept that individuals seek sexual orientation change of their own free will may be fallacious. Martin (1984) stated that "a clinician's implicit acceptance of the homosexual orientation as the cause of ego-dystonic reactions, and the concomitant agreement to attempt sexual orientation change, exacerbates the ego-dystonic reactions and reinforces and confirms the internalized homophobia that lies at their root" (p. 46). . . .

Discussion

Our understanding of human sexuality is entering a new era, one in which formerly sacrosanct assumptions and classifications are no longer applicable. A new generation of individuals, no longer self-identified as gay or lesbian but as "queer," is developing a perspective of sexual orientation more complex and fluid than what has historically been viewed along rigid lines. This new construction of sexuality, combined with the antiquated, unscientific hypotheses on which conversion therapy has been based, render traditional reorientation therapy anachronistic.

The lack of empirical support for conversion therapy calls into question the judgment of clinicians who practice or endorse it. The APA "Fact Sheet on Reparative Therapy" opens with the following statement: "No scientific evidence exists to support the effectiveness of any of the conversion therapies that try to change sexual orientation." A review of the literature makes it obvious why this statement is made. Psychologists are obliged to use methods that have some empirically demonstrable efficacy, and there is a paucity of such evidence relative to conversion therapy. Moreover, there is a need to understand fully the potentially damaging effects of a failed conversion treatment.

A next logical question, then, involves standards of practice for the treatment of lesbians and gay men that *are* compatible with scientific data. In 1991, the APA's Committee on Lesbian and Gay Concerns published the results of a survey on bias in psychotherapeutic treatment of lesbians and gay men. This survey is an initial step in providing the clinician with guidelines that are consistent with science and that promote the welfare and dignity of the gay or lesbian individual. More research is needed to refine these recommendations for the myriad of issues that gay people bring to therapy. It is the responsibility of psychologists to provide accurate scientific information, particularly as so much misinformation is currently being used to further stigmatize and justify, even legislate, discrimination against gay people. The current wave of antigay political activity is founded on the mistaken assumptions that homosexuality is a chosen way of life and an abnormal one at that. It may be impossible to understand why so many people would believe that lesbians and gay men would deliberately choose a way of life that puts them at risk for discrimination and violence. It is, however, well within psychology's purview to disseminate accurate information from our considerable database about homosexuality.

Even more significant than the practical considerations of conversion therapy are the ethical concerns. Psychologists are obliged to use methods that promote the dignity and welfare of humankind. Conversion therapies fail in this regard because they are necessarily predicated on a devaluation of homosexual identity and behavior. Some contemporary conversionists would claim a value-neutral stance, insisting that conversion therapy is simply a matter of the client's right to choose treatment, but what is the purpose of attempting to change sexual orientation if it is not negatively valued? How many dissatisfied heterosexual men and women seek a similar conversion to homosexuality? What message does psychology send to society when it affirms the normalcy of homosexuality yet continues to give tacit approval to efforts to change it? Murphy, summarizing his review of the conversion therapy literature, addressed this:

> There would be no reorientation techniques where there was no interpretation that homoeroticism is an inferior state, an interpretation that in many ways continues to be medically defined, criminally enforced, socially sanctioned, and religiously justified. And it is in this moral interpretation, more than in the reigning medical therapy of the day, that all programs of sexual reorientation have their common origins and justifications. (1992, p. 520)

This morality is at work in all aspects of homophobic activity, from the alarming increase in violent hate crimes against gay men and lesbians to the political and legislative agendas of antigay organizations. Perpetrators of violence and antigay political groups justify their actions with the same devaluation of homosexuality that is used by conversion therapists.

Given the extensive societal devaluation of homosexuality and lack of positive role models for gay men and lesbians, it is not surprising that many gay people seek to become heterosexual. Homophobic attitudes have been institutionalized in nearly every aspect of our social structure, from the government and the military to our educational systems and organized religions. For gay men and lesbians who have identified with the dominant group, the desire to be like others and to be accepted socially is so strong that heterosexual relating becomes more than an act of sex or love. It becomes a symbol of freedom from prejudice and social devaluation. Psychology cannot free people from stigma by continuing to promote or tacitly endorse conversion therapy. Psychology can only combat stigma with a vigorous avowal of empirical truth. The appropriate focus of the profession is what reverses prejudice, not what reverses sexual orientation.

References

American Psychological Association. (1975). Minutes of the Council of Representatives. *American Psychologist, 30,* 633.

Begelman, D. A. (1975). Ethical and legal issues of behavior modification. In M. Hersen, R. Eisler, & P. M. Miller (Eds.), *Progress in behavior modification* (pp. 175–188). San Diego, CA: Academic Press.

Bell, A., & Weinberg, M. (1978). *Homosexuality: A study of diversity among men and women.* New York: Simon & Schuster.

Bell, A., Weinberg, M., & Hammersmith, S. (1981). *Sexual preference: Its development in men and women.* Bloomington, IN: Indiana University Press.

Bieber, I., Dain, H., Dince, P., Drellich, M., Grand, H., Gundlach, R., Kremer, M., Rifkin, A., Wilbur, C., & Bieber, T. (Society of Medical Psychoanalysts). (1962). *Homosexuality: A psychoanalytic study.* New York: Basic Books.

Birk, L. (1980). The myth of classical homosexuality: Views of a behavioral psychotherapist. In J. Marmor (Ed.), *Homosexual behavior: A modern reappraisal* (pp. 376–390). New York: Basic Books.

Blair, R. (1982). *Ex-gay.* New York: Homosexual Counseling Center.

Cautela, J. (1967). Covert sensitization. *Psychological Reports, 2,* 459–468.

Cautela, J., & Kearney, A. (1986). *The covert conditioning handbook.* New York: Springer.

Coleman, E. (1987). The assessment of sexual orientation. *Journal of Homosexuality, 14*(1 and 2), 9–24.

Conrad, S., & Wincze, J. (1976). Orgasmic reconditioning: A controlled study of its effects upon the sexual arousal and behavior of male homosexuals. *Behavior Therapy, 7,* 155–166.

Curran, D., & Parr, D. (1957). Homosexuality: An analysis of 100 male cases. *British Medical Journal, 1,* 797–801.

Davison, G. (1976). Homosexuality: The ethical challenge. *Journal of Consulting and Clinical Psychology, 44,* 157–162.

Davison, G. (1978). Not can but ought: The treatment of homosexuality. *Journal of Consulting and Clinical Psychology, 46,* 170–172.

Davison, G. (1991). Constructionism and morality in therapy for homosexuality. In J. Gonsiorek & J. Weinrich (Eds.), *Homosexuality: Research implications for public policy* (pp. 137–148). Newbury Park, CA: Sage.

Faustman, W. (1976). Aversive control of maladaptive sexual behavior: Past developments and future trends. *Psychology, 13,* 53–60.

Feldman, M. (1966). Aversion therapy for sexual deviation: A critical review. *Psychological Bulletin, 65,* 65–69.

Feldman, M., & McCullogh, M. (1965). The application of anticipatory avoidance learning to the treatment of homosexuality: Theory, technique, and preliminary results. *Behavior Research and Therapy, 2,* 165–183.

Gonsiorek, J. (1981). Review of *Homosexuality in perspective,* by Masters and Johnson. *Journal of Homosexuality, 6*(3), 81–88.

Gonsiorek, J. (1991). The empirical basis for the demise of the illness model of homosexuality. In J. Gonsiorek and J. Weinrich (Eds.), *Homosexuality: Research implications for public policy* (pp. 115–136). Newbury Park, CA: Sage.

Hadden, S. (1966). Treatment of male homosexuals in groups. *International Journal of Group Psychotherapy, 16,* 13–22.

Haldeman, D. (1991). Sexual orientation conversion therapy: A scientific examination. In J. Gonsiorek & J. Weinrich (Eds.), *Homosexuality: Research implications for public policy* (pp. 149–160). Newbury Park CA: Sage.

Halleck, S. (1971). *The politics of therapy.* New York: Science House.

Hooker, E. (1957). The adjustment of the male overt homosexual. *Journal of Projective Techniques, 21,* 17–31.

Kinsey, A. C., Pomeroy, W. B., & Martin, C. E. (1948). *Sexual behavior in the human male.* Philadelphia: W. B. Saunders.

Lawson, R. (1987, June). *Scandal in the Adventist-funded program to 'heal' homosexuals: Failure, sexual exploitation, official silence, and attempts to rehabilitate the exploiter and his methods.* Paper presented at the annual convention of the American Sociological Association, Chicago, Illinois.

Martin, A. (1984). The emperor's new clothes: Modern attempts to change sexual orientation. In E. S. Hetrick & T. S. Stein (Eds.), *Innovations in psychotherapy with homosexuals* (pp. 24–57). Washington, DC: American Psychiatric Association.

Masters, W., & Johnson, V. (1979). *Homosexuality in perspective.* Boston: Little, Brown.

Mayerson, P., & Lief, H. (1965). Psychotherapy of homosexuals: A follow-up study of nineteen cases. In J. Marmor (Ed.), *Sexual inversion* (pp. 302–344). New York: Basic Books.

McConaghy, N. (1981). Controlled comparison of aversive therapy and covert sensitization in compulsive homosexuality. *Behavior Research and Therapy, 19,* 425–434.

Mintz, E. (1966). Overt male homosexuals in combined group and individual treatment. *Journal of Consulting Psychology, 20,* 193–198.

Murphy, T. (1992). Redirecting sexual orientation: Techniques and justifications. *Journal of Sex Research, 29,* 501–523.

Newswatch briefs. (1990, February 22) *Gay Chicago Magazine, 8,* p. 43.

Nicolosi, J. (1991). *Reparative therapy of male homosexuality.* Northvale, NJ: Jason Aronson.

Pattison, E., & Pattison, M. (1980). "Ex-gays": religiously mediated change in homosexuals. *American Journal of Psychiatry, 137,* 1553–1562.

Rangaswami, K. (1982). Difficulties in arousing and increasing heterosexual responsiveness in a homosexual: A case report. *Indian Journal of Clinical Psychology, 9,* 147–151.

Rist, D. Y. (1992). *Heartlands: A gay man's odyssey across America.* New York: Dutton.

Sansweet, R. J. (1975). *The punishment cure.* New York: Mason/Charter.

Silverstein, C. (1977). Homosexuality and the ethics of behavioral intervention. *Journal of Homosexuality, 2,* 205–211.

Silverstein, C. (1991). Psychological and medical treatments of homosexuality. In J. Gonsiorek & J. Weinrich (Eds.), *Homosexuality: Research implications for public policy* (pp. 101–114). Newbury Park, CA: Sage.

Weinberg, M., & Williams, C. (1974). *Male homosexuals: Their problems and adaptations.* New York: Penguin Books.

CHALLENGE QUESTIONS

Is Sexual Orientation Conversion Therapy Ethical?

1. Yarhouse bases his arguments on the notion that clients requesting sexual orientation conversion should be respected as autonomous individuals who are capable of making a free choice in this matter. What arguments can be made for and against the notion that the client is the most appropriate decision maker with regard to a particular clinical intervention?
2. Haldeman argues against sexual orientation conversion therapy on the premise that this treatment approach rests on homophobic ideology. What social forces might be at play in promoting people to value heterosexuality over homosexuality?
3. Imagine that you are a clinician consulting with a 21-year-old man who is distressed by his homosexuality because it runs counter to his strong religious beliefs. How would you develop a treatment geared to alleviating his distress while respecting his religious values?
4. Imagine that you are evaluating a study intended to assess the effectiveness of aversive conditioning (e.g., shock) in reducing homosexual responsivity in men exposed to homoerotic stimuli. What ethical issues would you raise about this proposed project?
5. The APA has been striving in recent years to develop guidelines for clinicians working with gay and lesbian clients. What aspects of therapy would you regard as especially important in this kind of clinical work?

Suggested Readings

American Psychological Association. (1998). Appropriate therapeutic responses to sexual orientation in the proceedings of the American Psychological Association, Incorporated, for legislative year 1997. *Americian Psychologist*, 53(8), 882–939.

Stein, T. (1996). A critique of approaches to changing sexual orientation. In R. P. Cabaj & T. S. Stein (Eds.), *Textbook of homosexuality and mental health* (pp. 525–537). Washington, DC: American Psychiatric Press.

Yeoman, B. (1999). Gay no more? Reorientation programs for homosexuals. *Psychology Today*, 32(2), 26–29.

Contributors to This Volume

EDITOR

RICHARD P. HALGIN is a professor of psychology in the Clinical Psychology Program at the University of Massachusetts–Amherst. He is coauthor, with Susan Krauss Whitbourne, of *Abnormal Psychology: Clinical Perspectives on Psychological Disorders*, 4th ed., updated (McGraw-Hill, 2005) and coeditor, with Whitbourne, of *A Casebook in Abnormal Psychology: From the Files of Experts* (Oxford University Press, 1998). His list of publications also includes more than 50 articles and book chapters in the fields of psychotherapy, clinical supervision, and professional issues in psychology. He is a board-certified clinical psychologist, and he has over two decades of clinical, supervisory, and consulting experience. At the University of Massachusetts, his course in abnormal psychology is one of the most popular offerings on campus, attracting more than 500 students each semester. He also offers this course annually at Amherst College. His teaching has been recognized at the university and national level: he was honored with the University of Massachusetts Distinguished Teaching Award and the Alumni Association's Distinguished Faculty Award and was also recognized by the Society for the Teaching of Psychology of the American Psychological Association. In addition, professor Halgin was the focus of a cover story in *The Chronicle of Higher Education* (May 9, 2003) on the topic of excellence in the teaching of large lecture classes.

STAFF

Larry Loeppke Managing Editor
Jill Peter Senior Developmental Editor
Nichole Altman Developmental Editor
Beth Kundert Production Manager
Jane Mohr Project Manager
Tara McDermott Design Coordinator
Bonnie Coakley Editorial Assistant

AUTHORS

E. JOANNE ANGELO is an assistant clinical professor of psychiatry at Tufts University School of Medicine, and she maintains a private psychiatry practice in Boston, Massachusetts. She is a corresponding member of the Pontifical Academy for Life, and her published writings have focused on abortion.

WILLIAM S. APPLETON is a professor at Harvard Medical School and a practicing psychotherapist. He is the author of *Practical Clinical Psychopharmacology* (Lippincott Williams & Wilkins, 1988) and *The Fifth Psychoactive Drug Usage Guide* (Physicians Postgraduate Press, 1991).

THOMAS ARMSTRONG, a former special education teacher, is a consultant on learning and human development in Sonoma County, California. He has published several articles and books, including *The Myth of the A.D.D. Child* (E. P. Dutton, 1995).

JOYCE ARTHUR is a social activist for abortion rights, evolution education, and wildlife preservation, topics on which she has written numerous articles.

RUSSELL A. BARKLEY is Director of Psychology and Professor of Psychiatry and Neurology at the University of Massachusetts Medical Center. He has authored or edited numerous articles, books, and newsletters on attention deficit hyperactivity disorder and related topics, including *The ADHD Report* (newsletter), *Taking Charge of ADHD, Revised Edition: The Complete, Authoritative Guide for Parents* (Guilford, 2000), and *Child Psychopathology, 2nd Edition* (Guilford, 2003).

DIANE L. BEARMAN works as a clinical health psychologist at the University of Minnesota Medical School. She sees patients with psychological issues related to both acute and chronic medical conditions. Her clinical interests include HIV/AIDS, coping with medical diagnoses, and effects of illness on family members and caregivers.

JONATHAN BIRD is associated with the Burden Neurological Hospital and the University of London Institute of Psychiatry.

SANDRA BLAKESLEE earned her B.S. degree at Berkeley, specializing in neurobiology. She is currently a science and medicine correspondent for the *New York Times*.

PETER R. BREGGIN is the founder of the International Center for the Study of Psychiatry and Psychology, a nonprofit organization concerned with the impact of mental health and practice on individuals. His background includes teaching at Harvard Medical School and a faculty appointment to the Johns Hopkins University Department of Counseling. He is the author of many books, including *The Antidepressant Fact Book* (Perseus Books, 2001) and *Talking Back to Ritalin, Revised: What Doctors Aren't Telling You About Stimulants and ADHD* (Perseus Books, 2001).

SUSAN BROWNMILLER is a social activist for women's rights. She has published numerous articles and books pertaining to the feminist movement, and her work has been featured in various forms of media, including *Newsweek, Ms.,* and *ABC Television News.* Her books include *Femininity* (Linden Books, 1984) and *In Our Time: Memoir of a Revolution* (Dial Press, 1999).

RHEA K. FARBERMAN is executive director for public communications at the American Psychological Association. She is also executive editor of the *APA Monitor.*

ANNE M. FLETCHER is a nationally known health and medical writer who has taught nutrition and biochemistry at Pennsylvania State University and was an assistant director of the Frances Stern Nutrition Center at New England Medical Center Hospital in Boston. Her books include *Thin for Life: 10 Keys to Success from People Who Have Lost Weight & Kept It Off* (Houghton Mifflin, 1994) and *Eating Thin for Life: Food Secrets & Recipes from People Who Have Lost Weight & Kept It Off* (Houghton Mifflin, 1998).

MAX FINK is a professor of psychiatry and neurology at the State University of New York at Stony Brook. He has been studying electroconvulsive therapy (ECT) since 1954, and he is the founding editor of the scientific journal *Convulsive Therapy.* He is director of the ECT Service at University Hospital at Stony Brook and executive director of the International Association for Psychiatric Research. His publications include *Electroshock: Restoring the Mind* (Oxford University Press, 1999).

MICHAEL B. FIRST is a research psychiatrist at the New York State Psychiatric Institute and in the Department of Psychiatry at Columbia University. He is coauthor of *Am I Okay? A Layman's Guide to the Psychiatrist's Bible* (Simon & Schuster, 2000); *DSM-IV Guidebook* (American Psychiatric Press, 1995); and *DSM-IV Casebook: A Learning Companion to the Diagnostic and Statistical Manual of Mental Disorders,* 4th ed. (American Psychiatric Press, 1994).

ALLEN FRANCES is a professor of psychiatry at Duke University Medical School. He has published extensively in the field of psychiatry, particularly on issues pertaining to the *DSM-IV.* His books include *Am I Okay? A Layman's Guide to the Psychiatrist's Bible* (Simon & Schuster, 2000); *DSM-IV Guidebook* (American Psychiatric Press, 1995); and *DSM-IV Casebook: A Learning Companion to the Diagnostic and Statistical Manual of Mental Disorders,* 4th ed. (American Psychiatric Press, 1994).

LEONARD R. FRANK, a former editor of *Madness Network News* and cofounder of the Network Against Psychiatric Assault (NAPA), is an outspoken critic of electroshock and all forms of psychiatric "treatment" applied forcibly or without genuine informed consent. He is the editor and publisher of *The History of Shock Treatment* (1978) and of *Influencing Minds: A Reader in Quotations* (1994).

JONATHAN L. FREEDMAN is a professor of psychology at the University of Toronto.

LINDA GANZINI is a psychiatrist at the Oregon Health Science University in Portland, Oregon, and director of genetic psychiatry at the Portland Veterans Affairs Medical Center.

JOSEPH GLENMULLEN is a professor at Harvard Medical School and a member of the staff of Harvard University Health Services. He also has a private psychotherapy practice in Cambridge, Massachusetts.

DOUGLAS C. HALDEMAN is a counseling psychologist in private practice in Seattle, Washington. He is the Division Representative of the American Psychological Association's Society for the Psychological Study of Lesbian, Gay, and Bisexual Issues.

EDWARD M. HALLOWELL is a child and adult psychiatrist on the faculty of Harvard Medical School and an authority on attention deficit disorder. He is coauthor, with John J. Ratey, of *Answer to Distraction* (Bantam Books, 1996) and the author of *Connect* (Pantheon Books, 1999).

E. MAVIS HETHERINGTON is a professor of psychology at the University of Virginia. She obtained her Ph.D. in psychology at the University of California at Berkeley. Hetherington is a past president of the Developmental Psychology Division of the American Psychological Association and of the Society for Research in Child Development in Adolescence. She has been editor of *Child Development*, associate editor of *Developmental Psychology*, and associate editor of *The Journal of Abnormal Child Psychology*.

L. ROWELL HUESMANN is a professor of psychology and communication at the University of Michigan as well as a senior research scientist at the Research Center for Group Dynamics at the Institute for Social Research. He is the past president of the International Society for Research on Aggression. His publications include *Development of Aggression From Infancy to Adulthood* (Westview Press, 1999).

JOHN KELLY is a writer in New York.

STUART A. KIRK has worked as a psychiatric social worker and as editor in chief of *Social Work Research*. He is coauthor, with Herb Kutchins, of *Making Us Crazy: DSM—The Psychiatric Bible and the Creation of Mental Disorders* (Free Press, 1997) and *The Selling of DSM III: The Rhetoric of Science in Psychiatry* (Aldine de Gruyter, 1992).

RICHARD P. KLUFT is a psychiatrist who brought international attention to the diagnosis of dissociative identity disorder during his tenure in the Department of Psychiatry at the Institute of Pennsylvania Hospital. He is the editor of *Childhood Antecedents of Multiple Personality Disorder* (American Psychiatric Press, 1985) and coeditor, with Catherine G. Fine, of *Clinical Perspectives on Multiple Personality Disorder* (American Psychiatric Press, 1993).

TERRY A. KUPERS is a forensic psychiatric consultant and the author of *Revisioning Men's Lives: Gender, Intimacy, and Power* (Guilford, 1993).

HERB KUTCHINS is a professor of social work at California State University, Sacramento. He is coauthor, with Stuart A. Kirk, of *Making Us Crazy: DSM—The Psychiatric Bible and the Creation of Mental Disorders* (Free Press, 1997) and *The Selling of DSM III: The Rhetoric of Science in Psychiatry* (Aldine de Gruyter, 1992).

JULIA LEWIS earned a Ph.D. in psychology from the University of California at Los Angeles and is currently professor of psychology at San Francisco State University.

ELIZABETH F. LOFTUS is a professor of psychology and law at the University of California and an adjunct professor at the University of Washington. An expert on human memory, eyewitness testimony, and courtroom procedure, she has also served as president of the American Psychological Society. One of her books, *Eyewitness Testimony,* coauthored with Gary Wells (Cambridge University Press, 1984), won a National Media Award from the American Psychological Foundation.

ROBERT MATHIAS has worked for numerous federal and state government agencies as well as nonprofit organizations. He has researched and written extensively about science and health-related issues and has served as a science writer and editor for *NIDA NOTES,* a publication of the National Institute on Drug Abuse that examines recent research findings about drug abuse.

PAUL R. McHUGH is a professor of psychiatry at the Johns Hopkins School of Medicine. He has a long list of publications, including *The Perspectives of Psychiatry,* coauthored with Phillip R. Slavney (Johns Hopkins University Press, 1986).

JESSICA MOISE received her Ph.D. in mass communication from the University of Michigan. She is currently a Research Associate for RMC Research, performing evaluative research on school-based violence prevention and substance abuse prevention programs.

MICHAEL MONTAGNE has investigated the social and cultural aspects of psychedelic drug use for more than 25 years. His research has also focused on the role of meaning, symbolism, and metaphors in depression and the use of antidepressant medications. He is currently the Rombult Distinguished Professor of Pharmacy at the Massachusetts College of Pharmacy and Health Science.

FRED OVSIEW is an associate professor of clinical psychiatry at the University of Chicago.

PATRICIA OWEN, Ph.D., is director of the Butler Center for Research at the Hazelden Foundation. She holds a doctoral and a master's degree in adult clinical psychology and an M.H.A. degree in health care administration from the University of Minnesota. Dr. Owen has published numerous articles on chemical dependency and has given presentations at many national conferences.

CRAIG T. PALMER is an evolutionary anthropologist at the University of Colorado at Colorado Springs, where he is a senior instructor and has been honored with several awards for teaching. His research interests focus on human sexuality, evolution, and behavior.

HAROLD ALAN PINCUS is the Executive Vice Chairman of the Department of Psychiatry at the University of Pittsburgh School of Medicine, Senior Scientist at RAND, and Director of the RAND-University of

Pittsburgh Health Institute. Previously, he was the Deputy Medical Director of the American Psychiatric Association (APA), founding director of APA's Office of Research, and Executive Director of the American Psychiatric Institute for Research and Education. Prior to joining the APA, Dr. Pincus was the Special Assistant to the Director of the National Institute of Mental Health.

FRANK W. PUTNAM is a psychiatrist who is an expert on multiple personality disorder. His list of publications includes *Diagnosis and Treatment of Multiple Personality Disorder* (Guilford, 1989).

ROBERT RESNICK has served as a professor of psychology at Randolph-Macon College since 1996. He is also a licensed and board-certified clinical psychologist. Dr. Resnick was the president of the American Psychological Association from 1995 to 1996, and has received numerous awards and distinctions for his research and contributions to the field of psychology. His publications and presentations include the areas of attention deficit/hyperactivity disorder and health policy.

JUNE RIEDLINGER is assistant professor of clinical pharmacy and director of the Center for Integrative Therapies in Pharmaceutical Care at the Massachusetts College of Pharmacy and Health Sciences. In 1985 she testified about the therapeutic effects of MDMA and later coauthored several articles on MDMA. Reidlinger has most recently been working in the field of complementary and alternative medicine, offering educational programs on topics relating to psychedelic drugs and MDMA.

WILLIAM N. ROBINER is currently at the University of Minnesota where he teaches in the Department of Neurology. He is a diplomate in Health Psychology through the American Board of Professional Psychology and is former Chair of the Psychology Standards Committee of the University of Minnesota Hospital. Dr. Robiner's clinical and research interests include AIDS, anxiety disorders, sexuality, and psychotherapy.

RUTH ROSS is managing editor of *The Journal of Practical Psychiatry and Behavioral Health*. She is coauthor of *DSM-IV Guidebook* (American Psychiatric Press, 1995) and *DSM-IV Case Studies: A Clinical Guide to Differential Diagnosis* (American Psychiatric Press, 1996).

DIANA E. H. RUSSELL is a professor emeritus of sociology at Mills College in Oakland, California. A leading authority on sexual violence against women and girls, she has performed research and written articles and books on rape, incest, the misogynist murder of women, and pornography for 25 years. Her publications include *Against Pornography: The Evidence of Harm* (Russell, 1994) and *Making Violence Sexy: Feminist Views on Pornography* (Teachers College Press, 1993).

NADINE STROSSEN, a professor of law at the New York Law School, is the first woman to become president of the American Civil Liberties Union. She writes and lectures extensively on constitutional law, civil liberties, and international human rights.

MARK D. SULLIVAN is an associate professor in the Department of Psychiatry and Behavioral Sciences at the University of Washington. He has written extensively on the topics of pain, death and dying, and physician-assisted suicide.

RANDY THORNHILL is an evolutionary biologist at the University of New Mexico in Albuquerque where he is a distinguished professor. Among his research interests are evolution and ecology of social interactions, especially sexual interactions and sexual selection. He has published numerous articles and books, several pertaining to the biology and evolution of rape.

E. FULLER TORREY, M.D., is a clinical and research psychiatrist and an ardent spokesperson for the appropriate treatment of people with mental illness. He is Executive Director of the Stanley Medical Research Institute, President of the Treatment Advocacy Center, and a Professor of Psychiatry at the Uniformed Services University of the Health Sciences in Bethesda, MD. His many publications include *Out of the Shadows: Confronting America's Mental Illness Crisis*, 2nd ed. (John Wiley, 1998) and *Surviving Schizophrenia: A Manual for Families, Consumers and Providers*, 4th ed. (HarperCollins, 2001).

FRANK T. VERTOSICK, JR., is a neurosurgeon in private practice at Western Pennsylvania Hospital in Pittsburgh, Pennsylvania. He is also the author of *When the Air Hits Your Brain: Tales of Neurosurgery* (W. W. Norton, 1996), which is an account of his training in surgery.

JUDITH WALLERSTEIN, a clinical psychologist, has developed an international reputation for her scholarship and research on the effects of divorce on children and their parents. For many years Wallerstein was senior lecturer at the School of Social Welfare at the University of California at Berkeley. She is the founder and executive director of the Center for the Family in Transition.

ROBERT WHITAKER is a journalist and author whose articles on the mentally ill and the drug industry have won several awards, including the George Polk Award for medical writing and the National Association of Science Writers' Award for best magazine article. Whitaker was nominated for the Pulitzer Prize for a *Boston Globe* series on harmful research involving the mentally ill that he co-wrote in 1998, which led him to write *Mad in America: Bad Science, Bad Medicine, and the Enduring Mistreatment of the Mentally Ill* (Perseus Publishing, 2002).

THOMAS A. WIDIGER is a professor of psychology at the University of Kentucky. In addition to serving on a number of editorial boards, he is a member of the National Institute of Mental Health's clinical psychopathology review committee, and he was a member of the American Psychiatric Association task force that developed the *DSM-IV*. He is coauthor of *DSM-IV Case Studies: A Clinical Guide to Differential Diagnosis* (American Psychiatric Press, 1996).

MARK A. YARHOUSE is an assistant professor in the Regent University School of Psychology and Counseling, where he specializes in marriage and family therapy, human sexuality, ethics, and the integration of psychology and theology.

STUART J. YOUNGNER is a professor of biomedical ethics, medicine, and psychiatry at Case Western Reserve University, where he has served as director of the Center for Biomedical Ethics and associate director of Clinical Ethics. He serves on the editorial advisory boards of *The Journal of Medicine and Philosophy* and *The Kennedy Institute of Ethics Journal*. He is coeditor, with Renee C. Fox and Laurence J. O'Connell, of *Organ Transplantation: Meanings and Realities* (University of Wisconsin Press, 1996) and coeditor, with Maxwell J. Mehlman, of *Delivering High Technology Home Care: Issues for Decisionmakers* (Springer, 1991).

PATRICK ZICKLER has served as a consultant for the National Research Council of the National Academy of Sciences. He has written extensively on scientific research in medicine and has been in a major editorial role for *NIDA NOTES,* a publication of the National Institute on Drug Abuse that examines recent research findings about drug abuse.

Index

DeLee, Debra, 69
Deniker, Pierre, 164
Department of Defense Psychopharmacology
    Project, 220
Department of Defense, 220–221
Department of Education, 63
dependent personality disorder, 22
depression, 85, 87, 88, 144
despair, 95
deviance, 353
Dexedrine (*d*-amphetamine), 61, 182, 189
diagnoses, 11
*Diagnostic and Statistical Manual of Mental
    Disorders, IV,* 178
discouragement, 95
discrepancy between the scientific consensus and
    anti-abortion beliefs, 98
discriminant validity studies, 46
dissociative identity disorder (DID), 107
dissociative service, 50
divorce, 300–302, 304–309, 311–319
Donnerstein, Edward, 288, 294
dopamine, 157
dread of dependency, 22
drugs, 152, 158, 179
DSM, 8, 11, 22
DSM-II, 8, 23
DSM-III, 7, 9, 19, 28
DSM-III-R, 9, 27–29, 32
DSM-III-R-Dissociative Module, 46
DSM-IV, 4–7, 10, 11, 16–17, 22, 23, 27, 28, 30, 34, 158
Duffy, Clinton, 339
DuPaul, George J., 189

Einseidel, Edna, 288
Elavil, 61, 142, 144
electrical stimulation, 198
electroconvulsive therapy (ECT), 240–244, 246, 247,
    249–251
emotional distress, 48
emotional intelligence, 57
end-of-life care and informed end-of-life
    decisions, 348, 357
end-of-life process, 346, 348–351
Epidemiologic Catchment Area (ECA) study, 229
EPS (extrapyramidal signs), 164
Eron, Leonard, 266
ethanol, 127
Ethical Principle D, 366
Ethical Principles of Psychologists and Code of
    Conduct, 228
event paragraphs, 118
examination for psychologists, 225
Examination for the Professional Practice of
    Psychology (EPPP), 226
EXIT of Melodyland, 388–389
Exodus International, 388, 389
Exodus International-affiliated ministries, 376

false memories, 116–118, 221, 222
family intervention, 360
Farberman, Rhea K., 346
father-daughter incest, recollection, 108
FDA, 157–158
feminine traits, variants, 28
Fiamberti, Amarro, 208
Fink, Max, 240
Finkelhor, David, 272
First, Michael B., 4
Fisher, Howard W., 99
Fletcher, Anne M., 130
Francell, Edward, 169

Frances, Allen, 4, 9, 27
Freedman, Jonathan L., 264
Freeman, Walter, 206, 208, 210–212
Freud, Sigmund, 49, 152
Friedrichs, Lynette, 265

gamma irradiation, 198
gamma knife capsulotomy, 200
Ganzini, Linda, 352
gay men and lesbians, rehabilitation, 382
"gay-affirmative" therapy, 366, 369, 372, 373
gay-affirmative therapists and reparative therapists,
    polarized, 377
gender identity disorder, 23
gender prevalences, understand differences, 27
gender stereotypes, 22
gender variations, 29
gender-biased assumptions, imposition, 29
gender-biased system, mislabeled as personality
    disorder, 28
generalized resistance to thyroid hormone
    (GRTH), 59
Gentry, Cynthia, 289
Geoffrey Knight National Unit for Affective
    Disorders, 200
Glenmullen, Joseph, 148
Goff, Lyn, 120
Gordon Diagnostic System (GDS), 66
Gottesman, Irving I., 232
Gouzoulis-Mayfrank, Euphrosyne, Dr., 82
Grob, Charles, Dr., 79
[G.W.F.] Hegel's, Master/Slave dialectic, 18

Haldeman, Douglas C., 382
Hall, James N., 76
Hallowell, Edward M., 56
Hamanne, Vynnette, 116
Hanson, Glen, Dr., 76
Hauser, David, 59
Hetherington, E. Mavis, 310
Hill-Burton legislative acts, 240
Hite, Shere, 275
homophobia, 19, 22, 368
homosexuality, 19, 20, 368, 370–372, 374, 376–378,
    383–388, 390, 393
Homosexuals Anonymous, 376, 388
hopelessness, 88
Hopkins, Johns, 51
Hubbard, L. Ron, 167
Huesmann, L. Rowell, 260, 266
Husban, Troy H., 118
Hyman, Ira, 118, 119
Hyman, Steven, 156
hyotena: concept, 50
"hyperstimulation", 156
hypnosis, 44, 109
hysteria, 21, 48, 51

iatrogenic dissociation, distortion, intrusive
    inquiry, 107
ICD-10; 1992 revision, 11; adopted, 12
ICD-9: *DSM-III-R,* 11; *DSM-IV,* 11; keyed, 11
imagination, 119–120
impossible memories, 120, 121
Industrial Revolution, 18
intermittent explosive disorder, 23
International Classification of Diseases (ICD), 8
interpersonal violence, 281
interseizure EEG, 241
Irvine, Rodney, Dr., 78